Fireball Lily

Christa-Maria's (Extra)Ordinary Travels
2000–2014

Memoirs, Part II

Christa-Maria Beardsley

Pen & Publish, Inc.
Bloomington, IN

Copyright © 2018 Christa-Maria Beardsley

All rights reserved. No part of this book may be reproduced or transmitted in any form or by any means, electronic or mechanical, including photocopying, recording, or by any information storage and retrieval system, without permission in writing from the publisher.

Published by Pen & Publish, Inc., USA

www.PenandPublish.com
info@PenandPublish.com

Bloomington, Indiana
(314) 827-6567

ISBN: 978-1-941799-78-9
Library of Congress Control Number: 2018930999

Printed on acid-free paper.

Travel is fatal to prejudice, bigotry, and narrow-mindedness. . . . Broad, wholesome, charitable views of men and things cannot be acquired by vegetating in one little corner of the earth all one's lifetime.

—Mark Twain

The author is proud to donate all proceeds from the sale of this book to the following charitable organizations.

Doctors Without Borders, in memory of my late, beloved husband, Major Wayne Roscoe Beardsley, MD, and his deceased son, Captain Peter Beardsley, MD.

Doctors Without Borders USA, Inc.
333 7th Ave., 2nd Floor
New York, NY 10001
Attn: Planned Giving
Phone: (888) 392-0392
Web: donate.doctorswithoutborders.org

The Carter Center, also in memory of my late husband.

The Carter Center
One Copenhill
435 Freedom Pkwy.
Atlanta, GA 30307
Phone: (404) 420-5119
Email: gayle.beckner@cartercenter.org

The Christa-Maria Endowed Scholarship Fund, created by the author, which will provide scholarships annually to college students enrolled in the Vienna music program offered by the Institute for the International Education of Students.

IES Abroad
Advancement Office
33 W. Monroe St., Ste. 2300
Chicago, IL 60603-5400
Phone: (312) 261-5069 (Jennifer Jerzyk)
Web: www.iesabroad.org
(IES Abroad is a 501(c)(3) organization.)

Contents

PREFACE — 21

MEXICO — 23
Cancún — 23

SOUTH AFRICA — 28
Johannesburg — 28

ZIMBABWE AND ZAMBIA — 30
Victoria Falls — 30

BOTSWANA – SAFARI — 32

SOUTH AFRICA — 34
Cape Town — 34
Stellenbosch — 35

KENYA – SAFARI — 38
Nairobi — 38
Maasai Mara Game Reserve — 40

EGYPT — 43
Luxor — 43
Karnak — 43
The Nile — 44
Edfu — 44
Abu Simbel — 45
Cairo — 45

NAMIBIA – FLYING SAFARI — 48
Windhoek — 49
Sossusvlei — 50
Swakopmund — 51
Etosha National Park — 54

ANTARCTICA, BY WAY OF ARGENTINA – MS MARCO POLO 55
Argentina 55
  Buenos Aires 55
  Iguazú Falls 56
  Ushuaia – Port of World's End 56
Antarctica 57
  Cuverville Island 57
  Port Lockroy 58
  Tierra del Fuego 59
Chile 60
  Santiago 60

NORTH POLE – NS YAMAL: THE ULTIMATE JOURNEY – 90 DEGREES NORTH – TOP OF THE WORLD 62
Russia 67
  Franz Josef Land 67
  The Compass 69

SOUTH AMERICA 71
Patagonia – Argentina 71
  El Calafate 71
  Bariloche 74
Patagonia – Chile 74
  El Chaiten 75
  Carretera Austral 76
  Coyhaique 78
  Punta Arenas 78
  Puerto Natales 79
  Torres del Paine 79
  Santiago 80
Argentina 81
  Mendoza 81
  Aconcagua 82
Chile 82

ANTARCTICA – MV POLAR STAR 84
  The Falklands – Islas Malvinas 84
  South Georgia – Scotia Sea 86
  South Shetlands 89
  Half Moon Island 90

Chile	93
Santiago	93

EASTER ISLAND – RAPA NUI 95

RUSSIA – TRANS-SIBERIAN RAILWAY 101

Saint Petersburg	101
Moscow	102
Kasan	104
Siberia	105
Novosibirsk	105
Irkutsk	106
Lake Baikal	107
Mongolia	109
Ulaanbaatar	110
South Gobi Desert	111
China	115
Beijing	116

JAPAN 118

Tokyo	118
Hakone	118

CHINA 120

Beijing	120
Shanghai	124
Suzhou	127
Wuhan	129
The Yangtze River	130
Chongqing	133
Xianna	134
Terra-Cotta Warriors	134
Guilin	135
Hong Kong	136

THAILAND 139

Bangkok	139

INDIA 143
New Delhi 143

BHUTAN 144
Paro 144

HEART OF INDIA 151
New Delhi 151
Old Delhi 151
Samode 155
Jaipur 156
Ranthambor 160
Agra 161
Varanasi 164

JEWELS OF ARABIA – THE MIDDLE EAST 168
Kuwait 168
Kuwait City 168
Bahrain 173
Manama 173
Qatar 177
Doha 177
Oman 181
Muscat 181
Nizwa 182
United Arab Emirates 186
Dubai 186
Sharjah 191
Ajman 192

AUSTRALIA – MS SAPPHIRE PRINCESS 194
Sydney 194
Ayres Rock 195
Alice Springs 196
Cairns 198
Sydney 198
Melbourne 200
Tasmania – Hobart 201

NEW ZEALAND – MS SAPPHIRE PRINCESS 202
Milford Sound 202
Queenstown 202
Mount Cook 204
Christchurch 205
Wellington 206
Tauranga 207
Auckland 209

SOUTH AMERICA – DÉJÀ VU 211
Bolivia 211
La Paz 211
Lake Titicaca 213
Peru 215
Lima 215
Amazon River 216
Iquitos 216
Lima 224
Cuzco 224
Machu Picchu – Déjà Vu 226
Ecuador 229
Quito 229
Galápagos Islands 230
Equator 233

SOCIETY ISLANDS – FRENCH POLYNESIA – MS RENAISSANCE III 235
Tahiti 235
Papeete 236
Huahine 238
Bora Bora 239
Raiatea 241
Tahaa 241
Moorea 242

BALTIC SEA – NORWEGIAN CRUISE LINE'S MS NORWEGIAN STAR 244
England 244
London 244

Germany	246
Kiel Canal	246
Estonia	246
Tallinn	246
Russia I	247
Saint Petersburg	247
Finland	251
Helsinki	251
Sweden	253
Stockholm	253
Denmark	255
Copenhagen	255
Norway	256
Oslo	256

TURKEY 259

Istanbul – Déjà Vu	259
İzmir	262
Kuşadasi	263
Turquoise Coast – *Gulet*	264
Marmaris	264
Göcek Bay	266
Gemiler Bay	266
Fethiye	267
Antalya	268
Aspendos	268
Lake Beyşehir	269
Konya	270
Cappadocia	270

RUSSIAN WATERWAYS (GOLDEN RING) – MS ROSSIA 274

The Siberians	274
Saint Petersburg – Déjà Vu	276
MS *Rossia*	278
Kizhi Island – Lake Onega	279
The Golden Ring	281
Yaroslavi	281
Uglich	282
Moscow – Déjà Vu	283

HOLLAND – MS RIVER CONCERTO   285
    Amsterdam   285
    Enkhuizen   285
    Aalsmeer   286
    Amsterdam   286
    Nijmegen   287
    Kinderdijk   288
    Rotterdam   289
    Middleburg – Zeeland   289

BELGIUM   291
    Antwerp   291
    Brussels   291
    Lier – Flanders   293
    Ghent   294
    Bruges   294

THE GREEK ISLES – MS STELLA SOLARIS   297
    Athens   297
    Turkey – Déjà Vu   299
    Patmos   299
    Mykonos   300
    Rhodes   300
    Crete   301
    Santorini   302

NORWAY – COASTAL VOYAGE ON THE MS FINNMARKEN   303
    Bergen   303
    Hurtigruten – MS *Finnmarken*   304
    Trondheim   305
    Arctic Circle Crossing   306
    Kirkenes   307
    Honningsvåg   309

AUSTRIA   312
    Vienna   312

NORWAY – COASTAL VOYAGE IN SEARCH OF AURORA BOREALIS 314
Bergen – Déjà Vu – Hurtigruten's MS *Lofoten* 314
Arctic Circle Crossing 315
The Big Storm 315
Honningsvåg 316

SCOTLAND 318
Edinburgh 318
Glasgow 320
Gretna Green 322

ENGLAND 323
Grasmere 323
York 324

WALES 326
Caernarvonshire 327

ENGLAND 330
The Cotswolds 330
Chester 330
Stratford-upon-Avon 331
Stonehenge 333
Bath 334
Oxford 335
London – Déjà Vu 336

NORTHEAST UNITED STATES 338
Massachusetts – Maine 338

CANADIAN MARITIMES 341
New Brunswick 341
Prince Edward Island 343
New Glasgow 344
Nova Scotia 345
Halifax 347

GOOD-BYE, CANADA – HELLO, USA   351
Portland, Maine   351
Boston   351

EASTERN EUROPE   353
Germany   353
   Hannover   353
   Berlin   353
Poland   355
   Warsaw   355
   Krakow   357
   Wieliczka Salt Mines   359
   Auschwitz II – Birkenau   359
Czech Republic   361
   Sedlec   361
   Prague   362
Slovakia   364
   Bratislava   364
Hungary   364
   Budapest   364
Austria   367
   Vienna   367
Italy   368
   Dorf Tyrol   368
Germany   368
   Bamberg   368
   Dwindling Friendships   369

EASTERN EUROPE – MS RIVER ARIA   371
Romania   371
   Bucharest   371
   Constanta   372
Bulgaria   374
   Veliko Tarnovo   374
Serbia and Montenegro   376
Federal Republic of Yugoslavia   376
   Belgrade   376
   Novi Sad   379
Croatia   379
   Osijek   379

Hungary	381
Budapest	381

BOSTON TO MIAMI – MS NORWEGIAN DREAM

BOSTON TO MIAMI – MS NORWEGIAN DREAM	382
Bermuda	382
Hamilton	382
British Virgin Islands	383
Tortola	383
US Virgin Islands	384
Saint Thomas	384
Saint John	384
Dutch Caribbean – Netherlands Antilles	385
Bonaire	385
Curaçao	386
Aruba	387
The Bahamas	388
Nassau	388

AUSTRIA

AUSTRIA	389
Vienna	389

CHRISTMAS MARKETS ALONG THE DANUBE – MS RIVER ADAGIO

CHRISTMAS MARKETS ALONG THE DANUBE – MS RIVER ADAGIO	391
Salzburg	392
Germany	393
Passau	393
Regensburg	394
Bamberg	395

SWITZERLAND

SWITZERLAND	397
Berguen	397
Davos	401

ITALY

ITALY	403
Tirano	403

SWITZERLAND

SWITZERLAND	404
Zermatt – Matterhorn	404

MEXICO 407
Cancún 407

HAWAII – ALOHA! 408
Honolulu – Oʻahu 408
Hawaiian Island Explorer – MS *Pride of America* 409
Maui 409
Big Island 410
Kona 411
Kauai 412
Honolulu 413
Pearl Harbor 414

JAPAN II 416
Tokyo – Déjà Vu 416
Hakone 418
Kanazawa 420
Kyoto 423
Hiroshima 427

THE UNITED STATES' MAJESTIC NATIONAL PARKS 432
South Dakota 432
Rapid City 432
Mount Rushmore 434
Wyoming 434
Cody 435
Yellowstone National Park 437
Grand Teton National Park 438
Utah 441
Salt Lake City 441
Bryce Canyon National Park 442
Zion National Park 443
Arizona 444
Grand Canyon 444
Colorado 447
Vail 448
Denver 448

THE GRAND FINALE 449

ACKNOWLEDGMENTS

My sincere thanks to all my worldwide friends who encouraged me to tackle this "magnum opus."

I am especially grateful to my sensitive, meticulous, and timely copy editor, John Rogers.

PREFACE

In January 2002, after I had returned from my first, and more extensive, trip to the African continent, I came to Cancún to complete the first part of my memoirs. Today, January 19, 2010, I am back in Cancún, ready to start where I left off and to recapture, if not all of my major experiences, then many that have occurred since the turn of the millennium. It will be Part II of my memoirs, and I will focus primarily on events relating to my worldwide travels to all seven continents – Africa, Antarctica, Asia, Australia, Europe, North America, South America – and out-of-the way regions and territories, such as the North Pole. I will also relate my interactions with some of the more interesting travelers I met along the way. After all, to quote my friend and favorite Middle East tour guide, the captivating Baroness Yvonne Buheiry Dialer von Fleschenberg, "While all places in the world are beautiful, it's the people who make the journey, not the places." Last but not least, I will invite my readers to what were most likely the last two Schubertiades at my residence, which I hosted toward the end of my travels.

MEXICO

Cancún

Since the beginning of the new century, I have continued to spend at least one or two weeks each year at the Sunset Lagoon and the Royal Sunset Hotel, in Cancún. It claims to be a four-star resort. Upon entering the Royal Sunset, I am always impressed by the 35' x 4' x 5' aquarium, which separates the lobby from the restaurant and is filled with colorful corals, algae, and Caribbean fish. What I enjoy most about the Royal Sunset is my room, a studio with an ultimate ocean view. Upon awakening, and without leaving my bed, I can look out toward the horizon and gaze in sheer ecstasy while the golden globe, surrounded by clouds with ever-changing pink and orange hues, rises out of the sea.

Almost two years have elapsed since my last visit, right after Katrina, the big hurricane in 2005. At that time, the hotel was badly damaged and the beach reduced to a width of only ten to fifteen yards. Today, Cancún's world-famous beach has been restored to its original width of about sixty yards. Indeed, it is back to its former seductive beauty, and I am fortunate to be among those who can once again fully experience this gorgeous strip of sugar-white sand. – Without the beach, Cancún is not worth visiting.

Whenever I stay at the Royal Sunset, I check out the place behind the big, lone rock close to the beach and look for the three iguanas, about thirty-five inches long, crawling around in the crevices of the rough, gray-colored rock. I was disappointed when I saw none at first. Yet two days later – lo and behold – I found one of them lying on the stone floor beneath the thatched roof of the pavilion, bordering the edge of the rock. I was happy. Now things were all right. Earlier that day, when strolling along the beach, I was equally excited to spot the pelicans that in previous years tended to perch on another huge rock stretching out from the beach into the turquoise waters, always sparkling when the sun was rising. This time, there were six or seven big, gray-feathered pelicans, gliding back and forth close to the rolling and splashing waves and darting into the water to catch some food with their long beaks. However, I did not observe any of them catching a fish, probably because as soon as they open their beaks beneath the surface, the catch slides directly into their throats. The pelicans blatantly ignored the seagulls that graced the atmosphere by happily sailing back and forth before landing on the white sand to pick up a morsel with their pointed beaks.

Twelve years ago, I befriended Cristian, the Chilean youth from Santiago, on this very beach. This time, I was content to chitchat with this and that guest and, as usual, was surprised at the mélange of foreigners who vacationed there. – I was again amazed to discover I had personally visited many of the places from which these visitors came. There were, among others, the stunningly attractive honeymooners from Argentina: a general surgeon and his wife, an ophthalmologist who did not like their country's Botox Evita, aka "the Botox Queen," President Cristina Fernández de Kirchner. –

Right away, the conversation drifted to Buenos Aires, Caliphate, Torres del Paine, Chile – in short, to one of my favorite regions on the globe, Patagonia. To my surprise, the young Argentineans had visited neither the Torres del Paine nor Mendoza in the north. Mendoza is the city I will forever remember as the scorching-hot place from which I ventured out to see the highest mountain in the Americas, Aconcagua. It was the trip on which I met my Polish friends Teresa and Jerzey Mirecki, who had lived and worked for years in Lybia, where they were afforded the "pleasure," if you will, of meeting Gaddafi before they exchanged life in the Sahara Desert for a more cooled-down existence in Toronto, Canada.

I found it difficult to refrain from discussing with the stunning MDs my bout with the weirdest of all weird afflictions, of which to date no one knows the cause: temporal arteritis. It had hit me out of the blue a year before and changed my lifestyle instantly. Until I took this trip, I was banned from traveling. It was without question the scariest experience of my life. I was within days of going blind. Fortunately I had the courage to pressure my doctor to put on his good-doctor hat, because something was definitely not right. When I enumerated the symptoms, such as a noticeable loss of weight, loss of taste and appetite, jaw pain when eating, double vision, and momentary blackouts in one or both eyes, he reacted with speed and ordered an immediate biopsy. It was positive. After four days in the hospital with one thousand milligrams of prednisone (a steroid) pumped into my arteries each day, I started on a gradual path toward – hopefully – full recovery. Thanks to the close supervision of my general practitioner, Dr. Bannec, my rheumatologist, the Romanian-born Dr. German, and Dr. Grogg, my optometrist, despite an occasional near-blind episode, I am optimistic all will eventually be well. It's the major reason I came to Cancún this time – to focus on my health by way of exercises in the gym, frequent massages, walks along the beach, and just relaxing in the shade and basking in the panorama of the ever-changing azure and turquoise waters of the Mexican Caribbean.

I met another Argentinean at my hotel. A tall, good-looking gentleman who farmed fruit trees and vegetable plants *en gros* surprised me by speaking German fluently. As is not uncommon for Argentineans, who in general boast a strong European influence, which I believe accounts for their good looks, his grandfather had emigrated from Germany in 1908. His attractive wife was of Italian descent and, like her handsome children, spoke English very well. – Each year, many Canadians flee from the cold up north to soak up the sun in Cancún. I get excited when I meet tourists from Calgary, since Lake Louise is one of my favorite spots to visit, especially in the winter. One Canadian was from Saskatchewan, the province to which my mother's cousin, Maria Silbernagel, had immigrated long before I arrived in America. She wrote a few letters in which she invited me to visit her on a huge farm, but we never connected. Later, I met a couple, also from Saskatchewan, who owned a 17,000-acre farm, thousands of cattle, a herd of some 150 bison, and over one hundred horses, some of which they trained for barrel races. – Italians from New Jersey flocked to the swimming pool, and we chatted about my wedding in Venice and my friend Marco in Anzio, whom I met on my first trip along the Norwegian coast, and two tall, handsome, and very polite young males of Dutch heritage turned out to be from Curaçao. Curaçao was among the islands where we spent a day in Willemstad when cruising to Bermuda, the Bahamas, and a string of islands in the Caribbean a few years before. Two pretty and very blond and blue-eyed women – masseuses – one of whom I had trouble conversing with in English, were from Siberia, Russia – and we talked about the times I took the Trans-Siberian Railway from Moscow to Beijing and the river cruise from Saint Petersburg to Moscow to tour the Golden Ring on the Volga and other waterways with Olga and Lubasha Belousowa. Agata, a beautiful young woman at the reception desk of the Sunset Hotel, had traveled to Cancún from Poland, where she had studied Germanic languages and literature. She had played the violin, lived, worked, and studied in Germany and England, where she fell in love with a handsome chap, half-English and half-Mexican, whom she followed to Cancún, where they both took jobs in hotels.

Of course, I ran into Mexicans from Acapulco, Mexico City, Veracruz, Mérida, and other regions besides Yucatán, but all came from places I had visited, and I therefore remembered what makes their towns special. I got really excited when I met guests from Bolivia, Brazil, Colombia, England, Germany, and even Cuba. – I then came upon the American couple Patti and John. I spoke with Patti on and off when passing by her lounge chair. She had an incredible dark-chocolate tan, a striking figure, and noticeably beautiful coiffed hair. No wonder – she was a hair stylist. In the one week she had been there, she had read eleven of the many romance novels she had packed in her suitcase. She forgot everything about a book as soon as it was finished. – John, her second husband, owned a bar, which she connected to the fact that he stood at the pool bar all day long, drinking beer. Once, probably after having had a bit too much, he stopped me and confided that his wife was on disability with some disease and that they had fallen on hard times and would have to declare bankruptcy after returning home. I was dumbfounded. He was probably in his late sixties, and Patty was fifty-nine or so. – There were only a handful of African-Americans from New York at the resort, happy to have escaped the snow back home. One of the African-American couples, a contractor and an MD, turned out to be quite interesting. In talking, we discovered that the wife's parents were from Cassopolis, Michigan, where Doc was a medical director at the hospital and also had a private practice. They knew of the Beardsley connection in Elkhart, Indiana, and had seen the statue of Doc's ancestor on Beardsley Avenue. They told me much about the portion of the Underground Railroad that went through Vandalia, Michigan, not far from the Croft, and when I told them Doc hired several

African-Americans to work for him in exchange for medical treatment, or treated them free of charge if they were very poor, they smiled.

Each time I visit Cancún, I marvel at the quantity of obese Americans. From afar, many of the men with protruding bellies look like pregnant women. This time, I chatted with a couple in their sixties. Spread out on a rattan couch, they reminded me of a couple of elephant seals loafing on the cinnamon-colored beach in the Galápagos Islands. Together, they boasted a solid mass of at least seven hundred pounds of blubber. It looked as though the couch might give way any minute. They were hardly able to get up and move around, but I guarantee they never missed a major meal and continued to stuff themselves in between with hamburgers, French fries, tacos, ice-cream cones, etc. at the pool bar. They were like those obese people on ocean cruises who load their plates so full the food threatens to spill over. This couple, who to my utter surprise turned out to come from my own neighborhood, bragged about their forty-two grandchildren, but complained about two daughters who unexpectedly ended up at their doorstep with a bunch of crying kids. They moved in because they could no longer stomach their husbands. And when the grandparents could no longer tolerate the move-ins? They escaped to Cancún. When I asked how they handled sending Christmas gifts to this army of grandchildren, Grandpa replied that when he asked his thirteen-year-old grandson whether he believed in Santa Claus and he said no, he stopped sending him Christmas gifts. – In contrast, I observed that guests from the Philippines, Taiwan, and Korea were much more disciplined when it came to their eating habits as well as the behavior of their toddlers. I was so impressed that once, on the way out of the restaurant, I stopped at the table of a Korean couple and complimented the parents on their well-behaved kids. They were most appreciative.

I always enjoy conversing with the locals in other countries and had chatted on previous visits with Mayan workers, who informed me how poorly they were compensated for building palace-like hotels. They had confirmed what I had read: that some twenty million Mexicans lived on less than $2 per day, which convinced me that the rich – in this case, the big hotel owners and contractors – were exploiting them. I was shocked when the woman who cleaned my studio each day told me she worked from 8:00 a.m. until 6:00 p.m. for a mere $6. Another woman said it did not pay for her husband to work, because the bus fare would cost more than what he would earn per day. I did not dare ask the workers whether it was true that the poorest, that is, those living in remote rural areas, often lived by going through garbage containers and frequently went to bed without having eaten anything. I knew what that was like, because I experienced it in Germany right after World War II.

This time, I chatted with a thirty-year-old Mayan Indian who was gatekeeper for the newly erected Ocean View, a glitzy glass high-rise on the beach not far from the Royal Sunset Hotel. Ocean View is a construction of two hundred units; they start at $1 million, and the higher up you live, the higher the cost. Each unit has a windowless, prison-cell-like room that houses a servant. Last month, in January 2010, one hundred units were still empty. Donald Trump reportedly owns a penthouse unit at Ocean View. The young Mayan was single and rented a two-bedroom apartment outside of town for $100 a month. He had no car and no health insurance, and earned $500 a month. With the exception of not liking his president, Felipe de Jesús Calderón, he had no complaints. I was somewhat surprised when I met an attractive Caucasian woman who had come from South Africa. She had been too young when the apartheid movement was going on in her native country. But just the fact that she came from Johannesburg, the country I had visited in 2001, triggered many mixed emotions.

SOUTH AFRICA

Johannesburg

On November 22, 2001, about two and a half months after 9/11, yet more than three decades after my first visit to Morocco, Africa, I ventured out to the African continent once more. This time, the journey would entail more than just a glimpse. It started in Johannesburg, city of more than three million, located in the northern part of South Africa. A handsome Afrikaans male, dressed in a black tuxedo loaded with colorful medals, sporting a black top hat decorated with yet more medals, and wearing white gloves, opened the huge entrance door to the rather posh Cullinan Hotel with a big smile. – I had trouble understanding our guide's warning not to leave the hotel, which was located near the airport and appeared to be located in a pleasant area, alone at night. – Following orders, I decided to order a pizza to be delivered to my room. It turned out to be a wise move. The short, middle-aged Caucasian pizza guy volunteered rather anxiously that Johannesburg was a dreadful and most dangerous place to live. He constantly had to barricade his house, never left it without a gun, and was saving every penny to immigrate, as soon as possible, to Australia, where he had family. Well, a not-so-nice welcome to Africa, I thought. In retrospect, I regret not having quizzed the handsome doorkeeper. Nevertheless, it got worse the next day. Luckily for our group, this particular Johannesburg outing was an unplanned add-on. It was a real shocker! In short, I began to understand why one would want to escape this dangerous and crime-ridden postapartheid metropolis for greener pastures. When the next morning, on the way to Soweto, our van stopped in downtown Johannesburg for a bird's-eye view from the city's highest structure, the Hillbrow Tower, we were told to rush across the street as quickly as we could. After stepping out of the elevator, which had transported a bunch of us at great speed to the top floor, some 807 feet high, we made the round of the tower – a continuous wall of glass and formerly a rotating restaurant, closed for security reasons – and I was shocked to learn from the guide how many of the high-rises I could see from there were former banks, apartment houses, hotels, etc. All were now empty or occupied by squatters from such neighboring countries as Somalia, Tanzania, and Uganda. – After this eye-opener, I befriended Lillian Boly, from Florissant, Missouri. She is a brilliant high-school teacher and historian, and she holds a master's degree in literature. I converse with her frequently by phone.

If I had assumed that the occupied buildings, with their broken windows and doors and unappetizing location smack in the center of the inner city, were bad, I had another thing coming. As our van left the city, what I saw along the highway left me in disbelief. Crammed together was a mess of the most devastating poverty, unlike anything I had seen up to that point, almost worse than the favelas I had encountered with horror and disgust on the mountainside in Rio de Janeiro. I shivered at the sight of virtually thousands of shanties, shacks, or whatever one should call these primitive and rather shaky propped-up sheds – often just four poles covered with plastic garbage bags or, if the residents were lucky, with corrugated sheet metal weighed down with rocks. One of these provided shelter for a family of six or more and a mutt. The shelters were so close together that children would have no room to play outside, as they often had in the rural areas in Peru. I noticed an occasional electric bulb dangling from a cord strung outside the shacks. An emaciated goat, its fur soiled from mud, was tied to a pole, presumably waiting to be auctioned off or butchered. I asked myself, "Aside from constant battles and confrontations, what has antiapartheid done for these poor?" It seemed that as in Brazil, the rich continued to get richer and the poor poorer.

Our visit to Soweto will remain embedded in my mind forever. It was at the same time sobering and heart-wrenching. After all, it was at that place that a major historical event began. On June 16, 1976, high-school students had protested for better education, and in turn police fired tear gas and live bullets into the marching crowd, killing at least twenty-three protesters (or many more, as others claim), mainly students. This criminal act took place while Mandela was serving his prison sentence, but ultimately set the antiapartheid movement into serious motion. Soweto was one of those places where I had to pinch myself to realize I was actually present at such a historic location. A most humble place, it was where the great civil-rights leader and symbol of resistance had lived until he was incarcerated in 1964 (he was released twenty-six years later, on February 11, 1990). To visit this family museum and get some insight, if only marginal, into Mandela's life was indeed an overpowering experience. I noticed that there were hardly any signs of the uprising. The fence bordering the yard of a nearby secondary school, one of the schools where it all started, was reinforced with barbed wire, and when we stepped inside the Catholic Regina Mundi Church, which had served as shelter for those fleeing the shooting police, I admired a large mural depicting a group of black and white protesters raising their hands. Four hands were without bodies. Each hand was painted in a different color: jet black, brown, yellow, or white. A black boy showed a fist. Standing high above the protesters were now Bishop Desmond Tutu, Nelson Mandela, and Steve Biko, three great civil-rights defenders.

A brief stop outside the more upscale whitewashed villa, where Nelson Mandela resided for a while after his release, was most welcome. Though surrounded by a big wall, the setting allowed glimpses of beautiful gardens with palm trees, a rich canapé of purple jacaranda, and bright red, yellow, and white flowering shrubs. I was overcome by a feeling of joy, relief, gratitude, and admiration.

June 30, 2013 – Today our president, Barack Obama, is visiting South Africa with his family to express his longtime admiration for Nelson Mandela, who at the age of almost ninety-five lies critically ill in the hospital in Pretoria.

ZIMBABWE AND ZAMBIA

Victoria Falls

We landed before noon at the Harare airport to see Victoria Falls. Expectations were very high. Another lifelong dream was about to come true. The African ambiance of the Kingdom Hotel set the mood for this adventure. Great! I could see the mist of the falls from the balcony of my room and was eager to follow our guides, an African-American and a Caucasian, who led us toward the spectacle. On the way, we stopped to marvel at the enormity of the gigantic baobab tree, some fifty feet in circumference and undoubtedly at least a thousand years old. I was ecstatic to encounter this specimen, which I had first read about in Saint-Exupéry's *Le petit prince* when studying in Aix-en-Provence. Saint-Exupéry's trees are in the Libyan Sahara Desert. The Prince pulls them out because they are constantly trying to take root and turn the little planet to dust, because, though he does not explain why, they can store up to thousands of gallons of water. Our baobab tree would have been even more enchanting had it been in bloom. The large white blossoms are known to have a pleasing, aromatic smell. – No monkeys were playing in the tree, aka the "monkey-bread tree," since it had not yet produced the fruits baboons like to feast on.

Nevertheless, as we approached the falls on the path through the rainforest, the baboons and blue-balled (vervet) monkeys entertained us splendidly. They were swinging from limb to limb, jumping and chasing each other or their little ones up and down branches and tree trunks, or just sitting quietly in the grass, cleansing or feeding themselves while staring emotionlessly at us perhaps otherworldly, perhaps familiar creatures. I don't know why I have always had a penchant for monkeys, especially little ones.

I could hear the roar of the falls and, as I got closer, wiped the spray off my glasses. My heart was beating faster and faster. I could not refrain from shouting "wow" at the moment the thundering waters of the Zambezi River – in the form of the magnificent Victoria Falls, a string of innumerable falls, some of which are 5,100 feet high, considered the widest in the world – came into full view. Awesome: the falls in their entirety, from the Devil's Cataract in the west to the Boiling Pot in the east, spread out before me. To raise the excitement, a radiant rainbow crowned the panorama, making it unforgettable. I clicked my little Canon with panorama zoom incessantly and had to work hard to keep it away from the mist.

Although everything we saw and did after the falls was anticlimactic, it was not without excitement. The impact of the beauty of the falls and the entire experience of the surroundings would have been greatly diminished had I not seen the monument built to commemorate David Livingstone, the Scottish missionary and great explorer of Africa, who in 1855 first discovered this natural wonder of the world and named it after his queen, Victoria. I appreciated the walk across the Victoria Falls Bridge, which links the Zambezi River with Zimbabwe just below the falls, and learned that Sir Ralph Freeman, the same man who designed the Sydney Harbour Bridge, which it actually resembles, designed it. As I stepped off the bridge, one of the two guides, with whom I had strayed from the rest of the group, stooped down and picked up a huge black scarab, placing it in the palm of his left hand for me to stare at. He explained that this ugly, jet-black, cockroach-like bug is also called a dung beetle. It places its egg in dung, which it rolls into a ball to be heated by the sun. In turn, this procedure creates an association with the life-giving powers of the sun and the sun god Ra. I remembered that the scarab is a popular amulet in Egypt and worn to protect people from the evil all around us. Who knows whether this beetle was responsible for my virtually stumbling upon what I considered to be one of the most stunningly beautiful flowers, the fireball lily. Its orange-red blossom, which looks like a pincushion the size of a tennis ball, sits on top of a tall and sturdy green stem, which is anchored in a bunch of lush, green, spear-like leaves. I had found what I had long searched for: this exotic red beauty, on a jet-black jacket, must grace the cover of Part II of my memoirs.

So much for the luck brought to me by a dung beetle. What really bugged me later, while strolling through the little town to find some souvenirs, were the herds of fat and scary-looking warthogs roaming around, their admittedly cute young trailing aimlessly behind or wandering off in all directions. Fortunately, at that time they were not as much of a menace as they were after our visit. Some ninety of these rather homely beasts were removed after causing an accident at the airport.

Warthogs are not and never have been my favorite beasts. I found much more thrilling the hippos, crocodiles, and elephants we spotted cooling off in a low spot in the river while cruising along the mighty Zambezi on a flat-bottomed boat to observe the promised "spectacular African sunset." The sunset kept us waiting. However, while waiting I chatted with a couple of professional gamblers from Almaty, Kazakhstan, the Las Vegas of Asia. Not knowing much about gambling and not being seriously interested in that vice, I was nevertheless dumbfounded to learn from these young Russians that the oil-rich country was thriving and that gamblers from all over Russia flocked to the scene with sacks virtually full of cash. I soon forgot about that conversation at the evening show, which was put on by the once-powerful Matabele tribe. It offered a mere hint of their lifestyle of years ago. The show was advertised as "spectacular," which I had a hard time agreeing with. The helicopter ride over the mighty Zambezi and Victoria Falls was much more rewarding. The panorama afforded a breathtaking view not only of the vast broadness of the river, but also of the numerous tributaries that, from up there, resembled arteries streaming toward a huge crevice and the many rifts of the cataracts.

BOTSWANA – SAFARI

The two-hour drive from Victoria Falls to Chobe National Park, in Botswana, was comparatively short. The border crossing was way out in the middle of nowhere and was a bit of a joke, I felt. We had to get out of the four-wheeler and cleanse our shoes in something like a puddle, which was filled with a chemical that killed any and all germs that could result in foot-and-mouth disease. The jeep had to drive through a similar puddle for the same reason. Our passports were checked in a little shack before we could continue. It was at this point that I learned Botswana is rich in diamonds. –

On our ride, we were constantly on the lookout for game. It seemed to take forever, but I finally spotted three giraffes in the distance. I saw them nibbling at the top branches of an acacia tree – somehow, I had not realized before then how endlessly long their necks are. It was an incredible experience to observe these gigantic mammals up close for the first time, instead of in a zoo. The same goes for seeing my first lion, which rested near a tree stump in the African bush, a small herd of slender, reddish-brown-colored impala roaming around in search of food, and antelopes and puku standing still and staring at us in broad daylight with blue skies overhead. Whenever a new bird specimen surprised us, our game ranger stopped for the obligatory photo moment. Within an hour, I added eagles, bustards, plovers, and rollers to my collection. Indeed, the drive to our posh Mowana Safari Hotel, right on the banks of the Chobe River, was great.

The Mowana Lodge itself was great as well. I fell in love with the place the minute I saw it. The entrance to the thatch-roofed Safari Stay was quite unique, because an eight-hundred-year-old baobab tree was incorporated into its main structure. The lodge stood out because of its bush setting as well as its location at the point where four countries – Botswana, Namibia, Zambia, and Zimbabwe – meet. To top it off, I was excited to notice a group of photos of the Clintons, who had stayed there in 1998. As soon as I had some time, I asked the concierge if he would kindly show me the Clinton suite. He led me there, and I was pleased to see that my own suite measured up nicely with theirs. Their double bed also had a mosquito net attached to the ceiling. Like mine, their balcony was on the side of the building that faced the Chobe River, and on the dresser stood a lamp with a huge stone elephant as its base. I would have liked to buy one, but it seemed too heavy to lug around so early on our trip.

The stay, however brief, was just the thing to put me in a safari mood. The dinner on the Bona Terrace was good, but I excused myself early to go to my room. As soon as I opened the door to the spacious suite, I was virtually overwhelmed by a swarm of insects. I had left the door to the balcony open and the elephant lamp burning. These little pests were covering the walls, the mosquito net, everything – not only everything in the suite, but also the walls in the bathroom, where I had left a light on. The white tiles were covered solid with these black insects. Fortunately I spotted a can with bug-killing chemicals. I closed the doors to the balcony and, for what seemed like forever, sprayed all the surfaces until all invaders had fallen to the floor. I swept the bugs into a pile with a bath towel. I pulled the string to the mosquito net after I got situated and made certain no cracks were left in the white veil, in order to prevent any malarial bug from intruding into my sanctuary. As a result of all this excitement, I don't recall hearing any lions, elephants, or other bush animals roaring or calling out to each other during the night.

That was quite an initiation to Chobe National Park. At least, living on the second floor, I was spared invasions by reptiles, monkeys, or other human-flesh-craving jungle creatures.

Two and a half days in the park was hardly enough to do it justice. However, for someone like me, who had come for the first time, everything was exciting. Our guides made the most of it with game rides in the morning, late afternoon, and evening, as well as late at night. They watched out for us rather keenly. At one point, we stopped for a break alongside the river to watch more hippos, a crocodile, and flocks of egrets, ibises, and herons. I wandered off a bit toward the bush. Immediately the guide came to fetch me, warning me never to take off by myself. A lion just might jump me. He also warned us not to approach the bunch of adorable little monkeys that were playing around and sitting peacefully on a fallen tree trunk while a group of impala grazed close by. Our evening game viewing by boat did not turn up any new animals, but it ended with an absolutely gorgeous sunset.

I guarantee that nobody in our group of twelve (eleven or more had canceled due to 9/11) was more disappointed than I. Up to that point, we had not seen a single elephant of the promised seventy thousand which supposedly inhabit the park. But the next morning after breakfast, on the way back to the airport in Zimbabwe, our ranger suddenly stopped the four-wheeler, turned around, and virtually raced across the bumpy terrain toward something massive and gray behind trees in the distance: elephants! We all jumped up in excitement but were told to calm down, which we did. Silently, with broad smiles and hushed-up voices, we snapped and snapped pictures of the group of four elephants feeding in the bushes, their trunks hanging down between huge white tusks, never once looking up at us, which was OK.

I was ready to move on toward more excitement – the next stop was Cape Town, South Africa.

SOUTH AFRICA

The wonders of nature tend to overshadow the sorrows of the people who live so close to and are an integral part of it. While sitting at the airport waiting for the flight to Cape Town, I talked to a white couple, in their forties and of humble means, about their life in Zimbabwe. They bent their heads and in low voices told me how repressively their president rules, evicting white famers from their farms and homes. It was no secret that he had reversed the practices of apartheid. This couple too was fearful of losing their home and hoped the coming elections would bring a new president and change for the better. I thought of them when Mugabe was reelected not long after my visit.

August 2, 2013 – Mugabe, at age eighty-nine, was again reelected. It was supposedly a rigged election. What else is new? Here, it's called "voter suppression."

The visit to Zimbabwe had a special interest for me. It was here in the old Rhodesia that the rich and powerful, yet controversial, English businessman Cecil Rhodes had established the Rhodes Scholarship at Oxford, from which President Clinton and my good friend General Bill Whipple, among others who had risen to fame and power, had benefited. One might wonder how Cecil Rhodes would have fared under Mugabe and vice versa.

Cape Town

The minute I stepped off the plane in Cape Town, I felt ever so much more free. While our bus drove to the truly world-class President Hotel, I began to realize why this city of more than three million, located at the southernmost point of the African continent, was considered by many, including several of my friends who had visited it, to be the most beautiful city in the world. How much more uplifting was this drive than the one in Johannesburg! It was like night and day. It seemed as though South Africa's gold and platinum mines had benefited this city more than others up north.

The buildings downtown, such as South Africa's oldest (built in 1666), once the residence of the governor, the classic baroque Great Synagogue, and Groot Kerk (Big Church), that is, the mother church of the Dutch Reformed faith, were noticeably well kept. They were whitewashed, had manicured surroundings, and were accented by royal palms reaching into a blue sky. The hotel itself was awe-inspiring, not only because of its location right on the azure Atlantic Ocean and the Platinum Mile, but also by virtue of its closeness to the playground of the rich, Clifton Beach, and the Victoria & Alfred Waterfront, which is situated between Robben Island, Mandela's longtime prison, and the domineering Table Mountain.

What really fascinated me in Cape Town, capital of Western Cape and parliamentary capital of the republic province, was Bo-Kaap, aka Cape Malay Quarter, a township on slopes with narrow streets. The restored buildings reflected a Cape Dutch and Edwardian architectural style. Their brightly painted facades, purple, pink, yellow, orange, and red, reminded me on the one hand of colors found in the flora I spotted here and there in gardens and parks throughout the city, and on the other hand of the colorful facades of houses in Buenos Aires that served as backdrops for the sexy tango dancers. These buildings were artisan houses, mosques, minarets, and the like and were still inhabited, we were told, by descendants of thousands of Javanese, Ceylonese, Indonesians, Sri Lankans, and Indians. They were captured in the seventeenth and eighteenth centuries and enslaved by the powerful Dutch East India Company, a trading company that established a major trading post in Cape Town. Indeed, we learned that as a result, the Afrikaans language evolved virtually by itself. It is a simplification of Dutch that came about so slaves could communicate with each other and the Dutch.

Stellenbosch

Stellenbosch is the second-oldest (after Cape Town) and best-preserved town in South Africa. It lies approximately thirty-five miles east of Cape Town and boasts one of the four top research universities in South Africa as well as some very interesting architectural and historical sights. On the way, I was pleased to encounter several of the extraordinary huge oak trees and blooming jacarandas that are spread around this town. Even more pleased were the true wine lovers in our group. The wine estate we visited was nestled between manicured vineyards and rugged mountains. Unfortunately, I have forgotten its name, but believe me, it was a delight to visit. I was surprised to learn that the reason climbing roses were planted alongside the mesh fences separating the vineyards from the road was to discourage animals from invading the vineyards. I had never seen such fencing in the vineyards in Europe or elsewhere. Our group spent a few relaxing hours at this well-kept winery. The wines were good, but I was more interested in watching two cheetahs resting in the shade on a bed of straw close to a wooden fence outside the winery.

Grand Circle Travel, or GCT, always manages to lend a special accent to the tours by including a visit to a local family. We were fortunate to be hosted by a very lovely Caucasian "lady," a divorcée from an MD with three children. The richly furnished home and well-kept gardens were flush with exotic flowers. The dinner, preceded by a cocktail welcome, revealed clearly that our hostess was not too much deprived. She subsidized her lifestyle by hosting these events. She enjoyed meeting people, and as I sat next to her at the table, we engaged in a lively conversation. For me, the high point of the evening was when I succeeded in convincing one of the daughters, perhaps ten years old, to play a few tunes on the upright piano I had noticed in the dining room. Everybody applauded the little girl. She was beaming.

Fireball Lily

The next day, I too was beaming when I saw the Cape of Good Hope. I could easily understand why Francis Drake described it as "the most stately thing, and the fairest Cape [he] saw in the whole circumference of the earth." The rock reaches two hundred feet at its highest point. As I looked down to watch the turquoise and azure waves crest and their white foam burst against the rugged coastline of the Atlantic seaboard, all under a clear blue sky, this natural drama held me spellbound. I had trouble breaking away for a stroll around the nature reserve, a part of the cape where we came upon the most beautiful flora, including huge pink proteas, and a variety of animals, such as elands, different kinds of antelopes – including rheboks, the namesake of the athletic shoe – and many more. We eventually landed directly in the world-famous and scenic Black Marlin Seafood Restaurant. It is located in Simon's Town and sits very close to the water's edge of the Atlantic Ocean, with an exquisite view. An extravagant lunch awaited us. This restaurant used to be a whaling station, and it had thus become a favorite place for whale watchers from July to November. – Each serving was presented like a piece of art, that is, garnished with flowers or arranged so artfully I hesitated to destroy the creation with my fork. One of their specialties was a fish kebab served on an iron skewer with a hook from which the kabab dangled. – As we left the place, I noticed a monkey holding on tight to the window frame of a van filled with tourists. I wondered whether these cute rascals might occasionally surprise the guests in the restaurant or chase each other up to the lighthouse, which we saw from down at the restaurant but did not hike up to. –

Earlier, we had taken the funicular to Cape Point, one of the world's great shipping beacons. It marks the turning point for vessels sailing between the Atlantic and Indian Oceans. Here, the warm Mozambique current meets the cold Benguela current and has a big impact on all forms of marine life in the vicinity and on the flora of the peninsula. – With not much further to go, we stopped at Boulders, also part of the national park and *the* spot where you can observe how, between 1982 and 2001, two breeding pairs of African penguins multiplied to over three thousand. They must not be compared to the "real" ones, the king or emperor penguins or other penguins of Antarctica. I had never seen these African specimens. After looking at and smelling them from the boardwalk as they hovered on the pinkish-white beach and on the huge boulders bordering the cape and sheltering the invaders, I tried to get closer to a small iguana on top of a rock. When the penguin's constant chatter and the stench began to annoy me, I was ready to move on. On this day, the big reward came on our way back to the hotel. Out of the blue, while I was looking out the window on the Atlantic side of the van, I saw a big black whale jump up out of the water, making a big splash and in no time disappearing again. It was a *wow* moment I will never forget. On my Alaskan cruise years earlier, I had looked for a whale for days, all in vain. I had seen several schools of dolphins jumping up and down as they accompanied our ship, but never a whale. But here, at the southern tip of the African continent, close to the Cape of Good Hope and exactly opposite

South Africa

Northern Alaska, a whale came into full view. I was not expecting or even hoping to see one.

And luck was with me once more on that day. I found my big, fat elephant carved out of ironwood in the boutique of our hotel. I had hunted for it ever since I arrived in Africa. Elephants bring good luck, and I had inherited a handsome group of elephants carved out of ebony and ivory. I had wanted a big one for the library. This elephant, about thirty pounds, was just perfect. I bargained the price down from $100 to $65. They wrapped it well in bubble plastic, and I carted it from safari to safari in my luggage cart. Thus, I can honestly claim that the big one in my library knows what it is like on the great Serengeti Plains.

Back in my hotel room that night, when I turned on the TV, I learned it was December 1 and World AIDS Day. All at once, the beautiful impressions and experiences of the days in Cape Town came crashing down. I learned that some twenty-eight million AIDS sufferers live in Sub-Saharan Africa and in the outlying provinces of the beautiful city of Cape Town. Here, as in Johannesburg, thousands of poor, black South Africans are growing up and dying young in squatter settlements in abject poverty, battling crime, HIV, and drugs on a daily basis. It is a remnant of apartheid and "hell on earth," as they say. It always amazes me that on these escorted trips, they frequently steer tourists away from locations that are living testimony to the darker side. I assume it is for security reasons, but it would be appropriate if at least documentary films were made available.

KENYA - SAFARI

Nairobi

The security concerns became all too obvious when, as soon as we had landed at Nairobi's Jomo Kenjatta Airport, we were ushered into a minibus. On the back seat sat an armed native guard who cautioned us not to open the windows. When our van began to struggle inch by inch through the streets of Nairobi, Kenya's capital, I could see why they warned us. It seemed as though most of the 1.5 million inhabitants of this city had gathered downtown on this sunny day, disregarding any and all street and traffic signs, if there were any, or any attempt by a traffic officer, if there was one, to control the flow. I did not know that during colonial times, Nairobi was a tent city and these paved streets were dirt roads. As we drove past the spot where terrorists in 1998 had bombed the US Embassy, which was rebuilt at another location, I did not see any trace of the attack. I don't scare easily, but I had strange thoughts about what it might have been like if our van broke down right there. – Never before had I been so aware of the contrast between black and white skin, black and blond hair, and brown and blue eyes.

I was much relieved when our minibus pulled up in front of the legendary, five-star, Tudor-style Norfolk Hotel, which according to GCT is known as the "nicest hotel in Southeast Africa." As our brochure claimed, "The Norfolk was the staging point for Theodore Roosevelt's safaris, home-away-from-home for Ernest Hemingway and gathering place for the celebrities and pioneers of East Africa – Beryl Markham, Isak Dinesen, Queen Elizabeth II, and the Prince of Wales. . . . 'Kenya Cowboys' the rugged (white) farmers and ranchers of the early 20th century used to ride their horses up onto the terrace and into the Lord Delamere Bar for a drink (or two)."

I can understand why GCT avoided a city tour of Nairobi and steered us instead through semiarid desert terrain in the direction of Kenya's highest and Africa's second-highest mountain, Mount Kenya, about 15,600 feet high. Kilimanjaro is, at 17,685 feet, the highest mountain in Africa, aka "the roof of Africa." Thus, instead of getting another glimpse of Nairobi's shantytowns, we were afforded a visit to the colorful market in Karatina. There, the natives were sitting on the ground displaying their crafts: rugs, necklaces, and bracelets of glass beads, carved wooden figures, and the like. They looked up at us with desperate eyes and pleaded with us to purchase a piece or two. – The stop at the equator at Nanyuki, at an altitude of 6,389 feet, was truly exciting. It was the first time I had personally witnessed how water swirls in one direction twenty paces north of the equator and in the opposite direction twenty paces south. I also have a genuine penchant for mountains and was glad we stopped at the small town of Timau. It is the starting place for thousands of ambitious climbers who want to conquer the snowcapped Mount Kenya with its permanent glaciers, which also straddles the equator.

On the way to Samburu National Park, we had the opportunity to meet a group of Samburu people, seminomadic pastoralists. They are cousins to the Maasai but still live traditionally, in round huts of plastered mud or grass mats stretched over a frame consisting of poles, which can easily be disassembled and transported to the next stop, as is customary with the yurts in Mongolia. Thorns to ward off wild beasts, however, surround their huts as well as their cattle yards. As soon as our vehicle stopped to cross the border and one of the guys in my group opened the window, three or four long and skinny arms forced their way toward our noses, offering bracelets and necklaces for sale. When we stopped at their camp to linger for a while, I observed that these *moranis* (warriors) wore red-and-blue or light-green *kangas*, which resemble skirts, and colorful beads around their neck, while the women stood out because of their elaborate, multibeaded necklaces, bracelets, and earrings. These men and women, with their shaved heads, looked rather serious. I was struck by the large, stretched holes in their earlobes and was told that the larger the hole, the more beautiful it is considered to be and the more respect is given its bearer. I was able to get one little boy to smile for a picture. I felt somewhat relieved to hear that the Samburu, who live off their cows, sheep, goats, and camels, pride themselves on defending their own and are content with their way of life. It was difficult to fathom what their education was like. The school was open-air, with a few wooden benches, and the walls were made of branches from thornbushes. I could understand why most children did not go to school. It was difficult to communicate with women, men, and children. One guy in my group, a very obnoxious bachelor from the East Coast whom I called "Hippo," was nevertheless successful in exciting a group of kids when he took pictures with his digital camera and then showed them to the children. He got so carried away that at one point – I could not believe my eyes – he opened the top buttons of his shirt and displayed the big red scars on his chest. He tried to explain to the Samburus that they were scars from a triple bypass. I do not think they understood. Maybe they thought a wildcat had scratched him.

January 22, 2015 – Cancún – As I review my manuscript, I simply must interject a description of what I just experienced in the lobby of Sunset Lagoon, a hub for Internet users where I have chatted with guests from around the globe, even Lebanon. Believe it or not, I met a French Canadian in her forties who spends a great portion of each year with her husband in Kenya. How exciting! Outside of Nairobi, this couple, while on safari in the Serengeti, "fell in love" with a group of children. They decided to use their reserves to build a school "with a roof" for the youngsters. They started with thirty-five students, and now, thanks to private donations and modest government assistance, they have 150 students, eager to learn. They attend this school through grade 8. Recently they hired a young woman to teach. Her records looked excellent. Not being able to pay very much, they asked her how much she expected to be paid. She answered, "Right now I have nothing, so whatever you can pay me is better."

The Samburu Serena Lodge, on the banks of the Uaso Nyiro River and adjacent to the Samburu Game Reserve, was much more to my liking than the Norfolk. I fell in love at first sight with the serene and scenic African ambiance of the lodge, the lush purple bougainvillea bushes and other vibrant flowers bordering the private veranda of my thatched-roof cabin, made of exotic African woods. In short, it put me even more in the adventurous mood for a safari. This place turned out to be even more exciting than the safari in Botswana. I found myself in a state of constant excitement during the game drive in the late afternoon and before sunset. The colors of the animals were much more vivid than in the morning. Thus, the stately group of giraffes, big elephants with their babies, the zebras, ostriches, gazelles, impalas, gerenuks, antelopes, buffaloes, baboon troops, waterbucks, and the many, many cute and tiny dik-diks all looked amazingly healthy as they leaped past us or grazed peacefully in the semiarid plains covered with scrub and thornbushes. But then there were the humongous and brutally scary crocodiles crawling toward us from the brown, muddy water of the Ewaso Nyiro River. No, they did not bite us.

I wondered whether any of those graceful gazelles, impalas, or dik-diks had ended up on the huge, circular Maasai barbecue which greeted us as we entered the famous Carnivore, a restaurant several miles outside of Nairobi. Huge spits of meat on Maasai spears roasted gently on burning coals. This all-you-can-eat restaurant boasted some twenty varieties of meat, such as giraffe, waterbuck, hartebeest, zebra, ostrich, beef, lamb, pork, and so on. To feast at this out-of-the-ordinary, open-air place was a unique safari adventure, which I had not anticipated but was game to try out. Each guest was provided a flag at his or her seat. As soon as I moved the flag into an upright position, the waiter appeared with a Maasai spear full of a variety of game meat from which I could select as much as I wished. He was a server and sliced the meat exactly – and exactly as thin – as I wished. At the end of the meal, I decided the slice of zebra meat was tastier than the others, including the dik-dik. After finishing my zebra, I laid the flag flat on the table to indicate I had had enough.

Maasai Mara Game Reserve

Our chartered plane was just big enough to hold our group of twelve. It awaited us at a small airport somewhere out in never-never land, outside of Nairobi, not at all my favorite city. – I eyed the small plane with a bit of suspicion. But no need to worry. Once in the air, I was fascinated by the vastness of the Maasai Mara, Kenya's seven hundred square miles of premier wildlife refuge, at the northern tip of the great Serengeti Plains. The area was spotted or peppered with acacia trees, and as *mara* means "mottled" in the Maasai language, the refuge is aptly named. The pilot flew low and tipped the plane on occasion so we could admire ostriches with long pink necks strutting through the bush, a couple of lions taking a siesta with all four of their legs stretched out and in plain view, two black vultures perched high in the top branches of a dried-out tree waiting to feast on a carcass, a coyote lying in wait not far away, and a fierce lion and lioness tearing into their victim, a poor impala, a bloody mess. Unfortunately, we did not see a sign of the thousands of wildebeest that migrate here in June and July to spend the dry season. We were too late, but I got a good idea of what it would have been like when watching a documentary on TV back home.

The plane dropped us off in the center of the Maasai Mara Reserve, where we were greeted and driven to our lodgings, the Mara Intrepids Camp along the Talek River, described in our guide as follows: "This Deluxe safari camp is the top choice of many a sheik, movie star, and royal-family member. Lavish accommodations are furnished with oriental carpets, Lamu (Kenya's oldest town on an island off the coast) chests, canopied beds, and private baths with shower. Each 'guest room' is actually a large walk-in canvas tent, built over a man-made floor; outside, there's a canopied 'porch,' with table, chairs, and lantern. Tent windows are fully screened." They forgot to mention the double zippers at the entrance and around the floor. You can imagine what the outdoors restaurant and the service were like. All of it blew my mind. I so appreciated the waiter's serving a pot of hot tea in my tent very early in the morning, before the game drive.

I will always remember this elaborate opening to our Maasai Mara safari, together with what was to follow, as a truly climactic experience!

If I had thought we saw a whole lot of game at the Samburu Serena Lodge, I discovered quickly that I had been mistaken. The safari drives at the Maasai Mara put all previous visits to shame. We watched herds of African elephants, giraffes, and zebras roam the rolling savanna, as well as buffaloes, wildebeests, hartebeests, impalas, and gazelles. Silver-backed jackals and hyenas crossed our path, not to mention different species of birds, too many to list. The black-and-white secretary bird seemed weird, and I had never before seen a giant black ground hornbill either. It resembled a turkey. I have a nice shot of a lilac-breasted roller in my album and several pages of sensational photos of lions. Once, we watched six or seven fat cats lying in wait in a big circle, ready to kill a zebra. On another drive, all twelve of us stood in utter silence for some twenty minutes watching a couple of lions mate. How could we be so lucky? We saw oodles of hippos in the brown Mara River. Actually, I would have preferred to see a cheetah or leopard up close rather than hiding in the bushes.

One day on our game drive, we were surprised by a picnic lunch in the bush. Rather unique and very nice! No disturbances by vultures or lions or such.

Each of the three days we spent in this extraordinary safari camp concluded with a late-afternoon game drive. The drives ended with a stop to observe a safari sunset, each of which was more beautiful than the next. Perhaps the most glorious and best-captured sunset in my photographs was the last. The setting sun painted the sky, in which remnants of fluffy clouds drifted by, ever so masterfully. It was a symphony of colors: yellow, orange, purple, lilac, pink, white, and blue, set off against the black silhouette of a canopy of acacia trees. I was overcome by a feeling of space and infinity.

The next day, I was definitely in the mood for a visit to the home of Danish writer Karen Blixen (Isak Dinesen), located at the foot of the smoky Ngon Hills, where she immortalized the farm in her book *Out of Africa*, and where she lived from 1914 to 1931. I had not expected the grounds that led up to the big house, with its red tile roof and veranda, to be so strikingly beautiful. Tall cypress and eucalyptus trees contrasted well with lush bougainvillea and other blooming tropical shrubs. The rooms inside were spacious and light. Mahogany wood paneling, paned glass windows with lace curtains, and tastefully selected period furniture projected an inviting ambiance. I could have stayed here for a while. Thanks to the Danish government for giving this landmark to Kenya upon its independence.

The visit to the Langata Giraffe Center in the town of Karen, named for Blixen, gave us an opportunity to observe from up close a bunch of rare Rothschild's giraffes, which were reared from five orphaned giraffes by the donors Jock and Betty Leslie-Melville, who purchased this property in 1974. For me, it lacked the excitement of searching for giraffes in the bush. –

On the way to the airport, we were given a very brief glimpse of Nairobi, which contrasted amazingly with what we witnessed upon arriving. I began to understand why Nairobi, aka "the City of the Sun," has a reputation as "Africa's most cosmopolitan and sophisticated capital." The high-rise office buildings and elegant boutiques are testimony to it. I would have liked to see more of it before heading north to the next stop on my African odyssey: Luxor, Egypt.

EGYPT

Luxor

Luxor is located in Upper (or Southern) Egypt and is the capital of Luxor Governorate. It is located on the site of ancient Thebes, which was called "the hundred-gated city" by Homer, the great Greek poet, and was the place where many festivals were held. The Arabs, impressed by its many beautiful palaces and imposing edifices, called it Luxor, meaning "city of palaces." The modern town of Luxor, along with its ancient temples, where the priests prayed to their gods, lies along the east bank of the Nile ("the City of the Living," where the life-giving sun rises). On the west bank of the river ("the City of the Dead," where the sun bids farewell to life) are the tombs of the pharaohs and their funerary temples. – During our visit to Luxor, no mention was made of the Luxor massacre on November 11, 1997, when sixty-two tourists, including seven Germans, were killed at the Deir el-Bahari, an archeological site across the Nile River from Luxor.

Visiting the Temple of Luxor, built by the pharaohs Amenhotep III and Ramses II, seemed like a field trip long overdue from the time I studied fine arts in Aix-en-Provence with the renowned Professor Dr. Dr. Bourde, a course of study that resulted in a trip to Athens, Greece. Egyptian art antedates Greek art, and I was finally in Egypt to make the connection. I understood fully why André Bourde became so excited when talking about Egyptian temples and their treasures. The Temple of Luxor was dedicated to Amun-Ra, whose marriage to Mut was celebrated annually, when the sacred procession moved by boat from Karnak to the Temple of Luxor. To be there in person was so overwhelming that I was in a state of "culture shock," if you wish. I walked slowly and silently past the gigantic pharaonic stone monuments, which were carved out of sandstone from Gebel el-Silsila, a region in Southwestern Egypt. I paused often, gazing upwards at the magnificent pylons flanking an entranceway and looking in awe up at the powerful columns and monoliths and the gigantic seated or standing statues of pharaohs carved out of stone. I gazed in wonderment at the Doric, Corinthian, and Ionic capitals and realized how the Greeks had refined them at their Acropolis in Athens. I was excited to finally see the huge scarab – Ra, the sun god, chiseled out of red granite – of which I had seen a live replica when visiting Victoria Falls earlier.

Karnak

When we explored the huge complex of shrines at Karnak – which the ancient Egyptians called "the most perfect of places," and which today is considered one of the most fascinating sites in Egypt – and saw the tallest obelisk (one hundred feet high) in Egypt in the impressive Hall of Pillars, erected by Queen Hatshepsut in honor of Amun, the god of fertility and growth, I was elated.

The Nile

We had embarked on our ship to cruise the Nile in the forenoon. During the night, I had trouble sleeping, and only after listening, forever it seemed, to the rather loud and wailing sounds of the Muslims' chants, customary at Ramadan, did I doze off. The cruise proceeded to the west bank of the Nile, the hilly area that was the Necropolis of Thebes, where we visited Queen Hatshepsut's ever-so-beautiful funerary temple before continuing to the Valley of the Kings, with its many tombs chiseled deep into the cliffsides. It is the place where Howard Carter discovered the treasures of Tutankhamen, some of which I had seen years before at a special exhibit at the Art Institute of Chicago. We set about to explore the tomb of Ramses, containing some of the best-preserved and most colorful hieroglyphs, with scenes from the reigns of Amenhotep III and Akhenaten.

We stopped at the pair of massive statues of Amenhotep, known as the Colossi of Memnon. They are the only remnant of a temple dedicated to Amenhotep III. It was assumed that an earthquake destroyed the temple. We were told the resulting cracks in the statues cause them to "sing" when the wind blows. I listened in vain.

Edfu

The ship sailed to Edfu through the Esna lock, which went rather smoothly. I welcomed the possibility of seeing the rural countryside, dotted with agricultural villages. Villagers did their laundry at the river's edge, and now and then children waved at us. The most fertile land in Egypt, a few miles wide, is found along the Nile. Behind it lies nothing but the desert. I had a somewhat disturbing conversation with a medical doctor who specialized in tropical diseases. He told me he had encountered the starkest poverty worldwide in Egypt.

We walked through the blistering sun toward the Ptolemaic Temple of Edfu, dedicated to Horus, the falcon-headed god of the sun and the planets, known as Egypt's best-preserved temple. The temple's vivid hieroglyphs and bas-reliefs were very imposing. They describe offerings to the gods. Thirty-eight columns surround the court, and a fine statue of Horus stands guard over the entry. We did walk to the dark inner recesses of the offering chambers, and I personally welcomed the shade.

The Kom Ombo Temple sits high on a hill overlooking a bend in the Nile. This Greco-Roman-style temple is unique, as it is Egypt's only double temple – dedicated to Sobek, the crocodile god, and Horus, the great winged solar disk. Everything is doubled and symmetrical along the main axis – twin entrances, twin courts, twin colonnades. It was the last stop along the Nile before we docked in Aswan.

Abu Simbel

I will forever be glad to have opted for an extra temple excursion, a short plane ride to the overpowering and massive Abu Simbel temples, south of Aswan on the west bank of the Nile in the land of Nubia near the Sudanese border. They were rediscovered in 1813. When the construction of the Aswan High Dam started in the 60s, and the rising waters of Lake Nasser threatened to flood the temples, UNESCO and the Egyptian government disassembled both temples and reconstructed them on top of the cliff, twenty feet above the original site. It was an achievement of historic proportions. The colossal monuments and seated statutes, which greet you from a considerable distance, were carved into solid rock three thousand years ago. The temple was built by the great pharaoh Ramses II as a tribute to the deities and his favorite wife, Nefertari. Four colossal statues, sixty feet high and directly facing the rising sun, are of the pharaoh himself, with his queen and daughters at his feet. More tremendous statues surround you as you enter the temple. And in the very depths of the temple, Ramses sits in state, flanked by the gods to whom the construction is dedicated. This temple trumped all those we had visited before. No words can describe it – *sublime*?

It was nice to see the Aswan High Dam, built in 1971, which created Lake Nasser, the Aswan Low Dam, built by the British in 1902, the lovely Temple of Isis, perched majestically on Philae Island, and the ancient granite quarries with their tall, unfinished obelisk. It was great to sail in a traditional felucca boat around Elephantine Island, where we had fabulous views of a fine example of Fatimid architecture, the Mausoleum of Aga Khan, the great Ismaili Muslim leader, which dominated the skyline of Aswan's west bank. Despite a gorgeous sunset on Lake Nasser, it all seemed for a while a tad anticlimactic – until we arrived in Cairo and set our sights on a visit to the Museum of Egyptian Antiquities, followed by an excursion to the Great Sphinx of Giza and the Giza pyramids, which the Greeks proclaimed to be among the seven wonders of the ancient world.

Cairo

I had looked forward to the visit to the Museum of Egyptian Antiquities with great anticipation and could hardly wait to enter the famed place, which seemed almost like a sanctuary to me. As is often the case when visiting museums, there was not enough time. Nevertheless, it is well worth the effort to see some of their most renowned exhibits and take a stroll through the halls highlighting each historical period. It goes without saying that the treasures of King Tutankhamen, unparalleled in variety, exquisite beauty, and sheer weight in gold, are indescribable. Seeing this treasure, consisting of more than 1,700 items buried with a young and relatively unimportant king, it is hard to imagine what the tombs of great and long-lived pharaohs must have contained.

I lack the words to adequately describe the many treasures displayed in the various chambers. I felt mesmerized by the most overwhelming piece of all, King Tutankhamen's famous burial mask. It was a profusion of gold and ebony. Once you have seen it in person, you'll never forget it. It's the same with the pyramids and the Great Sphinx of Giza.

July 8, 2013 – It is hard to believe that since my visit to Egypt, the Arab Spring has taken place and the democratically elected President Morsi has been ousted, little more than a year after his election. Cairo, Egypt's capital, with a population of over sixteen million and one of the biggest cities in Africa and the Middle East, which at the time of my visit showed no sign of turmoil on Tahrir Square or elsewhere, is today a place of protests and bloodshed. The world anxiously awaits the outcome . . .

The largest of three pyramids on the Giza Plateau is the Pyramid of Cheops, built probably more than two thousand years before Christ and standing 450 feet high. It is the only one of the seven wonders of the ancient world that remains intact. It was exhilarating and almost miraculous to stand next to the pyramid. When you look at the pyramids in pictures, the surfaces always look so smooth, as they must have looked originally, when they were enclosed in the marble which has since eroded and deteriorated. Today, the surface of the stones is coarse and brittle. But an up-close look will give an idea of the extraordinary labor and skills it took to construct these masterpieces. A total of 2,300,000 blocks of stone, each weighing two and a half tons, had to be transferred from Aswan and Tusa, but scholars still debate exactly how the Egyptians constructed this gigantic tomb.

More easily resolved is the "construction" of the inscrutable Great Sphinx of Giza, known in Arabic as Abu Al-Hol (Father of Terror). This reclining lion with a human head was carved almost entirely from one piece of limestone bedrock and is considered the first colossal royal sculpture. Viewing it was another sacred moment; I drifted away from the crowd to just sit, reflect, and contemplate how it was possible for me to be in the presence of this miracle, which has inspired and will continue to inspire so many artists and poets and all of mankind – indefinitely.

Saqqara is a pyramid complex, an immense necropolis west of the ancient city of Memphis. There, we focused on the stepped pyramid built by the engineer Imhotep for King Zoser. It is composed of six receding *mastabas* (levels or steps) placed on top of each other and is important insofar as the later pyramid builders adapted this concept to create the familiar even-sided pyramids. In Memphis, the oldest capital of Egypt, built by King Menes, we viewed another colossal statue of Ramses II in the museum. It is considered the most beautiful representation of the great

Egypt

pharaoh, made from fine-grained limestone, nearly thirty feet long and weighing 120 tons.

It was time to bid the Ramses II statues, and my cotravelers, farewell. Four weeks is a rather long time to spend with twelve people. I had given each one of them a secret name taken from the animals: elephant, zebra, gazelle, giraffe, lion, etc. – While cruising the Nile, we were asked on one occasion to dress like Muslim women and wear a hijab, which I thought ridiculous. I remember feeling extremely depressed at the sight of myself in the mirror and almost broke out in tears, which is so unlike me. I found out it was most likely a side effect of Malarone, the antimalaria medication. From that point on, I was careful to avoid that "poison" and asked for a substitute whenever I traveled to Africa.

While waiting at the Cairo airport for our flight home, scheduled to leave around 1:00 a.m., I chose to distance myself from my American cotravelers. I bought a pretty crystal-ball pendant, which sparkled like a diamond, for $12 at a souvenir shop, sat down next to a Muslim, and chatted with him in English about the 9/11 attack. He was convinced the Bush administration had engineered the incident in order to have an excuse to go to war against Iraq and oust Saddam Hussein. It was the first time I had heard of this controversial theory, which was making the rounds even in the States in the years following the attack.

NAMIBIA – FLYING SAFARI

If someone had told me during my first safari trip that I would return seven years later to Namibia, Africa, I would have thought they were delusional. Yet, sure enough – after having listened to several of my serious globe-trekker friends, especially my exuberant and widely traveled Italian friend Marco, whom I met on a trip along the Norwegian coast with Hurtigruten Cruises and who had not yet been there but had it high on his list, and after having seen plenty of documentaries and photos – I took the bait. Early in June 2007, I signed up with Nature Expeditions International for a comparatively brief, yet costly, flying safari to Namibia for October 4–15, 2007, without my Italian friend.

Just as my first trip to South America, in 1979, started out with major travel mishaps, this trip to Namibia, which started in Indianapolis and ended, after changes in Atlanta and Johannesburg, in the Namibian capital of Windhoek, situated in the center of the country, kept me in a panic for about two days.

For those who do not know where the Republic of Namibia is located, I quote from my travel documents: "It is in Southern Africa, the western border is the Atlantic Ocean, Botswana and Zimbabwe are to the East and South Africa is south. It is a country of stark contrasts, with two great deserts: the Namib (after which it is named) is the oldest desert on the planet, and its sea of red sand runs along the entire Atlantic coastline, while the Kalahari, in the eastern interior, is a vast and sparsely vegetated savannah that sprawls across the border into neighboring countries. In between lies the Central Plateau, with open plans and rugged mountains. It is the fifth largest country in Africa with a population of around 2.5 million people. Poverty is widespread with earnings of $1.25 a day and 15% of the adult population is infected with HIV. Namibia is dominated by desert and low rainfall, but it does have perennial rivers – the Zambezi, Kwando, Okavango, Kunene and Orange – which also constitute the political borders with its neighbors. It also has a multitude of ephemeral rivers, which can remain dry for many years and then turn into raging torrents in a matter of minutes. Namibia has passed through several distinct stages from being colonized in 1884 by the Germans until its independence March 21, 1990."

Having been born in Germany, I was embarrassed, as often on my trips to places where my forefathers had committed barbaric deeds, to discover that here too the Germans practiced genocide, eliminating between 60% and 80% of the native population. Indeed, it is believed these deeds may have influenced Nazi plans to conquer and settle Eastern Europe and may have been a precursor to Nazi colonialism and genocide. –

Windhoek

I had no choice but to change planes in Johannesburg – not exactly my favorite city, if you recall. Further, I had no choice but to spend a night at Pretoria, the airport hotel, because my flight to Windhoek had just taken off. – At 6:00 the next morning, I had to report back to the airline counter to pick up the rerouted tickets. They subjected me to a two-hour runaround that brought me to the verge of a breakdown – no kidding. Finally, at the very last minute, thanks to a helpful airline assistant who interceded to keep the gate open and after paying for a new ticket in full, I boarded the plane to Windhoek, where I landed one day late and, to top it off, without my luggage. The missing travel bag contained all of the allowed twenty-six pounds of safari gear. I was not happy when they told me at the hotel that it was not at all uncommon for tourists to arrive without their luggage from Johannesburg, where it was frequently either stolen or lost. Since I arrived on a Saturday, when the stores were closed, and the flying safari was to start the next morning, I wandered restlessly to and from my gorgeous room at the famous Heinitzburg, a castle built by some lovestruck count for his fiancée at the highest point in Windhoek, overlooking the Khomas Highlands, and converted into a state-of-the-art hotel with an African and European ambiance. I loved the four-poster bed. It took a footstool for me to climb into it. I had booked a two-night stay, of which I lost the first night as a result of my missed flight. I was unable to enjoy the second because I was worried about my luggage.

My guide picked me up at the Heinitzburg after a siesta and gave me a tour of the city, which reflected a strong German influence – very different from the architecture I had seen in either Johannesburg or Cape Town. He took me to the two contrasting suburbs, Ludwigsdorf and Katutura, to illustrate the difference between the higher- and lower-income classes of Windhoek. At Penduka, in Katutura, women produce and sell crafts, which were generously displayed. My tour guide also took me to the open market. Since it was Saturday afternoon, few people were shopping and many of the meat and poultry counters, a hangout for swarming flies, were almost empty. I recall a big smoked head of an ox or such lying on the table, flanked by two of its legs, with hooves on each side. I wondered what they might do with it. I am sure the Heinitzburg would not serve it at its fancy tables. Of course, you never know.

Somehow I could not get excited about any of the government buildings, the rather manicured parks and nice flowering bushes, or even my favorite jacaranda trees or a church, the interior of which I opted out of seeing. I barely glanced at the souvenirs (and did not buy a single one) at the Art Gallery shop, which was about to close anyhow. My lost luggage was constantly on my mind, even after returning to the hotel, where I pestered reception to keep calling to check for my bag. Seldom in my life have I been as relieved as I was when at 8:00 p.m., reception called to announce that my bag had arrived. It was a bit like the time I went to Peru and my suitcase was lost, only to show up waiting for me in the middle of the hall of the check-in counters at the airport in Lima. While I was eventually reimbursed for the new plane ticket I had to purchase, nobody was inclined to reimburse me for the night I lost at the Heinitzburg. That was not cheap.

Sossusvlei

I was happy that the guide picked me up the next morning to take me to the special small-planes airport and was even happier once I got on the plane, which had enough space for eight people. Only five were in the group, and everybody was satisfied. My window seat was perfect, especially for taking pictures. Michelle, twenty-four years old, multilingual, and rather pretty, was our designated pilot. I liked her right away. When we flew over the Namib Desert toward the Sossusvlei Wilderness Camp, it quickly became clear that she knew her stuff. Sossusvlei is one of the most remarkable sites in the Namib-Naukluft Park and the Namib Desert. The camp is built on a small mountain, and the views of the hyperarid gravel plains and dunes below were both serene and dramatic. I was reminded of similar plains in Mongolia, which after Namibia is the least populous country in the world. I was not surprised that the area where we stayed had been used to shoot many films.

A young man holding a pile of washcloths, which we used to refresh ourselves, greeted us at the entrance path of the lodge. Each of us was led to our en suite chalet, built from local rock and timber, covered with a thatched roof, and recessed into the face of the hill. These chalets were just beautiful. They were spacious, with a huge windowfront and a deck from which to view the plains, where wild horses grazed and sunsets of extraordinary beauty amazed us. Next to the unit, in the shade, was a plunge pool to cool off in when the heat was sizzling. That was not the case during our stay. Instead, as was the case during my trip to Mongolia, it got freezing cold at night, and had it not been for a heater and ample covers, I could not have slept.

Soon after our arrival, and after a refreshing lunch in an outdoor restaurant with a thatched roof, we climbed into our open-air four-wheeler safari vehicle to look for game and were rewarded quickly with a small herd of white rhinos and a bunch of zebras, elephants, and oryxes, but no lions. Especially nice was a late-afternoon picnic they set up on a plateau overlooking the plains, with golden-brown dunes on the horizon. It was close to a water hole where several species of waterfowl came to drink. When the sun began to set, we all stood in silence and drank in the awe-inspiring atmosphere. Another everlasting safari moment!

I could hardly wait to see the towering, beautifully sculpted red sand dunes, perhaps the highest in the world, which rise dramatically over one thousand feet above the surrounding plains. Their continually changing hues are highly captivating and attract photographers from around the world. I had signed up for a hot-air-balloon ride, which due to too-strong winds had to be canceled. Thanks to my driver, I was able to catch up with the others in time to take in the spectacular red dunes, the foremost reason for my return to Africa for a third time. I had been longing to see and photograph the remarkable Big Daddy and Big Momma, considered the oldest and highest dunes in the world. I was in a state of immeasurable ecstasy. Our guide gave a demonstration by picking up a spider in the sand and then putting it down again. As it ran uphill it formed many symmetrical ripples in the sand. Marvelous! – Unfortunately there was not enough time for me to climb Big Daddy. I did not even try – and I am sorry I cannot describe the experience here. However, I did climb a less challenging dune on the way to the white vlei (salt pan), with its intriguing petrified trees at the end of the Tsauchab River, a dry riverbed where water flows only in years of exceptional rainfall. It is another favorite site for photographers. The leafless trees on the white salt pan stand like pieces of sculpture, with a blue sky and red dunes in the background. Each one was different and unique and just fascinating.

These barren trees contrasted sharply with the baobab, or tree of life, that we saw on the way to our outdoor picnic. We were puzzled that this huge tree full of green leaves could survive in the middle of the desert, without a drop of water in sight. They had built a fence around it so no one could touch it. – The big acacia trees under which they had set up tables for an outdoor lunch provided ample shade for our small group, and we enjoyed the break immensely. Speaking of trees, I must not forget to mention the many trees in which massive nests, which resembled thick, thatched roofs and were constructed by hundreds of social weavers (small, like sparrows), hung and provided shelter for them, that is, protection against the midday heat and the freezing temperatures at night. – Quite clever, yet bizarre, I must say. We ended the day with a stop at a third geological phenomenon and a popular attraction of Namibia: the Sesriem Canyon, which is one hundred feet deep and one kilometer long. The Tsauchab River has carved it into the sedimentary rock for over two million years. I skipped the climb down into the canyon, which looked a bit challenging to me. My guide took a few pictures with my Sony so I would know what I missed. Somehow he found in that arid terrain a pretty white blooming flower, the name of which he did not know.

Swakopmund

The following morning we had a chance to admire the dunes from our plane, which flew intentionally low on the way to the coastal city of Swakopmund (from the German for "mouth of the Swakop"). We had an outstanding view of the skeleton coast, where here and there lay a stranded ship, completely or partially stuck in the sand and badly rusting. – Namibia has established 6,200 miles of the coast as Skeleton Coast National Park. – One cannot help but wonder what became of the prospectors who came this far to look for diamonds and gold, only to be stranded in a place where nothing but endless desert plains confronted them, leaving them with two choices: to drown in the sea or die of thirst in the desert. No wonder the survival rate of those stranded here was low.

Our plane landed in Walvis Bay (Whale Bay), at a smaller airport serving this deep-sea harbor town in the Erongo region of Namibia. Four-wheelers picked us up and drove us to Swakopmund, the premier southwestern holiday resort with a population of some thirty thousand, which gained its importance as a harbor during the German colonial era, beginning in 1892, when Walvis Bay was still under British control. We did not spend much time in this town, which reeked of German influence. I felt strange when I noticed the German names for buildings and palm-lined streets. The architecture was Wilhelminian and similar to Victorian. The customers in some of the upscale souvenir shops appeared to be very well-to-do. And it struck me as curious that all the salespersons spoke German perfectly. I began to understand why so many Germans like to come to Namibia. Considering the history, I personally felt a tad uncomfortable. The old feeling of collective guilt crept up again. – I purchased several ostrich eggs with artistic designs to take home, just in time to hop on the jeep to return to Walvis Bay and take a ride on a speedboat to go dolphin, sea lion, and pelican viewing, which is always exciting. We saw massive colonies of sea lions, thousands I swear, some of which jumped on our boat and were very wet and slick and sassy. They jumped off after having been fed a fish by the captain. Our boat was almost invaded by pelicans, and dolphins leaped incessantly alongside; finally, I succeeded in catching one on camera as it leaped close to where I sat. It was sheer luck. Others were disappointed because they missed and missed and missed. A more or less eerie sight was a big, ugly, rusting shipwreck stuck in the same bay. It was covered solid – up to the masts – with white birds, seagulls I believe.

It was a fun boat ride, and very refreshing, and it put us all in the right frame of mind for what was to follow: after having driven for a while, our driver asked us to close our eyes, which we did. We felt the jeep was negotiating rugged terrain, which went somehow downhill. The driver stopped, and we were asked to open our eyes. And voilà! The suspense ended: close to the sandy and stony beach of the Atlantic stood an elegant, large, tan-colored tent. Tables with white linen tablecloths and chairs with vinyl seat covers were set up. The crystal champagne glasses, white porcelain dinner plates, and silverware looked so inviting. Three waiters brought some of the tastiest food I had ever been served, starting with the best and freshest oysters I had ever tasted. They came directly out of the Atlantic – from Walvis Bay, right beside us. And they are justifiably famous! Don't forget the champagne. Delicious fish and meat dishes followed, and we all agreed the meal was fit for a king.

We were still a bit tipsy, I think, when Michelle called for us to take a pit stop at the little outhouse, set up close to the ocean. The walls reached up to my waist, but it was at the same time functional and amusing. Once we arrived at the airport, things got a bit hectic and scary. The winds were picking up, and sand clouds started forming. Michelle hurried us into her little Cessna, and off we went into the sky. I sat next to her and had the privilege of seeing whatever my pilot saw. I had enjoyed a similar experience a few years earlier in Patagonia. The difference was that here, there was sand and lots of it, which slowly blurred and almost eliminated visibility. If during our morning flight I could marvel at the endless desert and the mesmerizing dunes – more irregularly sculpted and not as red as the dunes in Sossusvlei – on this flight, they were becoming increasingly invisible. Boy, what if we crashed, like Saint-Exupéry in his *Le petit prince*?! There were no baobab trees out there. – Not to worry. Michelle set us down smoothly at Damaraland Camp, located on the north face of the Huab River Valley, fifty-five miles inland from Torra Bayon, on the Skeleton Coast. Throughout the flight no one made a peep, and everyone sighed with relief when we landed. Only then did Michelle announce, somewhat proudly and with a smile, that she had flown without instruments, just following her nose and her memory of previous flights. Mind you, for quite a stretch we flew alongside a rugged mountain range, which we could barely see. So much for that!

Damaraland Camp, an award-winning ecotourism accommodation, afforded us endless vistas: stark plains, ancient valleys, and soaring peaks. Just the kind of breathtaking panorama I liked. The tented rooms with en suite facilities and a front porch left nothing wanting. I found quite unique and intriguing the shower room, which featured open-faced rocks under an open sky and could be reached from the suite. Better to shower when the sun was still out, unless you wanted to freeze. – At night, the walks leading to the dining area under the stars were lit with lanterns. Indeed, lanterns were all around, creating a very warm, cozy, and romantic atmosphere. – One evening, the dining area had been transferred to a place under the stars, which required a ten-minute walk along paths also lit by many lanterns on the ground. Together with the entertainment, it was again an event one could not easily forget. Neither would I ever forget the many (but rare) desert elephants, black rhinoceri, oryxes, springboks, and other species we encountered on our various game drives into the Huab River system. Nor could I forget the Stone Age petroglyphs and paintings carved into the local sandstone by San hunters up to six thousand years ago at Twyfelfontein.

On the way to Twyfelfontein, we stopped briefly at a village somewhere in the middle of the desert, in a place where a bunch of trees were growing and a dried-up riverbed most likely provided some water when it rained. This village consisted of a handful of shacks and a round well. We did not see a single human being, only three or four elephants in the distance. – Later, back at the lodge, while relaxing on a comfortable rattan couch next to a large, low table on which a big, round basket filled with a dozen white ostrich eggs rested, I had an interesting conversation with our guide about life in his village. I found it hard to believe that they had received electrical power in their humble abode for the first time only a couple of weeks earlier. They had no school in their village, and if children were taken to school at all, they had to be transported by jeep – an hour or more away.

Etosha National Park

If you think each safari stop cannot be trumped, you are wrong. The flight to Ongava Lodge/Tented Camps, situated on a private, thirty-thousand-hectare reserve that borders Etosha National Park to the south, was short and nice, if you like to fly, as I do. Etosha is Namibia's premier wildlife park. And if you think they are kidding when they advertise that one will find "large concentrations of elephant, lion, leopard, black rhino, white rhino, springbok, gemsbok, and hartebeest and lions," you are wrong. We saw all of those and in addition plenty of bird life, such as ostrich, pygmy falcon, short-toed rock thrush, Hartlaub's francolin, freckled nightjar, and Meyer's parrot, to mention a few.

The game experience at Etosha National Park was overwhelming, even for me – I had thought Maasai Mara had a most impressive collection of game. What was so striking at Etosha was seeing herds of elephants, giraffes, zebras, wildebeests, oryxes, and other animals gather at the various water holes located here and there on the salt pans. It is so addictive; you cannot tear yourself away from the sight of so many different species of game animals drinking peacefully and gracefully side by side. This too was an experience of a lifetime.

Here we saw more rhinos than lions, which surprised me, because each night on the way to dinner, served underneath a canvas but close to another water hole, we had to notify our hosts to send a guard to pick us up and accompany us to the dinner table. He came with a gun, because lions were known to wander around the camp, especially at night. We waited for hours one evening for the lions roaring in the distance to come to the water hole, but in vain. No show while I was there. I was not too disappointed, since I had seen many lions in action at Maasai Mara. My only disappointment was that we saw no cheetahs.

Michelle flew us back to Windhoek without any problems, and we all thanked her sincerely before taking off in different directions. I personally returned to the Heinitzburg. My flight back to the States was leaving the next day. Great! I finally had a chance to enjoy not only their cuisine, but the beautiful grounds bursting with bright-red flowering bougainvillea, purple-blue blooming jacarandas next to a variety of palm trees, the swimming pool, splashing fountains, multicolored crawling salamanders, a tall and slender Afrikaans chambermaid balancing a basket of white linens on her head, always smiling, the amazing views of the landscape below and all around, and most of all, the spectacular sunset in the evening, which once more transported me into another realm! All in all, I could not have imagined a more perfect farewell from Africa.

ANTARCTICA, BY WAY OF ARGENTINA – MS MARCO POLO

Argentina

Buenos Aires

On February 27, 2003, I took off on a journey to another extreme climate: Antarctica. I decided to include a stop at Iguazú Falls, since I would be in the vicinity. I had to go by way of Buenos Aires, which is the major hub for anything that goes south or even to neighboring Chile. In that "Paris of South America," I filled in a few gaps left by my first visit, in 1979. After I had taken care of replacing a bunch of medicines and cosmetics, which I suddenly was unable to locate in my newly purchased backpack, I connected with the few people in my group who were sightseeing and found that not too much had changed in this beautiful city. I loved watching the pantomimes and tango dancers on the sidewalks of a narrow street where a big sign read "Centro Cultural de Los Artistas." It was attached to the facade of an old house with unsymmetrical squares, each painted different colors: pink, yellow, sky blue, cobalt blue, green, turquoise, burgundy, and so on. In a neighboring house with a rather dirty white facade, the words *Mujer = Hombre = Ser Humano* (Woman = Man = Human), printed in big red letters beneath the profile of a young woman, caught my eye and gave reason to reflect. – This more or less bohemian atmosphere stood in stark contrast to that of La Recoleta Cemetery, full of impressive mausoleums where such notables as Eva Peron and other rich and famous persons, such as the Duarte family, have been left to decay in style. Eva's husband is buried elsewhere. Using cemeteries, headstones, and mausoleums as status symbols is customary around the world. Think of the tombs of the pharaohs in Egypt or the more humble ones in Großförste, Germany, where my richer relatives went crazy with headstones.

While walking around Buenos Aires, I entered a small boutique where a pretty young girl greeted me with a smile. She was sipping maté with a silver metal straw from a hollow calabash gourd. I learned from her that yerba maté is an ancient tea-like drink dedicated to health and friendship, that it is made by steeping dried leaves of yerba maté in hot water, and that it is common in neighboring South American countries as well. They like to share this infused drink with others by just passing it around. She offered me a sip, and I gladly complied, smiling. It tasted very good. I ended up buying a silver straw and a maté gourd decorated with silver to take home. *Muchas gracias, señorita, and hasta luego, Buenos Aires.*

Iguazú Falls

Our Lan Airlines flight set down at Puerto Iguazú around noon, on the Argentinian side of the falls. Our four-star hotel was not far from the spectacle. Already, as we walked toward the falls through the lush flora, I got excited at the sight of my first toucan, with its orange beak, blue eyes, white chin feathers, and black wings, perched proudly in the canopy of a lush green tree. The sound of the thundering cataracts increased to a fortissimo as we came closer. And the continuously emerging clouds of spray could barely be avoided. But I did not mind the mist any more than I did when going for a ride on the *Maid of the Mist* at Niagara Falls. Once I could see the falls in their entirety, I was simply overwhelmed. The crescent-shaped falls were embedded in the most striking and luxurious vegetation on the planet. It is unquestionably one of the largest and most spectacular falls in the world, and definitely larger than Niagara and Victoria. – It is a network of 275 falls, one and a half miles wide and consisting of 450,000 gallons of water per second tumbling three hundred feet down into the Iguazú River. Sixty feet higher than Niagara, these falls are without question the most impressive in the world. The most dramatic – and somewhat frightening – fall is Devil's Throat, located at the border between Brazil and Argentina. You have to feel and hear the thunderous pounding of the water as it plunges into and crashes against the rocks and trees. – Yet, the rainbow at Victoria Falls easily trumped the one at Iguazú. – It was soothing to come upon white orchids and other colorful flora in this semijungle. And in the evening, another sublime sunset painted the sky a soft, purplish pink and was enhanced by the ethereal mists drifting up from the swirling pool of waters below. It was once more a farewell to my liking, and it ushered in what was to come.

Ushuaia – Port of World's End

We landed at Malvinas, Argentina's international airport, in the afternoon on February 8, 2003, in time to board the MS *Marco Polo*. It was a beautiful, sleek, 20,500-ton ship for 850 passengers, but as a result of environmental restrictions, only four hundred passengers were allowed on trips to Antarctica. That was probably the reason I had a hard time obtaining a green light to join the group. I found it very interesting to learn that Mathias-Thesen Werft, in East Germany, built this beauty as MS *Alexandr Pushkin* in 1965 for the Soviet Union's Baltic Sea Shipping Company. In 1993, Orient Lines took over and poured some $60 million into a major conversion project. The accommodations were excellent, and I was ecstatic to be a passenger on the cruise to Antarctica and the Chilean fjords. Several of my copassengers had traveled on the *Marco Polo* ten times or more.

After landing, we were transported directly to the ship, but on the way we got an idea of what Ushuaia, with a population of only 64,000, looked like. Once onboard, and after I had unpacked my suitcase and backpack, which miraculously produced the missing medicine and cosmetic bags, I headed for the deck. It was great to see the snowcapped Martial Mountains and a fleet of merchant ships, freighters, and yachts docked in the harbor and enhanced by the town behind. When the *Marco Polo* began to move and leave the harbor, the setting sun did his magic and draped the panorama with a pinkish veil.

Everybody onboard was a bit concerned when we headed toward the Drake Passage, named for the English navigator Sir Francis Drake. We had heard that this deep waterway, six hundred miles wide and comparatively narrow, is known as the roughest sea on earth. The Drake Passage is the strait between Cape Horn and the South Shetland Islands and connects the South Atlantic and the Pacific Oceans. The captain, a handsome young man from Norway, assured us that the ship, with its solid double hull, was fit to withstand any storm and break any thickness of ice. And sure enough, we sailed through the night completely intact and arrived in a timely manner at Deception Island (in the Shetlands). It was formed when seawater rushed into a volcanic crater. I declined the offer to go for a swim.

Antarctica

Cuverville Island

No, our vessel did not sail directly into the center of this restless volcano, but forged ahead toward Cuverville Island, where things got very exciting and intense. It was my first experience in a Zodiac inflatable boat, which took us to the desolate, dark, rocky island lying in the Errera Channel. A rookery of thousands of gentoo penguins covered the grounds. We were told to keep our distance. They were bigger than the penguins I had seen outside of Cape Town, but just as plentiful and equally smelly. But since everybody was enthralled to be entertained by the darlings, I too allowed myself to be enchanted for the duration of that stop, which was not really all that long. Much more exciting were the masses of glaciers and icebergs that floated past us or had to be avoided when we went exploring in our Zodiacs. The panoramas around us were exquisite, each one more so than the next. We were in Antarctica! It was freezing cold on deck, especially when the wind blew. But the sky was a solid blue, and the sun was shining. The red polar jackets, the woolen caps with eye and mouth slits, the thick socks, the high rubber boots, and the waterproof pants all came in handy. I wanted to be outside to take it all in. I did not know if I would ever be able to return to this magical landscape, which moved every fiber of my being. We all got excited whenever someone spotted a Weddell seal or an Antarctic fur seal floating on a piece of ice or navigating the freezing waters.

The ice magic continued, and it became even more glorious when the *Marco Polo* got the green light to enter the Lemair Channel. It is a steep-sided channel that is 5,250 feet wide and runs for seven miles between the mountains of Booth Island

and the Antarctic Peninsula. At times it is blocked by ice. We were lucky. And what an electrifying experience it was to see the majestic, snow-covered mountains all around us, set against a clear blue sky. We stood in silence. No words could describe what I felt. – The pictures I have in my album cannot do justice to what I felt when I took them.

Port Lockroy

After a three-to-four-hour stop at Port Lockroy, the British research station, now operated by the UK Antarctic Heritage Trust and containing the most southerly post office, where we had our passports stamped, mailed postcards, visited the museum, and chatted with a few stray penguins, we were off to Paradise Harbor, so called because of its serene ambiance. Some consider this harbor the most beautiful place in Antarctica. Our Zodiac trip was indeed exciting, because we got frighteningly close to the icebergs, some of enormous proportion. We were dazzled by their colors, shades of blue and green caused by refracted light. They were like sculptures floating gently across the glacial waters.

The scenic wonderland continued in the Neumayer Channel, between Anvers and Weincke Islands. On February 13, we stopped at Half Moon Island (in the South Shetland Islands), a minor Antarctic Island. Though I am not superstitious, the scariest moments in my life could easily have made me that way. The sea was rough, and the captain had advised us not to take a Zodiac to the island if we did not feel secure. Nevertheless, I was not afraid and looked forward to some excitement. I joined a group of the daring ones, and we were set ashore safely. The major attraction was a rookery of chinstrap penguins. By that time, I had seen plenty of these aquatic flightless birds (fish birds) but went along since it was the last opportunity to see them. Let's say I wanted to say good-bye to them and my beloved Antarctica.

The visit came to a rather abrupt halt. The sea had started dancing more wildly. The *Marco Polo*, docked in the harbor, was moving up and down. Dark clouds gathered on the horizon and above us. It started to rain sleet. Our Zodiac was rocking with the swells, and it took several attempts to steady it for each one of us to climb onboard. I went to the observation deck to observe our departure. While I stood up there and watched the island, the ship was suddenly heavily jolted. I was startled. The captain alarmed the mates and crew. We passengers looked at each other anxiously. Nobody knew what had caused this shock. Thoughts of the *Titanic* arose, and a certain feeling of helplessness overcame me. I smiled and joked a bit with my Belgian friends, with whom I conversed in French. The rather antiquated New Yorker socialite, always dressed like a million dollars, who used to have a prominent position at CBS and had called Dan Rather a prima donna when we discussed reporters at the dinner table, hurried to her cabin, and the senior bachelor from the Isle of Man, who had pestered me to dance with him and become his travel companion, was busy calming everybody. The *Marco Polo* was solid and could withstand any storm. Kathy, a slender pharmaceutical clerk from Wisconsin, a serious traveler, just smiled and was ready for any adventure. –

Little by little, the facts came out and were reported in their entirety. If you believed the captain, who had summoned us to the entertainment room, the instrument that measured obstructions on the sea floor had malfunctioned and the hull of the ship had hit a sharp rock that cut a seven-foot slit in the outer hull. Water was seeping in, but slowly enough to keep us from sinking. If serious danger persisted, they would transport us to somewhere in the Shetland Islands (I forget where exactly). The plan was changed an hour or so later, and we headed back to Ushuaia, where the *Marco Polo* was to dock for a couple of days while a repair crew flew in from Argentina and the United States. As a result, we would miss out on a couple of stops along the Chilean fjords, but we were offered a 40% discount on a future cruise. I was easily consoled and thought the captain deserved high praise for getting us out of the mess safely. Others were already contemplating a lawsuit. Later, I heard our captain had transferred to another cruise line. Too bad – I liked him.

Our ship docked around 9:00 a.m. in Ushuaia. The weather was perfect. Blue skies and sunshine welcomed us, and we were kept busy. At 10:00 a.m. we were to meet for our first consolation prize, a trip on a smaller vessel that sailed along the impressive shores of the Beagle Channel. It turned out to be a spectacular voyage. The Beagle Channel is the strait separating the islands of the Tierra del Fuego archipelago, at the southern extreme of South America. It is 150 miles long and three miles wide. We had the opportunity to admire a big colony of sea lions sunbathing on a stony beach and a rookery of gentoo penguins on another mount, as well as thousands of snowy sheathbills gathering on a rock; to please the lighthouse fanatics, we got a great photo opportunity at the famous Les Eclaireurs Lighthouse. And all of that was highlighted by the snow-covered mountain ranges that surrounded us.

After lunch, we finally had a chance to take a closer look at the picturesque and colorful town of Ushuaia. I combed the shops along the main street and bought a few souvenirs: little glass penguins, a few stuffed ones, and a large box of chocolate candy supposedly made in Ushuaia for my friend Cristian and his family in Santiago. The midday sun was so hot I began to perspire and decided to seek refuge on the ship. Nobody mentioned that Argentina had made this city a penal colony from 1884 to 1947, just as Australia had established penal colonies in the eighteenth and early nineteenth centuries.

Tierra del Fuego

Our second compensation was a bus trip to Tierra del Fuego National Park, about ten miles outside of Ushuaia. They wanted to give us a glimpse of nature's splendors in Patagonia, which is divided between Argentina and Chile. After all, two Patagonia land trips had to be canceled. The Tierra del Fuego National Park was on the

Argentinian side. And we were not disappointed. Much to the contrary – it was a splendid excursion into pristine territory.

We drove through lush forests, passed sparkling, sky-blue lakes framed by masses of tall lilac and yellow lupines, stopped to watch a Canadian beaver building a dam, and were amazed to see the enormous impact these imported critters have on the environment. Many fallen, decaying trees lay around. The beavers cut down the trees in order to build dams, which in turn cause flooding in other parts of the forest, where the trees then die in the excess of water. It's a vicious circle. At one point we got out of the bus and hiked on a narrow, rugged path through this rocky terrain until we reached a small log house near a crystal-clear lake. A huge pile of nicely cut firewood was next to it. We had already seen the smoke rising from the open barbeque pit near the log cabin. Four skinned and split calves were hanging over the fire, suspended by their hind legs from hooks in the roof covering the pit. It smelled so nice and reminded me of the barbeque I had when visiting Argentina in 1979. And it tasted just as good, tender and juicy. Nobody serves beef like the Argentinians. They are numero uno. We sat outside on benches near the lake and the clusters of lupines, soaking up the pristine Patagonian ambiance. I just loved it.

Chile

I also loved sailing in the Pacific, along the fjord-dotted Chilean coast, to Valparaiso, Chile, our next and final stop. Unfortunately, I had come down with a mild case of bronchitis that required a couple of visits to the ship's doctor, but it did not prevent me from observing what was going on along the sparsely inhabited coast. Channels, inlets, and straits dissected the region. Our captain navigated all of them with ease. Since the landscape consists predominantly of Andean mountain ranges, we enjoyed many photogenic panoramas accented with glaciers, waterfalls, and snowcapped peaks that one passenger compared to the fjords along the coast of Norway. He insisted that those in Norway were more dramatic. I was unable to argue the point but promised myself to check it out ASAP.

Santiago

We arrived early in Valparaiso, and my cold was gone! – The crew was anxious to transport us to Santiago. We drove past the old La Matriz Church in Valparaiso, dubbed "the Jewel of the Pacific" and recognized as a UNESCO World Heritage Site for being a leading merchant seaport. We traveled through many vineyards and arrived two hours later at the Sheraton Hotel in Santiago, Chile's capital, which boasts nearly five million inhabitants.

Santiago looked more beautiful than I could have imagined. The city lies at the bottom of a big bowl of mountains. The snow on top of the ranges seemed like a sugar coating on the rim. The weather was perfect – clear blue skies, no sign of smog. I was looking forward to seeing my young friend Cristian again; he had just graduated from a private high school run by Jesuits. After a sightseeing tour by bus to acquaint us with some of the architectural highlights of Santiago, such as churches, government buildings, and the like, I got in touch with Cristian through Edita, his nanny. The entire family was on vacation in their condo outside of Valparaiso. Cristian took the bus to Santiago to meet me. He was beaming, apologized for the absence of his parents, and presented me with a beautiful box of lapis lazuli and a letter opener with a lapis-lazuli handle. Both gifts were beautiful and very generous. I had already bought a lapis-lazuli pearl necklace with a matching bracelet for myself and other souvenirs for friends, and Cristian liked the stuffed penguin and the box of candies I brought for him. I invited him to dinner at the Sheraton, where we chatted until midnight. He joined me the next day for breakfast at the famous El Cid garden restaurant. A glorious day it was. Sunshine, blooming bushes, flowers, and palm trees surrounded us – and to top it off, a couple of violinists walked around serenading the guests, including us.

Cristian also took me to the Chilean Museum of Pre-Columbian Art, close to the main square. I was amazed at his knowledge of art in general. Maybe his mother, an accomplished architect with degrees from MIT and Harvard who had designed the plans of their house, as well as a fine artist who focused on still lifes of fruits and flowers in bold colors, had something to do with it. When Cristian took me to the family villa, built like terraces (split levels) into San Cristóbal Hill, I was taken aback at the sight of this absolutely gorgeous modern architectural masterpiece. The rooms were accented by tall tropical plants, modern art, light-beige furniture, Chilean pottery, and glass-top tables. The most striking asset was an entire glass wall in the living room that looked down on terraces with vibrant flowers and bougainvillea bushes, a swimming pool at the bottom, and Santiago with the mountains in the background. What a sight! Edita served cake and tea on the terrace, where Cristian introduced me to his white-furred pets, a cat and a rabbit. I would have loved to stay until dark to get a view of Santiago lit up at night, but it was time to think about the flight back to the USA early in the morning. Thus, *adiós*, summer, and hello, winter. *Hasta la vista*!

NORTH POLE – NS YAMAL: THE ULTIMATE JOURNEY – 90 DEGREES NORTH – TOP OF THE WORLD

Those who know me appreciate my fascination with ice and snow. I had been flirting with a trip to the North Pole for a while, and I simply could not resist when I discovered one was available with Quark Expeditions, Inc., aboard the icebreaker *Yamal*, from July 14 to July 29, 2005. I went into temporary shock when I discovered the price of this once-in-a-lifetime adventure, which at that time had been undertaken by a mere forty thousand humans. After I calmed down, I decided it was now or never. Also, the ice, which was in danger of melting at a faster pace, won me over. The high cost was due to the fact that I did not want to share a cabin with some stranger. – Friends and acquaintances questioned my sanity when I decided to undertake this expedition, but some really liked the article about it in the *Herald-Times*, printed on July 11, 2005. It appeared on the front page with a photo taken on the *Marco Polo* and was entitled "(EXTRA)ORDINARY Next Stop: The North Pole." Kurt Van der Dussen, the *H-T* columnist, interviewed me. –

When I called Quark last year, 2012, I was told the price had almost doubled. Lesson learned: don't procrastinate!

Preparing for the trip, including gathering the necessary clothes, was an experience in itself. Getting a visa for Russia required filling out a lengthy questionnaire probing into any and all details of my life, but I finally held it in my hand. I even had a frequent-flyer ticket to Helsinki, where the group of ninety or so met before flying to Murmansk, Russia, the next day. And as you will see, it was an extraordinary group of serious adventurers from seventeen countries. For obvious reasons, physical fitness was a strict requirement. The *Yamal* is no gin palace, as Tony Soper, the foremost ornithologist and England's "Mr. Birdwatch," who enriched the excursion with lively lectures about seagoing birds and mammals, used to say.

For those who are interested in the Arctic Ocean, I copy the following from the Quark flyer:

The Arctic Ocean is a big ocean, an area approximately twice the size of the Mediterranean. It is also very deep, plunging 4,000 meters in the center, although there is a wide continental shelf along the Siberian coast. It is mostly covered by pack-ice (frozen seawater) averaging three meters thick, but thicker where pressure ridges have developed. The ice drifts around the polar basin under the influence of winds and currents, breaking up during blizzards and then refreezing. Its only sizable escape southward is between Svalbard and Greenland. In the summer the ice is less thick and the edge of the pack retreats northward 100 miles or more. The maritime climate caused by this ocean explains why the coldest place in the Arctic is not at the North Pole but in Siberia.

The name "Arctic" is derived from <u>arctos</u>, the Greek for "bear." The heavenly constellation of the Great Bear – Ursa Major – points the way to the Pole Star, Arcturus. In classical times, the region was seen as deliverer of the north wind, Boreas, bringing ice and snow of winter to the south, a concept familiar to Mediterranean philosophers long before brave sailors ventured north to prove its existence.

Crossing the Arctic Circle when flying from Helsinki to Murmansk took about forty minutes. The weather was good, and from my window seat I could see the green, forested, rolling plains and the many lakes covering the Finnish countryside. The bus ride, which took us through dense birch and conifer forests as well as the sinister, concrete residential apartment blocks and industrial complexes of Murmansk, so typical of socialist countries, reminded me of my trip through Siberia a year earlier. When we entered the restricted area of the nuclear facility, which had a strict ban on photography, I felt a bit strange, and I felt even stranger when we pulled up alongside the monstrosity that was the 75,000-ton, nuclear-powered NS *Yamal* (a Nenets word meaning "end of the earth"), which Quark described as follows: "*He* was a very big ship. Icebreakers are masculine, breaking the normal rule for ships to be referred to as 'she.' As if to signal toughness and resilience, the bow hull was painted with a large, open jaw of white shark-like teeth, which stood out well against the black of the towering hull, and aroused much comment [I thought it looked tacky]. It was perhaps, a salute to the ice-munching capability of the ship [I doubt it]."

My cabin was plain and functional, with a monitor for films and high boards at the side of the bed to prevent me from falling out. I liked having the extra bed in the room and the luxury of being able to spread my things around.

At around 2100 hours, the *Yamal* began sailing past the submarine base at Plyani and into the Barents Sea. Laurie Dexter, our expedition leader, called us all together in the lecture theater at 1800 hours, for introductions to the senior members of the hotel staff and to meet the expedition team. According to the Quark literature,

Laurie is a polar skier of some note and vastly experienced in Arctic and Antarctic expedition travel; Mike Murphy, the Assistant Expedition Leader, has made many trips to the North Pole and dived in various remote parts of the world; Lea Williams, the historian, is an Emeritus Professor at Brown University in the USA; Kirsten Le Mar is a research zoologist who has been leading and taking part in Polar Expeditions since 1999; Tony Soper, the Ornithologist, is a veteran of more polar expeditions than most have had hot dinners [!]; Jason Roberts is an Arctic specialist and wildlife film maker who has extensive experience filming polar bears; Sue Currie, the Geologist, lives in Scotland and has worked in the Antarctic and offshore in the UK North Sea; Patrick Toomey, the Ice and Navigation Master, has some forty years of experience in Polar travel; Peter Sinden, the shopkeeper on the <u>Yamal</u> spends much of his time away from ships climbing and ice-guiding around Mount Cook in New Zealand; and an Artist-in-Residence, Nicola Murray hails from Edinburg, Scotland.

Indeed, a most impressive group of specialists. We had daily lectures, which were very instructive, fascinating, and entertaining. They were very well attended. I usually sat next to Professor Williams, from Brown University.

As is customary on cruises and sea expeditions, the activities of the first day focused on safety onboard the ship, the abandon-ship lifeboat drill, and use of the survival suit, which would keep us warm for up to twenty-four hours in the freezing waters of the polar seas. I loved my bright-yellow-and-navy-blue Quark Expeditions North Pole parka. In the afternoon, we were acquainted with the helicopter procedures. Always follow instructions! No Zodiac trips on this voyage! Our gigantic Russian captain, Stanislav Rumyantsev, who spoke no English, hosted a welcome cocktail party where we were introduced to the senior officers. The welcome dinner was superb, as were all the meals that followed. The executive chef, along with his crew, was at home at the Hotel Astoria in Vienna, Austria. On all my worldwide travels, I have yet to find a chef who surpasses Gunter Walder.

From then on, I focused on spotting ice. The temperature was 34 degrees Fahrenheit. At first, I observed small pieces of drift ice, which had broken from the pack ice toward which we were steaming. Before noon, the ship began to shudder, and Laurie announced that the *Yamal* had reached the southern tip of the pack ice and that from then on there would be no more open water. Sure enough, the pack ice continued to get thicker. Everybody got excited, and I spent much time either on the bridge or outside on deck looking down alongside the hull and watching the ship breaking up and forging ahead through the ice that piled up alongside it. We began looking for polar bears and seals. Our ice master pointed out an icebow – formed by light reflecting off of ice crystals in the air rather than off of water droplets, which produces a rainbow. There were also many polar-bear tracks on the ice, and we hoped we would soon spot one or two. Sure enough, when the Russian crew spotted the first bear, we all headed for the bow or flying bridge, as the ship slowed down. A very large male appeared in the distance, and we were ecstatic. The ship had slowed down a bit but then decided to give the bear its space.

Patrick's lecture on ice classifications was interrupted. Laurie had spotted a mother bear and her cub some distance from the bow of the ship, which slowed down. How exciting! Six bears were in our field of view – a subadult bear, a mother bear with her cub, and another female with two cubs. With binoculars, I saw an additional six bears in the far distance. The nearby subadult bear was eating a recent kill, probably a seal, and the smell of the kill was attracting other bears. The snow was red from the blood. We watched as the mother bear with the single cub chased away the adolescent bear from the kill and began to feed on it herself. The mother bear with two cubs then approached, but could not get close to the kill. Shortly afterward, the subadult bear came back, stole the kill, and was chased over the ice by the mother bear with the single cub until he (or she) dropped the kill. It was an amazing spectacle, which lasted some forty minutes. Thus, thirteen bears so far. We were told that on the previous trip, only three bears were sighted during the entire expedition. Indeed, a couple of years earlier, the *Yamal* had to turn around at 80 degrees north. The ice was so thick that there was not enough time to finish a full round. Several in our group had been on that trip. They were given a 40% discount to try again on a future expedition.

Each day we were treated to highly interesting lectures by the outstanding naturalists. On July 18, we all participated in the Neptune Ceremony on bridge deck 3 aft, where we greeted King Neptune and his attendants. Our captain asked King Neptune if we could travel to the North Pole, and after receiving a gift of a barrel of beer, King Neptune agreed to let us pass. King Neptune also wanted to "test our mettle" by observing a tug-of-war between a port-side team and a starboard-side team. In the end, both teams proved equally strong, and the contest ended in a memorable draw. There was a lot of dancing and celebrating, and then everybody partook of a scrumptious barbeque out on deck.

It was something quite otherworldly to eat such a great variety of delicious food and to dance to music against the backdrop of pack ice, green meltwater pools, dark-gray ocean water, and a calm, gray-white sky. We were actually lucky to have such tranquil weather in this climatically volatile part of the planet.

Believe me, the ice landscape through which the *Yamal* was moving was ever so beautiful and endlessly fascinating. At first sight, it looked white, but in the high Arctic there seemed to be at least thirty different shades of white and twenty shades of gray. Blue pools of meltwater formed a hundred different shapes on the irregular, undulating surface. As the *Yamal* broke ice in front of us, we heard the deep crushing noises of steel against frozen water and the growls of ice masses being pushed against each other.

I found climbing up and down and navigating through the vast engine room awe-inspiring and extremely fascinating. I had no idea as to how complex and colossal the engine of an atomic icebreaker would be. We were furnished much information and given handouts to read in case we were interested. They are filed away in my travel documents for posterity. Until then, I had been strictly opposed to nuclear power. After this trip I became more open-minded. It is clean and less expensive, if the waste is disposed of safely. The chief mechanical engineer informed us at one point that to reach the North Pole, we consumed three hundred grams of nuclear fuel, whereas if we were a diesel-powered vessel, we would have consumed three hundred thousand tons of fuel, worth well over a million dollars. In short, Alexander and all those operating this giant ship deserve much respect! We had a chance to chat with him and the captain at a predinner gathering, which took place before we arrived at our destination. Quark's literature described our arrival at the North Pole as follows:

After Lunch, Laurie called us all together to explain the arrangements for our approach to the North Pole. He said that we still did not know when we would get there, but that it might be later this afternoon. We would assemble on the Bridge and there would be champagne and canapés served. Although there were two navigation GPS receivers on the Bridge, the Captain had a further one on the port side navigation station, and this was to be our "official" position indicator. We waited, and wondered, and waited, and then at about 2120, came the news we had been hoping for – Laurie advised everyone to start dressing warmly and making their way to the bow, as we were only about two nautical miles away from the North Pole. The ship had entered an area of open water, so we were closing the distance fast. The dining room staff came around with champagne. We waited expectantly, watching as the Yamal inched forward with care. Then the ship's horn was sounded and we cheered and whistled. In calm and hazy sunshine, against a background of white, white, ice in every direction, we were here at last – 90 DEGREES NORTH! At 2140, on Wednesday, July 20, 2005, we were at the North Pole, and everywhere we looked, in every direction, was South.

Using a megaphone, Mike congratulated us and we cheered the Captain for getting us to this top-most point in the world safely. There was much laughter, photography, and sheer plain joy at having achieved our goal. Several called their family and friends back home to tell them we were here.

The total experience was almost surreal. I stole away from the frolicking crowd and stood in a meditative mood at the railing, looking out into the ice-covered sea glistening golden and silver from the sun. It was one of those moving moments when I feel so small and yet so blessed to be alive and able to feel the immense beauty of the universe.

I then went to my cabin to write a bunch of postcards to friends and family back home. I wanted them to know that while on top of the world, I was thinking of them.

They had intended for us to leave the ship for a celebratory dance on the ice at this point. However, the ice was too weak, and the captain decided to find a sturdier spot in which to "garage" the ship. The party was eventually postponed until the next day.

In the morning, we had our first helicopter flight. The pilot took us on a 360-degree tour around the ship at a low level, allowing us to watch the *Yamal* crunch through the ice. We got brilliant views across the bows of the painted teeth on the hull and across the anchor holes, which looked like eyes! – Some thought it looked rather fearsome from the front. We all took wonderful photographs of the vessel. It was great to see the red ship and the ice from the air. Later on, they found a place to park the ship in solid ice. The disembarkation process could begin. After some time for photographing, the ship sounded its horn. It was the signal to gather around the large rope circle that had been laid out on the ice. We performed a short dance, called the "hokey pokey," around the circle. After the dance, our captain came out and congratulated us all on arriving at the northernmost point on the planet. He presented Emiko Miura, the winner of our competition for the most accurate guess regarding the travel time to the Pole, with a bottle of champagne. I too had pictures taken of me next to the hull of the ship, holding the red "North Pole 90N" marker, and of the unbroken vistas of blue-white pack ice. The staff had set up a ladder at the ice edge toward the stern of the ship, and about twenty brave and hardy travelers took the ultimate cold-water swim. Experienced Russian crew members fastened a belt and rope around the waist of each "polar plunger." Each swimmer was rewarded with a large shot of vodka, courtesy of Bronwen, our bar supervisor. When some challenged me to take the plunge into the ice hole, which was a frigid 30 degrees Fahrenheit, I excused myself. I had forgotten to bring my bathing suit. Charles Veley, who had just turned forty and had proudly announced his inclusion in *The Guinness Book of World Records* as the most-traveled man, asked me to take a picture of him with his Sony digital camera. I was happy to comply. The plungers spent no longer than a minute in the water, and all survived the shock. Four young women were brave enough to jump. Tough!

May 27, 2016 – At this time, Charles has traveled to 833 countries, regions, and territories, leaving only forty-two unvisited (mosttraveledpeople.com).

One of our lecturers later pointed out that we had reached the North Pole on July 20 and stepped out of the ship on July 21, onto the pack ice. These events took place thirty-six years to the day after Neil Armstrong and Buzz Aldrin landed on the moon and became the first men to walk on its surface. For many of us, I am convinced, it was just as exciting. Meanwhile, our ship had drifted one nautical mile with the pack ice. –

We continued south and followed the track we had made heading north to the pole. The ice was already broken and presented less of an obstacle as we headed to Franz Josef Land.

Russia

Franz Josef Land

On Sunday, July 24, we arrived at Franz Josef Land, an archipelago of 191 islands in the Northeastern Barents Sea, totally uninhabited. It is named after the Austrian emperor. I had never heard of it. Polar bears are supposed to roam the island. Therefore, our crew had to bring along rifles.

The waters were calm and ice-free, and the temperature was 34 degrees Fahrenheit. The helicopter, from which we had wonderful views of a large glacier nearby, landed close to the shoreline of Champva Island. Thus, it was the first time in nine days that we touched land. There was quite a bit to explore, including volcanic rocks and boulders – basalt and dolerite. Vegetation colored the ground: pale and yellow Arctic poppies, purple saxifrage, and green moss "cushions" of many different hues. We spotted brilliant orange lichens that formed splashes of color on some large – around twelve feet in diameter – and very round boulders.

Susan explained that these boulders were cemented sandstones formed below ground over hundreds of thousands of years. They were now exposed at the surface only because glacier meltwaters had been eroding the surrounding, softer soil since the end of the last ice age (about ten thousand years ago). We saw territorial skuas and had to walk around their nesting areas, and we had to avoid the helicopter flight path on the way to some majestic cliffs by the shore. Many kittiwakes called these cliffs home, and were busy foraging as we walked. The big event occurred when one of the Japanese women sank almost to her waist into some swampy ground and two guys had to pull her out.

Our next stop was Alger Island, where we walked to a glacier that was located a little inland. Some of us stayed at the shore and looked at the ruined wooden building by the beach, with its remnants of barrels, rusting metal, and faded wooden signs attesting to the previous human occupation.

On July 25, 2005, we passed Rubini Rock. As we came within fifty meters of the rock and gathered on deck, we heard the cries and calls of the thousands of kittiwakes, little auks (dovekies), and Brünnich's guillemots that nest on the natural ledges of this column of basalt. The upper reaches of the rock were green with vegetation, and the lower part was solid black basalt, except where the bird guano stained the rock a pale cream color. Tony Soper was in his glory, and so was I. Wow!

Our stop at Cape Flora, known for its beautiful, green, vegetated slopes, took place in the afternoon. The cape also featured some historic remains. In the nineteenth century, Fridtjof Nansen, the famous Norwegian explorer, led an expedition to the North Pole on the ship *Fram*, which was the first ship in the world designed to sail on pack ice. We found amazing bird cliffs and encountered a kittiwake colony, fulmars, and little auks. Along the dramatic coastline, we saw snow buntings and purple sandpipers. It was our last stop before heading south to Murmansk.

The temperature was by now a balmy 55 degrees Fahrenheit, and after more lectures and recaps, a customary farewell cocktail party, and a most delicious farewell dinner, we were gearing up for the trip home.

On July 26, 2005, the sea was calm as the *Yamal* docked at Murmansk and we began bidding each other farewell. Some passengers stood out more than others, because of what they had told me about either their life or travels, and others were simply forgotten after a while. When oil prices rose sharply in 2008 and 2009, I remembered the Belgian who worked for big oil companies worldwide and foretold that the price of a barrel of oil would go up to $250. Two brothers from Hamburg traveled together with their sister and had some great stories to tell about their sailing ventures. One Italian and his Swiss lover of twenty-three years had hoped to marry on the *Yamal*, but due to some legal glitch were unable to do so. A journalist from France never touched a single dessert, no matter how tempting it looked. – Norman Goldberg, from New Jersey, entertained us whenever he showed up and generously let people call home on his phone when we reached the North Pole. He was the owner of one of the largest container companies in the United States. I found Charles Veley most fascinating because of his many travels. His wife was expecting their second child. When I said good-bye to him, I urged him, as I had on several other occasions throughout the trip, "Charley, stay happy, don't be greedy, and don't forget the poor." He always smiled, and at times we exchanged e-mails. I had never met a forty-year-old guy who had lost one hundred million bucks in the stock market when he was thirty-five. When I said good-bye to Professor Williams, he kindly claimed that without me, the trip would have been only half as nice, because I was always in good spirits. It made me feel very good inside.

The tour in Murmansk was somewhat anticlimactic. It was said that wedding parties tend to gather at the thirty-meter-high Alyosha Monument – a statue of a soldier overlooking the city. I personally could not find anything romantic about the sinister-looking monument carved out of gray stone. A tad more interesting was a stroll through the Regional History Museum. Regardless, this city of three hundred thousand inhabitants is the largest city in the Arctic and an important Russian naval base and commercial port. During Soviet times, World War II was known as the Great Patriotic War. Murmansk served as a port for Arctic convoys, and after the war it was the Soviet Union's most important submarine base.

The staff promised to mail our postcards in Helsinki. Eventually, those to whom I sent them, including myself, received them.

The Compass

One of the items dear to Doc was a pocket compass, which I sent to his grandson Wayne, a keen sailor, after he had tracked me down while browsing the Internet. Several months before I left for the North Pole, I asked him to send the compass so I could take it with me and then return it with a note indicating that it had been with me to the North Pole. I was very disappointed when he claimed he could not find it because they had moved to Florida and he did not know in which box it might be packed. Thus, during my visit to Brussels in April 2005, I purchased three pocket compasses to take along, with the intention of giving one each to Wayne's sons Peter and Eric after the trip. Both were avid sailors as well. – As soon as I returned to Bloomington on July 29, I took the compasses to a place where they engraved my name and the date on which I had reached the North Pole, that is, July

Fireball Lily

20, 2005, on the back of the compasses. It was sweltering hot that day. To make it worse, when I got home I noticed they had made a mistake in the printing. I took the compasses back, they corrected the mistake, and I was able to pick them up a few hours later. I hurried home, wrapped the presents, and made it to the post office just in time. – Very excited about my trip, I called both boys to tell them about it. I left messages on both machines. Eric returned the call rather promptly. Peter did not get back until several weeks had passed. I was extremely disappointed, found it rather disrespectful, and concluded that all the previous niceties had not been sincere at all. Being sensitive, I decided right then and there that I had misjudged Peter completely. Doc would have been very disappointed in him. To avoid further disappointments, I thought it best to distance myself from Peter. I just could not count on him for help in times of need.

SOUTH AMERICA

Patagonia – Argentina

After my return from the North Pole in September 2005, I took a minor trip by boat on the Danube called "Europe to the Black Sea," and on November 9, 2005, I headed south again to take a closer look at Patagonia. Several North Pole travelers had urged me to see more of that fabulous region, the Chilean and Argentinean Patagonia. My Chilean friend Cristian had sent an outline of places to see, which I forwarded to the tour operator of Ponce De Leon Travel. On November 9, 2005, I hit the trail via American Airlines to Buenos Aires, where I spent a night at the Hotel de las Americas before continuing south with LAN Airlines to El Calafate, Argentina. I had decided to engage private tour guides to avoid the hassle of getting from one place to another by myself. Thus, throughout the trip I had the luxury of being picked up by someone who transferred me to and from hotels, airports, etc.

El Calafate

El Calafate, a small town of six thousand inhabitants, is the glacier capital of Argentina and as such the point from which to visit Glaciers National Park. The town is settled on the southern shore of Lago Argentino. Its name stems from the little bush with yellow flowers and dark-blue berries common in Patagonia. I spent four nights at the ranch-style El Quijote Hotel. The rooms and reception area were decorated in an antique style and projected a warm ambiance, which I liked right away. I did not mind that the beds were comparatively narrow. I did not fall out! I also appreciated the downtown location, which made it easy to go for a brief orientation stroll shortly after my arrival.

The next morning, the driver picked me up in a 4x4 jeep and took me to the pier from which the cruise on Lago Argentina was scheduled to depart. The sky was blue; the sun was strong, as were the winds. Cruising amidst all of the spectacular white mountain peaks bordering the lake and mirrored in its striking milky-blue waters seemed made to order just for me. My panorama snapshots of the icebergs sailing past us like magnificent sculptures did not disappoint me. Wow!

Upsala is the park's largest glacier and is the ideal gateway to the huge ice sheet, the origin of the area's forty-seven ice floes. The glacier is fifty kilometers long and nine kilometers wide at the lake's edge, where large chunks calve and crash into the water, surfacing to become icebergs. The friction generated by the moving glacier and by the action of the water causes these ruptures. The visible height of these great lumps, which fall to the surface of the lake in the form of breathtaking natural sculptures, is an impressive seventy meters. I chatted with a number of tourists on the ship. Several were from Germany, Italy, and Spain. We disembarked at the harbor of Estancia Cristina, which has an important place in Patagonian legend, as it is still synonymous with unspoiled natural beauty and isolated from the worries of everyday life.

We continued traveling by Unimogs (specially adapted off-road vehicles) through rough, and at times scary, terrain. We had to hike over somewhat challenging rocky ground – that is, there were no paths – for about thirty minutes to Cascada de los Perros, a lookout point from which we stared in awe upon the magnificent Upsala Glacier. The glacier has two fronts; the main front faces the Argentina Lake, and the secondary front faces the Laguna Guillermo, which shows the receding and melting away of the glacier over the last thirty years. We trekked through marvelous landscapes, untouched nature, and exceptional rock formations carved and polished by the amazing force of the huge masses of ice. We paused occasionally to admire a geological treasure, a fascinating fossil, or a flowering bush, such as the yellow *calafate* and other flowers springing up in crevices of the colorful rocks. We felt blessed, because due to cloudless skies, we could see the only piece of land overlooking the Upsala Glacier. The view from the lookout point was spectacular. Before us was the entire bay area and the Estancia Cristina, where we eventually paused for an unforgettable lunch of Patagonian lamb, served in a sheltered addition to the main house.

In the afternoon, we took a trip around the Estancia Cristina, nestled in ultimate seclusion. It is a well-preserved former ranching outpost of the Masters family, early-twentieth-century British pioneers. They were also known for their hospitality and opened up their home to explorers and scientists such as Padre de Agostini and Eric Shipton, who explored the remote and then-unknown icefield. I found three graves marked with crosses in a small, fenced-in place while walking around on the grounds and looking for birds. The Estancia Cristina is loved for its name, for its "majestic setting," "gentle and rugged," "new and old"; in short, it's called "a gem." "The main buildings are located at the foot of the imposing, 2,730-meter Cerro Pared Norte. The estancia is surrounded by forests, lakes, mountains, and glaciers and is considered a nature lovers' paradise" (Brochure).

The Upsala experience will never be forgotten. The ship delivered us safely at Puerto Banderas, and after a sound sleep I was ready to go again early in the morning to spend another exciting day at the impressive, must-see destination of South America, that massive stream of ice, the Perito Moreno Glacier, named after Francisco Pascacio Moreno, the prominent Argentinian explorer and scientist (*perito* means "specialist, expert").

My guide, the young, handsome, and very enthusiastic Romiro Sebastian, a botanist, together with the charming Natalia, also a cook at a local ranch, picked me up in a 4x4 jeep driven by a jovial, young chauffeur, and off we went. The skies were blue, and I was elated at the first sight of this magnificent stream of ice. We walked around the balconies, a series of wooden platforms set up on the mountainside across the lake, and climbed some 160 steps to view the wonder from all sorts of angles. This glacier is famous for its movements; that is, it advances and recedes and in the process triggers much calving, which we witnessed spellbound. Though I had observed calving before in Alaska and Antarctica, it is always an experience that makes the heart beat faster. Whenever a chunk of ice falls, the waves race along the waterline and intensify the drama. Romiro talked about the huge *ruptura* in 2004, the big crash that occurred when a big chunk of ice broke off and caused the lake level to rise very high and cause unexpected danger. When we took a boat ride on the lake to get a closer look at the ice formations of the ice stream, I was amazed at the different shades of blue and turquoise in the cracks of the ice. It was changing constantly. The deeper the crevice was, the darker – that is, azure or cobalt blue – were the shades. I liked the dark-green forest along the east side of the glacier and, even more, the abundance of bright-red fire bushes, called *notros*, close to the icefield. For my photos, the predominance of the red flowers in the bushes against a blue sky above provided a striking contrast to the white ice.

The three of us were quite happy after our picnic lunch, sent along by the estancia. We sealed our friendship by sharing the maté tea, which Romiro prepared in the jeep by pouring warm water on finely crushed leaves.

After all that excitement, I welcomed the day at leisure in El Calafate. After breakfast I combed the main street and a couple of side streets crammed full of souvenir shops. I talked to a young blond and light-blue-eyed Russian beauty who offered hand-knit sweaters, caps, etc. and just loved the unforgettable trout dinner at a nice restaurant I stumbled upon on the main street. The fresh stream trout was pan fried and served with a unique blue-cheese cream sauce. It tasted more delicious than any trout I had ever tasted anywhere else in the world. A nice Chardonnay from Argentina tasted ever so good and gave me the courage to chat with a French couple at the next table in French, and after they left I had a pleasant conversation with two women – from Wales, of all places.

However, I had an even more exciting chat the next morning while waiting in the lobby of the Quijote Hotel for my driver to take me to the airport. Talkative as I am, and with a distinct penchant for musicians, I tried my Spanish and addressed a young, handsome Argentinian. Somehow I had overheard that he was a pianist. He told me he had recently graduated from the Conservatorio de Música Alberto Ginastera in Morón, Buenos Aires, and was looking for a job playing at hotels and such to entertain the guests. I asked him to play a tango for me, which he readily did. He seemed to ignore that the piano was totally out of tune. No matter; I thought he played quite well. I took it upon myself to tell the hotel manager to give this young man a chance. And I could hardly believe it when my young amigo Leonardo Eyhermonho (twenty-six years old), while I was still waiting, informed me that he had been hired. We exchanged e-mail addresses, but I did not keep it up. At the time, I had no idea who Alberto Ginastera was. Today, after getting to know the fabulous cellist Mark Kosower and his Korean wife and pianist Jee-Won Oh much better, I know a lot more about the great composer Alberto Ginastera. Mark and Jee-Won have recorded several of his compositions.

Bariloche

The flight from El Calafate to Bariloche with Austral Lineas Aéreas was brief. However, as we drove through Bariloche, a city in the province of Rio Negro, Argentina, situated at the foothills of the Andes and surrounded by lakes and mountains, I was immediately enchanted. Indeed, it seemed as though I was in an alpine village in Switzerland or Austria. I then learned that the first settlers had indeed come here from Austria, Germany, Slovakia, Chile, and Italy. When someone told me this place was also a haven for the former Nazi war criminals Erich Priebke, an SS *Hauptsturmfuehrer* (captain), and Adolph Eichmann, the place lost some of its attraction for me.

Patagonia – Chile

I spent only one night at the very nice Hotel Nevada, which was located about two hundred meters from the Lake Nahuel Huapi waterfront and had a distinct alpine decor. Already the next morning, I was picked up and transferred to the pier. The crossing of Lake Llanquihue also involved the crossing into Chile and therefore a serious inspection of passports. It's no love affair between the Argentinians and Chileans. While waiting, I met a gentleman from Mexico City, the owner of an amusement park who had been to the North Pole with his father. It was so exciting. He wore the same yellow-and-navy-blue parka provided by Quark Expeditions that I had. He too had traveled on the *Yamal*. Incredible. Upon entering their public bathroom, however, I was amused to observe a couple of rolls of toilet paper mounted on the wall next to the lavatories. A sign next to it asked prospective clients to help themselves to the paper prior to entering the stalls and to discard it into a basket instead of the toilet. This was a *novum* for me. Maybe they were afraid someone might hoard the paper?

The rather lengthy lake crossing was smooth, but since it was also rainy, many clouds in the sky obstructed at least partially the view of the Osorno, Calbuco, and Cerro Tronador Volcanoes. My overnight stay at the Hotel Cabana del Lago, on the hilltops of Puerto Varas, was memorable. I had a great panoramic view of Lake Llanquihue and could see the Osorno Volcano in the distance, less obstructed by clouds than the day before. The grounds of the hotel were particularly beautiful, with flowering shrubs, lupines, poppies, and rhododendrons. I could have stayed there for a few more days.

But, already the next morning, I was transferred to the small airport at Puerto Montt, where my private pilot was expecting me. He stood next to a small, eight-seater Cessna named *Tompkins Esprit*. The pilot informed me that the plane used to belong to the great and somewhat controversial North American businessman, environmentalist, and conservationist Douglas Tompkins. Tompkins established the Foundation for Deep Ecology and is the former owner of The North Face and Esprit clothing companies. He conserved over two million acres of wilderness in Chile and Argentina, more than any private individual. He is also the founder of Pumalín Park, which receives close to ten thousand visitors annually. I had never heard of Tompkins!

El Chaiten

The flight from Puerto Montt to El Chaiten was not for the faint of heart. As the only passenger, I sat next to the pilot and could see everything around, below, and above us. That is, as long as there was good visibility, which changed quickly after we had been airborne for about fifteen minutes. While we flew over the fjords, islands, and the Pacífico below, it began to rain, and soon we flew through big clouds that shed streams of rain. I could not see a thing, and my pilot, who kept telling me not to worry, was clutching a rosary and crossing himself repeatedly. But he landed the little plane safely on a narrow strip of land. Later, my very nice guide, Joos, born in Belgium but having resided in Venezuela, Bolivia, and Chile over a period of seven years, who spoke English, Spanish, French, and German, told me that each year several landings on that very strip in El Chaiten ended catastrophically, with fatalities. Only a few months earlier, four people had lost their lives in a crash landing on this landing strip, the most dangerous in the region.

It had stopped raining, but the drive in Joos's sturdy jeep to the lodging El Puma Verde was telling insofar as I did not see a single car or human being on the primitive gravel road. Though as soon as we entered the Hosteria, I felt safe and warm inside. Miriam, a pretty, young Peruvian hostess who spoke English, welcomed us into this small, rustic, and very tastefully decorated house, actually owned by Doug Tompkins. We were asked to exchange our shoes for felt slippers upon entering. Each room featured a wood-burning stove. All the floors and furniture were of light-colored wood and crafted by local carpenters. Copper trim was evident throughout, but mainly in the kitchen, where copper pots and pans were hanging on hooks on the walls. The bathtub was an original and stood on four legs. The blankets on the beds were made from white llama wool and very comfortable. Handcrafted area rugs, wooden bowls displayed on chests, and thick, fluffy pillows on the couch were inviting and looked ever so cozy. I could have stayed there for a month at least. Miriam was a superb cook, and the thick tuna-fish sandwiches made with bread she had baked in the wood-burning oven in the kitchen, and which she sent along for our picnic when we went to Los Alerces National Park, were as delicious as any I have ever tasted.

The visit to Los Alerces National Park, established to protect the *alerce* tree, a conifer that reaches 229 feet in height and up to 13 feet in diameter and can live for thousands of years, was another exciting experience. The place was totally deserted and appeared very pristine and wild, almost mystical. I could not get over the abundance of huge, rhubarb-like leaves spread throughout the forest. The giant redwood trees were totally unexpected. All plants were lush, vibrant, and of great aesthetic appeal – the ambiance of this rainforest was reminiscent of the Tanzanian rainforest, yet not hot and steamy. As Joos explained, it is a Valdivian temperate broadleaf evergreen forest, with an annual rainfall of twenty feet. No wonder. I could not have wished for a better introduction to what it is like to travel in a rainforest.

Carretera Austral

After I said good-bye to my new friend Miriam, who promised to stay in touch via e-mail, it rained almost continuously while we traveled south through thriving native forests and past Ventisquero Yelcho, a hanging glacier. We opted out of hiking up to the glacier, since I was not in the mood to get soaked by the rain. I was elated, though, to have traveled through the most beautiful scenery, regardless of the rough and bumpy road. There were cascading waterfalls, wild rivers perfect for white-water rafting, and not a glimpse of people. I got excited at the mere sight of a little house here and there, a few sheep grazing on the rugged terrain along the roadside, and a couple of cows with a calf in the middle of the road, making us wait until they reached the other side. We passed oceans of flowers – yellow *calafate* bushes bordering the road for endless stretches, orange-red *notros* at times covering an entire hillside, blue and pink lupines, buttercups, white, red, and pink flowering trees, which reminded me of Austria or Switzerland, meadows, snow-topped mountain peaks shining through clouds, bamboo trees covered with mosses, fences made out of tree branches, ibises appearing now and then, and fly fishers casting for salmon and trout on a lake. A gaucho on a horse posed for us to show off his poncho. And to top it off, a flock of black-necked swans were gathered close to the shore of a glacier lake. Truly a nature lovers' paradise!

Just as captivating was the drive from Futaleufu to Futaleufu Lake. We arrived at Puerto Puyuhuapi after a long drive, and the night I spent in the rustic, deluxe cabin 6 at El Barranco was heavenly. Again, a wide window provided a view toward a lush, green, gently rolling lawn of golf-course grass. There was a sprinkling of buttercups, and pheasant-like birds with shiny gold and brown feathers were hopping around. In the background was a steep mountain wall covered with evergreens and deciduous forests. One of the birds rested on a fuchsia bush while showing off its cobalt-blue feathers. –

It was a five-hour drive through more striking landscapes – mountains dusted with fresh snow. – We had a picnic lunch overlooking a meandering river and slowly passed by Lago Yelcho, which belongs to the Yelcho River system. It is a fly-fishers' paradise, where Redford and Clinton, among other rich and famous people, go fishing for salmon and trout while vacationing on this hideaway island in the lake and stay at the only existing dwelling, the Isla Monita Fishing Lodge. The view from there is exquisite: "The western horizon is crowded by jagged peaks, forests, snow fields, glaciated towers up to 6,300 feet high" (Brochure). How lucky I was to have found out from my little Chilean friend Cristian of this incredible trip along the Carretera Austral. Joos thought I was the only woman who had traveled alone on the Carretera Austral, the southernmost highway along the Chilean fjords. I was seventy-three years old at the time.

Our full-day excursion to Fultaleufu Lake was another venture on the Carretera Austral, and it was capped with a very pleasant night at the Cabanas El Pangue, Puerto Puyuhuapi. It is situated on the sheltered shores of Lake Risopatron. Local craftspeople had constructed my shingle-roofed cabana from native wood. I will never forget the bewitching singing of the yellow canaries in a huge cage in that unique, rustic restaurant, where I was served a delicious meal of wild salmon. –

The fourth day on the Carretera Austral was equally exciting and rewarding, with striking mountaintops, fields of purple lupines, and hills almost red with *notros*. – Some of the plains, light green with white sheep and brown cows grazing, were reminiscent of New Zealand. I asked Joos to stop for a photo shoot when I saw four white and gray geese marching along the roadside with six adorable yellow chicks. A cow with a calf forced us to stop until she was finished feeding it. We tried to ignore the extremely rough road – still under construction. Companies often folded in midst of the process and just left things unfinished. Huge potholes were filled with water and in the process of being washed out, so it was probable that the road would be closed at night. We passed a huge tree trunk that had fallen across the Carretera Austral the day before. Fortunately, it had been moved to the side of the road, so we were not stuck out there. There was no way to reach anybody by cell phone in this deserted countryside. Once, we had to wait some twenty minutes while a crew of road workers was trying to clear the road. We sighed with relief when our jeep reached a more even surface. Of course, there were no toilets either. Eventually, while picnicking close to a racing mountain stream, we found a little A-frame altar to St. Sebastian across from us. It stood about thirty feet high on the embankment, where I could hide without great embarrassment.

Joos told me that many Germans came to Patagonia to settle right after the war. Some prospered, as in Bariloche. I had spotted a German bakery in a small town somewhere, but we did not stop. Today, supposedly, more Germans than Americans travel to Patagonia. *Muy interesante*! Indeed, I could not believe my eyes when at one point I spotted a Condor Tours bus with the inscription *zu den Geheimnissen Suedamerikas* (toward the secrets of South America). The Germans actually slept on the bus for the entire trip!

Coyhaique

Our full-day excursion from Puerto Puyhuapi to Puerto Cisnes was equally awe-inspiring. We visited Ventisquero Colcante Queulat, the pendant bridge, and participated in a brief navigation of the lake, in which we saw falling glaciers. I was glad to arrive at the end of the day in Coyhaique at the incredibly gorgeous Mincho Lodge. Compared to all the previous lodgings, this place turned out to be the ultimate. My spacious room, exquisitely decorated with a picture window, offered a view of the snowcapped Andes, the Simpson River below, and birch, evergreen, and broadleaf forests all around. When the sun set and painted the panorama golden, I felt ecstatic and could not hold back tears. How beautiful is the world! – Victoria, a geologist, and her now-deceased husband, Mincho, a famous golfer, had designed the lodge. A life-size picture of him was displayed in the very cozy and artfully decorated lounge. Many photos of other famous guests, such as Nat King Cole, covered the adjacent walls, and wherever one looked, rare rocks and regional artifacts were displayed to catch a visitor's eye. Señora Victoria was a stunningly beautiful brunette with a captivating personality. I thoroughly enjoyed chatting with her. She spoke flawless English, and I could have stayed at the lodge forever. Yet, I spent only one day there and did not even get a chance to attend the lamb barbeque at the pit next to the lodge.

Punta Arenas

I had to bid farewell to Joos the next day. He drove me to the airport in Balmaceda, from which I flew to my next destination, Hotel Isla Rey Jorge, in Punta Arenas, the southernmost city on earth. Though this hotel was not state-of-the-art, the TV was excellent. I watched the Bundestag vote for Angela Merkel. The following day, I took the bus to Puerto Natales. It rained for the first thirty minutes, but then the sun came through, and I was happy when the snowcapped Andes reappeared. We passed a couple of Chilean villages with small, square houses and tin roofs – and finally, a big, house-like hotel appeared in the middle of these primitive structures. It seemed rather obscene and out of place – like an imitation of a small castle, most likely built by German pioneers. Yet, more importantly, we drove for a while along the famous Straits of Magellan. – The bus was rather nice, with reclining seats. I was glad to have a front seat at the window. Fortunately, an elderly French woman sat next to me, and we chatted away merrily in French. She lived on an island near Madagascar and was a retired scientist. Her hobby was scuba diving, and we had something else in common: a distinct dislike for G. W. Bush. She did not like Chirac either.

Puerto Natales

A private cab picked me up at the bus station in Puerto Natales and transferred me to Hotel Aquaterra Lodge, "a beautiful and warm place at the end of the world where water and land meet" (Brochure), for a two-night stay. It was an inviting place, constructed of wood from regional trees. I had a small, neat room with light-colored wood panels on the walls and a brand-new, all-white tiled bath. As the hotel was close to the Chilean Icefields, it was windy all the time. I took a long walk along Last Hope Sound, and since I was braving the strong winds, I was glad to have brought warm clothes. While exploring the small town and its town square, I thought it strange that many of the trees were clipped using the topiary technique common in Japan. The European influence was obvious as well. Several houses, inhabited by families of European origin, were much larger than those inhabited by native Chileans. I stopped to look at a big steam engine before visiting the small Historical Municipal Museum, where a collection of different objects, such as furniture, dishes, etc., brought over by the Eberhard family, pioneers from Selesia, Germany, caught my attention. I ran into a couple who were speaking English, and I learned that many English come to Patagonia to go horseback riding. It probably explained the noticeable absence of souvenir shops. As my pickup was scheduled for 7:30 a.m., I retired after a scrumptious dinner of king crab, which was recommended as their specialty. There was no TV in my room. I really did not care, because I was so excited about the prospect of seeing with my own eyes the magnificent Torres de la Paine the next day.

Guillermo, the guide, a real charmer, accompanied by Lorena, a young woman from a nearby estancia, picked me up at 7:30. Two more couples, one from Switzerland and another from Argentina, joined us. On the way, we picked up a couple of trekkers from the Netherlands, whose legs were hurting. Fifteen miles northwest of Puerto Natales, that is, miles from civilization, we stopped to explore the mysterious and huge Cave of the Milodon, where the remains of a prehistoric animal which looked like a huge grizzly bear standing on two very long hind legs – or a giant sloth, as others claim – were discovered. The hide-covered skeleton can be seen in the British Museum in London. The experience left me unexcited, to be honest. The good thing was that when we came out of the dark and eerie place, the weather had changed. The dark clouds slowly began to disappear.

Torres del Paine

When you travel to the end of the world to see the Torres del Paine, you definitely want to see them without clouds blocking the view. Thus, when the Torres appeared in the distance, stretching into a partially blue sky, we all cried out joyfully and left the van to take a picture – even if they had disappeared again, we would have been content. These three granite towers, seven thousand feet high and surrounded by snowcapped mountains, are just awesome – unlike anything else in the world. I would like to see them again. We were so fortunate to have reservations at the Grey Lake Glacier Restaurant, where we could stare at the Torres, mesmerized, while eating lunch. How lucky. I had waited for three years since my first trip to Antarctica to behold this natural wonder of the world. A genuine highlight! Blue skies hung above the granite wall, and fresh snow was sprinkled on it, like powdered sugar. We had a couple of hours to hike around Grey Lake and admire the glaciers and the rugged terrain at the foot of the towers. A few wild horses were grazing nearby, and the sun was shining bright. The trip back lasted three and a half hours. The Patagonian vastness held me spellbound. How could any place on earth be more exquisite? And I had seen many. We passed a herd of guanacos, a small, ostrich-like bird, two foxes, a flock of wild geese, and lakes shimmering emerald, turquoise, and blue green. Sparkling, meandering rivers rumbled past, and crimson *notros*, yellow *calafate* bushes, blue, white, and pink wildflowers, and oceans of lupines, as well as sheep, horses, and a proudly smiling gaucho on his horse, kept me smiling.

I was upset when we came upon a group of BMW motorcyclists from the Czech Republic who reported that they had accidentally started a huge brush fire when camping near the Torres. Ignoring warnings, they had attempted to burn down tree stumps. How stupid!

The good-byes were sad; but according to the guide, my Spanish had improved. I exchanged addresses with some of my cotravelers and began to switch gears. The next day, Thanksgiving, after a long bus ride, I would fly from Punta Arenas to Santiago to meet my friend Cristian once again.

Fortunately, I double checked the bus I had been told to take. Just before it took off at 9:00 a.m., I discovered it was the wrong one. With the help of a kind Chilean who retrieved my luggage, I ended up on the right bus, scheduled to leave at 9:15 a.m. I had a front seat next to another world traveler. The gentleman was a handsome Italian, traveled to exotic places in Africa, worked with foreign embassies, and lived in Trieste, not far from Venice, where I had gotten married in 1989.

Santiago

In Santiago, a chauffeur and representative of La Cocha transferred me from the airport to Hotel Neruda, a nice hotel with a poor view – against the walls of another hotel. Santiago looked as gorgeous as it did the last time I visited. The mountaintops were covered with snow, but the temperature in the city was 80 degrees Fahrenheit. It was hard to believe, but the papers were full of news about Pinochet, who had celebrated his ninetieth birthday while under house arrest in his mansion. After all, he was responsible, with the support of Nixon and Kissinger, for killing Allende and thousands of Contras, in addition to embezzling millions. I did not contact Cristian right away, as I was very tired.

I awoke early the next morning and set up a dinner date with Cristian, who was finishing his last day of classes. I spent the day strolling down the Avenida 11 de Septiembre, named after the day of Allende's assassination. The temperature was 80 degrees Fahrenheit, and the bougainvillea, jacarandas, and hibiscus were in full bloom. Everybody seemed happy and lively. Chile had made visible progress. I bought a pair of earrings for my Siberian friend Lubasha and treated myself to a *pequeño cono* (small ice-cream cone) at McDonald's while talking with a young woman who was breastfeeding her baby.

At 7:00 p.m., Cristian picked me up in his mother's very nice car. He had changed quite a bit. He had a well-groomed beard and short hair and had grown into a slender young man. He was happy and polite, as always. We embraced, and I handed over several of the little souvenirs I had gathered for him while traveling in Romania, Serbia, Croatia, and Hungary and also gave him the third engraved compass from the North Pole. He had tears in his eyes, and I thought to myself, "What a special young man!" Cristian had chosen a nice restaurant, specializing in seafood. On the way, I took a couple of pictures of him standing next to big, wooden horses similar to those I had seen in London. One had a huge dachshund face painted on his rear, and the body of the other was painted with big yellow, blue, red, and green squares. – The tuna steak tasted great. We talked until 10:00 p.m. Instead of just dropping me off in front of my hotel, Cristian insisted on taking me up to my room. A real gentleman. The next morning, my chauffeur transported me from the hotel to the airport for my flight to Mendoza, Argentina. I was determined to see Mount Aconcagua while I was in the area. It is the highest mountain in the western hemisphere, and since I had seen Mount McKinley, I just could not miss it.

Argentina

Mendoza

The flight from Santiago to Mendoza was fabulous! I just loved flying across the massive, snow-covered Andes. The sky was blue, the sun was shining, and the emerald-colored glacier lakes dispersed throughout the range lent the panorama a special appeal.

Mendoza is the capital city of the Mendoza Province in Argentina, located in the northern-central region, with a population of approximately 112,000 people. It is one of the largest wine- and olive-oil-producing regions in Latin America. The Hotel Aconcagua was modern and very nice and rather centrally located. Yet, I do not think I have ever visited a hotter place on earth. One could not go outside until 4:00 p.m., and even then I decided to hang out in the park nearby to admire the crafts displayed on the vendors' tables and seek out shady spots under huge, lush trees, some loaded with golden blossoms. Somehow, when I ventured a bit further while walking the streets, I got lost. Two lovely girls who spoke broken English offered to walk me back to the hotel. Both enjoyed practicing their English, and I always love chatting with young people.

Aconcagua

The guide picked us up at 7:30 a.m. for the trip to Aconcagua. I shared the ride with two couples from Gdansk, Poland, a brother and sister with their spouses, an architect, an MD, and an engineer. The architect and his wife had lived in Lybia for several years before immigrating to Canada, where they still lived, while the other couple still resided in Poland. On our trip, I became intrigued by the changing colors of the stones of the extremely arid mountain ranges. There were so many different shades of brown, tan, yellow, mustard, gray, and rust. Occasionally we passed a bunch of yellow flowers blooming on the roadside, and I got excited when a small herd of guanacos climbed along the Mendoza riverbed. The water of the river looked like cocoa, and we went by a couple of little huts. Our road was partially unpaved, and there were no resting stations until we reached the place from which we viewed the magnificent, snow-covered rock Aconcagua, unfortunately from about twenty-five away.

But there it was, some 2,521 feet higher than Mount McKinley (20,320 feet), the highest mountain outside of Asia. In comparison to the well-kept lookout points near Denali, which are crowded with tourists' cars and buses and offer helicopters that can be hired for a high price, this place was virtually deserted. We were offered a complimentary drink with a little alcohol in a shack-like shelter where, for those who just had to go, a very primitive outhouse was available inside a sort of bathtub. A few souvenirs were offered at dirt-cheap prices. I bought a knit cap for $3. It was not a place where one wanted to hang out for very long. The freezing wind blew fiercely. On the way back, we stopped at the Puente del Inca, a natural arch that forms a bridge over the Vacas River, a tributary of the Mendoza River. The bridge was formed naturally above some hot springs, high in the Andes. Nearby was a building, now rusty and mustard colored, whose color resulted from years of sulfur deposits from the hot springs; it was the remains of a luxury hotel built in this unique location. An avalanche of falling rocks and glacial floods destroyed this hotel and the entire village in 1965. Only the little church was not destroyed. It seemed like a miracle. I bought a tiny, mustard-yellow stone hat for my souvenir collection.

Chile

The ride home took about four hours. We very much appreciated that our guide had brought along an empty plastic bottle to demonstrate how the change in altitude (we had climbed 2,600 meters) affected the air pressure. The higher we climbed, the more the bottle flattened. It inflated more and more on the way down. Fortunately, I do not get sick at high altitudes. I was glad to have a few extra hours the next day to browse through some of the wonderful shops on the main street in Mendoza. I was surprised when I met my travel companions again the next day while awaiting my driver in the lounge of the hotel. I am still e-mailing with Teresa and Jerzey Mirecka.

The luncheon invitation to Cristian's gorgeous house in Santiago was a great finish to my Patagonian adventure. I have been a guest at many remarkable homes during my life, but none can hold a candle to Cristian's, designed by his mother, an architect. It's awesome!

My driver transferred me to the airport toward evening. Looking through the windows in the waiting area, I was captivated once more by a stunning sunset composed of a symphony of colors. *Adiós*, Patagonia! I'll be back.

ANTARCTICA – MV POLAR STAR

It is hard to believe that I would find myself in Ushuaia, Argentina, for a third time. However, the Great Antarctic Experience, from November 22 to December 10, 2006, on the MV *Polar Star* promised to be a completely different experience.

When I spotted the ship upon arriving in Ushuaia, I immediately realized, in comparing this icebreaker to both the *Marco Polo* and the *Yamal*, that he was a miniature. His gross register tonnage was 4,998, his length 86.5 meters, and his propulsion diesel electric, with 12,000 boiler horsepower. A Norwegian shipping company owned this former icebreaker. I felt very safe as soon as I came onboard and inspected my nice cabin, which had two big windows but no telephone. In the event of an emergency, I would have to look for a phone outside my cabin somewhere on the ship. Anyhow, the ship was equipped with ten Zodiacs and sufficient lifeboats. This was definitely a vessel for the adventurous.

The Falklands – Islas Malvinas

During the briefing and the welcome cocktail party, the *Polar Star* set sail for the Falkland Islands. The mandatory safety briefing took place in the Observation Lounge. Soon thereafter, dinner was served, and we got a good view of the spectacular scenery along the Beagle Channel. The channel was not new to me, since I had passed through it when I went to Antarctica the first time, but somehow it never looks exactly the same.

I was curious about what the Falkland Islands, an archipelago not quite four hundred miles due east of Patagonia and comprised of two main islands, East and West Falkland, would be like. I remembered quite well Mrs. Thatcher's 1982 war with Argentina. I did not like the Iron Lady, who had died a few weeks previously, in April 2013. Gary Kochert, with degrees in geology and botany from IU, as well as a long list of international experiences in academia, gave a fascinating description of the geography and geologic history of these South Atlantic islands.

It was early in the morning when we landed on the slipway on the eastern shore of West Point Island. This treeless island was covered in an ocean of golden-colored heather and shrubs such as *calafate*. Rod and Lilly Napier welcomed us to their island. After we had chatted with a group of soldiers and some teenagers, we walked over to the rockhopper and albatross colony at Devil's Nose. It was truly a sight to behold. Hundreds of black-browed albatrosses were huddled in the tussock on the rugged cliffs close to the blue waters of the Atlantic. Now and then an albatross spread its broad wings and gracefully sailed toward the ocean. "I now belong to a higher cult of mortals, for I have seen the albatross," said Robert Cushman Murphy. We did not linger very long, because it was rather windy and moist, and we were grateful for the mug of hot tea the Napiers served when we returned to their establishment and before we walked back to the ship, where a tasty lunch awaited us.

In the afternoon, after going through the tedious process, for the second time that day, of bundling up into umpteen layers of warm clothes and putting on those blasted rubber boots over a couple pairs of thick wool socks, which I still had from the voyage to the North Pole, we climbed again into Zodiacs. We went in search of a variety of avifauna on Carcass Island, the largest of the West Point Island group. We were lucky to see gaggles of geese, Magellanic penguins returning to their burrows, and a colony of gentoo penguins. Santiago Imberti, our expert ornithologist, told us that this is one of the few islands free of cats and rats and that it consequently boasts one of the largest populations of songbirds. However, I did not spot a single songbird or oystercatcher. As always on these trips, there is never enough time to see all the wildlife one might wish and pray to see. I really liked the pristine white-sand beaches.

Of course, whenever there was time between Zodiac trips, we attended lectures given by our outstanding naturalists and saw films about wildlife and everything related to our great Antarctic experience.

We landed early at Port Stanley, which has a population of about 2,200 people and a charming, Old World, Victorian feel. Guides were ready to point out the small museum and the southernmost Anglican cathedral in the world, and they steered us toward a couple of souvenir shops. "The town was established in the early 1840s. There was an ample supply of fresh water from Moody Brook on the western head. It was a snug, secluded harbor – perfect for sailing vessels to anchor and an abundance of peat for heating. The view to the west of Stanley harbor is dominated by mountains and hills, with Mount London and Mount Tumbledown lying north and south of the twin peaks of two sisters. The highest point in the horizon is Mount Kent at 1,504 ft" (Brochure).

I took in the museum rather quickly, as I had a chance to join one of the passengers and his son to visit one of the over one hundred still-uncleared minefields, though the English promised they would eliminate the mines. I had never before seen a minefield and found it hard to believe that after all these years, young and old would still be banned from walking there. The areas were fenced in and marked. Since many mines were laid on the main beaches, they too were off-limits. I had never seen a bomb-disposal unit either. Well, heaven knows the Iron Lady was lacking in compassion for the poor and less privileged. What would you expect? After all, the English won the war.

As we still had a little time before heading back to our ship, I went back to the little museum and admired especially the model of the SS *Discovery*. It was the late Captain R. F. Scott's Antarctic ship, which was reconstructed between 1923 and 1924. A special place was dedicated to the great polar explorer Wally Herbert, whom I had never heard about. I quote from the plaque: "During the course of his polar career he has spent 14 years in the polar regions; retracing the routes of some of the greatest explorers in history – Shackleton, Scott and Amundsen in the Antarctic, and Peary, Sverdrup and Cook in the Arctic." Though the people are very friendly in Port Stanley, it is not a place where I would choose to live!

In the afternoon I thoroughly enjoyed Brigitte Fugger's lecture in the Observation Lounge. She introduced us to the natural history of seals, focusing on elephant and fur seals. Brigitte was one of the most fascinating naturalists I encountered on my "ice trips." She had a great, full voice and a mesmerizing personality. Though she studied biology at Heidelberg University and was a native of Germany, her English was accent free. She had organized and led over 130 wildlife expeditions around the globe and really knew her stuff. Brigitte had also lectured on the *Yamal*, and I was stunned when she said that the *Marco Polo* was the worst ship for travel to Antarctica. In retrospect, I know what she meant. The *Marco Polo* is more a gin palace than an icebreaker. I found her so exciting because I had been to most of the places she had visited, such as the Amazon and Yangtze Rivers, the Caribbean, the Atlantic and Pacific Oceans, and the Arctic and Southern Oceans.

South Georgia – Scotia Sea

South Georgia was the main reason for my return to Antarctica. Someone once said, "If God went on vacation, he would go to South Georgia." When my stepdaughter Liesl was only eight or nine, she told me that someday she would like to go to South Georgia. At that time, I had no idea where South Georgia was. Of course, during my travels, this or that cotraveler would rave about it, and eventually I had no other wish than to see this wondrous island for myself, no matter how expensive it would be. After all, the cost did not exceed that of the North Pole trip.

Approaching South Georgia was incredibly exciting. Everybody onboard was keyed up with anticipation. Each iceberg we passed was more uniquely sculpted than the last and elicited oohs and aahs from us – or just silence. Suddenly, in the distance, four strange rocks, like pyramids, popped up out of the sea. Called Shag Rocks, they are outliers of South Georgia and 230 feet high. The snowcapped mountains along the shore grew higher and higher. Unimaginable panoramas, with a clear blue sky in the background and a blue sea at the mountains' feet, unfolded in slow motion and kept me awestruck.

After listening to several lectures – "Andes in the Ocean," "Penguins," "Whales and Dolphins of the Southern Ocean," "Shackleton – The Glorious Failure!" "Kings of South Georgia," and "South Georgia: Sub-Antarctic Jewel" – and viewing the film *Life in the Freezer: The Ice Retreats*, we were psyched up enough to embark on our first Zodiac adventure to South Georgia. We had arrived at Grytviken and Hercules Bay.

Antarctica – MV Polar Star

From a distance, the old whaling station at Grytviken looked rather picturesque. The whalers' white church, the museum, and the post office appeared well maintained, and on this clear day, November 29, 2006, the entire panorama, with the snowcapped mountains in the background, was mirrored in the calm sea.

My first stop at Grytviken was at the museum, followed by a visit to the post office to take care of mailings, buy little souvenirs, and most of all, get my passport stamped to prove I had been to South Georgia. I slowly made my way past sea lions loafing in groups along the shoreline and smiled at this and that penguin moving around or just standing straight up. I saw my first king penguins here! Somewhat reluctantly, I explored the old whaling station, which was closed down in 1964. I had no idea how extensive and brutal this industry used to be. Nevertheless, I looked at the crumbling structures of various buildings where different parts of the gigantic, dissected whales were processed. Four or five whaling ships, some larger than others, lay stranded and badly rusted on the shore. Very long, heavy, thick, and rusty chains and a huge, black iron whale claw lay discarded not far from a shipwreck. The seals did not seem to mind. Yet, they can be dangerous. Brigitte got quite mad at me when I once strayed from the marked path and did not notice that a big fur seal had started to chase me from behind. Brigitte had a friend who lost a leg to a fierce seal attack. After that scare, I was more careful.

My final and most memorable stop at Grytviken was the still-functioning whalers' church. I was impressed that it was the most southerly church in the world, prefabricated in Norway, together with its gray slate steeple and roof, before it was shipped to South Georgia, reassembled, and consecrated on Christmas Day 1913. I was interested in the church's cemetery not because many whalers were laid to rest there, but because on March 5, 1922, Sir Ernest Shackleton was buried there. His grave was oriented to the south instead of the east. I liked the Robert Browning quotation on the reverse of the stone: "I hold that a man should strive to the uttermost for his life's set prize." – I don't like to be photographed, but made an exception here. I asked one of my cotravelers to take a picture of me next to Shackleton's grave. Next to the grave lay a couple of still-fresh roses covered with a piece of transparent plastic and a commemoration, which I quote: "I had a dream to honor your life by placing roses on your grave. Your persistence and determination, your value of life has inspired our family, your distant relatives in New Zealand, to emulate your courage. 'In grateful memory,' January 2005, Karen Gaye Walker, Granddaughter of Francis William Shackleton, Auckland, New Zealand."

In the afternoon, we gathered for yet another Zodiac venture, which took us to Hercules Bay. We cruised along three-hundred-meter-high, snow-covered cliffs and small shingle beaches. Since I am comparatively short, I always had to be careful when climbing out of the Zodiac. It usually involved sliding into the freezing water and then making it to shore. Rubber boots are a must! Once, I jumped out of instead of sliding off the Zodiac. Brigitte, who was assisting with the descent, was furious with me. She later apologized, but I did not hold it against her. I realized it was stupid of me to be so careless. We climbed up and around this scenic inlet, admiring macaroni penguins with their distinctive yellow crests. The extraordinary, fat elephant seals looked scarier than the fur seals, even though it was a fur seal that had tried to attack me. Seals were resting on the rocky beaches all over, and not necessarily next to bushes of tussock grass on the bluff. They seemed to prefer to hang out along the shoreline, close to a waterfall, and to leave the penguins on the cliffs to themselves. I never looked for kelp beds in the crystal-clear water. Well, maybe next time!

On the morning of November 29, we were awakened at 6:30, and as early as 8:00, we landed on the beach of Husvik to view another crumbling whaling station. The weather was smiling. We walked to the cemetery, where some thirty-four whalers were buried from 1924 to 1959, and explored the very small but rather cozy manager's villa, aka "the Radio Shack." A small shelter with a generator was nearby. The villa, in addition to some other buildings, had been restored only a few months earlier by a team of Norwegian craftsmen. We were warned to stay some 650 feet away from the whaling station, as it was too dangerous. I opted out of a walk up the Husvik Valley, thus missing out on seeing glacial lakes, possibly reindeer, and unique vegetation. I let myself be amused by some resting seals and waddling penguins. I recall that the hikers did not see the reindeer either.

After lunch, we headed out again – to a whaling station at Stromness Harbor. According to my notes, it is the "historic site of Shackleton, Worsley and Crean's arrival in 1916 at the end of their crossing of South Georgia." Again, lacking the energy and the drive, I decided against hiking four kilometers up a trail to a waterfall at the head of the valley and sliding down the icefield, even though explorers supposedly did so. I did hike up by myself until I was forced to stop by the unexpectedly deep snow. I sank into a hole up to my hips, and the tip of the folding cane, which I had to support me, got stuck so badly that when I tried to pull it out, it collapsed into small sections along the elastic band inside. The bottom of the cane did not give. I laughed out loud since it looked so funny. A gentleman came to my rescue and pulled me out. A pair of gentoo penguins nearby did not even turn their heads.

That evening after happy hour, most of us went up on deck. We stood in silence and were spellbound by the most beautiful sunset I have ever seen. The rugged, snow-capped mountains reaching out of the sea shimmered like gold!

The next morning – a glorious day with sunshine and blue skies – we embarked on my most glorious Zodiac ride ever. It happened at the vast expanse of glacial outwash, the Salisbury Plain! A nature lovers' paradise unfolded before our eyes. Some sixty thousand, or even more as some claimed, dazzling-looking breeding pairs of king penguins occupied this enormous colony. We walked along the beach right into the heart of it, and I snapped more photos of these handsome creatures than I have ever taken of any other animal. They were so mesmerizing as they stood proudly in groups, in pairs, or alone amidst numerous fur seals and fat elephant seals. It was very hard to tear myself away from this wondrous sight. While walking around, I got stuck again in some sort of muddy hole in the swampy and very uneven terrain, but got out by myself.

The afternoon landing at Prion Island, where we saw the nesting site for wandering albatrosses and more fur seals, was for me rather anticlimactic, as were the 5:30 a.m. stop the next morning to view the Bertrab Glacier and the second morning landing at Cooper Bay to see more king, gentoo, chinstrap, and macaroni penguins, all four species in one spot. I guess, since this was my second trip to Antarctica, I had seen my fill of penguins. It was more exalting, I thought, to sail through the spectacular Drygalski Fjord – with its magnificent glaciers reaching into the sea – and wait for dramatic calvings.

I felt a bit sad listening to Bill's lecture, "An Introduction to Antarctica," as we bid farewell to South Georgia and sailed toward Elephant Island, on Antarctica. I was wondering whether I would recognize it, since I had been there with the *Marco Polo* a few years earlier.

South Shetlands

The Antarctic includes the continent of Antarctica (the fifth largest), the surrounding Southern Ocean, and the 19 peri-Antarctic islands. The limit of the Southern Ocean is the Antarctic Convergence. (Brochure)

We spent two full days on the Scotia Sea sailing to Elephant Island, in the South Shetlands. While sailing, we listened to lectures and watched a couple of films: *Moby Dick* and *Around Cape Horn*. On Monday, December 4, we cruised on a Zodiac around Cape Wild, Glacier Bay, Cape Belsham, and Elephant Island, where I recognized a building seen on my previous trip. Unfortunately, the weather was too rough for us to land at the historic Point Wild. "It was the place where the remaining members of Ernest Shackleton's failed attempt to cross the Antarctic continent were stranded for 135 days until they were eventually rescued by Shackleton in the Chilean tug *Yelcho*" (Brochure).

A quite memorable event occurred one morning. It had snowed, and the upper deck was all white. While the mates were busy sweeping the white fluff, we had fun tossing snowballs, and a couple of the younger women were hopping around in the snow wearing tank shirts, capris, and sandals. Amazing. Dr. Peterson's girls, Sarah (five years old) and Hannah (seven), just loved the snow. Looking back, I am so pleased to have met that nice family. Only a few years later, his wife wrote that her husband had passed away. I had no idea that he was already sick during the trip. He was much too nice and too young to leave his family behind. In fact, since he was quite interested in Hitler and the related history, I sent him the Mother's

Cross I still had. A silver cross with a swastika in the center, it was given to my devout Catholic grandmother because she had had more than four children. She had seven. My mother did not want it and gladly let me have it. I showed it to my students when lecturing about that period. – I wonder now whether "the Pest," a wealthy California Republican, then over eighty years old and accompanied by his younger Democratic son, has passed away. On the very first day, he started to pursue me, commenting on my nice cashmere sweaters and making it known that his wife had given him permission to have a fling with women while traveling without her. He was an arrogant b—d, and I tried to avoid him whenever possible. Fortunately, he avoided climbing up the rather steep stairway to the observation bridge, where I liked to hang out when we were sailing for long stretches. It was the place frequented by the younger and more interesting passengers. One young Japanese had taken a six-month leave of absence from a financial institution in California. He wanted to see the world. Actually, everybody in our group was a world traveler. These trips were not for the faint of heart.

Half Moon Island

On Tuesday, December 5, we landed at Half Moon Island, site of the Argentinean Antarctic polar station Camara, to which I had previously traveled. The chinstrap-penguin colony was still there, and not as smelly this time. I did not remember the remains of the old dory boat, and I skipped the rather long walk to the other side of the island. I was not the only one who did not go. – Of course, I made sure I was out on deck as we sailed into the caldera of Port Foster, on the volcanic Deception Island, and loved the passage through the precipitous, six-hundred-foot-wide Neptune's Bellows. Wow!

The afternoon landing at Whalers Bay entailed an encounter with yet another whaling station, operated from 1912 to 1931, and the BAS post destroyed by the eruption of 1969. It was the spot from which Herbert Wilkins took the first powered flight in Antarctica. The walk to Neptune's Window was nice but tiring. Sorry. Of course, as on my first visit, I forewent the swim in the thermally heated waters at Pendulum Cave. If you recall, I did not take a dip at the North Pole either.

The crew of the *Polar Star* truly did their best to make this trip special for us. Before heading to Port Lockroy and while maneuvering the icebreaker through ice and through the breathtaking soaring cliffs of the Neumayer Channel, they served breakfast in the observation lounge! What a treat! Thank you!

It was my second visit to Port Lockroy, located on Goudier Island, which some consider "the most exciting anchorage." It is a former British Antarctic station (Base A), which was closed in 1962 but is preserved by the UK Antarctic Heritage Trust as a museum and post office, where we had our passports stamped again. We were warned to be careful not to step on the moss on the way up to the PO, as it takes forever to recover. Somehow, I slipped, stepped on the moss, and had my head bitten off by a copassenger who noticed it. I made sure there was no damage. After all, I was petite and not at all overweight. Still, I have never forgotten it. I was sorry. – The museum was well-preserved, and I was amazed at the different canned foods on the shelves in the kitchen. Over the stove hung several sweaters – to dry, I suppose. Next to a storage room was a cozy bedroom combined with a radio-station room, crammed full of open boxes and instruments, not very neat. But there were curtains on the windows! – Somehow, I missed out on seeing the full whale skeleton on the beach of Wiencke Island. I was not upset. I had seen whale bones before.

In the afternoon, we landed more directly on the continent of Antarctica itself, at the "moth balled" Argentinean station Almirante Brown, in Paradise Bay. It is indeed a most stunning bay, with the most beautiful peaks and the Garzon Glacier. It well deserves to be called Paradise Bay! Most of all, I just loved the Zodiac cruise after the stop. We encountered some of the most striking sculptured icebergs and marveled at the massive ice wall, but searched in vain for any sort of wildlife.

We now sailed toward Cierva Cove and Mikkelsen Harbor along the Antarctic continent. I did not remember having been there on my first trip.

> *The ice was here, the ice was there,*
> *The ice was all around:*
> *It cracked and growled, and roared and howled,*
> *Like noises in a swound!*

(Samuel Taylor Coleridge, *The Rime of the Ancient Mariner*)

We were ready to board our Zodiac at 9:00 a.m., and we landed at Cierva Cove not too much later. This place was definitely new to me. I loved the icebergs, a seal here and there, and was happy to observe colonies of gentoo and chinstrap penguins. Fortunately, I also came upon a small, snow-white Antarctic flower embedded in a light-green bed of mosses. We were told that there are only two Antarctic flowering plants.

After lunch on the ship, we went through our last dressing hassle, this time for the landing at Mikkelsen Harbor, named by a "whaling captain after his wife Caroline Mikkelsen, who in 1935 [three years after I was born] was the first woman to land in Antarctica." Another large colony of gentoo penguins was gathered on this small island, located at the south end of Trinity Island, not far from the harbor where we landed. And if you have never seen whale bones, this is one of the places where you will see a big heap of them, dating back to the 1920s. The abandoned whaling station may still be near the shore. Slaughtering whales used to be big business on the Antarctic continent, as the rusting structures of defunct whaling stations will attest. This would be the last time I came upon penguins and whaling stations. We were leaving the Antarctic Peninsula to battle the challenging waters of the Drake Passage.

A deep strait (average depth of 11,000 ft and 620 miles wide) the Drake Passage is bounded by Cape Horn in the north and the South Shetland Islands, just north of the Antarctic Peninsula, in the south. . . . With stormy seas and icy conditions, the Drake provided a rigorous test of seamanship; "Rounding the Horn" was feared by mariners and travelers alike. (Brochure)

The entire crew of the *Polar Star* had already been somewhat nervous while we were out on the Scotia Sea. They knew the forthcoming passage would not be smooth. The closer we came, the more our little ship rocked, and we had to hold on to railings, walls, and chairs in the lounge and elsewhere. We were not allowed to go out on deck. A woman had fallen down a flight of stairs and broken her leg early on. She was stuck in her cabin. Fortunately her husband was there. The bull's eyes on the lower decks had been barricaded. One could not see out anyhow, because the water was splashing against the windowpanes. Since I had been on stormy seas before, I had learned how to navigate in situations like this. The drawers next to my bed in the cabin came rolling out constantly. Finally I just left them on the floor. While I sat on my bed, rocking and looking out the window, a loud scream came from the cabin next door. It was impossible for me to even walk to my door to look. It was too rocky, even for me. A bit later, I learned that the woman's husband had fallen just outside the door to the bathroom, where she was. As she tried to step down over him, she too fell, slid toward the chest of drawers in their cabin, and broke a rib or two, or so she thought. I have never heard anybody scream in pain as loudly as this woman did. – Instead of dinner, we were served sandwiches. And all beverages were served in paper cups instead of glasses. Many passengers just stayed in their cabins, and others were seasick. Somehow, I thought the situation was a bit amusing and really adventurous. I was really lucky not to suffer from seasickness and not to scare easily. After all, I usually travel by myself and have learned to discipline myself and be self-reliant. In retrospect, I must say that the captain and his crew did a superb job weathering the raging waves in the Drake Passage. Congratulations, and thanks!

I disembarked the *Polar Star* early in the morning on December 10, 2006. My driver picked me up and took me to the small airport in Ushuaia. My flight with Aerolíneas Argentinas took off at 9:50 a.m. and arrived in Buenos Aires at 2:20 p.m. My connecting flight to Santiago departed at 5:30 p.m. and arrived in Santiago at 6:45 p.m. I was expected by the driver, who transferred me to my hotel downtown. Again, the beauty of the Chilean capital, surrounded by snowcapped mountains, impressed me. The setting sun gave the mountains a golden glow. My upscale hotel was modern and comfortable. I was, of course, somewhat tired. Before retiring for the night, I called Cristian to announce my arrival and make a date for an early supper the next day.

Antarctica – MV Polar Star

Chile

Santiago

After breakfast, I ventured out for a stroll in downtown Santiago. It was a gorgeous day. The sun was shining, the sky blue, and the flowering shrubs and trees in bloom. I was amazed again by how much Chile had progressed. – At the hotel I decided to relax in the nice lobby, observe the people, and take a look at the newspapers. I could hardly believe the headlines, which announced the death of Augusto Pinochet, the Chilean Army general and dictator who assumed power in a coup d'état on September 11, 1973, resulting in the death of Salvador Allende and the end of his democratically elected socialist government. The CIA, of course, backed this coup. What a coincidence – a year earlier, I was in Santiago on Pinochet's ninetieth birthday. He was under house arrest while awaiting his trial. Now, this criminal dictator, who was responsible for thousands of deaths and tortured everybody who dared to oppose him, was dead. – I took advantage of the situation and walked up to the reception desk, where I started a conversation with a young female clerk. She told me that her father, as well as other family members and acquaintances, had disappeared under Pinochet's dictatorship and were never heard from again. I felt sorry for her and understood why she was relieved that the criminal was finally dead.

My meeting with Cristian was nice, but I excused myself early. I was invited for lunch at his parents' gorgeous house the next day. Cristian picked me up at the hotel in his mother's car. On the way, he asked me not to talk about Pinochet to his mother. I was surprised but kept my mouth shut. I liked his mother, who spoke perfect English. She had studied architecture in Chile and at MIT and Harvard. Edita was serving; the other maid and the two gardeners in charge of the beautiful grounds must have been on a siesta. Mrs. Lolas thanked me profoundly for being so nice to her son and to Edita, who had been their domestic help, as well as the nanny of their three children, for many years. I had wanted to do something nice for Cristian while I was still living. I had told him I would like to take him and a friend who would not be able to afford it on a trip to Easter Island. It was to be a graduation gift. I was surprised when he asked if he could bring Edita instead of a male friend, but I agreed. Later on, I realized that a young man like Cristian, brought up with a silver spoon, would most likely not hang out with youngsters from less privileged backgrounds. Of course, I had met Edita previously and liked her. She was always smiling, very respectful, and kind.

At one point, when Cristian was out of the dining room, his mother mentioned that they had a problem. Her husband had lost a huge amount gambling at the casino. They had to mortgage the house in order to pay off the debt. I was a bit shocked. I knew they owned a clinic, and even my driver knew of the family. But I was glad I knew about the problem. When the father drove us to the airport the next morning, I found him very nice and attentive, though he hardly uttered a sentence. It was probably because he did not speak English. But Cristian could have translated. In retrospect, it seems strange that he never thanked me for what I was doing for his son. Maybe he was embarrassed. I doubt they ever would have sent one of their servants to Easter Island. Maybe he was grieving the death of Pinochet, whom he obviously admired.

EASTER ISLAND - RAPA NUI

On December 12, 2006, after an approximately three-hour flight, the Lan Airlines plane landed safely at the rather humble airport on Rapa Nui, the Polynesian island in the Southeastern Pacific Ocean, a territory annexed to Chile in 1888. Upon deplaning, we were adorned with a lei of pink and white bougainvillea blossoms, and after having our picture taken, we met our driver, sent by Discover Latin America, for the transfer to our motel-like hotel, located at some distance from the little town close to the ocean. I was happy to see palm trees and bougainvillea and hibiscus bushes along the drive leading to the hotel, and we were pleased with our rooms. Cristian had suggested it would be proper for him to share a room with Edita. I was glad he had brought someone with whom he could venture out and who would look after him. The responsibility would have been a bit too much for me after the challenging trip to Antarctica. Moreover, I was not about to play nanny to a spoiled teenager. Since we had a plan that included breakfast and dinner, we did not have to worry about finding restaurants for the duration of our five-day stay. –

I had not read much about Easter Island before arriving, as I like the element of surprise. It immediately became obvious that the place was not overrun with tourists. Only a few flights, from Santiago and Tahiti, arrived each week. Most of the island is protected within Rapa Nui National Park. I noticed quickly that the island was lacking in trees and was in general dominated by a rather stark terrain, typical for volcanic rock. After a brief siesta, we explored the shoreline. It was just beautiful; rugged black rocks partially framed the inlets, and the blue waters within were splashing. One inlet, which resembled a swimming pool, was framed by rocks reaching as high as eighty feet where the ocean waves forced their way through a narrow opening. Cristian immediately dove into the pool to test the water. Edita and I laughed hard when the water suddenly began splashing as high as one hundred feet and the mist almost prevented us from seeing Cristian, who eventually waved at us from down there. Since his family owns a vacation condo outside of Valparaiso, on the coast, he had ample opportunity to swim. He was definitely happy and excited. I noticed a couple of weather-beaten palm trees close to the shore as we hiked back to our hacienda and got a chance to admire the grounds. They were beautifully landscaped, with palm trees, cacti, tropical flowers, and manicured lawns. Cristian then headed for a dip in the big swimming pool at the hotel and gave it his approval. It was a lot bigger than the pool at his home in Santiago. Later that evening, before dinner, we relaxed near the pool with a nonalcoholic drink and admired an intoxicating sunset. Also intoxicating, and quite exotic, was the young, dark-skinned waitress who served our pink fruit drinks. She wore a long, cobalt-blue sari, like a gown, and a pink hibiscus blossom was fastened in the thick black hair behind her right ear. She was happy to pose for a photo.

This trip was intended as a gift for Cristian, who was by then a freshman at the university. I told him I would appreciate it if he took over for me and engaged directly with our private guide, Dina, who appeared at 9:00 the next morning in a jeep with Roberto, the driver. Dina had studied history and anthropology, among other disciplines, in the States, met her husband during a visit to the island years ago, and more or less got stuck there. In short, she turned out to be extremely knowledgeable about everything we wanted to know about Rapa Nui, about which she had also published a book. Believe me, Cristian challenged her constantly. The bulk of my friends' conversation was in Spanish, though Cristian had a very good command of the English language. But Edita spoke only Spanish. After a while, I stopped insisting on translations and was content to see that my guests were happy. I felt sorry for Dina when I noticed that she climbed in and out of the jeep with difficulty and had trouble walking longer distances during our sightseeing ventures. She easily weighed more than 250 pounds, which at age 62 could not have been good. She occasionally had to stop and rest, and I was secretly hoping she would not have a heart attack. The weather was perfect. The sun was bright, and around noon it would get quite warm, even hot. The proximity to the sea, with a constant breeze, made it tolerable for me. I do not like being out in tropical climates. I welcomed the absence of humidity in Rapa Nui.

Our tour started with a visit to the ruins of the temple of Vaihu, which, Dina told us, was still as it had been for centuries. It was our first encounter with the mysterious, giant, monolithic moai, of which more than 880 are supposed to be scattered across the island. They are indeed fascinating sculptures. Though their features are similar, each one appears to have its own distinctive character. They are gigantic, weighing tons. Most of them wear a big, round, rust-colored "stone hat" on their heads. Many of the hats were supposedly thrown into the sea. When we continued to the Rano Raraku Volcano's quarry, which is the traditional symbol of the island and the original factory of the moai, we saw where they were carved in the rock in either an upright position or lying face down, abandoned on their intended road to the platforms.

Ahu Tongariki, aka Ahu, was our next stop. Among the moai platforms on the island that were destroyed by a tidal wave in 1960, it was the biggest. At this truly amazing sight, we were confronted with fifteen of these almost-majestic stone sculptures, all in a straight line on top of the platform, with their backs toward the blue sea, like soldiers. We were told that the moai were toppled during the island's civil wars and, in the twentieth century, by tidal waves.

Next to a small table, not far removed from that spectacular site, stood a woman and a young man selling miniature moai figures. I bought ten figures at a bargain price and was quite happy with my treasures. What was even more memorable at this spot was the appearance of the young man, the son of the mother. He was most likely a Chilean, maybe not pure-blooded. He was tall and slender and brown skinned. His features were striking and very handsome. He had an oval-shaped face and brown eyes, and straight, long, very dark brown hair hung over his shoulders. In profile, with a finely sculpted nose, his head resembled that of Jesus. His demeanor was gentle and somewhat humble. I asked him whether he would mind my taking his picture. He smiled and I thanked him profoundly. Nice.

At the archeological zone of Ahu Tahai, our guide pointed out the different sizes, smaller and larger, of the five moai and interpreted them as representing "an attempt to create some individualism in the statues." At some locations, we stared at just a huge head that seemed to have sat on the ground forever.

At the Father Sebastian Englert Anthropological Museum, next to wood statuettes and other displays, I found it quite interesting that the museum housed the only female moai with coral eyes. And it seemed a bit strange to me that the founder of the museum was a Bavarian missionary!

I thought it even more curious and exciting when, at Ahu Vinapu, I stumbled upon some rather striking stone walls, which immediately reminded me of the Incan walls I had seen when visiting Cuzco and Machu Picchu in Peru. The architecture of these walls – the carefully fitted slabs of basalt – displays the same extraordinary precision in stonemasonry as the walls in Peru and leaves little doubt that the early islanders came from South America.

At the Puna Pao crater, we saw where the red tuff stone originated – the stone from which the *pukao* (head knots) of the moai were made. Traveling nine miles from there, we visited Ahu Akivi, which featured seven moai of equal height. Still, it was quite a distance to transport these monumental stone giants. It is speculated that they were transported with the help of ropes and palm-tree stumps and by rolling, pulling, or sliding them down slopes and valleys. Either way, it was not an easy task. To think of the construction of the pyramids and monuments in Egypt!

We visited the Ahu Te Pito Kura mainly to view the supposedly largest moai ever finished, which at some point in history had tumbled, along with its topknot, to the ground. It lies face down and is called Paro. *Muy interesante*! We agreed that the hours spent at Anakena Beach and the Ahu Hekii site were more exciting.

Before driving to Anakena, we had lunch at a small restaurant a few meters from the seashore. We sat outside and chatted pleasantly with the nice young couple at the next table. They were from New York and were just loving their vacation here. Not far from our table, some local boys had fun repeatedly jumping from the shore into the water. A fisherman in his tiny boat boasted a lobster, just caught. I had no idea I would eat the very same lobster for dinner that evening at our hacienda. Not bad.

Anakena Beach is perhaps the most Polynesian-looking part of the island, very paradisiacal, with an unexpected grove of coconut palms on a white-sand beach in a calm blue cove of warm Pacific waters. It is quite a contrast to the otherwise rough, black-rock coastline. Cristian and Edita could not wait to go swimming. I opted to look at the ahu with six moai in the background. They had carvings on their backs, which struck me as very unusual, and they still had the red scoria on top of their heads. It is believed that Hotu Matu'a and his family first settled here. I am in no position to dispute that theory. It was nice to see a somewhat gentler side to this island, more or less devoid of any kind of shrubs or trees. We were told that at one time, forests covered portions of the island. Imagine that!

Cristian and Edita were eager to explore a couple of the many caves of the island, such as Ana Te Pahu, and the dramatic volcanic rock cliffs of Ana Te Pora and Ana Kai Tangata, which border the ocean. These caves are rather large and were once used by the Rapa Nui natives for living quarters. I did not crawl in – and forgot to ask whether they saw any wall paintings.

In the morning of our last day, we drove to the southernmost volcano of the island, Rano Kau. It was formed of basaltic lava flows, and we looked down on a reed-covered lake in the center of the crater. Since it borders the sea and is surrounded by very jagged basalt rocks, the view was both breathtaking and scary. I did not blame Dina for staying behind. We had a great view of the islets Motu Nui, Moto Iti, and Motu Kao Kao. I thought it a bit strange that the natives built their fifty-three stone houses in the ceremonial village of Orongo right on the crater's rim. The location at the edge of the crater is extremely dramatic. At that point, an approximately eight-hundred-foot sea cliff converges with the inner wall of the crater of Rano Kau. Careful!

It was here as well that Dina told us a bit about the birdman cult: "Each year leadership of the island was determined by the individual who could scale down the vertical slopes, swim out to one of the three islets in shark-infested water, and bring back the egg of the nesting sooty tern unbroken. The one who did this successfully was considered the birdman of the year and was bestowed with special honors and privilege." The cult is evidenced by the many petroglyphs carved with birdman and Makemake images into solid basalt. You are welcome to check it out yourself on this most isolated island in the world. You won't be sorry.

I do not recall seeing any birds while I was there. But never before had I seen more wild horses roaming around in search of nourishment than I saw on the already-overgrazed yet pristine yellowish-green meadows of Easter Island. I just loved watching them.

Dina insisted that we not miss a visit to the ruins of Vaihu and Akahanga. According to legend, the tomb of the first king of the island, Hotu Matu'a, is in this area. At both sites, Dina pointed out a few more knocked-over moai, which authorities were considering restoring. Personally, I felt they could just leave them as they were. By then I had a pretty good idea of what they would look like standing up.

Our good guide informed us that the early settlers called the island "Te Pito O Te Henua" (Navel of the World), and she made sure we saw the sacred navel of the world, located close to the coast. It was basically a very large, smooth, and round stone, considered very sacred by the ancients. She suggested we embrace it with our arms and see if we could feel anything. I did not feel the supposedly tingling sensation. I should have, as the stone is now thought to be a meteorite and hence magnetic. I personally got more excited when at this very location, I recognized a young man with whom I had chatted on the flight over. I asked Cristian to take a photo of us next to the sacred boulder. Still, I felt no tingling sensation. Sorry!

A visit to the colorful handicrafts market and a stop at the little grocery store where we picked up fruits and snacks for lunch, as well as our brief visit to the only Catholic church in Hanga Roa, were almost uneventful. Almost. – At the tiny grocery store, we stood in line for a while to pay for the goods. When it was my turn, in order not to hold up the people behind me, I handed my bills to the man behind the counter. He was quite upset and loudly complained about the manner in which I handed him the money. He said I should have placed the money on the counter instead of handing it to him directly. I did not really understand what it was all about. Once we were outside, Cristian reiterated that it was rude of me to hand the money to him like that. I turned around, went back into the store, and apologized to the man behind the counter. It must have been a cultural thing. To this day, I do not have a clue.

The church was small, and it had clearly been constructed with inexpensive materials. It was very well-lit inside, and I liked the carved wooden statues mounted here and there on the walls. I especially enjoyed a hand-carved fish and a wooden Madonna. Interestingly enough, neither Cristian nor Edita paid any attention to these pieces. Instead, they stood for a long time in front of a small Madonna dressed in a rather tacky, glitzy robe. Next to her stood a vase with a bouquet of equally tacky fake flowers. We attended Mass in that church on the morning of our departure. It made my friends very happy.

In the early afternoon, Dina took us for a good-bye to "the first ahu." On the way we passed a group of grazing wild horses. I noticed a gorgeous white stallion not far from the others. He really caught my eye. It was the only white horse I had seen on this mysterious island in the five days we had been there. Maybe it was a good omen? – This island really grows on you. It is a destination you must experience in person and, if possible, by yourself. It is eternally peaceful. The rugged shorelines formed by black volcanic rock, similar to the shorelines of Hawaii, take one's breath away. The blue waves breaking against the rocks and spraying white, foamy clouds of water onto the rocks and into the air are simply fascinating to watch. Easter Island is truly magical and enigmatic. It is like a good piece of art that leaves something to the imagination. Thinking about it brings a smile to your face and leaves a certain serenity within. A passenger on the plane told me she had heard that people like to come back and live out their lives here. I could see why.

We boarded the plane around noon on December 18. We were so lucky. They upgraded us to first class. *Muchas gracias.* The good-byes in Santiago were sad; Cristian and Edita thanked me a thousand times while a few tears trickled down our cheeks. Dr. Lolas picked them up, and I caught a connecting flight back to Indianapolis via Buenos Aires and arrived at home in the late afternoon. – Sometimes I wished Cristian's mother had not told me about her husband's gambling problems and that Cristian had not begged me to avoid talking with his mother about Pinochet. It definitely put a damper on the friendship. I have not heard from Cristian since the trip and am still waiting for a handwritten thank-you note from Edita, for which I had asked her. I have a thing about old-fashioned written notes, especially in Spanish. Regardless, I have not tried to contact Cristian for a long time. It was good to find out a bit more about his parents' philosophy. After a long silence, I made sure that neither Cristian nor Edita would benefit from any inheritance, which I had planned to leave for them.

To be fair, had I not known Cristian, I might not have gone to Easter Island, at least not at that time. – It is a place for savvy travelers!

RUSSIA – TRANS-SIBERIAN RAILWAY

Someone once said, "You have not traveled unless you have taken the Trans-Sib Rail." Thus, early in 2004, I started browsing the Internet for a Trans-Siberian Railway trip and ended up booking the grand tour with Lernidee, a German company. The trip went from Moscow to Beijing, with an optional seven-day detour to Mongolia (South Gobi Desert). Why not do it all, once there?

The Trans-Sib Railway, with almost six thousand miles of track, is considered the most complicated and longest railroad in the world. It had been a secret fascination of mine for a long time. I enjoyed reading the masterpieces of Russian literature during my college years and saw the movie version of Boris Pasternak's novel *Doctor Zhivago* several times. I would have loved to travel in winter to marvel at the snow-covered landscapes, but decided on a late-summer trip instead. I could always return, right?! Also, I had quickly fallen in love with Saint Petersburg when I first saw it on a Baltic cruise a couple years earlier, and I was curious to see what Moscow, the capital of Russia, which is after all the largest country in the world, was like. – But having developed a special liking for Saint Petersburg, I thought it would be foolish not to revisit it and combine it with the Trans-Sib Railway venture. Lernidee was glad to organize a pre-trip to this jewel of a city.

Saint Petersburg

On August 18, 2004, I flew from Indianapolis, by way of Frankfurt, Germany, to Saint Petersburg, where my private guide, Jurij Dudorov, who spoke perfect German as well as English, greeted me at the gate. I was treated like a VIP. We had a private driver with a Mercedes-Benz, highly polished and impeccably clean inside. My hotel was in a central location, and though not extravagant, it was nice and clean.

Without going into great detail, I want to relate that the itinerary Jurij had planned was just as I had wished. The reconstruction of the fabled Amber Room in the Catherine Palace, which was presented to Russia by Frederic Wilhelm I of Germany in 1719 and mysteriously disappeared during World War II, was completed in time for Saint Petersburg's three hundredth anniversary. Only one year after my first visit, I was determined to see it. In 2002, the city had been busy with restorations that would give the room a distinct face-lift, which now was obvious. Jurij had been able to obtain easy access to the famous and extremely flamboyant rococo summer residence of the Russian tsars, located about twenty-five kilometers southeast of Saint Petersburg. We walked past the long lines and, once inside, through many extravagantly decorated rooms right to the Amber Room, which struck me as somewhat over the top. It is also referred to as the eighth wonder of the world. The walls of the chamber are covered with a series of large, gold, shimmering amber panels, mosaics, and mirrors. We were told that several tons of carved amber and many gemstones were used to create the room. A German millionaire donated several million euros to the reconstruction. I was particularly interested in the room, because rumor had it that the chamber, or portions of it, had been hidden in the Wittekind Mine in Volpriehausen, where we lived in the big villa next door for seven years. My uncle, the tyrant, had been director of the potash mine before it was converted into an ammunition factory and underground storage place for some three hundred thousand tons of ammunition. I have written about that time in Part I of my memoirs. By the way, they are still looking for the treasure.

I had asked Jurij for a longer visit to the Hermitage, which he had arranged and which I thoroughly enjoyed. He had also included visits to a couple of smaller palaces and, more importantly, had secured a ticket for a perfect seat at a dazzling performance of Tchaikovsky's *Swan Lake* by the Kirov Ballet in the Mariinsky Theater. They picked me up at the hotel, and the driver, dressed properly in a black suit and carrying a big black umbrella to protect me from the rain, walked me to the entrance door of the theater. It was nice to have someone to talk to about the exquisite ballet performance on the way back to the hotel. What an evening!

Before I knew it, it was time to take my night train from Saint Petersburg to Moscow. I felt a bit uneasy. It had not been possible to reserve a sleeper compartment just for myself. Jurij accompanied me to my compartment, and I thanked him profoundly before he left. I almost forgot to tell you a bizarre story Jurij confided in me. Like many Russians, he did not trust the banks. Thus, he put all his cash in a coal-burning stove in their apartment. No, they no longer burned coal in the stove. – I had time to settle in before my compartment companion arrived. He was a tall, husky Russian who fortunately spoke English rather well and turned out to be very nice. We conversed a while, and he turned out to be a tattoo artist. He had trained in Germany and Italy and encouraged me to fix my lips so that they would look nice and full and red forever. No, thank you. He was very proud of his apartment close to the Kremlin, a choice location, from what I could gather. In the end, I was glad to have a strong and reliable guy with me, since he was sure to watch over things when I had to leave the compartment for a while in the middle of the night. I forgot to ask him where he put his money. I knew my Russian friends in Irkutsk, Siberia, kept their money in a plastic bag on the balcony. When their apartment was broken into, the burglars took the computer and some valuables, but did not find the money.

Moscow

I arrived in Moscow on the morning of August 22 and was met by a representative from Lernidee. She took me to the Renaissance Moscow Hotel, which was centrally located. The room was comparatively upscale, and I had nothing to complain about. The evening of our arrival, our pleasant and very knowledgeable female tour guide took us on a walking tour to the Kremlin and Red Square, where we had an impressive view of the architecture, since the buildings were brightly illuminated. It was exciting to see this historic fortified complex, with several palaces, armories, and churches, in real life instead of in books and on postcards. Quite striking, indeed!

Even more striking was a thirty-minute ride on the Moscow Metro. These "underground palaces" are simply out of this world. I lack the superlatives with which to describe them, so I quote from a brochure: "Used in their decoration are more than twenty varieties of marble coming from the Urals, Altai, Central Asia, the Caucasus and Ukraine, as well as labradorite, granite, porphyry, rhodonite, onyx and other natural stones. The magnificent festive looking halls and vestibules are adorned with sculpture, bas-reliefs, mosaics, paintings, stained glass panels and murals executed by the best artists." And all this exquisite construction took place during Stalin's dictatorship, among others. It started in the early 1930s. You just have to see it for yourself.

The grand city tour started at 9:00 a.m. in front of the hotel and took us back to the Kremlin, with a stop at St. Basil's Cathedral, which is simply splendid. It is also called "the Cathedral of the Intercession of the Virgin by the Moat." It was ordered by Ivan the Terrible to mark the 1552 capture of Kasan from Mongol forces and was completed in 1560. I did not know that at one time, Stalin had planned to have it demolished. I stood in awe in front of the cathedrals in the Kremlin: the Cathedral of the Annunciation, once the private church of the Tsar's family, built in the fifteenth century, and the Cathedral of the Assumption, the oldest church in the Kremlin. The gold-plated domes stretching upwards from the white, stained walls into the blue sky project something quite pure, somehow unexpected in Russia, at least when you think of the cruelties that were committed in that part of the world. The tsars were no angels either. Somehow their cathedrals struck me like fairy-tale castles. I must admit, whatever they showed us of Moscow was undeniably worthy of praise.

Toward evening, we were transported by bus to one of Moscow's major red-brick railroad stations: Kasan. Our special train, Zarengold, comprising twelve wagons that accommodated sixteen passengers each, awaited us. It was painted blue. I was curious to get a first look at my compartment in this train, which stemmed from Khrushchev's time and was used by Brezhnev when traveling to Siberia. My compartment was rather rich looking. The plush crimson- and golden-colored upholstery and the almost matching heavy curtains looked a tad tacky, I thought. The white daisies in a vase on the small table in front of the window made me smile. I had nothing to complain about. I had the compartment, which could hold two or even four passengers, all to myself. The sprinkle shower and toilet were only three compartments away from mine, at the end of the wagon. The luxurious dining room was three wagons away from mine. That dining room was something else and truly a place not easily forgotten. Someone called the decor "socialist baroque." All of the tables could seat four people. The booths and chairs had high backs, which prevented you from turning around and chatting with those at the table behind you. Furthermore, these seats were covered with thick, plush, dark-red upholstery. The floor was covered with a dark-gray carpet. The tables, with spotless white damask tablecloths and matching napkins, looked inviting. Good white china and sterling silver conveyed an elegant ambiance. Fresh flowers graced the tables throughout the seven- or eight-day trip. Since I did not spend time at the little bar next to the dining room, I do not remember much about it. Some Germans liked to hang out there, and I am convinced that travelers from Austria, Switzerland, France, Holland, and other European countries spent some money there. This does not mean I turned down the opportunity to partake when vodka and caviar were occasionally served before dinner. It had happened already on the second day of our trip, August 25. All in all, the food on the train was perhaps not exceptional, but good, if you like Russian cuisine.

Fortunately, my compartment was centrally located, and I took advantage of the opportunities to chat with various passengers, be they German, French, Dutch, or Swiss. It almost blew my mind when one of these passengers turned out to be from my mother's hometown, the tiny village of Großförste. – If you are interested, you will have to go back to Part I of my memoirs to find out why I severed all ties with that bunch years ago. Yes, I was the only American on this train.

Kasan

Around noon, our train stopped at Kasan, capital of the Republic of Tartarstan as well as of Russian Islam and the Tatars. We visited the Kasan Kremlin, listened to our guide's lecture about the sometimes-turbulent relationships between Tatars, Cossacks, and Russians, and got at least a glimpse of Kasan's museums, theaters, and other architectural highlights, such as the very nice university. More calming was the boat trip on the Volga, which offered a memorable panorama of the city. We were lucky. The sun was setting.

Never in my life had I dreamed of traveling through the Ural Mountains, yet here I was on the Trans-Sib Railway, glued to the window as I watched the rugged, and partially snowcapped, Ural mountain range, which runs roughly from north to south through Western Russia to Kazakhstan, pass by. Unbelievable!

Siberia

Novosibirsk

After the Ural excitement, the calm set in. Our train made its way at about eighty kilometers per hour through the vast, virtually uninhabited prairies of West Siberia, until we arrived a couple days later in Novosibirsk, the heart of Siberia. While we traveled, and while I stared out the window to avoid missing anything, rather interesting lectures were piped into my compartment, in German, of course: "The Conquest of Siberia," "Germans and Russians," "Life in Winter in Siberia," and "Procedures of Exile." These lectures were fascinating and extremely informative. I was glad to be by myself. Some of what I learned I had previously heard or read about. However, it is completely different to absorb this information while traveling in a train through the very places where these cruelties and tortures were committed. It turns your stomach. Just imagine the exiled human beings dragging their feet, heavy iron chains around their ankles, through the prairies of Siberia, often collapsing from exhaustion or freezing to death on the endless, torturous path. – Take a moment and think about it.

It was on the fifth day of travel that we arrived in Novosibirsk, Russia's third-largest city, after Moscow and Saint Petersburg, and the largest city of Siberia, with a population of well over a million. A pretty young girl and a handsome young man, both dressed in the costume of their region, greeted us holding a big, round loaf of bread on a tray. They went around, and each of us broke off a piece, which they sprinkled with salt. It's their tradition for welcoming visitors. In the background stood a group of women and men of different ages, also dressed in very colorful traditional costumes. While we were eating the bread, the group performed a few folk dances, which we all applauded enthusiastically. It was a refreshing sight after our long ride through rather barren country. – Rather sobering during the city tour was the humongous, gray, and aesthetically rather boring monument of Lenin standing in front of the opera, Russia's largest. I asked one of the passengers to take a picture of me sitting at Lenin's feet! Haha! I have no idea whether the Russian Marxist revolutionary with whom I share my birth date (month and day) had a special liking for opera, as Hitler did for Wagner's and I do for Mozart's.

We had a chance to briefly visit the local arts museum, of which I do not remember much. But several well-maintained old steam engines, which stood near the railroad station. made an impression on me. A bride and her groom standing next to a bridge along the Ob made an impression as well. The Ob, one of the greatest rivers of Asia, is Russia's fourth-longest and Western Siberia's major waterway. They were waiting to be married at that very spot. Fortunately it did not rain. For some reason, I did not go on the optional trip on the Ob, but took a nice photo of it as the sun was setting. I also photographed the Orient Express sitting on the tracks next to the Zarengold. After all, it was something I really did not expect to see play out in this part of the world. All in all, the Novosibirsk train station, with all its iron bridges, was rather imposing. Seeing it once in your life will do. At this station, I appreciated one of the women on the staff, who was washing the windows of our train. She did not object to my taking a photo. I always ask people before I take a picture. Thus, I asked two hefty blond and blue-eyed women at the market, where I purchased several jars of caviar to be served at my house during the forthcoming election night, whether I could take their picture. They did not mind. If they only knew that I never got a chance to serve the caviar – somehow, while in my suitcase, the lids opened and the caviar soiled several of my nice cashmere sweaters, which I purchased later on the same trip in Mongolia's South Gobi Desert for a bargain price. Well, maybe it was an omen. Bush was reelected. What a disaster! My party never took place. Also, I did not like the dried mushrooms I bought at the same market at a bargain price. To top it off, I heard later that a film about this trip, taken by a special crew, was nothing to write home about. As a result, I never saw the footage they took of me on the train during another vodka-and-caviar session. I had dared to make a pretty nasty crack about our so-called president. Too bad! The film was aired in Germany on some TV station.

Back on the train, traveling over the beautiful Jenisej River, I loved passing the quaint Siberian villages, with their wooden houses and windows equipped with shutters to protect them from fierce snowstorms and freezing winter temperatures. Some were nestled in the forest, and many trees stood in between the houses. – The Siberian landscape was very picturesque. All my life, I have admired the white trunks of birch trees and their dainty leaves glistening and trembling in the sun when a light breeze brushes through. For hours, we passed mile after mile of birch forests. The leaves were almost golden, because fall was approaching in Siberia. Also golden were the large fields of sunflowers which popped up now and then. On some stretches, mountain ranges were visible in the distance. It was never boring.

Irkutsk

After five full days on the train, we arrived at the main station in Irkutsk, the capital of East Siberia, with a population of more than six hundred thousand. Irkutsk is halfway between Moscow and Vladivostok, the end of the Trans-Siberian Railway. A bright-green-colored bus picked us up for the city tour. The sky was overcast and the streets still wet from a recent rain. Upon entering the bus, I noticed the rather tacky bright-blue curtains strung up above the windows. They reminded me vaguely of the buses in the former GDR. Never mind. While touring the city, I listened closely as the guide related, in perfect German, that early in the nineteenth century, many Russian nobles, officers, and artists were sent into exile here for taking part in the Decembrist revolt against Tsar Nicholas I. She pointed out that as a result, Irkutsk became the major center of intellectual and social life for these exiles. They were also responsible for the adornment and hand-carved decorations of these picturesque wooden houses, some with bright-blue painted shutters, which I took a particular liking to. They lent a warm, somewhat cozy ambiance to the city and stood in contrast to the overpowering and very boring-looking, standardized, gray Soviet apartment blocks, of which I had seen too many in the former GDR and other Eastern Bloc countries. The big department store looked bleak inside and out. I had a hard time understanding why they referred to this city as "the Paris of Siberia." Yes, the streets were wide, a certain portion of the architecture looked more or less Continental, and several, but not all, of the Orthodox churches boasted gold-plated, onion-shaped towers, but it was a far cry from Paris! Believe you me. To be fair, I must add that the city was rather clean.

We stopped briefly at the white Trans-Sib obelisk, which marks the border between Europe and Asia, and in the late afternoon we were all delighted to be treated to a tasty Taiga supper in a special Siberian restaurant in a remote, forested area. We had to tread carefully not to get our shoes muddy. The narrow path to the restaurant was soft and wet. I have forgotten what we were served – probably goulash and cabbage and borscht. I barely remember the night I spent at a hotel in downtown Irkutsk. But I vividly remember our tour guide, Olga. She spoke German like a native, was tall and slender, had very blue eyes and blond hair, and was a tad pale. Her very long hair lay in a thick braid around her head. And she was very knowledgeable. Since I traveled solo, she joined me at the dinner table, and we had a very lively chat about her experience as a student in Germany, her daughter, and the fact that one of her ancestors was sent here into exile by the Tsar and, like so many who survived the torturous journey, was banned from ever returning home. He got stuck in Siberia, where he started a new life. When we said good-bye, I gave her my card with my e-mail address and asked her to encourage her daughter Lubasha, who was also studying English in school, to write to me – in English, of course. I also gave her my chocolate dessert to give to Lubasha.

In the morning, our bus transferred us to a typical Siberian village near Lake Baikal, the largest sweetwater reservoir on earth. I admit I had never before heard of this natural wonder of the world. On a brief visit to a small Orthodox church nearby, which was rather sinister and dark inside due to its wooden walls and ceilings, I was struck by the array of beautiful, multicolored flowers in the churchyard.

Lake Baikal

The sky was overcast when we boarded a shuttle ship for the trip across Lake Baikal. It was quite cool outside. But, being one of the more adventurous in the group, I stayed outside on deck. I had brought warm clothes, just in case. I did not notice anything extraordinary during this two-hour crossing. The surface of the lake was smooth, a few ships were docked along the harbor, and in the background was hilly terrain covered with deciduous trees. Once, the sun came through an almost-foggy sky and painted the water in front of us silver golden. Lo and behold, perhaps fifty yards to the east, a tiny, maybe one-hundred-square-foot island, fenced in on one side with three or four evergreen trees and throwing a shadow on the water, appeared and disappeared within minutes. So much for excitement on this stretch of the natural wonder!

Much more exciting was the visit to the wooden houses on Baikal's lakeshore after we disembarked. The house I entered, after making my way to it on a path of flat stones and through beds of high perennials in full bloom, was surprisingly large. Against a big wall stood a wide wooden bench. The seat was covered with a plush carpet with a design of black and pink flowers. A huge Persian rug with dark-red and yellow-golden figures hung on the wall behind the seat from ceiling to floor. Against another wall stood a cabinet on which many of their thick china vases and other memorabilia were displayed. On the shelves beneath, they kept their good crystal goblets and the like. I was surprised to find such objects in these comparatively humble, but warm, surroundings. The women had prepared mountains of food for us, kept in huge china bowls on a sturdy table. I helped myself to some of it and thanked them profoundly for their hospitality before going outside to explore the grounds. Not far from the house, in front of a wooden picket fence, lay a pile of wooden boards, some rotting. Next to the pile stood a proud rooster with a smaller white chicken, maybe a hen?! A bit further away, close to a pair of beautiful birch trees, I came upon a couple of pigs in a primitive stall. It was in need of repair, as was most of what I saw out there. In a couple of months, they would be ready for slaughter. I remembered those screams and the squirting of all that blood from long before. A pond about one hundred feet away from the house was partially covered with some sort of mustard-green moss or algae. It looked idyllic.

Opposite the village was the lake, and some eager beavers simply had to go swimming in the famous Baikal. Definitely not me. They assured me that the water was actually freezing cold. I should have asked why smoke was coming out of a chimney that stuck out from one of the small shacks. After boarding the train that awaited us, we traveled for several hours along the lake, a real highlight of the trip. By then, the weather had improved vastly. The lake was in all its glory, accented by the snow-capped mountain ranges on the other side. Then, toward evening, the train stopped at Baikal's shores. The staff prepared and set up an absolutely fabulous picnic on the embankment next to the tracks. If everything up to this moment was a crescendo, the picnic was an awesome climax. The gods were truly smiling on us. A Russian tenor in a traditional shirt (red and white, with sunflowers) sung while another played an accordion. I wandered away from the crowd on a path along the lake. On one side grew high grasses and bushes with purple berries, and across Baikal were mountain ranges, capped with fresh snow. The sun was setting and painting the sky and the lake with rosy, purple, and orange hues. The atmosphere was heavenly and peaceful, such as I had never experienced before and never have since.

I joined other friends. All had split up into groups, sitting in the high grass along the embankment and enjoying their barbequed or fried meats, sausages, and the like. There was a generous supply of beer, wine, vodka, etc. After a while, a bunch of us formed a choir and sang German folk songs. We had so much fun. It was a great, joyous moment, as I recall. How lucky can one be?! I had to pinch myself.

It was sad to bid farewell to one of my new friends, with whom I had frequently sat during meals. Griseldis Henke, from East Berlin. She was a few years my junior, an inch or two taller than I, with short hair dyed chestnut brown, lively brown eyes, and a build somewhat sturdier than mine. Griseldis was a retired MD, a specialist in hygiene and epidemic infectious diseases, and impressively intelligent. She was well versed in world politics, especially regarding the former GDR and the Soviet Union. After graduating, she worked for a while at the University of Moscow. Her husband, a lecturer at the university in East Berlin, had stayed home. She had two daughters, a doctor and a dentist, and four grandchildren, and she spoke with pride about all of them. We were in touch for several years. She was always busy, still lecturing and conducting seminars in between travels to seaside spas in Europe and following the various popes with a passion that, unfortunately, bordered on the fanatical. Each morning, her husband, ten years or so older than she, reluctantly swallowed the cocktail of vitamins she placed in front of him at the breakfast table. She was a good wife, mother, and grandmother, but snoopy and rather domineering, if you allowed her to be. After Baikal, she headed back to her family. I continued on the Trans-Sib Railway via Mongolia.

Mongolia

The Trans-Sib snaked along another stretch of the mystical Baikal and then through more wild, vast, and lonely mountainous prairies in East Siberia. The lecture that day was about "Genghis Khan and the Invasions by the Mongols (1162–1227)." Genghis Khan was emperor of the Mongol Empire, which by the end of his life occupied a substantial portion of Central Asia and China. Massacres of up to forty million were part of it. By the time it all ended, his descendants, who continued the quest, had conquered substantial portions of modern Eastern Europe, Russia, and the Middle East.

I quote from one of my brochures: "Beyond his great military accomplishments, Genghis Khan also advanced the Mongol Empire in other ways. He decreed the adoption of the Uyghur script as the Mongol Empire's writing system. He also promoted religious tolerance in the Mongol Empire, and created a unified empire from the nomadic tribes of northeast Asia. Present-day Mongolians regard him highly as the founding father of Mongolia."

It was the ninth day of the trip. After a nice dinner, I went to my compartment to retire for the night. As always, the bed was ready, but knowing that we would be awakened later to submit our passports to the customs officer at the border crossing into Mongolia, I did not allow myself to really fall asleep. Though the procedure took about three hours, everything went smoothly.

Ulaanbaatar

On August 28, 2004, we did not go sightseeing in Ulan-Ude, capital of Buryatia, Russia, and the largest city in Eastern Siberia, and as a result did not get a chance to see the giant Lenin head surviving the fall of the Soviet Union. It was not the only noteworthy sight we missed. Not so important. The next stop was a must-see: Ulaanbaatar, the capital and largest city of Mongolia. One million of Mongolia's 2.8 million people live there. Naturally, it is the cultural, economic, and political center. Four sacred mountains surround it. Dense pine forests are on the northern slopes and grassy steppes lay to the south.

The bus tour of the city started in the forenoon. Among the places we visited was the imposing Buddhist Gandan Monastery, of which the Megjid Janraisig Temple is an important part. The temple houses the majestic, twenty-six-meter-high, twenty-ton, newly gilded statue of Megjid Janraisig. It is decorated with jewels. We stopped at the little museum where several steam engines were displayed. I preferred seeing Bogd Khan's Winter Palace, now a museum. It is the only one left from that period.

Bogd Khan was supposedly the spiritual leader and de facto king of Mongolia in the early twentieth century. We learned he had gone blind due to syphilis. Perhaps it was his punishment for being very greedy and corrupt. Mongolian architects erected the Choijin Lama Museum. It features, among other objects, art from Tibet, Nepal, and Bhutan, that is, Himalayan territories. You will not regret paying this place a visit.

Though we stopped at other noteworthy sites in the city – including climbing the many steps to the monument from which we looked down on the city and got a good look at the big cairns with predominantly blue prayer flags and at the temples, where we had a chance to spin prayer drums – I simply cannot cover it all in detail. As is normal for these sightseeing tours with buses, the constant climbing in and out of them leaves one pretty exhausted at night. So it was after this day in Ulaanbaatar. Instead of hanging out with others in one of the big beer gardens, I went to bed right after dinner at our hotel.

Soon after breakfast another bus tour started. It ventured out into the countryside. We finally got an up-close look at a typical *ger* (nomadic tent). Our destination was a settlement of yak breeders. It was a place where small herds of horses and gray, shaggy, long-haired yaks (Tibetan wild bullocks) were grazing near rugged, treeless, and hilly terrain. A very tasty picnic-type meal, somewhat like goulash, was served inside a wooden building. The meat was cut into chunks and cooked very slowly on top of a fire in a pit filled with gray stones. It was so tender and delicious it virtually melted in your mouth. They called it "Mongolian beef." It definitely bore no resemblance to the Mongolian beef served in our Chinese restaurant in Bloomington. It was probably from a butchered yak – or a horse, or a lamb? After lunch, we had a chance to watch a horse race and several pairs of skilled Olympic wrestlers, for whom the Mongolians are famous. One of the guys looked especially fierce. He had bleached his hair. I thought the yaks were very ugly and scary-looking beasts. I kept my distance. The horse show they put on for us was terrific. I bet they would compete well in a rodeo.

South Gobi Desert

After another night at the hotel, ten of us climbed into the van right after breakfast, anxiously awaiting what we were about to experience on this optional eight-day trip into the South Gobi Desert. We were heading toward the Bayangobi *ger* camp. What a trip! It was like riding over a washboard – for at least seven hours. Our van seemed like it would fall apart any minute. The windows were rattling constantly, and dust blew in through the cracks. I thought it was adventurous and a bit humorous. I think I was the oldest in the group. One of the much-younger German females was complaining about her seat in the front. Her back was hurting. Eventually, I offered her my seat, but warned her that its upholstery was loose and tended to slide down. These sissies would have been better off staying home. Things got even funnier when we stopped for a picnic way out on the barren steppe. The driver and our guide spread a blanket in the shade next to one side of the van. Everybody in our group was searching the area for a bush or an elevation for a pit stop. The highest bushes, or whatever vegetation could be found, were only about twelve inches high. Some walked quite a distance to find privacy. We had to decide whether to turn our backs toward the van or face it head on. A photo I took of the guys at this point is truly grotesque. Smile, you're on candid camera! The only living beings we encountered on the way were a herd of sheep at the foot of a mountain range and a rider on a horse watching them. Neither bush nor tree was to be seen anywhere. Since there was only one badly paved road through this desert, our driver, who eventually had to leave the road and venture out on the steppe, got lost so badly we had to wait around forever until he came upon the driver of another van, who pointed us in the right direction. Nobody dared to complain. After all, we were all supposedly adventurous and not fainthearted.

We arrived at our camp when it was already dark outside. And it was cold! I managed to haul my backpack and suitcase to my yurt, which was dimly lit. It actually seemed kind of cozy at first sight. The frames of the two beds were painted bright red, with round designs in yellow and green. The bright-blue blankets had white snorkel designs and were made of camel-hair wool. Inside, the walls were covered with some red and white cloth. A pretty thermos bottle with hot water and two glasses stood on a low wooden chest, which served as a table and was also painted red, with a white, blue, and green snorkel design. The miniature, barrel-like wood-burning stove stood close to my bed. Oh yes, near the door stood a bucket lined with a plastic bag in case you did not want to walk all the way to the facilities in the middle of the night in the freezing cold. It was a five-minute walk to the small building where meals were served. Next to it were showers, washrooms, and toilets. – The first thing I did was to ask the people in charge to start a fire in my *ger* and leave a box full of wood for the night. The food was OK, but nothing to write home about. They did not have much wood around either. That's the reason my small box was only half-full when I returned. Yet, the stove was on, and it was comfortably warm in my round camel-hair tent. Since my place had two blankets, I helped myself to the one on the spare bed and felt reasonably content. I had put the suitcase on the other bed and parked my backpack against a post near the stove, about five feet from my bed.

About three hours into the night, I was awakened by various scratching noises, not to mention the howling wind outside. I lit a candle to check my fire. It was dead, and I did not have enough wood left to bother rekindling it. Suddenly I noticed a couple of mice scurrying across the floor. I got up, gathered all of the towels they had put on the extra bed, and covered my face with them. I was in no mood to have mice crawling over my face. I eventually dozed off again, only to be awakened by the urge to take advantage of my bucket. Going outside my tent to take care of business next to it was out of the question, even though I believed there was no danger of snakes. But a five-minute walk to get to the facilities was also unthinkable. I was almost relieved when daylight peeked through a crack in the door to this windowless domain. When I looked in my backpack for clean underwear, I realized the mice had feasted down there on my granola bars. I had left the zipper open, and the bag was emptied out. That was not all. They had also chewed a hole in the bottom of the backpack. A quarter of one granola bar, still in a bit of the wrapper, was left on the floor. Thanks, mouse. You can have it!

This yurt camp was truly in a great location, that is, right in front of a group of huge, polished, tan-colored rocks, some over one hundred feet high. It was sheltered. Looking at the yurts' construction, it was easy to see how these tents were folded together and made ready for transport on camels or carts. At the end of my Mongolian adventure, I was told I could have a yurt sent to America for only $500. I was so tempted. It would be a unique guesthouse in my backyard. But I stopped myself and bought half a dozen tiny *ger* souvenirs instead.

On September 3, our rattling van took us to Karakorum to see the ruins of the ancient Mongolian capital, which date back to the thirteenth century. It was definitely a place I had never in my life aspired to see. The ruins are not far from the Erdene Zuu Monastery, which we also saw, and which I found more intriguing, as it is the most ancient surviving Buddhist monastery in Mongolia, built in 1585. I had never seen so many white-painted stupas in one place; at least one hundred of them surrounded the monastery. Also, the Laviran Temple, a big Buddha statue there, and the Golden Stupa are worth seeing. I have an excellent photo of the huge stone turtle with some ragged prayer flags at the center of its back, but I missed the stone phallus located on a hill outside the monastery. It is said to restrain the sexual impulses of the monks and ensure their good behavior. Something the Catholics might consider for their sex-driven clergy.

After another windy night in the yurt, and acquainted at that point with what happens at these camp events, we endured another rocky, dusty drive through impressive, somewhat mountainous regions followed by vast, barren landscapes in the southern part of the Gobi Desert. Finally, we reached our destination, near the ruins of the Buddhist Ongiin Monastery.

The following day was more eventful, as far as I was concerned. We got an extraordinary chance to stop at Flaming Cliff, the place in the Gobi Desert famous for the first-known nest of dinosaur eggs and other dinosaur fossils. The American paleontologist Roy Chapman Andrews discovered them in the 1920s. The name, we were told, came from "the surreal glowing orange color of the rock." Unfortunately, we did not spot a single egg, but as we drove on we did see an area where the scrubby-looking *saksauls*, trees endemic to Bayanzag, which looked more like bushes than trees, were growing. They call it the Forest of Saksaul. It's amazing how the Mongolians in this vast region survive with practically no trees.

The hike through Vulture's Gorge, located in the southernmost region of the Gobi-Altai Mountains, was a highlight of the trip. Vulture's Gorge is a mountain valley in the middle of the Gobi Desert and, as some claim, a spectacular natural wonder of the world. It was a rather challenging trip through extremely rugged terrain that involved about three hours of mincing one's steps over loose and often rolling stones and climbing over slippery rocks. A narrow creek barely flowed at the bottom of the gorge, where the sun did not reach. Occasionally, I welcomed a fellow traveler's friendly supporting hand. It was truly a gorgeous day, with blue skies, bright sun, and a very pleasant temperature. On the way, I stopped to buy a small wooden camel, hand carved by a lonely shepherd while herding some skinny sheep on a nearby slope. A picnic, which our driver and guide had prepared during our absence, was most welcome and tasted out of this world, if you know what I mean. *Vielen Dank*!

These tours are usually arranged in such a way that the sites increase gradually in beauty and drama, with a climax on the last day. After a while, we got used to sleeping in yurts, eating simple meals typical of the nomads, and riding in the shaky van. On September 7 we finally arrived at the place one fellow tourist had wanted to visit very badly all his life. Nothing else was more important to him than walking up the giant wandering dunes, aka the Khongoryn Els sand dunes, in the

Fireball Lily

South Gobi Desert. A seventy-year-old, short, and skinny Swiss traveler was just as eager to climb the dunes. Only a few years earlier, he had walked five hundred kilometers across Lapland. It was amazing to watch him go – and especially impressive, because a few nights earlier he had gotten deadly sick. They had to get a doctor, who lived in a nomad settlement and who miraculously healed him. His wife stayed at the foot of the dune. It was truly a sight to behold. My heart beat faster, and I climbed up a considerable stretch for the view. Unforgettable! One lacks the superlatives with which to describe these experiences out in God's, aka Mother Nature's, museum. The contrast between the vast, bright, blue skies and the light-brown ripples of the sand dunes is so striking and beautiful! What can I say? I had to pinch myself to make sure it was I who stood there. How was it possible? And then there were the two-humped camels gathered in a group not far from a herd of goats. I declined an invitation to ride the camel, since I had done it before in other places on the planet. –

I did not decline the invitation to visit a nomad family inside their *ger* and even drank the sour camel milk, which they passed around in a bowl and which I thought tasted better than the yak milk served at an earlier gathering. This particular family proudly showed off their little son when they posed for a photo outside their yurt's open entrance door, which was painted beautifully – orange with blue and yellow designs. This young couple wore simple Western clothes, jeans, shorts, and cotton shirts. Like most Mongolians, they were short people, not overweight, and I am sure super horseback riders. Young boys start riding at a very early age. There was no garden out there, as there was at a previous stop, adjacent to abandoned railroad tracks. At that settlement, which resembled a little village, they raised vegetables like beans, cabbage, potatoes, and tomatoes. I noticed a small TV, even though they were a rarity. Whenever we encountered Mongolians, they loved to gather around us. The children always smiled when they posed for photos, but they did not beg, as they do in China, Africa, and India. They appeared to be happy and healthy – at least for the time being.

As I write, I wonder what became of the female American tourist who hit her head on the entrance post to the *ger*. She insisted that they fly in a doctor from Ulaanbaatar by helicopter in the middle of the night, because she did not trust the Mongolian "medicine man." In the end, the rescue operation alone cost her some ten thousand bucks. We all thought she would have been better off trusting the native medicine man who healed the Swiss guy so miraculously.

After another night at the Gobi camp, we boarded a small plane, which flew us to Ulaanbaatar, where we spent a night in a real bed. The next day we were transferred to a regular train of the Trans-Sib Railway. I had to share the compartment with another passenger, who turned out to be one of the tour guides. He was a great talker and entertained me royally with all kinds of tales, which at times seemed a bit far-fetched. The ride to Beijing turned out to be anything but dull, starting with the ordeal of the unusual crossing of the Mongolian–Chinese border, at Erlian.

China

While waiting at the border crossing, I went outside to take a photo of our new train. I was right in time: the sky and the train were all aglow with golden and pastel-purple hues. A couple of elderly Chinese women, all dressed up, one in a bright-red woolen coat and matching turban and the other in a shiny, bright-purple, and silky-type coat and a turquoise felt hat, posed for me with big smiles. After a wait of approximately two hours, during which officials from China came, checked our passports, and looked under our seats for hidden treasures and/or passengers, our train went into the building dedicated to changing bogies (wheels). This procedure was totally new to me, unheard of. It was not an adventure to sleep through.

The wheels were changed because the Russian rail tracks are a different size than those in China (single versus double). In times of war, this trick comes in handy for transporting war paraphernalia. Just imagine: while we sat in the train, each carriage, one after the other, was lifted off its axles; cranes took away the Russian wheels, put on the Chinese wheels, and lowered the axles onto the narrower track. The carriages were then lowered back onto their axles. All this took place with a lot of noise. It must be a real nuisance for freight trains. Once the train started running again, I went to sleep on my side of the compartment. My companion snored loudly. Not so nice!

Much nicer indeed was the ride through China the next day. We passed many patches of blooming sunflowers. The fields were greener than those we left behind, and the greatest surprise came when suddenly, in more hilly terrain, a long stretch of the Great Wall of China appeared alongside the train. I was so excited. I had climbed a great number of the Wall's steps only four months earlier, while traveling in Japan and China, and had no idea we would see portions of it during the Trans-Sib Railway trip. The train stopped at a station to let us out for a while to admire the somewhat ruined Wall. "Wow" is all I can say. It was great to see it without tourists crawling all over. In fact, not a soul was to be seen. To top it off, the weather was again perfect. Sun, blue skies, and tolerable temperatures made us happier. In case you did not know, like Rome, the Wall was not built in a day. The construction of this four-thousand-mile-long architectural miracle began under the first emperor of China, Qin Shi Huang. Its completion took several centuries – and approximately one million lives. It was started in the third century because the Chinese feared Mongolian invasions, which ultimately took place anyhow. It was built along the northern borders of the empire. What was unusual to me was the fact that in between the outside walls were steps leading to the more than ten thousand watchtowers and beacon towers along the Great Wall. Thinking about the walls that have been built in East Germany, in Israel, and now in Arizona, I wondered why people are so obsessed with walls and actually believe they will last forever and keep them safe from whatever they want to guard against. Nuts!

One thing is certain, and so it was on this day in China. Toward evening we were blessed with another awesome sunset. I can vouch for it. Even along walls in other parts of the world, you may be surprised by a breathtaking sunset and, at least for a while, forget why these barriers were constructed in the first place.

I was extremely grateful to our guide on the Trans-Sib Railway, who gave me two long, rusty nails from the track. I sent them to Eric and Peter Beardsley as souvenirs. I think I was the only tourist on this stretch to get these rare nails.

Beijing

We arrived in Beijing in the forenoon, and after parking our travel gear in what they called a first-class hotel, which it was if you compare it to the yurts and my last compartment in the train, we were allowed to rest until the next day, when the sightseeing tours were scheduled for the morning and afternoon. I went along to some of the usual sights, all of which I had seen in April and which I will describe in the next chapter. Most importantly, I skipped the Wall and went hunting for a special souvenir instead, a twenty-four-carat gold necklace with a laughing-Buddha pendant. I had failed on my last trip to find a jeweler who would craft a replacement for a jade ring Doc had given to me. He told me at the time that he had it made by a Chinese jeweler when visiting Hong Kong during his stay at Fort Shafter, Hawaii, where he was chief surgeon at their military hospital. The very light green, oval jade stone was set in very soft, twenty-four-carat gold with a delicate design of the setting sun. It was a ring for my little finger and was the only piece of jewelry he had not passed on to his daughter. It somehow got lost or was possibly stolen by a playmate of Liesl's in South Bend, Indiana. Doc also had a special liking for Buddhist philosophy and had a fat and very heavy laughing Buddha made of brass in the library. Eventually, I found a very nice twenty-four-carat necklace with a laughing Buddha for about $200 and have worn it proudly around my neck ever since. – My companion travelers admired it at our fabulous good-bye dinner, where my favorite dish was served with great fanfare right at our table: Peking duck. While hunting for the necklace, I also let myself be persuaded by our guide to take a break and get my first foot massage ever. It was remarkably pleasant. But prior to the massage, a doctor examined my hand and tongue and presented me with a prescription for some defects he had detected. My doctor in the States felt it unnecessary, so I ignored the diagnosis of the Chinese MD. More importantly, when he was finished I asked him for a SARS mask, which he gladly gave me and which I have worn on many flights since. The massage cost a mere $2 plus tip.

I christened the SARS mask on the flight home from Beijing, which seemed endless. I spent a night in a modest hotel in Frankfurt and caught my flight to Indianapolis the next day. The limo picked me up, and I arrived in Bloomington during the early afternoon. While undressing, I couldn't find my little Buddha. I spent hours searching the house, looking in the driveway, and calling the limo company as well as both the hotel in Frankfurt and the airlines. My Buddha was gone, and I was quite sad. It was meant to bring me luck! You may not believe how the Buddha story ended. While I was on the phone two weeks later, relating the story about the necklace to my young friend Bettina in Berlin and adjusting the cushion on my chair, I felt a chain. Lo and behold, it was the end of the golden chain that held my Buddha. The clasp had unlocked and the necklace had fallen into the crack between the cushion and arm of the chair. Bettina and I broke out laughing. If that was not luck, then what was it? To this day, my Buddha goes where I go and has elicited many a curious comment from other travelers. Come to think of it, I have never met another traveler wearing a Buddha pendant. *Nadie*.

JAPAN

Tokyo

I never was big on celebrating birthdays, especially my own, and have written about it in the Part I of my memoirs. For years I had dreamed of a visit to Japan, if only to see snowcapped Mount Fuji at cherry-blossom time. Early in 2004, I took the plunge. GCT offered a pre-trip to Tokyo in connection with a major trip to China, where I had not yet been, and a post-trip to Thailand. This trip would bring me to my mountain precisely on my birthday. Strange as it may seem, seven years earlier to the day on which I am now writing about it, the trip began. I left home on April 7 and landed in Tokyo on the 8th. On the 9th, we toured the dazzling metropolis to see such sites as the Asakusa Kannon Temple, "the main site of the Sho-Kannon branch of Buddhism" (GCT). It was built in the year 645 and honors Kannon, the goddess of mercy. We also visited the Imperial Palace and its plaza, had a photo stop at the observation platform of the 330-meter, high-tech Tokyo Tower, and explored the famous Ginza shopping district, among other places I will not discuss in detail. I was predominantly interested in seeing the cherry and other flowering trees in full bloom. And believe me, it was like walking through a cherry-blossom paradise. Pink, purple, and white canopies and arcades were everywhere. Japanese families with their children were picnicking in the parks. It was sheer joy.

Hakone

Our Crowne Plaza Metropolitan Hotel was nice, and the food was good, as it was at all the places where we were nourished or pampered with tea, sitting on chairs or on floors in high-rise rotating restaurants and typical Japanese establishments. My mind was on the next day, the optional Mount Fuji and Hakone tour. The bus picked us up early for the drive to Hakone National Park. I did not breathe a word about why this trip was of such special importance to me. Already at a distance of a few miles, we all got excited. Mount Fuji, an almost perfect cone, 12,000 feet high and snowcapped, stood isolated beneath a clear blue sky in all its glory. Picture-perfect! I could feel my heartbeat increase as we came closer, and once there, standing at a miraculous elevation of about eight thousand feet, I was speechless and stared in utter amazement at my birthday gift. Here and there, cherry and plum trees were in white and pink bloom, and further away an entire snow-covered mountain range and the blue Pacific Ocean with an immaculate blue sky projected a sublime panorama.

After a minicruise on a catamaran on Lake Ashi, we were treated to a nice lunch at Schmit House, a restaurant on the lake, and continued to explore the beautiful Hakone region, known also for the hot springs in the volcanic Hakone Mountains.

We got a better look at the landscape in the Owakudani Valley and were rewarded with a few extraordinary views of Mount Fuji when riding the mountain train up to Mount Komagatake.

On the morning of our departure to China, I opted for the train/walking trip, which started with the impressive Tokyo National Museum, located in Ueno Park. It was my first time to experience a Japanese local train, which was just fine. From the museum we proceeded on foot to one of Tokyo's historic neighborhoods, Yanaka. It was a very quiet and peaceful district, an atmosphere created in part by a number of quaint wooden houses, still standing. There were hardly any people around, and blossoming trees gave the place an idyllic ambiance. Yanaka is one of the only sections of Tokyo that was not destroyed by bombings during World War II. The visit to the Asakura Museum of Sculpture was very special. Fumio Asakura (1883–1964) focused on modern sculpture, and the building, half-traditional and half-modern, was also his own studio and residence. I very much enjoyed walking around his house, looking at his sculptures and other exhibits of local art, and touring his immaculately kept gardens, one on the rooftop and others surrounding the house. They displayed the most artfully sculpted bushes and trees, that is, topiaries accented by thoughtfully placed rocks. It's amazing what the Japanese can create within the smallest spaces. It was so quiet and peaceful, and I was mesmerized by a couple of humongous, red-white-and-black-spotted goldfish in a small lily pond. Upon probing, I learned they are actually domesticated carp called koi. – Gray, slimy carp was served on New Year's Eve in Germany. Thus, these were a definite first for me.

My initial impression of Japan, though limited, was so positive that I was determined to return to see more of the beautiful and intriguing country and learn more about its history, culture, and people.

CHINA

Beijing

But at this point, I had to shift gears and fly from Tokyo to China, where I had never really wanted to go, even though I knew that it is, after Canada, the second-largest nation in the world in terms of land area, has a population of 1.3 billion, and offers an infinite reservoir of riches – historical, social, political, cultural, etc. – to explore. And before I knew it, I found myself in a pleasant hotel room in Beijing, capital of the People's Republic of China, with a population of more than twenty-two million. It was dark outside.

Fortunately, I did not suffer from jet lag and was ready the next morning to go to – where else? – Tiananmen Square (named after Tiananmen, or the Gate of Heavenly Peace, located to its north), which is said to be the largest and most imposing public square in the world. On this square, which was originally the gate of the Imperial Palace, aka "the Forbidden City," mass Red Guard rallies took and probably will take place forever. But many of us will remember it from the big pro-democracy demonstration which took place right after martial law was declared on May 20, 1989. Late on June 3 and early in the morning on June 4, military units were brought into Beijing and used armed force to clear demonstrators from the streets. Chinese were killing their brothers and sisters just as today, twenty years later, Libyans are killing their countrymen who are fighting for democracy. When will it ever end?! Not during my lifetime. When traveling in a group, one does not have much time to reflect on historic events, no matter how criminal they were.

Tiananmen Square lies in the center of the city of Beijing, as does the Forbidden City. "Beijing is not only the political and administrative center of China, it is also the single greatest repository of monuments and treasures from the imperial era" (GCT). I learned that in "traditional Chinese thought, the world was conceived of as square. A city, especially a capital, was supposed to be square, a geometric reflection of the cosmic order" (GCT).

While we were gathered around our very informative guide right on the square, she pointed out the various buildings of special interest surrounding it or right on it, like Mao Zedong's Mausoleum, the Great Hall of the People, which houses China's People's Congress, Quianmen, a gate in Beijing's city wall, and the Monument to the People's Heroes, which commemorates many of the uprisings that took place in China's history. One of the most obvious and imposing objects was the grandiose portrait of Chairman Mao Zedong at the center of the Tiananmen gate. It was hung there to commemorate the founding of the People's Republic of China, on October 1, 1949, and each year it is hung again on October 1. Here, emperors issued decrees, and I heard later that when Stalin died, they replaced Mao's portrait briefly with his. Our guide did not mention it.

More exciting, of course, was the huge complex of the Forbidden City, with some "800 ceremonial buildings, containing 9,999 rooms [I did not count] and a courtyard that can hold 100,000 people. It was completed in 1420 and the center of Imperial palaces for the emperors of the Ming and Qing dynasties was off limits to the general public for 500 years" (GCT). It was obvious that their favorite color was rusty red, almost like the red of the Kremlin. I climbed too many stairs and walked around leisurely in the sun to soak it all up, but was ready to leave it all behind when we were summoned. Back on the square, I chatted with a group of students from the States and watched others flying their fancy kites made of silk. Some looked like big butterflies. Enticing!

Also somewhat enticing, and highly amusing, was the chef's demonstration of Chinese noodle making after lunch in a restaurant close to the Forbidden City. I had no idea the noodle dough could be stretched out meters long so many times before the noodles were ready to be tossed into the huge pot of boiling water. The chef laughed, and we laughed, and I knew right then and there that I would never in my life attempt to copy him. Even more intriguing was the preparation of Peking duck that evening at our dinner table. It tasted divine, and I can honestly say I prefer the bird to their noodles.

The next day started with a tour of Beijing's hidden lanes, aka *hutongs*, ancient city alleys or lanes. "In the past, several thousand lanes, alleys, and quadrangles formed residential areas for ordinary people living in the capital" (GCT). After exploring the area on foot for a while, we took a rickshaw to Drum Tower. I was a bit worried about whether our driver could handle the load. My companion was, to phrase it delicately, a bit obese.

The Drum Tower area is also known for the narrow *hutongs* inhabited by the less-privileged citizens. It gave us an insight into the daily life of ordinary citizens. "Today, as the city develops into an international metropolis, its lanes and alleyways, occupying one third of the city proper, still serve as dwellings for half the total urban population" (GCT). A stroll through the local market was, as always on these visits, very enlightening. I did not know the Chinese could buy little songbirds at the market. They looked so forlorn in their cages. Some were singing beautifully, maybe because they were hanging close to the flower stands, of which there were surprisingly many. This attraction was completely new to me. I did not see any lingering cats.

I was amazed at how well the neatly dressed boys (aged eight to ten) at the school we visited behaved. They sang a song for us and even spoke some English. A big picture of Karl Marx hung on a wall in the classroom. Not a single American in my group of about twenty-five could identify the person in the picture. Hard to believe, right? Maybe not. When I educated them, they gave me a strange look. Since many of them were teachers, they were probably embarrassed. –

I had opted for the tour of the Summer Palace, "the former summer retreat for the imperial family during the late Qing dynasty and now China's largest and best preserved royal garden. It has an 800-year history, beginning with the creation here of the Golden Hill Palace during the Jin dynasty. Much later, in 1750, the Garden of Clear Ripples was built on this site. The garden has been restored twice since then, after being damaged by foreign military forces. This twelve-square-mile complex includes many pavilions, temples, palaces, and halls in a landscape of hills amidst open water. The Long Gallery measures over 2,300 feet long and offers paintings depicting Chinese legend, history, and natural settings" (GCT). This particular outing was to my liking, because many trees were in bloom and the place was not overrun by tourists. We had ample time to explore this aesthetically pleasing environment. It was the perfect place to get into the mood for the evening event: the Peking Opera at Chaoyang Theater.

"The Chinese opera is an ancient theatrical art, and the opera troupes in Beijing set the national standard for this highest expression of Chinese culture. This is not like the Western opera, full of arias and centered around singing. It's a beautiful and delicate blend of grand opera, ballet, song, drama, and comedy that spans the entire history of China, its folklore, mythology, literature, and culture" (GCT). I had long wanted to attend a Chinese opera, because I was aware of the effect it had on the German playwright Bertolt Brecht's theory of alienation. That is, in contrast to actors in Western plays, the Chinese actor rejects complete conversion of himself into the character he is playing. Moreover, according to Haiping Yan of Cornell University, "He expresses his awareness of being watched, and 'observes himself' consciously." I then better understood how and why Brecht had come to his conclusions. Indeed, the very elaborate and somewhat challenging opera performance struck me as extremely fascinating but indeed alienating, simply due to the nonmelodic music and the strange sounds of the instruments and voices.

Also, I very much valued the rare opportunity to observe some of the artists backstage as they put on their makeup and masks and went through the complex process of putting on the fantastic costumes. The entire stage boasted a luxurious array of colors, with bright red predominant. One could write a dissertation about the meaning of the various colors, masks, stage props, etc.

Early the next morning, we spent a couple of captivating hours at the renowned kung fu martial arts school. When we arrived, a gigantic red-and-yellow dragon was dancing around in the courtyard and got our full attention. Inside the school, the young male students performed a variety of highly disciplined exercises that held me spellbound – I was simply in awe the entire time we watched them. Before leaving, I talked with a couple of the boys and was impressed by their mastery of the English language. After this experience, nothing the Chinese do will ever surprise me. One understands why the Chinese train the best acrobats in the world. They go way beyond what is imaginable. This was a perfect introduction to the opening ceremonies in Beijing at the 2008 Olympics.

And just look at the fabled Great Wall of China, the construction of which began during the Warring States period (403–221 BC), with sections built in scattered areas. Only after China was united under the first emperor, Qin Shi Huang (221–206 BC), were some three hundred thousand men put to work connecting the segments into one rampart of brick, stone, and earth nearly four thousand miles long in order to protect China from foreign invaders. What would they say if they could see the thousands of tourists from around the world crawling around on this great structure?!

Fortunately, I still felt fit enough to start climbing the stairs of the Great Wall. It was a beautiful spring day, and the trees on the hills along the Wall were full of white blossoms. I climbed up to the fifth tower and could have kept going were it not that we had to be back at the meeting place in two hours. Only one other tourist in my group climbed as many stairs as I did. While catching my breath at one of the towers, I chatted with a family from Santiago, Chile. They did not know Cristian's parents. But it was nice to meet people here from a place I had visited. I learned on this trip that "the towers are built at a distance of two bowshots apart – meaning that the entire wall could be defended by the archers within it" and that "the wall snakes along such a winding path because Chinese mythology maintains that demons and evil spirits can only travel in a straight line, and the undulating wall effectively keeps them out" (GCT). I guess it did not always work out that way. Genghis Khan supposedly said, "The strength of a wall depends on the courage of those who defend it." Be that as it may, the Wall today brings in tons of hard cash.

I highly recommend that presumptive Republican presidential candidate Donald Trump acquaint himself with the facts about the Great Wall before he erects the Trump Wall to keep out "illegal aliens."

On the way back to the hotel, we stopped in the valley that the Ming emperors had chosen as their burial ground. It was so peaceful, and a special feeling of reverence came over me as I passed through the great marble gateway, more than four centuries old, and onto the Sacred Way, the Avenue of the Animals. Huge trees provided welcome shade. On both sides were massive stone statues of kneeling and standing elephants, lions, camels, and fanciful beasts. Not far from there, we saw "tombs housing the remains of 13 emperors and countless treasures. These 13 imperial tombs were built from 1409 to 1644, and are spread over nearly 25 square miles" (GCT).

The visit to a cloisonné (enamelware) factory was just what I had longed for. I found several special cloisonné gifts to bring back to the States.

On the way to the airport for our flight to Shanghai, I was wondering what Beijing would look like in five years or for the Olympics. Never in my life had I seen so many cranes going up into the sky. It was a forest of cranes, several thousand I am sure. And what would become of the *hutongs* and the poor people living there?

Shanghai

The four- or five-star Mayfair Hotel in Shanghai was perhaps a tad more upscale than the Jing Guang New World in Beijing. But I did not go to China to critique their hotels. One thing was clear; they can easily compete with the best in the world. Already on the way from the airport to the hotel, I was overwhelmed by what I saw just looking out the window of the bus! I knew this city would be overwhelming. And I was so right!

Whenever I think of Shanghai, which with a population of twelve million is the second-largest city in China and the fastest-growing city in the world, I see in my mind the dazzling, state-of-the-art Grand Theater. Truly, "the city's cultural and arts scene has been elevated with the advent of the Grand Theater. It is the nation's most eloquent statement of its commitment to the arts. This temple to culture glitters like a fantasy ice palace at night, its transparent walls and upswept eaves giving it a sense of otherworldliness. The clear walls are said to symbolize the new artistic openness that is sweeping across the country." I quote from the 2003–2004 edition of *China Welcomes You*, the book in my hotel room. For me, the Grand Theater is the ultimate in arts centers! Designed by France's Jean-Marie Charpentier, the building established the People's Square as the city's center of politics and culture.

You just have to see it at night – and if possible attend a performance in one of its theaters. We attended an acrobatic performance, which was as dazzling, fantastic, dramatic, precise, fast, disciplined, and all around as smashing as you can possibly imagine. No circus performance I had previously attended could be compared with the one at the Grand Theater. I did not expect it in a communist country. Not at that time. Today, I am no longer surprised. Think again about the opening of the Olympics.

August 3, 2013 – I just heard over the news that Shanghai now boasts the second-highest tower in the world (2,073 feet, according to German-born Peter Weingarten, Gensler's chief architect) after Dubai's Burj Khalifa (2,722 feet). Why am I not surprised?

We took the subway to visit the Shanghai Museum of Art and History, established on October 12, 1996, where we got a mere glimpse of some of the 120,000 artifacts of ancient everyday Chinese culture. I found the exterior of the museum to be quite fascinating. It is designed in the shape of an ancient bronze cooking vessel called a *ding*. Possession of a *ding* implied that one had power and dominion over the land. The museum has a round top and a square base and is said to symbolize the ancient

Chinese conception of the world as "round sky, square earth." – I doubt I will ever return to this museum, or to the most popular bazaar in Shanghai, or to the very large, engaging, and elaborately designed Yu Yuan Garden, located next to it. I loved the Grand Rockery, made of *huangshi* stone and twelve meters high. Due to the cliffs, peaks, gorges, and winding caves, it was very dramatic. Equally fascinating were the lotus pool, with a zigzag bridge and midlake pavilion, the Ten Thousand Flower Tower, and so much more. Much of the design reminded me of the Japanese gardens in Tokyo, but here it was all magnified.

I chatted with a couple of female Chinese vendors in the garden. One of them had assumed I was Chinese. We laughed. I was flattered, because she had also underestimated my age by fifteen years. Before we parted, we asked someone to take a photograph of the group. I always welcome the opportunity to communicate with the natives. Another attraction in the garden was a small group of musicians playing for half a dozen bystanders. They were interesting, because their instruments and the sounds they produced were so foreign to me. The sounds were more or less hollow, soulless, squeaky, and alienating. That's all I can say. The instruments at the Peking Opera were quite similar and had the same effect on me. I am glad I saw and listened to them, but I most likely will not travel to China again just to hear them. It's a far cry from the Vienna State Opera. Why was it that I did not see a single Westerner among the nine Chinese bystanders? I counted eight men and one woman.

Many more visitors flocked to the two jade Buddha statues brought to the lavishly decorated Jade Buddha Temple, an elegant structure that has stood for less than one hundred years. A monk brought the statues here from Burma around 1882. The statues, one a sitting Buddha (190 centimeters tall) and the other a recumbent Buddha (ninety-six centimeters), are carved out of whole white jade and encrusted with precious jewels. They survived the destruction of the temple during the revolution that overthrew the Qing dynasty and are considered rare cultural relics and fine works of art. In another place, there was a recumbent Buddha, four meters long and brought from Singapore in 1989. It was my first encounter with Buddha statues. Years before I had treated Hermann Hesse's *Siddhartha* in my literature classes. My students always loved it. And since my deceased husband had been quite sympathetic to Buddhist philosophy, I paid special attention to what our excellent guide had to contribute and engaged in a very "enlightening" conversation with two young men who were visiting from India. The atmosphere in the temple was in itself very calming.

Less calming was our ride along the famous Bund, a five-block-long riverfront promenade with many of Shanghai's banks and trading houses. I was struck by the various architectural styles, such as Romanesque, Gothic, Renaissance, baroque, and art deco. I did not know Shanghai is supposed to have one of the richest collections of art deco architecture in the world. The whole district underwent a major face-lift starting in the late 1970s and early 80s. It is a dazzling showpiece, a symbol of their past, their colonial legacy, which we from the West cannot help but admire. The Hongkong and Shanghai Banking Corporation, all illuminated at night, is alone a sight to behold.

Other sights to behold were offered by our night cruise, which began on the Huangpu River, aka the "Mother River" of Shanghai. Seeing the Bund in the old, eastern district again, all resplendent with lights, was magical. It seems almost unreal that most of these banks and trading houses originated in the UK, France, Italy, Russia, Germany, Japan, the Netherlands, and Belgium – and do not forget the good old USA. But the new and modern United States is showing off her modern high-rises not far away from the Bund, where building restrictions are still in effect. On the eastern shore, the slick steel-and-glass skyscrapers of the Pudong New Area point to a budding financial empire of the future. Their logos, each larger than the next, glare sharply in the black sky from the highest spots on their respective skyscrapers. They are all there: Siemens, Toyota, Epson, Bayer, TDK, and of course Citigroup. Alas, Trump had not made it yet.

We got a chance to enjoy a walk through the new and vibrant Pudong district, stretch our necks while looking up at the glitzy high-rises of the world's capitalist giants, and marvel once more at the billboards along the panoramic drive. You could not miss them if you tried. Maybe communism is not as bad as Reagan made it out to be? One thing is certain, the United States will never invade China unilaterally. Shanghai puts New York City in the shade! And, if you are fashion conscious, the dress code here is super elegant.

As we were ushered back to our bus to return to the hotel, I noticed that a group of Chinese women and men seemed to have waited for us tourists at the bus stop. While we stood in line to get on the bus, a couple of old women, emaciated and pale, with drawn faces and hollow eyes, stretched their bony arms out for a token or just an empty plastic bottle. A very old man, sickly and clad in rags, leaned against a pole for support. He was nothing but skin and bones. The whole experience was extremely heart-wrenching, and the situation seemed worse than what I had seen in Rio de Janeiro or Africa. It made me sick to my stomach.

It is always the stark contrast between the rich and the poor that is so troublesome. Somehow, I had expected that by now the Chinese would take better care of their poor. They always talk about it. –

One has to shift gears constantly on international trips, and more so in developing countries. Here too. Back at the hotel, a wedding was in high swing. The handsome couple did not mind posing for me. The beautiful, slender bride wore a sleeveless, bright-red chiffon-and-lace gown. Her skin was white as the feathers of a swan. The groom wore a black suit, white shirt, and pinkish tie and was probably a business executive and budding capitalist. Judging by the food and the flower arrangement on the table, set with a red tablecloth and white napkins, you would not find this crowd begging for plastic bottles at the bus stop. I wondered if they too were allowed only one child and what they would do if it happened to be a girl. Our guide told us that due to that rule, they were badly lacking in girls in China.

While it's on my mind, I would like to point out that red is a very popular color in China. All the dragons I saw were huge and red. In the West, we were taught that it is the color of communism, and in that respect red gained a negative connotation in parts of our world, while in theirs it stands for good fortune. In fact, red corresponds to fire and symbolizes good fortune and joy, except when it refers to hell. Red is forbidden at funerals and stands traditionally for happiness and love. Don't forget red roses on Valentine's Day and as a token of affection for those you love. Enough!

The next day, one woman in my group bought a very elegant bright-red silk jacket when we visited Suzhou, a five-hundred-year-old city located in China's renowned silk region. After a brief train ride, we were transferred to a boat and cruised on the Grand Canal. The waterway was crowded with strings of barges laden with vegetables, construction materials, coal, or fruit. We stopped at the Water Gate, which connects Suzhou to the southern end of the canal. It was used as a "toll gate" for the canal's commercial traffic.

Suzhou

Suzhou, part of the Yangtze River Delta region, has an urban population of 2.4 million, expanding to over six million in the broader metropolitan area. In case you did not know, the population of the state of Indiana is about six million at this time. While Indiana has problems with overflowing rivers and streams whenever it rains a bit more than usual, Suzhou prides itself on being called "the land of waters," "the Venice of the Orient," and "the land of fish and rice." Well, in Indiana we have no rice, but we do have fish – and lots of corn. Since I was married in Venice, Italy, and traveled to the church in the golden gondola, I felt the name "Venice of the Orient" much overstated. Nevertheless, the cruise was quite pleasant. I liked the graceful bridges over the water and the tile-roofed, whitewashed houses that sat close to the banks, as in Venice, Italy, or little Venice on the Regnitz in Bamberg, Germany – but they were less picturesque. This Grand Canal, according to GCT, is "second only to the Great Wall as a Chinese engineering feat, and was begun 2,400 years ago."

Our visit to the Wangshi (Master of the Fishing Nets) Garden, built in 1140, turned out to be a bit disappointing, because the section of the garden boasting a peony courtyard, which has been reproduced at the Metropolitan Museum of Art in New York City, was lacking in color since the peonies were not in bloom. However, all in all, the garden, along with its house and pavilion and ponds, was lovely, and I could see why its elegant style had inspired many a poet and why its original owner used it as a place to study. The huge, delicately wrought rock in the pavilion, we were told, "once embellished the residence of Tang Ying, a famous painter of the Ming dynasty." It reminded me of the Asakura Choso Museum, in Tokyo. I felt as peaceful here as I did there. It provided a perfect escape from the hustle and bustle of the crowded city. The ancients regarded these gardens in Suzhou and south of the Yangtze River as the "finest under heaven."

I had no idea what to expect from our visit to a silk-spinning factory, but was pleasantly surprised. Marco Polo had been here and reported, "So much silk was produced in Suzhou that every citizen was clothed in it." Also, at one time, "Suzhou guarded the secrets of silk making so closely that smuggling silkworms out of the city was punishable by death" (GCT).

We went to the No. 1 Silk Factory, built in 1926, and were given the deluxe tour, which began with a lecture informing us that silk is made from mulberry-munching silkworms in order to produce thread for fine textiles. A rather amazing process, when you consider that the silkworm creates its cocoon out of a single silk thread that is continuous for approximately 3,600 feet. It takes one week to make one cocoon! The spinners demonstrated the importance of cocoons in making skeins. One cocoon is attached to each spindle. We saw why the filament of each cocoon must be unbroken and finally how silk is produced with an old-style machine. In short, we witnessed the entire process of producing handmade silk quilts. After all that, how could you possibly leave the place without placing an order? And, I thought, at bargain prices. I simply could not resist. I ordered a queen-size quilt with silk duvet and silk pillowcases, all off-white. I had it shipped, and I unpacked it happily as soon as I returned home. So far, I have not regretted the purchase. As promised, my quilt is light as a feather, warm in the winter, and cool in the summer. At times, my dreams are pleasant; at other times, they are not.

I was disappointed when I asked someone how much these diligent workers were paid per hour. They were not allowed to give this information to us tourists. I wonder why. When I had asked the same question during a visit to the Meissen porcelain factory in the former East Germany, they too refused to answer. You can deduce that the workers were being exploited.

Grand Circle Travel always kept us on our toes. After breakfast, we strolled through a local market, which was similar to the one in Beijing: lots of fish, poultry with feathers and without, chunks of raw meat from a variety of four-legged animals, vegetables, and not too much fruit. I became distracted when I looked across the street and noticed the ten- or twelve-floor apartment buildings, concrete shells standing one next to the other and on the verge of crumbling. They had small windows and, in some cases, a tiny balcony, crammed full of clothes on lines. Clothes also hung out of windows to dry. Metal bars were affixed to the balconies – perhaps to keep laundry hung out to dry from flying away? I asked a guide if they had lifts in these houses. When she answered in the negative, I took a deep breath and wondered how the old woman carrying a bag filled with purchases from the market would be able to transport it to an apartment on the seventh or ninth floor. I remembered my mother, who had to take sitting breaks when walking up the stairs to the third floor.

Our visit to the senior-citizen house was informative. At least these women were taken care of fairly well, and they appeared to be content and enjoyed our visit. They performed a nice dance for us and wore pretty dresses they had made themselves. Of course, these places are showcases for Western tourists and should always be taken with a grain of salt. But maybe we can learn something from them. Not everything about socialism is bad. Don't forget, when tourists come to America, we too refrain from showing them the dumps and decaying districts in our towns and cities. Here too, tour guides avoid exposing tourists to the homeless, to crumbling, empty factories and houses, and to those living off the beaten track. You know what I mean.

Our visit to a local family was quite nice. Their apartment was sparsely furnished, but so clean and inviting that it was obvious the inhabitants were proud of what they owned. Instead of walls, a curtain separated a couple of rooms. Curtains come in very handy whenever you need to increase the space in one room. It's easier, cleaner, and faster to pull a curtain aside than to knock down the wall. Their TV was small but functioning. The meal was tasty, with rice, pork, noodles, several kinds of half-raw vegetables, tea, and watermelon for dessert. Nothing's wrong with that. To my surprise, no dumplings were served. One youngster even spoke some English, which was welcomed by us. None of us spoke a word of Mandarin. I am not about to start learning a new language this late in life. They were always smiling. If at this point you did not know how to eat with chopsticks, you were out of luck.

Wuhan

On the way to Wuhan, I had a perfect view of the Port of Shanghai from the plane. To see the thousands of containers down there was simply mind-boggling. But what else would you expect from a country of 1.3 billion people? This port ranks as the third-largest container port in the world and is considered one of China's most important gateways for foreign trade. It was a short flight to Wuhan, capital of the Hubei province, a modern metropolis known as the most important site of the revolution and as a gateway to the Yangtze gorges.

I was excited during our lunch, because we were treated to a variety of my favorite dumplings. We talked about the ensuing cruise on the Yangtze River, the third-largest river in the world after the Nile and the Amazon, which at that time I had not yet cruised. The Yangtze originates at "the top of the world," that is, on the Tibetan Plateau, where I had not yet been. Its waters "flow dramatically and productively for 3,900 miles through China, and empty into the South China Sea" (GCT).

The Yangtze River

Dinner was taken at a hotel before we boarded our nice ship, the *Princess Sheena* of Regal China Cruises. The cabins were small but air-conditioned, and the ship was big enough to accommodate our group of about one hundred. When I noticed another Chinese river ship as it passed us, I could hardly believe my eyes. This ship was very long, with four decks and a monstrous dragon head at the front. The cabins seemed tiny, and masses of people appeared to be squeezed into many of them, like sardines. One woman was on a lower deck washing clothes in a small tub. – I was not envious. We did not go sightseeing in Wuhan, though it is considered one of the most important cities in China. We all admired the modern and impressive Yangtze River Bridge when sailing underneath it. It rises 263 feet above the river and, including the various approaches, is over a mile long. It is regarded "as a symbol of China's modern industrial progress and self-reliance" (GCT) and is one of three bridges connecting Wuchang, Hankou, and Hanyang. "All three cities are situated on low, flat land, interspersed with numerous ponds, canals and natural waterways. Formerly vulnerable to flooding, Wuhan is today well protected by a newly reinforced series of dikes" (GCT).

I spent much time out on deck or at the window of my cabin while cruising the Yangtze River, known as "Mother River" because it feeds the big nation. The terrain on both sides of the river is rugged, and mountainous walls of stone stretch into the sky; the lower portions of the mountains are predominantly covered with trees. They lend the landscape its scenic ambiance. We followed the Ancient Plank Road, the walkway about two meters wide and sixty kilometers long, which is located on the cliffs of the Yangtze and is occasionally interrupted by a tunnel. Periodically, a pagoda popped up on top of a cliff, and from time to time a few small sailboats, probably used for fishing, were docked along the banks. If the Ancient Plank Road fascinated me, I was even more intrigued by the coffins that were hung on the limestone cliffs on both sides of the five-thousand-meter-long Bochuangou. How they got there and why is a mystery they are still trying to solve. A feeling of admiration and eeriness overcame me. Several coffins were hanging on the stone wall, and others were squeezed into tiny, oblong caves in the cliff.

We listened to very good lectures while on the Yangtze, either out on deck or in our cabins. Several focused on the controversial and truly amazing Three Gorges Dam project and others on traditional Chinese medicine or other cultural and social topics. I tried to imagine what it must have been like when, until some fifty years earlier, thousands of coolies towed vessels upstream by means of ropes and pulleys, and I could see why it was a very risky and dehumanizing undertaking.

Early the next morning, we arrived in the village of Sandouping to get a look at the dam project. Our ship had to pass the dam site via a temporary channel, which had been dug out of the south bank. At that time, we were told the project would be completed in 2009. And as is usually the case when the Chinese set a deadline for an unimaginable task, they do in fact meet it. Thus, the Three Gorges Dam, occupying an area of 5.8 square miles, four times larger than the Hoover Dam, and in fact the largest in the world, was completed in 2009, when it reached a level of 175 meters. "The construction of this massive hydroelectric project displaced 1.3 million people, submerged countless archaeological sites, 13 cities, 140 towns, and 1,352 villages. It created a reservoir equal in size to Singapore. It took 27 million cubic meters of concrete; 39 cubic kilometers of water have been stored. All that at a cost of about $88 billion" (GCT). Correction: while the water level has been raised to 175 meters, some construction projects are still in progress.

We still cope with the controversy. On the one hand, it brings benefits such as better flood control – and thousands had been victims of flooding. Though it improves power control, power generation, navigation, and tourism, it causes problems such as sedimentation, environmental disasters, migration, continued flooding, mudslides, and erosion, to mention a few. I leave it up to you, or more importantly the displaced Chinese, to decide whether it was worth the effort.

I walked for a few hours around the vast complex of the dam still in progress, marveling and photographing and thinking to myself about how frequently on my international trips it boggled my mind just to realize where I was. I was pleased to have traveled to the dam before the project was completed. I remember seeing, high up on the cliffs, a big white sign – the demarcation line – reading 175 meters. I wonder whether it is still visible. It should be gone.

I heard that a small farming village at Sandouping was preserved. Sandouping is now nestled behind a sturdy dike.

After witnessing the exciting passage of our ship through the locks at Sandouping, we continued on our way through Xiling Gorge, the longest of the three, known for its narrow, precipitous cliffs. I had to agree with GCT's assessment. We sailed through "some of the most dramatic scenery in the world – past tombs, shrines, and caves – through stretches of tranquil water and swirling rapids." We were lucky. Since the weather was clear, we actually saw the Twelve Peaks, Five Sisters Peaks, Three Brothers Rocks, the Needle, and Goddess Peak. The sunsets on the Yangtze were unlike those anywhere else on earth! Just gorgeous! However, I did complain to my very attractive Chinese guide that at least the roofs of the high-rises, often built in clusters on the higher elevations for displaced families, could be more aesthetically appealing and project a Chinese flair, similar to those on temples or pagodas. – Whenever I saw rice-field terraces along the banks or a small garden, I imagined that those who had labored hard throughout the years for their livelihood would not leave their land willingly.

The scenery along the Xiling Gorge was striking, but the strange peaks, bizarre rocks, a barrier of solid limestone ridges, and lush, green mountains along the Wu Gorge, 150 kilometers long and the second of the Three Gorges, looked equally spectacular.

And in the afternoon, just when it seemed the tour could not get any better, good weather permitted us to board an authentic sampan for an excursion on the Daning River, a tributary of the Yangtze, to the Lesser Three Gorges. It was a singular adventure.

I had no idea what a sampan boat looked like. It is a relatively flat-bottomed wooden boat from 11.5 to 14.8 feet long. I shared mine with five other passengers. Our captain steered the boat with a very long bamboo pole. Four trackers pulled our boat on long ropes when the water level was low enough to allow the bottom of the boat to touch the big boulders beneath. These gorges are narrower than the great Three Gorges, and indeed, their canyons are as overpowering as those of their larger counterparts. I felt sorry for the guys pulling us in their threadbare bathing trunks. Admittedly, they were young and very muscular. Their bodies were tanned, and their drawn faces reflected a hard life. I wonder what has happened to them now that the water level has risen so much that the sampans are likely motorized. The scenery cannot possibly be as dramatic as it was in 2004.

I relished the detour through the narrow, very rugged, and romantic gorges and was anxious when passing through another tough spot in our river ship. The captain had to navigate through the Qutang Gorge, the shortest and narrowest of the three. It is so narrow that it is a one-way passage, and upstream ships must at times wait for ships going downstream to clear the passage before entering. Many consider these gorges "the most spectacular" and "most beautiful" ones. The mountains on either side are as high as four thousand feet; the entire gorge is only five miles long, and it is five hundred feet wide at its broadest point. The sunsets on the Yangtze were awesome! You just have to experience it all to appreciate what I mean. I am sure the impact of the scenery has been altered since the water level reached its goal. Those who have cruised the great Yangtze both before and after the dam will be the judges. I am convinced that many will forever question whether it was worth it to tame nature in this fashion.

Since our visit to Wanxian, this city of millions has become a victim of the flooding project, and its citizens have been moved to the city that was in the process of being built on higher ground. At that time, we had to climb at least one hundred stairs from the pier to the location of the new living quarters, which consisted of the architecturally very boring multistory apartment houses so common in former socialist countries. I wonder how the family we visited in 2004 on the riverbank is coping with the forced evacuation. At the time, their new living quarters looked somewhat dark and primitive, with the exception of a small TV, and our guide informed us that this particular family was not at all happy with their new circumstances. To be fair, the new municipal building, the museum, and other buildings we saw were modern structures and of more pleasing architectural styles. Several had a big plaza in front of them, with well-kept lawns, flowers, and trees. At one point, some of us joined in to practice tai chi with a group of senior Chinese men and women. – If you like pig snouts, poultry, eggs, puppies, or vegetables as big as a football, the Wanxian Market is the place for you. I myself had a lot of fun interacting with the neatly dressed little boys and girls in a school courtyard. I made music for them by pressing my index finger against one nostril and humming a song for them through the other. They laughed and laughed and could not get enough of it. I finally had to tear myself away, because it was time to embark.

We continued our river journey on the upper Yangtze toward Chongqing, observing the old and the new of China. We learned that because of the rise and fall of the river over millennia, the terraced fields are among the most fertile in all of China. – Each year, new fields are carved out of the higher slopes to prepare for the future rise in the reservoir to be created here. While cruising, we got a good idea of the industry and commerce that drives the economy of this watery inland region. We also had a chance to see several coal mines on the slopes of the gorges. At one point, a good stretch of the slope was jet black with coal, and I wondered what it would look like once the dam and the flooding were completed. We were informed that the dam would facilitate the transportation of the coal. The barges now pull right up to the bank, and the coal is dumped directly into them. The Chinese rely on coal to produce over three-quarters of their energy. Now, in place of the highly polluting coal-burning plants, the dam provides clean energy. Fortunately, during my stay in China the air was not too badly polluted. But the flooding still occurs along the Yangtze and continues to endanger the lives of the coal miners.

Chongqing

It was the last stretch of our four-day cruise on the big Yangtze. We disembarked in Chongqing after breakfast and continued by bus to see the pandas at the zoo, considered to be the largest in Southwest China. It was a real treat to see these cuddly bears, with their thick white-and-black fur, walking around slowly in their Panda Ground, located at the foot of a hill by a little stream. Unfortunately, we saw only five bears; a few were hiding in their man-made caves. We were ushered in and out rather quickly and as a result did not have time to wander around. I saw a tiger sleeping in a stall next to a panda as well as a collection of big birds – don't ask me what species – that were perched on branches of trees inside big cages. That's all. Nevertheless, to observe a bamboo-eating panda in China was worth the visit. After all, they are one of the world's most endangered species, with an estimated one thousand surviving in the wild.

The visit to the mountain city Chongqing was comparatively brief. "Chongqing, with an approximate population of 31 million, is one of the five national central cities of the People's Republic of China. It was separated from Sichuan Province in 1977 and became an independent municipality, encompassing the entire Yangtze Valley between Wushan and Chongqing proper. It was the capital of China during World War II, and is the most important inland industrial city in China today" (GCT). We were allowed more time at the Stilwell Museum than at the zoo. Once inside, I understood why. The museum was the former residence of General Stilwell, aka "Vinegar Joe" Stilwell, commander of American forces in China, Burma, and India during World War II. I had never heard of him but was glad to learn about the colorful history of the American Volunteer Air Group, the "Flying Tigers," who were based in Chongqing during the war to fight on behalf of China against the Japanese. These Flying Tigers were actually mercenaries. They had lucrative contracts, with salaries up to three times more than what they had been making in the US forces. Since they were comparatively successful after combating Japan right after Pearl Harbor, they gave hope to Americans that they would help China succeed against the Japanese as well. – We now know what happened.

On the way to the airport, we stopped at the Painters' Village, and one of the artists demonstrated the art of painting and calligraphy. The speed with which he painted a wild horse was impressive.

Xianna

After a short flight to Xianna, one of the oldest cities in China and the eastern terminus of the Silk Road, and the transfer to our hotel, I was glad we would stay at the Sheraton Xian hotel for a couple of nights. I retired right after a good Western-style dinner and got a good night's rest before my anxiously awaited visit to the Qin Mausoleum, where China's greatest archeological attraction – the entire army of terra-cotta warriors, which the first emperor of China, Qin Shi Huang, had created and buried with him more than two thousand years ago – awaited us.

Terra-Cotta Warriors

When I entered the gigantic hall and looked down from the elevated walkway onto the entire legion standing in battle formation, set in the ground to guard and protect the great emperor's tomb, I was stunned. My eyes teared up. The eight thousand life-size funerary statues – archers, infantrymen, and cavalry, together with their horses and chariots – were individually sculpted from live models by some seven hundred thousand workers – and then painted. Farmers had accidentally discovered them in the early 1970s while digging a well. Since then, three large pits had been uncovered. It is truly "an exquisite and beautifully preserved symbol of an ancient era" (GCT) and was without question another climax of my trip to China and my worldwide travels more generally.

Before dinner at a restaurant, where we witnessed a demonstration of the preparation of the region's famous and tasty dumplings, we stopped at a lacquer-ware factory. It was more or less anticlimactic, but it gave me a chance to pick up a few more souvenirs in addition to the miniature soldiers I had bought at the Qin Mausoleum.

On the day of our flight to Guilin, we were taken by bus in the forenoon to see the Ming dynasty City Wall, built in the fourteenth century. It measures 11.9 kilometers in circumference, twelve meters in height, and between fifteen and eighteen meters in thickness at the base; a moat was also built outside the walls to protect a much smaller city. We were given about thirty minutes to walk on the wall – it was raining, and I decided to rush back to the bus and wait until we continued to the Jianfu Temple to see the Small Wild Goose Pagoda, one of the oldest pagodas in China. By then, it had stopped raining.

"Construction of the Great Wild Goose Pagoda began in 652. It was 64 m in height and built to store the translations of Buddhist sutras obtained from India by the Xuan Zang. Construction of the Small Wild Goose Pagoda began in 707 and measured 45 m tall at the time of completion but its tower was damaged by the 1556 Shaanix earthquake and reduced its height to 43.3 m. The pagoda has a brick frame built around a hollow interior, and its square base and shape reflect the building style of other pagodas from the era" (GCT). The gardens of the temple area were beautiful.

Guilin

After lunch, we flew from the dry, northwestern plateau of Xian to the moist, semitropical, mountainous region of Guilin, home to about six hundred thousand people. We boarded our local rivercraft and leisurely cruised the Li River. "Lijiang. As a tributary of Zhujiang River, it originates in Mountain Cat Xingan County in the north of Guilin. It winds and meanders its way for 437 kilometers passing through Guilin, Yangshuo, Pingle and Wuzhou. Between Guilin and Yangshuo, Lijian River traverses 83 kilometers like a jade ribbon winding among thousands of the hills. , the landscapes are so especially spectacular that the rocks and caves are fantastic, the deep pools, springs and waterfalls are wonderful. The reflections of the hills in clear and greenish water are like bright and beautiful pictures. 'A hundred miles Lijian River, a hundred miles Picture Gallery.' Numerous poems and literary works from modern and ancient times address her beauty. Hanyu, a great poet in the Tang Dynasty, had written a hymn to praise the beautiful scenery" (GCT).

Sailing on the Li was a memorable experience. We passed humped, cone-shaped, and phallus-shaped limestone peaks draped in emerald-green mosses, with shrubs and trees, fishermen astride bamboo rafts, washerwomen squatting on the banks close to their quaint houses, and leashed cormorants perched on rafts, awaiting their orders to go fishing. During our trip, a thin veil of fog covered the entire landscape. It gave our surroundings a certain mystique or eeriness, accompanied by a soft silence. Rarely had I experienced such a pristine ambiance. It felt ethereal. –

Thus, I experienced something akin to culture shock when only a few hours later, we made our way through the bustling market town of Yangshuo, producer of China's most famous inventions – tea and silk. Of course, I stocked up on scroll paintings for my friends and myself. Before returning to the hotel, I simply had to take a picture of a Chinese man showing off two big black birds perched on the ends of the wooden pole resting on his shoulders. I found his coolie hat so unique. It was worth a good tip. He gave me a big smile. A couple of teeth were missing. The schoolchildren we visited at the Children's Palace seemed doubly happy to chat with us Americans. They were a cheerful bunch and brave enough to practice their English with us.

As was to be expected, when we virtually invaded the home of a rice farmer, we realized quickly that neither he nor his wife spoke English. They looked very somber and could not even muster up a smile. I did not blame them. While their rice paddies, at that time more or less flooded, were presumably large enough to feed them, their living quarters were dark and extremely primitive, that is, in a state of dire disrepair, and I had a hard time understanding how humans could bear living like that for any length of time. When I spotted a small TV in a dark corner, I was glad to see they had at least something to entertain them. I am usually overcome by a feeling of guilt in these situations. I would have loved to visit a farmer living in one of the colorful floating villages we passed when cruising the Li River.

As I have said, one never has much time to reflect during these trips. Typically, these thoughts surface after I have returned home and when these places make headlines, are discussed in various media outlets, or come up in conversation with other travelers and friends. Thus, when my neighbors told me their daughter was adopting a Chinese orphan, I immediately remembered my visit to an orphanage in Guilin, where I was impressed by the comparatively good care these little children were given.

I was glad I opted to visit the Guilin Guangxi Teachers University for a lecture on Chinese painting by the well-published Professor Lue Ke Zhong. It was educational and fascinating, and I began to understand why Guilin's misty shores are so characteristic of this ancient art form. One of the women in my group – an artist – gave the painting technique a serious try during the lecture. She was quick to purchase a selection of fine brushes and other tools before we left.

Hong Kong

That evening, we flew to Hong Kong, the center of trade in Asia and the world's busiest port. It is located in the south of the South China Sea, which is part of the Pacific Ocean. "Starting out as a fishing village, salt production site and trading ground, Hong Kong would evolve into a military port of strategic importance and eventually an international financial center that has the world's sixth highest GDP (PPP) per capita, supporting 33% of the foreign capital flows into China. Its population is over 7 million people and thus it is considered to be one of the most densely populated places in the world" (GCT).

At Kowloon, the location of our hotel, we started our tour on the Star Ferry to Hong Kong Island, instantly feeling overwhelmed by the forest of majestic and impressive high-rises. We were told that even since 1997, when the lease with England ran out, they have continued to reclaim land from the sea in order to create more surface area on which to build. Several magnificent high-rise hotels and commercial buildings have been constructed on this reclaimed land. In addition to Hong Kong Island, Kowloon, and the New Territories, there are about 240 outlying islands.

A bus brought us to the Central and the Western District, the older part of Hong Kong, from which we were taken up to Victoria Peak. The view of the harbor, islands, and imposing skyscrapers from Tai Ping Shan (Mountain of Peace), 1,811 feet high, would have been much more spectacular had it not been so foggy.

We continued to Repulse Bay. Along the beach were several shrines amidst posh, prohibitively expensive high-rises.

A stark contrast to seeing the homes of the sinfully rich was my experience cruising through the floating fishing village of Aberdeen. The harbor village consists of some six hundred shacks that house over six thousand of the boat people in Hong Kong. I failed to see the magic in this kind of existence and felt embarrassed just looking into their houseboats or taking a photo. Rarely, except in South Africa or Rio de Janeiro, had I been confronted with such stark poverty. Most of the sampans and houseboats were in dire need of repair, yet their inhabitants seemed to be content. Some even had a pet dog on the boat. I learned that, on the one hand, people lived on the boats because they could not afford to rent the houses on the shore or nearby, but that, on the other hand, it was their chosen way of life. That is, their continuous presence was necessary if they wanted to make a decent living from fishing. It bothered me that even here, the divide between rich and poor was so obvious. Not too far away, I spotted several slick and huge yachts in the harbor. No ragged clothes were hanging outside to dry.

The next day, I took an optional tour through the eastern part of the New Territories, leased to Britain by China in 1898 for ninety-nine years. It is known as "the land in between." The peninsula across Victoria Harbor was a welcome respite. The coastline, bordering lush and hilly farmland, was rugged. More uplifting, if you wish, was our stroll through the local flower market, where if you could afford them, you could purchase the most beautiful orchids, roses, carnations, etc. – the market offered an amazing assortment of fresh flowers. Yet, I was even more excited and happy at the sight of the display of exquisite and colorful little pet birds, such as parakeets and parrots, in very nice cages. An entire street was filled with bird vendors.

We were afforded more local color when visiting the Wong Tai Sin Temple, a good example of a traditional Chinese place of worship. It is the big temple of Hong Kong and, because it has the reputation of answering one's prayers most of the time, among its most frequented shrines. "What you request is what you get." I forgot to ask for anything but enjoyed walking around, observing the people, and taking pictures of the main altar, the nine-dragon wall, and the huge cast-iron incense burner in the courtyard. I refrained from lighting one of the long candles and declined to have my fortune told. But I did not refuse the Chinese-horoscope handout. I had no idea what mine would be. I know now that my sign is that of the monkey. I am not kidding; it reads, "Extremely intelligent, diplomatic, tactful, clever, makes good friends, can sometimes be deceiving." I have no qualms about that, because I have had a fondness for monkeys ever since I was a kid.

If you like seafood, you must go to the Sai Kung fishing village. Go for a stroll along the shore and be amazed at the abundance of seafood restaurants. It is a seafood lovers' paradise. I spent quite a while just looking at the bizarre, slimy creatures of all shapes, colors, and sizes, still alive and wriggling around in aquariums, buckets, and big square containers – waiting to be chosen, fished out by their caretaker, slaughtered, scaled, fried, cooked, or whatever, and finally eaten right there at a sidewalk table with a view of the bay from which they originated. But I just wanted to watch and be entertained. There was no time to linger. Regardless, I would have preferred to eat my catch at one of the harbor's floating restaurants.

Our farewell dinner was Western style. But no steak. One guy in my group could not wait to get back to the States to eat a big, fat porterhouse steak with a knife and fork. He was sick and tired of rice, dumplings, and everything Chinese, especially chopsticks. He should never have come on this trip. I was glad he did not plan to join those who signed up for the optional four-day post-trip to Bangkok, Thailand.

THAILAND

Bangkok

We arrived in Bangkok (City of Angels), which has a population of nearly nine million and is both the capital of Thailand and its center of political, commercial, industrial, and cultural activity, in the late afternoon on April 30. The Dusit Thani hotel was uniquely Thai. Upon entering the lobby, I felt transported into another realm. The service was out of this world. We were welcomed with an herbal drink and cold towels. The strikingly beautiful Thai hostesses bowed gracefully whenever they passed by. They appeared and disappeared like butterflies. I was happy to relax in the lobby and took in the elegant and uniquely Thai ambiance. We were served a snack of wild salmon, presented artfully and accompanied by a crystal goblet filled with sparkling champagne. I had opted out of the trip from the hotel to a Thai dinner and classical dance performance and let myself be pampered by their royal-carpet treatment. At that point, I had been on the go for almost a month.

I was refreshed after a hot bath and a good night's rest, and at 8:00 a.m. on May 1, I was ready to go (no shorts, no sandals) for a visit to the Royal Grand Palace and the Temple of the Emerald Buddha in the old Kingdom of Siam.

In 1767, Burmese forces attacked the Thai capital of Ayutthaya, leaving it in ruins. King Rama I moved the capital to its present site in 1782, and the Grand Palace became the centerpiece of a new Thai capital called Krung Thep (City of Angels), known outside of Thailand as Bangkok. The original palace was constructed with some material brought from Ayutthaya, and each successive ruler expanded and refined the complex. It was King Mongkut (or Rama IV) who ruled from this palace, expanded trade with the West and was romanticized in the musical The King and I. (GCT)

I walked through the entrance gate to the Grand Palace, and was overwhelmed by "a massive square-mile complex of gilded *wats* (temples), elaborate ceremonial halls, and dazzling statues" (GCT). I could hardly believe what I saw. Everything, all of the facades, seemed to be covered with gold, cobalt blue, emerald green, dark green, and red mosaic. The temple roofs and pagodas were more ornate than others I had seen before. I felt like I was walking around in a magical kingdom. Each flight of stairs led me to another treasure. It seemed as though I ascended these temple steps without the slightest effort – as though I was floating on air. This complex is indeed authentic testimony to the creativity and craftsmanship of Thai people. It's amazing to learn that within its walls, the Thai war ministry, the state departments, and even the mint were housed. And within these ancient walls, the residence of the royal family and the government office still stand. It is definitely a place to which words cannot do justice. You must see it for yourself. It's magical. But it is also steamy hot!

Fireball Lily

No matter what, stick with it and follow me to the Temple of the Emerald Buddha. According to legend, the statue originated in India. It is considered the most sacred Buddhist temple in Thailand. The statue is carved from a slab of emerald-green jade. It's not something you see every day. The Buddha is only forty-five centimeters tall, but very famous. It dates back to the fourteenth century. I found it curious that His Majesty changes the robes on the Buddha every season. It is an important ritual in the Buddhist calendar. In case you were wondering, the robes for each season are made of gold. What else?!

On the way to a local jewelry shop, we came upon a very colorful May 1 parade. The participants carried blue and yellow flags, matching the colors of their shirts. A police force marching in step wore white jackets, white helmets, and black trousers with a red stripe. They carried their rifles in an upright position. Here and there, a huge portrait of the queen in a splashy round golden frame, modeled after the rays of the sun, was affixed to poles or propped up on a pedestal. They were erected in the flower isles in the center of the road. People lined the streets to watch. It was peaceful and pleasant at that time.

On May 2, a canal boat took us up the Chao Phraya River to Ayutthaya, the capital of Siam from 1350 to 1767. "During its time as the Thai capital, many kings of different dynasties ruled here until the grand city was invaded and destroyed by the Burmese in 1767" (GCT). Here, we also had the opportunity to see how the privileged and the very poor lived. Nicely kept apartment houses stood not too far away from primitive shelters and shacks on poles along the banks of the river.

On this particular trip, I met a young Indonesian student, a Muslim, who spoke perfect English. We really got into politics, and it came as no surprise that Ruciani had nothing good to say about G. W. Bush. She also told me she preferred to wear a scarf because it made her feel safer. Burkas and scarves, or whatever people choose to wear, do not bother me in the least. It's a personal choice. Leave them be – as long as no one forces their preferences on me. There are other things to get upset about. Ruciani also told me that Thailand's government exploits the poor and that it is corrupt, as is the case in Indonesia and so many other places around the globe. We e-mailed for several years after we met. She advanced in her studies after receiving an MA and had a baby girl, and her husband was promoted in his job. But by American standards they were poor. As far as I know, they were fortunately spared by the great tsunami and earthquakes. Eventually, Ruciani stopped writing, and I gave up trying to communicate. – Too bad. I really liked her. She was intelligent, caring, and a good Muslim.

We parted when I had to continue with my group to explore Ayutthaya's magnificent ruins: a beautiful ancient palace, pagodas, houses, and more temples. The highlights were Thailand's largest bronze statue of the reclining Buddha and a stroll through the beautiful palace grounds. The noticeably well-kept gardens were full of flowering shrubs, bushes, and trees. It was springtime! As we were leaving the ancient remnants of splendor, I stopped to take a picture of a stunning elephant, dressed up royally and with a red, upholstered chaise and canopy above it. If I had arrived earlier, I could have seen all those splendid ruins from the top of an elephant. Not to worry! I had ridden on elephants before.

Travel to Western countries is saturated with visits to chapels, churches, monasteries, cathedrals, etc. When you travel to Asia, you become equally saturated with temples, pagodas, Buddhist monasteries, places of worship, etc. And you simply cannot avoid the thousands of Buddha statues – bronze, emerald, jade, wood, and of course gold – that everybody insists you must see. And since I was there in the land of the Buddha, I signed up for my last optional tour, scheduled for May 2, 2004, to see the ultimate reclining golden Buddha.

"The Sukhothai Traimit Golden Buddha Image is the largest Golden Buddha image in the world. It is a Guccha image in the mara-conquering attitude, the typical artistic style of the days when Sukhothai was the capital of Thailand. It is made of pure gold. The image is unrivalled in beauty, measuring 12 feet 5 inches in diameter and has a height of 15 feet 9 inches from the base to the crown and it weighs approximately 5 tons" (GCT). We also learned that "the statue was covered with stucco and cracked open by accident during the transfer to the temple in 1955" (GCT). The Wat Pho is considered the largest temple in Bangkok and houses over one thousand Buddha images, including the reclining Buddha. Our guide called attention to the soles of Lord Buddha's feet. They were adorned with inlaid mother-of-pearl in beautiful designs "representing the 108 auspicious signs of the true Buddha" (GCT). I had seen other reclining Buddha images and found that they had one thing in common: they were extremely long and big and awkward in appearance. At first, I did not quite understand the significance of this position. Then I was told that it depicts the passing of the Buddha into nirvana. Thanks for enlightening me. According to the scholar Richard Gombrich, "Nirvana means 'blowing out' or 'extinguishing' – referring in the Buddhist context to the blowing out of the fires of greed, hatred, and delusion."

If you like Buddhas and temples, there are about five hundred in Bangkok alone. One of the long streets our bus drove through was crammed full of shops selling Buddha statues in all shapes and forms. The gold was blinding. I was relieved when our tour ended with a visit to the flower market, where you could find whatever flower you wished for and in the most exquisite and creative arrangements – more beautiful than any I had seen in China. Yet, even here a real downer interfered with my happiness in the flower market. Right across the street was a four-story apartment building that testified further to the harsh poverty that exists even in this almost Buddha-obsessed country. I would hope that if either the Buddha or Jesus knew what goes on today, they would be embarrassed.

At the farewell dinner, we exchanged our impressions of the country. Some had managed to have a jacket or suit tailor-made in no time at all. After the first attempt to walk through Bangkok's main shopping district, I soon lost my enthusiasm to forge ahead. The sidewalks were so crowded with people that it took a lot of energy and caution just to window-shop. Every second, I was afraid someone would snatch my purse and disappear into the crowd. What made it virtually unbearable was the suffocating heat, in the upper 90s. Since the temperature was coupled with 99% humidity, I felt as though I was stuck in a sauna. My only wish was to head back to the air-conditioned hotel and take a cold shower. I swore to myself that I would not leave the hotel as long as I was in Bangkok, which was one more night. And I decided right then and there that Thailand, with all its gilded, fairy-tale-like palaces, all its Buddhas, temples, and elephants, and all its admirable hospitality and well-spiced food, would thenceforth be a place on this planet to be avoided.

The flight home was long. And due to delays, the stopover in Tokyo seemed even longer. When we finally took off, it got a bit scary for several of the passengers. A Japanese businessman sat next to me. I looked out the window and could see nothing but brown dust or sand. We sat at the tail end of the plane, and the whole thing began to shake and tremble. The Japanese man broke out in a sweat. I told him not to worry and that it would be better to die in a plane crash than vegetating in bed. It failed to cheer him up. He was thinking of his children. Soon the plane began to stabilize, and everybody's face lit up. My neighbor wiped the sweat off his forehead and pulled out a paper to read. Eventually I arrived in good old Bloomington, Indiana, safe and sound as usual. No sooner had I gone to bed than the phone rang. It was my ex, calling to tell me who in his family had died. I told him I couldn't care less and not to call me again. It was the last time I heard from him. –

Maybe my experiences during World War II immunized me against fear of disaster. I was definitely not afraid of flying. Once bit by the travel bug, I kept forging ahead. After China, I cruised around Europe – to Holland and Belgium and the Black Sea – and treated my nonbiological great-grandsons to a Christmas cruise to Australia and New Zealand.

INDIA

On February 17, 2006, I ventured out on another big trip with Overseas Adventure Travel, this time to the hidden kingdom of Bhutan and to what OAT calls "the Heart of India." Knowing it would be a long flight with a stopover in London, I splurged on first-class tickets. We flew to New Delhi first and spent a couple of nights at Intercontinental the Grand, an "elegant oasis," as the hotel advertises itself.

New Delhi

Our guide was very nice and offered to show us around New Delhi a bit on the day before we flew to Bhutan. I always experience mild culture shock on my first day in a foreign place. But I love it. New Delhi is a far cry from Bloomington, Indiana. In fact, there are two cities: "Old Delhi, the capital of Muslim India between the mid-17th and late-19th centuries, is full of formidable mosques, monuments and forts. It's a lively area of colorful bazaars, narrow streets and barely controlled chaos." "New Delhi," on the other hand, is "the imperial city created by the British Raj, and is composed of spacious, tree-lined avenues and imposing government buildings, and has a sense of order absent from other parts of the city" (OAT).

Our "Namaste" orientation walk took place in Old Delhi. It was the equivalent of an hors d'oeuvre, if you wish. We would all return for the Heart of India tour nine days later, as you will see.

One thing was obvious at the start: in New Delhi, the most vivid colors commingled. Each and every person, man or woman, young or old, seemed to stand out – if they were men, because of their big yellow, purple, or green turbans, the length of their beards, or their multicolored robes, or if they were women, because of their even more brightly colored saris, which made them look like Madonnas. Adorable children with curly black hair and big brown eyes were everywhere. The city was vibrant, the architecture was powerful, ornamental, and impressive, and the visit to the local Sikh temple, where we had to take our shoes off before entering, was rather "enlightening."

"The Gurdwara – The Sikh Temple is a place for acquiring a spiritual knowledge and wisdom. It is open to everyone regardless of age, sex, caste, or creed. Here all men, women and children are treated as equal. It offers shelter and food to anyone in need. It provides care for the sick, elderly and handicapped. It is also a centre for promoting culture and health. Moral education as well as knowledge of the religion and history is often taught to children in the Sikh temple" (OAT). I liked the brief introduction to New Delhi and was convinced I would be ready for much more of this exotic country after a detour to the roof of the world: the Himalayan mountain range.

BHUTAN

Druk Air's plane was not very large, but it was immaculate inside, and the flight attendants were super friendly. We enjoyed perfect weather, with a blue and cloudless sky throughout. I had found a perfect window seat, where the wings would not obstruct my view. I was so excited when the pilot announced we would land for a stopover in Kathmandu, Nepal, since originally I had wanted to go to Nepal, but OAT offered no such tour. Bhutan was my second choice. In Kathmandu, we were allowed to step out of the plane for a few minutes only. No problem, though. What happened after we were back in the air was the ultimate! Our pilot announced that we were about to fly across the Himalayan mountain range, with a good view of the king of all mountains: Everest. At 29,035 feet and rising a few millimeters each year, it is the highest mountain on earth. I awakened the passenger in front of me, a guy from Germany, to point out Mount Everest below. He insisted that the particular mountain was not Everest, but Mount Gauri Sankar. When the flight attendant supported my opinion, he conceded the point. The pilot tilted the plane, and I swiftly snapped a series of picture-perfect photos of the majestic king and his proud entourage as they stretched out for miles beneath our wings, covered in blankets of immaculate snow. I never again felt as proud of my pictures as I did on that day. Congratulations, Christa-Maria. It could not get any better! I pinched myself! I really saw Mount Everest with my own eyes! Wow!

Paro

On February 20, 2006, I was in the right frame of mind for the descent into Paro, located in the wide, lush, and beautiful Paro Valley of Bhutan, aka "Land of the Peaceful Dragon" or "Land of the Thunder Dragon." This tiny but fascinating dragon kingdom, with a population of about seven million, prides itself on a unique development concept: gross national happiness. It aims to maximize happiness rather than solely economic growth. "The individual is placed at the center of all development efforts and it recognizes that the individual has material, spiritual and emotional needs" (OAT). It's tantamount to El Dorado.

Thanks are due to "his Majesty, King Jigme Singye Wangchuk, fourth in the Wangchuck dynasty, head of the state. His Majesty formally ascended the Golden Throne on June 2, 1974 and since then steered the country firmly towards the objectives of economic self-reliance, cultural promotion, regionally balanced development, environment preservation and good governance" (OAT).

In reading our OAT handout, I knew my appetite for Mother Nature's miracles, which awaited me in this Himalayan wonderland, would be satisfied. "Here the awe-inspiring vales and dales, daunting heights of the countless silvery massifs and towering black mountains, sprawling glaciers and huge moraines, stupendous waterfalls and crystal clear lakes, swift cascading gurgling, tumbling, falling rivers and flamboyant streams, deep gorges and seemingly unending series of beautiful valleys, verdant slopes and vast undulating flower studded Himalayan meadows, dense forests and scrub jungles and mysterious snow basins and whispering savannahs vividly illustrate the varying moods, modes and chores of mother nature." What more is there to say?

Our guide greeted us at the airport with a big smile. He was dressed in an impeccable *gho*, a long silver-gray robe made from a fine, handwoven fabric. His polished black leather shoes shone. His English was flawless as well. But my attention was focused immediately on the unique architecture of the buildings, already seen from the tarmac at the airport. They were strikingly beautiful. The shapes, colors, and decorations on the walls, doors, and window frames were unlike any I had seen before. They reminded me vaguely of facades seen on houses in Bavaria or the Black Forest in Germany. We went for a brief walk downtown to get acclimated. Paro had a population of about four thousand. It was a sunny day, and this new cultural environment fascinated me. Trying to communicate with a couple of cute little boys who were practicing archery on a sidewalk, I failed to pay attention to where I was going as I waved good-bye to them. Before I knew it, I found my feet and legs entangled in a barbed-wire mess on the ground next to the sidewalk. Fortunately, though embarrassed, I untangled myself rather quickly and emerged without damage.

The elevation at Paro is 7,300 feet, and I did not notice any uncomfortable effects due to the altitude. I did not take any medicine for altitude sickness. There were only nine persons in our group, and a van sufficed to transport us around Bhutan. From Paro, we headed to Thimphu, the capital and largest city of Bhutan (with 50,000 inhabitants), which sits at an altitude of 7,600 feet. The two-hour drive through the scenic Paro Valley to Thimphu was just gorgeous. We stopped at the confluence of the Paro and Thimphu rivers, and en route we visited Simtokha Dzong, the kingdom's oldest fortress. Our accommodations at the Hotel Jumolhari were excellent, and I had no difficulty falling asleep, despite the fact that an obese woman in our group had fallen quite sick, stayed in a room next to mine, and was coughing incessantly, even though the doctor in our group provided ample antibiotics for her. She was contemplating quitting the tour, but fortunately or unfortunately for her, she kept on going and eventually turned into a real nuisance. But I had long since learned to just ignore people like that and avoid them like the plague. I really liked the husband-and-wife MDs.

We spent the next morning exploring Thimphu, Bhutan's minicapital, and admired again the uniquely vibrant Bhutanese architecture and objects of art, as well as a group of archers practicing on the National Archery Ground. I noticed that this place was not yet overrun by tourists, and as I write, six years later, I wonder if the situation has changed.

The visit to the beautiful and very impressive National Library and Archives, established in 1976, was amazing. Among other collections, it holds a vast collection of ancient Buddhist manuscripts and what is considered the world's largest book, a compilation of photos of Bhutan. The librarian flips the page only once a month. I just stood there shaking my head. I was not sure this tale was true.

Zorig Chusum, the National Institute – aka "the Painting School," or the traditional school of the thirteen arts and crafts, which include painting, sculpture, carving, and calligraphy – gave more insight into their culture, as did the visit to the Medicine Institute, where centuries-old healing arts, such as acupuncture and herbal remedies, are practiced. The Textile Museum featured weaving demonstrations and rare glimpses into Bhutan's finest textiles and production techniques, such as weaving, dyeing, and spinning. Yes, we also saw firsthand how handmade paper is produced. As a matter of fact, I bought a couple of nice scroll-down wall hangings depicting Bhutanese dragons in local colors. We admired more of the exquisite artistry of traditional, local crafts and textiles at the Handicrafts Emporium, an extension of the Cottage Industry Division of the Department of Trade and Industry, and continued our afternoon excursion with a drive to the Memorial Chorten, a stupa built in 1974 in memory of King Jigme Dorji Wangchuck, the "Father of Modern Bhutan." It is a very large, Tibetan-style stupa, and as it is the focus of their daily worship, this chorten can be seen from far away and exudes the intended serenity and peace.

When traveling in Bhutan, it quickly become obvious that the Bhutanese are endowed with a profound faith. You will find chortens, small and large, all over Bhutan. I made sure to spin the huge and beautifully decorated prayer wheels to spread my prayers around the world and wondered silently how the monks who were present throughout Bhutan could possibly study and worship day in, day out throughout their lives in order to finally reach the state of enlightenment. I gained a deeper insight into Buddhist philosophy while reflecting on a selection of paintings and statues displayed in the multistoried chorten. I like their philosophy, which advocates peace, tolerance, and nonviolence.

I had reached a point of saturation when we were alerted that it was time for the drive up to the Takin Preserve to see the takin, the national animal of Bhutan. It is located in the Motithang district of Thimphu. The takin is the product of a miracle. "A Tibetan saint aka 'The Divine Madman' upon the request to be given a cow and a goat for lunch, after having devoured the meat of both animals leaving out the bones, took out the head of the goat and fixed it to the skeleton of the cow. He uttered abracadabra and the magic worked. With a snap he created a live animal, which had the head of the goat and the body of the cow" (OAT). If you don't believe me, go there and see for yourself. Weird-looking creatures they are. Their heads are definitely larger than those of goats. I wonder whether such miracles would pass the Catholic Church's test for sainthood. What seemed miraculous to me was that at this particular place, out of nowhere, appeared the German passenger from Druk Air who had insisted Mount Everest was not Mount Everest.

We hiked up to a place from which we had a stunning view of the valley. From up there, many colorful, tattered prayer flags, strung on a rope horizontally, scattered all those unscripted prayers to the heavens when the wind was blowing.

We saw another collection of more than one hundred prayer flags the next day, when driving over the fabulous ten-thousand-foot Dochula Pass. Seeing the 108 stupas at the monument dedicated to King Jigme Singye Wangchuck was thought-provoking, to say the least. It was almost too intense. Luckily for us, the weather was clear and gave us a good view of the magnificent, snowcapped peaks of Bhutan's northern border.

The drive through the valley where rice, the main crop, is harvested along the rivers Pho Chhu and Mo Chhu was lovely. The climate here is comparatively mild. Punakha held the title "Winter Capital" before Thimphu was declared the capital. Today, it is the winter seat of the Je Khenpo (chief abbot) and the Central Monastic Body.

I could not help but be impressed at the sight of the Pungthang Dewachen Gi Phodrang (Palace of Great Happiness), right at the junction of the Pho Chhu and Mo Chhu Rivers. Shabdrung Ngawang Namgyal built it in 1637. "This majestic Dzong served as both the religious and the administrative center of Bhutan in the past. It is representative of typical Dzong architecture found in Buddhist kingdoms of the Himalayas: Bhutan and Tibet. It is massive in style with towering exterior walls surrounding a complex of courtyards, temples, administrative offices, and monk's accommodations" (OAT). This one measures some six hundred feet in length and 240 feet in width and has a six-story, gold-domed tower. Walking around in the courtyards and taking a closer look at all the religious statuary, I began to understand better the depth of history and spiritual tradition resting here.

The *dzong* located on a ridge in Wangdue Phodrang, a nearly four-hundred-year-old town, which we visited the next day, was equally impressive. The young novice Buddhist monks present at the *dzong*, which was founded by the Shabdrung in 1638, particularly intrigued me. The guide explained that "the *dzong* is strategically located on a promontory overlooking the meeting point of the Sunkosh and Tangmachu Rivers." The view from up there was awesome. The rice terraces looked like golden sunrays on earth. Ethereal. Equally uplifting was the nature drive that followed. Camels surprised us, as did occasional herds of cattle, beautiful blossoming trees, shrubs, unusual flowers along the road, and endless breathtaking vistas. Since the road was winding, it was at times difficult for the driver to halt for a photo stop. But he did manage to pull over whenever we came upon a roadside stand, in order to give the locals a chance to sell their fruits or goodies, which someone in the group always bought.

Later that day, we hiked up to Chime Lhakhang Monastery. It is situated on a hillock below the village of Metshina. "The temple was built by Lama Drukpa Kuenley aka the 'Divine Madman' and is believed to enable conception to childless women who visit and receive a blessing. Lama Kuenley was known as the 'Mad Saint' for his unorthodox ways of teaching Buddhism by singing, humor and outrageous behavior, which amounted to being bizarre, shocking and with sexual overtones. He is also the saint who advocated the uses of phallus symbols as paintings on walls and as flying carved wooden phalluses on house tops at four corners of the eves" (OAT). – At the temple, you can see the wooden phallus decorated with a silver handle that Kunley brought from Tibet. If you play your cards right, you might get blessed with it – and even get pregnant, if that's what you're wishing for. Good luck! I learned that in Bhutan, symbols depicting an erect penis are intended to drive away the evil eye and malicious gossip. This reminded me of the evil-eye souvenirs in Turkey. I don't recall phallus souvenirs being available when we were visiting. They could make a fortune.

I could not help but grin whenever I spotted a huge phallus painted on the wall of a house in Metshina. However, the farmhouse of a rice farmer we visited in Metshina did not boast a phallus decoration. They obviously did not need one, because there were many children present, young and old. The family was most kind and hospitable. They led us around their three-story house, which seemed a bit dark because the windows were small. We were led around on the second floor, where they slept (on the floor) on heavy blankets. They had a special area where they gathered to talk, and next to the kitchen was a room in which many slabs of various butchered meats were hanging from the ceiling to age and other staples were stored. The walls were covered with colorful hangings. A huge Bhutanese flag, divided diagonally into a yellow upper triangle and an orange lower triangle, with a white dragon centered on the dividing line, was stretched across the entirety of the ceiling. In another corner of the room was a little altar where a Buddha stood, with candles to light when worshipping. Crops were spread out to dry on the loft below the roof.

In the courtyard stood a couple of scrawny-looking draft horses about to be taken to their stall on the ground floor of the house, where their feed was stored. I left with the impression that this smiling family lived in harmony and peace and was proud of what they owned. The rather big house looked inviting from the outside. The window shutters were colorfully decorated, and a couple of deer were painted on the facade. For once, I did not spot a TV. And come to think of it, not once during the trip in Bhutan did I encounter a person begging, and wherever we went, not a single souvenir vendor was to be seen.

Our Bhutan detour was approaching its end. After spending a good night in Punakah at the Hotel Zangtho Pelri, we returned to Paro via the Dochula Pass, which was by then familiar. We had a great view of the Himalayan mountain range, and I was ecstatic when I caught Gangkhar Puensum, the highest unclimbed mountain in Bhutan (7,570 meters), covered by a blanket of fresh snow and beneath a pristine blue sky! We did not see the famous black-necked cranes in Metshina. They had already left for the Tibetan plateau. What a shame.

But en route to Paro, we stopped and walked up and underneath the bridge over the paved stone path running alongside the imposing outer walls to explore Paro Dzong or Rinpung Dzong, aka "the Fortress on a Heap of Jewels." We could not argue with our guide's opinion – he considered this *dzong* the most impressive in Bhutan. "Gleaming white above the surrounding valleys, this Dzong was built in 1646 to defend the valley against repeated invasion from Tibet" (OAT). Inside Rinpung are fourteen shrines and chapels, as well as the district's monastic body, the government administrative offices of Paro Dzongkhag, and some two hundred monks. Each year they host a spectacular spring festival, the Paro Tsechu. It takes place in the courtyard and on the dance grounds on the hillside above. I was sorry to have missed it. I must admit that whenever I saw these *dzongs*, I was vaguely reminded of the fortresses, monasteries, and burghs across Europe, usually located in elevated places.

Our guide wanted to start early the next day to reach one of Bhutan's oldest temples, Kyichu Lhakhang, supposedly built in 659 by King Songtsen Gampo of Tibet. "Legend has it that it pins the left foot of an ogress so large that she covers Bhutan and most of Tibet" (OAT). We were also told that the two orange trees in the courtyard bear fruit throughout the year. I won't be back to check it out!

Housed in an ancient watchtower, Ta Dzong, the National Museum, had a fine and eclectic collection of ancient *thangka* paintings, textiles, weapons and stamps, birds and animals, and other historical artifacts. From the watchtower, the view of Mount Chomolhari (7,300 meters high), at the northern end of the valley, provided a perfect panorama shot for this mountain fanatic.

For some reason, and regrettably, I did not feel up to joining a handful of my travel companions to participate in a quite challenging hour-and-a-half hike to the Taktsang (Tigers' Nest) Monastery viewpoint, an extraordinarily captivating site. "It is built around a cave in which Guru Rinpoche (Padmasambhava) meditated and clings seemingly impossible on a cliff at 3,000 feet above the valley floor. For the local people this is a place of pilgrimage, but for tourists, a hike up to the viewpoint opposite the monastery is exhausting, thrilling and mystical. Legend has it that Guru Rinpoche flew to the site of the monastery on the back of a tigress from Tibet and meditated in the cave for three months. The main building of the temple was destroyed by fire on April 1998 but has been restored to its original splendor and glory" (OAT).

Some of us used the free time to purchase the collectors' stamps for which Bhutan is famous. I intensified my search for a Buddhist singing bowl, which was not as easy as I had thought. My guide pointed out a handful of shops on the main street of Paro. After inquiring at three or four shops without finding a single one, I came upon a store on a side street. They had a couple of ancient-looking bowls, seven inches in diameter, standing on the counter. Everything else in the shop looked rather dated and primitive. I did not even bargain for my bowl. I was elated to find it. Knowing these bowls can be very pricey, $40 was nothing to haggle over. It looked antique, and the thick metal with engraved patterns was most likely copper. It came with the essential thick wooden stick. The shopkeeper demonstrated how it works by rubbing the stick around the outer rim while holding the bowl in the open palm of his hand. It was like magic to my ears. The overtones were clear and penetrating and of long duration. These bowls are supposedly useful for vibrational healing techniques, especially when deep physical healing is required. I cannot vouch for it, but now and then I lift the bowl from my cocktail table and give it a try. The sound never fails to bring a smile to my face. It has an overall calming effect. Several of my companion travelers later regretted not having purchased one. Recently I befriended Kalie Porter, a young girl who majored in German and spent a semester in Heidelberg to perfect her language skills. Whenever she visits, I ask her to play the singing bowl. Every time she makes it sing, my soul resounds with joy. *Es klingt* (it sounds) so *schön* (beautiful)!

Later the same day, after having observed a team of adult archers practicing Bhutan's favorite sport on a field at least five hundred feet long, we took a ride to see the Drukgyel Dzong, an abandoned fortress built in the mid-1600s to commemorate Bhutan's victory over Tibet. The ruined *dzong* is located high in the mountains, at an altitude of 8,465 feet and in a spot where many long-distance mountain trekkers start their journey. At its foot a small village is nestled. But my focus was on a high, snowcapped mountain range of the Himalayas. The sun was setting, and I felt at peace with the world.

It was much noisier that evening at our farewell dinner in the hotel. As usual, our guide recapped our sightseeing experiences and had a surprise for us. We got to observe a demonstration of how to dress men, women, and ourselves in the local garb. "Men's clothing consists of a gho, which is a garment that wraps around the body like a coat that reaches the knee and is worn with a belt. The *kira* is for women. It is a garment that is made from a piece of cloth (in the shape of a rectangle) that reaches the ankles. It is secured at the shoulders with a clip, while a woven belt holds the garment closed and in place" (OAT). It was a lot of fun, and we much appreciated our guide's traditional gift, an oblong, white silk scarf, or *kabney*, worn by men as part of the *gho*, which he gave us to make sure we remembered forever our adventures in this peaceful gem of a country.

HEART OF INDIA

New Delhi

Druk Air flew us via Kathmandu and the majestic Himalayas back to New Delhi, where we arrived in the early afternoon and were greeted by Deep, our new guide. I was instantly impressed when I realized that in addition to perfect English, he had flawless German. He had a degree in history from Heidelberg University, in Germany. Deep gave us an hour to settle in at Intercontinental the Grand before taking us to New Delhi's National Museum, "which has over 2,000,000 works of exquisite art, both of Indian and foreign origin covering more than 5,000 years of our cultural heritage" (OAT). It is India's biggest museum, and I can confirm it is a remarkable place. It may interest you to know that "the cornerstone of the present museum was laid by J. L. Nehru, the Prime Minister of India, on 12 May 1955, and the building was formally opened to the public on 18 December 1960" (OAT).

After the museum, we traveled by bus to the "Akshmi Narayan Temple or the *Birla Temple* as it is more popularly known. It enshrines Lord Vishnu – the preserver of the Hindu Trinity" (OAT). Lakshmi is the Hindu goddess of wealth. A walk around the temple, with its many shrines and fountains and a large garden, had a somewhat dizzying effect upon me. There is too much to see and digest in a comparatively short time. After all, it is one of the biggest tourist and devotee attractions in New Delhi.

Old Delhi

The crowds in Old Delhi can drive you crazy. The streets are full of taxis, auto rickshaws, six-seater motorcycle rickshaws, and plenty of cycle rickshaws. Don't forget the overabundance of cows and goats strutting lazily and carelessly on the streets, roads, and sidewalks, or wherever they please. They know no fear, because their instinct tells them that since they are sacred, nobody will touch or hurt them. I noticed a bike vendor parked alongside the road. He had piled so many vegetables, sacks of grain, fruits, etc. on his bike that the wheels were hardly visible. Not once have I been in a country where people were able to transport huge loads of wood, iron rods, furniture, fencing, etc. on bikes or donkeys, as they do in India. There is no doubt in my mind that as India's population is increasing by leaps and bounds, so are traffic congestion, housing shortages, pollution, and cows. If only India's level of poverty would decrease as rapidly. I observed old, white-bearded men, emaciated to the point of looking like corpses, clad in long gray robes sleeping on rope beds on roadsides, protected merely by the branches of a tree above. Deep told us that while the cows are taken to a special place to die with dignity, the elderly are left to fend for themselves. One bright spot: you can buy a bottle full of antibiotics for a dollar, if you have one.

You need more than a dollar if you want to purchase spices at the exotic and very colorful spice market, which, after having missed it the first time and after our overweight companion encouraged us to visit it, we finally toured by rickshaw. Although the place was crammed full of countless sacks filled to the brim with different spices, they were neatly displayed. For some reason, the cows stayed away from these treasures.

In Old Delhi, you also need to have luck. When riding through the narrow streets and alleys, you cannot miss the entangled web of electric wires hanging down not far from your head. If that is not a life-threatening hazard, I do not know what is. It was downright scary. And then there are the little stores squeezed together in the alleys. Artisans galore were offering for sale anything you can think of. Thousands of pieces of gold and jewelry and trinkets of all sorts were squeezed into small spaces: necklaces, bracelets, pendants, earrings, broaches – you name it, it was there. Silk by the yard in every imaginable color for saris, shawls, etc. was stored up to the ceiling, and shoes, hardware, automobile parts, bikes, bananas, apples, and breads could be found nearby. Wherever you looked, there were heaps of stuff lying around and offered for sale. Next to each pile stood a young man dressed in a clean shirt – some were smiling, and some, it seemed, were totally disillusioned. In the midst of all this turbulence, I suddenly spotted a blue sign glued to the flaking facade of a building. "Bush Go Back," it declared in bold white letters. I asked my rickshaw driver to stop so I could take a picture. That really made my day! I doubt G. W., whom Trump called the "most stupid" president ever, came close to these places when visiting India, and I bet Palin avoided them as well. And The Donald would avoid them like the plague. Incidentally, though I do not agree with Trump on anything, I do agree with him about G. W.

And then there is "Chandni Chowk, the main street of Old Delhi, a magnificent bazaar and as fine a monument to congestion, colour and chaos as you'll find in India today. It's hard to believe that in the 17th century this used to be endowed with fine mansions and that a tree-lined canal was flowing down its centre and was renowned throughout Asia" (OAT). Deep elaborated at one point that "even when Bombay and Madras were mere trading posts and Calcutta a village of mud huts, Delhi had been the seat of an empire for five hundred years. In fact, through the centuries, eight cities have been built on this site, by Hindu, Mughal and British rulers, each adding their own flavor."

After this dizzying excursion, it was a welcome relief when we stopped at Raj Ghat, in the old part of Delhi. A simple but impressive black marble memorial to Mahatma Gandhi marks the spot on the bank of the Yamuna River where he was cremated following his assassination in 1948, one year after the British had granted independence to India.

Though Gandhi was unsuccessful at ending the strife between Hindus and Sikhs, remarkably, his death brought the country together. The period of violence ended, leading to reconciliation between the warring religious groups. When I walked around the museum dedicated to Gandhi, learning about the historical events and the principles that shaped this man and reading "India of My Dreams," his famous speech, I realized more strongly than ever before why I had admired this great statesman for so long. I wonder today whether this speech of Gandhi's influenced Martin Luther King Jr.'s famous "I Have a Dream" speech.

Jawaharlal Nehru was cremated just to the north, at Shanti Vana (Forest of Peace). It was a peaceful place in the park where such notables as Elizabeth II, Dwight Eisenhower, and Ho Chi Minh had planted trees in his honor.

To refresh your memory, I quote from OAT's literature: "Under the rule of Prime Minister Nehru, India undertook a policy of non-alignment, hoping to maintain peaceful relations with all nations. After Nehru's death, his daughter, Indira Gandhi, was elected Prime Minister. The first decade of Gandhi's time in office was highly controversial. She censored the press, had thousands of political opponents arrested, and sponsored a program of forced sterilization. In the late 70s Gandhi was removed from office and eventually imprisoned. Amazingly, she was reelected shortly after her release from prison in 1980, touching off a period of widespread civil unrest as small states attempted to break away from the country. Indira Gandhi was assassinated in 1984, and India's internal turmoil continued throughout the decade that followed."

The great mosque of Old Delhi, the Jama Masjid, was huge. Built in 1644 by Shah Jahan, the Mughal emperor who also built the Taj Mahal and the Red Fort, it is the largest mosque in India, with a courtyard capable of holding 25,000 devotees. Considering that India has a population of more than one billion, it's really not that huge – or is it?

Our cycle-rickshaw ride back through the crowded lanes of the Chandni Chowk bazaar was by now like déjà vu, with the exception that I got a better look at the Jain temple near the Red Fort and at the Fatehpuri Mosque, built by one of Shah Jahan's wives in 1650. I for one was happy when we returned to the posh hotel for a nap before the welcome dinner in a local restaurant, which it took forever to get to due to congested traffic and too many loosely straying gray-white cows.

We spent the next day visiting New Delhi. I will take the easy way out and quote from OAT's brochure: "The British laid out the broad, tree-lined avenues and neat street grid of New Delhi (in contrast to the narrow alleyways of the old part of the city). Today the former 'Imperial City' continues as the center of government for the world's largest democracy, and we see the buildings of India's Parliament and (from the outside) the residence of India's President, a palatial building called Rashtrapati Bhvan. Nearby we see the India Gate, where a popular park surrounds a memorial to Indian soldiers who served Great Britain in World War I and Britain's 19th-century war in Afghanistan. We also visit Qutab Minar, a spectacular example of Indo-Islamic architecture topped by a 234-foot-high brick tower. Begun in the 12th century, this is now a UNESCO World Heritage Site and the symbol of New Delhi."

I used the free time to walk around the beautiful park surrounding the memorial to Indian soldiers. It was a perfect day, about 75 degrees Fahrenheit, with the sun shining in a clear blue sky. Bougainvillea, as well as other bushes and trees, was in full bloom; families with their children had come out to enjoy the park. I noticed a young mother sitting on the stone walk, draped in a bright-yellow sari, and smiling down at her baby, who lay asleep on a yellow blanket on the grounds. In front of her was an area rug she had spread out. Behind her was a rolled-up Oriental carpet. I am not sure if it was for sale. Not far away, two women were playing with a group of five tan-colored puppies, feeding them bits of cookies. In a big group, over twenty seven-to-eight-year-old schoolchildren were laughing and singing and throwing their hands up in the air. I stopped to chat with them. They eagerly called out their names, asked, "How are you?" in good English, and waved cheerfully when I said good-bye. Another group of teenagers was engaged in having their arms and fingers painted. They proudly held out their open hands and bare arms to show off the paint job, which I found very nice and definitely unique and interesting. One woman in a white sari arranged her nine little children in a row so I could snap a good picture of all of them. Others passing by stood still and made sure they got into the picture as well.

On the way to the hotel, we stopped briefly to admire the well-known Lotus Temple, completed in 1986 and considered the mother temple of the Indian subcontinent. Having a penchant for lotus flowers, I simply had to add it to my collection of photos from India. Further on, several in my group insisted on stopping at a McDonald's for a taste of a hamburger. I had never seen the McDonald's clown. Here, I made sure someone took my picture cozying up to the funny man. Strangely enough, we were right in the neighborhood of the Judah Hyam Hall Synagogue. A couple of Jews in my group persuaded Deep to stop and even managed to get the keys to look inside. One in the group gave a little introduction, and the rest of us felt at peace, having been accommodating. By that time, I think I had convinced my Jewish travel companions that I had nothing to do with the Holocaust, since I was only six years old when it started. I liked them because one of them belonged to Doctors without Borders, which in addition to other charities, is a beneficiary of my estate, if anything is left after the lawyers, who belong to the greediest of all greedy professions, have taken care of themselves.

Samode

After breakfast, we started out overland to Jaipur, the capital of Rajasthan. En route we stopped for lunch at the magnificent Samode Palace, originally built by the Rajput ruler Jai Singh II's finance minister. If you have never heard of him, don't worry – neither had I. Samode is nestled in the hills, with the steep hillsides of the Aravalli Mountains rising immediately around the walls and an ancient fort on a hilltop. The palace is now a luxury heritage hotel, with all the interiors preserved in their original form. It is truly a memorable place and not to be missed. Be sure to go to Durbar Hall and look for its Meenakari, or inlay of glass mirrors and stones, and notice the adjustable louvers on the windows. This palace easily rivals some in Europe.

The beginning of the Samode experience was out of this world. We were treated like fairy-tale royalty. Already, when the bus stopped at a narrow entrance gate where a camel herder stood with a camel, I felt transported into another era. A handsome and gently polite Indian guided us through the most beautiful flowering gardens toward the palace, where we climbed many steps leading to a palatial dining hall. Handsome Indian waiters dressed in long white shirts and white turbans who spoke impeccable English served a most delicious meal.

On my way out, two of the youthful waiters approached me and asked if I would give them some advice. I told them that success in life depends on three important elements: education, education, and education. I complimented them on their English-language competency and advised them to use it as a foundation to build on. They were ever so thankful. I hope they followed the advice.

Outdoors, not far removed from the dining hall, was a group of natives. They had erected a colorful tent, a puppet theater, where they showed us their puppets in action. I did buy a couple for my young friends back home.

When we had to leave this paradisiacal fairyland behind to continue toward Jaipur, as soon as we passed through the narrow entrance gate, we noticed that some twenty Indians dressed in the most colorful saris, some of them fancy, had gathered outside the gate. One, dressed in a red-and-yellow sari, was balancing a big round bowl filled with stacks of round wheat flatbread, aka naan, on her head and caught my attention. Her golden bracelet and ring were glistening in the sun. A few yards down the same street, a group of young children, both boys and girls, were anxious to talk to us. Their black eyes sparkled. We were not allowed to give them money, because their parents might have used it as an incentive to have more children just to collect alms. And believe me, they already have more kids than they can handle. I entertained them with my old boarding-school trick. I closed the left nostril with one finger and made music by opening and closing the other with my right index finger while blowing air through one opening. The kids quickly began to copy me, and before we knew it, we had established a jolly little choir. By the way, I never saw a girl wearing jeans, only dresses or saris, no matter how poor they appeared to be.

As soon as we left the palace, we were confronted by poverty-stricken places. Of course, a lonely white cow strolled through the streets, bordered by houses with badly eroding facades. A man in my group, a Texan no doubt, tried hard to feed the cow an apple. It did not even raise its head. Poor thing. There was nothing but bare stones on the sidewalk. Maybe it had strayed from its home not far from there, that is, the senior cows' sanctuary, the weirdest of all places in India, where cattle are guaranteed to die with dignity even while great leaders are assassinated.

I must say that the women in India, especially those who appeared to me to be working the hardest, were amazingly proud and dignified. As our van passed alongside fields, I could not help but admire three women hard at work harvesting some sort of grain. A couple of women stood in the shade of a tree watching us go by. These women, as well as others I saw bent over and working hard, looked ever so dignified. I think it was partially due to their colorful saris, which they wore so gracefully. For us Westerners, these colorful scenes lent them an almost fairy-tale ambiance and had the overall effect of camouflaging the degree of poverty in their real lives.

Jaipur

When our minibus stopped in front of the Hotel Clarks Amer in Jaipur, located in a green residential area with a very inviting look, I almost felt guilty about being privileged enough to stay there.

Jaipur, with a population of over three million, is the capital of Rajasthan. It is generally called "the Pink City" because of the color of the buildings in the old city. "Jaipur is built on a dry lake bed, it is the city of forts, palaces, golden sands, a warm people and a rich culture" (OAT). – And I am not kidding when I tell you that the city was painted pink in 1876 to commemorate the visit of the prince of Wales. Thank God they refrained from repeating the paint jobs when Prince Charles and the late Princess Diana visited Jaipur during the annual royal polo matches.

The fairy-tale ambiance, which for me started at the Samode Palace, was sustained when only thirty minutes from our hotel, we approached the grandiose Amer Fort-Palace, perched high on a hilltop, in somewhat royal fashion. In case you were wondering, I sat on top of an elephant! If you think it was easy, think again. Definitely not royal was the fact that we had to wait in line for the elephant for at least an hour. Fortunately it was not yet hot. While waiting, I watched a group of Indians standing in line to fetch something to eat or drink. Someone must have delivered the big tin cans that stood near the food-distribution place, waiting to be emptied. A nice little boy held a very skinny black dog tightly, with its head resting on his shoulder, for me to photograph. We also got a good look at the elephants gathered at the foot of the hill, waiting to be chosen to transport us adventure-hungry tourists through snaking pathways up the hill. With some help, I managed to climb on top of the monstrous beast but had to share my seat with a marginally overweight male tourist who was constantly afraid of sliding off.

Here is what OAT had to say about Amer Fort: "The Fort is a classic, romantic Rajasthan fort-palace. Its construction was started by Man Singh I in 1592 and completed by his descendant Jai Singh I, and is a beautiful blend of Mughal and Hindu styles. Painted scenes of wars and hunting expeditions adorn the walls, which are set with precious stones and mirrors. The main attractions are the Sukh Mandir or Temple of Contentment, cooled by a stunning water cascade and the Sheesh Mahal or Mirror palace. In a tiny pitch-dark room with mirrors all over the ceiling, an attendant lights up candles and holds them for you creating a marvelous sight – twinkling stars on a clear night! In the foreground is the Maota Lake with stunning reflections of the splendid Amer Fort-Palace." Sorry, I have no memory of the candlelight demonstration in the Mirror Palace. I had heard that in Rajput times, a girl would hold candles while performing a dance of love for her maharaja. We also visited "the Temple of Kali, dedicated to the blue-black-skinned goddess of blood and destruction, as well as the Jai Mandir (Hall of Victory) and Sukh Niwas (Hall of Pleasure)" before returning to the hotel for lunch.

I do remember two completely forlorn elephants that appeared to be stranded on a very arid side street near a riverbed. Piles of crumpled newspapers were scattered around the place as well. The elephants were obviously on their way to join some of their companions, already cooling off in the shallow riverbed. In front of our little bus hovered an Indian with a multicolored turban, playing a flute to charm a snake in a basket on the ground in front of him. It was definitely something I had to catch on my camera, and I did – precisely when the snake raised its head out of the basket. How neat is that? Eventually, I bought a basket with a fake snake to bring home and amuse some kids.

We had the afternoon off, and I joined a group to visit a jeweler and learn about the gems for which India is famous. But mainly I wished to purchase some souvenirs and look for a special elephant, which I had decided to give Eric Beardsley and his bride as a wedding gift. I had decided not to attend the wedding and to give them something special instead. Doc had a small collection of elephants and claimed they bring luck and fortune, so I thought his great-grandson would appreciate it. I had been searching for one for quite some time and really lucked out in Jaipur, famous for its jewelry stores. Deep, our guide, arranged for me to be allowed entrance to a big antique shop. The owner specially opened the doors for me, and after looking at numerous elephants of all sizes, spread out across two floors, I found a very special one carved out of teakwood, beautifully decorated and very antique. It was locked up in a glass showcase. They wrapped it extra carefully, and I had to believe Eric when he said he liked it a lot.

We all appreciated the invitation from a "traditional, extended Indian family of noble lineage for dinner in their home" (OAT). The home turned out to be a small, tucked-away, walled-in palace. It was beautifully illuminated upon our arrival. The large rooms, which extended from a courtyard decorated with palm trees, statuettes, and big jug-like vases, were open. They were furnished with beautiful rugs, brocade-cushioned sofas, chairs, and colorful wall hangings. Our hosts were dressed in elegant garb and conversed with us in perfect English. This family consisted of parents, grandparents, and four children, three girls and a boy, all of college age. The son and his wife showed off their toddler son, and the girls talked about their lives at the university and how they had to be driven there by someone. They all had their quarters in the same palace. We were allowed to view some of their quarters and found that they looked relatively Western. They had a big TV and a computer. A couple of servants served the very tasty food. We all sat at an oblong banquet table. It was quite an experience. But I will never forget our departure. As we stepped onto the street outside the palatial home, we were confronted by stark poverty. Old people slept on the sidewalk, some cows were looking for something to eat, and a couple of vendors hoped to sell a few oranges piled high on their cart. When I asked Deep if he was bothered by the stark contrast between wealth and poverty, he claimed that one develops an immunity to it.

The next day, a sightseeing tour of Jaipur was scheduled, starting with a visit to the very pink Hawa Mahal (Palace of the Winds), which is not a palace, "but rather an impressive façade of 953 delicate, honeycombed sandstone windows used by the ladies of the palace to watch the outside world without being watched. . . . These openings also function to let the wind blow through and keep the rooms cool. It was built in 1799 by Maharaja Sawai Ptratap Sing, and designed by Lal Chand Usta in the form of the crown of Krishna, the Hindu god" (OAT). This royal grandstand is without doubt the centerpiece and main attraction of Jaipur. You cannot miss it. We also spent a couple of hours at the Jantar Mantar, an astronomical and astrological observatory built in the eighteenth century. Remarkably, the giant sundials were still accurate to two-tenths of a second, or so we were told. I forgot to check it.

Anybody interested in astronomy, I think, would find this tribute to medieval Indian astronomy uniquely fascinating. The instruments are in general huge structures. The scale on which they were built has been alleged to increase their accuracy, a finding that has been challenged. One warning: it gets very hot at this place, and the only shade I found up there was standing next to a wall. I was ready to go to the famous City Palace Museum, not just to get into the shade, but also to have a glimpse of its renowned collections of textiles, arms, carpets, paintings, and manuscripts. There, you will get a closer look at the lives led by the rulers of Jaipur, if you are interested.

I opted out of a trip to the local market that evening and decided to hang out at my posh hotel, the Clarks Amer. I skipped dinner and was happy to eat a banana, an orange, and a granola bar while catching up with the news by watching CNN.

On the eighth day of our Heart of India odyssey, we traveled through the rural countryside and into the low Vindhya mountain range. "It is a range of older rounded mountains and hills in the west-central Indian subcontinent, which geographically separates the Indian subcontinent into northern India and Southern India" (OAT). Deep warned us in advance that this five-hour drive would be quite bumpy, but assured us that we would break it up with stops along the way. Anybody who has traveled through the South Gobi Desert in Mongolia does not need to worry about these roads, not a bit.

Traveling through the countryside under blue skies in India is tantamount to a ride through fairyland, if you can manage to overlook the negatives. We stopped to chat with the children, watched one young boy make a jar out of clay, and asked groups of young women working in a factory next to a senior-cow facility – they were making dung patties and cigar-like sticks out of cow manure for alternative fuel purposes – to pose for photos. We showed them how pretty they looked in their bright-colored saris – pink, light blue, light green, yellow, orange, and purple – by letting them see the digital screens of our cameras. The heaps of dung patty were so high I could not look over them. I was afraid to ask the women about their hourly wages. I could not believe my eyes when we stopped next to a stretch of land bigger than a football field covered with small piles of red chile peppers, set out to dry. Several women – I never saw a man – were busy loading big, round baskets filled above the brim with peppers. They placed the baskets on their heads, balanced them, and then walked away while holding on with one hand or none at all. The peppers were loaded on a tractor and covered by a huge tarp, which was bulging so much that the whole mass seemed like it would fall off at any moment. Amazing. I genuinely admired the Indian women whenever I saw one walking along the roadside while proudly balancing a huge bundle of wood or straw on her head. They seemed to ignore us. I did not blame them.

When we reached the Sawai Madhopur (Ranthambore) tiger sanctuary, near the town of Sawai Madhopur, one of the eleven sites chosen for Project Tiger, India's national tiger conservation program and the largest such effort in the world, we all got excited. This was a huge site. "It extends over one hundred square miles of deciduous forest, and it includes several large lakes, and until 1970 it was a hunting preserve of the maharajas" (OAT). It was a peaceful day filled with sunshine, and no other tourists could be spotted as far as I could see. What we did see were lakes, rivers, grazing wildlife, large antelopes resembling cattle, spotted deer, black bucks with spiraling horns, dainty gazelles, wild boars, sloth bears, gorgeous peacocks, and many kinds of birds. Monkeys were frolicking in trees, and an ancient banyan tree (strangler fig) aroused our attention and great admiration. "Older Banyan trees are characterized by their aerial prop roots that grow into thick woody trunks which, with age, can become indistinguishable from the main trunk. Old trees can spread out laterally using these prop roots to cover a wide area" (OAT). I had seen this tree before, in Africa, and always found it intriguing. We learned that the Buddha is believed to have achieved enlightenment in Bodh Gaya, India, while meditating under a banyan tree of the species known as sacred fig. Unfortunately, we were ambushed by a fierce rain and had to take refuge. After that we gave up on our search for a tiger, of which not many survived. Neither did we spot a leopard. I was not too disappointed, because I had seen them while on safari in Africa. I felt compensated by the stunning peacocks that showed off their gorgeous feathers, and I bought a bunch of peacock-feather fans for a few friends back home, as well as for myself.

Ranthambor

A big surprise was the incredible stay at our luxurious Nahargarh Fort hotel, outside of Ranthambor. It was just like living in a palace, surrounded by sublime vistas, colorful birds, and fabulous wildlife, all visible from the terrace of my hotel room. Why should I tear myself away from this spot to see the ruins of the real Ranthambor Fort, built over one thousand years ago on a rocky outcrop and offering stunning views? I was just too tired to hike up there. I did not regret sitting this one out and greatly enjoyed the spectacular sunset, as my pictures prove.

After spending another day viewing game and encountering wildlife similar to what we had seen the day before (and again no tiger, though twenty-six supposedly still inhabited the reserve), I was ready to move on to the next stop, the retreat in the Lakeside Camp near Kalakho, located in a rural setting – a small island in a nearby lake – with an old Hindu temple. It was another bumpy, four-hour-long ride. In the last village en route to the camp, we were transferred into jeeps to continue over the next three miles of rugged terrain to the retreat, where I was assigned a rustic cabin with a porch, which I truly loved. This was indeed camel country and had the exotic ambiance of an authentic Indian village. The highlight of our stay at Kalakho was the camel safari to a remote local community.

It took some doing to convince the guide that I would not fall off the camel. He let me mount it, and I waved down to him happily from the lofty perch. I suggested that our overweight companion take the camel-drawn cart in my stead. I took many pictures in the village, of thatched-roof houses, of children and adults posing, of camels with colorful blankets on their humped backs lying in the grass, and of the mountain range in the distance. Three boys were lying on a rope bed partially attached to the trunk of a tree to take advantage of the shade, and a big pile of dried camel-dung patties was in the courtyard. We eventually ventured back to the camp on top of our camels while the golden ball, the sun, was setting behind the hills, painting the horizon orange. I got the distinct feeling that the villagers would stay there and make sure their various plots of land, where they grew a rich diversity of crops, were taken care of for generations to come. I am sure their life was not always easy and not without strife. But whose is?

That night, we were served an authentic Indian dinner, prepared by our camp cook with fresh, locally grown ingredients. After dinner we gathered around the campfire, where we were given an introduction to the history of the Mughals and watched Indian dances performed by rural villagers.

The overland journey to Agra gave us more exposure to India's vast rural countryside. We broke up the long drive with a stop at "Abhaneri to view an ancient *baolis* i.e. a step-well or waterway built to provide a constant water supply to local inhabitants" (OAT).

This huge well is actually considered an archeological wonder in Rajasthan, India. "It is one of India's oldest and deepest step-wells, Chanda Baodi and the eighth century Harshat Mata Hindu temple" (OAT). These stepwells, unique to India, were used as reservoirs for royal baths and provided respite from the summer heat. It was an impressive site.

Even more impressive was Fatehpur Sikri, the mysterious ghost city founded by the Mughal emperor Akbar the Great in the sixteenth century and capital of the Mughal Empire from 1571 to 1585. Its amazing monuments of red sandstone and marble will be etched into your memory forever. Fatehpur Sikri is considered one of the finest examples of Mughal architecture in India. The great Akbar Mughal, we were told, never learned to read or write, but supposedly "matured into a well-informed ruler with refined tastes in the arts, architecture, music and a love for literature with a tolerance for other religions." – "Although architecturally magnificent, the city suffered from a water shortage and was abandoned shortly after Akbar's death. The city occupies a sandstone ridge, and the area around it is enclosed within a 7-mile-long wall" (OAT).

Agra

The Jaypee Palace Hotel was so huge I had a hard time locating my room. Nevertheless, I slept well and, before sunrise, was ready to head to another much-anticipated wonder of the world, the Taj Mahal.

This white-marble Monument to Love, built by Shah Jahan between 1631 and 1653 to enshrine the remains of his beloved Queen Mumtaz Mahal – his third wife, who died during the birth of their fourteenth child – took twenty thousand workers and seventeen years to build. It was a sight to behold. I stood in silence as I watched the semitranslucent white marble turn light pink as the sun rose. The Taj is widely proclaimed to be the most famous example of Mughal architecture in India – who am I to argue? I spent much time exploring and photographing this grand edifice from all angles and all sides, as the building has four identical facades. I walked through the beautiful gardens, strolled along the walkways beside a long reflecting pool, where I spotted a sloth hanging in a tree, climbed many steps to see the inside, and stood in awe at Shah Jahan's cenotaph and Mumtaz Mahal's tomb. Both the Shah's tomb and his wife's were crafted out of semitranslucent white marble and inlaid with thousands of precious and semiprecious gems in the most striking patterns. I fell in love with the floral *parchin kari* work present throughout the Taj. It's amazingly beautiful, delicate, and sensitive – simply exquisite.

My fellow travelers did not stop coaxing me until I allowed the photographer who stood nearby to take a picture of me sitting on the stone bench with the Taj in the background. And, to my surprise, the photo turned out to be quite nice.

Later that forenoon, after breakfast, we visited the sprawling Agra Fort, located on the banks of the Yamuna River. "This immense fort and palace were the seat of power for four generations of Mughal emperors; they ruled all of northern India from the early 16th century until the consolidation by British colonial rule in the early 1800s" (OAT). It was rather strange to learn that Shah Jahan, the emperor who built the Taj, was "imprisoned by his son Aurangzeb in the Agra Fort where he had a view on the building erected for his deceased wife. He is said to have died in the Musamman Burj, a tower with a beautiful marble balcony. From there you probably have the best view on the Taj" (OAT).

Don't worry, I did buy a nice little souvenir at the marble-inlay factory. No, I did not purchase the beautiful tabletop for my winter garden, though it was hard to resist. I did pick up a Ganesha (elephant head) figure. I liked what Ganesha represents, that is, "the remover of obstacles, patron of arts and sciences and deva of intellect and wisdom" (OAT).

After dinner, I wrote postcards to my friends around the world and even pasted the appropriate stamps on them before handing them to the attendant at the reception desk. – As it turned out, someone must have removed the stamps and exchanged them for money. Not a single postcard reached its intended destination.

I had much better luck with the silk area rug I purchased at a carpet-weaving place. It was waiting for me when I returned home.

The train ride from Agra to Jhansi, center of the Chandela civilization, early the next morning turned out to be exciting. Even as we waited for the train on the platform, the ambiance was quite curious. I couldn't believe my eyes when I saw three men dressed in red jackets lugging up to three suitcases each on their heads through the crowds. An Indian man waved at me from the window of a train stopped next to the platform. His white teeth were shining. Vendors pushed their carts through the crowds, offering fruits, beverages, and beautiful peacock-feather fans. I ended up buying eight. Women, children, and men of all ages sat on boxes and suitcases while waiting for the train. Overhead, in the iron beams, three or four monkeys chased each other. Underneath were piles of big sacks, filled with spices or rice, I guess. A woman sat on one of them. On the train, I sat at a table with four Indians, three gentlemen and a young woman. We engaged in heated discussions about travel experiences, impressions, politicians, their families, and lots more. We laughed a lot and had fun. They all liked my laughing-Buddha pendant. My American cotravelers viewed me with a bit of envy, I think. One of them later suggested that I would make a good ambassador. My new "friends" and I exchanged e-mail addresses, and one of the young men, an engineer, when I told him I was writing about India, insisted on remaining anonymous and eventually faded away. I have no idea why he wanted to remain anonymous. It does not matter. He was a good and loyal friend, considering we met on a train. He was definitely climbing the ladder of success, and I wish him and his family the best. One of the businessmen tried to visit me in Bloomington not long after the train ride. Fortunately or unfortunately, I was out of the country.

In Jhansi, we were transferred to a van, and we continued for some four hours on a rather bumpy road through more countryside. In this particular area, we saw women and children picking potatoes in the fields and vendors who had spread out their sparse produce on newspapers or blankets on the roadside. We stopped to chat with children and took many pictures of them. One woman was dressed in a long black dress. She was walking on the paved road. On her head she was balancing a big bowl filled with flatbread. She pulled her veil over her face when she noticed we were watching. A cute toddler was resting on her left hip, while a three-year-old dressed in a turquoise sari held on to her left hand. On the other side of the street, a motorcyclist buzzed by. Further along a few guys stood in the shade of a tree with few leaves, trying to sell a couple of skinny goats. We stopped at a place where a brown and a white bull were turning a waterwheel to draw water from a well – definitely a *novum* for me.

I must not forget to mention that at one point during our safari, we had the chance to visit a rural elementary school. It was a very humble but very neat place. The children, about eight years old, wore uniforms and impressed me with their eagerness to communicate in English. I began to admire the competitive spirit of the Indians, just as I had admired the competitive spirit of the Chinese when visiting an elementary school in China.

"Khajuraho," Deep lectured, "in the tenth century was the center of the thriving civilization of the Chandelas. The magnificent group of temples [a UNESCO World Heritage Site] was built between the ninth and tenth centuries by the Chandela dynasty, which dominated Central India at the time."

Varanasi

We stayed at the Radisson Hotel and got up early again, in order to visit the east and west temple complexes constructed by the Chandelas. Much emphasis was given to the erotic stone carvings there, because they "have come to symbolize the important role of love and *pajna* energy in Hindu thought. British archeologists excavated these intricate stone carvings during colonial times, when they scandalized post-Victorian English sensibilities!" (OAT).

I had almost forgotten, but when wandering around this impressive park, I chatted with a young couple, Indians who were on their honeymoon, and ended up taking a few nice pictures not only of the attractive couple but also of the provocatively erotic and unmistakably explicit sculptures. Not much is left to the imagination, and one understands why some call this mountain crammed full of sculptures "the apogee of erotic art" and others consider it one of the seven wonders of India. I could not help but smile with the hope that this young couple got out of it what they were wishing for. Hopefully they achieved it all before they ended up on a funeral pyre on the banks of Mother Ganga in Varanasi, where we would be after another forty-minute flight.

Varanasi, dating back over four thousand years, has a reputation of being one of the oldest cities of the world and the holiest of Hindu cities. Already on the drive from the airport to the Radisson, I felt as though I was in a different sphere. Maybe just knowing that Varanasi is regarded as a holy city by Buddhists, Jains, and Hindus has a strange impact on one's psyche? Varanasi has "an intense, almost palpable atmosphere of spiritual devotion, a feeling of an unending religious festival. Hundreds of temples propitiate the thousands of deities in the Hindu pantheon. Pilgrims from every part of this vast nation crowd the narrow streets and the riverside *ghats*" (OAT).

The term Hinduism was introduced into the English language in the 19th century to denote the religious, philosophical, and cultural traditions native to India. Hinduism is formed of diverse traditions and has no single founder. It is nevertheless the world's third largest religion.

Around 1500 BC, a group of Aryan peoples invaded India from the North. Over the next two thousand years, many other groups from both Africa and Asia migrated into the area. Interbreeding between different ethnic groups was so common that it is nearly impossible to determine racial distinctions among the people of India today with any degree of certainty. The Aryans brought with them a religion called Vedism, which was based on a rigid social hierarchy or caste system. Vedism eventually combined with local religions and evolved into Hinduism. . . . According to Hinduism, the caste into which one is born depends upon one's karma – the accumulated good and bad deeds from past lives. Therefore, it is necessary for one to do good works on earth in order to reach a higher social status in future lives. Hinduism's rigid caste system, with its emphasis on accepting one's lot in life, has been the most important social influence in India for over 3,000 years. (OAT)

How, on this once-in-a-lifetime visit to Varanasi, could I not sign up for the optional evening Ganga *aarti*? It turned out to be another surreal experience, which began as soon as we stepped into the rickshaw and began navigating the bustling streets to the bathing ghats, that is, a series of steps leading down to the sacred River Ganges. I could hardly believe what I witnessed there. People flocked to the area in order to go down the many steps to bathe and to worship in the temples, shrines, and palaces, which rise from the riverbank for miles, tier upon tier. These ghats are considered one of the holiest places in Varanasi. It is where we see life and death together – where the soul separates from the body and where many come in old age in the hope of dying.

We boarded a boat to better observe the religious *aarti* performance. It is a Hindu religious ritual in which light from wicks soaked in purified butter is offered to one or more deities. What an experience – and what a spectacle! The sun was setting in the Ganges, opposite the temples. Thousands of lights on plates with flower petals, representing the earth (solidity), floated on the river while the priests performed the ceremonies at the brightly illuminated altar. The ceremony is also called the puja or Hindu honor ceremony. Incense, flowers, and candles are used to pay gratitude to Shiva and the river. A Hindu professor, who gave a brief lecture about the event and answered the questions we posed, accompanied us. A strange silence permeated the air as we watched the burning funeral pyres not far from where our boat was cruising. It was awesome – eerie and ethereal all at once.

I'll pass on OAT's comments about the funeral pyre: "The feet are positioned pointing south and the head points north, the god of wealth. Traditionally the chief mourner sets light to the pyre. It is done by accepting flaming kusha twigs from the Doms, who are part of the Untouchable Hindu caste responsible for tending to funeral pyres. The body is now an offering to Agni, the god of fire. After cremation the ashes are collected and usually scattered in water. The River Ganges is considered the most sacred place to scatter ashes." It sounds rather exotic, don't you think? Forget about the fact that this is the most polluted river in the world, and not only as a result of the ashes of the dead. Take a few minutes to meditate.

The rickshaw ride back was not so exotic. Vendors were busy packing up their unsold *aarti* candles and the like, but I was happy to have a pleasant place in which to spend the night, because the next day, before sunrise and before breakfast, we were up and on the go again for another exalting cruise on Mother Ganges, which despite the gorgeous sunrise looked rather muddy. But it did not deter the devoted or us. People kept on arriving, anxious to take a ritual dip in their river, perform Yoga asanas, wash clothes, or offer flowers and incense to their Mother Ganges. It is their religious way of life. I could not help but be in awe once more of the overpowering sight of the many riverside temples and ghats, bathed in a rich, golden dawn light under a pale blue sky. Where else on this planet can you have an experience like this?

The same afternoon, Deep walked with us to see a couple of local temples, but I was more excited when we drove in the afternoon to Sarnath, the nearby ancient Buddhist center of learning. The place seemed so peaceful and quiet. No other tourists were present, and I was so happy to stand at the very place where Gautama Buddha preached his first sermon to his disciples. Unfortunately, I did not see Bertolucci's film *Little Buddha*. But I had taught many times Hermann Hesse's *Siddhartha*, which my students just loved. I purchased a copy of an English translation for my young friend Cristian in Chile.

We were allowed enough time to walk around and to admire the Dhamekh Stupa, with a monastery built on the spot where, legend has it, the Buddha first turned the Wheel of the Dhamma. We saw the main shrine at the monastery and the shrine at Mulagandhakuti Vihara, as well as Ashoka's Lion Capital, the national emblem of India – and we saw the beautiful Teaching Buddha, among the most stunning sculptures in the world, housed in the Sarnath Museum. This sculpture surely put to shame many of the others I had seen around the world. And I could not have been happier to visit this special place, where again I learned much more about the Buddha and his philosophy. It was a perfect ending to a perfect journey, which started in Bhutan and ended in Delhi. At the farewell dinner in Varanasi, Deep handed me a beautiful silk scarf and a personal note extending an invitation to his home if I should return. It was a gesture I will forever remember. – When a group was planning to go out for dinner at the most expensive restaurant in Delhi, I politely declined. As it turned out, it was not worth the expense.

Flying home from India first class, thanks to frequent-flyer miles, was unimaginably wonderful. I had a fabulous window seat on the upper deck of the plane, with much space around me. A stunningly beautiful stewardess in an exquisite sari worked hard to spoil me. She was disappointed that I did not drink more champagne. We talked a lot, and since the skies were clear and blue, when we flew over the rugged mountains of Pakistan and Kabul, Afghanistan, she claimed that Kabul was her place of birth and that she had left ten years before. I had not given it a thought before I took off on this trip, but we actually flew over some regions of Iran and Turkey as well. I was very much impressed by my stewardess's impeccable English and her flawless demeanor, and I refrained from criticizing Afghanistan's corrupt President Karzai.

How do I determine where else I want to go? Let me give you an idea:

When flying over Turkey during the flight home from India, I decided I definitely had to take another trip to Turkey, which I did in 2007, followed by a Russian Waterways cruise. – Upon my return from Russia, I started sorting through my travel catalogues for something more exotic. And, voilà, I stumbled upon a 2008 Travcoa tour: Jewels of Arabia Rare Treasures in Ancient Worlds: Kuwait, Bahrain, Doha, Nizwa, Dubai, Sharjah, and Ajman. I began to check it out and, despite the rather steep price, could not resist booking it. But before that, I went on the flying safari to Namibia and spent a couple of weeks relaxing in Cancún.

JEWELS OF ARABIA – THE MIDDLE EAST

On February 5, 2008, I boarded my American Airlines flight, compliments of frequent-flyer miles, and headed to Kuwait via London (Dakar, Senegal) and Bahrain, where I had to change flights. We had some minor problems that caused delays, which did not bother me too much. As usual, I took it all in stride. I stood near the gate waiting for my flight to Kuwait, and I kept an ear on the primaries back in the States. I was rooting for Obama and not for Hillary. I looked quite scruffy with my backpack and my hair in disarray from the long flight, but I noticed that the place was full of travelers of all colors and nationalities. Then, all of a sudden, I spotted a gentleman surrounded by three or four others, all Caucasian. They were dressed in suits and neckties and clean-shaven. One of them looked so familiar. Lo and behold, it was Clinton's defense minister, Bill Cohen. Without giving it much thought, I zeroed in on him, expressing my amazement over seeing him in this part of the world. He looked surprised. I introduced myself, and it did not take long to get a lively conversation going. I asked about the election results, and he actually smiled when he stressed that it looked as though Obama was ahead of Clinton. I indicated that I was surprised by his happiness, since he was her husband's defense secretary. Of course, I knew he was a Republican. A guy in his group chimed in and asked me what I thought of McCain. I shot right back, raising my voice a tad and making sure he understood I considered him a complete bore and a zero. The guy retreated to a nearby bench. Come to think of it, I would not be surprised if the whole bunch was headed to Kuwait to cash in on some of the oil profits resulting from the 1991 Persian Gulf War.

I knew Mr. Cohen wrote novels, and when I told him about my autobiography, mentioning a few highlights of my not-so-boring life, he encouraged me to be sure and publish it. I thought this encounter was, on the whole, quite exciting. It really woke me up.

Kuwait

Kuwait City

I arrived late at my posh Marina Hotel in Kuwait City – capital of the tiny country of Kuwait, which has a population of 3.6 million and is located on the northwest shore of the Persian Gulf – so I missed the welcome dinner party at the Atlantis Restaurant, which by all accounts was superb. While I was waiting for my suitcase in my exquisite suite, my tour director, Baroness Yvonne Buheiry von Fleschenberg, showed up and greeted me with great enthusiasm, and with perfect German. It turned out that she was born and partially educated in Germany, and had lived in Rome, London, Paris, and in some Arabian country. She was fluent in seven languages, including Arabic, and turned out to be one of the most sophisticated and knowledgeable guides I have encountered to date. We hit it off just like that and have corresponded ever since. She was also very attractive and had exquisite taste in clothes. Extraordinary!

I liked her welcome letter, which started out like this: "Congratulations on choosing this adventure, in which the traditional survival skills of desert dwellers and humble fishermen live side by side with the dynamic of oil propelled modernity. Arabia evokes haunting mystery! We will meet people, who hold dear their intuitive beliefs, their practical art and respect for tradition."

I went to bed totally exhausted, even forgetting to set my alarm, which had never happened to me before. And to top it off, I overslept and was awakened by a call from the Baroness, alerting me to what was going on. I never got dressed so quickly. Thankfully, Yvonne arranged for a driver from the hotel to catch up with the group. He dropped me off in time for our visit to the Kuwait National Museum.

On the way to the museum, I got the impression that life in Kuwait City was rather normal. And since I had not seen the National Museum before it was badly destroyed and many of the art objects savagely stolen in 1990, it was amazing to see how well it was restored. In walking through the museum, we had a good introduction to Kuwait's history, culture, and customs. Among the many treasures there, you will find "living vestiges that go back to the first centuries of the Islamic era" (Museum brochure).

When we continued to the nearby traditional House of Weaving, the Al-Sadu House, located next to the Bayt Al-Badr House (built between 1838 and 1848), I was struck in particular by a woman dressed in a jet-black burka who sat on the floor weaving a carpet or wall hanging. When I approached her, she quickly bent down and hid her face so thoroughly that all I could see was her bent back cloaked in black and two bare hands clutching the weaving rod. The Al-Sadu House is known for displaying this traditional craft of the Bedouins. It is important insofar as the weaving stands out for its geometric designs, woven by hand with dyed, spun, and colored wool. Sadu weaving is still alive in nomadic culture. The Bayt Al-Badr House is also a good example of the desert-house architecture common before the discovery of oil. It is famous for the ancient front doors and the arched entrance. The Kuwaitis are proud of their architectural excellence.

This pride extends to their ultramodern Liberation Tower, which is forty meters taller than the Eiffel Tower and one of the highest telecommunication towers in the world. It is the symbol of Kuwait's multinational liberation and an unmistakable sign of the country's resurgence. Thanks to clear skies, we all took fabulous panorama shots of the city below, which also included the famous three Kuwait Towers made of concrete and prominent because of their big blue balls, which contain 4.5 million gallons of water. The main tower is 187 meters high and serves as a restaurant and water tower. Up there, I cornered several Arabs and asked if they would mind if I took their picture. Three gentlemen were happy to oblige. They were dressed in their *thobes*, ankle-length garments with a headdress consisting of a *ghutrah*, a large, square-shaped cloth, folded over the *taqiyah*, the ends of which are used to protect the face in the event of a sandstorm, an *ogal*, which holds down the cloth, and a double circlet of twisted black cord. A couple from Saudi Arabia, the wife in an all-black abaya, cloak, and niqab (veil) to hide her face, were just as kind, and I was happy to have one photo with me in the middle. Many thanks to my Arab friends. Many people in Kuwait wear Western clothes.

A local guide took us to the harbor to the must-see Arab dhows, moored in the vicinity of the famous fish market. We learned about the importance of the dhows before oil was discovered in Kuwait. They came in different sizes and were used for pearl diving, for delivering sweetwater and spices, and for carrying building materials like wood and coral. Some dhows, such as Al-Muhalab, were famous. She was burned by the Iraqis during the invasion, and in case you are interested, was made by Al-Estad Muhammed Al-Abdullah in 1937. These wooden dhows once transported fish and dates to East Africa and timber to the Persian Gulf.

The fish market was huge, nicely decorated, and so clean it did not smell fishy at all! – It was a fascinating experience. Never in my life had I seen so many exotic varieties of fish all in one place. They were either dumped in piles on the tile floor, displayed in big bushel baskets or buckets on ice, or laid out nicely according to species on long wooden tables. Hundreds of Arabs, dressed in their turbans and white or gray robes, stood in groups near the fish that were about to be auctioned off. Prices can go up astronomically, I was told. We left when the activities were about to start.

The next day we visited the Friday market in Shuwaikh, which starts on Thursday afternoons. It was a fun place to visit. Here you can find used and new things, designer and other clothes, various textiles, new and antique furniture, carpets galore, plants, and exotic kitsch, all for bargain prices if you know how to haggle. It all looked so tempting, but my house was already too full of stuff.

The privilege of seeing with my own eyes the Burgan field, in the desert of Southeastern Kuwait, was another highlight of my travels, simply because I remembered well the 1991 war in the Persian Gulf. It is one of the world's largest and richest oil fields, producing 90% of oil exports worldwide. What is so unique about these fields is that there are no rising and falling oil derricks, like the ones present in most other oil fields. Here oil practically flows to the surface on its own.

"In 1991, retreating Iraqi soldiers set Burgan Field on fire. Smoke plumes from the Greater Burgan oil field with over 700 wells ablaze extended for miles. From satellite observations the plume appeared like a black snake in the desert that extended parallel to the Persian Gulf. Despite the destruction there was no significant depletion of the oil reserves and production capacity, and most of the Burgan Field was rebuilt" (Brochure), as we saw. It took a team effort under the umbrella of the Kuwait Oil Company, joined by the United States, Europe, Canada, and Gulf Council Countries, to eventually, about ten months later, extinguish all wells. Among those fighters was Paul Neal "Red" Adair, a renowned American oil-well firefighter who at the time was seventy-five years old. Land mines had been placed in areas around the oil wells. They had to be cleaned off before the fires could be put out. Around six million barrels of oil were lost each day. I had no idea that some six hundred Kuwaitis were still imprisoned in Iraq.

Our visit to the very impressive and modern Display Center of the Kuwait Oil Company was extremely informative. The displays and explanations were state-of-the-art, and after spending a couple of hours listening to the guide's explanations and clear answers to our questions, I had a much better idea of what oil exploration, drilling, production, development, export, etc. was all about. Just as informative was the stop at the nearby Kuwait National Memorial Museum – the Not to Forget Museum of Saddam Hussein Regime Crimes. A tank and other weapons were parked outside, and above the entrance was a sign that read "KUWAIT A COUNTRY OF PEACE & FREEDOM." Inside, big dramatic pictures of burning oil fields mounted on the walls, as well as audio recordings, provided moving insight into the unfolding of the war. Another big plaque was mounted on the wall. It was addressed to "Sir John Major, The Previous Prime Minister of Britain, One of the Knights of Liberating Kuwait and the accompanying delegation. Your visit is a badge of honor for us. NBK." I can understand their gratitude. Thanks to its liberation, Kuwait once more has the highest per capita income in the world!

While driving back to the hotel, I became painfully aware of the domineering presence of oil. There were miles of pipes running through the desert countryside, and huge tankers were seen offshore, filling their bellies with about 110,000 tons of oil each. Ultralarge crude carriers move approximately two billion metric tons of oil every year. Think about it. Also, think about the Cheney–Halliburton–Kuwait connection. He was secretary of defense in 1991, when he managed to channel contracts to Halliburton resulting in millions of dollars of revenue. After leaving the administration, Cheney served as CEO of Halliburton from 1995 to 2000. As vice president of the United States, he maneuvered hundreds of millions of dollars of noncompetitive contracts to Halliburton in 2003 as part of the Iraq War. It goes on and on.

The Baroness had no sightseeing plans for the evening, and I enjoyed exploring this five-star luxury hotel located on Kuwait Bay, with two pools and a private beach. We were free to eat wherever we pleased, either in a restaurant connected to the hotel or elsewhere in the city. For meals taken outside the hotel, we were asked to save our receipts in order to be reimbursed later for whatever we spent. One couple spent an easy $500 each for one meal out, and the bill was reimbursed in full, including the tip.

We were immersed in luxury at the Marina Hotel. My spacious suite had a balcony overlooking Kuwait Bay, and when I went to the Six Palms Restaurant, I was stunned. It was shaped like a boat and overlooked the Kuwait Towers. Wherever I turned, I saw glass. The restaurant is located in an atrium with a large glass ceiling – just to give you an idea. You could eat whatever your heart desired and then some. It took me a while to get used to such opulence. Of course, our hotel, which earned top awards for best performance worldwide, was located in the part of town where the rich and famous do their shopping. At night, I found a poem on my pillow, next to a piece of chocolate. It read as follows: "Life is a powerful ocean churning beneath and above us. / We can drift on top, waiting for the calm, / waiting for a familiar motion. / Or, we can take a deep breath and dive in, / allowing the wave to push us ahead" (Anonymous).

Kuwait, being one of the richest countries in the region, also boasts many palatial homes, health centers, and housing projects. Though rebuilt in a hurry after the invasion, the buildings meld modern architecture with traditional design and construction. We had a chance to get at least a fleeting impression of this ambiance on the way to the Tareq Rajab Museum. It has a superb collection of Islamic art, books, ceramics, jewelry, costumes, and manuscripts that escaped destruction during the Persian Gulf War. Tareq Sayed Rajab, who studied in the United States, and his beloved wife Jehan Wellborne cofounded the collection. As I admired the very nicely displayed artifacts, I became very interested in the collection of Indian gold-filigree jewelry. In a display presented in a special small cabinet, I spotted a gold-filigree necklace identical to the one Doc bought for me in early 1957 in Mérida, Mexico, from our friend Maurice Goldstein. It was attached to a red velvet cushion and illuminated by a fluorescent light. I was so excited that at first I was speechless, but then I had to tell a couple of my friends in the group about it. I knew then that this gold necklace and the others, as well as the bracelets and earrings, had their origin in India. Incredible!

On the way back to the hotel we got an up-close look at the famous and striking blue Kuwait Water Towers. They were designed by a Swedish firm and constructed by a Yugoslavian company. Together, they hold 45,000 cubic meters of water. The rotating restaurant in one of the towers is, of course, a big tourist attraction, and we too enjoyed a fabulous lunch up there. When I asked our guide, who used to be a professor at the university in Baghdad, Iraq, what he thought of Saddam Hussein, I was surprised to hear him praise the Hussein era. I asked him about the location of our military bases, and he pointed toward the horizon of the vast desert . . .

Jewels of Arabia – The Middle East

Bahrain

Manama

We departed for Bahrain, an archipelago of thirty-three islands, on February 8. Thirty-four miles long and eleven miles wide, Bahrain, which means "two seas" in Arabic, is the largest of these islands, and it is situated to the east of Saudi Arabia, near the western shores of the Persian Gulf. It is ruled by the Al-Khalifa royal family and has a population of approximately 1,220,000. For centuries, Bahrain has been known for its superb, naturally occurring pearls, only one of its treasures. Today, the island group of Bahrain is an independent state and one of the most important crossroads in the Middle East, where oil is the principal commodity. The country sits on an amazing cache of important archeological treasures. Excavations reveal civilizations dating from 3000 BC. Bahrain also takes pride in many large structures, just like the rest of the Middle Eastern countries. The sixteen-mile-long and seventy-five-foot-wide King Fahd Causeway connects Saudi Arabia and Bahrain.

Since Qatar is to the southeast, across the Gulf of Bahrain, the planned Qatar–Bahrain Causeway will link Bahrain and Qatar and become the world's longest marine causeway. To date, it has not been started. Also in the process of construction is the 3,353-foot Murjan Tower. I learned that there is fierce competition between these Persian Gulf countries for the highest and largest structure. Since they don't have much space on earth, they have to go into the heavens or the oceans. If the oil should run out, what would they do?

As I write about my visit to Bahrain, I find it hard to believe that this country, which seemed so peaceful to us outsiders three years earlier, is today in such turmoil.

Their hotels are like palaces – and almost unimaginably extravagant and luxurious. We stayed three nights at the Ritz-Carlton in Manama, a seven-story, twenty-acre, and five-star luxury resort on the north coast of Bahrain, with access to a fabulous beach. Travcoa introduced it as follows: "Ringed by dazzling sand and washed by the warm, clear Arabian-Gulf waters, the Ritz Carlton is grand in scale, exclusive in style, and committed to luxury and comfort." The design is uniquely Arabian, and it hardly needs to be mentioned that the cuisine is out of this world. If you wish, you can dock your yacht right at their doorstep – so to speak. And there are a variety of spas and wellness programs at your disposal, if you have the time and money. Somewhere near Bahrain on the Arabian Gulf is our naval base.

We started out the next morning with a tour around Manama, the capital, and a visit to the National Museum, which is situated on the city's most prestigious plots. According to the Travcoa literature, "The design of the museum reflects high international standards and the modern building in which it stands honors Islamic architectural traditions. . . . It covers 7,000 years of Bahrain's history. From burial mounds to temples, art and culture, the museum captures all the life that continues to flourish on this very old site." Moreover, "the burial mound which was transported from its site in the desert and reassembled in the museum" struck me as rather unique, but to be honest, the old Quranic manuscripts, notes on astronomy, and historical documents and letters did not really leave a lasting impression on me.

I was looking forward to visiting the Al-Fateh Mosque the next day. If the mosques in Istanbul were impressive, the Al-Fateh Mosque, aka the Al-Fateh Islamic Center & Al-Fateh Grand Mosque, was simply awesome. As is characteristic of Arabian mosques, palaces, and private homes, these structures featured beautiful geometric tile work, which was developed by craftsmen of Arabia because the depiction of living figures is prohibited in Islam. The elaborate stars, circumscribed octagons, and fabulous free-form designs were aesthetically captivating. I did not know it is one of the largest mosques in the world, capable of accommodating over seven thousand worshippers at a time. "It is the largest place of worship in Bahrain and located next to the King Faisal Highway in Juffair, which is a town located in the capital city of Manama. The mosque is also very close to the Royal Bahraini Palace, the residence of the king of Bahrain, Hamad bin Isa Al-Khalifa. The huge dome built on top of the Al-Fateh Mosque is made of pure fiberglass. Weighing over 60 tons, the dome is currently the world's largest fiberglass dome. It is named after Ahmed Al Fateh, the conqueror of Bahrain" (Travcoa). Of course, it cannot compete with Mecca, Saudi Arabia, which is the holiest city in Islam and attracts thirteen million Muslims each year. If you are tempted to go, save the effort and expense. Non-Muslims are prohibited from entering the sacred site.

The Al-Fateh easily rivals the most intricate Christian churches of the West or Buddhist temples of the Far East. The tiles, floors, chandeliers, mosaics, and vaulted ceilings are out of this world. The spaciousness and openness of the mosque is liberating instead of confining – though to gain admittance we did have to adhere to a strict dress code. To make sure our shoulders, arms, and heads were covered, we were given a special robe and a scarf, and we had to take off our shoes and enter in just socks. Our nice, young, female Muslim guide, originally from Turkey but studying theology in Germany, lectured in perfect English, but also conversed with me in German. We exchanged e-mail addresses but unfortunately never connected. By the way, did you know that Muslim women are discouraged from visiting mosques during their menstrual cycles? I did not know that but did know that in the mosque, men and women have to stay separated. Be aware and never enter a room while men are praying.

We continued across the 1.5-mile-long causeway to Muharraq Island. Muharraq, located on the island, is Bahrain's third-largest city and has long been a center of religious practice. Muharraq is the northernmost island of the Bahrain archipelago, in the Persian Gulf. The city lies at the southwestern tip of the island. We visited Shaikh Isa Bin Ali's house. It was built in 1800 as the home of the amir's great-grandfather. Its structure provides a fine example of local architecture, complete with a wind tower, wall carvings, and latticework, and it is representative of traditional nineteenth-century life. The rather high wind tower was one of the early forms of air conditioning and is a traditional landmark of local architecture. It acts as a funnel, catching the breeze and drawing it into the cavities below, and it allows for the release of hot air, like a chimney. I had to admit that it was an ingenious way to keep cool. This type of architecture was common in the preoil period. The house is big and has huge walls and small doors, designed to protect inhabitants from heat in the summer and severe cold in the winter.

Most impressive was the square Arad Fort, built in the fifteenth century in Arab style – out of sea stones, lime, sand, and palm trunks. It has been restored, but no materials not in harmony with the traditional construction were used. The fort overlooks various sea passages of Muharraq's shallow seashores. It used to prevent ships from breaking through to the island where the fort is located. A small trench surrounded it. It used to be filled with water from wells that were drilled especially for this purpose. It is also believed the fort was used by the Omanis during their brief occupation of Bahrain in 1800, because of its location adjacent to the strategic waterways between Bahrain Island and Muharraq. It got pretty hot walking around without any shade nearby, and I was relieved when we departed for the museum.

Seeing ancient manuscripts and rare copies of the holy Quran at the Beit Al-Quran Museum in Manama, open since 1990 and one of the most renowned Islamic museums in the world, was another *novum* for me. That it was air-conditioned was a welcome bonus. The museum includes a mosque and a Quranic school in addition to the exhibition halls.

We walked to the Bab Al-Bahrain and from there to the Manama Old Souk & Gold Souk. *Bab Al-Bahrain* translates as "gateway to Bahrain," and the building was originally constructed by the British in the 1940s, close to the water's edge. The monument essentially consists of a huge arch below which runs a road, which is often referred to as the entrance to the Manama Souk. The souk (marketplace) lies in the older part of town. Its narrow streets and partly covered alleys are typical of Middle Eastern souks and quite different from the souks in India, Egypt, or Turkey. It's well worth it to take a stroll through the Gold Souk. This part of town has some of what little remains of old Bahraini architecture. It's exciting to experience the profusion of colors, sounds, aromas, cloths, gold, jewelry, traditional spices, and local produce. I had fun bargaining over a few sterling-silver camels and little brass oil lamps.

Yvonne took us to the big Bahrain Fort, "which marks the ruins of a large, ancient city. It is the site of 100,000 burial mounds, which made up the world's largest necropolis, and along with the relics in the National Museum, attest to the rich spiritual life of past inhabitants, and bears record to the prosperity and traditions and rituals of the past" (Travcoa).

We had been on the go for some eleven days at this point, and all along we did not feel a drop of rain. Nothing but clear blue skies, sunshine, 80 to 90 degrees Fahrenheit, and little humidity! We saw few trees and not much grass, since irrigation comes at a steep price. One almost forgets out here what trees other than palms look like.

After lunch at our ritzy Ritz-Carlton, we took off to travel on the King Fahd Bridge, the seventeen-mile-long causeway to Saudi Arabia. We stopped at the border into Saudi Arabia only to turn around, because we had been denied visas. I don't know what the big deal was. We had only wanted to spend a few hours in Al-Khobar, the commercial hub of the Eastern Province of Saudi Arabia. "Al Khobar was a small port on the Arabian Gulf, inhabited mainly by fishermen. With the discovery of oil, it was transformed into an industrial port, and still serves small ships carrying passengers and goods that are distributed throughout the Kingdom. It is also a local vacation center, with gardens, miles of relaxing beaches and a manicured corniche" (Travcoa).

The Baroness had a surprise consolation prize in store for us. She took us to the world's premier motor-sport facility – "the most modern, user-friendly and exciting venue in the high-speed, high-tech, high-adrenaline industry on the planet. By being the home ground of a sport that prides itself by demanding and achieving the highest standards of professionalism, Bahrain has linked itself in the international community to excellence, prestige and power. By linking with such a powerful and sought-after brand in the form of Formula One, Bahrain is reaping the benefits of being at the forefront of an elite club of 18 nations that host the premier motor sport events in the world" (Travcoa).

This $150 million track, designed by none other than the German architect Hermann Tilke, was definitely a first for me, because I was not at all into sports in general. I hardly ever paid attention to the Memorial Day Indy 500, where I was taken once by a former boyfriend, in 1960 I believe. I remember roasting in the heat, and out of desperation, I drank a cold beer, my first. The incredible Bahraini racetrack was, I think, more sophisticated. We went up into the grandstand and watched a guy, actually the Brazilian Felipe Massa, who had won the Grand Prix here in 2007, practicing in a Ferrari for the April 2008 Formula One Grand Prix event. The noise was so deafening I had to cover my ears whenever he raced past us down below.

You should have seen the sky-high, all-glass VIP tower. Sinfully grand! The Racing Circuit, which includes a formidable Grand Prix Circuit, looked dangerously challenging. The length is 5.475 kilometers, and there are sixteen turns. We watched the Ferrari for a while, and I began to find it all very exciting. Many a race fanatic would have envied me, I swear. But they would not have envied me when I suddenly could not find my billfold. I was getting really nervous and was reluctant to tell Yvonne about it. Eventually, I did. She immediately called the hotel. They searched the restaurant where I had eaten breakfast and eventually found it where it was supposed to be: in the safe in my room. I was so glad. Thank you, Yvonne! –

As I write, it strikes me as so bizarre that only some three years later, just this week, on June 11, 2011, the Formula One races were canceled for 2011 due to social unrest. Maybe if the crown prince, Shaikh Salman bin Hamad Al-Khalifa, had paid more attention to the people who do all the work, who sweat and toil, and who have a right to rebel against suppression and exploitation, times would have remained more peaceful.

Qatar

Doha

The next day, February 12, 2008, we flew from Bahrain to Doha, the capital of Qatar, a country of which I had never heard and which we learned had only opened its doors to visitors within the previous decade. How exciting to be one of those privileged enough to visit a country in the Middle East that has a meager population of about nine hundred thousand and that does not even appear on most foreign maps of Arabia drawn prior to the nineteenth century. It is very flat, and golden desert sands cover vast areas of the country.

Travcoa's introduction to Qatar reads as follows:

This tiny oil-rich sheikdom on the Persian Gulf is finally opening up to tourism. The government has been encouraging foreign investment, and Qatari women enjoy more freedom than their counterparts in some other Gulf States. Al Jazeera, the Arab world's version of CNN, broadcasts without censorship from its headquarters in Doha. . . . Qatar is on its way to becoming an appealing tourist destination. The country no longer regards the cultural influence of outsiders as a problem. However, Qataris adhere closely to the tenets of Islam: Women are seldom seen without a veil, and the country's justice system is based on a strict, literal reading of the Quran. . . . Historians have recorded from archaeological digs that the peninsula was inhabited as far back as the Stone Age, when the region's climate was milder than it is today. By the early 18th century, nomadic Bedouins from central Arabia settled in the peninsula's coastal areas, where they became fishermen and pearl divers. By the mid-18th century, Qatar was already well established as a pearling center. The introduction of cultured pearls in the 1930s, however, was the beginning of the end for Qatar's pearl workers. Fortunately, oil was discovered in Qatar around the same time, and it quickly replaced pearls as the country's biggest source of income. . . . Although the Gulf States traditionally act in concert on foreign policy, Qatar takes a more independent line. It hosts several major U.S. military bases, but also offered political asy-

Fireball Lily

lum to Saddam Hussein just before the second Gulf War in 2003 *[an offer he must have regretted not accepting].*

The Four Seasons Hotel Doha, with an exclusive beach and marina on the Arabian Gulf and, like our other hotels, embedded in supreme luxury, was our home for the next two nights.

After a very nice lunch in the garden restaurant, I got ready for our visit to the Doha Racing & Equestrian Club. "With years of experience of handling thoroughbred horses, the Club was the obvious choice as a venue for equestrian events at the 15th Asian Games. A new 1,050 capacity arena has been built, beside the racecourse, for show-jumping and dressage, along with a training area, extra stabling, and veterinary facilities" (Travcoa). It also had a floodlit grass track.

I like horses and have occasionally even ridden them. Doc had wanted to buy a horse for me while we lived at the Croft, but he did not pursue the intention when I got pregnant. I recall that my mother's father was very fond of horses and regularly attended races not far from where he lived. I still try not to miss watching the Kentucky Derby. The horses in the stables at the Doha Racing & Equestrian Club were impeccably cared for. Each and every one was just stunning. A young girl from France was staying at the club with her mother. She proudly introduced me to her horse, which she was riding regularly while there. What a life! Since I had never before seen a racing and equestrian club, I found this one most notable. The posters on the wall – "Qatari Riders Strike Gold," which depicted happy sheikhs and dignitaries, and "Get to the Excitement! Join Us at the 7th Qatar International Horse Jumping Championship 6–11 March 2007" – caught my eye. It was a nice, sunny day, and in the absence of other tourist groups, it was a terrific outing.

The stop at the market was almost as exciting, because never on my worldwide travels had I seen produce as lush, healthy, and huge in size. Cabbage and cauliflower heads were about eighteen inches in diameter. Onions and peppers – in short, all produce – were at least twice the size of those available in the United States or Europe. When I inquired about the source of their produce (it is very dry in Qatar), they said it came from Iran. Wow! I never would have associated any extraordinary vegetables or fruits with Iran. Back in the States, all we hear about Iran is their uranium and potential for developing nuclear bombs.

Not from Iran, however, were the falcons we saw in the falcon shop on the way to the hotel. The Arabs have a tradition of using falcons for hunting in the desert. They are treasured pets and can cost thousands of dollars. If you come to Qatar, you should go to the souk and pick one out. You can also buy all sorts of souvenirs related to falconry. For some reason, I did not think of buying an ornate falcon hood. I really was not into this aristocratic sport. Yet I would not have wanted to miss the experience at the shop. My compensation was a nice photo of five smiling Arabs, myself in the middle and an Arab showing off his falcon.

In the evening I decided to go for a casual stroll along the Corniche, the sweeping boulevard that skirts the waterfront on the balmy shores of the Arabian Gulf, very close to our hotel. The sunset was unforgettably beautiful, and the silhouettes of the palm trees on the horizon were a reminder that we were in the presence of one of Arabia's jewels.

At the camel racetrack in Al-Shahaniya, we watched hundreds of camels roaming around the desert racetrack. I had fun running from one camel to another, some resting on the sand and others, with a human or robotic jockey, getting ready for a race. Of course, I did not know a thing about the robotic jockeys and was pleasantly surprised to learn that Sheikh Abdullah of Qatar had them designed, mercifully, to replace the children formerly strapped to the camels for races. To monitor the speed of the racing camels, some Arabs and others drove alongside them in an SUV. They were practicing. All in all, it was a colorful scene out there in the desert. I would not mind returning for a real race, which strangely enough I saw on TV when visiting Vienna, Austria, later that year.

Come to think of it, I am convinced the Arabs have a fixation with races and sports of all kinds. And it should not come as a surprise that they maneuvered to host the 2022 World Cup, a challenging undertaking since they have to construct a stadium with a huge dome and sufficient air conditioning. Judging by the sophisticated, glitzy high-rises they already boast, I do not doubt they'll be ready by the time the World Cup starts, provided the oil continues to flow. I just hope they will treat the thousands of expatriate workers they will import from some of the poorest countries to build the stadium more humanely than they have treated them to date, June 2014. I have heard that thousands will die in the process.

Thanks to the black gold, Sheikh Faisal Bin Qassim Al-Thani (a member of the royal family) became so rich he was able to amass an enormous private collection of artifacts and house it in an impressive, large museum that looks like a fortress. It is accessible only by appointment, which we had. The sheikh accumulated his collection of Arabian and Islamic artifacts, weapons, Bedouin jewelry, manuscripts, numerous unusual fossils, and books during his extensive travels. It was bizarre to find so many vintage and classic cars, such as rare Ford T models, DeSoto models from the 1940s, Buicks from the 30s, motorcycles, and trucks, and stranger yet, a big collection of old registration plates, most of them from way out here in the USA. – I should have held on to mine from the '57 T-bird.

I do not know how, but Yvonne had succeeded in obtaining an invitation for a visit to Al Jazeera English. As soon as she mentioned it, I was almost ecstatic. Getting inside involved a somewhat complicated process and required the presentation of our passports. An attractive and bright young woman from the United States was one of our guides. The place was truly amazing, very modern and with state-of-the-art technology inside. It is somehow the counterpart to CNN. We watched reporters delivering the news in the impressive newsroom, where broadcasts appeared on many monitors. Al Jazeera's reporting is accessible in several world regions. It was amazing. I chatted with one of the executives about the forthcoming elections. He assured me, in an almost hushed-up voice, that Obama would not be elected. Well, he was wrong, wasn't he?

A male guide took us into a big, well-lit room in which hung large pictures of a couple of Al Jazeera reporters who were imprisoned in Guantánamo without being given a specific charge. I apologized and told him that I and many of my friends were for closing Guantánamo ASAP. I bet they are even more disappointed than I am that, thanks to our backward Congress, Obama has to date failed to keep his promise to close down that despicable place. After the completion of the tour, as we were waiting for some in our group in a large reception hall, I realized I had lost my passport. I thought I had lost my mind. Then, like a miracle, as I looked across the big, almost empty hall, I spotted my passport lying in the center of the polished marble floor. I ran, took a deep breath, grabbed it, and sighed with relief. Lucky me!

Outside, I made sure to take plenty of pictures and asked a cotraveler to take one of me as well – and to make sure the Al Jazeera sign was in clear sight. I could not understand why a handful of cotravelers refused to go inside the place. And I cannot understand why we cannot see Al Jazeera broadcasts here in the States. Surprise: right now, as the Arab Spring has started in Tunisia and Egypt, CNN and others have not hesitated to broadcast Al Jazeera reports. The Bush administration disliked the fact that Al Jazeera was the only broadcaster covering the Iraq and Afghanistan wars live. What ever happened to transparency?

On the way to the hotel, we stopped for lunch at a downtown restaurant and opted to be served at tables set up outside. It did not take me long to strike up a conversation in English with two attractive young Muslim women who were on their lunch break. And it did not take them long to render a not-so-flattering opinion about Bush and the Iraq War – and it gave me great pleasure to tell them I agreed with them wholeheartedly. Both wore fashionable Western clothes, with the exception of colorful scarves covering their hair. They were also puffing out clouds of tobacco from a long hookah, a water pipe, something I had not seen up close. This kind of smoking, or enjoying a *shisha*, is acceptable in Qatar, and when the lady offered me a puff, I gave it a try. It looked so cool, but tasted like nothing. It can supposedly be hazardous to your health. So watch it! I personally like to try almost everything at least once. How could I have an opinion unless I gave it a try?

Since we had no sightseeing plans the next day, I just relaxed on the inviting grounds surrounding the hotel. I took several pics of the spectacular restaurant, which featured a huge atrium, fountains, palm trees, and windows from floor to ceiling. The flowering shrubs were vibrant, and I lounged on a comfortable beach chair underneath a palm tree for quite a while. I was, as always when I am close to an ocean, mesmerized – this time by the blue waters of the Arabian Gulf. Can you top that? Pinch yourself, Chrissie.

I never talk much about the food in these luxury hotels, because words cannot really do it justice. Don't forget, I do count calories. I eat to live and do not live to eat. And the exquisite arrangements of flowers everywhere, including in our suites, never failed to soothe my soul immensely.

Oman

Muscat

If you thought the Four Seasons Hotel in Doha was the ultimate, you should have seen what awaited us after we landed in Muscat, Oman, after a short flight. We stayed at the ultraritzy Shangri-La Barr Al-Jissah Resort & Spa–Al-Husn Hotel, where none other than Bill Gates was hosting a business meeting.

Travcoa introduced the hotel as follows: "Exclusively located on the bay at Barr Al Jissah, the resort nestles against the dramatic backdrop of the rugged interior mountains and the spectacular waters of the Gulf of Oman. Set in 124 acres of distinct scenery, this deluxe resort complex comprises three hotels, with a total of 680 luxurious bedrooms, with an inviting décor inspired by royal Arabian palaces, accented by authentic Omani artworks, a large variety of food and beverage outlets, including six main restaurants, seven casual dining outlets and pool bars, three lobby lounges, two bars and a nightclub, a CHI spa, and three private beaches, along with many other activity options including saunas, steam rooms, Jacuzzi and plunge pools to aerobics classes at the gymnasium. The resort has 6000 square meters of swimming pools as well as a 500 meter 'lazy' river."

According to the hotel's literature, "The Al Husn Hotel, an exclusive six-star indulgence, offers our highest level of Shangri La (Garden of Eden, Utopia, paradise hidden from modern man) service, amenities and privileges to the most discerning of travelers. All of our expansive, richly appointed rooms and suites have direct views of the turquoise waters of the Gulf of Oman, with some offering a panorama of the resort and the surrounding coastline." I can vouch for it. They know what they are talking about.

Muscat, with a population of about one million, is the capital of Oman and an important port town in the Arabian Sea along the Gulf of Oman. What struck me as unusual in Oman were the rocky and very arid Western Al-Hajar Mountains, which dominate the landscape. The country's economy is driven by trade, petroleum, and shipping.

"Muscat is only a small part of a larger grouping of cities and towns strung along the coast of the Gulf of Oman, which is known locally as the 'Capital Area' or the 'Muscat Municipality.' These towns are sandwiched between the sea to the north and a very rocky, primeval-looking range of barren mountains to the south. A thriving and strategically located port of the Arabian Peninsula in ancient times, Muscat retains its somewhat medieval appearance. Two picturesque Portuguese forts, Jelali and Merani, co-exist with modern, commercial, and residential quarters of the neighboring coastal towns, and give Muscat a distinctive ambiance of its own. The seaside, ceremonial palace of H. M. Sultan Qaboos Said, nestled between steep rocky hills, offers a spectacular sight, especially at night" (Travcoa). We had to hurry a bit in order to catch the ride on a big, refurbished wooden dhow for a sunset cruise in the crescent-shaped harbor and a view of the Sultan's Palace. Several of us climbed around and examined the big dhow from up close. We missed most of the sunset, but it was a nice, refreshing, and peaceful evening cruise before dinner.

Nizwa

On February 15, Yvonne traveled with us from Muscat to Nizwa, capital city of the interior, to attend a live cattle auction and get a clear picture of daily life in the busy, colorful world of Omani commerce. It turned out to be quite an experience, uniquely interesting and exciting indeed. Walking toward the auction site, I was kept busy watching the approaching pickup trucks loaded full of nice, well-fed cows, cute black and white calves, and even cuter goats and lambs in various shades of brown, white, and black. Black-haired younger men and white-bearded elders all wore their long white dishdashas, tribal gowns, and, on their heads, white *muzzaras* or *kummars* (turbans) or intricately embroidered caps, either white or varicolored. Their white tribal garb contrasted sharply with their brown skin. All wore sandals on bare, suntanned feet. Not a single Omani, man or woman, was obese. Some were carrying baby goats or lambs in their arms. Others had tied them to the trunk of a tree, and cute little boys stood by, guarding them. A buyer was examining the animal carefully underneath and above, inspecting the fur and especially the teeth, while negotiating a price. The few women I noticed were all dressed in long black garments, abayas, and black veils or scarfs. Several groups of men sat on spread-out woven blankets or rugs, sipping tea or eating some dates while chatting and negotiating a trade. High palm trees dotted the scene and reached up into the blue sky. Another jewel of Arabia!

On the way back to the hotel we had another chance to bargain hunt for souvenirs at the bazaar, full of fascinating, traditional souks where silver, brass, local handicrafts, and a great diversity of art objects were displayed to tempt those of us who had a penchant for everything foreign or exotic. And some in our group eventually ended up with large packages and great treasures with which to adorn their mansions and vacation homes back in the States. And let's not overlook the roundabout in Nizwa, by way of which we set out to travel back to Muscat. A giant Arabic coffee urn surrounded by silver-lined cups, a symbol of Oman's legendary hospitality, stood in the center of the roundabout. We were told that in the center of another traffic circle, we would find a huge stack of books, an homage to the country's emphasis on learning. At least at the time of our visit, Oman did not boast the extraordinary oil wealth of its neighbor, the United Arab Emirates. The standard of living is still much higher in Oman than in many other Arab countries. It would have been nice to go to the Saiq Plateau of Jebel Akhdar (the Green Mountain), known for its seasonal fruits, like pomegranates, peaches, apricots, almonds, and walnuts, as well as for its roses. But one never can see everything on these trips. It's like skipping an appetizer.

After lunch, Yvonne took us to the famous Nizwa Round Tower Fort, which for three hundred years served as a palace, prison, and seat of government. It was built to protect this busy junction against fierce attacks on the caravan routes. The walls are rounded and robust, and the entire fort contrasts beautifully with the verdant countryside. Our local guide was lecturing in the bus while we were on the way. As on another occasion, I was astonished and impressed when Yvonne interrupted the guide in Arabic. She told him in a somewhat bossy voice to stop and start all over again, because he had gotten a few facts mixed up. I do not think he liked it, but he rather reluctantly gave in and continued. I thought it took a lot of guts on Yvonne's part, considering what many Arab males think of women.

The fort boasted an amazing interior and an exciting photo gallery. "The central tower is a colossal circular tower 115 feet above the rest of the fortification, but inside you will find a veritable maze of rooms, high-ceilinged halls, doorways, terraces, narrow staircases and corridors. This edifice – the largest on the Arabian peninsula – stands today, as a monument to this heady era in Nizwa's, and indeed Oman's, glorious history" (Travcoa).

When you look beyond the walls, you see a flourishing date plantation – a veritable oasis – which offered a welcome spot in the shade. While others were having lunch in a nearby restaurant, I joined a small Bedouin family, a father, a son, and two young girls, all in their customary garb, to rest in a tent-like shelter underneath palm trees. The son spoke English, and we had a pleasant conversation about their life as Bedouins and mine as an American. I learned that though they lived in the desert, they were no longer nomads, and instead of using camels for their daily sustenance (milk, meat, tents, transportation, etc.), they raised sheep and the son worked in a factory. He had learned English in school. The father offered to buy an ice-cream cone for me, but I declined politely. They were so nice and friendly and genuinely enjoyed chatting with me. When do you ever have a chance to talk to Bedouins?

After the date plantation, we were taken to a site that looked like a fairground. This was an unscheduled detour but turned out to be quite a treat. It was the end of the popular six-week Muscat Festival, which attracts visitors from neighboring Gulf countries. We were definitely the only Americans present. I did not notice any other Westerners, which was fine with me.

Fireball Lily

I wandered away from my group to get a closer look at the many different activities that took place on this fairground, peppered with a variety of palm trees. I watched several groups of locals, including men in white robes performing dances, others holding guns, and still others beating drums. Women in multicolored costumes performed a dance in slow motion. Each woman wore a rich, colorful, handwoven scarf, which covered her head and shoulders. Another woman, also dressed in a bright, long garment, balanced a big tin canister on her head. A stunning gold-filigree ornament hung down on her forehead. The canister was probably filled with some sort of soup, which she was en route to deliver to one of the six or seven women sitting in a row on the ground, next to big, round bowls filled with soups or lamb stews, all for sale. At another spot, underneath a big palm tree, sat a couple of Arabs stirring Omani halva in a big, round, flat copper kettle over a fire. Served with dates, it is a sticky, sweet, gelatinous substance made from sugar, eggs, honey, and spices. Another vendor offered date ice cream in a small plastic dish, which tasted so delicious.

I was surprised to see a demonstration that involved two oxen pushing a well wheel similar to the one in India. A white-bearded Omani looked on while leaning heavily on his cane. I thought it was a bit strange to see a whole bunch of women, most of them dressed in ankle-length black robes and veils (but with their faces visible), on the upper tier of a four-story, fifty-foot-wide cement structure. I don't remember seeing any Omani couples (male and female) just strolling across the grounds. I snapped a picture of a darling little boy looking somewhat forlorn. He was probably hoping someone would buy him a balloon. They were for sale at the entrance to the park, the meeting place for our ride back to the Shangri-La Resort.

A kind of melancholy overcame me as I paused to take a panorama shot, through the palm trees, of the orange sun as it was setting in the Gulf of Oman. That evening, we had dinner in the spacious garden restaurant. The ambiance was lovely and romantic. Lanterns were lit throughout the dining area, and as usual, the food was superb. I sat with some of my friends, whom I had gotten to know a bit better at that point. All of them were serious world travelers, and it was always exciting to exchange stories about places all of us had experienced. All of them also had their own unique stories to tell about how they had started out humbly and, either through hard work or by inheriting a fortune, had accomplished enough to reap the rewards and satisfy their thirst for traveling the world.

A tour of the Sultan Qaboos Grand Mosque was on the agenda for the next day. Since I have a special penchant for mosques, I was really looking forward to seeing Oman's biggest one, which was inaugurated on May 4, 2001. Even from a distance, the blue and gold domes so characteristic of Islamic architecture intoxicated me. Of course, I was impressed by its size, the manicured gardens surrounding it, the ornate interior, its exquisite chandelier, and most of all the prayer carpet! It is the world's second-largest handwoven carpet (70 x 60 meters) and was made by an Iranian carpet company. I wondered if it could have been the company owned by the parents of Mohammad Tabasian, my ex-boyfriend from Teheran. He was a medical student in Hannover when we dated (see Part I of my memoirs). The carpet "brings together the classical Tabriz, Kashan and Isfahan design traditions. 28 colors in varying shades were used" (Travcoa). Cobalt blue was the predominant color, just as the blue tiles stood out in the mosque in Istanbul. When walking on the vast, impeccable, open, and breezy marble floors in and around the mosque, I almost felt like I was floating. It was so uplifting and ethereal.

As on similar occasions, a profound sense of awe overcame me. I just loved it – and I would have been even more impressed had I not learned that less than a year after its inauguration, on March 16, 2002, none other than Dick Cheney visited the mosque and, of course, the sultan. All at the taxpayers' expense. It's no wonder that almost exactly one year after this visit, on March 20, 2003, the invasion of Iraq took place. I wondered if he too missed the call to prayer and if he knew the five pillars of Islam, which the Quran presents as a framework for worshippers and a sign of commitment to the faith. I will list them, in case you have forgotten: (1) creed, (2) fasting at Ramadan, (3) pilgrimage to Mecca once in one's lifetime, (4) almsgiving, and (5) daily prayer.

Our next stop was the Bait Al-Zubair Museum, located within the winding streets of Muscat, where we were treated to traditional Omani crafts and culture. "It houses one of Oman's finest and most comprehensive collections of artifacts from all over the Sultanate, such as weaponry, jewelry, costumes, domestic utensils and recreated urban and rural environments" (Travcoa). I noticed an elderly gentleman with a long white beard wearing leather pants and a Tyrolean felt hat. I zeroed in on him immediately, and we chatted for a while in German, since he was from Bavaria. I discovered that the Germans like to come to Oman. I think it has something to do with the mountains and, of course, the desert. I met a few more Germans in the parking lot. They were from the former East Germany. Since the fall of the Wall, many former-GDR citizens have started to travel to places around the globe that were once off-limits to them.

We continued along the beautiful waterfront corniche (Muscat lies in a natural volcanic bowl) to explore their fish market. The daily catch included quite a few varieties of fish, displayed on wooden platforms, and we were able to watch the workers prepare it. I wondered where the various yachts, boats, and ships anchored in the harbor came from. We continued to Muttrah, which was Oman's center of commerce before the discovery of oil and still is today. It is one of the largest seaports in the region.

A maze of pathways, the Muttrah Souk was dominated by household goods. By the way, *souk* is the Arabic word for a place where all kinds of goods are bought, sold, or exchanged, either with friendly haggling or without. Going to these local markets is always somewhat intoxicating and bewildering to me. Some consider this souk the most interesting or most famous one in the Arabian Gulf states. Others refer to it as a paradise for souvenir-hunting tourists or an *Arabian Nights* fantasy. You will find incense, perfumes, spices, dates, antiques, gold and silver jewelry, a unbelievable selection of electronic products, fluorescent flowers, fashion accessories, veils, black abayas (plain or embroidered), woven textiles, toys, gold, etc. You can watch people at work in small workshops while your senses are assaulted by exotic sounds, smells, and flavors, that is, by Arabian magic.

With all the stuff to see, the souk was dizzying. The magnificent Al-Alam Palace, the official palace of His Majesty Sultan Qaboos, flanked by the sixteenth-century Portuguese forts Al-Mirani and Al-Jalali, where we went for a photo stop, was much more calming. The facade was gold and blue, but we were not allowed inside. I was not disappointed. I took a picture, and since there was nothing but sunshine and blue skies, it was a given that it would turn out picture-perfect. – After having studied in England like other sultans, Sultan Qaboos rose to power by overthrowing his father in a palace coup in 1970. They sure have big egos. The sultan's birthday, November 18, is celebrated as a national holiday. To his credit, the standard of living, we were told, is still much higher in Oman than in many other Arab countries. Roads, electricity, water, health clinics, and schools have arrived in even the most remote mountain villages. When you get a glimpse of what these dictators stand to lose, you begin to understand why they would want to hold on to their power for dear life.

The last evening, we dined out at another very elegant restaurant. It was famous for lobster as well as other delectable dishes. And I for one never turn down lobster. I was late and had to hurry because all the rooms were on the ground floor. I had to walk through endless corridors to get to the expansive reception area, where the group was waiting for me next to a big room enclosed by all-glass walls and opposite a one-foot-high rectangular pool, one hundred feet long and twenty feet wide. As soon as I arrived, one of my cotravelers expressed regret that I was late. Had I arrived only a few minutes earlier, I would have had a chance to talk to Bill Gates. What a shame. I watched the wealthiest man in the world through glass walls as he sipped a glass of champagne (maybe it was water) while surrounded by a bunch of men in business suits. Thus, I did not crash the party as I had done at the airport in Bahrain, when I zeroed in on Bill Cohen. So much for that. The lobster was OK, but to be honest, I had had better in the States.

United Arab Emirates

Dubai

It was only a short flight from Muscat to Dubai. As we sat at the gate waiting to board, I realized I had left my sapphire-diamond ring on the nightstand next to my bed. I felt sick to my stomach and tried to persuade myself to just leave it. It would be a loss of about $6,000 – and perhaps more a sentimental than a monetary loss. It was a gift from my second and last husband, bought in New York. After I mentioned it to a couple of my new friends, they persuaded me to tell Yvonne, which I did. She turned around, called the hotel, asked for the tall, handsome manager from Bonn, Germany, whom I had talked to while at the hotel, and fifteen minutes later my ring was found; it would be forwarded to Le Royal Meridien Beach Resort and Spa, Dubai, UAE, where we would stay for three nights. Thanks again, Yvonne. – On the plane, I met another German couple, Kaethe and Seppel, from Dresden. We talked about traveling. They had toured Oman more or less on the cheap – they camped here and there in the desert – and had a great time. They were glad that since 1989, they could travel wherever their hearts desired, and I was impressed by the extent of their travels: the United States, Patagonia, Nepal, Africa, Namibia, etc. Their hobby was mountain climbing. They had tried their luck climbing Mount Kilimanjaro as well as in the Himalayas, the Andes, and other ranges. We stayed in touch via e-mail and telephone until not long ago, when family concerns, old-age ailments, and differing political ideologies led me to put a stop to it.

If you like luxurious hotels, you would love to stay at Le Royal Meridien. "Situated on a pristine stretch of private beach with stunning views of the Arabian Gulf and Dubai Marina, Le Royal Meridien Beach Resort and Spa is one of Dubai's premier resorts in Jumeira – the heart of New Dubai. With the clear blue waters of the Arabian Gulf literally on your doorstep, this resort offers a wonderful home for your visit to Dubai" (Travcoa).

It did not disappoint. It was absolutely opulent inside and out, and we were treated like royalty. However, I was more interested in Dubai proper than what this six-star Shangri-La resort had to offer, and I will share Travcoa's introduction to the Emirates before moving on:

Epitomizing an oil-rich sheikhdom isn't a bad life, but what Dubai really wants to be is an entertainer. Its act includes big-time horse races and sporting events, a month long shopping festival and a skyline that commands attention.

Until the 1800s, Dubai was a quiet settlement, and its people survived on fishing, pearl diving and agriculture. In the 1830s, it was taken over by the Bani Yas tribe led by the Maktoum family (who still rules the emirate today). When Sheikh Maktoum bin Hasher Al Maktoum, who was ruler at the time, granted tax concessions to foreign traders, development began and a trading empire grew, based on gold, silver, spices and pearls. A mix of Arab, Persian and Indian traders settled in the growing town and established Dubai's position as a serious trading center.

The importance of Dubai's large creek as a natural harbor was recognized, and the city began to specialize in the import and export of goods. Dubai and its neighboring emirates accepted the protection of the British in 1892, and the region became known as The Trucial Coast (Trucial States) among Europeans.

The discovery of oil in Dubai in 1966 led to improvements in the city's infrastructure, as well as the education, housing and health care of its citizens. In 1968, Britain announced it would withdraw from the region. The various ruling sheikhs recognized that they would be a more powerful force if they united. In 1971, the British departed and the federation of the United Arab Emirates (U.A.E.) were formed. . . . Dubai and the U.A.E. have been models of stability in a deeply unsettled region. . . . Crown Prince Sheikh Mohammed continues to push the city towards yet greater levels of ambition, and despite his absolute rule (the U.A.E. is the only nation in the region not to have introduced democratic representation at any level of government) he continues to enjoy high levels of popularity.

Though oil has been crucial to Dubai's development since the late 1960s, trade has always been a cornerstone of the nation's economy, which picked up speed in the 1970s and 1980s with the advent of the Gulf Cooperation Council (GCC) and the construction of major ports in the city. In the 1990s Dubai invested heavily in the tourist industry, building dozens of new five-star hotels and resorts and unleashing a massive marketing campaign that brought millions of tourist dollars flooding into the city. Over the past decade, a huge property boom – fueled in part by the announcement that expats were to be allowed to invest in real estate – has led to unprecedented levels of development. Flagship projects such as the Dubai Palms, the world's largest artificial islands, keep investment levels high, allowing Dubai the option of relying on the real estate market when the U.A.E.'s oil money eventually runs dry.

Dubai's rapid transformation has left it with a slice of old Arabia and a chunk of modern infrastructure. It also has a multinational population, attracting people from east and west. You'll find souks selling gold jewelry and traditional wares not far from modern shopping centers selling electronics and luxury items. You'll see wind towers and minarets rising up from old neighborhoods, dwarfed in turn by office and hotel towers. However, the biggest contrast can be seen in its landscape: A beautiful coastline and beaches are backed by an equally expansive desert.

We arrived in Dubai shortly after noon, and the first thing we saw on the way to the hotel was an impressive conglomeration of the glitziest architectural high-rises lining the streets. Wow!

My suite at the resort was spacious, with a king-size bed and satin sheets, a balcony overlooking the Arabian Gulf, and an immaculate white-sand beach with palm trees practically at the doorstep. Nothing was left to the imagination. It was all there, reeking of opulence. But my ring had not yet arrived, and after I talked with the German manager in Oman, it was decided that the ring would be delivered express to the States. They felt it would be safer. Indeed, I did receive the ring about ten days after I returned to Bloomington. Thank you, Yvonne!

Our morning tour began with a trip to the Madinat Jumeirah Souk, located on the beach next to the world-famous, sixty-floor Burj Al-Arab hotel. The souk is a new complex with traditional Arab-style architecture. The main purpose of our visit was obviously for us to have an ideal photo stop and relish the view of the "infamous" Burj Al-Arab, where a few in our group later opted to extend their trip just to spend a couple nights in the world's most luxurious hotel – for the bargain price of $2,500 a night. Why not, if you can afford the luxury of driving a Rolls Royce and a Bentley with the help of a chauffeur back home? The outlay for the Burj Al-Arab is chicken feed by comparison. Rumor has it that it is not really a seven-star hotel. Sam Wollaston, in the *Guardian*, described the hotel as "fabulous, hideous, and the very pinnacle of tackiness – like Vegas after a serious, no-expense-spared, sheik-over." I tend to agree with that description. They provide butler service, which we also had at the Royal Meridien for a few dollars less. I for one did not go into the Madinat Souk, which some had said did not really give you an "Arabian" feeling, whatever that means. But I took a bunch of fabulous pictures and am thus guilty of being one of those who give the hotel its reputation as the most photographed. I found the helicopter landing pad on the roof especially insane. The hotel, mimicking the sail of a dhow, reminded me very vaguely of the Sydney Opera House. We were told it stands on an artificial island 920 feet away from Jumeirah Beach and is connected to the mainland by a private curving bridge.

After the Burj, we took a step back in time, to the days before electricity and air-conditioning, by going to the oldest residential areas in the city, including the traditional Bastakiya district, where authentic wind-tower houses originally built by wealthy merchants were still present. We had seen wind towers in Kuwait, but this one seemed much bigger and taller. If I remember correctly, our attractive Russian guide explained that while the main door of the house was large, the inner door was short, because when men enter the house they should bend down so as not to face women directly. This district was named after Iran's Bastak County. Many of the residents had emigrated from Iran but moved back to Arabia later. The district also lies along the important Dubai Creek and features narrow lanes and the oldest existing building in Dubai, the Al-Fahidi Fort, which houses the Dubai Museum. The fort was built around 1787 to guard the desert approaches to the town.

The Dubai Museum was quite captivating. Life-size dioramas depicted traditional Arabian life before the discovery of oil, and a date palm caught my special attention. The museum also included local antiquities and artifacts from African and Asian countries that traded with Dubai. In front of the museum stood a big dhow and a couple of smaller dugouts. Leave it to Travcoa. They had arranged for us to ride in an *abra*, a traditional wooden boat used to transport people across the Dubai Creek. It was just big enough for our group, and I felt just like passengers must have (ten on each side) in olden times. Curiously enough, we all faced outward, and I appreciated that a canopy sheltered the short platform around the cockpit. We ended up at another souk oasis where, instead of gold, I stocked up on several boxes of juicy, plump Iranian dates to bring home.

That afternoon we climbed into Arabian Adventures' four-wheel-drive jeep for a sundown desert safari. It entailed a wild off-road drive through an area of hilly red sand dunes in the Dubai Desert. It was off the main road to Hatta. Just as we hit the dunes, one of our female passengers threw something of a fit. She did not want to continue and insisted that someone take her back to the hotel. I could not take it and distanced myself. I felt sorry for Yvonne and the driver. They finally calmed her down, and instead of sitting on a dune to wait for us, she came along. We had four jeeps. Our driver was excellent, and this roller-coaster ride up and down the dunes at sundown was great fun and for me ended much too soon. We stopped at a place where a herd of camels, along with their masters from a Bedouin camp, had gathered smack in the midst of the exciting rusty-red sand dunes. They were ready to give us a ride at sundown, which I, having ridden camels in India and Morocco, just could not miss. Taking fabulous panorama shots of the setting sun in the dunes from atop a camel is something one does not get a chance to do very often. Awesome! It was another adventuresome experience, which I cherished just as much as I did meeting the falconers who awaited us out there in never-never land. The young, very handsome Arab, after giving a brief introduction to the raising and training of falcons, performed a spellbinding demonstration with his beautiful bird. The falcon flew away and returned like an arrow, and we had the rare experience of admiring the proud animal as it stood in front of us on the desert sand, confident but quiet. I had learned earlier that this very expensive sport reminds many Emiratis of their Bedouin heritage. Out there, the Arab also told us that wild falcons are used to chase away pesky pigeons at airports, as well as crows and seabirds wherever they are not wanted. It makes sense inasmuch as falcons devour one pound of meat each day, preferably that of other birds. I forgot to ask whether the Venetians had ever haggled with them over their pigeons on St. Mark's Square.

While we were kept busy with the falcons, several Arabs were setting up a picnic on a Persian carpet nearby, and there was an opportunity to participate in henna painting and even take a "hubbly bubbly" puff on a hooka, which I had tried earlier. – It was great to relax and chat with fellow travelers and just to relish our shared adventure. The wine was a welcome beverage out there in the Arabian Desert. Thus, it was truly another Arabian Night! If you like to fantasize, imagine Scheherazade sitting in the center of the colorful Persian carpet, spinning her spellbinding tales.

I doubt one of her tales involved the indoor ski resort in Dubai. All you had to do was open your eyes. We did just that when, on the way back, we had persuaded Yvonne to take us to Ski Dubai, the first indoor ski resort in the Middle East, the construction of which began in December 2005. The resort covers an amazing 22,500 square meters, covered with six thousand tons of real snow, all year round. It is insane – especially when you consider that in the middle of the summer, the heat index rises to 140 degrees Fahrenheit; it is so scalding hot you can hardly walk across the street. Most Western expats go home during the summer. You have to see this miracle to believe it. It sits inside a huge glass bubble integrated with what is supposedly the largest mall in the world. Kids were snowboarding, teenagers skiing, and others tobogganing or just playing in the snow. If you get hungry, you can have a bite to eat at the St. Moritz Café at the entrance to Ski Dubai. What else?!

August 1, 2013 – The highest building in the world at 2,722 feet, Burj Khalifa, aka Burj Dubai, under construction when I visited, was completed on October 1, 2009, and is now up.

Sharjah

The next morning, which was actually the last day of the Jewels of Arabia tour, we traveled to the traditional cities of Sharjah (with a population of 678,000) and Ajman (260,000), capitals of two of the seven United Arab Emirates, both located about thirty minutes from Dubai (1,306,000) on the Persian Gulf. "Sharjah offers an impressive array of museums and beautifully restored heritage sites while Ajman embodies the calm and tradition of ancient Arabic culture and a pleasant blend of the old and the new" (Travcoa).

In Sharjah, designated "the cultural city of the Arab world" by UNESCO in 1998, we did not spend more than fifteen minutes at the Cultural Palace Square, on Al-Wahda Road. There, we stopped at the rather impressive King Faisal Mosque, the biggest mosque in Sharjah. We viewed the restored heritage area, which featured traditional local architecture. There were several old buildings, including Sharjah Fort, Sharjah Museum of Islamic Civilization, Sharjah Heritage Museum, and the Old Souk, and I was glad we had the chance to see the area, if only briefly.

Our lunch in a high-rise restaurant, from which we had a stunning view of the city below, was out of this world. It's easy to run out of superlatives in these Arab regions; they compete fiercely with one another, especially within the UAE. Each emirate wants to trump the next. And they have to show off their wealth through their skyscrapers, towers, hotels, and mega real-estate developments. The palm project goes way over the top, but it appears to attract those who themselves suffer from delusions of grandeur, like the flame-haired US real-estate and gambling kingpin Donald Trump, who has had big plans for Palm Jumeirah Island, the man-made archipelago off the Dubai coast. But it looks as though his bubble has burst, just as it has for others due to the economic downturn, which hit Dubai pretty hard. No problem – they'll survive!

May 12, 2016 – And survive he did. He is presently pulling out all the stops to be nominated as the Republican candidate for president of the United States.

Ajman

As we drove along the coast to Sharjah and Ajman, it was obvious that even these small emirates were on a roller-coaster building frenzy. The design of each skyscraper strove to top that of the next. They were round, triangular, square, rectangular, pyramid shaped, or whatever the imagination could concoct. As in Beijing and Shanghai, many cranes reached high into the sky, and construction will be in progress for a long time. While the high-rises and skyscrapers in the UAE can perhaps compete with those in Shanghai in terms of design, they cannot compete in quantity. Anyhow – that's about all I remember of Ajman.

I was glad to have the afternoon free, because I had invited my Indian "train friend" Prabhat, who had a good engineering job with one of the top construction companies in Dubai, for a visit. He was in charge of building large bridges, of which the UAE needs plenty. It was so nice to greet him in my room at Le Royal Meridian, and I really appreciated that he made the effort to visit, even if briefly. He had come with a company car and a chauffeur. He told me how difficult it was to pass a driving test in Dubai. We got to know each other a little better, talked about our respective families, travels, etc., and before he left I took a nice picture of him standing on the balcony with Dubai's skyscraper-dominated skyline and the Arabian Gulf in the background. So long, amigo. He was thirty-eight years old at that time and had come to Dubai to make big money, which he planned to save for a home for his wife and son in India. When the market crashed not long after we met, he too was worried about his job, but he eventually survived. I was not surprised, because I knew he was a superb engineer.

In the evening, we had a gala dinner, followed by a gala farewell meeting. The food and champagne – and whatever else one could wish for – were incredible. Everybody was dressed in their flashy, elegant best. Two gay travelers from California had too much to drink. One of them made a pass at me in the elevator on the way up to my room, which I thought a bit weird, but I managed to escape gracefully. This was the last Arabian Night of the Jewels of Arabia tour.

I wonder if the couple who owned the beef-jerky outfit somewhere on the West Coast, if the stunning model, TV actress, and beauty manager at *Vogue* magazine and her realty-group manager, also from New York, both of whom added a night at Burj Al-Arab, if the divorced Korean MD Kyoung, who had inherited a fortune from a Korean aunt and went on big shopping sprees, and if the bachelor patent lawyer from Hollywood, who continued to Yemen in a flashy black limousine, are still alive. And I wonder if any of my travel companions, many of whom had taken as many as twelve trips with Travcoa, had signed up for yet another adventure. I am constantly being bombarded with impressive catalogues from the exclusive travel agency, but so far have not found a trip that really excites me. Sorry, I have been to most of the places for much less.

On the flight home, which involved a dreadful stopover in London, where one always has to struggle through endless lines at passport control, I was tempted to check out the first-class section to see if any of the passengers were hiding a falcon under their seat to smuggle back as a souvenir. It's a story I had heard somewhere about first-class passengers – that is, that they like to bring back falcons to show off in the States.

AUSTRALIA – MS SAPPHIRE PRINCESS

Sydney

It was high time that I took a trip Down Under. Not long after I had returned from my journey to Japan, China, and Thailand, I began to entertain the idea of inviting Peter and Eric to join me on a Christmas cruise to Australia and New Zealand on the MS *Sapphire Princess*. They appeared to have liked our cruise to the Greek Isles in 2001, so why not go to the South Pacific? The boys were excited when I proposed the cruise and readily accepted the invite. The process of coordinating the trip was at times a bit complicated. I must say, though, that they were both very helpful, especially with flight and precruise arrangements, and agreed to pay for certain extras, such as alcoholic beverages and some shore excursions. Instead of joining me on a six-day precruise trip in Australia, they had opted to spend a few extra days in Sydney.

I left Bloomington on December 16, 2004, and flew from Indianapolis, via Los Angeles, to Sydney, where I arrived the next morning. Thanks to frequent-flyer miles, my round-trip ticket to Australia was free. The MS *Princess* had arranged for transport from the airport to the very nice Four Seasons hotel, located in the historic Rocks area. I had a breathtaking view of the Opera House and the Sydney Harbour Bridge from my room. What more could I have wished for?

After a brief lunch at the hotel, our group met with the guide for a four-hour sightseeing tour of subtropical Sydney, the thriving harbor-side metropolis with a distinct European flair, populated by around five million people. We learned that "the land was originally the preserve of the Aboriginal people of the Dharawal, Dharung and Kuring-gai language groups and that in 1770 Captain Cook took possession of Australia for the British when he landed at Botany Bay, and that in 1788 Captain Arthur Phillip founded the first settlement to the north of Botany Bay on the magnificent foreshores of Port Jackson, or Sydney Harbour as it has come to be known" (*Sapphire Princess* brochure). It was a special thrill to see the stunning Sydney Harbour on such a beautiful, cloudless day. The South Pacific mirrored the blue of the skies above, and the sailboats on the horizon, together with the white sails of the Sydney Opera, located near the Sydney Bridge across the harbor, provided the extra accent for a picture-perfect shot. It was easy to visualize Mrs. Macquarie, wife of Major-General Lachlan Macquarie, governor of New South Wales from 1810 to 1821, sitting on the sandstone bench located on a peninsula in this harbor and enjoying the great view while on the lookout for an approaching ship. It was a peaceful moment, and the flowers, shrubs, and lawns of the park were vibrant, lush, and well tended.

The guide took us to the kilometer-long Bondi Beach, one of Australia's most famous and one of the world's best-known beaches. It is extraordinary when you are actually there, walking on the immaculate white sand and watching the blue waves roll up on the gently sloped beach. It rivals Copacabana, Cancún, and several beaches in Hawaii. I treated myself to a tasty ice-cream cone, despite the fact that it was shockingly expensive.

I had arranged a brief get-together with Peter and Eric, who were not coming along with me to Ayres Rock, Alice Springs, and Cairns, after the welcome reception in the hotel. It felt great to see them again. Both had grown and matured since I last saw them, and I was proud to take them on this special trip. Eric was working for Starwood and had been able to get a very special deal at one of their hotels. We sat in the lobby, and after discussing our plans, we hugged and wished each other good luck until we would meet again on the evening of December 23, onboard the *Princess*.

Ayres Rock

Our Quantas Air flight landed in Ayres Rock in the late morning, and we were transported swiftly to our premium Sails in the Desert hotel, named after the soaring white sails that crown its roof. It simply took my breath away, because it was as unique a hotel as I had ever seen. The interior decor reflected Aboriginal heritage and culture, with a gallery in the lobby and striking artwork throughout the hotel, including our rooms.

Shortly after lunch, the minibus took us on our first Uluru (Ayres Rock) National Park sightseeing tour. Our guide made sure we all had the appropriate nets attached to our sun hats to keep away the millions of pesky little flies and mosquitos, which he was sure would annoy us. It goes without saying that it was scorching hot outside.

We could spot from far away the Red Centre Uluru, the great monolith, 5.5 miles in circumference and rising 377 yards above a wide, sandy floodplain. For some reason, Ayres Rock had not been high on my list of priorities, but since I was close enough, I did not want to skip it either. Somehow it grew on me, and eventually, the longer I observed it and the more I learned about it, it had an overwhelming effect. Most of all, I had no idea it was so gigantic.

I think everybody in my group decided against climbing the Rock. We were told that the Anangu prefer that visitors respect their culture and not climb it, but that they may if they wish. Instead, we walked around the Rock to study many of the caves and unusual rock formations and continued to explore more of Uluru National Park. We visited the thirty-six huge, mysterious domes and the spectacular rock formations at Mount Olga, a region leased by Australia from the Aboriginal people. Springs, water holes, rock caves, and ancient paintings, among other natural phenomena, surprised us. *Muy interesante!*

Of course, a visit to Ayres Rock is not complete without experiencing the magnificent sunset and the brilliant changes of color that take place over this gigantic sacred monolith. Taking as many pictures as possible of this quintessential image of the Australian outback is a must, and you can bet I did just that! – Quite a few people spread out opposite the Rock. I looked for and found a little stool, which I positioned for some picture-perfect shots. I also stood in line for a sampling of hors d'oeuvres and a glass of sparkling champagne, which I sipped while conversing with a nice young couple from France in French. They had plans to return in the morning to watch the sunrise.

When the sunset began to affect the color of the rock, and while I scanned the already darkened expanse of this remote, flat, arid area of Australia's outback with the eternal horizon in the distance, everybody stopped talking, pointed their cameras toward the monolith, and started clicking. It was magical to experience this fascinating spectacle. I wished I could have walked around it, but had to be content with being more or less stationary. Of course, there were no clouds and thus no rain. Ayres Rock turned out to be another high point of my travels.

On our Liru tour the next day, we spent a few hours meandering through bush land near the base of Uluru. We learned more about the distinctive Aboriginal way of life during a visit to the Cultural Centre; retraced the path of the Liru ancestors through unique bush land to Uluru, and saw the scar left on the Rock during their battle with Kuniua thousands of years ago. We listened closely as our guide spoke about the tragic fate of the emu thief Lungkata (the blue-tongued lizard man), whose body we saw lying at the base of Uluru. We paid attention to our guide's demonstrations of ancient bush skills, such as making *kiti* (bush glue), starting a fire without matches, and carving wooden tools with a single sharpened stone. Our guide explained and translated whatever the Aboriginals uttered. It was an informative and fascinating introduction to the region's native culture. Several in my group attempted to imitate a couple of their performances, but soon gave up trying.

Alice Springs

Shortly after an early breakfast at the Sails in the Desert resort, we were picked up by our air-conditioned bus for the five-hour drive through the "rugged beauty" of the Outback. I was a little baffled. The pesky flies had not plagued me at Uluru, and I did not spot a single kangaroo in that vast, arid countryside. We stopped at a place where a herd of camels stood ready for a brief ride, available for a small fee. I opted to walk around the grounds to look at the other camels and a couple of dingoes stretched out in a shady spot. A guy about to feed the "ships of the desert" told me that camels were used in central Australia during the construction of the Overland Telegraph Line. They were instrumental in supplying goods to Alice Springs and to cattle and sheep stations. I had no idea they even had camel races and camelback polo in Alice Springs (a small town named after a nearby spring). Why not?

Australia – MS Sapphire Princess

We stayed at the pleasant Crowne Plaza Hotel and rose early to be taken by bus to the airport for the flight to Cairns. We had a few stops to make on the way. One of the stops, after an overview of Alice Springs, was a visit to the best-preserved telegraph station in Australia. At the entrance was a sign that read, "Connecting Adelaide and the rest of Australia, through Darwin, with England by means of a single wire in 1872, the Overland Telegraph line was one of the greatest engineering achievements of the nineteenth century." Amazing.

After walking through the few humble rooms at the station, I stayed behind and chatted with an Aboriginal who spoke English very well. He had my undivided attention as he lamented the discriminatory practices against the Aboriginals pursued between 1869 and 1969. During those times, church missions and federal and state government agencies "removed" – that is, stole – children from their Aboriginal parents without having to establish that they were in any way neglected or mistreated. What happened to them after they were taken was too terrible to repeat here. I had never heard of these practices and was, of course, shocked, to say the least. I was equally shocked when I learned on this trip that a primary reason for the British settlement of Australia was the establishment of a number of penal colonies in order to alleviate pressure on their overburdened prisons. All of that happened during the late eighteenth and early nineteenth centuries. Depressing!

If I had not gotten so involved with the Aboriginal, I would not have missed what the others in my group saw: a bunch of kangaroos. I was ticked off because they could have called me.

To be fair, I must say that in Australia, discrimination against Aboriginals, although it has not been eliminated, has been greatly reduced. Thus, I was very pleased to see the Royal Flying Doctor Service facility in Alice Springs on the way to the airport.

The Flying Doctor, a not-for-profit organization, "is an emergency and primary health care service for those living in rural, remote and regional areas of Australia. It provides health care to people who are unable to access a hospital or general practice due to the vast distances of the Outback." And it is "the story of how medicine, aviation and radio have been jointly put to work in the service of the people who live, work and travel in the remote inland of Australia" (Brochure).

A representative gave a brief lecture, showed a film about the service in action, and answered questions. I was glad to have had an opportunity to hear about these very worthwhile services. It reminded me vaguely of Doctors without Borders.

Cairns

It was a comparatively brief flight to Cairns, and our five-star Hotel Cairns International was located right in the heart of the town of about 159,000. As my spacious room had a balcony overlooking the harbor, I was happy.

Cairns is a regional city in Far North Queensland, Australia, and was named after William Wellington Cairns (then the governor of Queensland). It is located about 1,500 miles from Sydney, by road. The temperature was in the lower 30s, which was about what I had expected. Cairns is known to experience a tropical climate.

We all took the precruise tour, because we knew we would spend at least a day seeing the Great Barrier Reef. A high-speed catamaran picked us up shortly after breakfast and took us to an island that would serve as our home base for various activities focused on what the Great Barrier Reef had to offer. I decided to first book a helicopter flight to Green Island. It was an amazing adventure. The aerial views from the rainforest to False Cape, and continuing over the Great Barrier Reef and Green Island, surpassed my expectations. The colors below, the shades of blue and green, were sublime and unlike anything I had ever seen. By the time we were ready to land, however, it began to rain cats and dogs. And when I arrived at the lounge, I was soaking wet. Someone brought a towel for me. Being so wet while eating lunch was not the most pleasant feeling. I should have brought a bathing suit. I did not bring one, because I had not wanted to go snorkeling out there, as so many tourists did.

To get closer to the corals and multicolored fish, I took a semisubmersible submarine. The *Princess* literature had this to say about the reef: "It is actually a network of over 2900 different reefs, each made up of 400+ different species of coral. We could find over 1500 different types of tropical fish, not to mention thousands of different mollusks, sea sponges and echinoderms." Well, I would have had to spend much more time out there to see all that. Instead, I saw comparatively few fish, and since the sky was overcast, the colors of the fish were not as vibrant as they would have been had the sun been shining. Nevertheless, I got a good feel for this natural miracle and what it had to offer. I was content just to have gotten a glimpse of what I had marveled at when watching documentaries about the Great Barrier Reef's marine life on TV. It is truly a wondrous and remarkable phenomenon, which many people on this planet will never be lucky enough to witness.

Sydney

Our flight from Cairns to Sydney arrived in the afternoon, and we were transferred directly to the *Sapphire Princess* to embark, according to plan, on December 23, 2004. I had booked outside cabins on this ship, a new one in their fleet. With an international gross register tonnage of 115,875, a holding capacity of 2,670 passengers, that is, seven hundred more than the *Dawn Princess*, on which I had taken my stepdaughter Liesl to Alaska in 1999, and some eighteen decks total, it was quite a monster of a ship and not exactly one I was crazy about, since I prefer the smaller versions. Be that as it may, I had had a good experience with Princess Cruises and thus received certain privileges as well. The deciding factor was the time, and this particular cruise was advertised as an inaugural cruise. I was quite certain the boys would find enough to entertain themselves without my input. My cabin was on Deck Plaza 5, with an ocean view, and I was glad it was not on the top decks. I had plenty of room since, as always, I paid extra for single occupancy. I had nothing to complain about. The boys were on the same deck but not directly next door to my cabin, which was how I had wanted it.

Having been on many cruises, I was not really surprised by the glitz and glamour this giant boasted, which were apparent the minute I set foot on it. And since I have already described the ship in some detail, I will refrain from being repetitive. An English naturalist on the *Yamal* quite fittingly termed these ocean cruisers "gin palaces." Be that as it may, I was happy to have pulled this trip off for the boys. And they were grateful for this gift: a stunningly beautiful bouquet, which they had ordered, greeted me in my cabin. As soon as we reconnected, we examined each other's cabins and proceeded upstairs to the deck, where the welcoming and inauguration party was scheduled to unfold.

While we sipped champagne at the party, the boys gave me a rundown of their days in Sydney. They had a marvelous time, a highlight of which was sailing the harbor with a father and his daughter, with whom Peter had connected via e-mail. It was ideal, since both boys were avid and accomplished sailors, just like their dad. I was so impressed that they had taken the initiative. They were also invited to their new friends' home for dinner, as I recall. Another highlight of their Sydney visit was climbing the Sydney Harbour Bridge, which is a steel through-arch bridge that spans the harbor and carries rail, vehicular, bicycle, and pedestrian traffic. It has spanned the harbor since 1932 (the year of my birth), took nine years to construct, and is one of the longest one-bow bridges in the world. Its nickname is "Coat Hanger" (Brochure). The boys were excited! – When they wanted to climb the bridge, the tickets were sold out. And they were very expensive. But lady luck was on their side. Two couples had two tickets, valued at $90 each, which they gave the boys as a gift. They were thrilled and swiftly proceeded to climb up the bridge, all the way to the top of the arch (440 feet from water level). As a thank-you gesture, they later invited the couples out to dinner, and a few years later they met with one of the couples in New York. I was jealous, because they also got to see the Opera House, a multivenue performing-arts center, from up close. The Opera House took a long time to build due to competition hassles surrounding both its design and construction, not to mention its astronomical cost of $102 million instead of the original estimate of $7 million. It was opened in 1973 instead of 1963. I would have loved to attend a performance in the impressive concert hall, but it was not meant to be. It's all right, because we experienced something very special that night. Since it was our ship's inaugural trip from Sydney, they stunned us with a most spectacular symphony of fireworks in the harbor, with the sails of the Opera House lit up in the background. It was a Christmas present I will never forget, and I can guarantee Doc would have been much pleased to see that two of his offspring and his widow had found each other and were happy.

Melbourne

December 24 was spent at sea, until the *Princess* docked in Port Phillip Bay of Melbourne, Victoria, early on the 25th. I was elated to see mountain ridges in the distance.

We had booked optional excursions for Melbourne and spent most of Christmas Day casually exploring this very clean city with many wonderful parks and gardens, all beautifully tended. We took Melbourne's Golden Mile Heritage Walk to see some of the city's historic buildings, great vestiges of nineteenth-century architecture that were built following the discovery of gold. They testify to a prosperous age, as do the Neo-Gothic skyscrapers on Collins Street, among others. And since very little traffic and few tourists occupied the streets and parks, we spent several hours exploring the Royal Botanic Gardens, considered one of the most significant botanical gardens in Australia ever since it was established in 1846. "The gardens are home to over 12,000 different species of plants and are a natural sanctuary for native wildlife" (Brochure). They are truly exquisite, and if you are a lover of nature, you will be stopped again and again by a flowering shrub, an unusual flower, a plant, grasses, or trees and exclaim, "How gorgeous!" If I should ever return, I will make a point of visiting their famous Arts Centre, which was closed. I would also have liked to visit Melbourne University, where one of my fellow students had accepted a position in the German Department and Liesl's mother had spent her junior year abroad.

Peter, Eric, and I had agreed not to meet regularly for breakfast and lunch but instead to do whatever pleased each of us. But we wanted to eat dinners together. The boys were responsible for selecting the restaurant, since there were many to choose from. I had told them to spend the evenings as they desired, since I was not keen on attending all the shows and activities the *Princess* had to offer. No complaints! I had given them a special amount to spend for shore excursions, which meant nobody felt the need to persuade the others to do what he or she wanted.

The *Princess* departed on Sunday, December 26, 2004. On that night, the deadly undersea megathrust earthquake and tsunami occurred in the Indian Ocean. Fortunately, our ship was not noticeably affected, but we watched in horror as the disaster unfolded on our TV monitors.

Tasmania – Hobart

The ship arrived safely at 7:20 a.m. on December 27, 2004, alongside her berth in Hobart, the capital of Australia's island state of Tasmania. Hobart has a population of about 212,000. In case you did not know, this island was once a penal colony. The climate is comparatively mild during the winter, but occasionally one can see snow on the adjacent Mount Wellington (4,170 feet).

I had signed up for the Natural Wonders of Tasmania tour, which started at 8:15 a.m. Our drive followed the scenic and historic Derwent River Valley past hop fields, farming country, and dense rainforest. The park was unusual in that it housed mainly native wildlife. It was commendable to create a park to aid orphaned wildlife. They have breeding programs for endangered species such as eastern quolls – a small marsupial – as well as wombats, wallabies, eastern gray kangaroos, golden possums, squirrel gliders, jet-black Tasmanian devils, and most importantly, a pair of adorable koalas. We were lucky to spot platypuses at play in the river flowing through the park. As we made our way through Mount Field National Park, I felt as though I was walking through a jungle. The world's tallest hardwood trees were amazing. In short, the Tasmanian rainforest, with the spectacular Russell Falls, was something I had not expected.

A brand-new experience was the visit to the Hamilton Sheep Centre, one of the oldest family-operated sheep stations in Tasmania. The meadows of the farm were beautiful, as was the pond on which a flock of ducks was swimming. Here and there in the distance, big herds of sheep grazed. After a good Tasmanian barbeque lunch and a glass of wine, the farmer showed off his two dogs; they rounded up the sheep just as he instructed. Fabulous! It was even more exciting to watch the men shear the sheep. I was amazed at the speed with which they clipped the animals and how they managed to hold them in such a way that they remained still throughout the process.

On the way to the ship, we passed the historic townships of New Norfolk and Hamilton, with their many quaint cottages and gardens, such as Glen Clyde House, built by convicts in 1840.

We spent December 28 and 29 cruising in the Tasman Sea and enjoyed exploring the ship and checking out all it had to offer. I had a chance to admire Peter and Eric playing golf on deck. Eric, who hoped he would come home with a tan, found a nice spot on the sundeck close to the pool and spent quite some time sunbathing. Peter had to avoid the sun because he burned easily. I chatted with the Japanese pianist in the lounge and made sure there was someone to listen to and applaud her very nice performances. When on big ships, I always look for a more or less secluded spot to hang out and just listen to the soothing sounds of the sea, watch the drifting clouds in the sky, and observe the seagulls sailing gracefully above and alongside the ship.

NEW ZEALAND – MS SAPPHIRE PRINCESS

Milford Sound

On December 30, the *Princess* docked briefly at Milford Sound, where those of us who had booked the three-day land excursion to Milford Sound, Queenstown, and Mount Cook National Park disembarked. I had been looking forward to this portion of the trip with great anticipation. New Zealand, in my imagination, was almost tantamount to El Dorado. We disembarked via launch, and I was immediately spellbound by the towering peaks in the sound's dramatic landscape. From our launch, I shot a few panorama pictures of the *Princess* with the mountains in the background. We were transferred to the motor coach for the drive to the small town of Te Anau, located on the South Island, on the eastern shore of New Zealand's second-largest lake. The road followed the swiftly flowing Cleddau River before climbing to the Homer Tunnel. After passing through the 1,200-meter tunnel and over the Homer Saddle, we entered Eglinton Valley and looked toward the beech-covered mountains that framed the distant peaks. The route then passed Lakes Fergus and Gunn before following the shore of Lake Te Anau to the town of the same name, where we enjoyed an early lunch.

We then departed from Te Anau and the Fjordland National Park and traveled across the Five Rivers farming locality to Kingston, situated on the southern tip of Lake Wakatipu. We followed the eastern shoreline of the lake in the shadow of the towering Remarkable Range, partially covered with snow, and crossed the Kawarau River at Frankton, before reaching Queenstown, nestled in the northern shores of beautiful Lake Wakatipu. If I were a skier, I would love to come back sometime to try out the slopes of the Remarkables.

Queenstown

Queenstown is truly a scenic resort town where I would not mind spending a vacation. The Gardens Park Royal Hotel was right on Lake Wakatipu, and I had a lovely room with a balcony and a stunning lake view. Great! During the afternoon, I wandered around Queenstown, and I was surprised to see so many young people, that is, students, out shopping (mainly in sporting-goods stores) or relaxing in sidewalk cafés. Toward evening, I walked a short distance from the hotel to the steamer wharf to board the vintage steamship TSS *Earnslaw*, aka *Lady of the Lake*, for a leisurely cruise to Walter Peak Station. We disembarked and walked to the sophisticated Colonel's Homestead Restaurant for a tasty carvery dinner. The setting sun painted a large area of yellow shrubs (broom) covering the hillside an even deeper gold. I had seen similar shrubs in the Falklands.

A word about the TSS *Earnslaw*: "Launched in 1912, she has been transporting goods for local run-holders and conveying passengers on beautiful Lake Wakatipu for over 90 years. The most visible link to Queenstown's past, the TSS *Earnslaw* is a true icon of Queenstown. Step aboard – watch the stokers fuelling the fireboxes and hear the sound of the steam engines working. Be transported in style on one of our regular departures to Walter Peak High Country Farm" (Brochure). We experienced all that and then some. I was fortunate once again to persuade the nice captain to have a picture taken with me. We were all smiles. Indeed, the evening meal at the Walter Peak High Country Farm Restaurant was unforgettable. Its setting – rolling meadows on which sheep herds were grazing and gardens bursting with pink, climbing rose hedges and many different flowers in full bloom – was exhilarating, as was the nighttime cruise back to Queenstown, her lights glowing in the distance. It was so romantic.

Very early the next morning, we drove to the Kiwi Bird and Wildlife Park for breakfast. A four-seat gondola "bubble car" carried us 1,500 feet up Bob's Peak to the Skyline Chalet for beautiful mountain and lake views. The chalet is tucked away in lush greenery and wooded surroundings. The Kiwi Park was captivating. It is a "hidden sanctuary of trees, bush and native trails" (Brochure). I saw my first kiwi here, which was almost like seeing my first panda. Curious. Since kiwis are flightless birds that spend their days sleeping underground, one has to go early to see them. I also had a chance to admire a tuatara, a reptile endemic to New Zealand, which looks like, but is not, a lizard. Supposedly they were around with the dinosaurs. (Yes, I now am the proud owner of a kiwi replica.) The scenery in the park, which is New Zealand's native forest, was much like the rainforest in Patagonia. The ferns, especially the tree ferns, were huge and lush, and the streams rumbling through reminded me of the glacier streams in the Andes.

After experiencing "Kiwi Magic," the Showscan spectacular, which captured the charm and breathtaking beauty of New Zealand, we returned down the cableway to continue the drive to Mount Cook. Our road went through Arrowtown, an old gold-mining boomtown. The Arrow River was the start of it all. Gold was discovered not far from where the town stands today. We did not pan for the precious metal but continued to our next stop through the dramatic Kawarau Gorge for lunch at a premium winery. After that, we lingered a while at the Kawarau Bridge. It is the world's first bungee site (142 feet high), but though bungee jumping was proclaimed very safe, it was not an exercise I was brave enough to try. To me it looked like sheer madness. However, it was a rather scenic spot. The river below did not look too treacherous, but to me it was not at all inviting. A couple of youngsters were waiting their turn to jump. I chose to take a couple of nice pictures of a patch of lupines next to the bridge and was ready to continue the trip along the Kawarau Gorge through Twizel. It is the closest town to Mount Cook, home to Lake Ruataniwha, Lake Benmore, Lake Pukaki, and Lake Ohau, a breathtakingly scenic region.

Mount Cook

The closer we came to the goal of this special trip to see Mount Cook – the highest mountain in New Zealand, reaching 12,316 feet and lying in the Southern Alps, the mountain range which runs the length of the South Island – the more anxious I became. I wanted to experience this mountain lovers' dream. But I could see nothing of Mount Cook, even when I stood directly at its foot. The thickest fog imaginable hid it. No matter how hard we stared, none in our group saw even a tiny portion of the rugged land of ice and rock, the nineteen peaks over three thousand feet high, not to mention Aoraki, Mount Cook itself. I could have cried, and I ended up buying a postcard of the snow-covered mountain, which I pasted in my album. I felt better when I heard that even Captain James Cook, who first surveyed and circumnavigated the islands of New Zealand in 1770, and after whom the mountain was named, did not see it either. He also missed the entrance to Milford Sound, "the entrance to one of the world's most dramatic wonders" (Brochure), which I saw in its fullest splendor.

I felt better when, later on the trip, the weather improved – but it did not improve enough for us to see the mountain. I began to focus on the countryside along the shores of Lake Pukaki. The further we left "the Cook" behind, the nicer the weather turned. In short, the countryside was so enchanting I quickly forgot what I had come to see in vain. Instead, I felt uplifted by the vast fields of purple, white, and yellow mountain lupines blanketing the slopes along the roadside. The lupines, as well as large patches of crimson fireweed and Indian paintbrush, made me smile. It all reminded me of the scenery I encountered when traveling in Patagonia and Alaska.

By the way, if you ever make it to Mount Cook, say hello from Christa. If you can actually see it, it will be a bewitching experience! If you can afford it, try to stay at the Hermitage Hotel, which is considered New Zealand's most luxurious mountain retreat; it is located in a "natural mountain amphitheater, Aoraki/Mt Cook" (Brochure). Judging by their restroom for ladies, where I had the pleasure of washing my hands in a marble, counter-like sink, the hotel must be supermodern all the way around. The water flows down on a long marble slab instead of into an old-fashioned sink. It was designed in a Scandinavian country. By now, such sinks may be common in upscale hotels. I thought it was super cool. Yes, they did have warm water, and it did not cost a dime.

We arrived in Twizel in time for dinner, and I am sorry, but I do not remember the name of the hotel, despite the fact that it was New Year's Eve. I might have remembered it if they had served us a complimentary glass of champagne. *Nada*! I do recall the drive from Twizel through Mackenzie Country to Lake Tekapo. Our first stop was at the Church of the Good Shepherd, a simple stone structure built in 1935 to commemorate the Mackenzie Country pioneers.

To give you a little insight into Mackenzie, I quote two excerpts from my brochure:

In the mid-1840s, James Mackenzie came to New Zealand by way of Australia, as many others did, to find "a pot of gold" at the end of the rainbow. He was the first European to discover the now-known "Mackenzie Pass," the "Mackenzie Basin," and the "Lindis Pass."

The Maori had known of these plains for centuries, which once were covered in ancient totara trees. In times past the giant flightless bird (similar to an ostrich), the Moa (who they hunted for food), had roamed these plains, feeding on the tussock, and various grasses, but had become extinct before the settlers arrived. Legend tells of how Mackenzie and his faithful dog Friday, who was trained (as legend has it) not to bark, stole whole mobs of sheep from the coastal farmers, drove them undetected through the secret mountain pass to the high country plains, then South to Dunedin, where he sold them for a handsome profit. A journey of some 300 or so miles, just he and his dog.

If you are interested in finding out what eventually happened to the red-haired roughneck Mackenzie and his dog Friday, dig deeper and enjoy! I guarantee it's quite a story!

I can also guarantee that the region is just beautiful. To see the yellow-green rolling pastures dotted with large, grazing herds of sheep is to experience a distinct, harmonious calm. The Church of the Good Shepherd, close to the shores of Lake Tekapo, is a sight to behold. The highland region in the background is equally soothing. I smiled as I sized up the famous sheepdog statue on the lake's edge, which commemorates the "hardy-mustering dogs without the help of which the grazing of this mountainous country would be impossible" (Brochure).

When you look through the altar window of the humble stone church, you will be stunned by its awe-inspiring view of the turquoise lake and rugged mountain ranges. The New Zealanders love to show off their merino-sheep station's trails and gardens, as well as their sheep dogs at work, their sheep shearing, and their wool spinning. Here, we were treated to another demonstration after a tasty country lunch at the station. Good job, doggies!

Christchurch

Our journey continued toward Christchurch by way of Geraldine through the Canterbury Plains farmlands, which looked like a patchwork quilt made with every imaginable shade of green, alternating with patches of bright yellow due to millions of thriving dandelions. To my surprise, we passed huge herds of deer raised for consumption, mostly in Europe. We had a comparatively brief sightseeing tour of Christchurch, the largest city on the South Island of New Zealand. The guide dropped us off to spend a couple of hours at the International Antarctic Centre.

I might have found it more interesting if I had not yet been to Antarctica. The exhibits, video presentations, laser holograms, and stereo sound brought the frozen continent to life. A walk into a real snow cave turned out to be moderately cold. Souvenir shoppers had an abundance of gifts, including stuffed penguins, to choose from. For me they had lost their appeal, and I was looking forward to returning to the ship at 6:00 p.m., before dinner and our departure.

I now regret that I had a rather superficial encounter with Christchurch, New Zealand's most English city, with an Old World ambiance. Only a few months ago, on June 11, 2011, another earthquake occurred in Christchurch, not quite a year after the quakes in September 2010.

Having myself been to Antarctica twice, I was interested to learn that Christchurch has a history of involvement in Antarctic exploration – both R. F. Scott and Ernest Shackleton used the port of Littleton, where the *Princess* was docked, as a departure point for expeditions.

It was nice to reconnect with Eric and Peter for a New Year's dinner, and we were all eager to relate our various experiences. The boys had taken a bus from Milford Sound to Queenstown, where they spent the night and watched fireworks over the lake on New Year's Eve. On New Year's Day, they rented a car and headed for their pipeline bungee jump outside Queenstown. On a scale of one to ten, Eric said, the scariest part was forcing yourself to jump, a seven on the scale. He was not sure if they pushed him, but remembered that it went fast and that "the part when you are in the air and falling isn't scary." Eric said it was the first time he ever drove on the "wrong side of the road" and that there were "lots of sheep and one-lane bridges and lupines."

Wellington

My minitour, called Wellington Town & Country, started at 8:30 a.m. on the dot. The weather was pleasant, and as we drove through New Zealand's capital and past such sights as the Parliament buildings, Old St. Paul's Cathedral, and the town hall, the guide had something to say about all of them.

He emphasized the unique blend of architecture of the four Parliament buildings, the Edwardian neoclassical Parliament House, the Victorian Gothic Parliamentary Library, the Beehive (also known as the Executive Wing), and the modern Bowen House, which accommodates many members of Parliament and their support staff. St. Paul's Cathedral, which is the church of the Anglican Diocese of Wellington and seat of its bishop, was completed in 1998 and is thus modern in style.

Our visit to the Southward Car Museum turned out to be more interesting than I had anticipated. It boasts a collection of over 350 vehicles, three aircraft, and various other exhibits, including motorcycles, bicycles, fire engines, etc. The collection was started by a successful businessman, Sir Len Southward, and his wife, Lady Vera Southward, and it opened in December 1979. I found Marlene Dietrich's 1934 Cadillac Town Cabriolet and a 1915 Indianapolis race car most exciting. Those who are curious will find an amazing collection of vintage household items. Maybe, if my 1986 baby Mercedes 190 E survives, someone there will be happy to acquire it once I depart. Curiously enough, Sir Southward died shortly after I visited his museum, on February 28, 2004. On December 16, 2010, someone stole his original driver's license and his private collection of old, commemorative coins and banknotes. I couldn't care less.

Like so many tours, this one led us to a sheep-shearing farm, an experience that was not as interesting as it had been on my first visit. I was much happier when they let us walk around and enjoy Lady Norwood's Rose Garden, which boasts over 1,200 varieties of the most gorgeous roses, blazing in many different shades of color. It was an intoxicating experience. No, I did not attempt to count the many varieties. It was out of this world, even though roses in New Zealand are nonnative. The Begonia House, a Victorian-style glasshouse, was just as beautiful, and I was drawn to Henry Moore's sculpture in particular. I declare, their ice-cream cones tasted delicious.

There could have been no better finale for the tour than our drive up Mount Victoria (or "Mount Vic"), about six hundred feet high, for an impressive panorama shot of Wellington from the very spot Peter Jackson had used twice as a location in his film trilogy *The Lord of the Rings*. It turned out to be a "stunning vista of forested peninsulas, a bustling waterfront, dramatic cliff-side homes and fine Victorian Buildings" (Brochure), all of it lying below us. I must agree with those who compare it to San Francisco, and I would have loved to see it at night.

The boys had decided to eat at the Italian restaurant that evening. Everything was very good, except for the focaccia bread, which revealed a big piece of tissue paper while I was chewing. I complained, of course, but without any result. That evening, the boys also succeeded in persuading me to join them at a trivia competition. I was very reluctant to go, because I am not good at that sort of game. But, surprise, I knew one of the answers and helped us win a bottle of champagne. Never say never. It was a nice ending to the evening. Before retiring to my cabin, I went to the sundeck to take in the sunset. The sky looked like an ocean of misty orange. Dark-gray strands of clouds above and the black sea beneath framed the descending golden globe.

Tauranga

At 7:43 a.m. on January 4, 2004, our vessel docked at the lovely port city of Tauranga. With 67,000 inhabitants, the city is situated on the "Bay of Plenty so named by Captain Cook when he first saw it in 1769 and replenished his ship's provisions, thanks to the prosperous Maori villages of the region" (Brochure). Tauranga is also the "gateway to Rotorua – a geothermal wonderland that is the heart of Maori culture" (Brochure). We started our Rotorua Maori Experience/Thermal Reserve tour at 8:30 a.m. A guide native to the Whakarewarewa Thermal Springs Reserve took us through Te Puke, the heart of kiwi-fruit country, past acres and acres of kiwi orchards. Kiwis grow on vines, and the orchards reminded me vaguely of vineyards in South Africa, Europe, and South America. The fruits, curiously enough, are shaped like the birds they are named after – they look like giant grapes.

We were surprised by the pools of boiling mud, spouting geysers, silica terraces, and steam vents of the "Whaka" thermal valley. They were reminders of somewhat similar places in Canada, America, Patagonia, and Europe, to mention a few that come to mind. But each one is different in kind.

The three of us split up, and I stuck with a Maori guide and listened to the fascinating local lore and legends of this homeland of the Tuhourangi subtribe. The reserve also featured a re-creation of an early Maori village. The gathering place for the war parties of Wahian turned out to be equally captivating, as did the New Zealand Maori Arts and Crafts Institute, established in 1967 and part of the complex. "The institute's mission is preserving the ancient skills of the Maori. Youngsters from across the country are selected as apprentices, studying skills ranging from carving to weaving along with creating flax skirts and patterned bodices" (Brochure). I remember especially the Rotowhio Marae, where we were welcomed with a traditional *powhiri* (welcoming ceremony) at the main gate of the *marae* (meeting grounds), before entering the *wharenui* (sacred meeting house), Te Aronui a Rua, and the Pikirangi Maori village (the pre-European village). Here, I got a feel for everyday Maori life in the past. I was impressed! One thinks back to the life of Native Americans for comparison. As we were about to leave the compound by bus, someone in our group was missing. Our regular guide ran back to look for him – what a nuisance – and about fifteen minutes later he retrieved the guy, who did not even see fit to apologize. What if he had sunk into one of the boiling mud holes and ended up in hell? – If he had been a female, all hell would have broken loose!

A visit to "New Zealand's most-loved tourist attraction" was a given. It was my third sheep-shearing event – I am not kidding – but I must say, this one turned out to be a deluxe version. The room was full of visitors, well over two hundred, all seated on long benches. Their sheep show featured live sheep shearing, a presentation of nineteen breeds of champion rams, cow milking, lamb feeding, dog demonstrations, and a complete New Zealand dog show. After all that, I joined the Organic Farm Tour, but just watched the hands-on experience with cattle, deer, alpaca, bison, ostrich, and sheep. Some children had fun feeding the lambs at the Farmyard Nursery. My boys had their picture taken as they stood on either side of a big ram mounted on a wall that boasted strong, curly horns. At the Woolen Mill, I was particularly interested to see how the Platt wool-carding machine, made in 1906, worked. It was used to demonstrate the final stages of wool production, "carding, spinning, weaving, and knitting with live educational demonstrations using wool straight off the sheep show stage" (Brochure). No, I did not buy a sweater. If Doc could have seen me with his great-grandsons, he would have chuckled.

It had started to rain, so I did not walk around outside. Soon after the ordeal, we took off for lunch and a Maori concert, definitely a first for me. The brochure had this to say about it: "Watch intricate hand games used to train young warriors; listen for songs that tell a story or deliver a message – poi dances suggest a flight of birds and the haka is a war dance designed to frighten the enemy." As I remember it, the *haka* posture dance was so wild, the screams so loud and ear piercing, and the decorated bodies of the performers so foreign looking that despite being done artfully, the entire spectacle almost drove me out of the room.

I felt better during the drive back to the ship. We went past a lovely rural and forested landscape, all of it pleasing to my eyes.

Auckland

The next morning, the vessel had docked in the Bay of Islands and began her tender service to Waitangi Wharf, from which I went on the Auckland City & Countryside Experience trip at 8:30 a.m. to see more of Auckland's countryside. It could not have turned out nicer and surpassed all my expectations.

The drive along the rugged coast, though the skies were overcast, was spectacular. The waves were crashing against the black rocks, foaming and rolling up on the long black-sand beaches. The big surprise was the dramatic cliffs of Muriwai Beach. We walked some four hundred yards to an overlook for a close-up of life in a seabird colony. Thousands of white and black gannets were breeding and nesting on the cliffs. Occasionally, one gannet or another would sail into the sky or glide above the turbulent and frothy waves of the verdant Tasman Sea. It was a sight to behold!

We continued through vineyards and farming districts and passed an occasional palm tree before arriving at a barbeque at Abbottsford, a large farm garden on the South Head peninsula, sixteen kilometers north of Parakai Hot Springs and an hour's drive from Auckland. All of a sudden, it began raining cats and dogs, but since big tents sheltered the picnic area, the Abbottsford stop turned out to be a highlight of my trip to New Zealand. When the rain let up, I strolled past a sizeable herd of sheep and walked around their idyllic garden, boasting such native flora as camellias, rhododendrons, and roses. It was an English garden ablaze with an array of colors, through which a path led on a slight incline up to the bungalow-style and comparatively simple but warmly furnished farmhouse. I chatted with the ladies in the kitchen and told them the lamb they had prepared for us with all the side dishes was very tasty. I felt so welcome in this newly discovered New Zealand paradise that I said to myself and others that if I were younger, this would be a place to which I would love to immigrate!

The boys had headed to Viaduct Harbour in the hope of sailing the NZL 40 or NZL 41 America's Cup yachts for at least a couple of hours. It would have been great, since they had sailed in Sydney's harbor. Unfortunately, bad weather prevented them from fulfilling that dream. Maybe next time. I personally was glad that I had not given in to Peter's coaxing to come along for a sail. The boys did not climb the impressive Harbour Bridge, which critics claim is an attempt to mimic the Sydney Harbour Bridge. Neither did they attempt the bungee jump from the bridge. Nevertheless, the coastal vistas, including those from the bridge on the way back to the ship after my country tour, were undeniably gorgeous. To be frank, I do not remember much of the city of Auckland itself. Sorry.

After a total cruise of 3,580 nautical miles, the *Sapphire Princess* arrived in Auckland Harbour at 0500 hours (5:00 a.m.). After breakfast, we were taken by bus to the airport to fly back to the good old USA. The boys were on their own, and as I was pushing my luggage cart toward the terminal building, I tripped over the cart and landed flat on my stomach on the wet pavement. A couple of guys helped me up, and I continued unscathed. The boys joined me at the gate, because their flight was leaving later than mine. I suddenly realized I had not gotten a New Zealand stamp in my passport, which was crammed full of stamps from all over the world. Peter grabbed it and disappeared, only to reappear with the passport and a New Zealand stamp in it. That was very nice. Thank you, Peter!

On the flight home, another shock came my way. The bin above my head suddenly opened because the male sitting behind me had not closed it properly. My heavy-duty metal luggage cart came crashing down on my head and hurt it badly. The stewardess brought a bag filled with ice cubes, which helped. The passenger responsible for the accident did not have the decency to apologize. – I must be accident prone. On my honeymoon with Doc, while we rode the train from Bolzano, Italy, to Hannover, Germany, the luggage cart also fell on my head. One thing is certain: I have a thick skull.

SOUTH AMERICA – DÉJÀ VU

Bolivia

La Paz

The travel bug did not stop biting. To satisfy its appetite, on May 28, 2006, after trips to Holland, Belgium, Europe, the Black Sea, and India, I took off once again for South America. I left Indianapolis at 2:29 p.m. to fly to La Paz, Bolivia, via Miami, and landed in La Paz, in the valleys of the Andes, on May 29 at 5:34 a.m. The OAT representative picked us up at the airport, and we were transferred by minibus to the very comfortable Plaza Hotel, in downtown La Paz. I loved my room, located on an upper floor, because I could see the majestic, snowcapped, triple-peaked Mount Illimani in the distance. At 21,122 feet high, it is the second-highest peak in Bolivia. Our guide had emphasized that although the official capital of Bolivia is Sucre, La Paz, at 11,975 feet above sea level, is the world's highest "de facto" or administrative capital city. Believe it or not.

It is not my intent to explore Bolivia's rather tumultuous history. Suffice it to say that since my visit, specifically since 2009, "this 'landlocked' Democratic Republic in South America, situated within the Amazon basin is known as the Plurinational State of Bolivia. It shares borders with Brazil, Paraguay, Argentina, Chile and Peru and has a population of about 10 million. It is multiethnic, representing Amerindians, Mestizos, Europeans, and Africans, speaking Spanish, Aymara, Quechua, as well as 34 other indigenous languages. Evo Morales, president of Bolivia has remained popular as he gives more power to the indigenous majority. The poverty rate in Bolivia is 60%. Its only access to the Atlantic is by way of the Uruguay River. They have a lease from Peru to build a port and a naval station on the Pacific. It was expanded in 2010 into a 99-year lease, but to date no port exists" (OAT). Judging from what I have observed while traveling throughout South America, it will be a long time before the Bolivians have a functional port on the Pacific. "Major sources of income are derived from natural gas, tin, agriculture, forestry, fishing, mining, textiles, clothing, refined metals and refined petroleum" (OAT). Compared to Chile, they have a long way to go.

Having arrived early in the morning, we were given some time to adjust to the altitude, but after lunch our explorations of La Paz on foot began, starting with the neighborhood of El Prado Avenue, Murillo Plaza, and San Francisco Church.

The main street downtown, El Prado Avenue is also known as July 16 Avenue. July 16, 1548, is La Paz's Founder's Day. We walked by bank buildings and department stores. The main sidewalk was lined with palms, deciduous trees, and well-clipped bushes. Whenever our guide stopped to elaborate, I was on the lookout for a nearby bench. The Government Palace reflected a strong Spanish influence, as did the rather impressive Palacio Legislativo de Bolivia. In general, colonial architecture dominated. I enjoyed the break, during which I walked around on the Murillo Plaza, located in the center of La Paz. It is named in honor of Pedro Domingo Murillo (1759–1810), forerunner of Bolivian independence. On July 16, 1809, he led a mutiny against the governor-general of Virreinato del Río de la Plata and proclaimed Bolivia's independence. As I sat on a bench in the park-like plaza, I observed a bunch of toddlers feeding the hungry pigeons and reflected on Murillo's fate. He was hanged at the Plaza de los Españoles the night he started the uproar. One cannot but admire such a hero, who is revered for starting the liberation movement of South America from Spain. Close by was the San Francisco Church, which is known for its "intricately carved façade, one of the finest examples of baroque-mestizo architecture in the Americas. It blends native and Catholic art and is decorated with indigenous symbols such as masked figures, snakes, dragons and tropical birds" (OAT). I found the neoclassical interior of the church interesting, but very confusing.

As we strolled through the *curandero* (medicine man) market, I became intrigued by the traditional garments – the brightly colored, multilayered skirts and the curious, felt-covered, hard bowler hats worn by the Andean women. We learned that there were up to thirty styles due to the different indigenous cultures. I snapped many photos of these women in their bulky *polleras*, with and without permission, and shook my head in disbelief when I was told that whenever the women needed to relieve themselves, they just squatted on the sidewalk or wherever they were, claiming they did not need toilets, and then went their way. It makes sense, then, that layered skirts were preferred to pants. Considering that 60% of the Bolivian population lacks proper sanitation, what else should they do? Use your imagination! Yet, it must be said that many Bolivians do not use a toilet even if one is donated. My friend Sally, who lived in Colombia, once told me that although her husband provided toilets for his workers, they did not use them. – Thus it is a matter of proper training as well?

I am always interested in finding out more about the use of indigenous plants, potions, and talismans for healing, especially when the plants are still used by indigenous people in remote areas. It came as no surprise that among medicinal plants, coca leaves are as much a favorite in Bolivia as they are in Peru. And if you are interested in this kind of stuff, you must go to a very bizarre market, a paradise for healers, shamans, fortune-tellers, etc. You will find an abundance of amulets, talismans, natural medicines, herbs, crystals, animal embryos for sacrificial offerings, and much more. Dried frogs guarantee you will be rich, and a dried llama fetus will protect your house. An estimated 99% of Bolivians have a dried llama fetus thrown under the foundations of their home for good luck. I should have brought home a dried snake to keep the Tea Party rats away.

After having been smitten by the bewitching stuff at the witch's market, we proceeded to Mirador, a location from which we had a fabulous view of the city, which is in fact shaped somewhat like a bowl. Curiously enough, the brick buildings and workshops and housing for the poor are perched on the rim, and the more affluent citizens have their mansions in the lower portions and at the bottom of the bowl. The higher you go, the less sanitation you find. I was devastated when I came face to face with the reality of these shantytowns, made up of dwellings which were mere shelters consisting of four walls, a dirt floor, and a piece of sheet metal for a roof. They are spreading quickly up the sides of the valley to the rim of the Altiplano. I just shook my head, as I always do when confronted with such stark poverty in developing countries across the globe. And I feel ever so helpless and ashamed at the same time. On the way to this poverty-stricken district, our guide stopped at the market, where all of us picked up a bunch of fruits and vegetables, which we presented to the women responsible for feeding the poor in the shanties.

The ride through rocky and very arid terrain to the Valley of the Moon was a relief from the depressing atmosphere of the shantytowns. "Moon Valley is a large collection of sandstone monoliths shaped over many thousands of years by the dry winds of southern La Paz. It is a rugged and fantastical landscape with deep gallies and oddly shaped outcroppings formed by centuries of erosion" (OAT). After traipsing around this unique territory, which was physically more challenging for me because the temperature was also higher, I was ready to retire as soon as we returned to the hotel. In retrospect, the valley reminded me vaguely of the badlands out West.

The next day, we drove to Bolivia's "most important archaeological site, Tiawanaku, a ceremonial location used by a pre-Incan civilization reaching back to 600 BC. The Aymara people of this ancient city were excellent artisans and left behind a series of mysterious monoliths, mostly in granite, as well as a pyramid, temple, and aqueducts. This was a well planned city, seat of one of the Americas' most powerful and organized civilizations" (OAT).

Much of the site was rather poorly preserved. I was taken by the monolithic (blocky and column-like) Ponce Stela and its huge, flat, square, carved eyes in the sunken courtyard of the Temple of Kalasasaya, because it reminded me so much of the moai statues on Easter Island. Having been to Peru previously, I immediately recognized the Incan connection. "Tiwanaku is recognized by Andean scholars as one of the most important precursors to the Inca Empire" (OAT).

Lake Titicaca

For my part, I was much more anxious to cross the border into Peru and drive to Lake Titicaca, my main reason for booking this pre-trip. The lake is located at the northern end of the endorheic Altiplano Basin. At 12,580 feet, it is the highest navigable lake on earth, and it covers more than 3,800 square miles. The western part of the lake lies within the Puno region of Peru, and the eastern side is located in the Bolivian La Paz Department. "Beyond its clear water, many islands, and the Andes Mountains that rise behind it, the lake holds a cherished place in Incan history. The Indian people who live in the small settlements around Titicaca believe that the lake and the Islands del Sol (Island of the Sun) and Islands de la Luna (Island of the Moon) are the sites of mythic creation of the Inca people. The views across the lake to the snow-draped peaks of the Andean range are magical, and the island people here have held onto their traditional culture and way of life. Fishermen still sail on reed boats made by hand, llamas are still herded along mountain paths to the hillside villages" (OAT).

On the way to the lake we had lunch at the village of Pomata on the south shore of Lake Titicaca. While there, we stopped briefly at the Dominican church, built in 1700 on top of a hill. On its facade was a carved puma. *Pomata* means "place of the puma." Our guide gave a brief introduction to the lake. While walking, we came upon a family harvesting totora in the shallows. Great!

But we had to wait until the next day to see life on the lake itself. Right after breakfast, we took a boat ride around the Uros Islands, where the islanders actually live on large and sturdy floating "islands," that is, handcrafted totora. About two thousand Uros live in this way, fishing in the lake for survival. Of course, we saw fewer than fifty during our exposure to their floating-island existence. Actually, the concept is rather clever. These islands could be moved if a threat arose. I was amazed by how solid and aesthetically attractive their reed boats were. It was highly interesting, and curious at the same time, to observe the Uro women, with their colorful full-length skirts, tall felt hats, and long, braided black hair, moving around or squatting on their reed-covered island floors. They showed us some of the more than eight hundred varieties of potatoes they grew, showed us where they raised the cute little golden-brown-and-white guinea pigs before they were roasted, and demonstrated how they crafted the reeds into mats and other utility items. They let us peek into their reed shelter, where a TV was turned on, and showed off the playground for the children. They even performed a dance for us. With their full skirts, it must be extremely cumbersome for them to squeeze through the narrow openings in the tent-like huts. The children were picked up by boats and transported to a floating school on one of the forty-four islands belonging to the Uros. We did not visit the small islands, such as Amantani or Taquile, on Lake Titicaca. That was OK. We got a pretty good idea of what life on these floats was like. If I were given a choice, I would rather live here than in a shanty in La Paz. We were not given the choice, as are tourists of different travel agencies, to spend a night in their shelter.

However, OAT had arranged a family visit in the village of Hatun Quilla for us. This visit turned out to be a real delight. I helped the women in the kitchen while the rest of my group chatted in the adjoining room, sitting around a long banquet table with Bolivian flair, simple but inviting. The Bolivians were noticeably friendly and cheerful. In addition to vegetable dishes, such as corn, beans, and potatoes, we were to be treated with golden-brown roasted guinea pigs. We had admired them previously in their open-air stalls in the courtyard, which was enclosed by high stone fences. I was chosen to carry in a big platter with the little roasted critters. When it was my turn to help myself, I reluctantly took a small piece, hoping it would taste like roasted piglet. Unfortunately, I had trouble chewing the leathery skin and in the end just swallowed it, hoping I would not choke on it. It did not taste like pork! I will avoid it in the future if possible.

After we thanked the family profoundly, and after having taken ample snapshots, we proceeded to Sillustani, where we had a chance to admire "the dramatic *chullpas*, or funeral towers, where the pre-Inca Colla tribe buried their dead. These large above-ground tombs have doors that face the east, where the tribe believed the sun was born again each day from mother Earth" (OAT). They built the towers around 600 AD to bury their nobility. Entire families, together with food and personal belongings, were buried in these cylinders. The tallest is some thirty-eight feet high. A vague comparison to the Egyptian pyramids, among others, came to mind. Though the round stone towers were deteriorating badly, their presence in this arid, hilly environment with the lake in the background was unusually striking. But it's definitely not a place where I would like to spend my postmortem existence – if I had a choice, which I don't.

January 21, 2015 – Cancún. I met two women, a mother and daughter, from Bolivia at the Sunset Lagoon, my resort. I was very much surprised. The mother was a prosecuting attorney, and the daughter was about to finish her law degree. While the mother did not like President Morales, the daughter was more supportive. They agreed in general with my way of thinking. The daughter planned to specialize in defending women's rights. Good for her. – They assured me that there are quite a few very wealthy people living in the valley of La Paz and that corruption in Bolivia is still present on all levels. The border dispute between Bolivia and Chile continues, and many refuse to use toilets even when they are provided free of charge. Maybe, if they started paying them in an effort to reduce poverty, they would comply?

Peru

Lima

On June 2, 2006, at 5:45 p.m., we flew with LAN Peru from Juliaca, Peru, via Arequipa, to Lima, Peru, where we arrived at 7:40 p.m.

I opted out of the trip to the Nazca Lines, which turned out to be a disappointment to those who went, because the weather was dreadful. Instead, I joined the guide for a sightseeing tour of Lima. Though I had visited Lima briefly in 1979, this trip, like many others, took me to places I hardly remembered, such as the Plaza de Armas, with the bronze fountain of José de San Martín, the place where he declared the country's independence from Spain in 1821. And as you can imagine, Lima boasts many churches in addition to its cathedral, the names of which I did not even try to remember. – However, I vividly recall the fish market along the Pacific. Lima's inhabitants claim it is the largest, and it is definitely one of the most curious markets I have seen while traveling the world. Dozens of pelicans were either floating along the shore of the Pacific or walking on the sand-packed beach, searching for fish. A whole bunch of the tall, gray, long-beaked birds waddled around in the marketplace itself. Really funny, I thought. I also thought it was funny, even bordering on the ridiculous, when further along on our shore drive, we stopped at the Love Park, located next to the Pacific on the cliff tops of the Miraflores district. The big attraction, and I mean really big, was an enormous pink sculpture of a well-fed couple in horizontal position – kissing, overlooking the ocean. It is a sculpture by Victor Delfin depicting himself and his wife. The mayor of Lima supposedly held a contest on Valentine's Day for couples who could sustain the longest kiss. This monument celebrates it. It is a favorite kissing spot for couples on Valentine's Day. More power to them!

Our stay at the Hotel Monte Real in Miraflores was pleasant, but not long, since my flight to Iquitos, Peru, departed as early as 7:45 a.m. on June 5, 2006, and landed in Iquitos one and a half hours later.

Amazon River

Iquitos

Before boarding our Amazon river ship, the *Aquamarina*, we were given a "get-acquainted tour" of Iquitos, the country's largest city in the Peruvian rainforest, with a population of 370,000 plus. "It was established in 1864 in the heart of rubber country on the Amazon's deep waters and is considered to be a major port in the Amazon Basin. Iquitos is an amazing 1,864 miles from the mouth of the Amazon at Belem, Brazil on the Atlantic and situated 78 mi downstream of the confluence of the Ucayali and Marañón Rivers, the two main headwaters of the Amazon River" (OAT). If you want to visit Iquitos, you can go by plane or boat. If you are adventurous enough and have a lot of time on your hands, you can take an ocean vessel of three thousand to nine thousand tons or a five-and-a-half-meter (eighteen-foot) raft originating in the Atlantic, some 1,900 miles away. That should be enough time to see all the wildlife your heart desires. I also recommend that you like tropical climates. Due to its average temperature of 85 degrees Fahrenheit plus humidity, this place gets steaming hot and stays that way without cease. It was obviously not too hot for the missionaries, who established a mission for the indigenous peoples in the 1750s.

By the way, you do not have to go to India to ride a rickshaw. In Iquitos, they are a bit more sophisticated. Instead of bicycles, they have modified motorcycles with a cabin behind that is supported by two wheels and seats three. These vehicles do not go to nearby towns, so you must travel via small motorized boats on rivers. "The architecture in Iquitos is a 19th century vestige of the era when European commercial barons held sway over life and culture here" (OAT). There are still some remnants of this era, such as magnificent colonial mansions constructed by the rubber barons. One of the landmarks is the Casa de Fierro (Iron House), designed by the man responsible for the erection of the Eiffel Tower, Gustave Eiffel. The building was imported section by section, carried through the jungle and reassembled on the Plaza de Armas. This plaza, a spacious square with a small, green park at the center and a dramatic fountain, sprays huge jets of water high into the sky and is worthy of one's admiration. You can sit on a bench and soak up the atmosphere while not ignoring the cathedral, a relatively modern structure from the early twentieth century. Some of the mansions were decorated inside and out with expensive azulejos, hand-painted tiles imported from Portugal.

I thought the Belén open market was a fun place to visit. I have never seen such a chaotic marketplace; it was unlike anything under the sun. Most of the goods were displayed in carts and on blankets or pieces of paper spread out on the ground. Of course, different cuts of meat, raw, dried, or whatever, as well as fish were arranged on small or makeshift tables or on sheets of wood. One fresh-meat display had a pig's head on the edge of the table. Several women and others showed off their chickens, ducks, turkeys, and multicolored roosters, all very much alive. Little kids were playing, and teenagers stood guard to make sure the birds did not take off. Next to the poultry flock hung a birdcage with three bright-green parakeets perched closely together inside. A few steps away, a man stood behind a little table on which he presented nicely arranged bundles of hand-rolled cigarettes. This was new to me. The tobacco was almost black. We did not stay, because the rain that blessed this quasi folk festival was intensifying.

I was keen to see our riverboat, which we boarded after the city tour. It looked somewhat like a cut-off portion of a floating motel, built out of wood. On its flat rooftop, meals were actually served underneath a kind of tarp canopy. It was about one hundred feet long and forty feet wide and had just enough cabins to house our group of fourteen travelers and a dozen or so crew members. My cheerful cabin was small but nice, with two beds; it was big enough for me since I paid a single supplement. I could look out the window from my bed. The boat was typical, and rustic rather than modern. Laundry was picked up daily and returned the same evening, and all in all I had nothing to complain about. I was ready to go.

Though they had advertised "time for leisure," as soon as we had viewed our cabins, we were summoned to join our guide for a boat ride on the Amazon, which at that point is actually the confluence of the Marañón and Ucayali Rivers. We were told that in Peru this confluence is generally considered the beginning of the Amazon River, if only in name – whatever that means. Amazon is easier to remember. The boat ride was something else. Fortunately, I had brought my rain poncho. Only eight or nine in my group had come, most of them without a raincoat, and we sat in a narrow boat powered by a motor. Pedro, the guide, was eager to show us the floating city of Belén on the Itaya/Amazon River, right outside of Iquitos. As it turned out, his motorized skiff provided an exciting trip. The second we took off, rain started to pour down in buckets. Instead of turning around, they sped up. The rain was so strong we could barely make out the floating houses. They were a sad sight indeed. Several other boats that we passed were laden with bananas and other tropical fruits, to be sold to villagers alongside the river. The thatched-roof houses were floating on rafts. Instead of doors and windows, they simply had openings of different sizes in the plywood walls. Owning a floating house seems to have the advantage over the more common stilt houses along the Amazon of not ever sinking! I for one was grateful that on this first day, our guide had provided us the singular experience of getting initiated to a snippet of life in the rainforest. *Muchas gracias*, Pedro. Those who climbed ashore drenched were not so grateful. I guess I was the only one in the boat who was overtaken with excitement. I loved it, but some of my cotravelers probably thought I was nuts.

Dinner on the upper deck was tasty, and the first night on this somewhat old-fashioned Amazonian riverboat was even better, especially since I was rewarded with a heavenly sunset before turning in. For some reason, I did not hear any strange noises originating from jungle animals. They too were most likely sound asleep.

We were out early the next morning for a special bird-watching launch, but in all honesty, I cannot recall exactly which kinds of birds I actually spotted. It could have been one or several of the following, which appear on my OAT list: "orioles, blackbirds, purple gallinules, yellow-headed caracaras," and others. I took enough pictures of treetops and of activities along the riverbanks, eroding and muddy in places. Young boys and others waved at us, and a little boy no older than five years of age paddled toward us in a dugout. He held onto the side of our boat with one hand and smiled at us with his big black eyes, not because he was begging, but just because he enjoyed seeing us strangers up close. Every now and then, Pedro showed us one of the slimy creatures he had fished out of the river – a turtle or something slippery. He was a bit overweight, and I was afraid he might tip our boat and send us all into that brown, and not very appetizing, sediment-laden brew in the great Amazon, the second-largest river in the world and first in water flow, as they claim. Remembering my boat trip on the Nile, the world's longest river, I could not have told the difference. At one point, a native fisherman pulled up close in his boat to show off an impressive bunch of silver-skinned fish floating in about six inches of water in the bottom of the boat. Nice catch, amigo – good for you! Quite a few fishermen were out that morning, trying their luck. The ambiance was simply captivating. The sunrise lent the vastness of the river a romantic, pinkish hue.

Later that morning, we walked on the banks of the Marañón at the Amazon Natural Park lodge to get a feel for the terra firma, or upland forest, which is never subjected to flooding. These forests support a very diverse and permanent population of plants and animals. It's also the place where we came upon half a dozen horses grazing next to a small rum factory. It was a sort of open-air facility underneath a tin roof, with mesh windows. We happily accepted the manager's offer of a shot glass of rum. The owners had obviously taken great pains to plant climbing pink rose bushes. I did not expect to see roses in this part of the world. Neither had I expected to see a snail such as the one Pedro picked off the ground – it was about six inches in diameter – when, later that day, we were hiking through the rainforest, which is a dense canopy that reaches as high as 150 feet and shelters a jungle floor thinly vegetated with palms, woody vines, ferns, bromeliads, and orchids, of which I did not see many. However, I did get a good view, for the first time, of a three-toed sloth hanging upside down high in a tree. A howler monkey climbed happily on the shoulders of one guy in our group, and someone spotted an almost nine-foot-long rusty-red-colored snake resting in the upper branches of a tree. Wow!

Back on the river, we stopped for lunch at a place called Las Palmas, so called because there happened to be a palm tree grove surrounding their small, open-air shelter, erected on stilts and covered by a roof of thatched palm leaves. As always, the native hosts in this rivereno house were all smiles, very hospitable, and grateful to have us partake of the regional foods they had prepared for us. The chunks of goat meat roasted in an open fire pit were delicious.

At our next stop along the riverbank, we were treated to a demonstration of the crafting of a dugout canoe. This particular canoe was made out of a single tree trunk about twenty-five feet long. It looked very new, because the wood had not yet aged and a pile of chiseled-out wood chips lay nearby. But it was ready to go. I personally would prefer a dugout canoe to a raft when navigating the Amazon.

Day 6 of our river trip was filled with more exciting experiences. It started out with a unique picnic breakfast at a quiet spot somewhere in the Pacaya-Samiria National Reserve's impressively diverse and unusual ecosystem. It is supposed to be the largest reserve in Peru and in the Amazon rainforest, the latter being the largest rainforest in the world. The temperatures range from 68 to 91 degrees Fahrenheit. The annual rainfall is between two and three thousand millimeters (about nine feet).

While we hiked through the jungle of the reserve, Pedro recommended that we look out for cocoi (hatted) herons, scarlet macaws, squirrel and howler monkeys, alligators, sloths, and many more primate, bird, and mammal species. We saw most of them, and others as well, which kept us in a constant state of anxiety and excitement, until I personally got tired. It's similar to safari trips, when after so many elephants, giraffes, hippopotami, monkeys, etc., the element of surprise diminishes. I think I was the happiest when we were lucky enough to spot a pair of scarlet macaws only a few yards from our boat. They were on the ground, close to a tree to which a gorgeous pink orchid was clinging, and they were unlike other macaws we had seen flying in the distance. I have always had a penchant for parrots of all colors – as well as for monkeys, elephants, and anything exotic.

When we returned to the riverboat, I was ready for the pisco sour, the Peruvian specialty which they served compliments of the captain, who had also been kind enough, as had many others on my trips around the globe, to let me be photographed with him at the steering wheel of the ship. *Muy amable. Gracias, señor.*

After dinner, we took off again, this time to pay a visit to a local shaman, aka a "mystic minister" or "healer." Having met shamans on previous trips but not in South America, I was curious to get a look at this one's magic.

Shamanism is practiced around the globe, and is universally distinguished by a trance state called shamanic ecstasy. In these "out of body" travels, the shaman enlists denizens of the spirit world to help him with a variety of duties, from healing the sick to assisting a deceased person's soul into the afterworld – and all the while, the shaman remains conscious. – He'll introduce you to his spiritual healing craft and tell you about rain forest plants that indigenous people have for untold centuries held to possess curative properties. (OAT)

We rode a catamaran and still had to walk quite a distance through the rainforest before we came upon a round and rather large thatched-roof shelter. It was so dark inside you could barely see. Nevertheless, we all sat on benches in a circle and watched as the shaman, dressed in a floor-length frock and sitting in front of a shelf stacked full of small bottles containing miracle potions, performed his "shams" on some of our volunteers. He also went around and touched each one of us on the shoulder with a palm branch before handing it to us as a gift, probably to purify us or chase away bad spirits. I had to agree that the experience was definitely out of the ordinary. But, to be honest, our shaman was so soft-spoken I could barely understand what he was mumbling. Yet we thanked him and swore that we felt better. We stood in line to have our picture taken with two of the shaman's assistants before heading back to the boat. Unfortunately, I lost my palm branch on the way back to the catamaran, and bad spirits have returned to haunt me ever since.

Day 7 meant getting up at dawn to watch the world awakening in the rain forest. Luckily, we came upon a couple of iguanas, a river turtle, and a pair of cormorants. I do not remember seeing a wattled jacana, a seven-inch-long, black-brown bird with yellow markings on its wings, which others saw walking over some plants in the marshes. It is not unusual for me to try in vain to see what others are seeing.

After breakfast we ventured out again. This time, we were treated to a new adventure, that is, a fifteen-minute walk on a swing bridge – a suspended walk through the canopy of the mysterious, lush rainforest. Each of us had to walk alone on the swinging walk. There were ropes on each side that one could hold on to if necessary. It was great fun. I was too excited by the walk to stay on the lookout for monkeys or macaws or sloths. Afterward, we attended a ceremony that emphasized the important reforestation efforts in this threatened ecosystem. To show our support, one by one, we planted a little tree right there in the jungle. I wonder if mine is still growing.

We were then treated to a rare and very memorable midday meal in the thatched-roof home of a family. The rather large habitat was, like all the others in the region, erected on stilts or poles. The roof was made of palm branches woven together tightly. One man demonstrated the procedure for us, while another showed off his skill in making baskets out of palm leaves. They also showed us the sleeping area. Mosquito nets were suspended over the so-called beds (cots, in fact), and clotheslines were strung across the room close to the roof to dry their few pieces of laundry. The cooking area was what we would call quite primitive, yet it was very functional, as the meal they served us amply proved. I was amused to notice a couple of chickens and a rooster resting peacefully on a bed of straw close to the stove, as though they could not wait to be slaughtered.

In the absence of a table, they arranged long leaves from banana trees nicely on the floor in the center of the shelter and then arranged platters and bowls filled with food on top of the leaves. The main dish was called *juane* (*bijao* leaves plus chicken, eggs, and olives). We had tin plates, but no forks or spoons. Fingers were OK. I sampled most of the dishes, but skipped the beverage. We visitors sat on the floor or on a long bench. While exploring the grounds below, I noticed they were drying some laundry underneath the floor of the shelter, not worrying about the piglets and cats and other domestic animals wandering around or enjoying their siesta. C'est la vie! Though we could communicate with the natives through gestures and smiles only, there was no doubt they genuinely appreciated the various gifts we had brought for them and their children, of which there were more than a dozen. In retrospect, I should have been surprised that there were no begging kids along the Amazon, as there were in Africa, China, India, and other regions in developing countries.

Not too far from the place where we were fed was a one-room schoolhouse named Libertad, also on stilts, but not without doors and windows. The children were waiting for the teacher, who lived a two-day journey away from their school and was obviously very late, that is, more than a day. An assistant introduced us, and we had fun listening to the children singing, chatting in broken English with us, and finally applauding happily when we too sang a song for them. They thanked us also after the assistant had handed out the pencils and writing pads we had brought for them. I always appreciated the stops that brought us into contact with the locals and that OAT always included in their itineraries for travel to parts of the world so different from ours.

If you like to go fishing and want to try your luck catching a piranha, take a trip up the Nawapa River, a tributary of the Amazon, and see what's biting. According to Teddy Roosevelt, piranhas are "the most ferocious fish in the world." They have very sharp teeth and a voracious appetite for meat and can easily bite one's finger off. Well, we went out in our speedboat and moored in a secluded, shady spot, and I tried my darndest to catch at least one of the golden, shimmering fish. The bait was simply chicken meat. Several guys in our group were extremely lucky. They hauled them in one after the other. All were rather small, but big enough to eat. Though I had been quite lucky fishing in the Upper Peninsula for sunfish and other fish, and in Germany for trout, I did not catch a single piranha. Fortunately, our group had caught enough so that each of us could be served at least one for dinner. They were delicious! The flesh is light and nutty tasting, most likely one of the reasons they are esteemed as some of the best-eating fish in South America.

The sundown that evening was again divine! The region's unique cloud formations make the sunsets on the Amazon very dramatic.

Day 8 was spent exploring another part of the Pacaya-Samiria National Reserve. I politely declined an invitation to go swimming and join the locals for a dugout-canoeing experience in a nearby jungle river. Instead, I followed Pedro to see local craftspeople creating goods made from natural forest materials and bought a miniature dugout canoe for my souvenir collection.

Later that day, we hiked for a long time through extremely muddy and soggy terrain and in sauna-like temperatures to an oxbow lake to look for hoatzins, one of the most primitive bird species in the world, as well as for the gigantic aquatic plants called *Victoria regia*. We did not see a single hoatzin, despite the fact that they tend to live in swamps and riverine forests, exactly the terrain we were in. They are a bit difficult to spot, even though they look like twenty-six-inch-tall brown pheasants. I was more disappointed that the *Victoria regia* plants, which were floating on the pond, were not as gigantic as I had imagined. I guarantee that, should they put a child on a leaf, it would not hold, as they claimed it would. We were all a bit stressed after stalking through the swampy forest. One guy sank knee-deep into a hole, which resulted in his rubber boot filling up with water; he had a hard time pulling it out. But, as nature is so often unpredictable, on the trip back to the big boat we were ever so lucky to come upon a school of bubblegum-pink dolphins, a first for me. These river dolphins were just as friendly as those I had seen along the coast of Namibia and on my cruise to Alaska. Quite a treat!

All of us were ready for another late-night skiff excursion to discover what comes out in the jungle after sundown. There was great excitement during our night outing on the skiff on the Marañón River when Pedro captured a black caiman. Its eyes shone red when Pedro directed his flashlight at them. It was about three feet long, and Pedro had caught it with his bare hands along the riverbank. It looked just like a baby crocodile to me, which it really was. Amazing! And a bit scary. Its teeth looked sharp. I kept my distance, getting just close enough to take another snapshot, one of hundreds. It seemed that every five minutes during our boat trips, Pedro would yell, "Take a picture!" Thanks to his big flashlight, we spotted quite a few big birds and owls in the treetops. But they were too far away to be captured by my digital. We did not encounter a jaguar, and again too far away for my Sony was the constellation of the Southern Cross, which, when we saw it in the skies above, triggered quite a conversation between two of our cotravelers. I for one was ever so grateful that they pointed it out to me, since I had never before even attempted to see it. *Vielen Dank!*

Our last day had come. It meant getting back to civilization and Iquitos. But before we docked, a few outings were planned.

We called on the town of Nauta, where the Ucayali and the Marañón – major headstreams of the Amazon – come together. We rode the local motorcars and hit the local market to browse for souvenirs, of which I bought several, such as small vases made of wood and hand-painted postcards depicting exotic jungle scenes in superbright colors. We gained another look into the tribes' customs in Nauta when we were taken to a large, round thatched-roof structure where a group of six or seven natives dressed in regional costumes, hula-like skirts for the girls and Native American–like costumes for the men, performed several native dances for us, some of them quite emotional. Regrettably, I do not remember the meaning of the dances. At one point, a pretty girl lay flat on her back on the floor while a young man waved his arms over her, which eventually brought her "back to life." The last show, during which a couple of our male companions joined in on the dancing, was an enjoyable way to finish up our adventure on the great Amazon.

After lunch, we had another chance to look for charapas and turtles on the Sapsipi River, and we concluded our hunt for rainforest flora and fauna with a final ride on the Marañón River.

The rather brief visit to the Amazon Museum, located on the riverfront, during our quick final tour of Iquitos allowed us a last look at the regions of many Indian tribes, as well as at photographs and artifacts from the city's affluent past.

The OAT farewell dinner and the party on our ship, complete with live music, was special. The crew put on a lively show before we retired, and the pisco sours were on the house. – To my horror, when I opened my suitcase to pack, the inside was covered with thousands of tiny brown ants, crawling all over and thriving on a few crumbs from a couple of granola bars I had left in the suitcase. Live and learn!

Lima

The next day was a Sunday. We left Iquitos in the morning, and after a brief flight, landed safely before noon in Lima.

Everybody in my group was heading back to the States, but I had decided to sign up for another trip while I was down in that region. I added Machu Picchu and the Galápagos to my itinerary, despite the fact that I had been to Machu Picchu in 1979 and was forced to spend seven days in Lima waiting for the group that had signed up for trip number two. They were due to arrive on the 17th of June. OAT had helped me find a hotel in a good and safe area at a decent price. Actually, I could not complain. I had a big suite, a bedroom, a living room, a kitchen, two TVs, and Internet access all to myself. I discovered a small market nearby, so what more could I want? I spent the days wandering through the busy streets in Lima, sitting on a bench in the big plaza, watching people, testing my Spanish with the natives, or taking a stroll down to the beach, which was not too far from my hotel.

When the regular group arrived, someone came to transfer me to their hotel, located fairly close to mine and actually the same one I had stayed in on the way down to La Paz, Bolivia.

I was the only person in my group who had been to Machu Picchu. I was not very eager to return, because I was afraid my first wonderful impressions would be tarnished.

Cuzco

We left Lima on June 20 at 10:05 a.m. and landed in Cuzco, at an altitude of 10,909 feet, at 11:20 a.m. Somehow, the city appeared larger and busier than when I arrived with Dele in 1979, and it seemed to lack the original charm. Maybe it all had to do with the fact that while we ventured out on our own the first time, this time it was all organized. Thus, the Hotel José Antonio was OK, but not as intimate or idyllic as the one where we stayed before. After a two-hour siesta, our guide, Eric, introduced us to Cuzco's history and walked with us from the hotel to explore Coricancha, a sun temple. "It is the city's most important ceremonial structure during the Incan era. Historical records of the time note that its walls were once covered with 700 sheets of gold studded with emeralds and turquoise; when the sunlight streamed through the windows, the reflection off the precious metals was blinding" (OAT). Right next to it is the Cathedral of Santo Domingo. Eric told us the courtyard was filled with golden statues and that when the Spanish required a ransom of gold in exchange for the life of the leader, Atahualpa, most of the gold was collected from Coricancha. It does not take a rocket scientist to figure out that the Spanish were obsessed with gold. Their cathedrals and churches still overflow with it. Let's not forget that Pizarro and his conquistadors pillaged the temples when they invaded the city in 1538.

The next morning, we drove into the hills surrounding Cuzco to see what is supposed to be the most significant ruin in the Cuzco area, Sacsayhua. This enormous fortress perched on a hilltop overlooking the city, of military and religious significance, was not new to me. I had not forgotten the three ramparts of zigzagging defense walls, supposedly forming the teeth of the puma. The stones were enormous, weighing up to 125 tons apiece, and what is so impressive is that each boulder was cleanly polished and so carefully cut with rounded corners that the boulders fit together tightly without mortar. At one time there were three immense towers and a labyrinth of rooms large enough to garrison five thousand Incan soldiers. Today, the interior buildings are gone, having been dismantled by the Spaniards for their stone. You'll never forget this wall. It's the Incan trademark and a must-see outside of Cuzco.

On the way to the sacred spring of Tambomachay, located in a peaceful sheltered valley, we stopped at a llama farm where a rather sizeable herd of llamas, brown, white, and black, were kept. We got a chance to feed the peaceful-looking, well-behaved animals with bundles of grass and other green stuff. A few steps further on, a couple of women sat with their children in a sheltered spot, spinning wool. Each and every one of them was decked out in the most colorful handwoven ponchos, big scarfs, and knitted caps. One woman in particular caught my eye. She sat on a stone step wearing a full black skirt, a short red jacket with an embroidered border, and a big black hat with white fringe. It looked Chinese, which was bizarre up there in the Andes. She was spinning alpaca wool into a thread, while another indigenous woman sat a few yards further down in the grass along the path, weaving a blanket. She did not even turn her head when a third woman driving two oxen and a horse in front passed by.

Tambomachay was a site I had not visited during my first trip to the region. It is at times referred to as the Bath of the Inca and was used for religious functions. It was fascinating to see that the fountains, fed by spring water, were still functional. Equally noteworthy was the Incan wall behind the springs. It was built with the big, black, square stones so characteristic of Incan structures. Along the way we passed a place where, for a long stretch alongside the road, a few men were busy making handmade bricks from adobe, a mixture of mud, clay, sand, and water. They created the mixture by stomping it with their feet into a mold, removing it from the mold, and then leaving it to dry with the other bricks in a long row. In case you didn't know, adobe bricks are an inexpensive and efficient building material, used the world over to make fireproof buildings.

As we continued through the mountains and watched the countryside pass by, I realized that these scenes, against the background of the magnificently sculpted terraces put in place by the Incas to protect the steep hillsides from erosion, had been and will continue to be indelibly imprinted in my mind. They are present everywhere in the rugged terrain. I saw the same pattern in the mountainous regions in Bhutan. They appear at times like big canvases of art spread out on the hillsides, both precise and creative.

Since I had witnessed a shaman ceremony on the Peruvian Amazon a few days earlier, I was not too keen on participating in another one. Yet, one conducted by an Andean *curandero*, or medicine man, was on the menu, and thus I went. Rather than explaining the procedure, I'll pass on OAT's comments: "This ancient healing tradition claims a head-spinning lineage, with influences as old as the classical medical writings of Galen and Hippocrates, with deep roots in Incan culture. The Spanish Renaissance saw a renewal of *curanderismo* practices, and today this healing art is an amalgam of medieval and European witchcraft; early Arabic medicine; Judeo-Christian beliefs, symbols, and rituals; scientific medicine; the Bible; and modern beliefs about psychic phenomena and spiritualism. . . . This twofold medicine practice is not simply a cure for illnesses, but a prayer for good health and well being with an offering to *Pachamama*, a deity associated with fertility and Mother Earth. Not surprisingly, then, great complexity accompanies the work of a *curandero*. Often, he will employ herbs and healing plants; while for other conditions he may conduct a religious ritual with sacred objects and shamanic chanting (called *icaros*). Thought to possess a gift from God to heal the sick, the *curandero* also sees himself as a front-line soldier in the battle between good and evil on earth – particularly when patients believe their physical ailments have supernatural causes."

Early the next morning, we traveled for about one and a half hours by bus to Ollantaytambo, located a bit above 6,500 feet, well below the elevation of Cuzco. On the way, we stopped at a small town and visited a bakery. They had a large paddle with an extension of about twenty feet that they slid into a large brick oven to pull out the pancakes within, which tasted good. (It was like a pizza oven.) Another stop involved a pottery place. There, a fellow molded adobe clay into pots and cups on a motor-driven turntable. He demonstrated the strength of the wares by hammering a nail into a board with a cup. After a brief walk through the Inca village, we boarded the train, which took us into the narrow and spectacular Urubamba Gorge and after about two hours delivered us to the foot of the Lost City of the Incas, Machu Picchu, which sat in the middle of a tropical mountain forest.

Machu Picchu – Déjà Vu

At this point, what I had feared when booking the trip materialized. The big disappointment was the missing train trip. In 1979, we traveled exclusively by the switchback, El Zig-Zag, which was only four wagons long and had wooden seats, but enabled the train to climb the steep incline out of Cuzco before it began its descent to the Sacred Valley and then continued down to Machu Picchu, with the last stretch ascending through incredible jungle flora to the entrance gate of the Lost City.

The Zig-Zag is a cheap way to travel, because it requires no tunnels to be built. It is also a much slower way to travel, and the number of passengers is limited to those who can fit into four wagons. In 1979, we had to book reservations for this trip many months in advance. But the entire experience was so much more exciting and adventurous. It was all much more pristine. Now, tourism has grown so much it has slowly destroyed the original ambiance. This fact shocked me when we were dropped off at the Machu Picchu Inn in Aguas Calientes, a village at the foot of Machu Picchu, which I had not heard of or seen during my first visit. It consisted of two narrow streets, too many hotels, souvenir shops, restaurants, and a street-side postal station.

When we were transferred to a bus to ascend, admittedly in zigzag fashion, through the jungle to the entrance of the ruin, I was ticked off because our guide, when I asked him what had happened to the old Zig-Zag train, repeatedly insisted that such a train never existed. Later, back in the States, I learned that that portion of the trip had been eliminated due to the danger of mudslides.

Of course, as soon as the fabulous ruins appeared, some twenty-six years after I had first seen them, I was once again mesmerized by the miracle. They had not changed, but this time, the panorama had a distinctly mystical ambiance, as white clouds were drifting past the emerald mountain peaks. Yet, while I climbed again up and down the many stairs to explore the fifteenth-century pre-Columbian site, including the Ritual Baths, the Palace of the Princess, and the Main Fountain, the sun slowly pushed the clouds ever so gently away. A glorious view appeared. There are no words to describe it.

I found a place up high, near the Guardhouse, to sit in the grass, relax, and contemplate. I felt so privileged to experience this remarkable wonder of the world for a second time. I was proud that at seventy-four, I still had the energy and enthusiasm to climb those many steps, at an altitude of almost eight thousand feet, by myself. Correction: my guide once helped a bit. He offered to carry my bag, and I let him.

Since we spent the night at the inn, I took advantage of the opportunity to see Machu Picchu at sunrise. Unfortunately, it was too cloudy and the ambiance more eerie and mystical than glorious. However, I came upon three or four grazing llamas and chatted for quite a while with a couple of young Israeli soldiers who were on an extended vacation and traveling in South America. – While waiting for the bus to return to the hotel, I struck up a conversation with a young couple who had hiked on the famous stone-paved Inca Trail to the Gate of the Sun, a small Incan ruin set in a mountain pass above the city. I then regretted not having hiked the trail in 1979, but at that time my friend Dele could not have done it. She also could not have hiked to the summit of Huayna Picchu, the sharp peak visible behind the ruins of Machu Picchu in many photographs. Maybe I'll return for a third time in another life, after I have risen from the ashes, like a Phoenix. Don't hold your breath!

The last day in Peru was spent in Písac and Cuzco. Písac is a small town not too far from Cuzco, set in the stunning Andes Mountains. We walked through the town, scrutinizing its colonial streets and artisan shops before browsing through their popular, busy market for unusual trinkets and authentic, handcrafted souvenirs. Next, we spent some time at a local school, where we handed over a box filled with useful gifts for the pupils in exchange for a song and simple conversation with the kids, who were dressed neatly in blue uniforms and who eagerly or bashfully answered questions about their daily life in broken English. We ended up at Písac's ruins on the mountain overlooking the city. These ruins gave us more insight into the advanced masonry skills of the Inca.

I had looked forward to visiting a Písac family. The family had prepared a typical lunch for our group. Though I had hoped for a delicious pink mountain trout, known as the Peruvian's best-loved dish, they had gone out of their way to spoil us with another favorite dish, two golden-brown, roasted guinea pigs, presented nicely on a large platter. I helped myself to a very small portion of meat but took more of the *papas a la huancaína*, cooked local potatoes covered in cheese and chiles. By then, I knew only too well that the first potatoes in Europe were imported from Peru, that there were hundreds of varieties, and that no meal in Peru was served without them. It was that way when I grew up in Germany. But I only remember one kind. Other common Peruvian staples are corn on the cob or in the dough, tamales filled with meat, vegetables, or fruit, and many kinds of stew. I was fortunate to have some knowledge of Spanish and pulled it out of my hat, to the obvious delight of our kind and smiling hosts, more women than men. *Muchas gracias, señoras y señores. Hasta luego.*

It was Sunday, and the Festival of the Sun, which lasts a week, was still in full swing in the Plaza de Armas. It celebrates the king (Sapa Inca) and the queen (Mama Ocllo). After much dancing, the queen was carried out on a throne of silver, followed by the king on a throne of gold, which weighed 140 pounds. The plaza was jam-packed with locals, wearing bright-colored (red, yellow, and blue) costumes. At night they wore masks, a bit like those worn during Mardi Gras. At the same plaza, two religious statues sat on platforms, decorated with bright-colored cloth and lots of beads to simulate gold. Someone told us they weigh up to two thousand pounds. About twenty-five strong men lifted the platform, together with the statues, and carried it to a church about one mile away. Every one hundred feet, they had to stop and put it down on another platform to make the lifting easier. Some in the group tried to return to the plaza after dark but turned around because it was too crowded and the tickets were sold out. I did not even try. Personally, I found all the glitter a bit offensive.

After breakfast at our Cuzco hotel, we flew to Lima, where we spent the day at leisure. We bid farewell to Pedro, who was glad to go home and rest, because, as he told me somewhere along the way, he was sick with a very bad cold. *Le pauvre* (poor guy).

On the way to the airport in Lima the next morning, I was irritated, as I was in 1979, when we passed the many unfinished houses with iron rods still sticking out at the top. I should have been used to them, because I had seen them all over South America. Supposedly, these houses were unfinished because it was always assumed that the next family member to get married would finish the floor and move in. Someone told me that as long as the houses were not finished, the inhabitants did not have to pay taxes. Well, considering their extreme poverty, I could understand that. Nevertheless, it offended my aesthetic sensibilities.

Ecuador

Quito

The flight from Lima to Quito, capital of Ecuador (Spanish for *equator*), lasted about two hours. Our Ecuadorian trip leader, a native of Ecuador and a certified naturalist, met and escorted us to our five-star Hotel Quito. The big attraction were the hotel gardens, praised as the "loveliest and largest" in the city. The panorama, which included a view of Pichincha, over 15,000 feet high and an active stratovolcano, was exceptional, and the garden boasted a wide variety of plants. In short, this hotel left nothing to be desired – and the cuisine was exceptional. The rooms were exquisite, with a view of the city, the neighboring valley, and the Andes mountain ranges surrounding Quito.

Quito, with a population of over 2 million is located in north-central Ecuador on the eastern slopes of Pichincha. It is also the second-highest administrative capital city in the world, after La Paz, Bolivia, and the highest legal capital (ahead of Sucre, Bolivia). Quito (a UNESCO World Heritage Site) extends to within about 0.62 mi of zero latitude. (OAT)

We had lunch in colonial Quito, South America's oldest capital city, founded by Sebastián de Belalcázar on December 6, 1534, before walking through San Francisco, the first (and very imposing) Catholic church in South America. It is quite an architectural monument in that it is at once a temple, a series of chapels, and a convent – where we admired remarkable artwork, wood carvings, paintings, sculptures, and period furniture. Ernesto La Orden supposedly called it "the Escorial of the Andes." I found it interesting, and disturbing, to learn from our guide that the San Francisco Convent was constructed, as were quite a few other churches, during the colonial period, when the Spanish forcibly converted the indigenous population to Christianity, that is, Roman Catholicism, and used them for slave labor. Our guide did not speak too highly of the Franciscans who had settled in Quito at that time. Another church we visited was the Jesuit Iglesia de la Compañía de Jesús (Church of the Society of Jesus), which, being the richest church in the western hemisphere, featured seven hundred pounds of gold leaf decorating the interior. It's disgusting. I was sorry to never have discussed with the Jesuits, who were my close friends during my younger years, what they thought of these infamous practices of their Spanish "ancestors." The Jesuits definitely collaborated with the Spaniards back home to impress the Peruvian natives with this extravagance in an effort to convert them to Catholicism.

A refreshing and moving experience was the performance given by the Sinamune Disabled Children's Orchestra. A group of handicapped youngsters (some blind and some mentally deficient, but all of them musically inclined) performed classical and folk music for us. The performance brought out the creativeness in each and every one of them. Keep up the good work!

Galápagos Islands

The last evening, we had a welcome dinner in downtown Quito, which looked quite nice lit up at night, and I slept well until the wake-up call the next morning. After breakfast we flew from Quito to the Galápagos, which OAT praised as "an enchanted archipelago that straddles the Equator some 600 miles west of the Ecuadorian coast, and a UNESCO World Heritage Site." The archipelago is 1,730 nautical miles north of another favorite destination of mine, Easter Island, and is also the result of volcanic eruptions. I was happy to hear from our guide that the Spanish sailors who discovered the islands in 1535 named them after the abundant tortoises. The Spanish word for tortoise is *galapago*.

We landed in a small bay of the Baltra/Santa Cruz Islands, from which we were transported by another small boat, a *panga*, to our ship. *Corina* was the name of the ship on which we would spend the next four days, exploring the islands with a naturalist as our guide. She slept sixteen passengers and a crew of ten. She had three decks and a large dining room, where generous and delicious meals were served. My cabin was just fine. The next days were spent boating from one island to the next, always in the motorized *panga*.

Each island was unique, and several of my cotravelers genuinely enjoyed snorkeling in the coves, even though a couple of them were badly stung by jellyfish. – During our stop at Santa Cruz Island, we saw our first marine iguanas sunning themselves on the sand, and a whole bunch of brightly colored Sally Lightfoot red crabs crawled around on the rough black lava flow near the coves.

Bartolomé Island, shaped like a moonscape with its black lava rock, volcanoes, and lava flows, and home to Pinnacle Rock, was explored before we landed on Santiago Island (Sullivan Bay), with its abandoned salt mine at Puerto Egas. The tidal pools revealed a profusion of octopi, starfish, and other undersea life. Rare fur sea lions, which were once on the verge of extinction and which I later saw in South Georgia, cavorted nearby. We spotted an oystercatcher and a couple of blue herons, but no yellow-crowned night herons. Rábida Island stood out because of its reddish beach and steep volcanic slopes. I stood and watched the sea lions relaxing on the red sand while others played around close to the beach. On the same beach, I spotted a huge, gorgeous sea star spread out on the red sand. I was tempted to pick it up and take it home.

I had hoped for more flamingos in the Flamingo Pond, but a group of land and marine iguanas, which seemed to be plentiful on the island, had claimed their territory. Iguanas were just as plentiful on South Plaza Island, where we marveled also at ice plants and a multitude of different birds, such as frigates, swallow-tailed gulls, brown pelicans, blue-footed boobies, etc. I could not get enough of the blue-footed boobies. They looked somewhat like ducks, with brown coloring and a pointed tail. Most importantly, their webbed feet were strikingly light blue. They circle the sky looking for fish in the water and dive straight down as soon as they spot one. Of course, so do many other sea birds.

Our launch at Santa Fe Island involved a hike through a forest of opuntia cacti (prickly pear), an incense-tree forest with fifteen-foot-tall scalesia, or "daisy trees," many birds, including the Galápagos hawk, and dozing land iguanas. We were lucky to find a pair of Galápagos penguins, relatives of the African and Magellanic penguins, both of which I had seen on previous travels. It is the only penguin that lives on the equator in a tropical environment, and it survives due to the cool ocean temperatures resulting from the Humboldt Current and the cool waters brought up from great depths by the Cromwell Current.

Some of my cotravelers raved about their swim with turtles and stingrays, in the midst of which sea seals darted suddenly through the stunning blue waters. I almost regretted not having brought my swim gear.

At Lobos Island, a few pelicans hovered not far from a sea-lion colony. And Española Island (Hood Island) did not disappoint either. Its galaxy of birds, such as Hood mockingbirds, blue-footed and masked boobies, and especially Darwin's cute, sparrow-sized finches that hopped about on the black lava flow, was particularly impressive. The rugged terrain was much harder for me to navigate than it was for the lively finches. Even though we were all given a cane for the duration of the trip, this excursion was more challenging, because the sun was beating down on us mercilessly.

Fireball Lily

We headed back to Santa Cruz Island and took a tour of the Darwin Research Station, where we were introduced to pioneering ecological studies and the giant Galápagos tortoise-breeding program. I did not need to be persuaded to believe in Darwin's theory of evolution and was happy to note that I was not the only one in the group. No Tea Party nuts in this group! Next we were off to the Tortoise Reserve, where we hiked through the highlands in the meadows with giant tortoises that live for about 150 years and weigh a ton. The tortoises were simply amazing and a sight to behold. People driving on the roads must stay on the lookout for tortoises, which wander about and across the road as they migrate to and from the ocean shore to the highlands, where the grasses and plants are lush and green.

We spent two nights at the best five-star hotel I had ever stayed in, even including those in the UAE and the Royal Palm Hotel in Santa Cruz, Ecuador. It is an exclusive retreat on five hundred acres of lush tropical forest. I had a gorgeous, thatched-roof Villa Jacuzzi suite, located not far from the ocean, all to myself. It was huge, with a living room and fireplace, a king-size bed in the spacious bedroom, a special Jacuzzi room with a thatched roof, and a spacious bathroom with extra dressing rooms, one with a bath and another with a huge shower. All the fixtures, including those in the lavatories, were copper, and the woodwork and paneled walls were dark mahogany. And there was a front porch. On the property, we had access to all the amenities one could wish for, including a library, Internet service, a swimming pool, a sauna, hiking trails, tennis courts, etc. If you did not want to walk to the dining room, a golf cart would pick you up. The meals were served in an exquisite dining room where the next morning, at breakfast time, I noticed a strikingly beautiful young woman. She was tall, slender, blue eyed, blond, evenly tanned, and dressed in a sexy white sporting outfit. Her little boy was not too well behaved, as he ran around the restaurant wildly. The nanny had a hard time catching him. When I asked our waiter about the lady, he volunteered that she was the wife of an "important" Russian politician who was expected to arrive at a later date. So much for that. This was a place where I missed having a husband or a red-hot lover. Unfortunately, we spent only two nights there, and overcast skies and an occasional drizzle dampened my spirits a bit.

July 24, 2013 – If I were Snowden, the heroic leaker who is presently stuck at the airport in Moscow, and Ecuador offered me asylum, I would take it.

Nevertheless, despite the weather we took our last excursion via boat to North Seymour Island, where we saw more of my favorites: frigates, blue-footed boobies, lava lizards, fur seals, etc.

If by then I had fallen in love with the blue-footed boobies, I was even more intrigued by the large colony of frigate birds, aka pirate birds, which are related to the pelican on North Seymour. In addition to admiring the nesting site of my blue-footed friends on the cliffsides and the sea lions riding the waves, I found the jet-black frigates simply awesome when they spread their long wings (on the males, as wide as seven feet) and inflated their bright-red gular pouches to attract a mate. I was spellbound whenever they sailed through the air above us and darted down to catch a fish, sat perched in bushes and trees, or sat nesting on the ground. The females have a white underbelly. I wish you could see my shot of a sailing frigate. Awesome!

While spending a couple more days in Quito before flying home, we visited more churches and were given time to explore the town by ourselves. I went souvenir shopping and got stuck with fellow travelers watching the second half and overtime of the Fútbol World Cup, between Brazil and Germany. It took place in Berlin, and fortunately or unfortunately, Brazil won 2 to 1. I always liked the Brazilians, because in 1979 I watched a *fútbol* game in Rio's famous stadium, Maracanã.

Equator

The final day was taken up by a visit to the open-air Intiñan Museum, not far from the Mitad del Mundo Monument. In this interactive museum, we witnessed, more dramatically than had been the case for me in Africa, the change in the water's swirling direction between the northern and southern hemispheres. They used a small tub of water with a few leaves in it to demonstrate the Coriolis effect. When they placed the tub drain directly over the equator and pulled the plug, the leaves drained straight down. When they moved the tub to one side of the equator, the drain created a small whirlpool that moved in the counterclockwise direction. After that, we visited the more traditional Middle of the World Monument, where they also had a red line marking the equator and where we attempted to do certain balancing exercises with one foot on each side of the line. Surprisingly, no one could keep their balance, since the opposite sides of the globe pull your body at a latitude of 0° 0' 0". It was also very hot up there. To perform the egg trick, you took a raw egg and balanced it on the head of a nail hammered into a board. If you could do it, as three or four people in our group could, you received a certificate. I could not, and like everybody else, I failed the balancing exercise that involved walking straight on the red line. I did not even attempt the strength test. I was not too disappointed that I did not receive a certificate. I had obtained one when I was at the equator in Kenya without performing all those tricks. Of course, we all had our photo taken as we stood behind the "Middle of the World" sign, and I personally was elated to see from up there one of the highest active volcanoes in the world, Cotopaxi Mountain, which is 19,000 feet high, known as "the Neck of the Moon," and worshipped as a rain sender and a sacred mountain by the indigenous people. Fabulous! Do not forget: on a previous trip, I was at 90 degrees north – on top of the world, that is, at the North Pole.

During the flight home, I realized I had forgotten to buy a shrunken-head souvenir. We were told that the shrinking of heads was practiced in the Amazon watershed as an act of revenge. They were actually quite civil about it. If two parties met on a trail, they both determined the ancestry of the person in question to decide if revenge was necessary for some trespass committed by a relative some two hundred years ago. They had to remove all the bones from the skull and then boil what was left and add some preservatives. If revenge was required, the head was shrunk after being removed from the body to which it belonged. I have been unable to discover whether they shrunk any missionary heads, since it is obvious that the missionaries did not always treat them kindly. Today, the souvenir heads are made of leather.

SOCIETY ISLANDS - FRENCH POLYNESIA - MS RENAISSANCE III

Tahiti

During the summer of 2000, while surfing the Internet, I came upon an announcement by Renaissance Cruises, Inc., inviting interested travelers on a cruise to Tahiti, in French Polynesia, which would start shortly before Christmas. A trip to exotic Tahiti had always been a dream of mine. "Come with Me to Tahiti, to Tahiti in the Ocean" was the title of a song that had caught my fancy as a teenager in Germany. I had good memories of a luxurious 1996 cruise with Renaissance in the Mediterranean when I was studying in France and of another one in the Caribbean, on an even more lavish Renaissance ship, with Tonio over Christmas in 1993. I did not think twice, called Renaissance, and asked for their brochures. As soon as I had gone through the details, I booked the trip, which required that I fly to Papeete, Tahiti, in time for embarkation on December 13. I flew over LA and arrived on time and without a hitch. The only trouble at the time was happening in the States in connection with the Gore versus Bush debacle, which had me glued to a TV wherever I could spot one, such as at the airport in LA. Since I had been a staunch supporter of Democrats ever since Nixon, I was among those hoping against hope that Gore would make it. When the courts sided with Bush, I could hardly believe it.

The *Renaissance III* was a midsize ship, about double the size of the ship I took to the Caribbean in 1966, but almost as elegant. It had room for 648 passengers. My cabin, which had a big window, was just gorgeous, and I spread my wings – that is, my belongings – because I had the extra space for a partner whom I had opted not to bring along, as there was none.

I did not read up on Tahiti and the Society Islands before I took off, knowing full well that all cruise ships bombard their passengers with informational flyers. As their information is always rather reliable, and since I have gone to the trouble of retaining all the info-flyers, if you do not mind, I will now take advantage of their courtesy and pass it on to you:

Comprised of volcanic peaks (the highest 7,337ft/2,236m) and surrounded by barrier reefs, the island of Tahiti is a breathtaking study of contrasts. Due to the high elevations, most of the island's population of approximately 160,000 people makes their homes along the coastal area of the island.

Tahiti is part of the Society Islands in the South Pacific, one of the five archipelagos that comprise French Polynesia. An overseas territory of France since 1946, French Polynesia covers a land area of approximately 1,600 square miles which although less than 1/3 the size of Connecticut spreads out over an area of roughly 2,000 square miles.

Discovered in 1767 by European explorer Samuel Wallis, it was not until Captain Cook made his voyage in 1769 that Tahiti became a destination of importance to the French. The arrival of missionaries as well as explorers greatly altered the lives of the native population. Archaeological studies date civilization back to 900 AD or sooner. However, there is still a great amount of mystery and speculation as to who the original Tahitians were and where they migrated.

Papeete

According to one of the informational flyers, "Papeete, capital of French Polynesia, is a cosmopolitan, 20th-century city. Although bustling and congested, one can still feel a certain Polynesian charm. Journeying to smaller towns on Tahiti can put one in touch with the tropical, romantic tales of the South Seas and the 'old' Tahiti that has become familiar through years of literature and Hollywood depictions. Home to many artists and writers, if only for a brief time, the world has long been exposed to the many wonders of French Polynesia."

All the information provided by Renaissance intensified my appetite for what I was about to experience. The suggested attire for the welcoming dinner was "country club casual." I had chosen to wear my newly acquired navy-blue silk "sailing suit," with golden anchor buttons which the rather distinguished-looking captain complimented as he shook my hand for the usual photograph. I was lucky to connect right away with several very nice and intelligent tourists, with whom I stayed in contact long after the trip was over. Professor Dr. Peter Breit, a German political-science specialist, and his equally intelligent and charming wife, Olive, were among them. Like me, they were retired and had emigrated from Germany, but unlike me, they were Jewish and from the East Coast. They did not have children and liked to escape over the holidays to a place far away. Both were devastated about the outcome of the election. I could go on and on, but prefer to zero in on the exotic ambiance, which had lured me to the South Pacific in the first place.

I had signed up for the Circle Island Tour of Tampeete in an air-conditioned minivan. Going through a much-too-busy downtown perplexed me. The place was unsightly and downright dirty. So much so that I forgot to look for the much-anticipated oceans of tropical flowers and exotic flowering shrubs and trees. The overcast skies made it worse. Fortunately, as we traveled east on the not-so-great roads, peppered with potholes, my searching eyes were finally rewarded. On both sides of the road stood magnificent royal palms, lush rainforest ferns, flowering shrubs and trees, huge poinsettias, orchids, and other unusual tropical plants, the names of which I have forgotten. The coast leading up to Point Venus, the landing site from which Captain Cook, Tahiti's first explorer, observed the transit of Venus in

1769, was beautiful. We lingered to see a memorial that listed the members of the London Missionary Society who landed there in 1797, and we admired the nineteenth-century lighthouse. I thought the black-sand beach looked striking next to green lawns and shady casuarina trees, and I felt uplifted while watching the white foam of the gentle waves caress the beach.

We continued through ever-more intoxicating rainforests toward Tiarei's Arahoho Blowhole, located at the base of a steep cliff on the roadside. It was quite dramatic to watch the waves crash against the rocks and to be showered by the geyser-like plume of seawater. Over countless years, the battering surf had undercut the basalt shoreline and eroded a passage to the surface beneath the road, creating this big roadside attraction, the blowhole. We could hear the roar of the sea erupting from the lava tube as we walked back to our van to continue the adventure.

We crossed the narrow Isthmus of Taravao, which connects Tahiti's two volcanic peaks, the spot where the big isle meets its peninsula, and continued west to Papeari. It is considered by some to be Tahiti's oldest village. We did not stop at the museum dedicated to Paul Gaugin. I did not complain, because the place did not look very promising, and I had heard it did not house any remarkable originals. Our guide showed us the cascading Valpahi waterfall before taking us to the romantic, ferny Maraa Grotto, where overhead springs seep through ferns and giant elephant-ear plants into a cool romantic cave by the sea. We returned to the ship via Puna'auia, an overseas territory of France where Gauguin lived in the late 1890s. He is said to have painted his masterpiece – *Where Do We Come From? What Are We? Where Are We Going?* – right there. We continued along the Taina Marina coastline to Papeete, where the *R3* was waiting for us and served a delicious dinner. I spoke to a Chinese couple from Vancouver who swore the *R3* served the best food of the thirty or more cruise ships on which they had sailed.

On December 14, I decided to take it easy and join Anne Eglise, who escorted us to the Robert Wan Pearl Museum, located in downtown Papeete. I had always been interested in pearls and halfway believed that a gift of pearls from a lover would lead to tears down the line, which was the case with the first pearl necklace I ever received. The second strand of pearls, though bought by me prior to my marriage to Tonio, also failed to bring me luck. The museum was quite impressive, and upscale. "Robert Wan, who dedicated his life to the Tahitian cultured pearl, had opened this museum in 1999. It is the only museum in the world dedicated to pearls in general and Tahiti's gem in particular" (Brochure). In short, he is the largest pearl producer in the country. It was a dazzling experience and very tempting. I had never seen so many pearls crafted into such incredibly artistic pieces of jewelry made of platinum, silver, gold, etc. In the end, I did purchase a little broach – a black pearl set in platinum shaped like a bat. I paid too much for it, but knew it would probably be much appreciated by my newfound step-relative Diane Beardsley. She seemed pleased. That's the last time I bought a pearl for someone else. I had heard that black pearls in particular bring bad luck. And, to prove the point, the Diane friendship turned out to be quite superficial and slowly evaporated into thin air. During the visit to the museum, I learned that Tahitian keshi pearls are composed entirely of nacre, that is, mother-of-pearl, and that they are collected after the larger pearl has been removed from the mother shell. When back on the ship and sorting through my brochures, I realized I had totally overlooked a coupon that would have entitled me to a free gift of one Tahitian keshi pearl with a natural-colored shell jewelry case. Too bad.

On the way back to the ship, the guide pointed out the Catholic Notre Dame Cathedral of Papeete, built in the late nineteenth century. I would call it a minicathedral, Neo-Gothic plain and simple, but it was obviously a place of worship and a point of pride for those who built it.

In the afternoon, we had the mandatory general-emergency and lifeboat drill, and at 7:15 p.m. we filed in, in more or less dressed-up attire, to join Captain Michele de Rosa for the Renaissance champagne reception – with music, of course. I enjoyed the dinner, during which I chatted with newly made friends, but preferred to skip the show in the Cabaret Lounge to watch *Erin Brockovich* with Julia Roberts and Albert Finney in my very nice cabin.

Huahine

The *R3* dropped anchor the next morning in Maroe Bay, Huahine, 108 miles northwest of Tahiti. "Huahine is known for its serrated coastline, long beaches, ancient maraes, picturesque main town and independent spirited residents. Painters and writers have repeatedly and unanimously bathed this island in a special light. It is a kind of 'Provence of the South Seas.' It is part of the Society Islands, but belongs more precisely to the Leeward Islands (Illes sous le Vent). . . . Huahine consists of two volcanic ranges, the larger, Huahine Nui, is in the north and the small, Huahine It, in the south. The two are joined by a kind of natural bridge and embraced by a protective coral reef. About 4000 people live on the two islands and most of them earn a living growing cantaloupes, watermelons and harvesting copra for the Papeete market" (*R3* brochure).

A 4x4 open jeep picked us up to take us on the Huahine Highlights safari. Though the temperature was near 90 degrees Fahrenheit and it was already drizzling, we were ready to brave the not-so-promising weather. No sooner had we started than the rain turned into a heavy shower. Our guide stopped and pulled out several plastic sheets to put over our heads and along the sides of the vehicle. It was quite an adventure, because those plastic covers were flapping happily in the wind, which allowed the rain to settle on our faces and bodies. It was both exciting and amusing when our driver navigated the jeep around or through very muddy, bumpy, and water-filled potholes in the road. Our seats were wooden benches on each side; thus, the rough ride shook us up quite a bit. By the time we reached the vanilla-orchid farms, where some in the group were anxious to purchase a package or two of the precious spice pods (it is the second most expensive spice, after saffron), the sun had come out. I could barely smell the otherwise intoxicating aroma. The rain had obviously dampened it. I had no idea that the vanilla orchids grow like vines on a pole or tree. Since I am not very interested in baking, I did not buy vanilla beans.

More curious were the three-to-six-foot-long slithering, blue-eyed freshwater eels, which we fed with mackerel from a can at the old stonefish traps beneath a bridge that crossed over a stream. The eels are deemed sacred by local mythology. I am not sure whether these eels are the same as or related to those we used to buy smoked at a lake not far from Hannover. Those were so delicious – definitely not "divine," but very special and very expensive. They hung on a line between two poles with baby-blue or bright-red ribbons and price tags tied around their necks.

Our guide retraced the ancient paths through Maeva, home to the largest and best-preserved coastal *maraes* (ancient sacrificial stone temples) on the island. The village resembled an open-air museum and dates back thousands of years. After that stop, we continued to Maroe Bay and Huahine Iti, where we were stunned by the most spectacular ocean views. The crystal-clear blue waters of the South Pacific contrasted harmoniously with the lush green mountain ranges in the background.

Each day I spent cruising the islands, I became more bewitched by the paradisiacal ambiance, and the abundance of tropical flowers was overwhelming. As flowers play an important part in the lives of the islanders, I will quote a passage from my *R3* brochure:

You will never see a race of people so enamored with putting flowers in their hair as the French Polynesians. Fresh flower tiaras or hibiscus blossoms are always worn behind the ear or braided with palm fronds and other greenery into floral crowns. Tradition has it that if a woman or man tucks the flower behind the left ear she or he is taken. A flower placed behind the right ear means the person is available. Tahitians joke that if someone waves a flower behind their head it means 'follow me!'

I liked the "thought for the day" on our flyer: "Some people come into our lives and quickly go. Some stay for a while and leave footprints on our hearts. And we are never, ever, the same."

Bora Bora

On December 16 and 17, the *R3* set anchor in Bora Bora, which, according to the *R3* brochure, "ever since its depiction as a Garden of Eden by the 19th century romantics has together with all the islands surrounding Tahiti attracted not only missionaries and vagabonds, but artists and writers as well." These artists and writers, according to the brochure, had the following to say about the island:

The reason why I am leaving [Paris] is that I wish to live in peace and to avoid being influenced by our civilization. I only desire to create simple art. In order to achieve this, it is necessary for me to steep myself in virgin nature, to see no one but savages, to share their life and have as my sole occupation to render, just as children would do, the images of my own brain, using exclusively the means offered by primitive art, which are the only true and valid ones. (Paul Gauguin)

There were none of the thousand sources of irritation that the ingenuity of civilized man has created to mar his own felicity. There are no debtors, no orphans, no destitute, no lovesick maidens, no grumpy bachelors, no melancholy youth, no spoiled brats and none of the root of all evil – money. (Herman Melville, *Typee*)

The languor of this island, the Polynesian playfulness, the contractive sexuality that abounded there, could not save him from his ultimate and wretched fate. That of course was Gauguin's predetermined course of tragedy. (W. Somerset Maugham, *The Moon and Sixpence*)

Bora Bora enjoys the reputation of being the most beautiful island in the world. This tropical paradise covers less than fifteen square miles. Its high volcanic peaks, translucent blue lagoons, and lush landscape will remain imprinted in my memory forever.

I did not sign up for another tour, because I preferred just to explore this jewel, located 166 miles from Tahiti and first sighted by Captain Cook in 1769, by myself. Bora Bora was under its own rule until 1888, when she became a territory of France. World War II brought over four thousand soldiers to the island after the attack on Pearl Harbor. It was a US air base, and in 1977 the island was inundated by film crews, including Marlon Brando's crew for *Mutiny on the Bounty*, which I watched one night in my cabin. To watch *Mutiny on the Bounty* with Mel Gibson and Anthony Hopkins at the very place where the action took place on April 28, 1789, when Lieutenant Bligh's cruelty resulted in the mutiny, was a surreal experience, strange and exciting. The second night, I watched another favorite, *South Pacific*, filmed in Hawaii. A cotraveler from Hawaii told me Bora Bora can easily be compared to some Hawaiian islands.

I leisurely explored several small, palm-covered islands (*motus*), took off my sandals, walked on the white-sand beaches, and relaxed in the shade of a palm tree, gazing toward the sea until it was time for a picnic served in the shade of a palm-tree grove. I chatted with several of my new acquaintances and somewhat regretted that the Bloody Mary restaurant, named after the song in *South Pacific*, was closed.

The next day, I ventured out again and was enthralled when on one of the *motus* I came upon the overwater bungalows of the Hilton Bora Bora Nui Resort and Spa, in which anyone can watch the multicolored fish frolicking in the crystal-clear turquoise waters through a glass floor. It was definitely a place where I would not mind spending a last honeymoon. It seemed almost bizarre when eight years or so later, Doc's great grandson Eric spent his honeymoon in an overwater bungalow in Bora Bora with his bride.

Raiatea

We spent December 18 and 19 on the Leeward Society Islands, the sister islands Raiatea and Tahaa. Eighteen miles west of Huahine, they are separated by a narrow strait with many small reefs, but share a barrier reef that has a few passages through which their many harbors can be entered. Legend has it that they were once one island but split when a sacred giant eel swallowed a young maiden. Her spirit enraged the eel, causing it to break through the surface of the earth, merging the two bodies of water. "Raiatea, the most sacred island (as well as the largest) in French Polynesia, is the religious, cultural and historical heart of the Polynesian Maohi, ancestors of today's Tahitians. Raiatea, more precisely the Faaroa River, was the departure point for the Maohi who left to establish settlements in New Zealand. The Faaroa River is the only navigable river in French Polynesia" (*R3* brochure).

The volcanic mountains, crystal-blue lagoons, and awe-inspiring temples make this place the quintessential South Seas destination. Today, Raiatea is undergoing a renaissance of sorts. Careful planning is underway to renovate Uturoa, the island's capital and the port where we docked, with particular attention to preserving the island's character. Although relatively devoid of beaches, the relaxing and secluded surrounding *motus* can add an element of adventure to the typical beach-going experience.

Tahaa

Tahaa, approximately 2 miles to the north of Raiatea, is an even more unspoiled destination. The 4,000 residents live a modest existence, making their living through agricultural endeavors such as raising livestock and fishing. Copra (coconut) and vanilla are produced commercially. Tahaa is the number one producer of vanilla in the Society Islands. Black pearl farming is also a thriving industry. (*R3* brochure)

I had decided to spend the forenoon by myself and just soak up the tropical atmosphere of this enchanting island, where Gauguin had sought to find peace as an artist. But I had signed up for an afternoon trip to a private, family-operated black-pearl farm on Tahaa's main island. It was fascinating to see how this family of pearl farmers practiced the craft of grafting and culturing pearls in Pacific oysters. I had heard the black pearl is known as "the pearl of queens" and "the queen of pearls" and that long before Western man discovered Tahiti existed, the black pearl was known for its exceptional value and rarity. I did not know that the process of raising a pearl oyster is very lengthy and, because the species is quite fragile, requires extraordinary care and attention. The pearl farmers watch over the black-lipped oyster constantly. If the weather is stormy, the oysters are immersed more deeply in the lagoon. If it is warm, they are moved to a cooler place. It is a process that takes several years, and I will remember the experience of observing a part of it whenever I come upon pearls.

While reading my *R3* literature, I came upon the following information about "how waves are formed": "Most waves are formed by winds which move across the ocean's surface, mile after mile. As the winds shift, the waves come from several directions and form a changeable pattern. These seemingly endless waves that ripple past our ship's hull, could have been created several hundred miles away. Three factors interplay to create waves. The first is the force of the wind. The second is the duration of the wind. And the last is the amount of uninterrupted sea over which these winds continue to slow. When winds blow at a rate faster than the waves, the waves soak up the winds' energy and continue to grow in size. That is the reason waves in the Pacific Ocean are generally larger than those in the Atlantic, they have greater distances over which they can build. The sea covers nearly three-quarters of the earth's surface with an average depth being more than two miles. The average ocean wave is between 150 and 300 feet in length and moves at an incredible speed. Interestingly, a wave breaks whereas a swell does not."

Moorea

Our cruise was nearing its conclusion when, on December 20, the *R3* threw anchor in Cook's Bay of Moorea. Moorea sounded almost more alluring than the previous islands: "Here is an island so stunningly beautiful that Hollywood often uses stock shots of its jagged mountains, deep bays, and emerald lagoons to create a South Seas setting for movies that don't even take place in French Polynesia. Geologists say Moorea is twice as old as Tahiti and once contained a volcano that reached 1,000 ft. Moorea's magnificent beauty covers an area of 136 square miles, which is the south rim of a crater that was formed following cataclysmic explosions eons ago. Cathedral-like Mount Mouaroa, Moorea's trademark 'Shark's Tooth' or 'Bali Hai Mountain' shows up on innumerable postcards and on the 100 CFP coin. Most of the island's 11,000 or so residents live on its fringing coastal plain; many of them in small settlements where lush valleys meet the lagoon. Vanilla was the island's big crop early in the 20th century, and clapboard 'vanilla houses' built with the profits still stand, surrounded by wide verandas trimmed with Victorian fretwork. Vegetables, pineapples, and copra are still grown and shipped to the market in Papeete" (*R3* brochure).

It may interest you to know what Renaissance shared regarding Polynesia's history: "Polynesia was populated as the result of successive waves of migration, coming from Southeast Asia and starting over 30,000 years ago. The Marquesas were the first islands to be settled by these fearless sailors on their large seafaring canoes. For 300 years they remained cut off from the rest of the world until the arrival of the first Europeans. Wallis was the first European to reach the shores of Tahiti in 1767, but Cook, Bligh and Bouganville, a Frenchman, were right behind him" (*R3* brochure). I thank *R3* for their flyers. They saved me a lot of time researching.

At times, when you write about your travels around the world, it is hard to think of new words to describe the wonders you have been privileged to behold. It is true that words often fail me in my efforts to paint the incredibly dramatic sunsets that stunned me each evening on this cruise. It is equally difficult to describe to you in detail the performance of the exotic Polynesian dancers on our ship. Wherever I looked, it was a profusion of the most vivid colors. Their costumes, the flower leis around their necks, and the orchid wreaths on their heads were as intoxicating as the abundance of fruits and vegetables displayed on the market stands behind which women stood, showing their beautiful white teeth as they smiled. Each of them wore a wreath of orchid, hibiscus, or bougainvillea blossoms on their head, like brides on their way to the altar. I asked several of the ladies who had a white blossom stuck behind each ear if I could take a picture of them. One was sitting on a stool immersed in an ocean of the most vibrant tropical flowers, another was showing off the baskets she had crafted, and a third was engaged in butchering a huge, fat fish lying on the table in front of her. The flesh of the fish was as dark a pink as some of the blossoms arranged at the neighboring stand.

That evening, the captain invited us to the farewell party. I wore the Bagshaws skirt Tonio had bought for me in Saint Lucia while cruising the Caribbean. In terms of attire for this paradisiacal utopia, the distinct tropical floral design was as colorful as I could have wished for. I almost looked like a native due to my nice tan and the white blossoms behind each of my ears.

We disembarked on December 21, during Hanukkah, and I said good-bye to my friends Peter and Olive Breit, who had suffered with me through the extremely disturbing results of the election, disturbing because we now had to cope with a president as stupid as the one the Supreme Court had favored. Before I had to deal with that reality, I would spend a couple of days at Universal Studios, where I had to wait in line for at least two hours to get in. While waiting, I got a good idea of what it is like to be virtually the only non-Latina as far as I could see. I felt a bit strange, because my Spanish was not good enough to strike up a conversation. – Universal Studios was fascinating all around. I questioned the winter scene with pine trees and fake snow. That too was strange. – I was anxious to return home, where I would have just enough time to get ready for my next escape: Cancún, Mexico.

BALTIC SEA - NORWEGIAN CRUISE LINE'S MS NORWEGIAN STAR

England

London

On August 2, 2002, I took off on an American Airlines flight and headed, not for the first time in my life, to London. I had booked a Baltic cruise with Norwegian Cruise Lines on their *Norwegian Star*, which was to start on August 5 from Dover, in the United Kingdom, some seventy-five miles from London. Never in my wildest dreams had I thought I would ever get a glimpse of Dover, which I remembered from the bombings during World War II and the jokes we played in boarding school. We held up a box of matches, lit one, held it over someone's head, and said, "Fire over Dover" (*Doof*, pronounced with an *o* like the one in *stove*, means "stupid" in German).

I flew to London a couple days before the start of the cruise to meet with my young friend Bettina, who by then was a successful attorney in Berlin. We stayed at London's Thistle Tower Hotel. It was wonderful to hang out, talk until the wee hours, and enjoy a city sightseeing tour by bus and another by boat on the Thames during which we saw popular tourist places like Buckingham Palace, Westminster Abbey, London Bridge, Tower Bridge, Windsor Castle, etc. New to me was the London Eye, which we admired from a distance, but due to long lines and heavy rain, we opted out of the $50 ride that would have taken us closer. Since neither one of us had seen the Crown Jewels, we scheduled a separate visit to the Tower of London, home to the treasure as well as the legendary beefeaters (prison guards). We had to wait in the rain there as well, but at least, once we had entered this impressive fortress, which had in its time served as a royal palace, prison, armory, and even zoo, it was dry inside.

The Tower of London was constructed over nine hundred years ago by William the Conqueror and was then expanded by other medieval kings. I witnessed reenactments of the beheading of three queens of England and the torture of numerous prisoners. The big attractions were the queen's dazzling Cullinan Diamond, the exquisite Koh-i-Noor, which became part of the British Crown Jewels when Queen Victoria was proclaimed empress of India in 1877, and the infamous ceremonial beefeaters. They have the duty of guarding the treasure but in practice act as tour guides, outfitted in their striking uniforms. Supposedly, they were paid in rations that included beef, mutton, and veal. Their preference was beef. If you are interested in arms, you will find a vast collection in the White Tower. It houses an exhibition of Tudor, Stuart, Hanoverian, and Windsor arms and armor "fit for a king." I was particularly interested in seeing the spot where Mary Stewart was beheaded, because I was gripped by Friedrich Schiller's portrayal of her in his play *Maria Stewart*.

I might add that "the largest polished gem from the stone is named Cullinan I, or the Great Star of Africa, and at 530.4 carats was the largest polished diamond in the world until the 1985 discovery of the Golden Jubilee Diamond, 545.67 carats, also from the Premier Mine. Cullinan I is now mounted in the head of the Scepter with the Cross. The second largest gem from the Cullinan stone, Cullinan II or the Lesser Star of Africa, at 317.4 carats, is the fourth largest polished diamond in the world. Both gems are in the Crown Jewels of the UK" (NCL brochure). Once you have seen them, you will never forget them!

It was a nice start for the Baltic cruise, and it was even nicer that I had seen Bettina. We waved our good-byes, and she stood outside the bus until it left and took me to the port in Dover, where I embarked around noon. The ship departed at 4:00 p.m. on August 5, 2002. I was grateful for my ocean-view cabin on the MS *Norwegian Star*. Since I had traveled previously with NCL, I was familiar with the glitzy ambiance. This ship was renamed in 1998 after a two-month project to "stretch" the ship in Bremerhaven, Germany. For $69 million, they lengthened it by 133 feet, for a total of 754 feet. I liked the *Star*, because with a gross tonnage of 50,764, it was smaller than others of NCL's fleet. By the way, Diana Ross had christened the ship on December 6, 1992. I welcomed their open-seating policy, which gave me a chance to choose my table companions and thus to meet people from all walks of life and many countries. As usual, I was up on the sundeck when we left the harbor and was elated when I watched the setting sun cast a golden shimmer over the White (chalk) Cliffs of Dover!

Since Roman times, there has been a landing place in the southeast corner of England called Dubris by the Romans. Dover is situated at the narrowest point on the English Channel, and has always been a natural port of entry into Britain as well as a witness to history.

The ancient road from London to Canterbury, known as Watling Street in Chaucer's Canterbury Tales, continued on to the coast at Dover. King Richard I embarked from here on the Third Crusade in 1190. Dover Castle, on the heights above the town, was regarded as 'the Key to England' and was captured by the Parliamentarians in 1642 during the English Civil War. Eighteen years later the Restoration began here with the return of Charles II.

In more modern times, Woodrow Wilson became the first American president to visit England when he landed at Dover in 1918. The city played a prominent part in the evacuation of Dunkirk and was one of the first places bombed during the Battle of Britain. From the 11th Century, Dover was one of the Cinque Ports, a series of five harbor towns on the southern coast of England charged by the Crown with supplying ships of the Royal Fleet. (NCL)

Germany

Kiel Canal

I regarded this cruise more or less as an appetizer for a part of Europe I had not yet visited. Not long after embarkation, our ship headed toward Germany, where the next day we passed through the Kiel Canal, in German the Nord-Ostsee-Kanal, known as the Kaiser-Wilhelm-Kanal until 1948. I stood on deck waving cheerfully at onlookers along the shoreline, where cows and horses grazed peacefully. As a result of the stretching project, the ship's funnel and radar mast had been hydraulically equipped to allow a large portion of the mast to be lowered and the top third of the funnel to be flipped, in turn allowing our ship to pass under bridges in the canal. Though the canal transit took about eight hours, the canal saves travelers 250 nautical miles by obviating a trip around the Jutland Peninsula and avoiding potentially dangerous, storm-prone areas. It is considered the most heavily used artificial seaway in the world.

The canal was built between 1887 and 1895 and initially served the German military. It was enlarged between 1907 and 1914 to accommodate large naval ships. Prior to World War I the German government owned the canal, but in 1919 the Treaty of Versailles laid down new regulations that internationalized the canal while leaving it under German administration. Traffic on the canal was subject only to general police, shipping, sanitary, and customs regulations. These provisions were repudiated by Adolf Hitler in 1936; however since World War II, the canal has been in the State of Schleswig-Holstein, and the conditions of the Treaty of Versailles guaranteeing freedom of navigation have again been practiced. (NCL)

Once our long and varied passage was completed, the *Star* stopped to pick up several tourists who had gone sightseeing in nearby Hamburg.

Estonia

Tallinn

Wednesday was spent cruising the Baltic Sea, and on Thursday, August 8, 2002, at 12:00 noon, we docked at Tallinn, in Estonia Harbor, for a six-hour sightseeing tour on foot through the small Estonian capital, which has a population of 414,940 and is situated on the southern coast of the Gulf of Finland, not more than fifty miles south of Helsinki. I was pleasantly surprised by my first encounter with this beautiful medieval city. The cobblestones and alleys and the well-preserved historical architecture reminded me of German medieval towns, an association that was confirmed when our well-educated, pretty, blond-and-blue-eyed guide explained that the upper town was traditionally inhabited by German aristocrats. I will always remember the fourteenth-century Viru Gate, the entrance to the Town Hall square. It is the gateway to the heart of the city, where the Tallinn Town Hall, with its striking Gothic architecture, stands. It is admired as "the only one of its kind in Northern Europe" (NCL). Just as memorable were the Great Guild Hall, the Estonian History Museum, and St. Olaf's Church, which used to be the tallest building in the world. From there, we were granted a fabulous panoramic view of the Tallinn Old Town. Another highlight was Toompea (Upper Town) Castle, the impressive medieval fortress that houses the Estonian Parliament and the Russian Orthodox Alexander Nevsky Cathedral, which was built during the period of the Russian Empire on a site that formerly housed a statue of Martin Luther.

Of course, one cannot overlook Tallinn's amazingly well-preserved city walls. It came as no surprise that Tallinn is considered a European Capital of Culture. Tallinn became the capital of an independent, democratic Estonian state in August 1991. I had an intense conversation with our young guide while we walked through the cobblestone alleys. She was not sure whether it would be good for Estonia to join the EU, and I wonder how she feels today. Estonia became a member of the EU in the spring of 2004 and adopted the euro on January 1, 2011. In short, the stop in Tallinn was very pleasant. The city is definitely worth a trip. The people are hospitable and the places are neat, not overrun by tourists, and full of opportunities for picture-perfect photos. If I were younger, I would plan a return visit.

Russia I

Saint Petersburg

We left Tallinn at 6:00 p.m. on Thursday and docked at 8:30 a.m. the next morning, August 9, at Port Saint Petersburg, Russia. We had two days to explore this city, referred to, like many others around the globe, as the "Venice of the North." I had signed up for a three-hour excursion, which was announced by NCL as follows: "It is an introduction to St. Petersburg. The mighty Neva River curves through the central city, and some 360 bridges arch above the extensive waterways and canals, lined with palaces and onion-domed cathedrals. You'll see the Academy of Arts, the university, the monumental Rostral Columns, the famous Winter Palace and the *Aurora*, the ship that fired the blank round signaling the start of the 1917 Bolshevik Revolution. You will also see the Admiralty and the famous Bronze Horseman statue depicting the city's founder, Peter the Great and immortalized in the poem by Pushkin. Just beyond the statue is magnificent St. Isaac's Cathedral, one of the world's largest domed structures. You will also view the Peter and Paul Fortress, the oldest building in St. Petersburg. Until 1917, it was used as a political prison."

I fell in love with Saint Petersburg instantly. We soon learned that the government had heavily invested in sprucing up the city for its three hundredth anniversary, on May 27, 2003. Indeed, they were still in the process. As I think back, and in looking at my photos, each building stood out in one way or another. Peter the Great (Peter I), the city's founder, had succeeded, together with Alexander Menshikov, the city's first governor, in making Saint Petersburg the new capital of Russia. The city does not pale in comparison with any other European capital in terms of splendor and importance. One can easily recognize why Saint Petersburg symbolizes the European part of Russia and is one of the most venerable capitals in the world. I was glad the city had restored its original name, that is, changed it back from Leningrad, as the city was subject to the Soviet Republic from 1931 to 1993 and has since then been a city of federal importance, a separate administrative unit of the Russian Federation (like Moscow). I will never forget that President George W. Bush, when visiting Saint Petersburg, embarrassed us when he revealed his ignorance of the fact that it was the same city as Leningrad. In short, the city held me spellbound throughout my all-too-brief stay. "The greatest reigns and architectural chefs-d'oeuvre of the 18th and 20th centuries are embraced in one chronicle of St. Petersburg" (NCL).

Our excellent guide spoke in detail about the suffering imposed on the population during the Civil War, in 1917–1922, and especially during the Second World War, in 1941–1945 (nine hundred days of the German blockade, famine, and ruin), and about the harsh winters and the millions who froze to death and died of postwar hunger until 1947. Of course, I could easily relate to that, as we Germans struggled hard during those years and often went to bed hungry. My uncle Karl was among the German soldiers who never returned from Russia. Casualties from the Siege of Leningrad totaled over six million. It was one of the longest and most destructive sieges in history and one of the most costly in terms of casualties. It resulted from the failure of the German Army Group North to capture Leningrad in the Eastern Front theater of World War II. We learned that Hitler was so confident about capturing Leningrad that he had the invitations to the victory celebrations, to be held in the city's Hotel Astoria, printed in advance. Some fantasized about renaming the city "Adolfsburg" and making it the capital of the new Ingermanland province of the Reich in Generalplan Ost. Leave it to the Germans to suffer from delusions of grandeur.

I was quite impressed by the late-neoclassical Byzantine Greek-cross cathedral on St. Isaac's Square, ordered by Tsar Alexander I. Its main cast-iron dome rises 333 feet and is plated, like most Russian onion-shaped steeples, with pure gold. The columns, pilasters, floor, and statue of Montferrand, made of multicolored granites and marbles from all parts of Russia, were stunning. Eight columns of semiprecious stone frame the iconostasis: six of malachite and two smaller ones of azurite. Somehow I felt strangely overwhelmed while trying to digest this imperious splendor. I felt more uplifted when I finally stood in front of the striking baroque hermitage, that is, the Winter Palace, located along the Palace Embankment on the Neva River. It is a complex of six historic buildings housing nearly three million items, including the largest collection of paintings in the world.

The history of the Hermitage as a museum began with Peter the Great, who himself bought a number of works of art – among them Rembrandt's David and Goliath and the Tauride Venus. In the reign of Catherine II the imperial collections occupied rooms in the Hermitage of the Winter Palace, which gave its name to the museum. The museum is considered to have been officially born in 1764, when in payment of a debt the Berlin dealer Gotzkowski sent the Empress of Russia 225 paintings intended for Frederick II of Russia. Catherine bought many more works of art (including many complete collections) in Paris, Dresden and London.

A fire swept through and devastated the Winter Palace in December of 1837. The imperial collections were saved. It was decided in 1839 that a New Hermitage should be built to house the collections properly and display them to the general public. Nicholas I opened the museum in 1852. (NCL)

It is impossible for me to do justice even to our comparatively brief visit to the Hermitage. Suffice it to say that the overall impression was highly exhilarating. I was awestruck and promised myself I would return some day. No doubt, the Hermitage rivals the Louvre, the Cairo Museum of Art, and any museum in New York, Berlin, Munich, Dresden, Florence, Rome, or Milan, etc. It's a must-see! I did not know that the Oscar-winning Soviet adaptation of Leo Tolstoy's novel *War and Peace* was partially filmed in the Winter Palace. Tolstoy's novels are among my favorites. And, lest I forget, another highlight was Catherine the Great's functioning golden-peacock clock, designed by James Cox, which took the Russians some nine years to assemble. It is displayed in a special glass pavilion and considered the only large eighteenth-century automaton in the world to have come down to us unaltered and in a functioning condition. It's just gorgeous! They supposedly play it every Wednesday. We missed it.

But I did not miss a most memorable performance of the ballet *Giselle*, written in 1841 by the French composer Adolphe Adam, that evening at the Mussorgsky-Mikhailovsky Theatre. It was an exhilarating performance, and during the intermission I struck up an exciting conversation with a couple from Rostock, in the former German Democratic Republic. Liebich was a shipping engineer and his wife an MD. We e-mailed for a number of years, but eventually drifted apart. I got sick and tired of their constant whining about the fact that in many ways, life for them in East Germany had been so much better than it was at present. The one positive, though, was the fact that they were now free to travel the world, which they do.

We spent almost half of the following day at the captivating, baroque Peterhof: "Peterhof (also known as Petrovorets), one of the oldest summer palaces in the St. Petersburg region, was named after the first Emperor of Russia. Peter the Great built a preliminary residence here in 1710. Then, in place of this small wooden building, he proceeded to construct a far bigger palace in 1714. . . . The Great Palace still has the exterior planned by the Empress Elizabeth I. After 1745, she had the initial building altered by the architect Bartolomeo Rastrelli (the initial architect of the Hermitage). After he enlarged Peter I's original palace, he added a couple of single-floor galleries to it. He also surrounded the Upper Park with a long railing punctuated by broad pillars, later designing formal enfilade in the purest Baroque style. The wide variety of fountains at Peterhof is the principal feature of the park. Elsewhere, all surviving fountains are classical in design; not so at Peterhof, where their extravagance and sheer playfulness give us a vivid idea of the atmosphere that must have reigned in a park of this kind during the early 18th century. The Great Cascade, with its Samson Fountain, is the most impressive of all. Peterhof covers 2,500 acres and remains one of the main attractions of St. Petersburg today" (NCL). The sun was shining while I walked around the grounds, snapping many, many photos. The golden statues next to the active fountains were sparkling! One felt transported into a realm completely disconnected from the poverty-stricken residential sections of this glamorous city. On the way back to the ship, we saw only a fraction of the stark poverty still prevalent in Russia. Not all is what it appears to be, in Saint Petersburg as in other grandiose cities around the globe. Unfortunately, those of us who are more privileged too frequently forget this fact.

I almost forgot to tell you about our stop at the Church of the Savior on Spilled Blood. One of the many stunning Orthodox cathedrals and churches in Saint Petersburg, it is also the spot where, after a number of unsuccessful attempts, Alexander II was assassinated by a group of revolutionaries, who threw a bomb at his royal carriage on March 1, 1881. Alfred Parland designed the church in the style of sixteenth- and seventeenth-century traditional Russian Renaissance churches, and it represents a stark contrast to its surroundings, dominated by baroque, classical, and modernist architecture. Over the years, the church was subjected to looting, used as a garbage dump, and, during the siege, severely damaged and threatened with demolition. But it survived, and following a major restoration, which took thirty years and cost almost five million rubles, it was reopened to the public in August 1997, six years after the fall of the Soviet Union. The collection of mosaic icons in this church, and especially the extravagant shrine on the spot where Alexander II was fatally wounded, are amazing! I felt ecstatic when I walked toward the church on Nevsky Prospect and saw it from about 150 feet away in all its dazzling glory, with the six onion-shaped steeples decorated in blue and gold and sparkling like giant jewels in the blue sky. Of course, everybody is familiar with this picturesque church on the Kanal Griboedova, which strongly resembles St. Basil's Cathedral in Moscow. It always seems to me like a fairy-tale castle. It's magical.

I wish I could remember the intimate concert hall in a palace where a group of string instrumentalists performed a selection of Mozart compositions for us. It was a wonderful end to our brief stay in this Russian city, where the arts reign supreme.

Finland

Helsinki

On Sunday, August 11, 2002, the *Star* made a scenic approach toward Finland's Helsinki Harbour, where it docked gently at 8:00 a.m. The sky was blue, and the sun looked promising. After a good breakfast, I happily joined the guide for a walking tour of Finland's capital-by-the-sea, which has 560,000 inhabitants and is known as "the Daughter of the Baltic." In 2000, the NCL flyer described it as "Europe's city of culture," adding that "there is a lot to see here: architecture from different periods, parks, museums, galleries, boutiques and shopping centers."

We were also introduced to a bit of Finland's history: "During the age of the Vikings the Finns became exposed to both eastern and western influences. Vikings from Sweden used the Åland Islands (colonized by Swedes in the 6th century AD) as a base for their journeys of pillage and trade into Russia as far south as the Black Sea. Although they did not actually participate in these Viking expeditions, the Finns benefited by the growing contact and the establishment of trading colonies in their country by merchants from Sweden and Gotland. At the end of the 11th century, three Finnish tribes had spread as far north as the 62nd parallel: The Finns proper in the southwest, the Tavastians in the interior lake district, and the Karelians to the east. Saami were also living in the wilderness to the north. No unified government or state existed" (NCL).

Finland, which has a rather flat landscape, few hills, and even fewer mountains, boasts thousands of lakes and islands as well as the largest forested area in Europe, predominantly coniferous taiga forests. Finland became an EU member in 1995 and joined the eurozone in 1999.

Since it was Sunday, the city seemed almost empty. I was impressed by the iconostasis of the Uspenski Orthodox Cathedral, built in 1862–1868 on top of a hill on the Katajanokka Peninsula. It is considered the largest Orthodox church in Western Europe. I climbed the many steps to the Evangelical Lutheran Helsinki Cathedral, aka St. Nicholas' Church, built in 1830–1852. It stands in the center of the city and displays a tall green dome surrounded by four smaller domes, and it was designed by Carl Ludvig Engel with the intention of making it the climax of the entire Senate Square. The connection with Saint Isaac's Cathedral in Saint Petersburg, which I saw a couple of days earlier, was obvious to me.

From the top of the stairs in the center of the Senate Square, I had a perfect view of the statue of Emperor Alexander II on a pedestal, surrounded by figures representing the law, culture, and the peasants. On the eastern side of the square was the Palace of the Council of State, which now houses the offices of the prime minister of Finland. On the opposite side of the Senate Square was the main university building, constructed in 1832. At the time of my visit, around 35,000 students were enrolled in degree programs. The university interested me insofar as, years ago, the father of my friend Telle Bayerle (aka Tellervo Ravila) was president of the institution. It ranks in the top one hundred worldwide.

Prior to visiting Temppeliaukio Kirkko (Rock Church) in Helsinki, we had a chance to appreciate the controversial, yet striking, Sibelius sculpture, which is dedicated to the Finnish composer Jean Sibelius (1865–1957) and stands in Sibelius Park. It is made up of more than six hundred hollow steel tubes resembling organ pipes. In case you did not know, Sibelius did not play the organ.

I was more intrigued by the Rock Church, designed by the architects and brothers Timo and Tuomo Suomalainen and opened in 1969. With persistence and lots of luck, I gained entrance through the square, cave-like opening to this unique piece of architecture. The church is frequently used for concerts due to its excellent acoustics. The interior was excavated and built into rock but is bathed in the natural light entering through the glazed dome. The unique and impressive organ has forty-three stops mounted against the rock wall. The acoustic quality is ensured by the rough, virtually unworked rock surfaces. I persuaded a custodian to unlock the door for me so I could go inside for just a few minutes. I was totally enthralled by the interior, especially the rock walls and the underside of the copper roof of the temple, and I will forever remember the experience. Hearing a concert performance in this church definitely would have been a memorable climax. I can easily understand why the idiosyncratic choice of form for the Rock Church makes it a favorite among architecture professionals.

An hour or so before lunch, our tour bus took off for a trip to Haikko Manor, which is situated in a natural setting of tall evergreens and deciduous trees outside Porvoo, Finland's second-oldest town. It was once a manor house of distinguished heritage and frequented by many royals. Now, it is a beautiful place for guests of some means to visit, enjoy the setting, and relax, provided they have the time. Our group had about two hours to enjoy a good lunch and explore the hilly terrain. I admired the impeccably manicured grounds, a beautiful pool, and the small ponds, and I sat for a few minutes on a bench to gaze out at the blue sea before it was time to continue with a stroll through the picturesque city center, consisting of wooden houses. The small town dates back to the thirteenth century. It was fun to take a leisurely walk through hilly, cobblestone alleys without stumbling, and eventually I ended up in a candy store specializing in licorice. I could not resist stocking up on salt-dipped black-licorice fish, my favorite, and bought one package for my friend Telle. I did not know soft licorice was developed in England in the nineteenth century and that the craft was taken up in Porvoo over one hundred years ago. To satisfy my penchant for rustic and picturesque sites, I spent some time exploring. I crossed the river to the park on the other side and took advantage of a picture-perfect view of the iconic red warehouses, as my photos will attest.

Heading back to Helsinki, I absorbed once more the idyllic countryside. Rolling through the vast, flat forest taiga, I imagined how incredibly beautiful the forests must look in winter after a fresh snow. Truly, it is perfect terrain for cross-country skiing and a place to dream about when life turns hectic back home. I wonder what has become of the Australian I met on the Trans-Siberian Railway, who had walked five hundred kilometers across Lapland at the age of seventy. It was not during the winter.

Sweden

Stockholm

On Monday, August 12, 2002, at 8:00 a.m., our elegant cruiser arrived in Stockholm, Sweden. It is known as "the city that floats on water" and is believed by many to be one of the most beautiful cities in the world.

Stockholm (852,000) is located on a small strategically located island on Sweden's East Coast where the waters of Lake Malaren join the Baltic Sea. Stockholm's harbor opens into an archipelago of 24,000 islands and inlets. It is the Baltic's largest port. Because of its northern position, the city enjoys as many as 270 hours of sunlight per month between June and August.

People have lived in the Stockholm area for 4,000 years and the waters around the present-day city were filled with Viking longboats a thousand years ago and its ancient roots are still quite visible in the waterfront area known as Gamla Stan, or Old Town. During the 13th century, merchants from Lubeck used the islands as storehouses for the goods they were exporting from Sweden, notably iron. It was Gustav Vasa, however, that created Stockholm as the capital of Sweden in 1521. But it was not until the 17th century that Sweden had its greatest period and the city of Stockholm expanded into the countryside outside the islands for the first time. Because of this expansion, by the 19th century the Gamla Stan became little more than a slum as more and more people moved to the suburbs. Sweden's geographic and political isolation also helped to spare it from the ravages of World War II. In 1977 an architectural appraisal of Old Stockholm resulted in the area being put under a preservation order and buildings were cleaned and refurbished. Today its narrow streets lined with houses, churches, and other buildings over a hundred years old are the most popular area of the city for a stroll. The easy-going, liberal Swedes complement the city as well as making it both fun and fascinating. (NCL)

I am quite grateful to NCL for these useful introductions and hope my readers will forgive me for taking the easy way out by just passing them on. Like so many other beautiful cities, Sweden's capital is referred to as "the Venice of the North." As our ship navigated the archipelago of the thousands of islands that stretch for eighty kilometers east of the capital, which with 1.65 million people is the largest of the Baltic port cities, I became increasingly enthralled by the panorama of striking buildings along the shore. They are indeed a testimony to Sweden's reputation as one of the richest countries in the world.

One of the most exhilarating architectural monuments is the exquisite Royal Palace, the workplace and official residence of the popular royal family. Though the country is ruled by a constitutional monarchy, it is highly socialized, and the taxes here are among the highest in the world. There is also the Royal Dramatic Theatre, where Ingmar Bergman, Greta Garbo, and many others got their start. It was a real thrill to see City Hall, where Nobel Prizes are awarded each December (all except the Peace Prize, which is given out in Oslo). On October 21, 1833, Alfred Nobel, chemist, engineer, innovator, and armaments manufacturer (that is, the inventor of dynamite), was born in Stockholm. It was a breathtaking encounter! "The city is made up of 14 islands connected by some 50 bridges on Lake Malaren, which flows into the Baltic Sea and passes the archipelago with some 24,000 islets" (NCL). I would not mind owning an islet with a summer cottage there.

At 8:15 a.m. we had to meet in the Stardust Lounge for our Stockholm and Vasa Museum tour. Our well-informed guide provided us with succinct information about the most important sites as we forged ahead toward the island of Djurgården, where we entered an enormously spacious, yet rather dark, hall at the Vasavarvet, a museum where we stood in awe of the largest warship in the world, the *Vasa*, built in the seventeenth century. What a sight! And what a story! And what a coincidence: the *Vasa* sank on August 13, 1628, and I was there on August 10, 2002 – 374 years later! She capsized in Stockholm Harbor a few hundred feet from the spot where she was launched on her maiden voyage.

The Vasa was to be one of four ships built in the Stockholm shipyard. Large quantities of timber went into the building of the ship. Oak was the principal wood used, and many of the timbers had to be found growing in just the right shape. These pieces were carefully checked against molds during felling.

A multitude of people gathered on a beautiful August afternoon to see the new addition to the royal fleet. She had four sails set when leaving the docks. As she left the shelter, a breeze caught the canvas. She heeled, then righted herself and then heeled again hard over to port. The water gushed in, and she sank swiftly in 110 feet of water in the harbor.

The wreckage of the Vasa was not discovered until 1956. In addition, since then more than 24,000 items from the ship have been recovered. To accomplish this, divers had to sift through some 40,000 cubic yards of mud in the Vasa's grave. The hull is amazingly well preserved and elaborately decorated. Experts were faced with the stupendous task of piecing together 14,000 fragments recovered from the deep. (NCL)

Of the 150 people onboard, thirty to fifty drowned. We learned that King Gustavus Adolphus, traveling in Poland at the time, wanted the guilty parties to be punished. But it was found that the ship had been badly proportioned. It was built with two gun decks, both of which had heavy artillery. Normally, lighter artillery would have been placed on the upper deck.

The incredible national treasure has rightfully become a national monument. It is a must-see, and Stockholm is a city to revisit when one has plenty of time for exploration.

Denmark

Copenhagen

Our ship departed at 4:30 p.m. on Monday, August 12, cruised the Swedish archipelago, and docked in the harbor of Copenhagen, Denmark, at 7:00 p.m. the next day. Copenhagen is the second-largest metropolitan area in the Scandinavian countries and, with a population of 1.5 million, the largest city in Denmark.

"Copenhagen came from the word KOBENHAVN, meaning 'merchant's harbor'" (NCL). It grew in size and importance because of its position on the Øresund (the Sound), the body of water between Denmark and Sweden, guarding the entrance to the Baltic. Since its humble beginnings in 1167, when Bishop Absalon of Roskilde was given the village by King Valdemar and a castle was built to protect the community and its harbor, Copenhagen has become the largest city in Scandinavia and home to the oldest kingdom in the world. In 1445, it was made the capital of Denmark. "Over the centuries, Copenhagen suffered more than its share of disasters. In the 17th century the Swedes repeatedly besieged it and in the 18th century it endured the plague and two devastating fires. The British attacked twice during the Napoleonic Wars in the early 1800s. Its last major disaster occurred in 1940 when Nazis overpowered Denmark and held it in their grip until 1945 when the British army moved in again, this time as liberators" (NCL).

I had signed up for a boat trip on the canals, which turned out to be a delightful experience. The architectural sites that we passed and that were duly commented upon by our guide did look particularly striking due to the blue skies and sunshine. Though there were no glittering skylines or special sights, as in Stockholm, it was just as thrilling to pass the many boats and yachts, their masts crowding the canals. Some were more luxurious than others. After the sixty-minute boat trip, we were taken on a walk through the famous pedestrian precinct in the downtown area and on Strøget, Denmark's most famous shopping street. I loved the old-town area of winding cobblestone streets, stuccoed houses, and curio shops. Truly, a somewhat "magical quality pervades the city with its 17th century green copper roofs and domes, a royal legacy of Denmark's great builder, King Christian IV" (NCL).

We were not given time to see the Crown Jewels, housed since 1606 in the Renaissance Rosenborg Castle, which I am certain do not rival the queen's in the Tower of London. In retrospect, I should have ventured out to Kronborg Castle, in the town of Helsingor, the setting for *Hamlet*. Anyhow, it would have involved a trip of twenty-five miles. Maybe I should not have opted out of the evening visit to the romantic, one-hundred-year-old Tivoli Gardens. I would have loved to see the multitude of flowers and the more than one hundred thousand lamps in different colors illuminating the old garden, but I was not crazy about the amusement part and the tourists packing the park. Due to lack of time, we also missed the changing of the Royal Guard in the octagonal courtyard of the wonderful residence of the queen, considered the greatest work of Danish rococo architecture. We had a glimpse into the royal abode and enough time to walk around Christiansborg Palace, which houses the Danish Parliament, Supreme Court, and Ministry of State and is used by the royal family for certain functions and events. It is the place where foreign ambassadors and heads of state are welcomed by the prime minister and the queen.

To satisfy my penchant for fairy tales, including those by Hans Christian Andersen, I took time before our departure to stroll for a second time along the seaside to linger and delight to the fullest in the city's most famous symbol, the bronze *Little Mermaid* statue. She sits on a small rock, is polished by the winds, shimmers in the sun, and gazes longingly out to sea, waiting for her prince to return.

Norway

Oslo

We left Copenhagen on August 14 at 4:00 p.m. and docked in Oslo, Norway, the City of Light, on August 15 at 8:00 a.m. An hour later, I joined the group for the Oslofjord, City & Folk trip.

Oslo, the tenth largest city in the world, but only a tenth of its 175 square miles making up urban and town districts, is located at the head of the long, low Oslo fjord. Oslo in contrast to Stockholm and Copenhagen, does not boast magnificent architecture, sweeping boulevards of imposing buildings. It is a rather green city with hills, parks, forests, fjords, mountains, meadows and well-shaded streets that give it the reputation of being one of the "greenest" cities in the world.

People are believed to have lived in the area 7,000 years ago, but the known history of Oslo dates from 1048. The city was founded by King Harald Hadrade (Hard Counsel). Medieval Oslo reached its high point during the reign of King Haakon V. Magnusson (1066–1093), who built the majestic Akerhus Castle and Fortress and decreed Oslo the capital of Norway. [It was also chosen as headquarters for the Nazis during the Occupation.] After Haakon's death, the city went into decline, Norway united with Denmark, and Oslo lost its importance as a capital. Several times the city was devastated by fire and in 1624 all of its wooden buildings were destroyed. During the Napoleonic Wars Norway and Denmark were separated and there followed a 90-year union with Sweden. Oslo's main street is named after the first of the Swedish-Norwegian kings, Karl Johan. The union dissolved in 1905. Since 1917, Oslo has been Norway's most important maritime city. Its harbor has more than 8 miles of quays and the world's largest tourist ships can dock here. (NCL)

On the way to Norway's largest open-air museum, the Norwegian Folk Museum, we were treated to a fabulous lunch on a huge yacht with all the shrimp you could eat, bucketfuls if you wished. We all had a great time. The skies above were blue, the sun was shining, and the beer did the rest. I hung out with the LeCounts, David and Arla. David was a teacher and prizewinning haiku poet and Arla a university administrator at the University of California–Berkeley. We talked a lot about politics, since we were all proud liberals. David, who had also lived in China and Japan, was very interested in my memoirs and suggested I give them the title *Not Hitler's Child*.

Without exception, the travelers in our group took a special liking to the Folk Museum, where we walked around the grounds on winding paths to see some of the more than one hundred buildings dating back to the seventeenth century, such as barns, stables, and raised storehouses, all made of wood and logs. I personally found curious the rough-timbered and mostly raised farmhouses with sod roofs sprouting wildflowers. The restored stave church, built around 1200 in Gol and moved to Bygdøy in 1885, was a definite highlight. I chatted with a lovely young girl dressed in a beautiful folk dress, long black skirt, and white, long-sleeved blouse with colorful embroidery and learned that the buildings were mostly from the seventeenth and eighteenth centuries. They were brought here from around the country, rebuilt, and organized according to region.

Another impressive site on the way back to the ship was the Holmenkollen ski-jumping hill, which I remembered well from the televised FIS Nordic World Ski Championships. It is the longest jump in the world, and from the top it looks as though you are going to jump into the city, hundreds of feet below. It is super-modern and has been rebuilt several times since my visit. Wow!

Fireball Lily

Our captain navigated the Oslo Fjord after our 4:00 p.m. departure, and we beheld one last sublime sunset. On the way to Dover on August 15, the North Sea was calm, and we enjoyed the time by sunbathing on deck. The white cliffs seemed ever so much whiter than at the time of our departure. After having listened to more reports about the devastation my former countrymen had caused in this beautiful land, I felt once more relieved that peace now reigned in this part of the world. I vowed to myself that someday I would return to Norway and see more of it than just Oslo. I kept my word. I returned twice.

TURKEY

On November 7, 2006, I decided to book an Overseas Adventure Trip: Turkey's Magical Hideaways – Reverse (April 29 to May 16, 2007). I had heard about the trip from fellow OAT travelers. They all claimed it was perhaps the most physically challenging in OAT's repertoire. By the time of the trip, I would be seventy-five, and who knows how much longer I would last or be fit enough to meet the challenge. I had visited Istanbul and Ephesus a couple of times before – rather briefly in connection with Mediterranean cruises, in 1967 and 2001 – but since both places were part of the deal and worthy of being seen again and again, I did not mind.

I was never keen on mountain climbing, but welcomed the opportunity to invest in and get properly equipped with some serious hiking gear, such as boots, portable poles, etc. I followed OAT's advice and kept in mind that we were to explore Istanbul, Antalya, Cappadocia, and many ruins on foot, which would involve treks ranging from three to six hours. Many would include rough, uneven, or steep steps with rubble. I felt confident and was up to this adventure.

Istanbul – Déjà Vu

On April 29, thanks to another frequent-flyer ticket, I flew business class from Indianapolis via Chicago and New York to Istanbul, known historically as Byzantium and Constantinople, where I connected with the rest of a group of ten. I was lucky to hitch a ride with them on the bus from the airport to the rather fancy Divan Hotel, located near the historic Sultanahmet neighborhood in bustling "Istanbul, a sprawling city of more than ten million people, partly in Europe and partly in Asia, its geography defined by three famous waterways, the Sea of Marmara, the Bosporus Strait, and the Golden Horn. The Sea of Marmara lies to the south. The Bosporus Strait divides the European and Asian sections of the city and forms the route from the Marmara to the Black Sea. The Golden Horn divides European Istanbul into the modern Beyogly section to the north and Old Stamboul (Eski Istanbul) to the south. The famous Galata Bridge spans the Golden Horn to link these two parts of the city" (OAT).

After lunch, we met in the lobby for the usual orientation walk and followed the guide through the Sultanahmet area, one of the oldest areas in Istanbul. It is a very picturesque district of small row houses of traditional Ottoman design, old churches, and mosques. We passed by a myriad of small cafés, stores, and restaurants as well as lots of people, tourists, and eager vendors. Our goal was the Sultanahmet Sunken Palace. We walked to a small park near the old Hippodrome chariot grounds, the site of a former circus and the social center of Constantinople. In ancient times, horse and chariot racing were popular pastimes. We entered a little doorway to descend beneath the streets to the Yerebatan Sarayi (Sunken Palace), formerly known as the Basilica Cistern. "The Emperor Justinian built this cavernous space as part of Istanbul's elaborate water system – a forest of columns and walkways" (OAT). It was a somewhat eerie place and definitely damp due to the water on the grounds. We even spotted a group of ugly, fat carp swimming around down there. It was rather dark, but we did not miss the two heads of Medusa, which, so the legend goes, were brought here from some ancient pagan site and placed upside down as bases for two columns. One head was upside down and the other turned on its side, supposedly affirming the belief that Christians put the heads there. However, others speculate differently. We all touched the heads for good luck before continuing on the wooden planks that were laid down along the decorative columns and the beloved fragments of the Roman capitals that once crowned them. They were toppled to be salvaged for their marble, as the guide explained. The basilica is a popular tourist attraction and a place where classical-music concerts are occasionally performed. I wondered what the moisture might do to the instruments. After dinner at a local restaurant, of which I remember nothing, we were taken by bus back to the hotel.

The next morning, right after breakfast, we were summoned and set off on the scheduled walking exploration of Eski Istanbul. We headed straight to the famous Ottoman Turkish Topkapi Palace, which I had visited twice before. It was built by Mehmed the Conqueror in about 1459 and served as the royal palace of the Ottoman sultans until 1853. I was impressed by the riches housed by this museum, that is, the staggering collection of jewels, arms, porcelain, sculpture, manuscripts, and more. I walked around the grounds and courtyards, which boasted many magnificent trees and bushes full of spring blossoms, and tried to imagine what it must have been like when, for some four hundred years, the palace served as the primary residence of the Ottoman sultans and some four thousand people. The palace was rebuilt after an earthquake in 1509 and after a fire in 1665, which destroyed mosques, a hospital, bakeries, and a mint. I did not like that we were barred again from viewing the innermost (fourth) courtyard, the secret passageways, and the harem, the private domain of the sultan, but felt somewhat compensated by the gorgeous cobalt-blue İznik glazed tiles of variegated design, which decorated the walls above the windows in the library as well as the walls of the privy chamber of Ahmed III. Cobalt blue is my favorite color. Thus, I was kept in a state of intense delight while viewing a sampling of the hundreds of rooms that used to fill the palace.

I made sure that this time I could spend at least thirty minutes enjoying the view from the promontory overlooking the Golden Horn and the Sea of Marmara, with the Bosporus down below in plain sight. This view is from one of the highest seaside points and is without doubt another one of the most exalting and unforgettable sights on the globe!

Just as unforgettable is the Blue Mosque (Sultan Ahmet Camii), so called for the more than twenty thousand blue, shimmering İznik tiles that line its interior, including the ceilings. Of course, its six soaring, symmetrical minarets and eight cascading domes, along with the main one, visible from far away, make it one of the defining elements of Istanbul's skyline. This classic of Ottoman architectural design was constructed under the patronage of Sultan Ahmet I, from 1609 to 1616. He was a very religious-minded king and became a monarch at the very young age of fourteen. He was laid to rest in the mosque, to which one is inspired to assign such attributes as magnificent, exquisite, awe-inspiring, and overwhelming. Though we had to take off our shoes before entering, we had to stand back from the thick red carpet with blue floral designs covering the vast prayer area. The flickering oil lamps that hung from the ceiling on a huge, round frame motivated us to just be silent and whisper. The numerous stained-glass windows in the walls of the mosque, letting in sunlight, endowed the interior with an inspirational glow.

After a lunch break, we made our way through crowded streets to the Turkish and Islamic Arts Museum, located in the sixteenth-century palace of Ibrahim Pasha, once the largest private residence of the Ottoman Empire. It's not far from the Blue Mosque. While walking through this monument of Turkish history, we were introduced to several choice displays of gorgeous Seljuk carpets from the thirteenth century and as well as very old illuminated manuscripts, carved Quran cases, and amazing calligraphy. Our visit to this great little museum convinced me that I must not return to the States without acquiring a couple of Turkish carpets!

We made our way through the dazzling, overcrowded Grand Bazaar on the way to the dock near the Sirkeci boat station, where we started the much-anticipated two-hour Bosporus cruise. It was wonderful to see the European district of Galata to the north and the Asiatic side of the Bosporus and the Maiden's Tower, a twelfth-century Byzantine fortress. "In ancient times, the Golden Horn could be closed off to warships with a giant chain stretching from here to Seraglio Point" (OAT). We passed several Ottoman palaces, went under the Bosporus bridge that connects Europe and Asia and cruised the Northern Bosporus. While going along the southern shores, we got a glimpse of the Selimiye Barracks, where Florence Nightingale worked, several other palaces, mosques, and the Topkapi Palace. I found the sights along the Northern Bosporus, such as the wooden seaside mansions, a little rococo palace, and the Fortress of Anatolia, equally captivating. By the way, the Dolmabahçe Palace, on the European shore, is a perfect symbol of the decadence and magnificence of the nineteenth-century Ottoman Empire.

That night, I skipped dinner to rest up for a tour the next day of "Istanbul with emphasis on the great architectural achievement, which was the largest cathedral in the world for almost a thousand years, the magnificent Hagia Sophia (Church of the Divine Wisdom) former Orthodox patriarchal basilica, cathedral of Constantinople, a Roman Catholic cathedral under Latin Patriarch of Constantinople also a mosque and in 1934 the revolutionary leader and founder of the Republic, Kemal Ataturk, proclaimed it a museum" (OAT). As on previous visits, the decorated interior, with stunning mosaics, marble pillars, and coverings, despite the fact that much of it was in need of restoration, indicated how breathtakingly beautiful it once was. Unfortunately, as on my last visit, the scaffolding erected for various renovation projects (which was removed in 2010 after seventeen years) prevented me from fully appreciating the splendor. I tried hard to rely on my imagination. The dome is simply grandiose: the forty windows placed around its base lend it a distinct mystical quality of light, which reflects everywhere in the interior of the nave, above which the dome seems to hover. It is shaped like an umbrella, with ribs that extend from the top of the dome down to the base. I stood in awe before the loge of the empress, located in the center of the upper gallery, and imagined what it might have been like to watch the proceedings down below. A green stone marks the spot where the throne stood. On the way out, I tucked my scarf into my bag and was glad to find my shoes, which we had to take off prior to entering at the same spot.

The Ottoman military band that gave a matinee concert at the Ottoman Empire's Military Museum was colorful, entertaining, and plain interesting, yet at times so loud I stuck my fingers in my ears and was tempted to leave early. In short, I could have done without it. More interesting was the ride on the Old Tram down İstiklal Street to the heart of art-nouveau Istanbul and the hike up to the medieval stone Galata Tower, where we had a 360-degree view of Istanbul as well as a tasty meal in the restaurant. The tower was built as a watchtower for the Genoese colony of Galata in 1348, and later became useful in spotting fires. Ironically, the structure itself caught fire twice, in the eighteenth and nineteenth centuries! – To be honest, I would have been content with street food, like their delicious kebab and fresh bread, or a *gözleme*, a very flat pancake, cooked fresh on the street with endless choices of delicious fillings.

I never get tired of people watching in other cultures. On this visit, I noticed that fewer women wore the "controversial" headscarves and fewer men covered their heads with the very colorful woven caps I observed on my previous visit. The streets seemed more congested with traffic, and the crowds on the sidewalks, including women pushing baby carriages, were maddening. I was careful not to get lost this time, since the last time I had trouble finding a person who spoke English. I stayed close to the group, and even when navigating the various streets in the Grand Bazaar – where gold is as much in abundance as spices and the Turkish treats, dating back to Ottoman times, made of sugar, starch, nuts, or dried fruits – I made sure to keep someone familiar in view.

İzmir

I was looking forward to getting out of this megacity and boarding the one-hour flight to İzmir, in the seaside district of Kuşadasi, the next day, May 3. We were dropped off in the center of İzmir to find something to eat before venturing out with our new guide to tour the city, in particular the old section of town, which

Turkey

meant climbing up Mount Pagos to Kadifekale (The Velvet Castle), the panoramic castle of Alexander the Great built around 340 BC. It is a fabulous vantage point from which to see the entire town of İzmir, a large metropolis in the western extremity of Anatolia with a population of almost four million. İzmir, located on the Gulf of İzmir, an inlet of the Aegean Sea, is not a place one can cover in a couple of hours, which is all the time we spent in Turkey's third-largest city – formerly known as Smyrna, in case you did not know.

Kuşadasi

I loved the two-hour ride from İzmir to Kuşadasi, the resort town on the Aegean coast. This was the first time I approached it on something other than an ocean liner; it is also the port of call for cruise ships. The purpose was, of course, to visit Ephesus, the famous ancient Greco-Roman site, one of the largest and best-preserved ancient cities in the world. It was déjà vu for me. Again, we were blessed with a sunny day and blue skies, although I could not help but notice that this third time, the tourist crowds seemed to have at least tripled since my first visit in 1967. But the site is forever miraculous, just like other great monuments or wonders of the world. They never lose their magnetic force. It is just awesome to walk the remarkably well-preserved, wide marble streets, flanked by columns and temples. The Library of Celsus, a tiered facade decorated with exquisite statues, is mesmerizing each time you see it. I noticed a young, blond Russian woman in an unusual, bold, and fashionable blue dress standing on the steps to the library. A light breeze was blowing the chiffon skirt and her long strands of hair. She wore very big sunglasses and a wide-brimmed straw hat. Together, they made it impossible to see her face.

I am always a bit amused at the sight of the latrines, that is, the city's public toilets, built in the first century AD as part of the Scholastica Baths. They are rather well-preserved, aligned side by side along the walls with a drainage system underneath them. For an entrance fee, men could sit on the toilets and chat with each other about daily events, as they did in the Roman baths. A stray cat was taking a nap on one of the openings. The floor used to be paved with mosaics. – I lingered a while at the ancient theater where St. Paul preached to the Ephesians and wondered what the Temple of Artemis, one of the seven wonders of the ancient world, which is no longer standing, must have looked like – it was one of the most colossal temples ever built. I wandered off by myself and was overjoyed when I discovered a patch of bright-red poppies growing in a pile of sun-bleached rubble. I asked a guy to take a picture of me.

Before returning to the hotel, we visited the Ephesus Museum, in Selçuk, to view numerous rare finds from Ephesus, including the marble statue of the multibreasted Great Artemis, which Professor Dr. Dr. Bourde had raved about when I studied in Provence in 1966–1967. We also explored the nearby ruins of the sixth-century Basilica of St. John, constructed over St. John's grave during Emperor Justinian's reign. The sight was a welcome déjà vu for me. Back in the hotel, while gazing down on the stunning harbor from my balcony, I contemplated contentedly. I knew this visit to Ephesus would definitely be my last. After all, how many people in the world have come here three times in the course a lifetime?!

Almost as unforgettable as Ephesus was our stay at the famous and enchanting Kismet Hotel, owned by the children of the Ottoman imperial family and sitting on a peninsula that protrudes into the sparkling, turquoise Aegean Sea. This place boasts a long list of distinguished guests, such as kings and queens from Europe, including her majesty Queen Elizabeth II of England, renowned artists, academicians, and President Carter, which would account for the superb dining experience we relished in their elegant dining room, where I had a seat with a glorious view of the sea. I spent some of my leisure time walking the immaculately kept grounds, and I sat on a bench under palms and near pines, soaking up the ambiance of lush, vibrant flowers, especially the dark-purple blooms of massive bougainvillea, which contrasted strikingly with the turquoise sea below. The yachts in the harbor led me to anticipate the forthcoming adventure in a *gulet* along the turquoise coast. Here was an abundance of picture-perfect panoramas right at my feet.

Day 7 represented the big change in the program. I do not mean the visit to a craft demonstration by local artisans at a rug-weaving cooperative, which was interesting but not new to me, since I had seen silkworm cultivation, spinning, and dyeing as well as traditional patterns and weaving techniques in other countries. Nevertheless, I could not resist and bought an area rug in burgundy red, tan, and black shades. It arrived home before I did, and I derive pleasure each time I look at it.

Turquoise Coast – *Gulet*

Marmaris

After the carpet event we drove for about five hours along the coast to the beautiful natural harbor of Marmaris, which has reputedly attracted everyone from the Crusaders and Mark Antony to the denizens of the numerous luxury charter yachts that invade the port each day. It was the place for us to board our Turkish *gulet*-style yacht. "A traditional Turkish gulet is a teak and oak beauty with two sails and a motor, an outdoor eating area, and comfortable cushions for relaxing on the observation decks, fore and aft" (OAT). I had one of the eight snug cabins with a private shower and loved it the five nights I spent onboard.

Our first stop was at Ekincik Cove, on the Dalyan River. It is a small but scenic bay lined with pine trees. We were met by "a small riverboat that took us on a side trip upriver on the Dalyan River through a maze of small channels lined with bamboo and cattails. Named for dalyans, the fishing weirs that have supported locals for centuries, the river reveals an abundant birdlife" (OAT). A fishing weir or fish trap is an obstruction placed in tidal waters or wholly or partially across a river to hinder the passage of fish.

Our riverboat brought us to İztuzu, a 4.5-kilometer-long beach. It is a narrow spit of land that forms a natural barrier between the freshwater delta of the Dalyan River and the Mediterranean. We had hoped to discover loggerhead sea turtles, which have nested here since the age of the dinosaurs, but were not so lucky. It was all right as far as I was concerned. I enjoyed the outing and cruising through the peaceful landscape and the lunch in a local tavern before we proceeded to visit the ancient Lycian site of Kaunos, where we clambered around to view temples, baths, the nymphaeum, and an ancient theater. Along the way, we had striking and rather intriguing views of Lycian temple tombs, the last resting place of the kings of Kaunos, which hugged the rock face.

In the morning after breakfast, and after several had gone for a swim, we cruised to Aga Limani, or Friendship Cove, a lovely spot to moor. It was a perfect day to go for the much-anticipated big and very challenging hike. I was ready to go. Our young female guide sized me up several times and asked whether I thought I could do it. I was the oldest in the group. I said, "Let's go!" The narrow path that wound around and up the hill was quite rugged. It was steep and had lots of loose stones, so it was hard to get a good footing. We went slowly, and at times, when I turned my head to the right, it looked a bit scary, since the drop went straight down. It was hot, but the shade was welcome when we hiked through forests, and the meadows felt refreshing. We stopped frequently to rest and admire the spectacular coastal scenery, the Göcek Lagoon and the Bay of Fethiye. At one stop, I walked past a couple of grazing goats and a seemingly starving horse toward a hut where a young goatherd and his wife, with a toddler sleeping in her lap, were selling strands of old, weather-beaten bells. I bought one of the two strands available, since we had heard their ringing in the distance and I liked to support the locals. Goats and even a few camels favored our hiking path. We saw them earlier in the morning from our *gulet* as they trekked slowly on the narrow track.

Our trail brought us to the Greco-Roman ruins of Lydia. After checking out the ruins rather briefly, I found a shady place to rest while some in the group more curious than I went on to explore more thoroughly. We began our descent, which was almost more challenging than the ascent. At each step the stones rolled beneath our feet, and I had to wait for them to stabilize before I took the next step. I hate to think of what it would have been like had it been raining. Except for a couple of young and eager hikers, the rest of us took our time and breathed a sigh of relief when we reached the spectacular cove that shelters the sunken Baths of Cleopatra, built for her by Mark Antony as part of his wedding gift, that is, the entire Turquoise Coast. I was so happy to have made it, and instead of going for a swim, I sat on a bench waiting for our *gulet* to pick us up in this intoxicating scenic cove. I was unable to see the Old Hamman (baths) but could fancy what they may have been like. Why not? Use your imagination!

Göcek Bay

The following day, we cruised along the coast to the large and strikingly beautiful Göcek Bay, the center of yachting, lined with small coves and surrounded by pine-clad mountains. I opted out of a hike on the shores and lounged around on the yacht, relaxing on the nice green cushions present throughout the seating areas. I chatted with fellow travelers, gazed out on the Aegean, mused when goats or horses offered a sound as they grazed along the shore, and admired the stunning yachts that cruised with hoisted sails among the twelve islands in the distance. At one point, some of us succeeded in persuading our forever-grinning little captain, whose name I have long since forgotten, to hoist our main sail. I probably made a mistake when I asked someone to take a picture of him and me at the ship's wheel. While I lounged on the cushions, he approached me several times uttering the phrase "I you marry." If you think he was a gorgeous guy, you could not be more wrong. He was short and all skin and bones, he had silver-gray hair and dark-brown, deeply wrinkled, sunburned skin, and worst of all, when he grinned, he showed an almost toothless mouth. I think there were perhaps four teeth remaining. At one point, he wanted to take me to shore to go fishing with him. I had a hard time getting out of that invite. At dinnertime he offered me a fried fish on a platter, which I declined in the hope that he would finally give it up. This one was a far cry from the captains I had met on previous boat or ship adventures.

Gemiler Bay

On day 11, we continued our cruise along the craggy Mediterranean coast and made our landing on a small beach in the Bay of Gemiler. I was overjoyed when I noticed that, in lieu of breakfast on deck, a small boat had pulled up next to us. A man and his wife were preparing *gözleme* on the boat, and I was quick to order a couple. I shared one with a cotraveler who for some reason was still unfamiliar with this Turkish pastry dish (flat pancakes). This traveler was the guy in his sixties who at the onset of our trip was full of energy and always the first to go. He went on early hikes, exercised whenever he found an appropriate spot, such as a parking lot, and after the big hike was so sick that he was incapacitated for several days.

From Gemiler Bay we drove to a spot near Kayaköy, a Greek ghost town. For some reason, a bunch of us opted out of the hike to Kayaköy and decided to hang out in the small town, the name of which I have forgotten. What I do remember is that I had a wonderful time walking around and hanging out, if you wish, with the locals. A few carpet vendors were lined up along a sidewalk across from their stores. They had many beautiful carpets of diverse sizes hanging on clotheslines. I sat with them, chatted about this and that in English, and enjoyed sipping the tea one of the men offered. He had fetched it from his store. The sun was shining, the sky was blue, and the Turks were ever so friendly. I ended up following one of them to his store, where I bought a small, wool area rug with vibrant colors, woven by locals from Kirşehir, a small province in Central Anatolia. They wrapped it up for me, and from then on it was a constant companion; at home, it serves as another reminder of my worldwide travels.

Fethiye

On day 12, after breakfast, we disembarked in the harbor at Fethiye on the Mediterranean, which was full of yachts. I murmured my good-bye to the little captain and was glad to get into the van, in which, after a two-hour drive through beautiful countryside, we arrived in the tiny fishing village of Üçağiz, where we saw Lycian tombs half-submerged in the sea. From Üçağiz we hiked across the Simena Peninsula. The area is known as the Kekova Archipelago and is acclaimed by many as one of the most beautiful places in Turkey. There were few roads. We saw ruins of the ancient city of Theimussa, fishermen mending their nets, women curing olives or drying figs, and little kids playing. At the end of the hike, we boarded a small boat and sailed to the Sunken City and Çayağzi. We sailed past old village houses, tall, stone Lycian tombs more than two thousand years old, and marble ruins of a Roman "sunken city." Geological movements of the island caused the city on the island to be submerged, such that the city is half under water and half above. The scenic beauty of the area is amazing and exhilarating.

After a leisurely lunch in Demre, we went to explore the ancient Roman ruins of Myra, once a leading city among a group of ancient Turkish cities known as Lycia, and admired the conspicuous Lycian house-tombs carved into the cliffs in the fourth century BC. They contain some of the earliest examples of Lycian script and funerary bas-reliefs. We climbed around the rock-cut tombs and sat on the marble seats in the amphitheater to better appreciate the mask friezes scattered around the elaborately decorated stage area, which is still used for festival productions.

Our next stop was at the Church of St. Nicholas in Demre. "In the 4th century AD, Saint Nicholas was the bishop of this area and was known as a protector of children, adorning them with gifts at every opportunity. He was later declared a saint, and is the model for Santa Claus or Father Christmas. Christians from as far away as Italy and Russia come here to attend a special annual festival mass" (OAT). Indeed, while walking around the rather dark interior, I was surprised at the presence of many Russian tourists. Some lit candles at altars for a charge; of course, others kneeled in front of altars, praying. On the way to our van, we stopped to take a picture in front of a gigantic Santa Claus statue – it stood on a cement island, on an elevated white pedestal with three steps. A bit kitschy, if you ask me.

Antalya

It was an eventful day, and I was seriously looking forward to finding a place to rest up, which turned out to be Antalya, "set on a wide bay with mountain views all around. Once an old fishing village, it is now a popular resort that combines unspoiled beaches with an award-winning restored harbor and an architecturally interesting old city" (OAT). We were scheduled to spend two nights at the Dogan Hotel, located in the Kaleiçi district, aka "Old Antalya." The hotel comprises four authentic buildings and has a total of forty-one nicely furnished rooms. The district is famous for its narrow cobbled streets, and for good reason. We actually had to get out of the bus somewhere downtown, gather our luggage, and lug it up a steep street and through some alleys, aka tiny streets, where our "particularly nice, small hotel . . . was nestled" (OAT). I liked my room, which had a distinct Ottoman ambiance, even though I did not have a Mediterranean view.

Day 13 started with a walking tour of Antalya, which focused on what is left of Hadrian's Gate, and the Yivli Minaret. This "ornamental, well-preserved monumental triple-arched portal, which connects with the ancient walls and marks an entrance into the city, was the project of the Roman Emperor Hadrian, 130 AD" (OAT). As I walked through the arch, I was overcome by a feeling of awe. Perhaps the experience was so powerful because hardly any tourists were there to interfere with it. The mosque's Yivli Minaret is hard to miss. It is in the center of the city. Built in the thirteenth century, it is fluted, and though many of the formerly blue and turquoise tiles that used to cover it in a checker pattern are missing, the thirty-eight-meter-high minaret is a striking piece of architecture because it is different from the more common Ottoman minarets. It is the symbol of Antalya. No, we did not climb the ninety interior steps to the top. And we did not have enough time to truly appreciate the numerous artifacts in some fourteen exhibition halls and an open-air gallery of the prizewinning Antalya Archeological Museum, which "earned a worldwide reputation for its extensive collection of artifacts" (OAT). I spent most of my time looking at sculptures and sarcophagi. The ancient city of Perge, in Asia Minor, was of special interest. St. Paul visited the city in 46 AD and preached his first sermon. After that, Perge became an important city, especially for Christians during the Byzantine period. For me, the many spots displaying an abundance of spring flowers or bougainvillea bushes were, as always, refreshing and rejuvenating! If they cropped up between ruins or along the roadside, in alleys or on hotel grounds, I always exclaimed, "Oh, wie schön!" (Oh, how beautiful!).

Aspendos

But I also voiced my excitement the next day, when, after a drive from Antalya of about one hour, I saw the incredible open-air theater and aqueduct of the ancient Roman city Aspendos, which was built in the second century AD and seats 15,000.

It is one of the best-preserved amphitheaters in the world, and perhaps the finest, and is still used for large concerts and events. As I stood in awe while looking down on the stage from higher up, I could not have imagined that only a few months later, the 2006 Grammy nominee Corey Cerovsek – the world-renowned violinist, pianist, and mathematician who at age twelve was the youngest student to receive a gold medal from the Royal Conservatory of Music and who had performed in the Aspendos amphitheater – would play at one of my Schubertiades and take my breath away. Corey was a student of the famous Josef Gingold. Julien Quentin, also a graduate of the Jacobs School of Music in Bloomington, was his pianist at the Schubertiade.

Lake Beyşehir

From Aspendos we continued across rolling hills, fields, and grasslands toward several small villages near Lake Beyşehir: Akburun, Budak, and Kuşluca. The lake is strikingly beautiful and lies at an altitude of 1,121 meters. It is Turkey's largest freshwater lake, and the Dedegol mountain range, which runs along the western shore, was so gorgeous because the highest peak, Dippoyraz (2,992 meters), was covered with snow. The lake's pale-blue waters contrasted beautifully with juniper and black-pine forests, creating a scenic backdrop. A number of islands dotted the water of the lake. – In the absence of tourists, it was one of the most peaceful places on the planet. I was elated when I found out that our home visit would be in one of these villages, and within walking distance of the gorgeous lake.

Our home stay in this hamlet turned out to be a highlight of the trip. A number of women and men greeted us in the cobblestone courtyard when we arrived in the late afternoon. Their house was built of wood and stone. Inside, the rooms were somewhat dark, furnished with more or less simple furniture, and had a strong Turkish ambiance. I took lots of pictures of women, young and old, all wearing scarves, and of men, young, old, and very old, wearing caps or hats. Their faces looked robust and sunburned. They made their living as farmers and herders. One young man was also a teacher and spoke English, which really helped when we sat around the long banquet table partaking in the generous meal they served. Most of the dishes originated from their gardens and fruit trees and from animals that were raised nearby. The children were eager to have their pictures taken, just like the kids in the light-blue uniforms who happily posed when we visited their school in another village. I was lucky not to have to share a room and had no trouble falling asleep on the futon-like floor mat with a comfortable quilt. A colorful area rug lay next to my futon, and in the corner of the room stood a small wood-burning stove.

A rooster awakened me early. I showered, dressed, and went out for a morning stroll through the small town, which nevertheless boasted a nice mosque with a minaret. The sun was shining; a farmer picked up a couple of milk cans in a cobblestone courtyard and put them on his cart. I took a peek into the barn, where a couple of well-fed cows stood. One cow looked at me sort of stupidly. Funny. On the way to the lake, I passed a woman herding a few goats. I sat for a while on a bench and gazed out at the mirror-like, shimmering surface of Lake Beyşehir, with the snowcapped mountain range on the horizon. *Ach, wie schön!* When I look back, memories of Lake Baikal in Siberia surface.

Konya

After a pleasant breakfast, during which we drank tea instead of coffee while chatting about our experiences, it was time to head overland to Konya. It was a comparatively long drive, interrupted by several stops to break it up. Somehow, I never get tired of even long trips through the countryside, and I never fall asleep. I am always afraid I might miss something. The guys tend to snore louder than the females.

Konya is a town built on the site of an ancient Phrygian city. It was the capital city of the Selçuk Empire and the hometown of Mevlana, founder of the Whirling Dervish sect. We traveled south from Cappadocia to the Konya Plain, crossing open farmland for about four hours to reach Konya. It is a rich city, with great mosques from the Selçuk period, wonderful museums, and most of all the burial site of Mevlana. We spent some time at the Mevlana Tekkesi (1550–1557), the founding monastery of the mystical Sufi order of the Mevlevi. "This sect, known as the 'Whirling Dervishes' for their ecstatic ritual dance, was founded by Mevlana Celaddin Rumi (1207–1273), a lyrical poet who preached of tolerance, forgiveness, and enlightenment" (OAT). I felt particularly intrigued by the marble tombs of several Dervish abbots. They were covered with rich and colorful brocades. In walking through the monastery, judging by the many Turkish visitors, it was obvious that many outside the sect itself hold the Muslim Mevlana Dervish mystics in high regard. The famous green conical roof of the Mevlana Mosque is one that attracts countless Turkish pilgrims, who come to pay their respects to one of Turkey's greatest mystics.

Cappadocia

When approaching Cappadocia, located in Central Turkey, a region known for its exceptional natural wonders and characterized both by a bizarre landscape with fairy chimneys sculpted by the elements over time and a unique historical and cultural heritage, one cannot help but be astounded by the unique rock formations that, collectively, look like a forest of stones. The natural fortress of Uçhisar, the tallest point in Cappadocia, is riddled with man-made dwellings and dovecotes that dominate the skyline. It is a most striking and unforgettable panorama, with blue skies as a background. I felt transported into another world – the surroundings looked like an imaginary lunar landscape. Fairy chimneys consist of relatively soft rock topped by harder, less easily eroded stone that protects each column from the elements. (They are shaped like totem poles.)

Our hotel seemed almost otherworldly as well. Lykia Lodge is advertised as a "fairytale kingdom" where you can relax among the lush greenery, with the hotel's architecture reflecting the natural environment. Lykia's brochure describes Cappadocia as "a magical place which the Persians called Katpatuka, 'Land of Beautiful Horses' and which carries the traces of the Hittites, Phrygians, Romans and many more ancient civilizations; a place that is unique in the world with its beautiful nature, cultural and historical richness and embellished with fairy chimneys."

Several of my globe-trekker friends had raved about Cappadocia, and I was glad to have followed their advice to be there in the flesh. Another dream had come true. I signed up right away for the hot-air-balloon flight very early in the morning and did not care how much it costed. In Africa, I had tried to go on such a flight, but the winds were too strong. Three others from my group and I were picked up early and driven to the site. The weather was perfect, and after watching the crew spread out the colorful balloon on the field, I was quick to go when they called us to climb into the basket. Wow – all ten of us were so excited when they fired up the gas and the balloon was gradually lifted upwards. We drifted ever so gently through the air and waved at others – who stood in different balloons further away. But the most exciting part of the flight was when we sailed past the forest of fairy-chimney rock formations and came so close that we could almost touch them. If we had had an emergency landing in this region, we most likely would have ended up in the tops of apricot trees, which are so plentiful there. Apricots, tomatoes, peppers, and other regional fruits are often dried on rooftops before they are exported. When we did return to earth, even though it was a rough landing because the basket ended up on its side so that we had to crawl out, we were happy to be safe and toasted each other and the crew with one or two glasses of champagne. Back at the hotel, we all received a photo with a balloon, certifying that we had successfully participated. Great!

After breakfast, we walked through a few of the small village lanes of Uçhisar and began a hike downhill on a narrow trail. It was semichallenging. We hiked among terraces and along a meandering streambed. It was a small, rocky canyon, away from the roads and tour buses, and it provided an entrance to an ancient world, serene and startlingly beautiful. At one point, I decided to stay behind and wait for the return of those who had forged ahead. It was only a ten-minute wait, and I did not miss too much. For some reason, I had not worn my boots and had left my hiking stick at the hotel. I no longer take risks on these trips.

I liked this rural region. People still dwell in cave homes next to their vineyards and apricot orchards. Irrigation channels and carefully cultivated fields were nestled between narrow canyon walls, and tufa rock cones up to 250 feet tall loomed over us. We readied our cameras quickly when a local man rode by on a donkey, and we

Fireball Lily

asked a woman sitting in front of her stone house making *yufka*, the traditional, large flatbread of the region, if we could photograph her. She nodded and smiled. Thanks!

If you desire to see an underground city, take this trip. After another sixty-minute drive, we arrived in the underground city of Kaymakli. "During the Hittite era, as successive armies swept across Asia Minor, underground cities were built as a uniquely defensible community, approximately eight stories underground" (OAT). It was mind-boggling. Of the hundreds of rooms, we explored only a few. We wandered the many narrow, sloping passageways between kitchens with enameled food-storage areas, and we saw water cisterns, storage areas, stables, and living spaces – all well ventilated by air shafts. Mind you, it was rather dark down there and reminded me vaguely of the catacombs in Rome. Just imagine: we were told that at one time, several thousand people lived there. They kept the animals on the first and the church on the second floor. The cemetery was outside. This is a place I will not return to.

In the parking lot, area vendors had set up stalls to display their crafts. Our trip was nearing its end, so I decided to stock up on souvenirs. On the dry branches and twigs of a big bush hung many evil-eye pendants of all sizes, necklaces, bracelets, earrings, etc. It looked rather amusing. I bought a bunch of pendants in different sizes to send to friends and a big one for myself. I also acquired a glass tennis-ball-size evil eye. It is cobalt blue, with white and light-blue circles around a dark-blue iris in the center. This home-protection amulet now dangles down on a sturdy string from the lamp above my kitchen table to chase away those who would invade my territory uninvited. I wore the big pendant on a string around my neck when my doctors were treating me for temporal arthritis. And it worked: I did not lose my eyesight.

Our next stop was the open-air museum, Göreme. We climbed around among a group of ancient churches carved from the rock in the tenth and eleventh centuries and admired the well-preserved, colorful frescoes inside some of the small chapels. It was a hot day, and I was constantly hunting for a shady spot in the rocks, which was quite a challenge. I was ready to return to the hotel and relax before taking off again that evening to see the Whirling Dervishes whirling.

We were picked up around 8:00 p.m. and, after some twenty minutes, dropped off at the Sarihan Caravanserai prior to the ceremony. Camel trains stopped by night at inns known as caravanserai (caravan palaces). It's the place where merchants traveling the Silk Road used to spend the night and stable their animals – a kind of motel.

I had no clue what to expect and was surprised to see such an impressive complex. It was already dark, and we did not have too much time to walk around before we were ushered into the big hall where the Dervishes would perform the Sema ritual.

Turkey

OAT enlightened us as follows: "The Semazens, the so-called Whirling Dervishes, believe that the fundamental condition of our existence is to revolve. From the smallest cell to the planets and the farthest stars, everything takes part in this revolving. Thus, the ones who whirl participate consciously in the shared revolution of all existence. The Semazen (with their camel's-felt hats representing tombstones and wide white skirts symbolizing shrouds) stand with their arms crossed, ready to begin their turn. As they whirl, their motions represent a spiritual journey." Great silence reigned in the room, which was dimly lit from the beginning to the end of the ritual. It was another climactic moment of my trek around the globe and one that you have to see for yourself to fully value it. We all appreciated the glass of sweet Turkish sherbet, served in the courtyard after the ceremony. Hardly anybody uttered a word on the way back to the lodge.

We took Turkish Airlines from Kayseri to Istanbul the next morning at 10:00 a.m. and were taken from the airport to the Divan Hotel, where we arrived around noon. In the evening, we gathered for a delightful farewell dinner, where at one point we engaged in a serious discussion about a topic which had been avoided for the duration of the trip: the Armenian Genocide, which was carried out by the Young Turk government of the Ottoman Empire in 1915–1916. Out of a total of two and a half million Armenians, one and a half million were systematically killed. Many claim it was in some way a model for Hitler's atrocities against the Jews. I always feel somewhat ashamed of my German heritage when such topics as genocide and the Holocaust are discussed, because the feeling of collective guilt never fails to creep up. However, it would be worse if we were to ignore the subject. I strongly agree with George Santayana, who said, "Those who cannot remember the past are condemned to repeat it."

I arrived home safe and sound, spread out my rugs, positioned little souvenirs on the shelf, and hung the blue-and-white ceramic electric clock in the kitchen close to the EVIL EYE!

RUSSIAN WATERWAYS (GOLDEN RING) – MS ROSSIA

The Siberians

I had a couple of months of breathing space to manage my domestic affairs and get ready for the next trek with GCT: Russian Waterways. A river cruise from Saint Petersburg to Moscow on the MS *Rossia*, it would take place from July 26, 2007, to August 10, 2007. It would be another of my so-called charity trips, the recipients being Olga Belousova and her daughter Lubasha, from Irkutz, Siberia. You may recall I had befriended Olga on my Trans-Sib trip and developed a rather close relationship with her and especially with Lubasha, her teenage daughter. We e-mailed regularly, and I called them weekly to give Lubasha an opportunity to practice her already near-native English skills. I was impressed with her intelligence. In the process, I learned a lot about their life in Siberia. The more I learned, the more I sympathized with them and their comparatively tough life. I began to send them many packages with clothing, gifts from my travels, and well over $1,000 toward Lubasha's education – and a keyboard, since she had developed a liking for music. I felt sorry for them when they told me about Lubasha's father, who drank too much vodka, a major concern since his own father had died early of drinking-related causes. In addition, Olga's sister, a divorcée with four kids, lived with a guy much younger than she. She was rather lazy and an alcoholic. She worked as a cleaning lady. Her mother lived with them to help out, though she too had a sparse monthly income of about $100.

The Belousovas were hard up as well. Lubasha at times complained about their long trips to the countryside in order to help with the watering and harvesting of the potatoes, cabbage, and other vegetables in her grandmother's garden. They had to transfer water to the garden by carrying it with them on the bus, which seemed rather crazy to me. They also had a very old car in need of major repairs. Olga worked in an office, and her husband was a night-shift maintenance man at the same company. Both earned some money, though a very modest amount. Olga earned a bit extra in the summer as a tour guide, and her husband did some odd jobs as a repairman. They were always afraid of losing their jobs. A couple of times, I sent them $500 via Western Union, and each time Olga had a hard time receiving the money, because they required additional information. She had to run back and forth and send more e-mails until they were satisfied. They were very grateful. Once, they were very upset because someone had broken into their tiny three-room apartment and taken the computer, a necklace, and some other items. I was worried about their savings, which they hid in a plastic bag on the balcony. They did not trust the banks, because on a couple of occasions, when for some reason all accounts were frozen, they had been unable to withdraw money. The thieves did not find the cash.

For Christmas, Lubasha sent a couple of handcrafted gifts, a pillow and slippers, which I really appreciated. She was a very gifted and attractive young girl, fifteen years old when we first got acquainted. Olga was very thin, had light-blue eyes (like Putin), and hair that reached down to her waist. Of course, I was always anxious to find out how they were coping with the freezing temperatures during the winter, which started as early as September or October and lasted until April. The city would turn off the central heating now and then, which meant they had to put on many layers of clothes to stay warm. The windows were frozen over, so they could not look out. I remembered similar times from my childhood in Hannover, Germany. The sidewalks were always very slick during the winter, because they did not put sand or salt on them. At one point her father fell, broke a foot, and was on sick leave for a long time. I was a little disappointed that despite my occasional requests, Lubasha never told me about her grandparents' experiences during World War II. I would have liked to know more about those experiences in order to compare them to my own. One thing was incomprehensible to me: how could someone with Olga's intelligence (she had also studied in Germany for a while) earn such a small monthly income ($500)? When possible, they liked to go camping at the nearby Lake Baikal in the summer, and once they went to adjacent Mongolia and stayed in yurts.

Lubasha, whom I had never met in person, would graduate from high school in the summer of 2007. As I had developed a special love for Russia and some of the Russians – their culture, great writers, composers, and of course Saint Petersburg – I decided it was high time I met Lubasha face to face. They had invited me to visit them in Irkutsk on various occasions, but that sounded too complicated to me. Instead, I took the plunge and invited Olga and Lubasha for a river cruise as a graduation gift for Lubasha. She seemed most deserving, because she had graduated with high honors and also won a gold medal. We were all excited. I did not include the father, since I had gotten the impression that the marriage was not perfect and I was not in the mood to deal with an alcoholic onboard the MS *Rossia*. I had also heard about the Golden Ring, northeast of Moscow. The cities are known to feature unique monuments of Russian architecture of the twelfth to eighteenth centuries, such as kremlins, monasteries, cathedrals, and churches. They boast the most picturesque towns, in which the famous, and often golden, onion domes excite visitors from around the world. I thought this would be a good time to see this part of Russia together with my two Russian friends. I wanted to get to know them better, especially in view of the fact that I had plans to help Lubasha with tuition at the university, where she wanted to study architecture. It would be a bit like a family trip.

Organizing this adventure turned out to be quite a challenge, because GCT would not help me with arrangements for my Russian friends' travel inside Russia. But in the end, I managed to make sure the two would be reimbursed for any money they had to advance for flights from Irkutsk to Saint Petersburg and from Moscow to Irkutsk. In short, I footed all of their travel costs, including some optional trips but excluding expenses incurred for their private telephone conversations. While planning their inland travel, I thought it was considerate of Olga to reassure me that since she had good connections through her work as a tour guide, she was in a better position than I to find reasonable flight tickets as well as cheaper rates for one night of hotel accommodations in Saint Petersburg. As it turned out, however, she really did not try very hard and left it all to me. Thus, there was no help from the Siberians.

Saint Petersburg – Déjà Vu

I left home on the morning of July 26, 2007, flew via Chicago and Frankfurt to Saint Petersburg Pulkovo Airport, and arrived in the early afternoon at our downtown hotel, where we were to spend four nights. My friends had not yet arrived. I settled in, checked out the hotel, and asked the guide in charge, as well as the receptionist, to let me know as soon as my friends arrived and to inform them of my room number. I was both tired and anxious and stuck close to my room, waiting for their arrival. Hours went by and nobody contacted me. I went for the umpteenth time to the reception desk and was finally told they had checked in – some time before. I went to their room and found them happily settled in, and we embraced cordially. Lubasha had brought all kinds of things, such as books, pictures, and most of all, the golden medal, which she proudly showed me. She was a lovely young lady. About 5'2", she had a perfect figure and thick, very long brown hair, large brown eyes, and a beautiful smile. She was overflowing with excitement. Her English was perfect. Olga was just as happy. I handed her the envelope with the money, which I owed her for reimbursement of flights, etc. Since it was getting late and I was so tired (and frankly, a bit disappointed that they had not tried to locate me as soon as they arrived at the hotel), I made sure they understood the plans for the next day and then went to my room to go to bed. I was pleased with my first impressions of Lubasha.

After breakfast in the hotel, we all participated in GCT's Panoramic City Tour of Saint Petersburg, which Pushkin called "Peter the Great's window to the West" and which is known today as the Venice of the North, with more than forty picturesque islands, over sixty canals, and hundreds of lovely bridges. We viewed "the Admiralty, the immense fortress built in 1704 on the banks of the Neva River to showcase the might of the Russian navy. Embellished with a tower in 1711 and with friezes and statues in the early seventeenth century, it remains a beloved symbol of Russian pride to the local people. Between Admiralty and St. Isaac's Cathedral stands the Bronze Horseman statue, a tribute to the city's founding father, Peter the Great" (GCT). Olga and Lubasha appeared to like all these treasures of their country very much. I had visited these sites twice before, and since the trip was a gift, I tried to stay in the background, with the exception of meeting for meals.

The same afternoon, we visited my favorite museum, the Hermitage, and saw a portion of the "staggering collection of art and paintings ranging from ancient Egypt to early 20th century Europe, set in a complex of buildings magnificently and lavishly adorned with gold leaf, malachite, jasper, agate, and marble. We marveled at masterpieces by da Vinci, Michelangelo, Raphael, Rembrandt, a full range of French Impressionists, van Gogh, Rodin, and many more of the world's great artists" (GCT). It would have taken many years of daily visits to see it all.

The next day, I opted out of a visit to Catherine's Palace and Park, but sent my friends to see this striking example of Russian baroque architecture, which was heavily damaged during the Second World War. The restored building is said to be the finest replica in the world. "Its grandiose façade stretches 978 feet and glitters in all its former glory, with elegant white columns and ornate gold moldings set against a background of brilliant blue sky" (GCT). I gave them my digital camera, and they brought back many pictures, in most of which they stood in front of statues or the like.

I invited my friends for a superb ballet performance at the Mussorgsky-Mikhailovsky Theatre, since they had never seen a live ballet. They were as exhilarated as I was.

On day 5, we all went on another optional tour, this one of the splendid Yusupov Palace, once owned by one of the wealthiest families in Russia. The nineteenth-century palace stands on an embankment of the Moyka River, beyond the Bridge of Kisses. Built by Vallin de la Mothe in 1760, the palace's claim to fame is as the place where Prince Yusupov murdered Grigori Rasputin, a controversial figure in Russian history, in 1916. We saw where it all took place and could let our imaginations go wild, since the place was dimly lit and seemed a bit eerie. More uplifting was a performance by the Soloists of Saint Petersburg, a chamber-music ensemble, in the palace's beautiful private theater, renowned as one of "the most beautiful of its kind in all of Europe" (GCT). They played compositions by Mozart, Vivaldi, Rossini, and Tchaikovsky, and we were delighted.

On day 6, we visited the chief monument to Peter the Great's reign, the Peter and Paul Fortress, which I had visited before but wanted to see again. "On May 27, 1703 (considered the city's birth date), Peter the Great laid the foundations of the fortress on an island in the Neva River to protect the city and Russia's access to the sea from the Swedish armies during the Northern Wars. Within the fortress is the St. Peter and St. Paul Cathedral, whose lovely spire is topped by a golden angel holding a cross. This figure is the symbol of the city. Peter the Great and all the Russian emperors and empresses are buried there. The Cathedral made headlines when the remains of the last Romanov family (Nicholas, Alexandra, and their children) were laid to rest here" (GCT).

I had made reservations for my friends to take the optional Peterhof tour, which I considered a must. It also gave them a chance to cross the Gulf of Finland by hydrofoil in order to see this "Versailles by the Sea." I will never forget the remarkable Grand Cascade, the extraordinary fountain ensemble made up of three waterfalls, nearly 150 fountains shooting more than two thousand jets of water, and myriad statues and sculptures. The sun was shining, and the two were impressed. It was a nice finale for them prior to boarding the MS *Rossia*. To celebrate our forthcoming voyage, we met, nicely dressed, for the captain's reception and welcome-aboard dinner.

MS *Rossia*

As was usual at these welcome dinners, all those sharing a table introduced themselves, and before you knew it, a vibrant conversation was underway. There were some 185 Grand Circle tourists on the ship. Olga and Lubasha were the only Russian guests onboard, and it did not take long before we were much talked about. – Everybody spoke about their travel experiences, and I was no exception. We had much fun when one of the fellow travelers at our table asked me about the places where I had been. He went down a very long list, and when I assured him again and again that I had visited the places he mentioned, some shook their heads in amazement. Others, I think, were a tad envious, and all seemed to sigh with relief when he asked if I had been to Timbuktu, Mali, and West Africa, and I had to answer no. – My Siberian friends seemed proud to be my guests, and I was pleased to see that everybody liked them. The passengers were impressed with their knowledge of the English language. I was astounded to find out that Olga too spoke English almost fluently. She had never told me, as we had always conversed in German. Several passengers who got to know us expressed their amazement that I was generous enough to treat mother and daughter to this cruise, since we were not related.

We cruised all night, and after breakfast we went to the observation room to look at the countryside along the forest-fringed banks of the Svir River. I was not really surprised to see so much wooden architecture, similar to what I saw when traveling on the Trans-Sib Railway in 2004. We went to the Discovery Series talk on Russian handicrafts and learned about the skills and creations of Russian artisans. They had arranged a most impressive display of *matryoshkas* (nesting dolls). Olga and Lubasha really got into painting *matryoshkas*, because they hoped to eventually win a prize, which Lubasha did. She won second prize. I forfeited the chance to learn Russian phrases.

In the afternoon, we disembarked at our first port of call, Svir Stroi, a remote village on the Svir River, 280 miles south of Saint Petersburg and halfway between Lake Ladoga and Lake Onega.

Though the town is best known for the orphanage for troubled children, we visited the homes of local residents, which seemed a bit awkward to Olga and Lubasha, though we did not really talk about it. We were served Russian tea and very tasty *pirozhki*, that is, pastries with chicken, fish, fruit, beef, and cheese fillings. I had brought a couple of souvenirs from the States, and I gave them to the hostess. She thanked me with a big smile. Most importantly, I took a bunch of pictures of the clan in front of their rather modest wooden house, painted in vivid green, and of the wildly mixed pink, blue, and yellow flower garden next to it. In case you are interested, nobody in the group engaged in a heated discussion with any of the hosts. Across the road was a gray, wooden, shed-like hut with a rusty tin roof. An old man rested on a low stool next to the narrow entrance door. Instead of flowers, a big patch of high weeds had taken over. A guy from our group in a blue-red-and-white parka stood next to the man, but they neither talked to nor looked at each other. – So much for Russian–American relations! I did not spot a single goat either.

Kizhi Island – Lake Onega

The evening before our arrival, GCT always gives a briefing about what we will see the next day. The guide reiterated that we would dock at Kizhi Island, in the middle of Lake Onega, the second-largest lake in Europe between Lake Ladoga and the White Sea. It is a popular summer resort for Russians, one of the "most ancient inhabited sites in Russia, an early pagan center and now hosts an open-air architectural museum and reserve. It was opened to visitors in 1966 and offers an array of architectural monuments. Over 80 wooden monuments represent folk wooden architecture, ancient Russian pictorial art, and cultural items of Karelia's various ethnic groups. The museum's precious collection includes many wooden churches and shrines brought from other parts of the Russian north" (GCT). The major and highly remarkable attraction is the eighteenth-century "Church of the Transfiguration, with its 22 timbered onion domes" (GCT). I walked around it and got a quick peek into the very dark interior, where all of the walls were covered with icons. I tend to get claustrophobic inside these Orthodox sanctuaries, but was nevertheless pleased to be fortunate enough to see it in the flesh. As I strolled around the village on this sunny day, I noticed that some of the quaint wooden houses, which have tiny windows and painted shutters and are badly in need of repair, are still inhabited by locals. – The guide emphasized that the Church of the Resurrection of Lazarus, built in the late fourteenth century, is the oldest wooden church in Russia. No nails were used in the construction. Pieces of wood were notched together to form a highly intricate structure. Amazing! The location of this treasure, in the middle of the lake, which on this day shimmered magically, was simply picture-perfect. If you doubt it, you are welcome to browse the pictures I took of these unique architectural treasures on this glorious day.

We continued to talk about the outing when we were sitting in the ship's lounge, at tables on which glasses for the vodka-tasting demonstration were lined up. GCT called this event a "Discovery Series presentation on the beverage that has been integral to the Russian culture for over 600 years: vodka. Distilled even before it was named vodka (from the Russian word 'voda,' or water), vodka was once believed to be a miracle-working medicine." I recall that on one of my trips, when I came down with a very bad cold – I think it was in Mongolia – someone recommended I buy a bottle of vodka. Regardless, Olga did not drink a drop, and understandably, neither did Lubasha. I tasted a couple shots and found the stuff extremely strong. It was a far cry from water. I was glad Mr. Belousova had stayed home, since he most likely would have made up for all of us. Actually, we never talked about him. – Weird.

I felt rather relaxed and enjoyed the smooth, pastoral countryside surrounding Lake Onega as the MS *Rossia* sailed for all of day 9 on the big lake toward the next port, Yaroslavi. Of course, I held my little Sony camera at the ready to catch the sinking sun before he disappeared on the horizon.

While sailing, we were treated to another Discovery Series presentation, a *blini* party. They taught us the art of creating *blinis*, small Russian pancakes that are served with sour cream, caviar, or smoked salmon. I really liked them, because I had tasted *blinis* with caviar and vodka on the Trans-Sib trip. If you are interested in the recipe, you can look it up in a cookbook. Sorry.

That evening, we gathered for the usual port talk before dinner, and a handsome young pianist entertained us afterward with compositions by Chopin and Tchaikovsky. It was nice even though the baby grand was a tad out of tune, which most of the guests failed to notice. The pianist found it annoying, but what could he do? I bet they did not even pay him well enough.

On day 10, we finally started to cruise the Volga, the greatest river in Europe, "twisting, meandering, and flowing from the Valday Hills to the Caspian Sea for almost 2,500 miles, draining an area of a million square miles, and linking five oceans and seas to Moscow through its canals" (GCT). The Russians call it the Volga Matushka (Dear Little Mother).

The Golden Ring

Yaroslavi

Since I am relying more or less on GCT flyers and my numerous pictures, which complement each other, I quote from one of the flyers: "After lunch, you'll arrive in lovely Yaroslavi, a thousand-year-old trading center rich in monuments and known for the fine architecture in its churches. Here you have entered the region around Moscow called the Golden Ring, an arc of cities where magnificent pieces of Russia's past have been preserved. . . . On your included tour, you'll see the Church of Elijah the Prophet (Ilia Prorok), which contains some of the finest 17th century wall paintings and icons in Russia. This church was built in 1650 at the expense of the Skripkin brothers, who were wealthy local merchants. It contains an extraordinary treasury of historic Russian art and represents the talents of master architects, painters, goldsmiths, and carvers. The tour also takes you to the Savior-Transfiguration Monastery, where you'll enjoy a bell choir performance," which we appreciated.

In this austere Orthodox cathedral – founded in the twelfth century and, by the sixteenth, part of one of Russia's richest and best-fortified monasteries – all of us had to wear a scarf. It was there that I realized how devoutly religious both Olga and Lubasha were.

Almost everybody on the MS *Rossia*, especially the young, had been busy getting ready for the big postdinner event on day 10, a talent performance. I had encouraged Lubasha to come prepared and perform one of her songs, which she had supposedly composed. I had not heard her sing before, except once briefly over the phone. She practiced with the young pianist, and I was quite anxious for her to appear. She also participated in a group dance, which was very nice and earned much applause. When it was her turn, she made a nice entrance on the set-up stage. To my utter surprise, she sang the theme song from the movie *Titanic*: "My Heart Will Go On." I thought I did not hear right, because not only did she sing out of tune, but her voice was equally disappointing. That was not the worst part. Once she stopped, she shouted out toward me at the top of her voice something to the effect that she appreciated all I had done for her and all I was going to do in the future. Olga, who stood next to me, seemed elated. The crowd applauded politely. I had a hard time being polite.

I guess it finally must have sunk in, because Lubasha reportedly went to their cabin to cry. I later discussed the matter with the pianist, who had tried in vain to stop her from singing that song. It was so embarrassing. The next day at the breakfast table, one of the ladies remarked, "Was that necessary?" Another woman thought it "took a lot of guts" for Lubasha to sing that song. In a way, I had to agree. I was surprised that Olga, who knew about Lubasha's plans, did not try to stop her, but perhaps she was just as ignorant about music. And what about that composed song?

I wondered why she let me send her the money for a keyboard and piano lessons. Regardless, we all got over it, but the glass had suffered another crack. The first crack occurred when they failed to contact me the day of their arrival, the second, when Olga informed me on the way to our first meal together that Lubasha could not eat certain foods, meats, vegetables, fish, etc. For breakfast, she could only have oatmeal. She had experienced a problem with her stomach from the time she was born, etc., etc. I was disappointed, because I had informed Olga before the trip that GCT had to be made aware of any special dietary needs in advance. I asked her to take care of it, which she did. It meant Lubasha could not join us for dinner most of the time and had to eat in their cabin, which I regretted, because mealtimes were important to me. Another crack had already occurred on the first day, when we sat at the dinner table with other passengers. Out of the blue, Lubasha, who was very talkative, which I did not mind, announced that she had written a book. I told her I was surprised to hear it, since she had never mentioned it. When I asked about the title, length, and where it was published, she blushed. I decided to steer the conversation in another direction. Olga was very quiet. It was then that I began to realize we had a problem with honesty.

Uglich

On day 11, we continued our discoveries in the Golden Ring, and we were quick to click our cameras when the striking Church of St. Dmitry on the Blood appeared. It has red walls and a cluster of beautiful, spangled blue domes. It was built around 1690 and named in memory of the spot where Prince Dmitri, the youngest son of Ivan IV, "the Terrible," died in the late sixteenth century. He supposedly stabbed himself in the throat during an epileptic seizure. Others say he was murdered. Who knows? I liked the stone edifice of the church and was awed by the red Uglich fortress, or kremlin, as it is called. Together with its beautiful churches, it looks ever so striking on the banks of the Volga. The long history of Uglich is reflected in these ancient buildings, of which the monumental Cathedral of Transfiguration, built from 1700 to 1713, is a part.

We walked the streets of Uglich and admired the center of the town, which is renowned as a historical and architectural landmark. The streets were noticeably wider, and all the churches boasted distinctive domes and belfries, which I will refrain from describing in detail. There is just too much to absorb. I have seen more churches on this trip than I could have imagined. The three of us split up when we were given time to browse around the handicraft market near the center of the town and where we found a trinket or two to take home.

In the evening, we all got dressed for the captain's farewell dinner.

Moscow – Déjà Vu

After docking in Moscow the next morning, we wandered around the city, looking at upscale shops along the well-known Tverskaya Street, and then met onboard for lunch. After lunch we set out for a city tour, which included the famed Moscow State University. I had an informative discussion with our tour guide, who was well connected with the university. She had valuable information about the rigid entrance requirements, tuition costs, scholarships, etc. I was interested, because I was entertaining the idea of supporting Lubasha financially, should she be accepted. I had trouble understanding why Olga did not exactly like the idea. That morning, she was more excited about some news she had received from Irkutsk. She had been informed that they might have discovered the remains of her grandfather, who had died somewhere in Germany during World War II. I thought it was insane to look for the remains of a fallen relative some fifty years after he had died. I too had a cousin who never returned from the war in Russia. It never occurred to any of my relatives to locate his remains. –

Our tour also took us to Krasnaya Ploshchad (Red Square), which I had seen before. The guide explained that in the sixteenth century, *krasy* meant "beautiful," but its meaning changed over the centuries to mean "red," referring to the beauty of the city square, which became a place for state ceremonies. After a ride on the metro, we were let off at Arbat Street, a pedestrian area.

On day 13, we toured the Central Armed Forces Museum, which chronicles the history of the Russian military. I was particularly interested in seeing the banner raised in Berlin in 1945 to signify victory over the Nazis. There was Josef Stalin's coat and a desk blotter used by Hitler, which looked a bit different than the blotter on my father's desk. The documentary film, which favored the victories achieved by the Russians decidedly more than those achieved by America and her allies, was especially telling. The tour got more interesting during a meeting and discussion with a select handful of Russian World War II veterans. It took place in a very large hall and was preceded by a brief performance by a Kremlin military orchestra. It soon became clear that the Russians rather than the Americans emerged from the war as the great liberators and that the Germans were the great killers. The name Stalin was carefully avoided – until I pulled myself together, stood up, and asked whether they knew how many people Stalin had killed. There was a great silence, followed by a murmuring among my fellow travelers. Some turned their heads, casting looks at me that could have killed. Then, the guide came back with an answer: two million. And I sat down. I had heard and read that the number was as high as fifty million, but decided to shut up. After all, why quibble over a few million? My Russian friends never commented on the situation, and neither did any of my travel companions. It was only on the flight home that a man, sitting a few seats in front of me, turned around and said he was glad I had asked the question. I thanked him profoundly and felt relieved.

We spent two more nights at a hotel in Moscow, and my friends and I said goodbye. Instead of taking the Trans-Sib back to Irkutsk, as I had suggested, they spent a couple of days with Olga's friend, an MD, and flew back to Irkutsk.

A few days after I returned home, I received a very nice thank-you letter from Olga in perfect German. We telephoned occasionally. At one point, Olga told me her husband had asked her why I had done this for them. I said, "Because I felt sorry for you and just wanted to do something special." I never quite understood why Olga led me to believe her marriage was more fragile than it was. I gathered during the trip that they stayed in touch with the father by telephone. He complained at one point that they had not left enough money to buy food for their pet cat.

The story developed further. Lubasha started at the university, and since I had promised to support her by financing her tuition, which would be about $1,000 annually, I said I would mail $100 each month in a letter. I sent the first installment with a pair of silver earrings. A couple of weeks later, the phone rang, and Lubasha said that although the letter had arrived, the money and earrings were missing. In the meantime, I had asked Lubasha to make a translation of the book she had written. I thought it would be a good exercise for her, and I offered to pay her for the work. Since she ignored my question, I decided she had lied about the book. When I made her aware that I was disappointed and stated that she was obviously not very honest, she wrote back rather nastily. Meanwhile, I had told Olga I preferred to reimburse her for tuition at the end of each semester. A letter arrived in which she stated that tuition had to be paid in full for six years, right then and there. That sounded very questionable. When I inquired into the matter at the Russian Cultural Center in D.C., I was informed I could pay tuition one semester at a time and that it was not in fact the case that everything had to be paid six years in advance. Enough is enough! I cut off all connections, changed my will, in which I had been rather generous to them, and have not heard from them in five years. – Thus it goes. I was glad I had taken the Russians on this trip, mainly because I got to know them better. It was worth the investment, and in addition I got to see the Golden Ring.

HOLLAND – MS RIVER CONCERTO

Amsterdam

In the fall of 2004, I decided to treat myself to another birthday present and booked GCT's Holland & Belgium river cruise, which would take place in the springtime and included a post-trip extension in Belgium. It was to start in Amsterdam on April 13, 2005, and end in Bruges on April 27, 2005. I liked the name of the cruise ship, MS *River Concerto*, a lot! It was to be a leisurely trip, because for July 2005 I had planned a big adventure to the North Pole. Fortunately, I had enough points for a frequent-flyer ticket, and on April 12 I left Indianapolis on Northwest Airlines and flew, after a stopover in Detroit, directly to Amsterdam, where I landed on April 14 (Doc's birthday) at 5:55 a.m. A few hours later, I settled into my nice cabin, #311, and again, since I was one of GCT's frequent travelers, I enjoyed their customary VIP treatment. I had traveled with them to Japan a year earlier to see the cherry blossoms and Mount Fuji on my seventy-second birthday, and since I love spring flowers, why not celebrate my seventy-third with a visit to Holland while the tulips are in bloom? It would be exciting to experience the Low Countries abloom in a riot of floral colors via the waterways. It is common knowledge that water has shaped Holland, that over the centuries "its lands have been flooded, claimed, reclaimed, and even created with an ingenious system of dikes and canals" (GCT). These waterways are the source of one of Holland's gorgeous treasures: flowers.

Enkhuizen

The *Concerto* sailed that evening to the nearby historic village of Enkhiuzen, of which I had never heard before, but which we got to explore for a few hours the next morning after breakfast. This well-preserved town was established between 1000 and 1200 and became a city in 1355. It prospered as a result of its herring fishing industry and trade with the Dutch East India Company, and it reached its peak in the seventeenth century, when it had the largest herring-fishing fleet in Holland. Today, the town derives part of its fame from its open-air Zuider Zee fishing village, which I would have liked to visit, because I am a great herring lover. But we ran out of time.

"The thriving port sat on the edge of the Zuider Zee, an inlet of the North Sea until it was enclosed in 1932 [the year of my birth]. Now, Enkhuizen sits on the Ijsselmeer, the large inland lake created by the damming of the sea outlet. With a population of about 16,000, this historic city retains its old charms, and its harbors attract thousands of pleasure boats" (GCT). – When I walked through the streets, I became aware of the rather peaceful ambiance of this small town, with its small, red-brick houses, their tile roofs, and the arched bridges across a narrow canal, in which a boat was anchored. Some houses had a little flower garden in front. I came upon a functioning smokehouse full of hanging herrings. I could not find anybody who would sell the fish. At the entrance to the harbor were quite a few pleasure boats and the dromedaries, an old defense tower and many warehouses originally used by both the East and West India Company, of which I had heard during my visit to Cape Town, South Africa. They too were involved in the slave trade.

I attended an informative lecture on modern Holland before lunch and enjoyed the walk through the charming town and the brief visit at the home of a local family. We sat around a coffee table like those I was accustomed to when living in Germany, and I just loved the *stroopwafel* – a thin, waffle-like cookie sandwich with a sweet, chewy center, which they served with coffee. Though we tried to avoid talking politics, since the Iraq War was going on, it was difficult not to mention it. I was relieved to discover that our hosts were decidedly against it.

Aalsmeer

I did not stay long after the welcome dinner. I had signed up for the trip to the Aalsmeer Flower Auction (the world's largest) very early the following morning. And it turned out to be quite a fascinating experience. It took about thirty minutes for our bus to arrive at the huge facility. The auction started at about 7:30 a.m.

"Holland produces more than 9 billion flower bulbs annually, and throughout the country more than 23,000 acres of land are dedicated to greenhouse production. In Aalsmeer, the auction house itself comprises about 160 acres. Stationed at the visitor's gallery, you'll witness buyers from all over the world making deals at a lightning pace. Each day 19 million fresh flowers are sold during a computerized auction. As the clock for a group of flowers to be auctioned ticks down, the price lowers with it. Bidders bid by pressing a button (which is linked to the main computer) when the price of the flowers reaches what they are willing to pay – if someone hasn't already pressed their own button first. So here is only one bid: the highest. Once purchased here, they're loaded onto airplanes and transported to florist shops across Europe and the U.S., to be sold usually the same day" (GCT). The whole process – workers moving the crates loaded with flower boxes and bidders glued to their computers – is amazing and definitely worth seeing if you are in the area. In case you did not know, the "tulip mania" reached its peak in Holland in 1637, when tulip bulbs were sold for ten times more than the average hourly wage.

Amsterdam

After breakfast back on the ship, we joined our fellow travelers for the morning canal tour and a visit to the Gassan diamond factory.

It was a rather gloomy and rainy day, and at times we had to open our umbrellas, because it was really pouring down. The umbrellas partially blocked our view of some of Amsterdam's landmarks, such as the seventeenth-century Royal Palace, one of three at the disposal of Queen Beatrix, and the Mint Tower, which has retained its name even though gold and silver coins were minted there for only a couple of years. We passed the wooden double drawbridge, the Skinny Bridge, which reminded me of van Gogh's bridge paintings. It is one of over 1,200 bridges that cross the Amstel River and one of the city's outstanding structures. Amsterdam too is called the Venice of the North, because many curved bridges cross the canals that divide the city into ninety small islands. I much prefer Italy's Venice! These canals were full of houseboats, some in rather poor condition, similar to those I had seen in the Hong Kong Harbour. It's definitely not my preferred lifestyle. –

I was glad when we left our small boat, whose top did not cover all of us, and sought shelter from the rain to see the brilliant Gassan diamonds in one of Amsterdam's many diamond factories. I had seen such demonstrations in other places, but I am always curious to see them again. After all, Amsterdam has been a center of the world's diamond trade since the sixteenth century. The world's largest (the Cullinan) and the world's smallest (0.00012 carats, with fifty-seven facets) diamonds were cut there. And we were treated to a deluxe tour. We watched the men cut and polish loose diamonds, and if you were interested, you could also purchase one or two. "The Cullinan Diamond is the largest gem diamond ever discovered. It weighed about 3,106 carats in rough form when it was found in 1905 at the Premier mine in Transvaal, S. Af. Cut it is 530.20 carats" (GCT).

Upon leaving, I noticed a couple of three-wheeled Wielertaxi "bicycles" (a kind of rickshaw) going by and would have loved to take a ride. It's their latest form of taxi transport, offered at a rather reasonable cost. They looked quite sturdy and had a modern design. Not bad.

Nijmegen

In the afternoon, upon arrival in Nijmegen, Holland's oldest town, some of us joined the program director for a stroll to check out the town's charming old buildings. After dinner, a traditional Dutch shanty choir entertained us with songs of the sea.

The next morning, while cruising from Nijmegen to Gornichem, I opted to relax onboard. – Maybe, having lived through World War II in Germany, I should have participated in the optional tour of the Liberation Museum, but for some reason I do not like to relive those times, which eventually led to my immigration to America. Since Nijmegen was practically on the border of Germany (Emmerich), I could see why it had been a perfect strategic location for the German invasion of Holland. According to GCT, "The Liberation Museum chronicles life in the Netherlands in the years before World War II, the Nazi occupation, and during liberation and postwar reconstruction. Located in hilly woodlands, the museum uses exhibits, interactive presentations, dioramas, film, and sound to honor the sacrifice of the Allies and the underground. Among the items displayed are many related to the British, Canadian, and American forces that fought here during Operation Market Garden. In September of 1944 the Allies captured bridges over the main rivers of German-occupied Netherlands, eliminating their last major obstacle in their advance into Germany. Market Garden was successful up to the capture of the Rhine (Waal) bridge at Nijmegen, but the final bridge also crossing the Rhine at Arnhem could not be held." I remember well that on April 10, 1945 (my birthday), the Germans failed to explode the bridge next to my aunt's mansion in order to prevent the Americans, who approached on that road with heavy tanks, from invading our village. I have written about it previously. Several fellow travelers spent some time at the Anne Frank Huis, the secret annex to a nearby house where her family hid. The small museum details the daily life of the young girl and her family before their betrayal by Dutch collaborators and their subsequent deportation to Nazi death camps. Others went to the Rembrandt House Museum, which features over two hundred of the artist's drawings and etchings.

Kinderdijk

The afternoon trip to the "UNESCO World Heritage Site of Kinderdijk, which takes its name from a sixteenth-century legend involving a baby, a cradle, and a cat that all survived being tossed into the raging waters" (GCT), was much more heartening. I had seen a random windmill in the countryside before arriving there and was delighted to see a whole bunch of them in Kinderdijk. "For centuries, the Dutch were at the mercy of frequent floods. In about 1740, 19 windmills were built in Kinderdijk. These innovative structures drained the excess water from polders – the reclaimed land that is situated below sea level – and pumped it into nearby rivers and canals, helping to evenly distribute water levels and lessen the threat of devastating floods. Nowadays, modern engines do this vital job, yet the country still has a unique bond with, and affection for, its many windmills. They have been well preserved, and the historic structures became protected by UNESCO in 1997" (GCT). We were fortunate to have a chance to see the giant windmills spread out in front of us as we walked toward the area – and fortunate to stand in amazement so close to one of them and snap pictures to our hearts' content. Indeed, another one of my childhood dreams had come true. I climbed up inside one and listened carefully to the guide's presentation. Actually, people still live in some of the mills. We were given a flyer with drawings of a mill and its interior and an explanation of how its mechanism worked. Quite ingenious and *hochinteressant*!

Back on the ship, we were invited to a Discovery Series demonstration and to try our hand at the renowned Dutch art of Delft porcelain. Now I know how the Delft porcelain breakfast tablet that hangs in my kitchen was made.

Rotterdam

On day 6, we docked in Rotterdam Harbor, the world's largest cargo port, of which I did not have very fond memories, since several students from my summer abroad program in Bonn had ventured to Rotterdam without permission, reportedly to buy drugs. That was another dramatic event I have related in Part I of my memoirs.

The MS *Concerto* cruised the Rotterdam Harbor later that afternoon, at high-tea time. Our guide told us that Hitler's Luftwaffe bombed the city rather badly in 1940, that the Dutch gradually rebuilt it from the 1950s through the 1970s, and that in the 1980s they began developing an architectural policy that resulted in a new skyline. The Kop van Zuid was built in the 1990s on the south bank of the river as a new business center.

Middleburg – Zeeland

The next morning, on day 7, our ship docked in Middleburg, the provincial capital of Zeeland, which dates back to the late eighth or early ninth century. It has a population of 48,000. – After breakfast, we went for a stroll through the town and the traditional market square, built in the sixteenth century. We paused at the splendid Gothic Town Hall, which is now a university, and looked briefly at the "picturesque" cathedral. Its foundation was laid in the tenth century, but construction continued through the Middle Ages. It is one of two pre-Reformation cathedrals in the Netherlands.

We had some free time to venture out on our own, and I finally spotted a vendor in a pedestrian park who sold *maatjesharing*, which I had been dying to try – and dying to eat their way, that is, taking the fish fillet by the tail, dangling it over your backward-tilted head, and then lowering it – gradually letting the fish slide into your open mouth and devouring it with gusto. I assure you, it was delicious. I struck up a conversation with a couple of young students at a street display, who hoped to make some money selling handcrafted earrings, necklaces, and the like. I bought a pair and wished them good luck. I was lucky to find the department store, where I was able to buy the last five of their very unusual Albert Heijn bottle cleaners, which our guide had demonstrated for us and which I distributed among my friends back home.

The afternoon was spent visiting the incredible Delta Works: "Originally, Zeeland province was a collection of islands that were easy prey to the sea. Now the islands are connected and protected by a series of dams, dikes, and bridges. Spurred into action by the 1953 flood that claimed the lives of nearly 2,000 people, construction was begun on a system of giant dams to provide more technologically advanced flood control along the coast of Zeeland. An innovative engineering feat, the Delta Works was 32 years in the making and cost $6.5 billion. . . . With a series of sophisticated dams and barriers to close off the coastline, the Delta Works complements the ecosystem and protects a vast area of vulnerable lowlands. This tour shows you several of its ingenious technical achievements and gives you an impressive idea of how the Dutch have claimed, reclaimed, and protected their homeland from the threat of the sea. You'll get a fascinating perspective on this life-and-property-saving wonder" (GCT). This trip was well worth the extra $50. You have no idea how often I have thought about this project since Hurricane Katrina devastated the Mississippi Delta and New Orleans with catastrophic floods. I hope the United States will finally wake up and learn from the Dutch how to broaden coastal dunes, strengthen sea and river dikes, and do whatever it takes to prevent future disasters.

Back on the ship, we had a farewell drink, the usual port talk, dinner, and a show performed by the crew as we cruised to Antwerp, Belgium, in the region of Flanders.

BELGIUM

Antwerp

On day 8, after breakfast, we had a guided walking tour of Antwerp, a city with over half a million inhabitants located on the banks of the Schelde River. It is Belgium's major port and has been commercially important in European trade since the eleventh century. Like Amsterdam, Antwerp is one of the world centers for diamond trading. It was not spared during World War II either, but like all of the bombed cities in Europe, it turned out to be a city of beautiful architecture dating back to the sixteenth century. I have a penchant for old towns, whether in their rebuilt or original forms.

In the heart of the city, we explored the Grote Markt (Town Square), with its lovely old Town Hall, a 315-foot-tall structure that boasts a twelve-foot statue of St. Michael slaying a demon, the Bread House (King's House), and other beautiful guild houses. Grote Markt was voted the most beautiful square in Europe in 2010. Every two years in August, an enormous flower carpet is set up in the Grand Place for a few days. A million colorful begonias are displayed in patterns that cover a large area (19,000 square feet). The spires of the Cathedral of Our Lady are elegant, and the masterpieces by the great painter Peter Paul Rubens, who lived here in the seventeenth century, must not be ignored. We made our way along the Meir (the main shopping street) and appreciated the elaborate patrician mansions from the sixteenth century. They rival those in Northern Germany.

The afternoon was spent packing, resting, and chatting with new friends.

Brussels

On day 9, we disembarked and were transferred by motor coach to Brussels, the capital of Belgium: "Brussels is a district with its own government (with restricted powers). It is the headquarters of both NATO and the European Union (EU). The city has architecture and museums to rank with the best in Europe, a well-preserved medieval center, and an energetic street life and night scene, especially in its immigrant quarters; indeed European bureaucrats and business people, together with immigrants from Africa, Turkey and the Mediterranean region constitute a quarter of the population. The population of Brussels is 1 million and the population of Brussel's metropolitan area is just over 2 million. Belgium is divided into two semi-autonomous regions, Flanders and Wallonia" (GCT).

I was very disappointed that on our city tour, we did not stop to look more closely at the enormous EU complex and the steel construction of the Atomium, constructed in the form of an iron atom with nine spheres connected by corridors. We passed by the impressive Cinquantenaire Arch, the Chinese Pavilion, the Japanese Pagoda, and the Royal Park and saw much of the beautiful architecture of the city, including the art-nouveau structures associated with the famous architect Victor Horta. About ten minutes were spent in front of the famous *Manneken Pis*, on the Rue de l'Étuve. "It is the legendary statue that embodies the irreverent spirit of Brussels: a very small 17th century bronze statuette of a young boy urinating. He is believed to be nothing more than a decoration on the top of a fountain that provided fresh water in the Middle Ages. During the course of the centuries he has been hidden to protect him against bombs of invading armies and has been stolen several times by plundering soldiers. Every so often he is given a costume by the city authorities, and now possesses a wardrobe of more than 500 . . . Elvis Presley and Mickey Mouse costumes among those" (GCT).

We spent about an hour at the Grand Place, the famed market square and heart of medieval Brussels. I can easily agree with those who consider this "one of the most beautiful town squares in Europe, if not the world" (GCT). It is awe-inspiring. The ornate guild houses that dominate the square are as magnificent as the fifteenth-century Town Hall, with its hundreds of little statues and the King's House. I stumbled upon a festive event, a marriage, which was about to start. I talked with the mayor, congratulated the bride and groom, and chatted with several of the musicians. They gladly posed for me. *Merci beaucoup*!

On day 10, after a good night at our hotel in Brussels, we took off to visit Louise Verschueren's Real Belgian Lace Manufactory, housed in two lovely fifteenth-century almshouses. According to GCT, "Lace making has a long history but came into its own in the 15th century. Lace was intended to replace embroidery. Unlike embroidered clothing, lace pieces could be changed as fashion changed, and attached decoratively to different articles of clothing. Belgium soon gained a peerless reputation for fine lacework. In the 17th century, Brussels lace – a favorite of Queen Elizabeth I – was prized throughout Europe. . . . Lace making endures as a 'cottage industry,' employing about 1,000 workers, most between the ages of 50 and 90, and there are numerous family-run businesses throughout the city." I found this visit especially fascinating, because I had inherited a beautiful Brussels-lace banquet tablecloth from Doc, which he brought back from Belgium after completing his postgraduate work for surgery in Montpellier, France. He used to tell me with great pride that five women had worked on it for an entire year. When I described my tablecloth to the owner, he implied that today it would be priceless. I purchased half a dozen white-lace butterfly broaches for several of my friends back home. I liked them, because years ago, when I visited Belgium briefly at the age of nineteen or so, I had bought such a butterfly broach for myself.

Of course, we did visit the Chocolaterie Duval to see how fine Belgian chocolate is made. "Chocolate arrived here in the 1870s, following Belgium's colonization of the Congo and its cocoa plantations. Traditional Belgian chocolates are filled with creams, liqueurs, nuts, or a special dark chocolate called ganache. Today the finest chocolates, characterized by a smooth, velvet quality and a rich flavor, are produced in Brussels" (GCT). We stood around a large, fenced-off square and watched how chocolate was made in big kettles and then poured into molds, etc., until it finally ended up in various shapes, sizes, and shades of brown or white on a conveyor belt, which rolled past us. Though tempted, we were advised to refrain from helping ourselves to a piece from the conveyor belt. Not to worry – we were all treated to a generous sample or two (or three), enough to tempt me to line up to purchase a bagful for friends at home. That chocolate was the best!

Lier – Flanders

I skipped lunch and hopped on the bus to tour the Flemish town of Lier, with a population of some 34,000 and located on the Nete River. We praised their thirteenth-century architecture, which stood close to the river, and explored the market square, taking note of the rococo style of the old Town Hall, constructed from 1740 to 1745. It has a beautiful pediment, which bears the coat of arms of the city. Against the Town Hall stands the belfry (built in 1369), which is the symbol of the city's power and autonomy. To take in the city's sights from another perspective, we took a boat tour on the town's quaint canals. It was peaceful to glide for some forty minutes through the small town's idyllic scenery, devoid of tourists.

If you have a penchant for clocks, the Zimmer Tower is a must-see in Lier. "Originally part of the 14th-century city wall, it today houses a 75-year-old clock named for a famed clockmaker, astronomer, and inventor Louis Zimmer (1888–1970). He built this Jubilee clock for the Brussels World Exhibition in 1935. In 1938 the clock was sent to the States for the 1939 New Yorker World Fair. Every day, at noon, a hatch in the side-façade opens, showing personalities from both local and national histories between 1830 and 1930. This masterpiece is 16 ft. high and weighs over 4500 lbs. It contains 93 dials and 14 automatons" (GCT). It did not turn me on, if you know what I mean.

Back in Brussels, I packed my suitcase for the optional post-trip extension to Bruges and ventured out once more to the Grand Place. Instead of dinner, I treated myself first to Belgian French fries, which I purchased from a vendor on a side street. I decided on two different sauces for the fries, mustard and garlic-flavored mayonnaise. Simply *délicieux*. After all, French fries originated in Belgium! I sat at a small table outside. When finished I found my way back to the Grand Place. At a waffle stand, I bought a nice, thick, freshly-baked Belgian waffle. The deep pockets and large squares were filled with fresh, juicy strawberries, and the waffle was topped with whipped cream. I sat down at an outdoor table with a young couple and their kids and chatted about this and that. Later, I spent a while at the Royal Museums of Fine Arts of Belgium to see paintings by Pieter Brueghel de Jonge (1564–1638) and Hieronymus Bosch (1450–1516), since I always had a special liking for both.

Although postcards are admittedly a poor substitute for the real thing, I picked up a few for my album. I bet you don't own postcards of the two Flemish painters' art! When finished, I walked back to the hotel, where I joined the group for a farewell drink. *Adieu, mes amis*!

Ghent

It was 9:00 a.m. on Sunday, April 24, 2005, when we boarded the bus for the transfer to Ghent: "In the 16th century, Ghent was the most powerful city next to Paris. Now it is the lively core of a large area (population 350,000) with a historic center, which breathes out history and sociability. Cozy corners are alternated with busy shopping-streets. The citizens of the medieval city certainly did their best to turn Ghent into a rich showcase of beautiful civic gothic buildings" (GCT). I was struck by the city's architectural wealth and idyllic charm and loved the guided city walk. Though our time in Ghent was all too brief, we stayed long enough to compel me to put it on my mental "come again" list. I'll mention just a few outstanding sights: "Saint Bavo's Cathedral was named after a 7th century local nobleman who was canonized after he had given away his possessions to the poor and entered a monastery. The mighty uprising tower of the cathedral, which combines different architectural styles: the Romanesque, the high Gothic and the late Gothic is perhaps the most visible sign of the pride of the citizens of Ghent" (GCT). We had time to go inside to view Jan van Eyck's famous altarpiece *The Mystic Lamb* (1432) for a $4 ticket and Rubens's *The Conversion of St. Bavo* (1623). The Gravensteen – the Dutch name for the castle of the counts of Flanders, built in 1180 by Philip of Alsace – looked rather impressive thanks to extensive restorations. The belfry, so typical of medieval Flemish architecture, was as eye-catching as the Town Hall, built in the fifteenth century. We ended our tour at the Graslei (the Street of Herbs and Vegetables) and Korenlei (the Street of Wheat), which are considered to be among the most beautiful parts of the city. They lie along the quays of the old harbor of Ghent, right in the middle of the city. The names of the streets indicate that these specific products were traded or stocked in that area.

I regretted not seeing Ghent in her prime, when flower growers from the region sell their beautiful begonias and azaleas all over the world. Every five years, in spring, the successful Gentse Floraliën (Ghent Flower Show) attracts thousands to the city. Well, we saw Holland's tulips, so we really had no reason to complain.

Bruges

Our bus left Ghent at 3:00 p.m., and we arrived in Bruges, at the centrally located Novotel, at about 4:00 p.m. Its decor is modern, and it is set in a quiet courtyard, thus away from traffic noises. We gathered for a walk through the vicinity not long after having settled in. I was ready to get started; I had booked this optional extension to the trip primarily because I wanted to see Bruges and in particular the house of the lace makers. I own an oil painting by the Indiana artist Homer Gordon Davisson that depicts the house of the lace makers at an idyllic spot on one of the canals in Bruges. It was a wedding gift to my ex-husband Tonio, which I bought for $2,000 at Bradley Vite Fine Arts, at Beardsley Crossing, 1600 West Beardsley Avenue, Elkhart, Indiana. It hangs above the fireplace in the library.

It was a curious coincidence that I had inherited the Belgian-lace banquet tablecloth from my first husband, Dr. Wayne R. Beardsley, who shared the painter's birth date, that is, April 14. Davisson, born in Blountsville, Indiana, in 1866, was a painter and a teacher. He made ten trips to Europe, painting mostly in France, Holland, and Belgium. He studied at DePauw University, where I taught as a doctoral student. Among other honors and awards, he received the 1927 Indiana University Award: Hoosier Salon. Not bad for a Hoosier.

Bruges is another canal-based town in Northern Europe, connecting Belgium to the North Sea, and is thus also called the Venice of the North. Its medieval architecture is still intact and is obviously the reason why Bruges' historic center has been a UNESCO World Heritage Site since 2000. Bruges, with its 117,000 plus inhabitants, and thanks to its port, was once upon a time the "chief commercial city of the world" (GCT).

We went on another walking tour the next day and, among other sites, visited the twelfth-century Basilica of the Holy Blood, the Bruges City Hall, built between 1376 and 1420, the Country House, and the Provost's House, a baroque structure built in 1665–1666.

I took the guide's advice and followed the path along the canal, via Steenhouwersdijk and Groenerei, to see two of the oldest stone bridges in town (Meebrug and Peerdenbrug) and went down to Groenerei to have a look at the quaint De Pelikaan, a typical almshouse built 1714. It is such a pretty stretch of canal. Calm waters mirror the medieval bridges and skyline. – Later on we took a boat ride and liked cruising past the idyllic Old World houses, including the one depicted in my painting. And that is all I wanted.

On the way back to the hotel, I window-shopped and could not resist taking a photo of a seductive display in a chocolate store. Three pairs of voluptuous, dark-brown, white, and light-brown chocolate breasts, I kid you not, were staring at me with their dark nipples. I had a lot of fun showing the shots to a handful of male friends back home. I also bought three compasses in another shop to take to the North Pole later that year. I planned to have two of them engraved for Doc's great-grandsons upon my return.

On our next (and last) day in Bruges, we were free to do whatever we wanted. I took another walk, checked out a couple of lace stores, talked to the salespersons, and visited a *béguinage* on Wijngaard Street. It was founded in 1245, and Sisters of the Order of Saint Benedict have taken the place of the former *béguines*. "The béguinage is a collection of small buildings used by béguines, i.e. various lay sisterhoods of the Roman Catholic Church. The béguines lived like regular nuns, but did not make the same binding vows that nuns normally made. They vow obedience and chastity, but not poverty and they were free to break their vows and leave whenever they wanted. In the middle ages, it was not a religious movement. Poor and needy women as well as girls from rich and noble families joined the community. The rich often lived in the nicest houses and the poorer béguines lived in the 'convents' where several sisters lived together" (GCT). Having lived in a boarding school run by Ursulines where the rules were extremely rigid, but equally discriminating, I found all of this very enlightening. For some reason, I missed the Comic Strip Route, where famous artists have painted a series of giant comic-strip murals around the city and add new murals each year. If you go there, send me a postcard. Pray for me if you stop at the Basilica of the Holy Blood (of Jesus). It's amazing to realize that since 1150, thousands of visitors have come to Bruges to attend the mile-long Procession of the Holy Blood on Ascension Day. Another real moneymaker!

During the trip, I heard a lot about the fabulous seafood in Belgium and especially about mussels, which I like a lot. Therefore, the last day I was prepared to treat myself to a mussel dish at the famous La Civiere D'or, located in the market square, which I chose for its location. It is surrounded by impressive architecture, such as guild houses from the fifteenth to seventeenth centuries. I had heard that Audrey Hepburn, King Albert, Marcio de Oliveira Dias, and other celebrities raved about the place. I found a nice table outside, ordered their specialty, a huge terrine of mussels, a glass of wine, etc., and got a chance to chat in French with a nice couple at the table next to me. The mussels were delicious, as was everything else, but the waiter turned out to be a rude bastard – pardon me. I have forgotten the particulars, but the nice couple who observed the dispute wanted me to report the guy in order to have him fired. That I did not do. Instead, I withheld some of the tip, which triggered another screaming dispute, which left me speechless. I got up, folded the place mat, wished the kind French couple *au revoir*, and left. When I recently checked out the restaurant's website, I discovered I was not the only one who had bad things to say about their waiters. C'est la vie! I will stay away from La Civiere D'or – even during my next life!

I arrived home safe and sound in the evening on April 27, 2005, and began looking forward to my big trip to the North Pole, which I have already mentioned.

THE GREEK ISLES - MS STELLA SOLARIS

After having gotten to know Doc's offspring rather well and having become very fond of them, especially Peter and Eric, and after Eric was officially accepted to the Junior Year Abroad Program of Hamilton College in Paris, I thought it would be a great gift to both to treat them to a cruise to the Greek Isles. Peter would graduate that year from Amherst, and Eric, enrolled at Bowdoin College, was deserving of an early graduation gift. I had treated myself to a Mediterranean cruise during my junior year abroad in Aix-en-Provence and thought it was one of the best educational experiences one could have. I wanted to do this for the boys out of gratitude to Doc, who had laid the foundation for me to pursue my own studies. Both accepted happily, and after searching for the ideal itinerary as well as figuring out the best time frame for the boys, I booked a trip with Royal Olympic Cruises on the MS *Stella Solaris*, which was scheduled to depart from Piraeus, Athens, on June 8, 2001, and return on June 15, 2001.

Athens

I suggested that we meet in Athens a couple of days earlier and booked sightseeing tours for Delphi and Athens. The boys came from Paris by way of Corfu, and I flew directly to Athens via New York. It was just great to greet them on June 6 at the Divani Palace, a very nice hotel with a choice view of the Parthenon. I invited the two for dinner in the very romantic rooftop garden restaurant, where lush pink and white oleander was in full bloom. The dinner was superb, and the view from our table of the fully illuminated Parthenon was out of this world!

Early the next day, June 7, a private guide picked us up at the hotel to take us to the archeological site of Delphi, located on the southwestern spur of Mount Parnassus, in the valley of Phocis. I could hardly wait to finally visit the place from which the most famous oracle in the classical Greek world originated. But Delphi is also the major site of the worship of the god Apollo, particularly for his slaying of the Python, the dragon who lived there and protected the navel of the earth. – The weather was perfect, only a handful of people were present, and we had plenty of time to explore the theater, climb around the ruins of the Temple of Apollo and of the circular Tholos, and visit the treasuries of the Athenians and the Scythians. We stood in front of the few remaining Doric columns to pose for snapshots beneath cypress trees and admired the surrounding rolling mountains and the red-tile rooftops of the town of Delphi (two thousand inhabitants) below. How lucky we were to come face to face with this foremost archeological site of Greece, dating back to between 380 and 360 BC. Oracles, as centers of the religious and political world, influenced affairs for more than a thousand years, because they were presumed to be accurate predictions given by Pythia, the priestess. She muttered incomprehensible sounds in a state of trance. They were translated into comprehensible language for those who had come in search of answers. I remembered Professor Dr. Dr. Bourde's incredibly captivating lectures about Greek art when I studied fine arts in Aix-en-Provence.

Among other treasures in the Delphi Archeological Museum, the 5'11" Charioteer, a unique bronze sculpture from 470 BC, caught our attention before we had to leave.

I had fallen in love with Athens during my first visit in 1966 and was determined to give the boys at least a chance to see some of its highlights. We had only half a day before embarkation. Without going into detail about the places on the tour, here are the sites in the order in which we visited them: "Tomb of the Unknown Soldier – Royal Palace – Panathenian Stadium – Temple of Olympian Zeus – The Acropolis (site and museum). Thesseum – Greek Orthodox Cathedral – Monastiraki (Flea Market) – Modern Market – Patission Ave. – Alexandras Ave. – Vas. Sofias Ave. – Panepistimiou Ave. – University – National Library – Omonia Square – terminal" (Itinerary).

Of course, I think the Parthenon is and will always be the ultimate Greek monument. The boys were impressed. However, perhaps an even more memorable experience, and a *novum* for me, took place at the Panathenian Stadium, considered one of Athens' most significant remodeled historical monuments. It stands on Ardettos Hill and dates back to between 336 and 330 BC. The stadium can hold some fifty thousand spectators. Most seats were white marble, and others were carved from rocks. And then we saw the significant marble structure, the *propylaea*, or entrance gate!

I observed at the stadium that the boys were highly competitive. They agreed to race each other. I forgot who won, but found out that Peter suffered from asthma. I admired him for not allowing it to hold him back in the least. It was an event I will always cherish – I just wish Doc could have been there with us.

We boarded the MS *Stella Solaris* (Star of the Sun) at Piraeus on June 8, 2001, at 2:00 p.m., but had a bit of a problem during embarkation, because Eric could not find his passport. They were kind and let us onboard anyhow. He located his passport when unpacking. We all sighed with relief. Our cabins were nice, but not extravagant, as they are on bigger and newer cruise liners. The boys had been upgraded and were content. The *Stella Solaris* was built in 1953 and refurbished in 1973. She had a gross tonnage of 17,832, room for between 545 and 700 passengers, a service speed of 20 knots, and a length of 545.1 feet. The ship reflected a "traditional European charm with mellow wood paneling accented by continental furnishings and a refined décor. Public rooms are beautifully laid out and include the Main Lounge, decorated in warm autumn tones; the Monte Carlo Bar, a club-like salon with dark wood and deep leather chairs; and the Piano Bar, with huge windows overlooking the stern. Staterooms are notable for their spaciousness" (Brochure). I read recently that she was scrapped in India in 2003, one year after our trip. How about that? I liked that she was much smaller than other cruise ships and could see why she was a favorite of young people during spring breaks. Indeed, there were quite a few young people onboard, which was nice for Peter, especially since he ended up inviting a bunch of them to celebrate his twenty-first birthday.

Turkey – Déjà Vu

Peter, Eric, and I stood on deck when the MS *Stella Solaris* left Piraeus and happily watched the harbor, with its ships and the town, fade away as the sun set. Our ship cruised through the Straits of the Dardanelles, which like the Bosporus separate Europe from the mainland of Asia. It is an international waterway and, together with the Bosporus, connects the Black Sea to the Mediterranean Sea. Our next port was Istanbul, Turkey, where we had a full day to explore the city once known to the Greeks as Byzantium and to the Romans as Constantinople – and finally to the Ottomans as Istanbul. As I have already discussed Turkey and had decided to let the boys discover the city on their own, I will skip writing about Istanbul and Ephesus. Though I must say, I could hardly believe the extent to which tourism had increased in both places since my first visit in 1966.

Patmos

After Istanbul, we cruised to Patmos, a small Greek island with a volcanic landscape in the Aegean Sea, where we docked at about 6:00 a.m. on June 11 at the port of Scala. It was the first stop on our seven-day island-hopping odyssey. Homer's *Iliad* was always a mental companion when I wandered off by myself through the hilly and narrow lanes flanked by whitewashed houses on this little, yet ever so enchanting, island. I reached the top of Prophet Elias Hill, where the snow-white stone church that shared its name with the hill stood. From there, some nine hundred feet above the blue sea, my eyes wandered from one island to another in the distance. Not a cloud could be seen – the sky was a radiant blue.

The *Stellar Solaris* was docked in the wide, sheltered harbor below and, with the rolling hills in the background, looked stunning. I was curious to see the grotto and monastery where St. John the Divine supposedly wrote the Book of Revelation and had a vision of fire and brimstone. I mused at the Cave of the Apocalypse and the rock where the book was written by his disciple while in exile for some eighteen months. The monastery towers, with their massive fifteenth-century walls, were imposing. Seventeenth-century battlements top them. The bell tower is a favorite of photographers, including me. A couple of ancient and sinister-looking Orthodox priests with long, untrimmed white beards, floor-length black undercassocks, black overcassocks with wide sleeves, and black chimney-pot hats were kind enough to pose for me in the cobblestone courtyard. On my walk, I ran into Eric, who smiled and let me snap a picture of him in front of a lush bougainvillea bush creeping up a whitewashed wall. Pretty neat. On the way back to the ship, I checked out the colorful jewelry and ceramic and leather souvenirs, including those having to do with St. John, that the vendors in the narrow streets offered for sale.

Mykonos

We left Patmos at 11:00 a.m. and arrived in Mykonos, at the port of Chora, at 4:00 p.m. Mykonos, primarily composed of granite, spans an area of thirty-three square miles and reaches 1,119 feet at its highest point. It is one of the Cyclades islands, which surround Delos in the Aegean Sea. In Greek mythology, the island was named in honor of Apollo's grandson Mykonos. It was the location where the battle between Zeus and the Titans took place and is only 1.2 miles from Delos, the birthplace of the gods Apollo and Artemis. As in Patmos, the white houses, some of which used to accommodate pirates, dazzled me while I made my way through the narrow pedestrian streets and alleys with trendy boutiques and quaint tavernas. Of course, a main attraction of Mykonos included the windmills. Only seven of the more than twenty original lower mills remained. All were circular and painted in white, with a conical roof made of wood. They are located close to the harbor, still function, and are brought to life by the wind that blows between two hundred and three hundred days per year. Mykonos was on a major trade route. Therefore, the grain production needed to be refined and compacted for sea transport. Today the mills are used as museums or dwellings, much like the windmills in Holland!

I wandered off to look for a seaside restaurant, where I sat down at an outside table. I relaxed and relished a heavenly Aegean sunset while sipping a glass of Chardonnay instead of ouzo.

Rhodes

We departed from Mykonos at 10:00 p.m. and docked in Rhodes at 9:00 a.m. the next morning. In Greek mythology, Rhode, also known as Rhodos, was the daughter of the sea god Poseidon and thus a sea nymph and the goddess of the island of Rhodes. The myth relates that the sun god Helios became enamored of Rhodos, named the island "Rhodes" after her, and made the water which had covered it disappear.

On June 13, Peter's birthday, we were given the choice of exploring the historic Old City, with its ramparts and palaces built by the Knights of St. John during the Crusades, or joining an optional excursion to the Temple of Athena at Lindos.

We opted for Athena's Temple (sixth century BC). It's just wonderful now to look at the photos I took at the time. How nice to see Eric and Peter sitting on the steps beneath the remaining columns of the Temple of Athena with the immaculate blue sky in the background and the tantalizing azure waters of the Mediterranean at its feet. Lindos is a charming village with white, cube-like houses dating back to the fifteenth century and located at the foot of a vertical rock protruding from a barren landscape. The ancient Acropolis crowns the rock. Narrow, winding cobblestone streets give the town of eight hundred inhabitants an unforgettably quaint look, so typical of these picturesque islands, which I dearly love. We were lucky not to run into too many tourists on this comparatively hot day. – On the way to the ship, we had a chance to see the ramparts and palaces of the Knights of St. John in the distance. So long, Rhodes! Let the party begin.

Crete

The boys were busy preparing their cabin for the birthday party, and I retired early to rest up for the excursions scheduled for the next day: a bus trip to explore the island of Crete, which separates the Aegean from the Libyan Sea, in the morning, and a visit to Santorini in the afternoon.

The *Stella Solaris* docked at Heraklion, on Crete, at 7:00 a.m. I spent a three-month pre-honeymoon on Crete with Tonio and have written about it, including the visit to Knossos, in Part I of my memoirs. The bus excursion turned out to be something of a disappointment to me, and I was glad not to have booked a trip to Knossos. Peter was obviously suffering from a hangover. He kept falling asleep in the back of the bus, and we had to coax him to get up whenever we stopped at various places along the way. I am not sure Peter remembers much. Eric seemed to be more awake. I was glad we had a stop at a place in the country where the owner of an olive-tree orchard let us taste a variety of olive oils with baguettes, for which I had developed a great fondness during my last visit to Crete. In the distance, we saw several of Crete's beautiful sandy, pebbly, and rocky beaches that attract so many tourists to this, the largest of the Greek islands. And you could not miss the many olive-tree orchards in this forever-changing landscape. It is harsh and barren in one place and wooded and gentle in another. I liked the palm trees, the bougainvillea, the lush greenery in the villages, and the old stone farmhouses. Cretan men sat on chairs next to small tables in front of the houses, chatting, reading a paper, smoking pipes, and sipping coffee or an ouzo. A very peaceful ambiance, I thought. Although their attitude toward us seemed friendly, they did not smile.

Driving back through Heraklion, and recalling that years ago the Venetians were occupiers, I noticed that the architecture clearly reflected the island's Venetian past. And then there were the walls, more than four and a half kilometers in length. They were so strong that they withstood a siege that lasted twenty-one years and resulted in the loss of many Cretan, Venetian, and Turkish lives. When I visited Heraklion before, I had no idea that someday I would get married in Venice. – C'est la vie.

Santorini

The ship departed from Crete at 11:30 a.m. and arrived in Santorini, where people have lived since 3000 BC, at 4:00 p.m. It is the largest island in a small, circular archipelago of the same name and spans an area of twenty-nine square miles. It is also the remnant of a volcanic caldera, caused by one of the largest eruptions in recorded history. This Minoan eruption destroyed the earliest settlements on a formerly single island, creating the caldera of today. The sight of Santorini from the ship was a singularly exhilarating experience! Wow!

There are three ways to get to the village of Thera, which has a bow-shaped rim and is the remaining, eastern half of the exploded volcano. We could either climb 588 steps on foot, let a mule take us up in the blistering sun, or do what I did: find a shady spot and wait in line to ride up in a cable car. Peter and Eric virtually raced up the steps. None of us had signed up for a special tour, which meant we were free to do whatever we preferred.

I had heard from someone that red-wine grapes were grown in Thera and that the village was an exporter of pumice, a porous, frothy volcanic glass used for cleaning and scouring, but was more interested in a few choice photo opportunities. I headed directly to the top of the cliff, where I just stood for a while losing myself in another one of the most beautiful views in the world! I loved the blue domes on the whitewashed Orthodox churches and the dark-purple bougainvillea clinging to the white facades of houses and to the fences along the hilly streets. I checked out a mule standing on a cobblestone path, ready to carry someone or something. I took a picture of another mule carrying a basket filled with root vegetables. Its head was bent, and it looked tired or perhaps bored. How could anyone get bored while looking past the rocky cliffs out at the sparkling blue waters of the Aegean, where yachts and sailboats glide back and forth and an occasional seagull darts through the air?

That night, we bid farewell to our cotravelers at the customary farewell dinner. We shared discoveries, and I smiled when one of the passengers at our table asked me if Peter was my son.

Ever since I took the trip with the boys, who are both excellent sailors, I have hoped that one day they will return and navigate the islands themselves. That's all I have to say about our odyssey to the Greek Isles.

NORWAY – COASTAL VOYAGE ON THE MS FINNMARKEN

Not long after I returned from my trip to Antarctica on the *Marco Polo* in February 2003, I began surfing the Internet for a trip along the Norwegian coast. A fellow passenger on the ship had spoken with great authority when we cruised along the Chilean fjords. He proclaimed that the fjords in Norway were much more dramatic. I was determined to check them out myself ASAP and booked a trip that was to start with a train ride from Oslo to Bergen on August 6 and to continue from Bergen to Kirkenes on August 7 on Hurtigruten's MS *Finnmarken*, with a return date of August 18. I was scheduled to fly from Bergen to the States on the 19th.

It all sounded very good, but the trip itself quickly turned hellish, to put it mildly. My flights were booked on Continental and Scandinavian Airlines. The agony started when my flight from Indy was delayed by more than four hours and arrived in Newark after my flight to Oslo had already taken off. I spent hours waiting on standby – in vain, because a pilot and his family had taken my spot, which resulted in my running around from one airline counter to another in an attempt to book another flight and recuperate my suitcase. Finally, at 1:00 a.m., I found a taxi ride, which took me to a vacant room at the Hilton Garden Inn in Edison, New Jersey. The next day at 5:00 p.m., instead of flying to Oslo, I had to skip the train trip and fly directly to Bergen, where I arrived on the 6th, in plenty of time for embarkation in the late afternoon on the 7th. Of course, all of my trips had been prepaid, and I was much relieved when the travel agency assisted me in reorganizing my travel by reversing the train portion. I was to take the train from Bergen to Oslo at the end of the cruise and return home a day later.

Bergen

The Neptune Hotel is located in central Bergen and has a quayside location. I liked it, because from there it was easy to get around on foot. We were lucky. It did not rain, and I thoroughly enjoyed exploring this charming, hilly town (or city) with a population of some 266,000, located on the southwestern coast of Norway and sometimes referred to as the "Atlantic coast capital of Norway" or "gateway to the fjords." I loved the seven mountains which surround Bergen and regret not having taken the Fløibanen, a funicular that goes up to Ulriken (320 meters), the highest mountain of Fløyen, for the panorama view so many tourists have raved about. My fondness for the quaint and old was satisfied when I strolled among the eighteenth- and nineteenth-century wooden houses, along the quay and in neighboring alleys. They were painted lovingly in rusty red, mustard yellow, olive green, white, or khaki and gave me a true sense of Bergen's charm.

I spent quite a bit of time at the famous fish market near the quay. It was just wonderful, unlike any of the many fish markets I had visited before. Shellfish, crabs, chunks of smoked wild salmon, mackerel, and other types of fish were on display in an attractive, colorful combination on small pieces of ice. I tasted the best smoked wild salmon and mackerel and was determined to buy several packages for my friends on the way back. The vendors were ever so friendly.

Later that day, I visited the Edvard Grieg Museum, Troldhaugen, and the hut where Norway's most famous composer wrote many of his most popular works. His original villa and the hut sit perched on top of a hill close to beautiful Lake Nordås, where a rowboat lay anchored at a stone pier. I reflected a while by the statue and the tomb, hewn into a cliff, where Grieg and his wife were buried, and I passed by the old buildings and gardens with blooming shrubs, all well taken care of. An idyllic and inspiring spot! I was envious of those who had time to attend a concert at Troldsalen, the intimate concert hall located on the grounds.

Hurtigruten – MS *Finnmarken*

A cab transferred me from the hotel to the MS *Finnmarken* in the early afternoon on August 7, 2003, and since the ship, built only a year earlier in 2002, was comparatively small, that is, 15,000 gross tonnage, 138 meters, and capable of a speed of eighteen knots, I found my outside cabin rather quickly. I liked the modern decor a lot.

The Hurtigruten's Norwegian Coastal Voyage around the majestic coastline of Norway has been described as the world's most beautiful voyage. It departs daily from Bergen and travels north across the Arctic Circle and beyond as it meanders among the dramatic splendors of the Norwegian coast. "The Hurtigruten carries passengers, mail and supplies to over 30 ports along the Norwegian Coastline, most never visited by commercial cruise liners" (Brochure). Many tourists traveling by car store their vehicle onboard for the duration of their trip.

The Norwegians were quick to remind us that great thanks must go to the warm waters of the Gulf Stream, which facilitates the development of the Norwegian coast. The fjords would otherwise be blocked by ice for several months in the winter. "The Gulf Stream arises at the point where the Equatorial Stream presses its warm water into the Caribbean, moving north into the Gulf of Mexico and then south past the southern tip of Florida. At this point it is 100 m wide and transports 25 million cubic meters of warm water eastward across the Atlantic ocean every second. Part of the stream continues north of the British Isles and approximately 4 million cubic meters per second turn in towards Norway, flowing along the entire coastline past the North Cape. It also flows into the fjords, ensuring that ports as far away as Murmansk in Russia remain free of ice all year round. During severe winters, ice sometimes forms in Kirkenes harbor. Thanks to the Gulf Stream, 4.5

million people live in Norway. Fish have always flocked towards the coast in the same way as millions of sea birds do. Naval commanders have always wished for ice-free ports in the deep fjords, where even the largest warships can anchor close to the side of the cliffs" (Brochure). The Gulf Stream safeguards the sea, the life-supporting environment of both humans and animals.

I booked this trip mainly because I wanted to see the fjords and the mountains along the Norwegian coast. When I looked at the time schedule, which I found in my cabin, there was little doubt that I would not be disappointed. I counted sixty-seven stops. However, while our ship would stop briefly – that is, long enough to drop off mail, etc. – at all ports, it would stop at only twelve ports long enough for us to get off for some sightseeing on this twelve-day trip. That was fine with me. I spent a lot of time on the panorama deck, looking at the intoxicating scenery and chatting with passengers who had come from different parts of the world to participate in this seafaring adventure. Not your average tourists, I must add. Another big attraction was the food served on the ship. Each and every dish – a vast array of seafood – was superb! You would not be disappointed, and neither was I!

The MS *Finnmarken* took off at 8:00 p.m. on August 7. After a delicious dinner, I retreated to my cabin to get a good rest for the next day. The ship was crossing the open Stadthavet, heading for Torvik. En route, we stopped at Ålesund rather briefly, for a forty-five minute look at the beautiful art-nouveau town. And we were lucky to stop at Geiranger, in the Geirangerfjord, to see the beautiful Brudesløret (Bridal Veil) and Friaren waterfalls as well as the spectacular Seven Sisters waterfall. Molde was next, and it was just exhilarating to see the magnificent Romsdal Alps, where Henrik Ibsen, so we were told, loved to vacation. On the panorama deck, I was glued to the window while the captain navigated skillfully the Hustadvika, a belt of islets and skerries, before docking at Kristiansund. Dramatic and exciting! Kudos to the captain.

Trondheim

At 8:15 a.m., we stopped in Trondheim, a city with a population of 176,384, where we had about four hours to explore Norway's first capital during the Viking Age, which lasted until 1217. I did not know that the first Viking sale of goods from "the new found land" took place at this spot in about 1000 AD. Timber from Leif Erikson's Vinland estate was sold to a Bremen merchant. I knew of Erikson from my graduate work, when I struggled through a course in Old Norse, for which I earned an A-. *Trondheim* stems from Old Norse, meaning "home of the strong and fertile ones." How about that? I walked across the old city bridge after having sat for a while by the peaceful harbor, and I took a few very nice pictures of the restored wooden buildings in Bakklandet before walking to the great, Gothic Nidaros Cathedral, where the new kings of old Norway at one time received their official blessing.

We stopped in Rørvik for thirty minutes. It is the port where the southbound and northbound coastal ships meet, but I did not leave the ship. It was already 9:15 p.m. when we resumed our journey.

Arctic Circle Crossing

Exactly on time on the fourth day of our trip, the MS *Finnmarken* crossed the Arctic Circle. We spotted the big globe on Vikingen Island from the port side of our ship and docked at Bodø at 12:30 p.m. We had about three hours to explore the North Cape on the island of Magerøya. Its steep, 1,007-foot cliff is frequently referred to as the northernmost point of Europe, located 1,306.3 miles from the North Pole. I went to the Nordkapphallen, a large, round building, to look at the exhibits on the cape's history, purchased postcards in the tourist center, and had them stamped before mailing. Though the sky was overcast, I managed to get a few nice shots of the globe and the disks of the Children of the Earth monument, but since it was daytime, I have no picture of the midnight sun at the North Cape, which would have been fabulous. Next time! Nevertheless, I too was presented with a Polar Circle Certificate, which reads as follows:

I Njord, Ruler of The Seven Seas, hereby witness that Christa-Maria Beardsley, onboard MS "Finnmarken" crossed the Arctic Circle on 8/10/2003. Signed Captain so-and-so.

May good luck and happiness follow you on this voyage and forever after.

The Children of the Earth – a monument of hope – "stands as a witness to the ability of children to work together and understand each other across all boundaries. Since its erection in 1989, this monument and the North Cape Hall have been the scene of the annual award ceremony of the Children of the Earth Prize" (Brochure).

After Bodø, the ship headed out to the open sea for the highly anticipated Lofoten Archipelago, affording us "exciting panoramic views, majestic sights of the ragged Lofotveggen 'wall' of 100 km of peaks and snow-clad granite and volcanic ravines rising defiantly from the sea, and delight us with views of their picturesque cabins on stilts and weathered wooden racks with drying cod" (Brochure). The captain navigated the narrow Raftsund Strait, passed the looming crags of the Trollfjord, and docked in Stamsund at 7:00 p.m. Well done, Captain. The trolls did not bewitch us. "Lofot fishermen often had to spend the night in the open, sometimes sheltering under their upturned boats. Eventually, simple wooden fishermen cabins were built" (Brochure).

On day 5, we arrived in Harstad at 6:45 a.m. and had an hour before taking off again. I was in a good mood at breakfast and chatted with passengers, and I spent more time on the panorama deck, watching the scenic Vågsfjorden and the great island of Senja, with its diverse countryside of pine trees, plunging peaks, and farmland, pass by. When we stopped at Tromsø at 2:30 p.m., I got off, since we had four hours to kill. It was called "the Paris of the North," because in the nineteenth century, Russian, British, Dutch, and German ships called here before heading off on Arctic expeditions for hunting whales, walruses, and seals. It is almost two hundred miles north of the Arctic Circle and Norway's seventh-largest city.

While on a brief offshore tour through the arid, rugged, hilly terrain, I got excited upon seeing a couple of rather skinny reindeer with huge antlers feeding next to a Sami, an indigenous (Lapp) farmer dressed in a black frock down to his knees. The frock's red trim complemented the crimson trim on his pirate-like, three-corner headdress. He posed for me proudly with a grin.

On the panorama deck, I had made the acquaintance of a young man in his forties who was traveling by car with his wife and a little three- or four-year-old son. They traveled only for a couple of stations on the ship. Marco Bertagni turned out to be a very exciting man. Not only was he extremely handsome, tall, dark, very charismatic, and charming, but he had so much sex appeal that it was difficult to stop talking with him. He was from Italy and the director of a company in Rome with a house in Anzio. He had a PhD in economics and spoke English, French, and Spanish (in addition to Italian) fluently, and I am sure one could add others to the list. In short, he was intellectually brilliant and a conversationalist unlike any I had encountered in a long time. – Thus, meeting Marco on this trip was a big plus, and it boosted my enthusiasm, since he was also a world traveler. What more is there to say? We still e-mail now and then. The last I heard from him was a message from Uzbekistan, which was followed up by a picture of the Registan, in Samarkand.

On day 6, we spent three hours at Honningsvåg, capital of the North Cape, walking around and getting a sense of the austere landscape. I searched in vain for rookeries of puffins and spotted no gannets nesting in cliffs, as I had in New Zealand. We cruised past the unique fishing villages of Kjøllefjord, Mehamn, and Berlevåg and were on the lookout for Finnkjerka, a graceful sea cliff in Norway, formed in the shape of a church. As the story goes, it used to be an ancient place of sacrifice for the Sami people.

Kirkenes

On day 7 at 10:30 a.m., our ship docked at Kirkenes (3,300 inhabitants), our trip's northern terminus and turning point. We had three hours to go sightseeing, and I had signed up for a bus trip. This place was truly at the end of the planet, and due to the sparse population and rugged terrain, this seemed to be the case here more so than in Ushuaia, Argentina. It also turned out to be a rather depressing experience, for me at least. At one point, while we waited at a bus stop, a bus with Norwegian tourists stopped. The first person to step out of the bus was a gray-haired woman who exclaimed in loud, clear English, "I hate the Germans!" Though I consider myself to be an American born in Germany, I was a bit shocked. To be fair, I am not sure it was directed at me personally. As our group continued to visit some of the sites, I began to understand why the woman, after all these years, was still so full of hatred. – Our guide informed us of the extreme cruelties Nazi Germany committed there. Kirkenes suffered some 320 air attacks. The Germans destroyed most of the infrastructure and houses. Only thirteen houses survived their scorched-earth attack. I looked silently at the dark hole – the entrance to the Bjørnevatntunnelen, a cave in a mountain in which 2,500 inhabitants of Kirkenes sought shelter for two months in the autumn of 1944, before the Soviets liberated the area on October 26, 1944. Ten children were born there during this period. Germany invaded Norway strategically, to secure ice-free harbors from which naval forces could establish control over the North Atlantic. The English and Americans burned our houses and cities in Germany, and the Germans burned entire Norwegian villages. It's too depressing for me to discuss in detail, and others have written much about those horrors. I was surprised to learn that several thousand Norwegians volunteered for combat duty on the Nazi side, and I did not know that at the end of the war, Norwegians joined forces with Russia to defeat the Germans. How much more confusing can it get?!

The landscape of Kirkenes, a place where iron used to be mined, now looked rather dismal. We were about ten miles from the Russian border and not far from Murmansk, a major shipping port that also benefited from the warm Gulf Stream. We were not allowed to go there. I took a picture of a post with five signs that listed distances from Kirkenes: Helsinki 1,154 kilometers, Roma 5,102 kilometers, Oslo 2,202 kilometers, and Bergen 2,626 kilometers. None pointed to Moscow or any other Russian city. – Interesting. It is not a place where I would want to vacation, with the exception of perhaps a brief stay in the winter. One positive: tourists had not yet overrun the place! And it does not get too hot up there in the Finnmark region.

At that time, I did not think of ever coming to Murmansk to board the icebreaker NS Yamal for a trip to the North Pole. Neither did I think of repeating the same trip in 2008 to see the aurora borealis.

After having docked in Kirkenes for a few hours, the MS *Finnmarken* departed for the southbound half of the voyage, calling during the day at ports passed at night on the trip northward. We crossed Varangerfjord, Norway's only east-facing fjord and a "fabled bird-watching site" (Brochure), though we looked in vain for birds, and arrived at Vardø, the easternmost point of Norway, at 4:45 p.m. – The *Finnmarken* rounded the Varanger Peninsula, and the commentator explained that archeologists excavated a community in this area believed to date from 9000 BC. Who knows?

At 8:45 p.m., we docked in Båtsfjord for a mere thirty minutes, but I did not leave the ship to stretch my legs, as some always do. Neither did I look for the remains of a Stone Age settlement. When we docked at Berlevåg at 11:00 p.m., I was sound asleep, thus missing the steep, 270-meter-high Tanahorn, a mountain peak which was supposedly a Sami sacrifice site! It also entailed a four-mile walk from the ship.

Honningsvåg

On day 8, we arrived at Honningsvåg early in the morning, docked for thirty minutes, and continued to Havøysund for a fifteen-minute stop. After stopping at the island of Hammerfest at 11:45, we had until 1300 hours to check out the town, which claims to be the northernmost town in the world, with over nine thousand inhabitants. It is also one of the Sami capitals (Laplander culture). I spent my free time looking at the Hammerfest Church, with its characteristic triangular shape. Fish flakes – used for drying fish, since the traditions of fishing are important in the region – inspired the shape. Also, instead of an altarpiece, the church had a huge stained-glass painting. In front of the Royal and Ancient Polar Bear Society is a wooden portal with carvings of the meridians. It is crowned with Hammerfest's coat of arms. The two polar bears on the ice floes symbolize Hammerfest's history as a center of Arctic hunting and fishing. In the museum, I focused on displays of town traditions related to fishing and hunting in Arctic areas, as well as on the northern lights and polar bears. Notably, Hammerfest was the first Norwegian town to have electric city lighting and its own power station.

We left Hammerfest at 1:00 p.m. and went south to Øksfjord, whose glacier calves directly into the sea but failed to do so in our presence. After crossing open water, the ship called at the old trading post of Skjervøy for thirty minutes, at Tromsø from 11:45 to 1:30 a.m., at Finnes from 4:15 to 4:45 a.m., and finally, on day 9 at 8:00 a.m., at Harstad for thirty minutes – barely long enough to get a glimpse of the town. If you think I overlooked a stop, I apologize.

Back onboard, in the panorama room, I watched again with excitement as the island groups of Lofoten and Vesterålen boasted some of the most stunning scenery of the trip. We passed Risøy Channel, Raftsund Strait, and the breathtaking Trollfjord before arriving in Svolvaer and Stamsund at 9:00 p.m.

On day 10, we traveled from Ornes through crystalline waters and lush agricultural fields, crossed the Arctic Circle again, stopped at Brønnøysund, admired the Seven Sisters mountain range, which had a light dusting of snow on the peaks, and arrived in Rørvik at 8:20 p.m.

We arrived in Trondheim on day 11 at 6:30 a.m. and had almost four hours to check out the town, this time in a more leisurely fashion. By then, I had decided to really splurge and spend a small fortune on a black leather silver-seal vest and matching seal fur bedroom slippers at the boutique on the ship. They should last forever. You are only young once! (Today, almost ten years later, they still look like new.) Why do some things hardly age while we humans shrivel away day by day?

Fireball Lily

On day 12, during the night, our ship called at Torvik, Måløy, and Florø, but in the morning we took a last good look at mile after mile of spectacular West Norway scenery: holly trees on Svanøya, the mouth of the Sognefjord, and the beautiful archipelago. We arrived in Bergen at 2:30 p.m.

I headed back to the Neptune Hotel, dropped my luggage, and hurried to the fish market to buy half a dozen packages of smoked wild salmon to take back to my friends in the States.

At 8:30 the next morning, I boarded the express boat to Balestrand, where I was to spend a night at the historic, wooden Kviknes Hotel. It was a very scenic cruise through the Sognefjord. And since I never get tired of looking at mountain cliffs, cascading waterfalls, meadows where horses or cattle graze, and quaint villages with picturesque churches, I can assure you that this highly praised trip met all my expectations. I arrived in Balestrand about four hours later, was picked up at the pier by the hotel, and was ushered to my room in style. It was very, very nice and measured up to its reputation as one of the most distinctive hotels in Scandinavia.

I was so happy to have a room with a balcony and a view of the fjord. After a nice lunch in the elegant dining room, I ventured out to take a look at the little town. The inhabitants are very proud of their Anglican St. Olaf's Church, which was built in 1897 in the style of a stave church (a medieval wooden church with post-and-beam construction, similar to timber framing). I sat on a bench on the fjord and wondered if any of the royalty, emperors, presidents, prime ministers, movie stars, or artists from many countries who used to spend their holidays here, not to mention Kaiser Wilhelm II of Germany, might have sat at this very spot and gazed at the stunning panorama, which reminded me vaguely of that on Lake St. Moritz in Switzerland. It was so peaceful in Balestrand and surprisingly devoid of tourists. –

The dinner in the evening surpassed many I had eaten in other renowned hotels in different parts of the world. The food was superb. Before I retired for the night, I explored the hotel grounds, admiring their art and treating myself to a beautiful hand-knitted Norwegian cardigan.

After a good rest, I had to catch the train to Flåm and then continue to Oslo by another train. The Flåm train is virtually a must if you go from Bergen to Oslo or vice versa. And the trip by way of Flåm and Myrdal on the Flamsbana was a scenic highlight! "The Flåm Railway with a maximum gradient of 5.5 percent is one of the world's steepest rail lines on normal gauge. The Flåm Line is 12.6 mi long, has 10 stations and 20 tunnels with an elevation difference of 2,831 ft" (Brochure).

In Flåm, the MS *Maxim Gorki* (Nassau) was docked in the small harbor. Of course, I was glued to the train window with my camera ready to click and was thrilled when the train stopped for a special photo opportunity at the powerful Kjosfossen waterfall. I walked out to the edge of the platform to fully appreciate the fall's forceful gushing. It was breathtaking!

I changed trains in Myrdal, and my trip continued on the modern Bergen Railway through more beautiful Norwegian scenery toward Oslo. The gods were kind and provided this trip finale with a most memorable and awesome sunset.

I arrived in Oslo after midnight and had to pull my suitcase up a hill to a very expensive hotel, because no taxi was in sight. Once checked in, I could not find anybody anywhere to help me figure out the complicated mechanism of the hotel's elevator. I ended up sleeping a couple of hours and taking off without breakfast at 5:30 a.m. I reached the airport by train, and after asking umpteen people for help and being totally surprised when I was told that I had been upgraded to business class, I was ever so relieved when this last leg of my trip was completed. – After writing a two-page letter of complaint to the airlines about this troublesome ordeal, and after receiving the reimbursement they owed me, I was happy and ready to start all over again. –

AUSTRIA

Ever since the journey along the Norwegian coast in 2003, I had dreamed of a return during the winter months. I wanted to see what it looked like covered with lots of snow, and above all, I had longed to experience the drama of aurora borealis, the northern lights.

On May 9, 2008, I booked my second Hurtigruten voyage, this one on the MS *Lofoten*, not realizing at the time that it is not only one of their oldest ships, built in 1964, but at 2,661 gross tonnage also their smallest, accommodating fewer than two hundred passengers. Its speed is fifteen knots. She was refurbished and refitted in 2003, preserving most of the original style, with no stabilizers. "With unique lounges and panoramic decks this 'old lady' is simply unparalleled" (Brochure). Get the idea?

While planning my trip, I knew I would be in the mood for music inasmuch as it would follow another Schubertiade at my house on October 31, 2008. Why not treat myself to a ten-day Christmas gift in my beloved city Vienna prior to the twelve-day round-trip cruise, which was scheduled to leave Bergen on December 31, 2008, and to return on January 11, 2009?

And all this during the 2008 stock-market crash, starting on October 6.

Vienna

A former travel companion had given me an excellent tip on a hotel in downtown Vienna, where I secured a reservation well in advance. Shortly after noon on December 21, 2008, my taxi let me out in front of Hotel Kaiserin Elisabeth. As soon as I entered the elegant lobby, I felt welcome. The gentlemen at the reception were without question Viennese from the old school. I was addressed as "Frau Professor Dr.," and the welcome was accompanied by a gentle kiss on the hand.

I had to wait some thirty minutes for my room to be ready and used the time to look around a bit. I came upon the golden plaque in the entrance vestibule and read the long list of famous and remarkable people who, next to the Empress Elisabeth, had over the decades and centuries stayed at this rather elegant yet intimate hotel. Mozart, Liszt, Wagner, and Grieg were among the many composers, artists, and renowned dignitaries. I knew instantly that this hotel, located right around the corner from St. Stephen's Cathedral, was the one for me. "Our hotel encapsulates what is typically Viennese. This is reflected in its ambience of unobtrusive cordiality and discreet expressive style. Traditional charm unfolds in a timeless setting, underlying the hotel's sophistication, exceptional service, genuine attentiveness and superior quality. The Hotel 'Kaiserin Elisabeth' is an expression of lifestyle in its most elegant form" (Brochure). I could not have said it better.

Austria

Though I had not felt 100% prior to my departure and suspected that I had a mild flu or something related, I proceeded with the trip when my doctor, after various tests, gave me the green light. I decided to take it easy, but took full advantage of Vienna's fairy-tale-like Christmas ambiance. The Christmas decorations and lights, especially downtown, were intoxicating. I explored the Christmas Market in front of the town hall in the evening and sipped a *Glühwein* (hot red wine with seasonings) before attending a performance at the Burgtheater. The hotel had made reservations for me for a performance of *The Nutcracker* at the Staatsoper, where I had previously seen a superb ballet performance of Rudolf Nureyev's *Swan Lake* with the incredible solo dancer Shoko Nakamura as Odile. I attended a lovely performance of my childhood favorite, Humperdinck's *Hänsel and Gretel*, at the Volksoper and another memorable Johann Strauss concert at the Musikverein. I spent several hours at the Albertina museum and, among other outings, took a cab to the Museum of Modern Art. As the Stephansdom was right around the corner from my hotel, I attended several outstanding orchestra, quartet, and choral performances free of charge and watched, somewhat amused, when on Christmas Day all the church clergy, trailed by altar boys and the like, paraded through the center aisle of the cathedral decked out in their most elaborate gold- and silver-brocaded robes, mitras, and whatever else, spraying lots of incense while pretending to look sinister and as though they occupied another realm. The organ played fortissimo, of course, and the collection baskets were overflowing with euro bills. For the poor – in case you were wondering.

At the hotel, I chatted with other international guests – mostly at breakfast or when reading the paper in the lobby by a cozy fireplace. For some reason, the loss of appetite I had experienced before leaving the States persisted, and I regretted it, since the breakfast buffet at the hotel looked so tempting. I ate despite the fact that nothing seemed to taste quite right. My friend at the reception desk offered to make a doctor's appointment for me, but I decided just to keep going. Thus, on December 30 I flew to Bergen as scheduled and checked into the hotel where I was to stay until December 31, at which point I would board the MS *Lofoten* in the late afternoon, in time for the New Year's Eve party onboard.

NORWAY – COASTAL VOYAGE IN SEARCH OF AURORA BOREALIS

Bergen – Déjà Vu – Hurtigruten's MS *Lofoten*

During the day on December 31, I killed time in the hotel's restaurant area, which had access to TV. It was gloomy and raining, and I was in no mood to walk around the bay area. When it was time, a cab took me to the pier, and since there were only a handful of passengers, I settled into my nice cabin in no time at all. I was the only one of the four or five passengers to do the entire stretch, that is, Bergen to Kirkenes and back. The few companion passengers had chosen this particular ship, the MS *Lofoten*, because it was one of the oldest and known for its charm. Since it was New Year's Eve, a big event was scheduled for the evening. I put on my extra-nice Norwegian cardigan and was pleased to notice that several of the Norwegian guests who showed up for the special dinner also boasted colorful sweaters.

The buffet dinner looked incredibly inviting, and everybody raved about how delicious everything tasted. But I was somewhat disappointed, since everything was lacking in taste. I sampled different dishes, and some desserts tasted a bit better. I tried not to think about why it was thus, since on my previous voyage, in August 2003, I had just loved all of their seafood dishes. – The champagne did not taste normal either, but I did enjoy the fireworks and the lit-up city of Bergen as we cruised around the harbor waiting for midnight, at which point the fireworks reached their crescendo. On deck, I chatted with a couple who lived in Bergen and had come onboard to celebrate. The lady, a beautiful blond wearing a purple evening gown and a mink coat, was an immigrant from Russia. They were praising the dinner and especially one of the seafood dishes, a rare and very costly delicacy in Norway and served only on special holidays. I think it is called *lutefisk*. It is lyed fish – stockfish that has been steeped in lye. I did not know what they were talking about, because to me everything had tasted the same. – Enough food talk. I never went on trips for the sake of the food. I just wanted to see and enjoy nature.

Since we were scheduled to hit the same ports as in 2003 and I had not signed up for any off-shore trips (because it was winter), I will focus only on the events and adventures that made this trip so different, more exciting, and at times downright dangerous.

The next morning, January 1, 2009, when all the locals had left the ship, I was pleased with the table assigned to me, which was next to a window and close to the buffet. Before each lunch and dinner, an attractive young waitress served a special soup or appetizer and stood ready to wait on me hand and foot. Each dish she served looked like a piece of art. My only regret was that I had to explain repeatedly that I had already eaten enough. I simply lacked an appetite. She understood. – At the neighboring table sat a couple from Germany with whom I chatted quite a bit, and at the other side of the dining room, an elderly, bearded man had his place near a window. We did not converse too much, and he did not stay the entire trip. –

I spent much time near the front of the ship or in my cabin looking out the window, and I got excited when, little by little, as we moved further north, the landscape began to turn white. Mind you, up there it's rather dusky almost all day long. About five to six hours of sunlight is all you get. Of course, since everything is white, it compensates a tad for the lack of sunlight. That's why I took this trip in the first place! And I was happy. Especially impressive were the snow-covered mountains and cliffs of the Lofoten. The villages were blanketed in snow and looked cozy due to the lights inside the houses.

Arctic Circle Crossing

On January 3, 2009, the handful of passengers onboard gathered in the lounge to be christened by Njord, ruler of the Seven Seas. We kneeled down to have a cup of water dumped on our heads, and after the ritual I was presented with my second Certificate of the Arctic Circle Crossing. Thanks!

The further north we cruised, the more the wind picked up. The snow was drifting fiercely, and at times I had a hard time distinguishing anything outside. But I loved it. We had a couple of hours in Tromsø. I bundled up to venture outside and feel the snow blowing, at least for a short while. Next to the gangway stood a mate. I took a few steps, and the wind blew so forcefully I had to hold on to the rope to brace myself. The mate stopped me cold. He told me not to continue because the wind would blow me away. It was too risky. I agreed, returned to my cabin, and took off the layers of sweaters I had put on. So much for that.

The Big Storm

As we continued toward Honningsvåg, it got so stormy that our little ship was wildly cradling up and down and sideways. The crew looked concerned. We all were ordered to stay put in our cabins and not walk around. I sat on the bed, looking out the window. The space heater – for which I had asked, because it was rather cold in my cabin – kept tipping over and the *Rauschgoldengel* (Christmas angel from Nuremberg), which the Segebrechts had sent to me in Vienna, kept sliding off the windowsill and onto the floor, together with my alarm clock. The waves were so high they splashed against my windows, completely obscuring my vision.

When the sea calmed down a bit, the huge snowflakes stuck to my windows like cotton balls. I loved that particular decoration, because it looked like Christmas. In the distance, two smaller ships were drifting and navigating the swells. – The whole scene reminded me of my experience in the Drake Passage when returning from South Georgia and Antarctica and of my first trip to Antarctica on the *Marco Polo*, when she hit a sharp rock on the ocean floor. – The captain said they rarely encountered such fierce storms, calling the one we were then facing a hurricane. Fortunately, I never get seasick. – Suddenly, the swells lifted our little ship so high that most of the dishes, plates, glasses, silverware, pots and pans, etc. slid off the shelves in the kitchen and shattered into thousands of pieces, crashing on the floor with a big bang. Two women from the Netherlands who had been onboard for only a couple of ports had had it. They were so scared – especially the older one – that they insisted on being flown home from the nearest airport. It was extremely complicated, since a charter flight had to be arranged, but Hurtigruten took care of them. The younger woman was so disappointed, because they had looked forward to this trip for a long time. One of the waitresses fell and injured her back. She was sent home as well. –

This storm was so fierce that at the end of the trip, we were presented with a storm certificate that stated, "It is hereby declared that the passenger holding this certificate was on board the MS *Lofoten* during a storm between Havoesund and Hammerfest on January 7th 2009." That, I must say, was definitely a first for me. A stamp was affixed, and Captain Truls Bruland, who had been kind enough to pose with me for a photo on the bridge, signed it.

Honningsvåg

We stayed in Honningsvåg for more than a day, because the captain had been advised against continuing all the way to Kirkenes. It was much too stormy, too dangerous, and very dark. Indeed, one of their fleet, the MS *Richard With*, named after Hurtigruten's founder, had run aground at Trondheim and taken water, so that the passengers had to be evacuated. The ship was about five times larger than ours, with a capacity to accommodate seven hundred passengers. It was sent to Germany, where it was built, to be repaired. – I was not too disappointed, since I had been to Kirkenes in 2003. My only regret was that I never got to see the northern lights, because the skies, instead of being clear, were always overcast. I did get to see a fabulous show of the aurora borealis on a big screen TV in the lounge. In desperation, I took a bunch of pictures of them and must say that they did not turn out too badly. At one of the ports, a couple who had flown in a small plane from Kirkenes to Honningsvåg, I think, boasted about having had a glorious view of the aurora borealis when flying above the clouds. At that point I was jealous!

While stuck in Honningsvåg I did get a chance to go outside, look around, brave the drifting snow, and relish the freezing winter atmosphere. I bought a couple of souvenirs and took a few pictures of unusual things, like a kicksled, also known as a spark, in front of a store. It is a small sled consisting of a chair mounted on a pair of flexible metal runners, which extend backward to about twice the chair's length.

Kicking the ground by foot propels the sled. It was a neat invention, I thought. You could use it for shopping or hauling toddlers around. With the exception of two ladies in the souvenir store and two female crew members, I did not spot a single human being on the totally deserted street. Mind you, it was also very dark outside, even though it was daytime.

I did spend quite a bit of time in the lounge watching CNN and talking with a young, honeymooning couple from Scotland, and I had an extremely interesting conversation with a young Palestinian. The war between Israel and Hamas seemed to be heating up. I thought it quite unusual to meet a rather attractive, very well-educated young man – a student of Dr. Hanan Ashravi, the prominent spokeswoman for the Palestinian cause who was frequently seen on CNN – speaking flawless English on a ship cruising the coast of Norway. I had never met anybody who lived in the Gaza Strip and had no idea how badly the Israelis treated them and how dire their life circumstances were. Their living accommodations in Gaza sounded like prison camps, and worse, they had no hope for any change anytime soon, if ever. The wars between Israel and the Palestinians have been and probably will continue to be imbalanced. He did not think that even Obama would be able to improve their lot, which at that time I did not want to believe. Unfortunately, today I can see that he was right. We exchanged e-mail addresses. I wrote, but I have yet to receive a reply. I am no longer surprised.

I was glad when we arrived in Bergen. Though we did so much later than scheduled, we were still in time for me not to miss my flight back to the States the next morning. When the MS *Lofoten* docked, it was raining buckets. I got on the transfer bus in a hurry and ran, pulling my suitcase through splashing puddles, as fast as I could from the bus to the hotel. As soon as I had my key, I went to my room, which was very nice and very modern but had very narrow beds. I took a hot bath, fell asleep quickly, fell out of bed once, jumped out of bed at about 6:00 a.m., skipped breakfast, climbed into the cab the hotel had ordered for me, and caught my flight in time. I returned home on January 12, 2009, as scheduled. – That was the last time I went to Norway! Today my only connection to Norway is the mechanic who takes care of my 1986 baby Mercedes-Benz 190 E: Joern from Oslo.

SCOTLAND

On April 27, 2006, I booked another trip with GCT: Scotland, Wales, & England. The journey included a three-day pre-trip to Edinburgh from August 3 to August 21, 2006. It was high time for me to go to Scotland, because as you may recall, during the occupation right after World War II, Sergeant Rorrison from Scotland had virtually saved my life by stealing eggs, butter, sugar, and cocoa from their kitchen for me to eat. I simply wanted to pay his country a visit out of gratitude, if you will. And ever since I had met two very likeable Scottish naturalists on the NS *Yamal*, during my excursion to the North Pole, I was even more inclined to go to Scotland. I had been to Ireland and England but never to the other British Isles. It was time to complete that list. Last but not least, I wanted to escape the steaming heat that invades Indiana in August. I had enough miles for a free flight, but had to leave one day before schedule.

Edinburgh

Around noon on August 4, I arrived in Edinburgh. I checked in at the Hilton Edinburgh Grosvenor, located in the Haymarket area and within walking distance of most of the major attractions. The hotel was built in the nineteenth century. They had only one single room left, and at an astronomical price, but I was in no mood to start shopping around. The room was at the lowest level, a half basement. I had to step on a chair to look out the window, and for safety reasons several iron rods secured the window on the outside. Thus, I paid $300 a night only to feel somewhat imprisoned, although a tolerable breakfast was included. The room was rather small but very tidy; it had a TV but no fridge. –

My assigned guide, Ronnie, had left a welcome note announcing a "panoramic sightseeing tour of Edinburgh," a half-day outing that would start at 9:00 a.m. on the 5th, that is, a day after my arrival, which meant I was on my own until then. No problem. – It did not take me long to discover that Scotland's capital was celebrating its annual festival, which revolves around the famous Festival Fringe, an arts festival, and the Edinburgh International Festival. Usually in August, internationally accomplished performers in classical music, opera, ballet, and drama come to Edinburgh, and the Fringe presents some two thousand shows at nearly 250 venues. Anybody who is interested can put on a show there. It's just great. Moreover, the Fringe usually kicks off the event with a big parade called "the Cavalcade," which is comprised of cars, horses, marching bands, acrobats, dancers, clowns, lots of glitter and color, etc. I spent an entire afternoon watching the parade and ended up completely boxed in among the crowd of onlookers, so that I was unable to find an opening to cross a road. But I would be lying if I said I did not have fun. Occasionally, the parade stopped and goodies were handed out. I came away with half a dozen colorful glass-pearl necklaces, which I later sent to several of my younger friends around the world.

I spent quite a bit of time on the famous stretch that leads up to Edinburgh Castle, not far from the Royal Mile. I applauded young bagpipers, acrobats, charade artists, two teen violinists, and guys on ten-foot-long stilts, and I chatted with several young artists who had set up booths to promote their plays. One intrigued me in particular; its focus was the assassination of JFK on November 22, 1963. They wanted us to find out what really happened through "the majesty of song"! That would have interested me, but I would be long gone by the time of their performance, which was from August 7 to August 18. Sorry! If it had not been so sinfully pricey and had not been sold out a decade in advance, I might have gone to spend an evening listening to the Royal Edinburgh Military Tattoo, which was put on by the British Armed Forces, Commonwealth, and International military bands and was famous for being the most spectacular show in the world. Oh well! To be honest, military tattoos do not interest me very much.

When I returned to the Royal Mile the next day to explore the impressive Edinburg Castle, I did see the area where the tattoo takes place, and believe me, they could not have chosen a more spectacular setting. Awesome! Since it is out in the open and the seating consists of simple bench and scaffold structures around the north, south, and east sides of the castle, accommodating over seven thousand spectators, it would be a shame if it rained. But I was told it had never been canceled because of bad weather. The Scots are a tough bunch.

During our Panoramic Sightseeing Tour of Edinburgh, I found the stop at Edinburgh Castle, the instantly recognizable fortress perched on an extinct volcano, to be the most memorable. I admired the Scottish Crown Jewels, the oldest royal regalia in Britain, and the Stone of Destiny, displayed in the same room. The latter is the coronation stone for the Scottish kings. I spent some time visiting the new Prison of War, where among other people, American citizens of the newly independent USA were jailed, shook my head at the giant medieval siege gun, and tried to imagine what was going on way back in the room where Mary Queen of Scots gave birth to James VI. If you are interested, its history goes all the way back to 638 AD. Indeed, "within the castle are many reminders of the country's rich and turbulent past" (Brochure).

On the way back to my hotel, I walked down a few steps from the street level to see the Princes Street Gardens, known as the "most scenic city center gardens in Europe" (Brochure). I just loved it and found a park bench on which to rest and reflect a while. Could one wish for a more ideal place? From this spot, I had a perfect panorama view of the castle. The gardens run along the south side of Princes Street and are divided by the Mound. Vast areas of manicured lawns lay at my feet. Here and there, a family had spread out a blanket to enjoy a picnic. Others played with their children, tossing balls back and forth or just lying on the ground to bask in the sun or relax in a shady spot underneath a tree. An embankment filled with lush, vibrant flowerbeds stood behind the park benches along the pedestrian walk and instilled within me a sense of sheer delight.

I spent the last day exploring the Scottish National Gallery, the Scottish National Gallery of Modern Art, and the Scottish National Portrait Gallery. I much appreciated their free shuttle-bus service, which ran every hour between all the galleries (five buildings). Just great! I skipped the portraits and focused on a few special exhibits: *The Paintings of Adam Elsheimer (1578–1610): Devil in the Detail, Van Gogh and Britain: Pioneer Collectors*, and an exhibit of the hyperrealist sculptures of Ron Mueck, who was born in Melbourne in 1958 but worked in the United Kingdom. Each artist touched me to the core in different ways and gave me much to reflect upon when, on the way back to the Hilton, I stopped once more at Princes Street Gardens and found a bench where I relaxed and browsed through the brochures. I was grateful to have stumbled upon these art treasures, up to then unfamiliar to me. Edinburgh is a city which I added to my "go back to" list.

Glasgow

With six hundred thousand inhabitants, Glasgow is Scotland's largest city. The bus ride from Edinburgh, which featured lovely countryside, took less than two hours. I do not recall the name of our hotel. It was somewhere downtown, not far from the shopping area. After settling in, we went on a customary orientation tour. Glasgow is a busy city, and the River Clyde, the ninth-longest river in the United Kingdom and the third-longest in Scotland, goes right smack through Glasgow. The Clyde has a fascinating history, especially regarding its development and importance in connection with England's shipping industry. But I will refrain here from talking about that aspect. The one thing that interested me was the fact that the *QE2*, our honeymoon ship, and the *Queen Mary* were built in Clydebank. *C'est tout.*

The main group had arrived from the United States, and we all got acquainted with each other over drinks at the welcome briefing, after which I retreated to my room to catch up with the news.

On the following day, day 3, we all got on a bus for the tour of the city. It was interesting, but somewhat anticlimactic after picture-perfect Edinburgh. Glasgow does not boast a castle on top of a rock. Actually, I would say it reflects a mélange of architectural styles, which, with the exception of the quaint private houses typical of the city and the gray stone buildings, one can find in other major cities in Europe. Some buildings date back centuries, and others are supermodern or contemporary creations. And I must point out that the Scots love to adorn their facades, front yards, balconies, and any nook and cranny with flowers. Hanging baskets bursting with the most beautiful arrangements of vibrant flowers were everywhere. Of course, all such beauty is the direct result of their incredible climate. I hope it lasts forever.

Our tour included a visit to the eclectic Burrell Collection. I liked Edgar Degas' *Ballet Rehearsal* (1874) and *The Green Dress* (1897–1901) in particular. The unique L-shaped museum, which one enters through a sixteenth-century stone archway built into a modern red-sandstone gable, was established in 1944 by Sir William Burrell, a wealthy Glaswegian shipping magnate and art collector. It houses some nine thousand works and is most deserving of a visit. Before we left, I located a bench under the branches of a huge tree at the border of adjacent woodland in Pollok Country Park, where the museum is located. I looked out over a big, formal lawn in front of the museum, away from the hustle and bustle of Glasgow! I am not a city girl and was happy there.

The dinner, which took place at an eighteenth-century coaching inn, was a genuine Scottish experience. We were greeted by a bagpiper dressed in proper Scottish attire, who stood close to the inn's entrance and played his bagpipes with great enthusiasm until he had no wind left. We liked the welcome, loved the Scottish ambiance of the upscale restaurant, and relished the delicious meal. And we fit right into the setting. The proprietors of the roadhouse welcomed us as warmly as their ancestors did before them. I assume thus.

Day 4 our journey included a cruise on the twenty-four-mile-long and five-mile-wide freshwater Loch Lomond, not famous for a monster, in case you were curious. I can assure you, though, that monsters are not far away, maybe hiding on the many green, tangled islands. They lie like big emeralds upon this loch, and contribute significantly to its beauty. We welcomed the peaceful cruise and listened quietly when, in the bus on the way to Inveraray Castle, the guide played a well-known song: "Oh, ye'll take the low road, / And I'll be in Scotland afore ye, / But me and my true love will never meet again / On the bonnie, bonnie banks o' Loch Lomand." I personally was no longer as obsessed with castles as others were, especially if they had not traveled much. After all, no castles were built in the States with defense and armaments in mind. – Those "castles" built by rich guys to show off are better called "manor houses." I once heard that an American imported an entire castle – from either Germany or France, I forget.

Be that as it may, Inveraray Castle was built in 1744–1771 by the third duke of Argyll and is still the home of the chief of the Campbell clan, aka the duke of Argyll. It is a forceful piece of architecture, and if you join the tour conducted inside, you may be intrigued by some of the portraits hanging on the walls. To be honest, I do not remember a single one. Neither do I remember their heirlooms. We got a glimpse of the center of Inveraray, and I thought the white buildings designed by the renowned architects John Adam and Robert Myline were rather nice and somewhat memorable. They are considered one of the best examples of an eighteenth-century new town in Scotland. It is hard to believe, but I did not see any bagpipers around, not even at the restaurant where we had dinner.

On day 5, we took off for York via the Lake District and rolled past lush, green meadows accented with well-fed, grazing cattle or small herds of sheep and partially covered with wild purple flowers. Now and then a small pond or a bigger lake caught my eye. A pair of white swans, and a duck trailed by adorable ducklings, swam gracefully by. And lo and behold, at one point another bagpiper stood on the roadside piping away, loud enough for us to hear in the bus. At another stop, an entire bagpipe army started piping the second we stepped off the bus. They made so much noise I decided to retreat to a bench some one hundred yards away. –

Gretna Green

The stop at Gretna Green, the location of the old blacksmith's shop, was much more exciting. I had never heard of it and wanted to find out all about it. I bet you do not know that "it is one of the world's most popular wedding destinations, hosting over 5000 ceremonies each year, with one of every six being a Scottish union" (Brochure). It is known for its runaway weddings. Unlike in England, here boys can get married without their parents' consent when they are as young as fourteen, and girls can do so at a mere twelve years of age. How about that? Since Gretna Green was right across the border, it was a haven for elopers coming from England. Since anybody had the authority to conduct weddings, the blacksmiths in Gretna became known as "anvil priests." Keep it in mind.

I remember this place also because up to then, I had not bought any Scotch whiskey. At their gift shop, I spotted a huge basket full of tiny Scotch-whiskey bottles (one and a half inches tall) for five euros each, which I thought exorbitant. But on the way back to our bus, I spontaneously changed my mind, ran back, and bought a tiny bottle. I am now glad I succumbed. It found a place on my souvenir shelf, and it is a nice conversation piece. This was actually my last chance to buy a bottle of Scotch in Scotland, because the next stop was the charming English village of Grasmere.

ENGLAND

Grasmere

Grasmere is located in the center of the English Lake District, in the county of Cumbria. It was William Wordsworth's place – Wordsworth, who was one of my and Doc's favorite English romantic poets. He lived here for fourteen years and described it so fittingly as "the loveliest spot that man has ever found." It's a place where one might wish to die, if one had the choice. Its special charm must be attributed to its location on the River Rothay, which flows into the rather small Grasmere Lake. This place attracted other poets as well, including Samuel Taylor Coleridge, who befriended and collaborated with Wordsworth and is so well known for *The Rime of the Ancient Mariner*.

I headed straight to Dove Cottage, the home of Wordsworth and his sister. And a cottage it was, but a lovely place with rose bushes clinging to whitewashed walls, flagstone floors, and dark wood paneling. Indeed, an idyllic spot where poetry flowed and where Sir Walter Scott, Thomas De Quincey, and Samuel Taylor Coleridge must have felt right at home. I was deeply moved and promptly remembered the many times Doc quoted the first and last stanzas of Wordsworth's 1807 daffodil poem: "I wandered lonely as a cloud / That floats on high o'er vales and hills, / When all at once I saw a crowd, / A host of golden daffodils; / Beside the lake beneath the trees / Fluttering and dancing in the breeze.... For oft, when on my couch I lie / In vacant or in pensive mood, / They flash upon that 'inward eye' / Which is the bliss of solitude; / And then my heart with pleasure fills, / And dances with the daffodils."

The poem came fully alive at this spot. It was this poem that had inspired Doc to plant a field of daffodils on the grounds of the Croft. And it inspired me to plant a large bed of daffodils on the hill in my backyard. Curiously enough, I discovered later that a belt of daffodils the poet and his sister came across on April 15, 1802, triggered the poem. Doc's birthday was April 14; thus, we three romantics were born in April! When I spotted the daffodil-poem postcards in a small gift shop, I hurried to buy a few. Before I continued my stroll through the charming village, I asked a guy to take a picture of me in front of Dove Cottage!

I did not stop at Sarah Nelson's famous Gingerbread Shop, but did spend some time browsing in the Beatrix Potter gift shop. Many customers, mostly female, were looking for items related to Peter Rabbit and other Beatrix Potter characters, who were quite foreign to me, since I had grown up in Germany. Across the street, on the banks of a narrow stream, was a rustic restaurant where I would have loved to sit and sip a cup of coffee in the midst of nicely placed, red clay pots bursting with bright-colored flowers.

York

Our drive continued toward the walled city of York through the lovely Lake District – never-ending acres of lush, green countryside – and in the late afternoon we settled in at the Quality Hotel York, a nice contemporary establishment in a good location. We had dinner at the hotel and got a good night's rest before the activities on day 6, when we would take a tour of the center of York, with a visit to the York Minster and lectures by a local expert on it.

York played a central role in British history – under the Romans, Saxons, and Vikings – for nearly two thousand years. We saw the well-preserved medieval city walls, aka Roman walls, with five "bars" or gateways. I did not have two hours to circumnavigate York along the walls. But, trust me, the center of York is a rich tangle of intriguing, historic alleys and streets. I always like to see the half-timbered, whitewashed houses, because they remind me of good old Germany.

Even when I spotted the York Minster from a distance, I was amazed at the sight. "It is the largest gothic cathedral in Northern Europe. In fact, it is both, a cathedral and a minster. It was originally a Roman Catholic Church, but has been part of the Church of England since the break from Rome initiated by King Henry VIII in 1534. The 128 stained glass windows in the minster are of special interest. Among them is the ornate Rose Window c. 1500, which commemorates the union of the royal houses of York and Lancaster. After the 1984 fire this window and the roof needed extensive restoration." Moreover, "the Great East Window, 1405–1408 contains the world's largest area of medieval stained glass in a single window. It depicts the beginning and end of the world using scenes from the Book of Genesis and the Book of Revelation, the first and last books of the Bible. This scene shows the temptation of Adam and Eve" (GCT). They are even ranked among the wonders of the world. When visiting the shop of the artisans working with stained glass, we were told that it could take over six hundred man-hours to complete the restoration of medieval stained glass.

That afternoon, we were introduced to a traditional English "cream tea" at Betty's Tea Room. The various scones, with clotted cream and strawberry jam, tasted almost as good as Belgian waffles.

We took off early to tour Whitby Abbey and Castle Howard and, at about 10:00 a.m., arrived at the ruined Benedictine monastery (657 AD) overlooking the North Sea on the East Cliff, high above the charming coastal town and former herring and whaling port. It was a rainy day, which had a special appeal since the gaunt and imposing remains of the monastery looked both eerie and romantic. The site was even more beautiful because the ruins were mirrored in the abbey pond, on which two white ducks were floating. I went right to the edge of the ruin to gaze out on the stormy sea below and lingered until our guide summoned us to the bus, which took us to the famous Quayside Restaurant in Whitby, where we were treated to

England

the most delectable meal of fish and chips. I asked the cooks behind the counter if I could take a picture, and they were happy to comply. Instead of walking around Whitby after lunch, I waited for our bus in front of the restaurant beneath an awning. It was raining cats and dogs. Remember – we were in England.

The skies were still overcast when we arrived at Castle Howard in York, built mostly between 1699 and 1712 and considered "one of the grandest private residences in Britain" (GCT). Who am I to say that this castle is not a true castle but, together with its manicured formal gardens, more a working estate of ten thousand acres in the Howardian Hills? It operates such businesses as farming, forestry, real estate, retail, and a holiday park. One hundred permanent and up to 150 seasonal staff members are employed by the family who has lived in the castle for more than three hundred years. Actually, a portion of the formal garden was sectioned off for growing vegetables like cabbage and herbs, with a few sunflowers mixed in. A pair of proud peacocks made their rounds on the grounds. Unfortunately, they did not show off their feathers, as they did in India.

WALES

After sunrise on day 8, we crossed the English border and drove through the rugged Welsh countryside toward Snowdonia, Wales. On the way, we stopped briefly in Llangollen, a small town in North Wales steeped in legend. With a population a little over three thousand, it is a community in Denbighshire, northeast of Wales, on the River Dee and on the edge of the Berwyn Mountains. The brick houses with slate roofs give the town an ambiance of unity. The town supposedly took its name from St. Collen, a monk from the sixth century who also founded a church beside the river there. We arrived in Snowdonia in time for dinner.

On day 9, some of us went to Portmeirion, a tourist village in Gwynedd, North Wales, on the Celtic Sea. The village is surrounded by seventy acres of exotic woodlands with nice trails and coastal walks down to the rugged beach. It is a place for vacationers with or without kids and is a welcome spot for shooting movies or TV series. It was designed and built by Sir Clough Williams-Ellis between 1925 and 1975, inspired by an Italian village, and intended to reflect the atmosphere of the Mediterranean. While navigating the grounds, I sized up the various pieces of architecture gathered from other places in Europe, all of it intended to dazzle the visitor. At first, I had trouble falling for the diverse architecture, despite the attractiveness of the trees, flowering shrubs, and swimming pools in between the buildings, cottages, etc. I appreciated the place more and more when I walked on the forest trail high above the gentle western coastline.

When after an exceptional lunch I ended up in one of the elegant tea rooms in this iconic hotel to sip a cup of tea, I was delighted to discover that the English couple I chatted with were also world travelers. – I sat next to a large window from which the panorama view of the sea, with several islands here and there, was sublime. When I was told that several of my favorites, like Gregory Peck, Ingrid Bergman, and Frank Lloyd Wright, were much inspired by Portmeirion's exotic location, I could understand why.

I felt great when I got out of bed on day 10, because we were heading to the Snowdonia National Park for a true Welsh experience. The park covers 823 square miles and is the largest national park in Wales. It encompasses diverse landscapes and boasts the highest mountain (3,085 feet) and the largest natural lake in Wales. I was lucky we did not have to speak Welsh, which is really a very weird language. Nevertheless, the Welsh are extremely proud of it. Not many people on this planet even attempt to learn it.

Our first stop was at the Llanberis National Slate Museum, located in a dramatically beautiful landscape on the shores of Llyn Padam. Unfortunately, the weather was not too rosy, but the overall experience was truly fascinating. I had never set foot in a slate quarry and did not know that slate played a very important role during industrialization in the eighteenth century. The place was not so much a museum as a slice of open-air history, designed as though quarrymen had just put down their tools and left the courtyard for home. The refurnished chief engineer's house; the *Una*, a 0-4-0, sixty-one-centimeter-gauge steam engine from 1905; a waterwheel – the largest on the British mainland – that made the tools for slate quarrying; the workshops and buildings; and the slate-cutting demonstration were extremely informative and really interesting. (Wales produced over four-fifths of all British slate in this period.)

While waiting for the guide to pick up the tickets for the ride on the bright-red Ffestiniog Snowdon Mountain Railway, a cog or rack railway – that is, a railway with a toothed rack rail between the running rails – that runs several times a day to the summit of the mountain, we all tried our best to read a Welsh word posted over the door of James Pringle Weaver's souvenir store. This word was a single row of fifty-eight letters without a single break: LLANFAIRPWLLGWYNGYLL-GOGERYCHWYRNDROBWLLLLANTYSILIOGOGOGOCH. Translated, it means "the church of Mary in the hollow of the white hazel near the fierce whirlpool and the church tsilio by the red cave" (Brochure). If this is not weird, what is? By the way, the name of the town where the train started is Lanberis. It has a population of 1,954, of which supposedly 80% speak Welsh fluently. Good for them! I could do nothing to change it, just as I could not change the weather. The skies remained gray the entire time our train crawled up to Mount Snowdon's peak. No matter, it was a beautiful ride through the wild land of peaceful valleys, brooding mountain skylines, and heather meadows – until we reached the top, at which point we had torrential rains. I tried to ignore the downpour and struggled toward the pinnacle of the rugged mountain, navigating each step carefully to avoid slipping on the "slippery slopes." I was proud to have made it intact, had my picture taken, and bragged about it to some of the males in my group who had stayed below because they were a bit overweight.

Caernarvonshire

It was miraculous, though, that by the time we arrived at our hotel, the sun was shining! Hurrah! We had all been invited to a home-hosted dinner to learn more about life in Wales. And I was extremely lucky, because they sent me, together with four others in my group, to Cochwillan, Nr. Bangor, Caernarvonshire, out in the countryside, aka the sticks, close to the Menai Straits and with views over Puffin Island. It was an absolutely gorgeous ride, and the visit turned out to be exceptional as well. We were hosted by three sisters – one divorced, one a spinster, one temporarily separated from her husband, and all of them unique characters. William Gruffudd, who was believed to be of considerable means, supposedly built Llys Cochwillan around 1465. "Today, Llys Hynafol Cochwillan, one of the finest hall houses, retains many of its original features such as the hammer beam roof of three open bays, 30 ft. high, an almost entirely original west screen of oak beams still retaining the master carpenter's numberings. . . . The hall has a side-mounted fireplace with its original huge oak lintel, an innovation for the time. Most houses of that era had a central fire with a hole in the roof for smoke to exit" (Brochure).

This place was something else. The interior resembled a small church. I had never seen living quarters quite like these. I must say that the three sisters put together a very tasty meal, making use of a small burner in a dark place in the area next to the ladder, which led to the loft. – The dining table stood at one end of the room or hall. It was somewhat elevated but not blocked off by a wall. At the other end was a seating area with couches and a cocktail table, where dessert was served. The enormous, empty fireplace in one wall was so huge that three or four tree trunks, each about two feet in diameter and twelve feet long, would have to burn in it for a long time to warm the place up. How one could get such logs inside I forgot to ask. During dessert, it got rather cold in the hall. –

I could hardly believe my eyes when one of the elderly sisters got up, walked over to a trampoline in a corner of the hall, and started jumping up and down to warm up, as she proclaimed. I tried my best not to laugh. – We were told that the bedrooms were up high at one end of the hall, like a loft, and could be reached, if I remember correctly, by climbing a ladder. Without heat up there, they used several hot-water bottles at night and went to bed very early. I did not see a TV. They said it snowed quite a bit in the winter, and when our driver, who was very late, finally picked us up, they pleaded with us to write. Sorry, I lost their address. As fascinating as the place was, I do not think I would want to vacation there. They did have a young female Korean voice student living with them, and we enjoyed listening to one of her recordings. I should have asked them if they went swimming in the nearby Menai Straits and if they ever saw puffins. I saw none.

Before the trip, I had been totally unaware that Wales began with the arrival of human beings in the region. Thousands of years ago, Neanderthals lived in what is now Wales.

I should perhaps mention that we stayed at the Celtic Royal Hotel Caernarfon, located not too far from the famous and impressively massive Caernarfon Castle (1284), which unfortunately, due to lack of time, I could not explore.

The hotel management was kind enough to hand each of us a welcome letter, on which they explained what was special about the hotel and its Victorian architecture. It was built in 1794 and refurbished in 1997.

As the letter explained, Caernarfon Castle "was built in 1283 by King Edward 1st in order to defend his Country. Here, Prince Charles was officially invested as the Prince of Wales in 1969. In 1832 [one hundred years before I was born and when Goethe died] Queen Victoria stayed in Caernarfon with her mother, and in her honor the Hotel was renamed the Royal Hotel." I took a nice photo of the Welsh flag, with its red dragon symbolizing Welsh heritage. Incidentally, the daffodil is the national flower of Wales.

ENGLAND

The Cotswolds

On day 11, we departed for Gloucester, located close to the Welsh border on the River Severn, with an en-route visit to Chester, England's best-preserved walled city. "The Romans first settled here in AD 97 and the 20th legion (1 of 3 in Britain) was stationed here protecting the fertile North-West from Welsh tribes and sea pirates" (Brochure). It was a lovely day, and I walked on the walls, which date from the sixteenth century, for about thirty minutes, admiring the beautiful parks and the vibrant flowerbeds below. When I reached the Eastgate Clock, erected in 1898 to commemorate Queen Victoria's diamond jubilee, I took a picture and descended the steps to return to everyday life below.

June 2, 2012 – This weekend, England is celebrating Queen Elizabeth's diamond jubilee, and the country's media are widely reporting on it (how time flies).

Chester

Chester boasts an array of the most fabulous, large, well-preserved, and unique timbered and Tudor architecture I have come upon in England. Dating from the fourteenth century, the buildings are known as "the Rows" and dominate Watergate Street (no kidding), Eastgate Street, and Bridge Street. "It is thought early inhabitants built their homes in front and on top of old Roman buildings. . . . God's Providence House in Watergate Street dates from 1652 and was the only house to be untouched by the plague in the 17th century. It was restored in the 19th century" (Brochure).

Another major attraction is the Chester Cathedral, in the heart of the town. "It was dedicated to St. Werburth, a 7th century Saxon princess and founded in 1092. Some of the Norman Architecture still survives, although many additions and restorations have taken place over the centuries. In the choir there are interesting fourteenth-century wood carvings of dragons, kings, angels, human caricatures and monsters while leering out from the North side of the clerestory, in the nave is the 'Chester imp' (carved bearded devil in chains) an example of the way medieval church thought of evil spirits" (Brochure). I think the choir carvings in the cathedral are among the finest medieval wood carvings I have seen to date. Amazing!

I was happy to check into the Thistle Glasgow Hotel early enough to freshen up for dinner. Early to bed after a bit of English TV, and up at dawn for an optional tour to Warwick Castle.

England

The visit started with an upbeat welcome at the entrance of this Norman castle, the first to be erected at Warwick. The Anglo-Saxons built this earthen rampart in 914 to protect their hilltop settlement overlooking the Avon River from invasion by the Danes. The castle has a reputation as one of the best in Britain and Ireland. – Several jovial jesters who awaited the visitors, ready to entertain them by clowning around and eager to be photographed with them, staged the upbeat welcome. I readily complied, joined two jolly jesters, and had a photo taken with me in the middle. Thanks!

The castle is set on beautiful grounds, and since it was not raining, I made the rounds and saw quite a few, if not all, of the interior attractions to get a good feel for the place and what it must have been like during medieval times: "Gradually changing from the impregnable medieval fortress to the sumptuous home of the Grevilles, Warwick castle can boast a truly gruesome past. It has witnessed murder and violence, suffered attack, experienced wars, and been involved in royal and political treachery. Caesar's Tower is an incredible wall-tower, five stories high, with a double parapet, rising to some 150 ft. from the base of its plinth. In the lowest chamber was the vaulted dungeon, a grim and daunting place for prisoners facing any length of confinement" (Brochure). The great hall was impressive. The displays, high towers and ruins, dark dungeons, and stately rooms were presented in "living history" style, which younger visitors will find exciting.

I made sure not to miss the medieval trebuchet, the largest in the world, in motion, and I sought out a perfect spot on the vast lawn from which to watch the event, scheduled for 11:30 a.m. I sat on a big stone and happily watched a bunch of youngsters rolling in the grass and almost colliding with a family of young geese trying, I assumed, to get down to the river intact. Many had spread out blankets and were picnicking. Meanwhile, our guide had given us some information about the machine's incredible engineering, and we became conscious of the fact that witnessing this event in an authentic medieval setting, with the castle as a backdrop, was very special. This deadly machine stands eighteen meters high and weighs twenty-two tons. The trebuchet propels eighty-pound cannon balls, which are dipped in oil and set ablaze, some twenty-five meters into the air and sends them hurtling for distances up to three hundred meters. It takes eight men half an hour to prepare and load the machine. When the monstrous machine finally went off, it happened so fast I almost missed it.

Stratford-upon-Avon

What I would not dare to miss was the next stop, which I had been awaiting for what seemed an eternity: the Elizabethan playwright William Shakespeare's birthplace, Stratford-upon-Avon (25,000 inhabitants). On the way, we stopped at the hamlet of Shottery, one and a half miles from Stratford, to see the cottage of Anne Hathaway, Shakespeare's wife. He was eighteen and she was twenty-five when they met. Shortly after they met, she became pregnant, and to avoid a scandal for both families, the two supposedly married on November 27, 1582, six months before the birth of their first child, Susan.

I was more than just surprised when I saw the very large, twelve-room, part-timbered, thatched-roof cottage. If the house looked charming, the beautiful English-style flower and vegetable gardens that surrounded it contributed much to the effect. There was no time to go inside, but that was all right with me, because the peaceful setting and ambiance were ever so much more poetic in their own way. Sometimes, knowing too much destroys the effect and leaves nothing to the imagination. I did not care to see the much-talked-about bed inside the abode.

Our ride to Stratford-upon-Avon, a pretty market town in south Warwickshire that dates back to medieval times, took us through a lovely countryside of rolling hills and meadows. We were let out for a lunch of typical British fare at The Dirty Duck, which I remember because I took away two beer coasters as souvenirs. The pub has two names; the older is The Black Swan, I assume because the pub is across the street from the River Avon – which runs through the town and on which I actually spotted a few snow-white (not dirty) swans gliding proudly and gracefully downstream. A couple of ducks, trailed by a flock of the cutest ducklings, waddled on the riverbank, and a slow-moving canal boat caught my attention as well. The American GIs who camped over the river in World War II were responsible for the new name. I liked the rustic ambiance of the pub, and the food – though I do not remember what I ate – was guaranteed to be excellent.

The Swan Theatre and, more importantly, the Royal Shakespeare Theatre were within short walking distance. This is no doubt why the Dirty Duck is a favorite postperformance hangout for many of the Royal Shakespeare Company actors. How great would it have been to meet and chat with some of them, as I did years ago in the former East Berlin with actors from Brecht's Berliner Ensemble? The Dirty Duck ranks in the top 1% of English pubs.

Strolling through the streets downtown, I found the predominantly Tudor houses attractive and got very excited when I noticed a sign for The Garrick Inn. Doc would have liked this one, since we owned an antique porcelain jug with Garrick's picture. David Garrick (1717–1779) was the greatest actor of his time and perhaps one of the greatest of all time. Among other pubs with famous names was Marlowe's. But when I arrived at the Royal Shakespeare Theater, I stood quasi-spellbound when looking at the many billboards advertising an array of Shakespeare's most famous plays. I secretly wished that one day I could return and attend one performance after another for a couple of weeks. Dream on, Chrissie . . .

We stood in line for quite a while before we finally gained entrance to Shakespeare's birthplace, a restored sixteenth-century half-timbered house on Henley Street, where he spent most of his childhood years. "Shakespeare was born (in

1564) and died (in 1616) on the same date – April 23. England's greatest poet and playwright was the son of a tradesman, alderman and glover of Stratford, John Shakespeare originally from Snitterfield, and Mary Arden, the daughter of an affluent landowning farmer. William, the eldest son, and third child (of eight) was probably educated at Stratford Grammar School, but little is known of his life up to his eighteenth year. He did not go to University. . . . Five years after his marriage to Anne Hathaway, he left for London and worked at the Globe Theatre and appeared in many small roles. He started writing plays in 1595, 'Love's Labor's Lost' and 'The Comedy of Errors' being among the earliest. When he retired from writing in 1611, he returned to Stratford to live in a house, which he had built for his family. His third child Susanna married a Stratford Doctor, John Hall and their home 'Hall's Croft' is today preserved as one of the Shakespeare Properties and administered by the Shakespeare Birthplace Trust. In 1616 Shakespeare was buried in the Church of the Holy Trinity where he was baptized in 1564. Tradition has it that he died after an evening's drinking with some of his theatre friends" (Brochure).

As I write, it occurs to me that Doc might have named the property in Michigan "the Croft" after "Hall's Croft." Though the Michigan property was smaller, similarities do exist.

Not knowing what to expect, I must say that the house itself, the well-restored interior (including the chamber where the great playwright was born), and even the little garden were rather humble. Thus, it served as further proof that the place of your birth often has very little to do with whether or not you will succeed later in life. I had fun in the gift shop looking for souvenirs and found a refrigerator magnet that quoted Dick the Butcher, a character from *Henry VI*: "Let's kill all the Lawyers." I was going to send it to Peter Beardsley, a lawyer married to a lawyer, but stuck it on my refrigerator instead to remind me of my visit to Shakespeare's birthplace.

Day 13 – still in the Cotswolds, which "conjures up a vision of honey coloured stone, pretty villages and a cultivated upland landscape. . . . 'Cotswolds' is derived from the word for the stone sheep shelters or 'cots' (we still use the word in dovecote), plus the word 'wold' for the rolling hills. That tells us about a time in the past when sheep were the mainstay of the economy. The limestone from this area has been quarried to build the houses, cottages, stone field walls. The lovely stone has travelled further afield, to build St. Paul's in London, Melbourne Cathedral in Australia, and many of the Oxford colleges" (Brochure).

Stonehenge

It was delightful to travel through the Cotswolds landscape toward Britain's greatest national icon, symbolizing mystery, power, and endurance: Stonehenge. Whenever I see it, it reminds me vaguely of Easter Island (Rapa Nui) and the moai statues. The original purpose of Stonehenge's erection is unclear, as are the reasons for the erection of the moai. "Some have speculated that it was a temple made for the worship of ancient earth deities. It has been called an astronomical observatory for marking significant events on the prehistoric calendar. Others claim that it was a sacred site for the burial of high-ranking citizens from the societies of long ago. . . . Only something very important to the ancients would have been worth the effort and investment that it took to construct Stonehenge" (Brochure). I leave you to speculate – have fun!

Annoyingly, it was raining when we stepped off the bus and walked toward the starkly dramatic monument of the Neolithic and Bronze Ages, located about one thousand feet away. It consists of forty-ton granite rocks, which have stood without supports since they arrived five thousand years ago. It is situated in the vast Salisbury Plain and is surrounded by many round barrows, or burial mounds. The closer I came to the site, the more I forgot about the rain – I was awestruck by the miracle in front of me. There it stood, solid and proud, gray stones against gray skies. I will always remember it as a high point of my trip to the British Islands.

Silently I stared and wondered. I felt exhilarated and intrigued while contemplating the composition as well as the magnitude, weight, shape, and height of the stones. I walked around the circle to get a view from all angles, and when the guide summoned us to return to the bus, I could barely tear myself away from the monument, which represented yet another goal of my worldwide quest. It had stopped raining by then.

Bath

We arrived in Bath (84,000 inhabitants) early enough to explore – what else? – the Roman Baths. They are fed by hot springs, dedicated to Sylis Minerva, the healing goddess, and believed to be sacred. In front of the entrance, we had to cope with too many tourists, but we eventually got inside the "sanctuary" and rather quickly arrived at the main attraction: the hot-springs pool, aka the King's Bath, constructed in the twelfth century. The water looked green and mossy, and I am sorry to admit I could not imagine any king or even commoner bathing in that very uninviting pit. I walked through the museum and found several of the displays quite interesting, but not so impressive that I would remember them without looking at my pictures.

I liked the Pump Room Restaurant. Once upon a time, the Romans gathered in this ornately designed place. The ceilings were lofty and high and the walls stone pillared, and the windows, almost reaching the ceiling, provided a view into the old baths, which seemed elegant and decadent. A string quartet played adequately. But the glass filled with the famously healing Bath water, which is a must-drink on your first visit and is served elegantly from the spa water fountain, somehow put me off. Once is enough. I am still waiting for a miracle.

England

I should add a footnote from my brochure: "Visitors to the baths were first covered with oil and sand. After vigorous exercise and a sauna they were scraped clean by slaves. This was completed by a refreshing dip in the mineral waters." There you are. What they used slaves for never ceases to amaze me.

After visiting the Roman Baths, we continued on a city tour in order to admire the carefully manicured parks and gardens, bursting with lush, colorful flowerbeds, and the impressive architectural masterpieces from post-Roman and medieval times, such as the Bath Abbey. The Circus (1754–1768), whose name means "ring," "oval," or "circle," and the Royal Crescent (a residential road of thirty houses built in 1767–1775), which are so strikingly beautiful due to their honey-colored classical facades, will not be forgotten. Who am I to question the guide's proclamation that "Bath is without doubt England's finest Georgian City"? Kudos to John Wood the Younger, the architect of these beautiful structures.

Oxford

After traveling through the charming Cotswolds – which offered breathtaking views of open countryside, accented with herds of sheep, cattle, a random pair of horses, dry stone walls, unique market towns with magnificent Perpendicular Gothic churches, and a pond or small lake here and there – we reached Macdonald Hatherley Manor, our hotel in Gloucester. It was advertised as "a lovely 17th century manor house nestling in rolling green countryside within 37 acres of mature gardens and grounds" and turned out to be delightful. We all loved our stay and got a good night's rest before heading to Oxford, whose university is the oldest in the English-speaking world. The university is known for its fine architecture – honey-colored stone buildings set around ivy-clad quadrangles. I was so glad that Oxford (165,000 inhabitants) was included in our itinerary, especially since my good friend General Bill Whipple, a Rhodes scholar, had spent three years at Oxford in connection with his studies at West Point. At the age of ninety-three, he had volunteered to proofread my manuscript, and he very much enjoyed receiving my postcard from the "city of dreaming spires," home of his alma mater. May you rest in peace, good friend!

We had about three hours to explore the city, but we spent most of our time on the campus of the University of Oxford, the second-oldest surviving university in the world. Did you know that in 1167, Henry II banned English students from attending the University of Paris, a fact that resulted in Oxford's speedy growth? "Undergraduate teaching is organized around weekly tutorials at self-governing colleges and halls, supported by classes, lectures and laboratory work organized by faculties and departments" (Brochure). Not all of the colleges were open to visitors. Our guide had been able to gain access to the College of the Blessed Mary and All Saints, Lincoln, one of the constituent colleges, next to Exeter College. It was founded in 1427 and is the ninth oldest of the university's thirty-eight colleges. The facade is completely covered with Virginia creeper, dark green in the summer and changing to scarlet in autumn, and bare in winter. We were allowed to walk around the chapel, which dates back to the seventeenth century, and the wooden figures of St. Peter, St. Paul, Moses, and Aaron were still on the front pews. The carved ceiling, installed in the late seventeenth century, was nicely preserved as well. On the way out, I picked up a flyer announcing that a Jennifer and a George were to be married in Lincoln College Chapel on August 19, 2006. It would be a lovely place for a wedding. The big front lawn was manicured, and beneath each window and between the creepers covering the facade, lush beds of purple petunias thrived.

I wandered off by myself after the visit to Lincoln College and took pleasure in the ambiance of the architecture of several Oxford complexes. They are not all confined to one area, as is commonly the case on US campuses. I did not seek out the colleges where President Clinton, my friend Bill, and my former professor Brion Mitchell had studied. While others in my group retreated to pubs or restaurants, I sat down on a bench, chatted in French with a visitor from France, and was content to snack on a banana and a granola bar. I paid a brief visit to the world's first museum, the Ashmolean Museum of Art and Archeology, built in the 1600s, and peeked into the Bodleian, Oxford's central library, which houses more than eight million volumes, that is, twice the number housed by IU–Bloomington's Herman B. Wells Library. Oxford left an indelible imprint on my memory.

London – Déjà Vu

Back on the coach, we journeyed toward London. We arrived at the Millennium Gloucester Hotel, in the heart of the prestigious Kensington Town district, in the late afternoon. After settling in, we were treated to a royal farewell dinner.

The hotel was ideally located, that is, within walking distance of several fabulous museums. But before I embarked upon a museum tour, I participated in the London sightseeing tour, which hit almost all of the major attractions I had seen on previous visits to London, one of my favorite cities on the globe. I am in no mood to cover them again. Anybody who is marginally educated knows the unforgettable Tower of London (located, along with the drawbridge and the London Eye, on the banks of the River Thames) as well as Westminster Abbey, the House of Parliament, Big Ben, Buckingham Palace, Trafalgar Square, etc. – but wait:

Saturday, June 2, 2012 – Just now, the activities in connection with the queen's Diamond Jubilee are starting. What a coincidence!

Sunday, June 3, 2012 – And today, I watched a broadcast of the queen's festivities, with the one-thousand-boat flotilla on the Thames. The very rainy weather was endured stoically by the royals, who occupied a huge barge with a roof, and the cheering crowds, which sported thousands of umbrellas. I saw on TV what I failed to see a few years earlier, when

England

my husband and I stayed at a hotel nearby: the opening of the drawbridge. On this joyous day, as I sift through my notes on the trip, I am reminded that London, like Dresden, Warsaw, Berlin, my hometown of Hannover, and a thousand other towns and cities, was nearly flattened by the fierce carpet bombings initiated by the Germans during World War II, against which the Brits and Americans retaliated brutally. And here we are, all of us intact. Reborn like a phoenix from the ashes. – Queen Elizabeth was inaugurated in 1953, a year before my immigration to America. Time heals all wounds – or does it?

After the city tour, I spent my free time on a brief visit to Harrods – just out of a sense of tradition. I am not a fan of the tube and walked many blocks to the Natural History Museum, a Victorian-style, cathedral-like structure, and was lucky not to have to wait in line for a long time. I was eager to finally see the museum's world-famous dinosaur skeletons – which you could not miss if you tried. As soon as I entered, I was overwhelmed by the gigantic *Diplodocus* skeleton, some seventeen meters long and weighing four hundred kilograms. It was so awesome and overpowering that even though I spent quite some time looking at the other exhibits, all of which were excellent and extremely interesting, what I remember today is this humongous skeleton, one of the first sauropods to be discovered. It is a must-see!

The Victoria and Albert Museum, the world's largest museum of decorative arts and design, was next on my list. It houses a collection of more than 4.5 million objects. My focus was on Islamic art, because I had been told the V&A features one of the most important and renowned Islamic art collections in the world. After spending about two hours relishing this extraordinary collection, at which point I finally departed, I was dazed and exhilarated all the way back to the hotel. (And this after seeing only a few of the millions of objets d'art.) I felt content and relaxed and even enjoyed some English TV while in bed. How much more sophisticated and unbiased their reporters were than their counterparts in the United States, and I was surprised to notice that they had several channels reporting in Arabic, including Al Jazeera. I fell asleep while listening to a Verdi opera performed by the members of the Royal Opera. If ever I return, I must make sure to attend a performance at the fabulous performing-arts venue in Covent Garden.

And thus, I say good-bye to London, past and present.

The river festivities ended in pouring rain. But you have to hand it to the Brits – they stuck to their program. Though it was soaking wet, the choirs sang, the orchestras played (maybe a bit out of tune?), and everyone smiled except the queen, or did she? She departed underneath a huge, transparent umbrella dressed in snow-white attire. "Long live the Queen." Yes, she smiled a lot the next day while standing on the famous balcony and waving to the cheering crowds, despite the fact that it rained again and that her husband, Prince Philip (ninety-one years old), had been hospitalized for a bladder infection, which did not surprise me at all.

NORTHEAST UNITED STATES

Massachusetts – Maine

For years I had been thinking about a trip to the northeast coast, in order to get acquainted with a few states still missing from the long list of states I had visited and, more importantly, to see firsthand the landscape and the shores about which Doc had spoken with nostalgia so frequently. He had been stationed at Fort McKinley, on Great Diamond Island, long before I met him.

I booked GCT's Nova Scotia & the Canadian Maritimes trip, and on May 31, 2008, I flew from Indianapolis, Indiana, directly to Boston, Massachusetts, where our group stayed at the Back Bay Hilton Hotel. Our suitcases were loaded the next morning, and I was eager to finally get at least a glimpse of Boston, a city I had not yet seen. Our guide took us to charming Back Bay, where we saw the nineteenth-century brownstones and the gilt-domed State House atop Beacon Hill and then continued to the impressive Leonard P. Zakim Bunker Hill Bridge. It is the widest cable-stayed bridge in the world, we were told. The guide pointed out the "big dig," which looked as though it would take ages until it could lay claim to being the city's crowning achievement and most extensive artery-reconstruction project. Four years later, as my research revealed, the fifteen (or more)-billion-dollar project had turned out to be full of pitfalls and more problematic than those responsible had anticipated. What a mess.

I genuinely relished the scenic drive from Boston to Bar Harbor. Rugged as well as smooth seashores, wooded areas, lush meadows, and rolling hills captivated me as I looked out the window, trying to see what Doc, the great lover of nature, had fallen in love with on these shores along the Atlantic. We did not stop in Portland, Maine's largest city, with a population of some 66,000 people. At the time of my trip, I did not know exactly where Doc had been stationed, but now that I know it was at Fort McKinley, on Great Diamond Island, I understand, when I look at my photos, why he loved living on the island. I closely observed the shingle-covered houses along the way, because Doc had told me that when building the Croft on the same spot where the log cabin in which he was born had stood, he had intended for the house to resemble those in Maine. And it did. If only I had known then that the shingles were meant to age naturally, I never would have painted them dark brown prior to putting the place up for sale. Doc would have been so upset with me. Sorry.

For lunch on our own, we stopped in the little town of Freeport in front of the famous headquarters of L. L. Bean, which really did not interest me as much as it did a few of my cotravelers. After a quick look at jeans, boots, backpacks, etc., all displayed in a big building on a couple of floors, I went outside to explore their small park area, where I found a spot on a bench underneath a big shade tree. I then strolled down the main street for some window-shopping and was glad when our bus took off again.

I liked the Bar Harbor Grand Hotel, because it was close to the waterfront. It is situated on Mount Desert Island, home to beautiful Acadia National Park, and I had an ocean-view room that reflected the charm of the late nineteenth century. Our guide insisted that the island had a reputation as "the most beautiful island in America" and that it was "Maine's summer playground for artists, yachtsmen, and outdoors enthusiasts." Who am I to argue?

Well, we would spend only two nights at this delightful hotel, but we were most anxious to be treated to Maine's specialty, an authentic downeast lobster bake with all the fixings. "The seafood, fresh off the boat and out of the cold, teemed with waters of the Gulf of Maine give it the true taste of New England. A lobster bake steams the ocean's tang into the lobster, fresh mussels, and corn on the cob" (Brochure). Now I know. – The lobster treat was superb, and I finally understood Doc's love of these fruits of the sea. He told me that when stationed at Fort McKinley, he always had an icebox filled with fresh oysters and that lobster was his favorite. It is mine too. I have never forgotten that when Doc treated me to my first lobster dinner at Niagara Falls, he ordered two for me. How about that?! Come to think of it, we learned on this trip that years ago, lobster was a poor man's food. As a footnote, I should add that the Maine lobster was superior to the lobster I had on Easter Island, even though that too had just been caught.

After breakfast on June 2, the third day of the trip, we set out to explore Acadia National Park, America's easternmost national park and the centerpiece of Mount Desert Island (pronounced "Mount DeSERT"). As our guide explained, "The island owes its moniker to the French explorer Samuel de Champlain, who in 1604 named it the Island of Barren Mountains [l'Île des Monts Déserts], for the bald appearance of its hills from the sea." I shouted a resounding "wow" at the sight of Thunder Hole, where the thunder of the sea splashes forcefully against the rocky shores of Mount Desert Island! I spent a while sitting not far from Jordan Pond, taking in the spectacular landscape surrounding the oligotrophic tarn, and regretted not having enough time to hike the hills known as "the Bubbles." The ride up to the summit of Cadillac Mountain (1,532 feet – the highest point along the North Atlantic seaboard) was special. We had an awesome view from the bare summit, encompassing the Blue Hill on the mainland, all of Acadia National Park, Bar Harbor, Schoodic Peninsula, the Cranberry Islands, numerous other offshore islands, and the Atlantic Ocean. A sunset would have been climactic. Artists, we were told, have been drawing and painting the sunset-spattered pink granite and lichens for years.

I walked leisurely through the town in the late afternoon along the Shore Path to watch a four-masted schooner glide between the Porcupine Islands and checked out several of the stately "cottages." "Wealthy Eastern families like the Astors, Vanderbilts, and Rockefellers found this glacier-carved island of rocky shores, gentle lakes, and meadows an ideal spot to spend their summer vacations, and built these grand summer 'cottages' here at the turn of the century. The area is still a favored location, with Martha Stewart being one of the more visible recent residents" (Brochure). I did not spot any celebrities, but was not sorry.

CANADIAN MARITIMES

New Brunswick

On June 3, day 4 of our trip, we departed for Saint Andrews, New Brunswick (one of Canada's three maritime provinces, and bilingual – French and English), and after passing through Canadian customs, our first stop was Campobello Island, where we visited Franklin D. Roosevelt's favorite summer hideaway, a thirty-four-room Dutch-gabled Victorian cottage. This visit was definitely a high point of the trip, simply because I had never before taken the time to learn much about this president. As 2008 was an election year, it was high time I learned more about our history. The cottage sits in the lovely Roosevelt Campobello International Park and is truly "an everlasting symbol of the good and neighborly relations between the people of the US and Canada" (Brochure).

I took my time passing through the rooms in the museum, looking at photographs and reading the comments. The more I read, the more pleased I was. When I finished my rounds and walked through the park alongside vibrant flowerbeds, I was proud to be an American. I was amazed at some of the similarities between FDR and Obama, as far as their education was concerned. FDR had a college degree from Harvard and a law degree from Columbia, whereas Obama had a bachelor's degree from Columbia and a law degree from Harvard. Of course, their ideologies were the same, but FDR had set in motion what was, in 2008, in danger of being destroyed. And to think of the physical handicap FDR had to endure. What a character! Unlike Obama, however, he was white and came from a very wealthy family. I could go on and on, but you know what I mean.

I took quite a few pictures of the Mulholland Point Lighthouse (built in 1885), the only one shared by the United States and Canada. But it was nothing compared to the Head Harbor Lighthouse, which we saw on a nature cruise across the Bay of Fundy, "one of the Marine Wonders of the World" (Brochure), on the way to New Brunswick. The East Quoddy Lighthouse, as it is also known, is an isolated home with a lighthouse standing proudly out on a rock in the sea. We wondered whether someone would take up the cause and preserve it for others to see in future years. It is supposedly the most photographed lighthouse in the world, yet like other monuments, it too may become a victim of technology.

After disembarking, we continued to Saint Andrews By-the-Sea, "a historic town that exudes colonial charm. Its English-American heritage is reflected in the historic buildings on almost every street. Wealthy Bostonians and New Yorkers used to stay at the gabled Algonquin Hotel, a summer playground. The King's surveyor mapped out the town in 1783 and divided it into 60 perfect square blocks separated by wide, tree-lined streets. The town boasts 100 houses that are more than 200 years old and many more dating from the 1800s. The central business area has been designated a National Historic District and has remained virtually unchanged since 1800" (GCT).

I could not have said it better myself! And to top it off, we would spend two nights at the renowned, century-old Grand Hotel, surrounded by beautifully manicured gardens and right on the sea, which you can watch endlessly – if time permits – from their rooftop terrace. When there is no fog, it is exciting to spot the Bay of Fundy. The second floor of the hotel is half-timbered, which reminded me instantly of England and Canada. It has the ambiance of a big manor house and is similar to the Fairmont Hotels at Lake Louise and Banff National Park in Alberta, Canada.

On day 5, June 4, after a tour of picturesque Saint Andrews By-the-Sea, we boarded a local coach for a short drive across the ocean floor – that is, on the bar at low tide – for a tour of Minister's Island, the former summer home of railway builder Sir William Van Horne. We saw "Covenhavene, Van Horne's summer cottage, the bathhouse (which features a tidal pool), the livestock barn and had a spectacular view from Shea Mountain" (Brochure).

The whole venture struck me as something strange. We had to wait for low tide to get in or out. It is a 690-acre island that stands several hundred meters offshore. I would not care to live on this geographical oddity. Well, if you spent only the summers there, it might be OK. It is unquestionably "the most spectacular of many palatial summer homes in St. Andrews" (GCT). Granted, there is not enough room for competition.

To satisfy my penchant for flowers, I had signed up for a special tour of the beautiful Kingsbrae Gardens. It was a bit rainy, but I did not let it stop me from wandering around and appreciating the various gardening traditions on display at the White, Rose, Knot, Perennial, and Cottage Gardens. I would have loved to transfer their wildflowers to my backyard to find out whether the deer would eat them. I ended the rounds with lunch at the Garden Café, located in a former turn-of-the-century home on the property. It was not at all overcrowded, and a couple of my travel companions asked me to join them at their table. One of the couples had come all the way from Kula, Hawaii, and I found it ever so exciting that they had known Barack Obama during their teens. The Mrs. spoke about him with great pride and related that he had won a scholarship to a very good private school. The Buetlers had immigrated to Hawaii from Switzerland and owned a restaurant in Hawaii. They were big-game hunters and spoke with great enthusiasm about their experiences in Africa. I was not impressed. On this trip, they ordered lobster whenever we stopped at a restaurant with lobster on the menu.

Canadian Maritimes

Prince Edward Island

After breakfast on day 6 – June 5, 2008 – we set out for Prince Edward Island, with a stop at Saint John. It is the place where the 450-mile Saint John River meets the Bay of Fundy at the Reversing Falls.

Observing the unique phenomenon of the Reversing Falls, caused by the enormous tide in the Bay of Fundy, was captivating and intriguing. "At low tide, the St. John River empties into the bay through a rocky gorge. Once the tide is higher than the river, the reversal of the current occurs and continues until high tide" (Brochure). You have to see it to believe it. These are the world's highest tides, we were told. We stared at the phenomenon for some thirty minutes but failed to see a single whale, porpoise, seal, or eagle. I won't be coming back. Once is enough!

On the way to Salisbury, we stopped briefly in the lobster capital of the world, Shediac (6,053 inhabitants). Unfortunately, we did not have a chance to eat lobster there, but we did get to view the largest lobster sculpture in the world for about ten minutes. We were told that the biggest lobster ever caught weighed some forty-four pounds. The sculptured lobster was about twelve feet long and three feet wide. The claws were enormous, as you might guess.

After lunch in the village of Salisbury (2,208 inhabitants), which is nestled on the banks of the Petitcodiac River, we crossed the Northumberland Strait on the spectacular Confederation Bridge, the world's longest bridge over salt water that freezes. The nine-mile span takes ten minutes to cross and joins Borden-Carleton, Prince Edward Island, and Cape Jourimain, New Brunswick. It joined the Canadian Confederation in 1873. This bridge was really something else. I wondered what it would be like in winter. To cross it by car is not cheap. I was busy photographing the bridge, the monument, the bronze Quartermaster statue, and the surroundings and was happy we had blue skies!

We arrived in Charlottetown on Prince Edward Island in the late afternoon. "Canada's smallest province, Prince Edward Island (called PEI by the locals) is known for its sandstone cliffs, blossoming gardens, and wide beaches. When the French explorer Jacques Cartier landed on the island in 1534 the native Mi'kmaq people who still live and flourish here called the island home. Later, French-Acadian, Scottish, and Irish settlers landed on PEI – creating the rich heritage that's evident today. Though tourism and fishing are important to the PEI economy, much of the island is carpeted with farms – this tiny province produces most of Canada's potatoes, hence its moniker of 'Spud Island'" (Brochure).

We stayed at the elegant Rodd Charlottetown Hotel, where I had a beautiful room with a view of the harbor. I had no complaints and went to bed early to watch TV.

I had been very much looking forward to our next stop, the Anne of Green Gables Museum, and was thrilled that the sun was shining bright in the blue sky on this seventh day of our trip, June 6.

As soon as we arrived at the museum in Silver Bush, I felt transported back into those riveting pages of the novel. I broke away from the group to take in the ambiance of the place that inspired Lucy Maud Montgomery to write the beloved tales of Anne Shirley, the gregarious, feisty, adventurous orphan girl. After the death of her mother and abandonment by her father, Anne's maternal grandparents raised her in their PEI home. She called the place "the wonder castle of my childhood" (Brochure). I happily climbed into the horse-drawn carriage for a ride on the grounds, which took us past farm buildings, the house, and the manicured, hilly lawns surrounding it. I walked to the pond and sat on a bench, meditating while looking at the silent water on which a couple of ducks were paddling in harmony. On our way back to the white frame house with a porch, one of my fellow travelers had her picture taken with a woman wearing a red-haired wig with long braids. After having checked out the rooms of the house, which were pleasant and bright, I walked across the lawn to the gift shop. I could not resist buying a nice hardcover edition of the novel commemorating its one hundredth anniversary, and after returning home, I sent it to my stepdaughter, Liesl, who loved the book and the TV series when little – but she never acknowledged the gift. Back on the bus, we were happy to watch a video version of the novel.

Our guide, a local of the island, told us much about its history, culture, and industry. We passed through quaint towns and villages on the island en route to "Prince Edward Island National Park, a 25-mile ribbon of white beaches, spectacular dunes, sandstone cliffs, and salt marshes" (GCT).

New Glasgow

The tour ended with a visit to the "Prince Edward Island Preserve Company in New Glasgow. Founded by owner Bruce McNaughton in 1985, the store features a cornucopia of foods and condiments including preserves, vinegar, fruit sauces, syrups, and barbecue sauce, all made mostly from local produce" (GCT). It was a lovely place. A handsome chap in Scottish attire greeted us at the entrance, sans bagpipes. I bought a jar of blueberry preserves to take home. Yummy! It would have been great to spread out a blanket on the well-kept lawn and enjoy a picnic. The flowers on the grounds were thriving.

A stop at the Province House National Historic Site was scheduled on the way to the hotel. Though PEI is the smallest province in the land, the most significant event in Canadian history took place there. In 1864, the Charlottetown Conference laid the groundwork for the establishment of the Canada we know today.

After relaxing at the hotel for a while, I took off again to explore Charlottetown, the smallest of Canadian capitals and the oldest city in the province, a bit more. I have not made a secret of my penchant for old country-town atmospheres, and the beautiful Colonial and Victorian buildings along Charlottetown's restored waterfront were no exception.

Dinner was included in a tour called the Prince Edward Island Experience. For a lover of lobster, this was a must-do. We learned all about the lobster business and history during a demonstration with live lobsters, the traps, the boats, and more. The demo was followed by a delicious seafood buffet featuring seafood chowder, mussels, lobster, and Atlantic salmon. The chowder was so good I picked up a few cans to take home. Try it – you'll like it.

Nova Scotia

In the late morning of June 7 – day 8 – we gathered for a ride of about an hour to the pier, and near lunchtime we boarded a ferry that took us from Wood Islands, PEI, to Caribou, Nova Scotia, a transit of less than an hour and a half. I stayed on deck the entire time, chatting with passengers and taking in the marine vistas, including the Caribou Lighthouse, until we disembarked and continued by bus, driving through the towns of Antigonish and Pictou. "The port of Pictou is renowned as the spot where the first Scottish settlers landed in 1773. In late afternoon we arrived in Baddeck (2,000) located on the shores of the lovely, expansive Bras d'Or Lake. Cape Breton Island is the northeastern part of the Province of Nova Scotia, separated from the mainland by the Strait of Canso" (GCT). We checked in at the inviting Auberge Gisele's Inn, and at dinnertime, I noticed right away a sophisticated European ambiance. The hostess, who spoke French, German, and English, treated us with an elegant flair. I welcomed the food, which had a European flavor and was superb. Not far from the park-like grounds was the lake. I was so enchanted by the sufficiently secluded spot, I thought to myself that if I ever wanted to escape the hot summers in Bloomington, I would choose this place as a hideout.

Elizabeth LeFort Gallery, in Cheticamp, was on the itinerary for day 9. The gallery housed a one-of-a-kind collection of hooked rugs that bear the likenesses of politicians, pontiffs, and royals from around the world and that I found a bit unusual. Nevertheless, this stop prepared us for the next one. Truly, I had no idea as to what this visit to Les Trois Pignons would be all about. But there it was, nothing out of the ordinary: a small museum out in the country in a big white frame house, with a big sign: "Welcome to Les Trois Pignons." We soon discovered what was so special: a stunning collection of hooked rugs and antiquities, a genealogy resource center, and a library. And we got some insight into Acadian culture and the history of Cheticamp, a small fishing community on the Cabot Trail. And lest I forget, a woman gave us a hands-on rug-hooking demonstration before we visited the

Fireball Lily

Hooked Rug and Homelife Museum. I will never be tempted to return to Les Pignons!

I perked up as soon as we came upon the amazing, winding scenic coastline, with its jagged peaks rising straight out of the sea: the fabulous Cabot Trail on Cape Breton Island, Nova Scotia. We passed seaside settlements strung along the trail, which reminded me of my trip to Scotland. This roadway was full of sublime, breathtaking, and incomparable vistas of mountains, valleys, forests, and waterfalls, which required many photo stops. This coastline also prompted me to think of others I had seen along the coasts of New Zealand, Easter Island, and Hawaii. Just awesome! Our guide said that many consider it one of the world's most scenic destination areas. The trail passes through part of the Cape Breton Highlands National Park, and we felt exalted when we stopped in the midst of the pastoral beauty for a picnic lunch.

At one point, we paused at a souvenir store and restaurant called the Atlantic Restaurant Birch Tree Shop, where I had enough time to walk through the park and take in the atmosphere. It was near the shore, and the path led through birch trees, which reminded me of the birch forests I saw from the Trans-Sib Railway. Lush, purple rhododendron bushes were planted here and there, and forget-me-nots, daffodils, and blue pansies shone brightly alongside the path. I loved the peacefulness and harmony that radiated all around me, at least for a while.

On day 10, we had another remarkable experience at the Alexander Graham Bell Museum. "It houses some of the great inventor's personal effects and documents as well as some of his remarkable inventions" (GCT). The site is located on twenty-five acres of beautifully landscaped land. And I will never forget sitting on a bench after I finished my rounds in the museum, marveling at models, replicas, photo displays, artifacts, and films describing the inventor's life and work, and looking out on the blue, shimmering Bras d'Or Lake. The great inventor and humanitarian lived and worked there for thirty-five years. I found his inventions and his history fascinating. I had not known Dr. Bell was born in Edinburgh, Scotland, and came to Canada by way of London – and then to the United States in 1870. In 1877, he married Mabel Hubbard, ten years his junior. She had been his student for many years. She became deaf due to a bout of scarlet fever at the age of five. They moved to Cape Breton Island in 1885, because it reminded Bell of his native land, and built an estate on a point across from Baddeck that overlooked Bras d'Or Lake, where they spent many years inventing and enjoying life, up until the time of his death on August 2, 1922. Bell left behind his widow, who died two years later, and two daughters. After having been to Edinburgh and having traveled through Scotland, I could easily understand why he felt drawn to this spot. What an incredibly gifted man. What would the world be like without the Bell telephone, and what would its inventor have said about its evolution into the cell phone, the iPod, and so on?

We traveled from Baddeck to Auld's Cove, where the causeway crosses the Strait of Canso and connects Cape Breton Island to the peninsula of Nova Scotia, where we stopped to eat. As soon as we stepped out of the bus, a piper dressed in Scottish attire and standing next to a fake lighthouse welcomed us with ear-piercing noise. I quickly located a bench some fifty yards removed from the restaurant to which others were rushing to eat. I sat down and, while munching on a banana and granola bar and drinking a bottle of tap water, gazed at a small lake on which a family of ducks was swimming. Sorry, I did not throw granola-bar crumbs to feed the ducks and ducklings.

We arrived at the Lord Nelson Hotel & Suites, a pleasant, renovated historical landmark near the waterfront and Halifax Public Gardens, in plenty of time to rest before dinner.

On June 10, we headed to Peggy's Cove, which according to our guide promised to be another extraordinary spot: "According to local lore, the cove got its name from 'Margaret,' the sole survivor of a schooner that sank off its shores in the early 1800s. This scenic fishing village, with its historic lighthouse, may be one of Canada's most photographed sites and many travellers cite this visit as a trip highlight" (GCT). I agree. Only some forty-five people live in this tiny rural community. I carefully navigated up and down the rocks to the wharf to watch a couple of fishing boats come and go and to view one that had returned from a lobster catch. They had spread traps and fishnets along the pier. Then, all of a sudden, I saw a huge flock of white seagulls sailing a few feet above the water. The ancient boulders that had been shaped and polished by glaciers thousands of years ago, some weighing many tons, were wet and slippery, and I had to be careful not to stumble. After I sat on a rock for a while – just reminiscing, looking out to sea, and gazing, of course, at the octagonal lighthouse high on the summit of a huge boulder – I got up and walked closer to take pictures of the lighthouse, and I had one taken of myself in front of it. The wind was blowing hard, but I did not mind. It was an exhilarating and rejuvenating experience. (After boarding school, I worked at the Kommerzbank in Hannover, Germany. As soon as they found out I was planning to immigrate to America, they nicknamed me "Peggy.")

Halifax

Our tour continued to Halifax, the capital of Nova Scotia and the largest city in Atlantic Canada (390,000 inhabitants). The driver went directly to the star-shaped Halifax Citadel, Fort George, which was completed in 1856 and is today a national landmark, commemorating Halifax's role as a key naval station of the British Empire. The weather was not favorable. It was foggy, and the view down to Halifax was less than perfect, but the bus driver made sure we saw the row of cannons facing down toward the harbor, the second-largest natural harbor in the world. We had missed the "noon gun" at 12:00 p.m., which supposedly makes quite a noise. I was

Fireball Lily

not sorry we missed the thundering report, a ritual upheld since the mid-nineteenth century, made by one of the six-pounder guns.

On the way to the Fairview Lawn Cemetery, we passed some of the city's main landmarks, including the famous Old Town Clock Tower, commissioned by Prince Edward in 1803. By the time we arrived at the cemetery, the weather had improved and the sun was shining. This cemetery, which holds the gravesites of those who died on the *Titanic*, was definitely another climactic stop on our journey. "Halifax sent three of her ships to recover those lost in the tragedy, and brought many more back to their final resting place in Halifax" (Brochure). – It was a heart-wrenching experience to walk along the more than one hundred grave markers, laid out in gentle curves. Many were laid to rest unidentified, and many graves bore the names of young crew members. I remember several markers in particular: "Alma Paulson, aged 29 years, wife of Nils Paulson, lost with four children, April 15, 1912 in the Titanic: Torbur Danria Aged 8, Paul Folke Aged 6, Stina Viola Aged 4, Costa Leonard Aged 2."

I skipped the Maritime Museum of the Atlantic, which features a special exhibit on the Halifax Harbour explosion of December 6, 1917. It must have been a devastating detonation. "The *S/S Mont-Blanc*, a French cargo ship loaded with massive ammunition collided with the Norwegian *S/S Imo* in a part of Halifax Harbor called 'The Narrows.' Debris, fires, and collapsed buildings killed some 2,000 people and injured about 9,000" (GCT). I was impressed when I learned that Alexander Graham Bell and his wife Mabel had actively participated in the rescue operations.

In the evening, I joined a group to visit Alexander Keith's, a historic brewery founded in 1820 and thus the oldest working brewery in North America. Though I am not a beer drinker, I thought it could be educational to visit a brewery at least once in my life. And it was a lot of fun. Our tour guides were pretty good actors, and they dressed in period costumes that dated back to the Halifax of 1863. They told us about the history of beer brewing, sang, joked with us, and took us to Stag's Head Tavern, where the tour climaxed when they let us taste different kinds of Alexander Keith's fine ale. I actually thought it tasted quite good and ended up having another big glass with my three-course dinner at the Waterfront Warehouse, where the tour ended. All that for $85.

On June 11, after a good night's sleep (the beer had helped), we set out along the 180-mile historic and very scenic Evangeline Trail. It is named after the main character in Henry Wadsworth Longfellow's famous poem *Evangeline*, which up to that time was not known to me and therefore represented another hole in my education. Our first stop was the Grand Pre (meadow) Historic Site. It commemorates Le Grand Derangement, the Acadian expulsion by the British in 1755, which is the subject of Longfellow's poem. Grand Pre was the largest of all the Acadian settlements in the Annapolis Valley – until September 5, 1755, when the Church declared that all Acadians (French settlers, originally from Port Royal) would be deported. More than ten thousand Acadians had to leave Nova Scotia. Their plight was heart-wrenching. They were sent to the British colonies in America and to France, among many other places. Families were torn apart, and many died along the way or were imprisoned. The British thought the French in Nova Scotia would never be good British subjects to the queen. – All of this history was new to me, and I found it very disturbing, to say the least. I easily understood why the early descendants of the Acadians cling tenaciously to their heritage and still predominantly speak French.

FYI: Henry Wadsworth Longfellow's heroine, Evangeline, an Acadian girl, is on a quest to find her lost love, Gabriel. He disappeared during the expulsion. She searches for him throughout America for years and eventually, as an old woman, settles in Philadelphia and takes care of the poor as a Sister of Mercy. When an epidemic breaks out, she finds Gabriel among the sick. He dies in her arms.

The National Historic Site of Grand Pre is a large park with marshland and commemorates the Acadian settlement, which lasted from 1682 to 1755. A small memorial church stands at one end and serves as a museum. A large statue of Evangeline stands to the right of the beginning of the path leading to the little church. A plaque in the church reads, "Over half the Acadians deported from the Minas Basin area in 1755 were children." I found it commendable that the Acadians were also instrumental in helping with the construction of the dikes along the Minas Basin. Rich pastures for their animals and fertile fields for their crops were thus created, resulting in Grand Pre becoming the breadbasket of Acadia. As I left the park, which consisted of manicured lawns accented with lush, blooming flowerbeds, I came upon a group of young children picnicking on the lawn with their teacher. We chatted in French, and one of the little girls showed off her acrobatic skills for me. She leaned backward and touched the ground with both hands. Not bad! *Adieu*!

Port Royal, site of the earliest-known French settlement in North America, is in Digby, one of the first areas in Canada to be explored and settled. The town is located on the western shore of the Annapolis Basin and close to the entrance of the Digby Gut, which connects the basin to the Bay of Fundy. The town is famous for its scallop fishing, and GCT had arranged a stop where those of us who liked scallops would have a chance to savor them. – After a two-hour drive, we arrived in time for dinner at the Rodd Grand Hotel, in the small town of Yarmouth.

On June 12 – day 13 – I spent part of the forenoon exploring the town and taking pictures of the port, where yachts and fishing boats had docked, and got excited when I spotted a huge, freshly caught lobster on one of the boats. After all, Yarmouth is at the heart of the world's largest lobster-fishing site and boasts Canada's highest lobster catch. – We were told that Yarmouth is also known for some of the most beautiful examples of Victorian-house styles in the Maritimes. They were inhabited by wealthy captains and ship owners of the town's golden age of seafaring. I took a special ride to the main street, where I got a good look at the Lovitt

Fireball Lily

and Eakin/Hatfield Houses and the Killam Brothers Building, which is preserved from the sailing era, on the waterfront. At the end of the little trip, we were taken to the large Cape Forchu Lighthouse, a beacon to Canada and the first "apple core" lighthouse in Nova Scotia. It is a modern-style light tower, perched atop picturesque volcanic rocks. I was glad to have taken the little tour, and in looking back, I appreciate, perhaps more than I did at the time, our stay at the Rodd Grand Hotel. The largest building in town, it is located on the site of the original Grand Hotel, which was built in the French-inspired Second Empire architectural style and was Yarmouth's key landmark for many years.

GOOD-BYE, CANADA – HELLO, USA

Portland, Maine

After lunch, we were transferred to the dock, where we boarded the *CAT*, a high-speed ferry, for our cruise to Portland, Maine. "The CAT is a milestone in naval architecture: it's a stable, safe, and very fast 300 ft.-long boat designed for comfortable ocean travel. Water jet powered, the boat skims the water and can breeze right over the lobster pot buoys that would snare the propellers of normal powerboats" (Brochure). I had been on a cat, a high-speed catamaran (hydrofoil), in 1989 as we crossed the English Channel on the way to our Venetian wedding. This trip took about five hours. I spent most of the time chatting with new friends. We had to clear customs upon arrival in Portland, Maine, and stayed at the historic Eastland Park Hotel, designed by the architect Herbert Rhodes and opened in 1927. It became famous for being the largest hotel in New England, and its fame grew when aviator Charles Lindbergh stayed there after returning from his solo, nonstop flight across the Atlantic Ocean.

Boston

On day 14, our tour would come to an end in Boston at the Back Bay Hilton, where we arrived toward lunchtime and met again an hour or so later in the lobby for a Boston sightseeing trip with a step-on, that is, a local guide, a retired Harvard professor. We passed some of the sights we saw briefly on the day of our arrival. Most importantly, this time the professor took us to the Harvard campus, which I had longed to see for years – ever since, when I was pursuing my PhD at IU, Professor Dorit Cohen, who had recommended me for the Woodrow Wilson Scholarship and had accepted a position in comparative literature at Harvard, wanted me to complete my studies there. At the time, I decided to stay in Bloomington instead, because we had the number-one department in the United States. – I found the Harvard campus most impressive and remembered a former student, Carlos Enrique Cavelier, who had done his graduate work there. And since it was an election year, I was proud of the fact that Barack Obama had earned his law degree there. Anybody who gains admission to the most prestigious and oldest (375 years old) institution of higher learning in the United States can truly be proud.

I was particularly impressed by the library and took a good look at the controversial John Harvard statue, on the west side of University Hall. He was the major benefactor, a fact theretofore unknown to me. I also did not know that John Kerry and his wife Teresa Heinz owned the gorgeous, multimillion-dollar, Federal-style row house the guide pointed out in Beacon Hill, one of the most desirable and expensive neighborhoods in Boston. It is a beautiful, quiet area, enhanced by lush, green flowering bushes, flower beds, trees, etc. I would not mind living there. Security is guaranteed!

We saw MIT from a distance, but did have time to spend a couple of hours downtown after learning much about the history surrounding the Episcopalian Old North Church, built in 1824. It is the oldest church of Georgian architecture in Boston. Much emphasis was placed on the steeple, the maiden peal of bells, the weather vane, and their historic importance. The steeple touched off the War of Independence in 1775. Paul Revere had asked the sexton, Robert Newman, to climb the steeple and hang two lanterns, which warned the colonists that the British were approaching by sea, and not by land, to seize their stores of gunpowder. I was in awe to see the first bust of George Washington. We were told it was an excellent likeness of the president. And then there was the monument of Paul Revere high on a horse near the church, a must to be photographed. Most American-born students of history, I am sure, know Henry Wadsworth Longfellow's poem "Paul Revere's Ride."

We were dropped off in the heart of Boston, near Quincey Market, and I headed directly to the fabulous food court, which offered a great variety of international dishes. I walked by the shops for a while, but eventually found a shady spot on a bench, from which I watched the people, licked a strawberry ice-cream cone, and chatted with a group of youngsters who happily posed for me. They had come to Boston for a day to walk the 2.2-mile-long Freedom Trail, which passes some thirteen historic sites and is marked by a red line. Curiously enough, in looking at my pictures, I have just realized I was there almost four years ago today – Father's Day. Not far from the bench where I sat, a group of photographers got ready to film the statue of Arnold Auerbacher, coach and manager of the Boston Celtics. Not interested in sports, I had never heard of Auerbacher or the Celtics. They were to play a week or so later for the NBA championship. Well, the photographers were successful in talking me into standing next to Auerbacher and having my picture taken. – I bragged about it to my travel companions at the farewell dinner that night and continued to brag about it to Eric Beardsley and others obsessed with sports. When the Celtics played, I rooted for them, and they did win! How about that? I guess Auerbacher inspired me, too.

EASTERN EUROPE

Germany

Hannover

Late in the spring of 2003, I decided it was high time to take a look at the former Iron Curtain and see in which way countries and cities such as the former East Berlin, Poland, the Czech Republic, and Hungary were faring after the fall of the Wall in 1990. Indeed, I had never visited Poland, the Czech Republic, or Hungary and was curious to see what they were like. In addition, I owed my German friends a visit and thought it would be ideal to combine it with GCT's the Best of Eastern Europe trip, scheduled to take place from October 25 to November 16, 2003. I booked the trip and made my own travel arrangements using frequent-flyer rewards.

I started out with a visit to my friends Father Tukay and his housekeeper, in Hannover. As usual, they were very hospitable. His housekeeper was a superb cook, and it was nice to indulge in my favorite Hanoverian *Gerstenbrot*, delicious cold cuts and what have you. They also showed off their brand-new Mercedes, raved about the latest worldwide trip, and drove with me to Hildesheim to show me their very nice future retirement house. I thought to myself, "Where do these Catholic priests get the money to afford such luxuries?" As I think back, I remember being secretly amused when his housekeeper showed me a burning candle in a red glass on top of the armoire in her bedroom, explaining that she kept it lit in the hope that the Father would not stray. Well, on the way back from Hildesheim, the Father stopped by in Großförste, my mother's place of birth, to say hello to my relatives, who were surprised to see me with the priest. He made sure I said a prayer at my parents' grave before I continued, the next day, by train from Hannover to Berlin to spend a few days hanging out with more friends.

Berlin

Bettina Segebrecht and I went theater and museum hopping. The Liebischs, from Rostock, whom I had met in Saint Petersburg, came to see me, and I made sure to get together with one of my young music friends, the pianist Sabine Simon. GCT had assisted with reservations at the Sofitel Hotel in Berlin, which turned out to be just fine. The Sofitel had a pretty decent restaurant, which came in handy. One day, I invited Sabine and her father for lunch at the Sofitel, and another day, the Liebischs were my guests. Mr. Liebisch presented me with a long-stemmed red rose, which I thought was very nice. He had virtually forced me to invite his friends as well, which I did not like. In contrast, I found it a bit strange that Sabine, to whom I gave an envelope with $1,000 in cash as a thank-you for all the concerts she had played at my house, never thanked me.

Bettina and I were busy shopping for a Yamaha upright piano, which I had promised her, and we were glad when we found just what she wanted, that is, one that could be silenced so that the neighbors would not be disturbed. Each day we had something cultural planned: We had a lot of fun at the Bar jeder Vernunft (Bar beyond Reason), a well-known cabaret in Berlin, and laughed hard at their political jabs, directed at German and American politicians, especially Bush. We attended a great performance of *Les Miserables* at the Theater des Westens and a so-so performance of *La Traviata* at the Komische Oper and squeezed in visits to my favorite museum, the Pergamon, and another at the new Nationalgalerie, where we saw the exhibition *Kunst in der DDR* (GDR Art). A special event took place at a big store selling Steinway pianos, to which Simone had been invited to play Schubert and Chopin for a select group of friends. We were all impressed and applauded enthusiastically. It was great!

Bettina drove me around Berlin to show me what had been accomplished since the fall of the Wall. I was awed, to say the least, and found noteworthy the architecture boasting a conglomeration of huge glass domes at the Potsdamer Platz and the changes to the Reichstagsgebäude, which featured another glass dome. I wondered quietly what kind of dramatic impact a terror attack by air, similar to 9/11, would have here in Germany's renovated, glass-domed capital. There was not much left of the infamous Wall, but once you looked beyond Unter den Linden, the famous boulevard, plenty of evidence was left in the form of drab *Plattenbau* (gray-panel facades), GDR apartment complexes, etc. It was uplifting to see the Brandenburg Gate free of remnants from the postwar obstructions erected by the GDR regime. I stepped into the nearby lobby of the famous Hotel Adlon Kempinsky just to get a glimpse of its luxurious ambiance! Wow! – In short, Berlin exhibited major improvements since I had been there with Toni right after the fall of the Wall in 1990. And I must not neglect to mention our stop at the United Buddy Bears, located at the Pariser Platz and Brandenburg Gate. It was a circle of more than 140 two-meter-tall fiberglass bears, in an upright position, holding hands and painted in bright, cheerful colors. They were on a global tour, promoting peace, love, tolerance, and international understanding. UNICEF sanctioned the exhibit. What a nice idea!

Eastern Europe

Poland

Warsaw

Bettina and I bid each other farewell on the evening of October 29, and the next morning, after I joined my GCT cotravelers, we were taken by bus to the train station, where we caught the InterCity train that took us to Warsaw, Poland. We arrived in the capital in the afternoon and were taken to our hotel, the Victoria, in the heart of the city, close to the famous Krakowskie Przedmiescie Street and Old Town. I liked my quiet and elegant room, which had a view down on the eighteenth-century Saxon Gardens and the famous Pilsudski Square. The location was perfect, that is, within walking distance of Old Town, the Grand Theatre, the Royal Palace, and fashionable shops.

We met our program director, a native of Poland who spoke English fluently and tried his best to be nice to us. He welcomed all of us just before the welcome dinner at the hotel.

After a good rest, a hearty breakfast, and the usual orientation and briefing at 8:30 a.m., we met at 10:30 a.m. in the lobby, ready for our half-day tour of Poland's capital and largest city. Warsaw, with a population of over one and a half million, is located on the Vistula, the queen of Polish rivers.

We soon learned about the devastating effects the Germans had on Warsaw during World War II and especially after the Warsaw Uprising in 1944, when they virtually destroyed this once-vibrant and glorious capital. To give you an idea, the pictures we saw were not unlike those of my hometown Hannover, or Berlin, or Dresden. It was worse than I had imagined. After all, 85% of the buildings were destroyed. It never ceases to amaze me how miraculously these cities have risen from their ruins. An excellent example is the reconstructed, historic Old Town, surrounded by fourteenth- and fifteenth-century walls located on the left bank of the Vistula. I loved the narrow, winding streets, the charming houses, the churches, and the old, cobblestone-covered marketplace, which reminded me of similar quaint provincial towns back home. Here too, Old Town was closed to all traffic except pedestrians and horse-drawn cabs.

We traveled down the Royal Road, which boasts the Baroque Royal Palace. One end of the road was totally obliterated during World War II, and the beautiful, huge Lazienski Park, with wide lanes overshadowed by trees, small lakes, and sculptures here and there, lay at the other. I was overjoyed when I spotted a beautiful monument to the Polish composer Frederick Chopin at one of the park's entrances. It was a lovely, sunny fall day, and consequently, the photo I took of one of my favorite composers turned out to be equally lovely. "Chopin was born in 1810 in Zelazowa Wola, near Sochaczew. His family moved to Warsaw only a few months later, i.e.

after graduation from the School of Music, linked to the Warsaw University. He spent many years in Paris, never losing his love for Warsaw. He died in Paris in 1849 of tuberculosis. His body rests in the Parisian Cemetery Pere-Lachaise, his heart as he wished returned to Warsaw and is kept in an urn in one of the columns of the Church of Holy Cross" (GCT). Looking at the monument that had been destroyed by the Germans on May 30, 1940 – and where Boy Scouts had put up a sign on the empty pedestal saying, "I don't know who took me down and why, but I know whose funeral march I will play" (GCT) – triggered intense contrasting emotions when, later that day, I stood before the Heroes of the Ghetto Memorial, a large but simple slab of dark granite in the heart of the prewar Jewish ghetto. The main bunker of the Jewish Fighting Organization was located at that very spot. One of the fiercest battles in human history took place there.

Since November 1 was All Saints' Day, our guide made sure we did not miss a visit to the main and very huge cemetery. It was our first stop that morning, and I was completely blown away by the ocean of flowers that covered the entire cemetery. The place was virtually overflowing with mums in every color imaginable – a virtual carpet of flowers. I have never seen anything like it in my entire life and could hardly understand how poor people could afford to purchase all those flowers. Until that day, I did not know just how devoutly Catholic Poles were. At the time, around 90% were Catholic, and I was told their "fanaticism" was in part their reaction to the communistic regime. I am not so sure.

What a relief it was when, in the afternoon, we were driven to a nineteenth-century manor house out in the country and welcomed by a local family to a typical and tasty Polish meal. The manor house, including its furnishings, looked humble, and the hosts were plain and simple. They treated us very politely. I refrained from talking about possible shared war experiences. The highlight of the evening occurred when the hosts led us into an adjacent music room where a grand piano stood and about two dozen chairs were set up for us to sit and listen to a piano recital performed by Eugeniusz Chudak-Morzuchowski, a graduate of the Music School in Warsaw. He played ten Chopin études with great sensitivity, and we all thanked him with generous applause. I spoke with him after the concert, congratulating him and mentioning my connection with IU's Jacobs School of Music, which he knew. I carefully hinted at the fact that the piano was a tad out of tune, which he admitted apologetically. Maybe I should have kept quiet. Sorry. Eugeniusz had enjoyed a rather successful career, playing internationally but predominantly in Poland. It was a nice finale to our day in Warsaw.

Day 4 – November 2 – started with a lecture, "Poland, My Home Away from Home," given by an American who lived in Warsaw. He gave us some insight into life in Poland after World War II.

It was obvious that the Poles we met, including our guide, were very pro-American and even pro-Bush. When I asked the guide why, after having been through World

War II, initiated by Hitler and costing so many lives, Poland would send soldiers to Iraq to fight a war initiated by Bush and based on a lie, he responded that these soldiers would be handsomely compensated. It's always about money, money, money . . .

I spent the day resting and reading a bit about the places we were to visit the next day on a two-hundred-mile trip: Czestochowa and Krakow.

On day 5, we got another early start. – I never get tired of looking out the bus windows when traveling through the countryside. It was a scenic ride and not very dramatic; that is, no mountains were to be seen, just farmland, meadows with grazing cows, sheep, and horses, an occasional pond, and villages with houses that were definitely in need of repair or sprucing up. Not much had happened since the turn, and I felt a bit sorry for them. Much of it looked like the countryside in the former East Germany. (My Canadian Polish friends assured me a couple days ago that much had been done since my visit and that today I would hardly recognize it. Good for them. All I remembered about Poland was an unplucked goose my father sent us for Christmas when he was fighting in Poland during World War II.)

After our lunch stop, we visited the old, Pauline Jasna Góra (Bright Mount) Monastery to marvel at the site of the Eastern Orthodox *Black Madonna Shrine*, a revered painting of the Virgin Mary with child, said to have curative powers. There are too many legends surrounding this icon for me to get into here. However, one of the legends claims that the presence of the sacred painting saved its church from being destroyed in a fire. But not before the flames darkened the flesh-tone pigments. Whatever. It's another big moneymaker for the Catholic Church. No, I did not light a candle. Oh yes, it is a pilgrim's favorite, as it is Poland's most famous shrine! Pauline monks from Hungary founded the monastery in 1382. Benedict XVI drew big crowds in Jasna Góra in 2006.

Krakow

After a long drive, we were happy with the choice of the five-star Radisson SAS hotel in Krakow. It was within walking distance of Planty, Wawel Castle, Collegium Maius, Old Town, Main Market Square, and Wawel Cathedral. Get the picture?

We had no plans for the evening, and since the skies were clear, after freshening up, I ventured out by myself to take a look at the city. I fell in love with it instantly, especially with the Main Market Square. It is supposed to be the most important market square of Krakow's Old Town, and it dates back to the thirteenth century. It is actually the largest medieval town square in Europe. Historic churches, palaces, and townhouses surround it. There is the impressive Cloth Hall, rebuilt in 1555 in Renaissance style, the Church of St. Wojciech, from the tenth century, the Adam Mickiewicz Monument, from 1898, and the stunning Gothic towers of

St. Mary's Basilica, with the unforgettable Veit Stoss Altarpiece. This magnificent monument of medieval oak and linden sculptures, which dominates the interior, left me breathless.

On November 4 – day 6 – we were properly introduced to Krakow, which happens to be the seat of Poland's oldest university and was the capital of the country until 1596. The city was designated a UNESCO World Heritage Site in 1978. It boasts an abundance of cathedrals, churches, and sacred art, with more than eighty existing churches and, at the time of our visit, nearly thirty more under construction. Krakow fortunately survived World War II with little damage. However, I am sure the main reason was the establishment of the new German General Government, which was seated in Krakow. "Krakow was one of five major, metropolitan Jewish ghettos established by Nazi Germany for the purpose of persecution, terror, and exploitation of Polish Jews during the occupation of Poland" (GCT).

After a historical introduction to the Market Square, center of Krakow life for more than seven hundred years, and after another glimpse at the more than life-size sculptures of humans without heads erected at various spots in the center of the square (sorry, I do not remember the name of the artist), we traveled by way of the Jewish quarter of Kazimierz, home to a Jewish community from the fourteenth century until World War II, and along the Royal Road (along which the kings of Poland walked) to Wawel Castle and Cathedral, where the former cardinal Wojtyla (Pope John Paul II) preached. We stood atop Wawel Hill, the beautiful Gothic-Romanesque castle complex, on a bend in the Vistula River and felt exalted at the view of the lovely cityscapes "punctuated with picturesque bridges" (GCT). The bell tower of the cathedral, which is surrounded by many exquisite chapels, contains the Sigismund Bell, one of Europe's greatest bells, according to the guide. It weighs 12,600 kilos and, with a diameter of 2.42 meters, is the largest of the five bells in the tower.

During our personal lunch break, I came upon a quaint little restaurant. It was just around the corner from the square on a narrow street. No more than fifty guests could be seated at the solid, wooden picnic tables. The menu was written on a board on the wall. *Schmalzbrot mit Harzer Käse* (an open-faced pumpernickel sandwich with pork lard and hand cheese – extremely stinky) and *Gemüsesuppe* (vegetable soup) was one of their specialties. I ordered just that with a mug of draft beer. It tasted divine! Just as if Mutti had prepared it. (No ordinary American would touch this meal, and none could be spotted in this place). I sat and chatted with a couple of Polish but English-speaking businessmen. A young couple from the Czech Republic joined us. The young man was a PhD student who had taught at the University of Tokyo off and on, and his girlfriend was an artist and interior decorator. We talked for a very long time, and before I left we exchanged e-mail addresses.

Wieliczka Salt Mines

In the afternoon, we visited the Wieliczka Salt Mines, a UNESCO World Heritage Site located 250 feet underground. These working mines have provided the world's most popular and important seasoning for more than seven centuries. "Dating from the eleventh century, the mines still produce about 700 tons of pure salt per day. These fascinating mines are considered one of Europe's great wonders and are protected as a historic monument. Here are more than 2,000 caverns of underground beauty on nine main levels – breathtaking chambers, galleries, and salt lakes" (GCT).

I was so glad I opted to take this tour. It turned out to be a genuine underground miracle. We walked more or less silently through the different chambers full of carvings and statues and through the late-seventeenth-century St. Anthony's Chapel and the enormous Chapel of St. Kinga, which is made completely of salt and decorated with salt bas-relief wall carvings. They were fashioned by talented miners, depict scenes from the New Testament, and display an amazing dimension and realism. I was totally awestruck. There was a salt lake that holds more than three hundred grams of salt per liter and a hall big enough to fly a hot-air balloon in. At the end, five persons per ride had to squeeze into a rather ancient and rattling high-speed mining lift. We prayed the cage would not get stuck, since it was very dark in the shaft, and that it would deliver us back into daylight intact, which it did. *Deo gratias.* I sure would have loved to attend a concert down there. The acoustics in this European wonder are said to be phenomenal.

I skipped dinner that night and snacked on a banana and an apple while sitting on a bench in Krakow's largest park, Planty. It is the green ring that encircles the old town and marks the former location of the medieval city walls, which stood until the early nineteenth century. It was close to my hotel. An artist had displayed a long row of paintings in the park. It was a neat idea, I thought, as long as it did not rain. Unfortunately, I do not remember any specifics. It's not the only thing I have forgotten. Nevertheless, one thing was clear: I could never tire of Krakow and thought that if the occasion should ever arise, I would definitely return and spend more time there. That night, I slept like a baby.

Auschwitz II – Birkenau

On day 7, we traveled by bus to Oswiecin, the location of the Auschwitz-Birkenau State Museum. "It is the largest of the WWII concentration camps, memorializing the millions of Jews, Gypsies, and 'enemies' of the Nazi regime who died here" (GCT). I had previously been to Buchenwald and Sachsenhausen and was seriously debating whether I should go. I decided to join the group, because I felt that unless I saw it for myself, I would not be able to comment objectively. Suffice it to say that, like my visits to Buchenwald and Sachsenhausen, Auschwitz was a heart-wrenching experience. If I was shocked by the motto at the entrance gate to Buchenwald – "Jedem das seine" (to each his own) – I was shocked even more deeply by the motto in big metal letters at the entrance gate to Auschwitz: "Arbeit macht frei" (work sets you free). The irony is mind-boggling, especially when you know that prisoners who understood the craft of welding made the words. The same motto was found at many other camps throughout Germany and Poland, we were told. And whenever I hear the term *concentration camp*, I cannot help but remember what an older student of mine, a Republican, said to me years ago, when I first started teaching at the university: "We should do to the blacks in America what Hitler did to the Jews." At the time, I thought I did not hear right. And after years of observing the racism still in existence in this country, even though the Declaration of Independence states that "all men are created equal," today – forty years later – it saddens me deeply to admit that the student meant what she said.

July 30, 2013 – In the middle of the night, when I turned on my TV because I could not sleep, I watched a portion of a documentary on public television. I was shaken to see that the KKK admired Hitler because he detested African-Americans and Jews as much as they did. Live and learn. I am ashamed to say that it is a known fact that even today, KKK members continue to live in my state.

After visiting Auschwitz II, one of about forty satellite camps surrounding Auschwitz, we visited Auschwitz itself. After touring the camps, we had a moving lecture by Mr. Kazimierz Smolen, an Auschwitz survivor and the director of the Auschwitz Memorial Site, who, I just read, died on January 28, 2012, that is, on the sixty-seventh anniversary of the death camp's liberation and about ten years after my visit. He was ninety-one. That's all I am going to say about Auschwitz. The experience reinforced my conviction that it must never be forgotten. Unfortunately, looking at the state of the world today, not enough has been learned from it. It's downright scary.

I was sorry not to have a chance to spend some time at the University of Krakow, aka Jagiellonian University, or JU. I had heard about its status as the oldest university in Poland, the second oldest in Central Europe, one of the oldest in the world, and among the world's top five hundred universities. I did not know at that time that following the Nazi invasion of 1939, 184 professors were arrested and deported to the Sachsenhausen-Oranienburg camp and that the university was closed until the end of World War II, when the Soviets continued to suppress the faculty's activities.

The next morning, we attended a lecture at the university by Dr. Pawel Pencakowski, a lecturer in the Art Conservation Department of the Krakow Art Academy. He had studied in Egypt, Paris, and Rome and earned an MA and a PhD at JU. The lecture was entitled "Krakow in the Time of Copernicus" and took us "back in time to the end of the 15th century – The Golden Age – of Polish Art and Culture, a time when Krakow was the capital of a great and powerful empire. It focused on

Wit Stwosz, German late Gothic artist who created the famous main altar and the impressive stone crucifix in St. Mary's church, Filippo Buonacorsi, Italian poet and writer who became a diplomat, political adviser and teacher of the King's sons and Mikilaj Kopernik, the famous astronomer who studied at Krakow's famous university" (GCT). We learned that "Krakow was a multinational and multicultural metropolis inhabited by Jews, Germans, Italians, Hungarians, Scottish, Dutch and others." To be honest, I really do not remember much of the lecture and took this information from my GCT flyers. *Danke schön!*

I managed to spend some time in the afternoon at the Czartoryski Museum Library, mostly to see Leonardo da Vinci's masterpiece, *Portrait of a Lady with an Ermine*, circa 1485. And she was flawlessly beautiful! I liked this portrait more than the *Mona Lisa*, located in the Louvre. The *Lady* depicts a teenage beauty, assumed to be Cecilia Gallerani, the mistress of Milan's ruler Lodovico Stora il Moro, the artist's patron. Da Vinci supposedly painted her some twenty years before the *Mona Lisa*. I was fortunate to see her in Krakow, since a few months later this portrait, among others, was exhibited in Houston and San Francisco. – A folkloric show at dinnertime provided some time to unwind.

Czech Republic

Sedlec

On November 7 – day 9 – I showed up early for the 370-mile bus ride through the heart of Moravia, so named after the Morava River in the northwest part of the region, to Prague, Czech Republic. We traveled past vineyards and through some lovely river valleys and stopped for lunch in the Moravian town of Olomouc, the sixth-largest city in the Czech Republic. After lunch, our guide asked the driver to guide us on a brief tour through Olomouc. The tour offered a couple of photo stops, one at Saint Wenceslas Cathedral, founded in 1107, and another for a panoramic view of Olomouc from the Gothic, fifteenth-century Church of Saint Maurice.

GCT often had a surprise in store for us. On this day, about an hour away from Prague, we stopped in Sedlec, a suburb of Kutna Hora, to see the Sedlec Ossuary, aka the Church of Bones. This was perhaps one of the most bizarre and macabre sights I have ever laid eyes on. "The small church at All Saints is located in Sedlec in the center of a picturesque cemetery in the vicinity of the grandiose structure of the Church of Our Lady. As the cemetery failed to provide sufficient space for the victims of plague and the Hussite wars, during which the monastery was burnt down and its residents murdered, the bones from the graves were piled up in the lower chapel" (GCT).

I entered reluctantly and could not believe what I saw. I will not touch upon all the details, but the place was crammed full of human skeletons. Skulls and bones from all parts of the body were neatly arranged. The big chandelier hanging in the center of the church included at least one of every human bone, we were told. I did not attempt to verify it. The coat of arms of the Schwarzenberg family, also made of human – not animal – bones was also remarkably appalling. As if it were not enough that thousands of human skulls stared at you with hollow eyes wherever you looked, the ceiling was crammed full of them as well. Although I had time to further examine, yet not admire (?), the site, I quickly turned around, left, and sat down on a tombstone in the cemetery, where I waited until my cotravelers had their fill. If you believe in a life hereafter, you must ask yourself why, if it looks anything like this, one would want to be stuck there. I can do without the angels and harps.

Prague

Our afternoon drive took us into Bohemia and its capital and largest city, Prague. We stayed at the Diplomat Hotel, not far from the city center. After a welcome drink, I sought refuge in my very nice room, where I treated myself to a snack and a beer from the bar and just relaxed and watched TV from my very comfortable bed.

The next morning, we walked to the metro, which I must admit can easily lay claim to being one of the world's most efficient subways. We went to the Institute of Economics, where Professor Jiri Amort gave a lecture entitled "From Forty Years of Communism to Free Market Economy." He tried to help us understand the transition and transformation of the country's economic system by explaining the historical and economic background of the Czech Republic and by giving examples from real life. A very lively Q&A session followed. Afterward, our guide led us on a get-acquainted tour of the Golden City, which was left virtually intact throughout World War II. During the reign of Charles IV, the king of Bohemia and Moravia, Prague was the seat of the Holy Roman Empire. Later, it was the vital center of the Habsburg Monarchy.

I had wanted to visit Prague for many years, and words fail me when I try to express how grateful I was that another dream had come true. It was a love-at-first-sight experience. Awesome! Our guide took us to Stare Mesto, the Old Town, with its many wonderful Gothic and baroque buildings. We arrived at the famous fifteenth-century astronomical clock at the Old Town Hall in time to join the crowds that had assembled below to watch Christ and the twelve Apostles appear at two little windows above the clock face, followed by the skeleton of Death tolling the bell. Fantastic! Yet another great experience, enhanced by blue skies and a bright sun! – We walked across the Charles Bridge, which goes over the Vltava River (the longest in the Czech Republic) to Mala Strana (Lesser Town). It was lined with statues and ornate lampposts. The bridge was reserved for pedestrians, and we appreciated the wonderful views of the castle and the skyline of the medieval city as we walked across it. Our tour ended at Prague's best-known landmark, Wenceslas Square, located at the edge of Old Town. On this square, a horse market in the Middle Ages, which can hold some forty thousand people, demonstrations against the communist government took place. At the top of the square stands the equestrian statue of St. Wenceslas, the patron saint of Bohemia. The Duke was sainted for bringing Christianity to Bohemia. The monumental National Museum, situated behind the square, provided a great backdrop.

After lunch, I passed along the waterfront of the river to see the Theater on the Balustrade, the center of Prague's theater scene in the 1960s. Former president Vaclav Havel worked there as a stagehand and later as the resident playwright, a fact that always impressed me. I did manage to look at Franz Kafka's memorial marker on the structure in Franz Kafka Square, which now stands at the location of the house where the great writer was born. The original building was destroyed by a fire in 1897. I reminisced for a while, thinking about the many times I had lectured on this all-important and influential twentieth-century author. His writings never ceased to challenge those eager to understand his philosophy and his message. He died at an early age and, unlike his two sisters, escaped the horrors of the Holocaust.

I had planned to take advantage of the cultural scene whenever possible. In looking over my notes, I find that while in Prague, I went to the famous Rudolfinum on November 7 to hear the Ceska Filharmonie play, with Zdenek Macal conducting. It goes without saying that I was very happy. The following night I had a ticket to the State Opera for Verdi's *Un ballo in maschera*, and the next evening I saw Mozart's *Così fan tutte*, again at the State Opera. I was in seventh heaven. All the performances were sublime and sparkling.

Indeed, they were more sparkling than the crystal we were shown on another day in Prague, when we went to the well-known Moser, "the jewel of Bohemian glass artistry" (GCT). I eyed their elegant display chambers curiously, looking for crystal. I can say that my stemware, when freshly cleaned, sparkles just as brilliantly as Moser's creations.

On November 10, we set off on a tour of Prague, featuring a visit to Hradcany, the Castle District, where the Prague Castle is perched on a hill. At a length of 570 meters, it is known as one of the largest castles in the world. "Centered around Castle Square, this is a massive complex including palaces, churches, museums, and the soaring Gothic St. Vitus Cathedral. The Prague Castle, whose construction commenced in the late 19th century is the city's crowning glory, and the area surrounding it is filled with Baroque palaces and Romanesque and Gothic churches that span nearly six centuries" (GCT).

On day 12, after attending a cooking class on marinating Czech cheese, given in the basement of a small restaurant, about which I remember only that we were served a mug of tasty Czech beer, I spent the afternoon exploring the Bertramka Museum, a villa where Mozart stayed in 1787 and 1791 as a guest of the Czech composer F. X. Dušek and his wife. It was there that Mozart composed the famous overture to his opera *Don Giovanni*, one of my favorites.

That evening, we were both treated to dinner in the local village of Nosalov and invited to join a local group of polka dancers, which I watched from my place at the table. It was fun!

I was a bit sad when it was time to leave this fabulous city of stone and spires, which today still ranks as the thriving center of the country and is proud of its "artistic community reminiscent of Paris in the 1920s" (GCT). So they say.

Slovakia

Bratislava

On November 12, we began our daylong ride to Budapest (about three hundred miles). We stopped for lunch in Bratislava, the capital of Slovakia, whose history goes back to Celtic and Roman times. "Though the Czech Republic and Slovakia were united as Czechoslovakia for nearly 75 years, they each have distinctive personalities, languages, and landscapes" (GCT). And we did get a taste of Slovakian culture during our lunch in this city, which has a population of 460,000 and sits on the banks of both the Danube and Morava Rivers. It borders Austria and Hungary, two independent countries. Though Bratislava Castle was, from the end of the ninth century, an important fortified settlement, we had to be content to view it from a distance. Fortunately, it sits high on a hill above the Danube! I would have loved to attend a theater performance up there during the Shakespeare festival or a summer concert under a starlit sky. No time . . .

Hungary

Budapest

We arrived in Budapest, the capital of Hungary, in the early evening and checked in at the Courtyard by Marriott. I retired to my very nice room, where I enjoyed a snack with a beer while watching CNN.

Our city tour started on November 15 with a stop in Buda, on the right bank of the Danube, and a visit to the turreted Fisherman's Bastion, which offers a grand panorama of the entire city. The Bastion is a viewing terrace with many stairs and walking paths in Neo-Romanesque and Neo-Gothic style (1892–1902). It is located on Castle Hill near Matthias Church, where the Hungarian kings were crowned. The seven towers resembled sugar cones, I thought. Regardless, the view from up there down on the Danube, Margaret Island, and Pest to the east, as well as Gellert Hill, was awesome. We took a picture of the bronze statue of Stephen I of Hungary (1906) mounted on a horse and then crossed the Danube by way of the famous Chain Bridge to visit the imposing Parliament Building in Pest, an Austro-Hungarian masterpiece. We crossed the more modern Elisabeth Bridge to Heroes' Square, with statues of Hungarian kings and governors and other Hungarian historical figures inside the niches of the two semicircles that compose the monument. High above the monument is the 118-foot-tall Millennial Column, topped with a statue of the Archangel Gabriel, symbol of the Roman Catholic Church. It's a perfect place for demonstrations and celebrations. In front of the monument is the Tomb of the Unknown Soldiers.

In the afternoon, I spent several hours at Budapest's immense Central Market Hall, Vasarcsarnok. The building displays a beautiful tiled exterior and an airy iron and glass interior. It opened in 1897 and has three levels. I spent most of the time on the main floor, where I bought paprika, goose liver, and Hungarian salami for my friends back home. Upstairs, I found some nice hand-embroidered tablecloths, and after that I treated myself to a very tasty and very fresh *lángos*, a huge, savory yeast doughnut, deep fried, sprinkled with garlic powder, and topped with sour cream. My mouth waters as I think of it. Try it – you'll like it! Oh yes, I also had a small beer.

Before we ate dinner at a place somewhere in Budapest, where a group of enthusiastic Gypsy fiddlers entertained us, we had a lecture from an expert on "Hungary's Political Past & Future."

On day 15, I headed to the Parliament building, where I had to wait for a long time to get a ticket. But it was worth it. I enjoyed seeing the inside of this magnificent place, walking up the many steps, and listening to an excellent introduction to the history and events surrounding this architectural gem.

In the evening, I splurged and went to a highly recommended Biedermeier restaurant, known for its Biedermeier ambiance and on the fifty-best-restaurants list. It was a small, rather intimate place in a subterranean location, but very elegant, with antique baroque-style furniture, white linen tablecloths, sterling-silver tableware, fine china, sparkling crystal glasses, background music by composers of the period, from Vivaldi to Mozart, and dishes prepared according to recipes from the 1830s.

I chose the gourmet menu: "Pate de fois gras with truffle, almond soup with quince dumplings, stuffed quail with spinach risotto, fillet steak with a piquant oyster sauce, served with couscous and wild mushrooms baked in rice paper, sweet polenta with peach, served with praline ice-cream and goat's cheese specialties." (*C'est tout.*)

It was superb. The waiter spoke German, and since the restaurant was not yet full, I truly enjoyed chatting with him.

For day 17, I had signed up for an optional tour to Holloko (Raven-stone), which was recommended by GCT as "a typical Hungarian village dating to the turn of the century. The architecture, lifestyle, and culture from the early 1900s are still very evident here and are thoroughly charming. There are many historical buildings located in this village, and the ruins of a 14th century castle remain on one of the highest hills surrounding Holloko."

Upon arrival, we were ushered into a large room in which a row of wooden tables was set up. Several women, dressed in local costumes, welcomed us before we found our seats at the table. The meal they served was out of this world. It started out with a bowl of potato soup, and as I remember it, they then served their chicken dishes with rich and very tasty gravy (a far cry from dry chicken breasts). All the dishes, as well as the potatoes, cabbage, and goulash, were served on big platters and/or in stoneware bowls. Their home-baked rye bread and the apple strudel were delicious. We had a choice of beer or wine, and before we left, we were surprised by a group of singing locals dressed in regional costumes. We were in superb spirits when we left the place, thanking our hosts profoundly and then following our guide for a stroll through this quaint and well-preserved one-street town, one of UNESCO's World Heritage Sites. It is idyllically located in a peaceful, green valley. I was quite enchanted by their whitewashed wooden-towered church and the sturdy, traditional peasant architecture. We stopped briefly to watch a couple of elderly women at work on their colorful embroidery. Our cobblestone path ended up on top of the hill where the ruins of the medieval castle were perched on top of a rock on one of the highest hills surrounding Holloko. Yes, the view from up there was fantastic. Even more fantastic was the Operalia evening with Placido Domingo at the fabulous Hungarian State Opera House. What more could I want?

I spent day 18 walking around, just enjoying gorgeous Budapest and thinking about how nice it would be to tell my Hungarian friend Professor Gustav Bayerle that I had finally been to the place of his birth. I took my time packing the suitcase and got dolled up a bit for the farewell dinner at a restaurant outside the hotel. The dinner was excellent, and the Gypsy musicians succeeded in pleasing all of us. Several in my group even joined the dancing crowd. Our guide, however, surprised us all profoundly when, on the way back to the hotel, he directed the bus driver to make a detour to Fisherman's Bastion, illuminated by a special floodlight, so we could marvel at this magnificent place, also known as "the Paris of the East." I will never forget looking down on the Danube, with the panoramic view of the historic buildings now bathed in floodlights and the lit-up Chain Bridge reflected in the river's flowing waters. Could anything be more romantic?

Eastern Europe

Austria

Vienna

On November 20, after cordial farewells, I took the two-hour train from Budapest to Vienna. I checked in at my favorite hotel, Kaiserin Elisabeth, quite close to the Stephansdom. It was intimate and elegant; the gentlemen at the reception desk, genuine Viennese, greeted me, *comme il faut*, with "Frau Professor Dr." and a kiss on the hand, and they were more than happy to find opera tickets for me to keep me in high spirits during the three-day stay in Vienna. This hotel was very special, because such prominent guests as Mozart, Clara Schumann, Franz Liszt, Richard Wagner, Anton Rubinstein, and Edvard Grieg, among a long list of others, used to lodge there. The hotel was the best you could find in Vienna and thenceforth became my favorite.

The hotel secured two reservations for me at the Staatsoper, one for Mozart's *Magic Flute* and another for the ballet *Swan Lake*, and a third for Bernhard's *Elisabeth II* at the Burgtheater. During the day, I went museum hopping and soaked up the Christmas ambiance at the big Christmas Market in front of the Town Hall. Since it was already a bit chilly, I ordered a *Glühwein*, the typical Christmas drink of hot red wine with cinnamon and other spices. It put me in the right mood for the incredibly humorous premiere of Thomas Bernhard's *Elisabeth II*.

The theme for this Christmas was "Magic of Advent in Vienna." And it was magical indeed! Vienna was covered with the most gorgeous Christmas lights I had ever witnessed. The minute I stepped out of my hotel, I felt as though I had entered a fairy realm. Since the State Opera was not far from my hotel, I walked there to attend performances. For the last night, I had a choice ticket in a VIP loge to Rudolf Nureyev's *Swan Lake*, with the Japanese dancer Shoko Nakamura, a guest performer, as Odette/Odile. It was sensational. The audience – including me – felt exalted. We stood up at the end and called out in jubilation our bravos and bravissimos while a sea of flowers covered the stage at the dancer's feet. The standing ovations lasted at least fifteen minutes. Two young women in my loge were so excited that when I started to leave my seat, they invited me to join them for a glass of champagne. They thought I was such an enthusiast. I would have loved to accept their kind invitation. Unfortunately, I had to decline, because I had to get up at 6:00 the next morning to catch the train to Merano, my next stop. The train ride from Vienna to Merano was just what I had hoped for. The mountains were covered with fresh snow. I felt exuberant and was so happy. I could not tear myself away from the train window – the panoramas were picture-perfect.

Italy

Dorf Tyrol

I had a reservation at Hotel Erika in Dorf Tyrol, outside of Merano. They had a special and quite glamorous Advent-Christmas event planned, which promised to be extravagant. And I was not disappointed. The entire place was decked out with Christmas lights, ornaments, candles, and what have you. The food – Christmas cookies and beverages – was superb. As usual, they went all out. A highlight was Santa Claus sliding down their wide entrance stairway and distributing all kinds of gifts to us. I found a few special Christmas gifts the next day in Merano while admiring their Christmas Market. On November 30, after a couple of days at my favorite hotel in Northern Italy, I took a train ride through more snow-covered mountains to spend a few days with my friends Wulf and Ursel Segebrecht in Bamberg.

Germany

Bamberg

The Segebrechts treated me with warm hospitality. The day of my arrival, Wulf was in Frankfurt to be honored as the recipient of another one of the many literary prizes he so richly deserved. Ursel and I took off for the PX the next morning to buy a TV for their guest suite, and in the evening we explored the Bamberg Christkindlmarket. On December 3, they took me to Nürnberg, famous for having the number-one Christmas market in Germany. It was especially nice because Bettina, who had arrived from Berlin at midnight on December 2, joined us. I bought several nutcrackers and two Rauschgold angels (unique to the region) for my music kids, and we all had a glass of *Glühwein* before returning home.

My friends hosted a good-bye party at their beautiful home on December 6. They had invited several couples, professors, and friends for a unique dinner, which two of the young male professors cooked for us. They had prepared unusual gourmet dishes, utilizing both kitchens in the house, and we praised them and their creations abundantly. I was not so happy when Wulf decided to challenge our literary brains with a test after dinner. We had to draw a piece of paper out of a hat and correctly attribute the quote on the slip we had drawn. I was a nervous wreck, because I knew the minute the game started that, since I had been out of touch with literature for so many years, there was no way I could compete. And I was right. I was glad when the torture ended.

My friends dropped me off at the train station the next morning for my trip to Munich. Ursel presented me with a very nice nativity, which she had bought in Nürnberg. I boarded the InterCity to Munich, where I had booked a reservation at a hotel for a couple of nights, since my flight back to the States was scheduled for the 9th, Wulf's birthday. In all the excitement, I left the nativity in the luggage net above my seat on the train. I was quite distraught and called several lost-and-found places from my hotel, without results. Fortunately, I found a nativity much like the one I lost when exploring the Christmas market in Munich. I spent another day museum hopping and went to bed early for a good night's rest, feeling extremely relieved to have survived this very long trip in pretty good shape. The plane was on time, and I arrived safe and sound in Bloomington the same day I left Munich. *C'est tout.*

Dwindling Friendships

I had planned to be home a few weeks before Christmas, because I had promised two of my Korean music kids to fulfill their wish to experience a genuine German-style Christmas with me at my house. And believe me, I came home well prepared. I had bought Christmas ornaments for each of the girls at every Christmas market where I spotted them: in Poland, the Czech Republic, Hungary, Austria, South Tyrol, and Germany. I spent much time wrapping them all nicely and hours decorating my tree with German wax candles, beautiful ornaments, etc., and I sent the girls tickets for their flights from Washington, D.C., and Santa Barbara, California. I bought a nice duck to roast, a head of red cabbage, etc., and I was deeply disappointed when a week or so before their scheduled arrival, Hoo-Ryoung, the soprano, canceled her trip because she had fallen madly in love with some singer – who later turned out to be more gay than straight, as I recall. Thus, Hee-Kyung, the pianist, came alone, and I tried my best to present her with a German Christmas, which she seemed to like. But when I served the roasted duck, she became rather picky, and I ended up tossing the bird into the garbage. I still get upset when I think about it, because in my opinion the duck was just fine. I believe she then cooked something Korean. But I really don't remember. I let her drive my car to some church on Christmas Day. Something got damaged and cost about $300 to repair, which was not the worst thing about her visit. The longer she stayed, the more annoying she got. She had nothing positive to say about her friend Hoo-Ryoung and filled my head with a lot of rumors. I asked her to wrap the gifts for Hoo-Ryoung so we could send them to her. She wrapped them so sloppily I could not believe my eyes. Instead of cutting the paper she just tore it. Need I say more? I had looked forward to her playing the piano now and then, which she hardly did, and the violin professor whom I had agreed to let her invite never showed up. When she was ready to fly home and left my house in the limousine I had ordered for her, she turned around and said, "Good riddance." That was the last time I saw her, and all the letters and attempts by her to contact me ended in the wastebasket. So much for dissonances. It took me years to figure out that some musicians think we enthusiasts owe them something. I have fallen for them again and again. You'll see.

No sooner had the pianist left than I got busy contacting several of my friends who lived either in or not too far from Berlin. I encouraged them to attend a piano recital which Sabine Simon was scheduled to give in the Chamber Concert Hall of the Berlin Philharmonic on February 12, 2004, at 8:00 p.m. She would perform compositions by Schoenberg, Beethoven, and Chopin. Several of my friends went, including the Liebischs, who drove all the way from Rostock. Their reports were enthusiastic, and they were glad they had made the effort. And I was grateful as well. What more can one do? I was confident Simone would not disappoint. By then, she had completed another year at the Mozarteum, in Salzburg, and the last time I had heard her play – a few months earlier – as well as when I had invited her to spend a weekend with me at Hotel Erika in Dorf Tyrol, where she gave an impromptu performance for the much-delighted guests, she had definitely improved. – I was disappointed when she stopped writing, and when I heard she had gotten married without notifying me, I thought it was time to let her go and spent a generous amount of the money set aside for her wedding gift on another trip. She attempted to reconnect when she had given birth to a baby girl, but I decided to leave them to lead their own life and hoped they would be happy.

EASTERN EUROPE - MS RIVER ARIA

In July 2005, I had been to the top of the world, that is, the North Pole. Though I had taken GCT's the Best of Eastern Europe trip in 2003, I felt I should go a bit further to the east of Europe, since it had become accessible after the turn. So I booked Eastern Europe to the Black Sea, a thirteen-day GCT river cruise and a more or less take-it-easy trip. Cruising on the Danube would be just what I needed. I did not want to seriously explore those countries formerly under communist rule, but just to get a glimpse, a general impression, of each of them. I had always been curious to see how these countries compared to the former GDR, which I had gotten to know well during my years as a professor, when I took or sent my students to the GDR for a week every year.

On a Continental flight bound for Newark, I left Indianapolis on September 27, 2005, and continued with Air France via Paris to Bucharest, known as "Little Paris" in the early twentieth century, before communism. We landed in Bucharest at 7:20 p.m. on September 28 and stayed at the Sofitel, where I skipped the welcome dinner and went to bed early to rest up.

Romania

Bucharest

After breakfast on September 29, the third day of the trip, I was ready to tour Bucharest, the capital of Wallachia and, since 1659, of Romania. The city is located on the banks of the Danube River. I immediately noticed the unusually broad tree-lined boulevards and the city's eclectic architecture. The architecture combines neo-classical structures with monumental twentieth-century edifices which, we were told, were built for the most part to satisfy the late dictator Nicolae Ceauşescu's program of systematization. He ruled from 1967 to 1989 and is reputed to have implemented the most Stalinist, that is, the most brutal and repressive, regime in the Soviet Bloc. During my travels through other Eastern European regions, it had become clear to me that the communist leaders of the various countries had a penchant for building big, colossal, and monumental architectural structures, which were klutzy and aesthetically unappealing, in my opinion, compared to the palaces, parliaments, cathedrals, opera houses, etc. designed by their predecessors. In case you did not know, he and his wife were executed shortly after the December 1989 Revolution.

The Arc de Triomphe, which commemorates the exploits of World War I soldiers, made a favorable impression. The original had been constructed out of wood in 1922, but over the years, due to the wear and tear caused by wars and the like, it ended up being finished in Deva granite. It strongly resembles its counterpart in

Paris, just as it was intended to. – Victory Square, with its huge government-office buildings, and the Natural History Museum were indeed grandiose, and even more so was Revolution Square (Palace Square), where the National Museum of Art of Romania, the Athenaeum, Athenee Palace Hotel, and the University of Bucharest Library, among other buildings, are located. The building of the former Central Committee of the Romanian Communist Party stands there, and it is of special interest to me because it is the place from which Ceauşescu and his wife fled by helicopter on December 22, 1989. But they were later executed in this very building.

There is no way you can overlook the Palace of the Parliament, the world's second-largest building after the Pentagon. It is neoclassical in style, started in June 1984 and completed in 1997. There was no time to go inside to see the reputedly luxurious furnishings, velvet and brocade curtains, embroideries in silver and gold, etc. Much was unfinished when the dictator's reign ended, but the plans left no room for doubt regarding the excessive luxury in which he would have lived. Again, all this is not so different from what I have seen in capitalistic regimes around the world, not excluding the riches of the Catholic Church, the palaces of kings, etc. Here too, the people living in poverty have little choice but to endure it. I am sure that by now, almost ten years later, though much more slowly, the Romanians are trying to restore their "treasures," just as their neighbors have. – My advice: lift up the people first and then – with their help – renovate. And compensate them fairly for their work.

I would like to include here the information GCT provided about the Palace of Parliament: "Begun in 1984, initially it took 20,000 workers, 7000 architects and uncountable billions of Lei to build. But when the dictator died, only the exterior and three rooms had been finished. Work continues on it to this day. What is seen from the street level on Bulevardul Unirii is a monolith rising 276 feet above ground level but it is nearly as deep under ground, rumored to hold a nuclear bunker big enough to contain the entire government, although its actual function has never been revealed. Inspired by North Korean Communist architecture, which reflected Ceausescu's political leanings, it is 1,082,677 square feet in area and the second-largest administration building in the world (after the Pentagon). . . . It is now the seat of Romania's Parliament and headquarters of the International Conference Center, although it has also been used as a film set, imitating the Vatican."

Constanta

We took the train to Constanta later that afternoon and were transferred to our ship, the MS *River Aria*. After dropping off our luggage, we gathered for a briefing, followed by drinks and the welcome dinner, after which I retired to my cabin, as I usually do. I read through some of GCT's flyers, and I will pass on what they said about "the River Danube, Europe's second longest river, rising on the eastern slopes of the Black Forest in Germany and eventually flowing into the Black Sea via its delta in eastern Romania. It has a total length of 1,776 miles. . . . Vital to trans-European communication, the Danube is now part of the Rhine-Main-Danube Waterway, an inland waterway which links the North Sea at Rotterdam with the Black Sea on the Ukrainian/Romanian border. The inland waterway communication system also provides a link to the Mediterranean via the Rhine-Rhone Waterway. The Black Sea Canal cuts through the Dobrogea platform to link the Danube directly to the Black Sea, south of Constanta, thus avoiding the delta area."

On day 4, after breakfast onboard, we gathered for the city tour of "Constanta, aka Tomin, Romania's second largest city and an ancient crossroads, 185 miles from the Bosporus Strait, a place where people from many of the Eastern European cultures and religions mingled and mixed through the ages. It has been a sixth-century BC Greek colony, a Roman outpost in the first century AD, and as recently as the late 20th century a coveted Soviet port" (GCT).

We were lucky – the sun was shining while we made our way through the narrow streets of Old Town and saw for the first time places in this port town where "Greeks, Romans and Turks had settled since 600 BC. It is after all, the oldest extant city in Romania, with a population of over 387,000.00. The port is the largest on the Black Sea, and one of the largest ports in Europe" (GCT).

We toured the National History and Archeological Museum, which emphasized artifacts from Greek, Roman, and Daco-Roman civilizations, among others. Two statues are highlights of the museum: the Glykon Snake (second century AD) and Fortuna and Pontos (which depicts the god of the Black Sea next to the goddess Fortuna). Both are revered as protectors of Constanta and her port and were fitting highlights of the exhibit. We drove past the Orthodox church and stopped in briefly to look at the Orthodox icons on the ceiling of the nineteenth-century Eastern Orthodox St. Paul and Peter's Cathedral. After trying to appreciate the remnants of the 9,150-square-foot, and once very colorful, mosaic-paved Roman Edifice of Ancient Tomis, which dates back to the fourth century, we ended up at their pride and joy, an art-nouveau-style casino built between World War I and World War II. The casino stands at a prominent spot, and one can easily see that it once looked rather flamboyant. Yet, at the time of my visit in 2005, the place was in need of some serious attention.

I walked on the promenade in front of the casino and went down a flight of stairs to the beach, hoping that eventually the Romanians would be able to restore this truly lovely spot, a favorite for vacationers, to its original beauty. I must not forget to mention Ovid's Square and the statue of the Roman poet Publius Ovidius Naso, designed by the sculptor Ettore Ferrari in 1887. The emperor Augustus had exiled Ovid to Tomis in 8 AD. I have a volume of Ovid's poems in my library, and when standing in front of the statue I reminisced about Norbert, my very youthful student friend whom I met during my student years in Hannover. When we parted, he handed me this volume of Ovid's poems as a token of friendship. Like many of my other friends and lovers, separated from me by an ocean, he too faded away little by little. But the memories return like the ebb and flow of the seas. Here it is, the Black Sea!

After lunch onboard the MS *Aria*, while I unpacked my suitcase in my comfortable cabin with a big window, we entered the Black Sea Canal and continued cruising toward Ruse. During the afternoon sail, I listened to the commentary on the Black Sea Canal, a forty-mile waterway praised as an engineering marvel and one of the most important commercial links in Eastern Europe, connecting the North Sea to the Black Sea via the Rhine–Main–Danube Canal. It became notorious in the 1950s, when communist Romania sent thousands of political prisoners to labor camps and forced them to work on the canal's excavation using shovels and pickaxes. Many lost their lives in the process. The main reasons for building the canal were to facilitate navigation by avoiding the delta of the Danube and to shorten the distance to both the Black Sea and the Soviet Volga–Don Canal and Central Europe. In looking at the rocky terrain from the ship, I shuddered to think how difficult the excavations must have been.

"Nicolae Ceausescu's devastating dictatorial rule was brought to an end by the people's revolt of December 1989, which closed the historical gap Romania had been living in for 45 years, and opened a new page in Romania's contemporary history.... The period between 1992 and 1996 can be seen as a transition towards a new political, economic and social environment. In a national referendum, 85% of the population voted for joining the EU" (GCT).

Bulgaria

Veliko Tarnovo

Early on day 5, we passed through customs at Ruse, Bulgaria's fourth-largest city and main port on the Danube, and as I had signed up for an optional tour of Veliko Tarnovo and Arbanassi, the motor coach took us directly to Veliko Tarnovo, the capital of Bulgaria from 1186 to 1394, located high on hills, with a good view overlooking the Yantra River.

We started out at the great fortified wall of Tsarevets Hill and passed through the old city, whose ruins date back to the Byzantine and Ottoman empires. Veliko Tarnovo struck me as a rather unusual city. The stone houses were perched one above the other on the steep bank of the Yantra River. "Tzarevets is the place of the patriarchal church and royal palaces. The Tsarevets Citadel was the strongest Bulgarian Fortress during the 12th–14th centuries until it came under Ottoman rule in 1393–1878 and the fortress was destroyed" (GCT).

The lunch at a local restaurant was special. A group of locals, dressed in their regional costumes, richly and colorfully embroidered, surprised us with a dance on the lawn in front of the restaurant. Nice!

We continued to Arbanassi, a village in the Veliko Tarnovo municipality, set on a high plateau and known for seventeenth- and eighteenth-century churches and examples of Bulgarian National Revival architecture. "Arbanassi is one of the most historic towns in Bulgaria. Over 80 houses as well as several churches and two monasteries reflect massive architectural styles of the 17th and 18th centuries in this region" (GCT). Four of the friendly Orthodox priests posed for me in front of the monastery.

Back on the ship, we gathered to listen to music before dinner.

Day 6 was a welcome intermission. We could just sit and relax in a comfortable deck chair and observe life along the banks of the Danube while listening to a bridge commentary that focused on Iron Gates I, II, and III.

The section of the river at this point has a reputation for hazardous whirlpools, currents and rocks just below the surface. Until the 1970s, passage through this section was limited to 200 or so days of the year when the water level was high enough, and even then experienced captains had to be taken on board. Substantial deepening and widening of sections of the Iron Gates took place in 1896 but the river did not become easily navigable until the 1970s with the construction of the Iron Gates. The Kazan gorge, 10 miles upstream of Orsova, has cliffs which fall 1,968 feet into the Danube.

River traffic passes through a double lock system to descend the 108 feet to the Drobeta side of the dam. There are locks on both the Serbian and the Romanian side of the river. . . . Cazanele Mari and Cazanele Mici represent the final narrowing of the gorge. They are cut in Cretaceous limestone. Cazanele Mari is 650–1,000 feet wide, dominated by the steep slopes of the Ciucarul Mare Hill. Here the river has its greatest depth in the gorge (147 feet). The Sirbatu Mic is the narrowest section of the gorge (492 feet). (GCT)

Going through locks was not new to me, but I took enough pictures to satisfy my curious friends back home. I must say this particular stretch was a bit more dramatic, that is, rugged. Up to that point, the countryside had lacked excitement (no *wows* or *ohs*). There were few villages, farmhouses, or herds of cattle or sheep to see. Once, I noticed a farmer crossing a ditch with an empty horse-drawn cart, going toward a wheat field, I think. – No one was working in the fields, and as a result nobody waved to us as we sailed past. The dwellings we saw in the distance were all in need of some repair, it seemed. They reminded me of those I saw in the former GDR or while traveling on the Trans-Sib Railway in Russia. Of course, we have an overabundance of run-down houses throughout the United States as well – and without communistic regimes, mind you.

That night, we cruised along a stretch of the Danube where the river once raged and pounded its way through deep gorges. "In the 1960s Yugoslavia and Romania cooperated on a joint venture that raised the level of the Danube with a series of hydroelectric dams called the Iron Gates . . . which put the once spectacular 2-mile long gorge under water" (GCT). – I thought about the Three Gorges hydroelectric dam across the Yangtze River in China, which I had seen in 2004 and found mind-boggling. I wondered what they would say about this disappearing gorge. I was glad I saw the gorges on the Yangtze before they all vanished.

Serbia and Montenegro

On day 7, our ship passed Iron Gate I during the night, but we were awake when we sailed through the cataracts route, the narrowest and deepest part of the Danube, which was exciting to see and quite striking. At this point, the gorge lies between Romania to the north and Serbia to the south. The river separates the southern Carpathian Mountains from the northwestern foothills of the Balkan Mountains. Amazing!

After lunch, we docked at Veliko Gradiste, a charming town of some seven thousand inhabitants, and took a motor coach to Belgrade, the capital of Serbia and Montenegro, one of Europe's oldest cities, and the center of political and cultural life in the country. "Belgrade and the rest of Serbia-Montenegro were just emerging from many years of repressive rule" (GCT).

Covering 39.517 square miles and with a combined population of eleven million, the Federation of Serbia and Montenegro is slightly smaller than Kentucky. It has four different geographic zones: to the north, fertile plains; to the east, limestone ranges and basins; to the southeast, mountains and hills; to the southwest, an extremely high shoreline with no islands off the coast. – "During WWII, all regions of Yugoslavia united under the strong hand of Josip Broz Tito. Tito was leader of the partisans and became, after the war, the lifelong president over SFRJ (Socialistic Federal Republic of Yugoslavia). Tito died in May 1980" (GCT).

Federal Republic of Yugoslavia

Belgrade

"In 1992 Serbia and Montenegro declared a new 'Federal Republic of Yugoslavia' (FRY) and, under President Milosevic, Serbia led various unsuccessful military intervention efforts to unite Serbs in neighboring republics into a 'Greater Serbia.' In 1999, massive expulsions by FRY forces and Serb paramilitaries of ethnic Albanians living in Kosovo provoked an international response, including the

NATO bombing of Serbia and the stationing of NATO and Russian peacekeepers in Kosovo. (Belgrade was also bombed in April 1941 and occupied by the Germans from April 1941 to October 1944.) ... The UN Interim Administration Mission in Kosovo has governed Kosovo since June 1999, under the authority of UN Security Council Resolution 1244. ... In March 2003 presidential candidate Zoran Djindic was assassinated in Belgrade, a sign that Serbia is still in a period of political disarray, turmoil, unrest, chaos and instability" (GCT).

Belgrade is one of Europe's oldest cities and the center of political and cultural life in the country. As we drove through the city of over one million inhabitants, we saw signs that she was beginning to emerge from the years of repressive rule. The local guides were especially kind, I thought. The city was built centuries ago along important east–west trade routes and used as a gateway to Western Europe from the Balkans. We stopped at Kalemegdan Castle, with its impressive fortress overlooking the rivers, and continued with visits to the old Town Hall and St. Sava Orthodox Cathedral, considered one of the ten largest churches in the world. Sava was the founder of the Serbian Orthodox Church. It was refreshing to see many parks throughout the city, and I appreciated that we had time for a walk downtown on Knez Mihailova Street, the main pedestrian and shopping zone in Belgrade. It gave me time to chat with a student couple selling earrings, necklaces, etc. at a nearby stand. I saw very few shoppers. – I did not have time to go inside Princess Ljubica's well-preserved residence. It was built in 1831, during the reign of Prince Milos Obrenovic (1783–1860) and is one of the best-preserved historic houses in Belgrade. It is now a museum.

In the late afternoon, back on the ship, I attended the Discovery Series lecture "Serbia-Montenegro: Past and Present." We learned more about this historic region and the situation of the Balkans since the end of the war in the former Yugoslavia. I was somewhat familiar with some of the events taking place in Yugoslavia and welcomed this opportunity to hear more about it.

Day 8 began with a visit to the Tito Memorial, erected in honor of Josep Broz Tito, born in 1892 in what was then the Austro-Hungarian Empire. He held Yugoslavia together as an independent country during the turmoil that followed World War II and the subsequent Cold War. This visit was an emotional experience for me, because I was a semiadmirer of Tito's during the Cold War. Yet, when I actually stood at his mausoleum, the House of Flowers, I was amazed at the unwavering devotion of the thousands of visitors that flock to his tomb annually. "The tomb includes an exhibition of gifts sent to Tito, including paintings, love letters, and crocheted tablecloths. It's located on the grounds of the Museum of Yugoslav History, home to more than 200,000 items from Yugoslavia's 20th century history, most emphasizing Tito's life and work" (GCT).

According to GCT's literature, "Tito rose to power during World War II. After the Nazis invaded Yugoslavia in 1941, the Yugoslavian monarchy fled the country.

Tito's communists organized the Partisans, a resistance group who fought fiercely against occupation. Post-war Tito became Prime Minister and worked to rebuild the country and unite its six republics (Croatia, Slovenia, Serbia, Montenegro, Bosnia & Herzegovina, and Macedonia). The war had stirred up ethnic tensions between republics, which Tito suppressed – through sometimes brutal means – under the Yugoslavian national slogan of 'brotherhood and unity.'... The ethnic and nationalist tensions Tito had held back for half a century exploded a decade after his death, leading to the Yugoslav wars that killed 125,000 people in the 1990s. Many in the former Yugoslavia blame Tito's repressive and autocratic regime for covering lingering ethnic hatred with a veneer of communist ideals. Today, Yugoslavia is gone and its former republics face uncertain futures as independent countries, leaving Marshal Tito's dream of 'Brotherhood and Unity' a relic of the past. He pursued a lifelong policy of 'non-alignment.' His funeral was the largest state funeral in history, attended by dignitaries from 128 countries."

As I write, I realize it was only a year later, in 2006, that I stood in much greater amazement at the tomb of Mahatma Gandhi, on the banks of the River Yamuna, in Delhi, India.

I remember Tito's tomb very well, but what struck me even more during this visit was what I saw along the roadside when heading back to the ship. I think the bus driver and even our guide did not want us to see the huge garbage piles at the foot of the embankment on our right-hand side, where I sat. Men, women, children, and an emaciated mutt were crawling around among the many piles of trash, junk, and waste covered up with plastic bags, tarps, tin roofs, and the like. Eventually, we were told the people were Roma (Gypsies) and that these places, where they tried to survive, were colonies that existed in and around Belgrade. One of the excuses for the problem was that they preferred to live this way and that, when they were given improved living spaces, they would look just as run-down before long. – It's the same explanation and excuse I have heard in other third-world countries. It is almost impossible to change certain habits, so why even try? – I heard that one of their means of survival is to collect and shrink cartoons, which they then sell. This devastating site reminded me of the stark poverty I saw outside Johannesburg, South Africa. It was sickening. For some reason, I had long romanticized the Gypsies and their culture. I had heard of them traveling through the countryside with all their kids and possessions in plane wagons, stealing chickens or such in villages, but also playing the violin rather well to entertain villagers in exchange for a few pennies or food. In Part I of my memoirs, I wrote about the time my mother's older sister was mistaken for one of them because of her curly black hair. Her brother spotted her on the Gypsies' wagon as they were leaving the village. The Roms belong to the millions of "forgotten children" around the globe.

Novi Sad

The driver dropped us off at the ship, and we sailed for Novi Sad (New Seed), a city northwest of Belgrade on the Danube River, which we toured after an onboard lunch. It is the capital of the autonomous province of Vojvodina and one of the largest economic and cultural centers in the region. I assure you I was not the only person in our group who had never heard of Novi Sad. I had no idea it was the second-largest city in Serbia and Montenegro and the center of a Serbian literary revival in the eighteenth and early nineteenth centuries.

Here is what we saw in this rather lovely town, still untouched by heavy tourism: "Some of the great monuments and buildings on the Square of Liberty are the monument to Svetozar Miletic, the work of Ivan Mestrovic, the old City Hall in neo-Renaissance style (1894), and the monumental cathedral in pseudo-Gothic style with the inner Tyrol woodwork and several interesting icons. This structure was designed by the architect Djordje Molnar and built by the end of the 19th century. Behind the cathedral there is the old Deanery built in 1808" (GCT). Fortunately, the site was not destroyed during the war.

A most interesting fact for me was that on the Square of Liberty, some ten thousand people gathered to demonstrate against President Milosevic, who is no more. The former president of Serbia (originally the Socialist Republic of Serbia) from 1989 to 1997 was found dead in his cell in The Hague on March 11, 2006, thus ending his trial for crimes against humanity.

We liked the onboard show put on before dinner by a local group from Vojvodiana, but we were on deck later that evening when we approached the Novi Sad pontoon bridge, stretching across the Danube. They opened a section of the bridge for our passage. A temporary pontoon bridge, it replaced the original bridge spanning the river, which was destroyed during a NATO bombing raid in 1999. It was completed in 2006, not long after we had sailed there.

Croatia

Osijek

On day 9, we docked and passed through customs in Vukovar, site of the worst artillery shelling of the Croatian-Serbian war. We saw the ruins briefly in passing, and the driver slowed down so we could take a picture, which I did, even though I detest the sight of war ruins. Once you have lived through wars, you have had enough. On the way to Osijek, the guide explained that it was the fourth-largest city in Croatia, with a population of over 128,000, and the site of the war between, on one side, the Croatian National Guard and forces loyal to the Croatian government and, on the other, the Army of the Republic of Serbian Krajina, supported by the Yugoslav National Army and other Serb paramilitary units (from July 1991 until the spring of 1992, and beyond).

We attended the Discovery Series lecture "Croatia: Past and Present," which provided a historical framework for our city tour.

Situated on the Drava River, about 15 miles from the mouth of the Danube, the area of the city was populated even in prehistoric times, and the first urban settlement was erected by the Romans. But the area's advantageous geographical location made it prey to assault throughout the centuries. It was destroyed by the Huns, rebuilt in the Middle Ages, destroyed by the Turks, and rebuilt again in the 18th century. As a result, Osijek boasts an eclectic architectural heritage . . . such as the Tvrdja, a unique and military complex that lies in the center of the city and was built between 1712 and 1721 by the new Austrian authorities; a neo-Gothic Cathedral of Saints Peter and Paul, with a 290-foot spire, and a striking, 690-foot modern pedestrian bridge that rises over the Drava.

Reliving its own cruel history in our era, Osijek was heavily damaged during the Croatian-Serbian war of 1991–95. (GCT)

It was depressing to drive past the houses that had not been repaired or rebuilt since the war. They reminded me of the bombed houses, including our own, in Hannover, Germany. Though I must say, while Hannover was almost totally wiped out, Osijek was not.

At one point, when the bus drove through farmland, I spotted a very amusing sign on the roadside. It read, "Americans Sorry but we could not wait for you any longer! Storks – Croatia." A stork was painted next to the text. We did see a stork's nest on one of the rooftops in Croatia. I was reminded of Germany, where storks also like to nest.

At the time, peaceful Osijek appeared to be experiencing a rebirth of civic pride and cultural and economic achievement. We had a sense of this new, and hopefully lasting, era of peace when we visited a school where a large group of youngsters had gathered in the gym to greet us with a song. A similar ambiance prevailed when we sat around a table in the small house, nicely and humbly furnished, of our Croatian hosts, who had invited us for lunch. Somehow, no one broached the topic of the recent war. We chatted with them about their work in the fields and about the children and the subjects they studied in school. The host was a teacher who spoke English. It was obvious that he very much appreciated the opportunity to host us Americans and thus to show off his English-language skills. It was nice.

The bus took us to the ship, which docked in the Hungarian port of Mohacs, the place where a battle was fought in 1526 between the Hungarians and Bohemians on one side and the Ottoman Empire on the other, which Sultan Suleiman the

Magnificent won. Of course, it eventually ended up in Hungarian hands. I will spare you the details of how it all happened. As a footnote, I add that in talking to some of the Croatian crew on the ship and to people who had traveled in other parts of Croatia, I realized that if ever I return, I should definitely go to Dubrovnik and other scenic spots along the Adriatic Sea!

On October 6 – day 10 – we were happy to have finished the cruise portion of the trip and looked forward to hitting Budapest.

Hungary

Budapest

Since I had visited Budapest before, I skipped most of the sightseeing tours. I had invited my young friends from the Czech Republic, whom I had met in Krakow in 2003. They had borrowed a little car and driven to Budapest to meet me. I treated them to a couple of nights in our very classy hotel, which almost overwhelmed them. They had never experienced such "glamour," if you wish. I was pleased to see them again, but let them go sightseeing on their own. We met for breakfast and in the evening for dinner, and before we knew it, it was time to say good-bye. We corresponded for several years, until they got married. Then, little by little, we lost touch. Thus it goes in life – friends come and go.

By the way, if you think the Danube River is as blue as the lyrics to the Strauss waltz claim, you are dead wrong; it is milk-chocolate brown and looks like café au lait! And I am sorry to say it, but the portion of the Danube from Constanta to Budapest is anything but romantic. We saw few idyllic villages (or even houses) along the riverbanks, and even fewer people. I think it stems from the fact that for so many years, people were banned from living too close to the river, which must have been a tempting escape route. Or perhaps they refrained from living too close to the river to avoid the dangers of extreme flooding.

June 2013 – Germany's rivers – the Elbe, the Danube, and the Saale – are devastating many of the towns that lie alongside them. They are calling it the flood of the century.

On October 9, the thirteen-day adventure ended, and I returned home from Budapest fairly relaxed and in one piece.

BOSTON TO MIAMI – MS NORWEGIAN DREAM

My newly discovered Beardsley relatives, who were avid sailors, had told me about the biennial sailing regattas from Newport, Rhode Island, to Bermuda, in which Doc's grandson Wayne had occasionally participated. It was one of the reasons why, on July 16, 2002, I booked NCL's Boston to Miami cruise, for which their MS *Norwegian Dream* would set sail on October 25, 2002. Another reason was a positive experience with their line in 2002 on the Baltic. It was a cruise to Bermuda and other islands in the Caribbean, which up until then I had only heard about. These megaships are a bit over the top, but for solo travelers like me, they are a tolerable alternative. On October 25, 2002, I flew from Indianapolis to Boston and embarked on this 46,000-gross-tonnage monstrosity in the late afternoon. The gin palace, with a 1,750-passenger capacity, was christened by superstar Diana Ross in 1992 with champagne and cost some $240 million. She was later "stretched" by 133 feet in Bremerhaven, Germany, for an additional $69 million. I do not have to tell you it was a dazzling affair, and as a Latitude Member I was assigned a very nice outside cabin with a big window, which was great.

The ship left Boston Harbor on Friday, October 25, at 4:00 p.m. After unpacking my suitcase, I explored the ship and looked for a spot on deck where I could hide out and read, sunbathe, just stare at the sea, watch the seagulls sailing overhead, and dream . . .

Bermuda

Hamilton

After a day at sea, we docked at King's Wharf, the original cruise-ship berth in the Royal Naval Dockyard of Bermuda, at 1:00 p.m. on Sunday, October 27. This docking facility is for ships too large for the docks in Hamilton and St. George.

I did not sign up for any shore excursions scheduled for Sunday and just walked around King's Wharf for a while, taking pictures that were nice but not exactly awesome. The seashore was interesting, but there was too much going on, and the architecture was OK but not impressive. –

The next day, Monday, October 28, I joined a local Bermuda driver/guide for a three-hour sightseeing excursion in the capital city, Hamilton. Even though we came upon some pink-sand beaches on the South Shore and saw the Gibbs Hill Lighthouse and Somerset Drawbridge, the smallest of its kind in the western hemisphere, I had a hard time getting excited. If you like pastel-colored two-story houses, you'll find some of those along the shore. But all in all, this glimpse of Hamilton taught me that Bermuda is not a place where I would want to spend a honeymoon, as one of my ex-friends had in the early 60s. Unlike the Romneys or others of their clan, or even Doc's yacht-racing, well-heeled grandson, I was not looking for a bank in which to hide any of my nonmillions. It was probably the reason this place had become so well developed since the British moved in. After all, Hamilton is the capital of the British Overseas Territory of Bermuda and its financial center. I could, if I owned a yacht, think of more enticing places to go racing. I am sure I would have liked the place more in its pristine state, when its namesake, the Spanish sea captain Juan de Bermúdez, first spotted it in 1505.

British Virgin Islands

Tortola

I was not exactly sorry when we took off for Tortola the next morning around 6:00 a.m. After another day at sea, we docked there at noon, to get at least a whiff of this largest of the more than fifty islands comprising the British Virgin Islands.

On the southern shore of this twelve-by-three-mile island is Road Town, the capital and largest city, whose population is only half of that of the entire British Virgin Islands. "Christopher Columbus discovered what are now known as the Virgin Islands during his second voyage to the New World in 1493. Faced with the task of christening dozens of quays and islets, he wisely named them in honor of the legendary army of 1,100 virgins who were martyred along with St. Ursula by an angry pagan prince who wanted Ursula to marry him. Though Columbus claimed the islands for the Spanish Crown, Spain's interests lay with the continent's richer colonies" (NCL). I was quite surprised to find out how the islands got their name, because I spent four years in an Ursuline boarding school in Germany. A bunch of the nuns at Sankt Ursula would have deserved to be victims of the Spaniard. If only I had known then what I learned on this trip – half a century later! Darn!

We did not stop at Virgin Gorda, the third largest of the BVIs, but were told it was a favorite of those who love to hide out on the many deserted beaches that fringe the island. Maybe next time.

I liked what I saw of Tortola when traveling through Road Town, where we saw the humble police headquarters, the old prison destined to be a new museum, a couple of churches, a high school, etc. We stopped briefly at their botanical garden and admired a colorful array of tropical plants before ascending the hillside of Great Mountain for photo stops. We had ample opportunity for more pics on top of Sky World. I declare, the 360-degree view of the island and its neighbors from up there was truly breathtaking. The skies were so clear we could see Saint Thomas and

Jost Van Duke, birthplace of William Thornton, who, we were told, designed the Capitol Building in Washington, D.C. The island trip required travel on winding, picturesque roads with forever-changing vistas of the crystal-clear turquoise waters hugging pristine, powdery-white beaches and rugged shores. The hills were covered with lush meadows, trees, and bushes, which gave this small island a rather exotic sheen – accented, of course, by the abundant palm trees. We ended up at Pusser's Landing before heading back to the ship via the scenic Drakes Highway. Judging by the fancy yachts in the harbor and the ritzy villas in the hills, this place was on the way to being taken over by upscale international tourism. What a pity. Anyhow, I prefer this place to Bermuda and would not mind if someone invited me for a sunset sail. I could easily have found a secluded cove in which to anchor and sip a glass of champagne, preferably with a hot lover. As it was, I snapped a sunset photo from the upper deck of the *Dream* before I retired to my cabin. No, I did not dream.

US Virgin Islands

Saint Thomas

We left Tortola at 8:00 p.m. and docked at Saint Thomas, US Virgin Islands, at 7:00 a.m. on Wednesday, October 31, to spend a day getting acquainted with that romantic island, which, combined with Saint Croix, Water Island, and Saint John, is a county and constituent district of the USVI (unincorporated district), of which I had heard much. At the time of our visit, the population of Saint Thomas (31.24 square miles) was a bit over 51,000. The MS *Dream* had anchored at this harbor, claimed by many to be one of the world's most beautiful, and we were afforded a nice view of the capital, Charlotte Amalie, an idyllic-looking village that spreads into the lower hills. Unfortunately, few traces remained of the era of the Danish settlers, who came in the 1600s. Harbor development and trade in indigo, tobacco, and cotton had been replaced by silk and leather, now stored in stone buildings.

Saint John

Saint John (named after John the Apostle?) had been praised as one of the most romantic islands we would see on this trip. Thus, I had signed up for the Saint John Island Tour, which NCT advertised as follows: "Cruise by ferry along St. Thomas, southeast coast, then across Pillsbury Sound to St. John. This mostly-undeveloped 20-square-mile island is two-thirds national park, with verdant hills, isolated bays, gorgeous white sand beaches, crystal-clear water and incredible scenery. Once ashore, you will have a tour of some of the island's highlights. Back on the coast road, you'll stop at several breathtaking overlooks: Cinnamon Bay, Trunk Bay, Caneel Bay and Hawksnest Bay. The tour concludes in Cruz Bay, where you will board the ferry back to St. Thomas."

When I close my eyes and think about Saint Thomas, I see some of the most gorgeous beaches I encountered while traveling the globe. At that time, few people could be spotted on the beaches. I was secretly wishing to return sometime – alone or with company. There is nothing like the turquoise waters cuddling pristine white-sand beaches, with palm trees in the background. It's so intoxicating, and definitely seductive. Use your imagination!

On Friday, November 1, we cruised the turquoise waters of the Caribbean, doing whatever pleased us.

Dutch Caribbean – Netherlands Antilles

Bonaire

On Saturday, November 2, at 8:00 a.m., the *Dream* docked in Kralendijk (which means "coral reef"), the capital city and main port of the Caribbean Netherlands island Bonaire. We had ten hours to explore. I neither windsurf, a sport for which this place is famous, nor snorkel. I would have loved to take a trip to Venezuela, the place from which, around 1000 AD, the Caiquetio, a branch of the Arawak Indians, sailed some fifty miles to settle in Bonaire. For ridiculous political reasons, Venezuela was off-limits. I signed up for the Scenic Combo excursion, which sounded like something I would enjoy. FYI, Bonaire is the B of the ABC islands, Aruba and Curaçao being the other two sisters in the Dutch Caribbean.

We departed from Kralendijk and traveled along "the rustic northern coastline with a first stop at '1,000 Steps,' a limestone staircase of 67 challenging steps to reach the beach carved into the beautifully landscaped seaside cliff" (Brochure). The place is famous for its dive site. We looked in vain for pink flamingos at Gotomeer, the scenic inland salt lake, even though this saltwater lagoon is one of their few nesting places in the world.

Rincon, a small town with clusters of red-roofed houses and the oldest Spanish settlement on the island, dating back to the sixteenth century, was our next stop. I was not very happy to hear the place had been home to many slave families, who labored in the nearby plantations and salt fields. They often had to walk seven hours to get there and to return home. On the way to Seroe Largu, which is nearly four hundred feet above sea level, we stopped at a place where aboriginal Indian inscriptions could be seen, and from Seroe Largu we could see Klein Bonaire (Little Bonaire), which, in contrast to the northern part of the island, lies to the south and is flat. It is home to natural salt pans that feed a salt-processing industry. The color contrasts between the azure sea, pinkish salt pans, snow-white mounds, and clear blue skies are out of this world.

The old wattle-and-daub houses, which slaves built centuries ago and which sit amidst century plants, aka agave, looked strange. Century plants take decades to flower, an event we unfortunately missed. An iguana was crawling around in the holes of a huge, dark boulder. We passed Pink Beach on the way to the four or five stone huts that served as shelters for the slaves who worked in the salt pans. These huts measured 6 x 8 feet and held twenty-three slaves each. Today, they are whitewashed to hide the crimes against humanity they enabled only some 150 years ago. They look rather nice (although the appearance is deceiving) with the white salt mounds in the background and a clear blue sky above. Why was I not surprised to find out that Americans in World War II also used Bonaire? A soccer field served as an airfield where bombers took off in pursuit of Nazi U-boats. They say these islands are paradise, but when you learn about their history, it never fails to put a damper on the total experience. It is slavery, war, greed, and power, again and again. It will not stop during my lifetime . . .

Curaçao

We took off on Saturday, November 2, and docked on Sunday, November 3, at 8:00 a.m. in Willemstad, the capital of Curaçao, located in the Southern Caribbean Sea and a constituent country of the Kingdom of the Netherlands.

The influence of the Netherlands as well as Spain became obvious as soon as the pastel-colored facades of the houses in the harbor came into view. Indeed, the fanciful arcades, gables, and bulging columns are stark reminders of Dutch and Spanish colonial burghers. Curaçao, largest of the Netherland's Antilles, boasts a fascinating mix of settlers. They came from Portugal, Africa, Arabia, Europe, etc. and left their distinctive mark on this island, situated only seventeen miles from the northeast coast of Venezuela. Here, Dutch is the official language, but English is spoken by all as well. In case you did not know: since the natural harbor of Willemstad seemed to be an ideal location for trade, the infamous Dutch West India Company founded the capital of Willemstad and was responsible for establishing Curaçao as a center for slave trade during the seventeenth and eighteenth centuries. To make a long story short, they too became prosperous through exploiting millions of slaves, becoming sinfully rich by forcing them to labor. Once I start digging deeper into the crimes against slaves, I get sick to my stomach!

It was Sunday, November 3, when I joined a group for the Discover Curaçao trip. We drove west into the country past the salt flats, again absent the pink flamingos, to San Willibrodo, the rather sizable Catholic church named after the patron saint of the Netherlands and neatly painted in light yellow. We stopped to get a good look at an old *conuco* (farm) house built some 150 years earlier, when Aruba was under Spanish, French, and Dutch occupation. The house seemed solidly built and well-preserved, as the fresh coat of deep yellow testified. We climbed some fifty steps to see the Hato Caves: "Deep within the cliffs, overlooking the north shore of the island, is a dramatic collection of grottos filled with stalactites, stalagmites, and crystal clear pools, centuries in the making. At the foot of the caves we easily negotiated the Petroglyph Trail. A short stroll took us past an ancient shelter for slave shepherds and the guide pointed out exceptional 1,500-year-old religious scenes carved into the rock walls. From the Hato Caves we continued to the Curaçao Museum in Otrabanda, founded in 1946 and housed with a former military quarantine hospital. The museum displays contemporary art and an exhibition of life in Curaçao during the mid-nineteenth century" (NCL). We had time for a magnificent photo stop when crossing the Queen Juliana Bridge, two hundred feet above the capital, and then drove through Punda, in the heart of Willemstad, and past the Mikvé Israel-Emanuel Synagogue, the oldest Jewish synagogue in use in the western hemisphere, before returning to our *Dream*.

Aruba

On Monday, November 4, at 8:00 a.m., we docked at Orangestad (Orangetown), the capital and largest city of Aruba.

In the morning, on the 4x4 Country Crossing Trip, I was thankful that this island adventure actually delivered what it promised. It took us to Aruba's most exotic sites: "the Casibari Rock Formation, Bushiribana Gold Mill Ruins, ocean-carved Natural Bridge, picturesque Alto Vista Chapel, a stunning variety of lush tropical flowers, i.e. bougainvillea, hibiscus, shaving brush, flower of gold, different blossoming trees as well as a stop at the town square with time to admire the charming Dutch-Colonial architecture with pastel colored facades and ornate gables" (NCL). My favorite photo of Orangestad was the tall, white, round California Lighthouse, named for a steamship that wrecked nearby in 1891. It looked picture-perfect with the turquoise sea in the background and the blue sky above. Our trip ended with a stop at the famous Arashi Beach, where I did not splash but just sat in the shade of a palm tree, mesmerized by the azure waters of the Caribbean and thinking about how lucky I was to bask in such natural beauty all by my lonesome self.

I felt so joyful that I ventured toward Little Switzerland, a jeweler, to take a look. I had to pass three or four emaciated mutts, which, by the way, can be a real nuisance in the Caribbean Islands. I sighed with relief when someone restrained one that seemed inclined to follow me right into the upscale store. I heard that these mutts end up, more times than not, on some islander's dinner table. – After spending plenty of time looking and bargaining, I treated myself to an emerald-and-diamond necklace. When leaving the store, I noticed the exact gemstone globe I had bought for myself a few years earlier at T. J. Maxx for $300 – but here the price tag was $3,399 (at least it was tax-free). How about that? When I received my Diners Club bill a month later, I discovered that someone in that store had had the audacity to charge $2,400 for a plane ticket to Africa. Fortunately, Diners Club caught the fraud in time.

The Bahamas

Nassau

On Thursday, November 7, after two relaxing days at sea, we docked at Great Stirrup Cay, in the Bahamas. It is the northernmost island in the Berry Islands chain, and NCL purchased it specifically to treat their passengers, including yours truly, to "an uninhabited tropical island. . . . It is an unspoiled paradise of magnificent white sandy beaches, majestic coconut palms, and calm, pristine waters where an abundance of colorful marine life inhabits the surrounding coral reefs" (NCL).

We also had the chance to sail over to the monstrosity called "Atlantis," on Paradise Island, which we saw from up close. As I did not want to sunbathe in the hot sun, I decided to see what this massive, red stone structure, which sticks out of the sea like a sore thumb and is constantly advertised on TV, is all about. The guide explained that the bridge suite joining the Royal Towers cost Michael Jackson a mere $25,000 per night. – I liked the huge aquarium most of all, and was not in the least surprised by the glitz inside. It reminded me somewhat of casinos in Las Vegas and Atlantic City and of the luxurious ambiance of mega cruise liners. Such obscene kitsch is not my cup of tea. I am certain, though, that kids love all the excitement this megaresort has to offer.

August 24, 2012 – SOS! As I write, everybody is watching Storm Isaac zeroing in on the Caribbean and Florida, where on August 27 the GOP convention will start in Tampa. I just noticed that NCL is adjusting their schedules in response to a possible hurricane. The coincidence seems so bizarre.

Why? Because when NCL docked on schedule in Miami, on November 8, 2002, at 7:00 a.m., I wished they had paid closer attention to my schedule. As it turned out, they put me on the wrong airport-transfer bus. Instead of sending me to Miami for my 12:05 ATA departure flight, which would arrive in Indianapolis via Chicago at 5:50 p.m., they put me on the bus to the Fort Lauderdale airport, a mistake I noticed when I saw the green stickers on the luggage of the other passengers. I quickly got off this bus, retrieved my luggage from underneath it, and was taken to the bus to Miami, where, despite everybody's assurance that I would arrive in time, I was thirty-five minutes late, missed my plane, and had to reschedule my flight, which involved taking a shuttle bus, at my expense, back to Fort Lauderdale and notifying the limo in Indianapolis about the change. I was pretty disgusted, to say the least. I landed in Indianapolis after midnight and arrived home at 1:30 a.m. A week later, I sent a long letter to NCL, blasting them and their services. I asked for a refund for my extra expenses, but do not remember whether I ever received a dime. I have steered clear of NCL ever since.

AUSTRIA

In August 2010, I decided to cancel a trip to Vietnam, Laos, and Cambodia, which I had booked earlier that year with OAT, and to replace it with Christmas Markets along the Danube, a leisure cruise. Scheduled for November 23–30, it would take me from Vienna, Austria, to Nuremberg, Germany. I was reminded that in Asian countries, temperatures are tropical, and Bangkok, Thailand, had been too hot for me. I planned to start out in Vienna, my favorite city, on my own and join the group a few days later, on November 23, for the cruise. I wanted to visit my good friends the Segebrechts in Bamberg for a few days at the end of the trip and planned to fly home from Munich on December 6. I was very happy when Mr. Johnny Pour at Hotel Kaiserin Elisabeth answered my call. He remembered me from my stay in 2008 and was only too pleased to reserve a room for me for November 18–23, 2010.

Vienna

I flew from Indianapolis to Vienna via London with American Airlines and British Air and arrived rather punctually at the hotel in the forenoon on November 18. I liked their VIP treatment, loved my room, and was ever so grateful when Mr. Pour informed me that he had been successful in securing tickets for me to a performance of Verdi's *Rigoletto*. The distinguished cast, including Vargas, Hvorostovsky, Ciofi, and others, made this opera experience as memorable as any I have ever had. Hvorostovsky is an incredible and legendary singer! A very attractive young Russian woman who had lived in Vienna for some sixteen years sat next to me, and we engaged in an exciting conversation during intermission. The performance of *The Nutcracker* at the Vienna State Opera, though the ballet was superb, was a bit disappointing. The modern set design dampened the magical ambiance I was used to. The concert with the Wiener Symphoniker at the Musikverein, where Georges Prêtre conducted a piano concert by Poulenc, with the sisters Katia and Marielle Labèque as soloists, was superb. However, I found the *Struwwelpeter* at the Burgtheater with Birgit Minichmayr somewhat shocking. In between, I spent an afternoon at the Albertina Museum, where I met a top administrator of the Vienna State Opera and his wife, decked out in a stunning fur coat. She had noticed my Tiffany solitaire diamond and admired it so much I decided to hide it for the duration of the cruise. They walked with me back to my hotel and were quite impressed when I told them about my musical friends Mark and Jee-Won Kosower. They, of course, knew Franz Welser-Möst, conductor of the Cleveland Symphony Orchestra and music director of the Wiener Symphoniker, but did not know that Mark was solo cellist at the CSO. I told them how sorry I was to miss *Don Giovanni*, to be performed at the Vienna State Opera a few weeks later, with Franz Welser-Möst conducting.

I took a cab to the famous Christkind Market, located in front of the grandiose Vienna City Hall, which I had visited a couple of years before, and went to Vienna's famous Sacher Hotel, built in 1832, one hundred years before I was born. I ordered several Sachertorten in their elegant café/restaurant downstairs, which I would mail to my European friends in time for Christmas.

CHRISTMAS MARKETS ALONG THE DANUBE – MS RIVER ADAGIO

On November 23, a driver for the Hotel Kaiserin Elisabeth dropped me off at the pier in plenty of time to get settled in on the MS *River Adagio*. The ship was decorated tastefully with Austrian and German Christmas ornaments, and a beautiful Christmas tree stood proudly in the center of the lounge, next to a baby grand. Soft Christmas music was audible in the background. It was a cozy welcome. *Wie schön*!

In my room I found an invitation from Captain Boris Car to join him at his table during the welcome dinner. After the port talk and before dinner, we were to come to the library to get to know him better, which in my case meant a chance to boast about some of my more exotic ship adventures, that is, my trips to the North Pole and to Antarctica. He was visibly impressed and I think a tad envious.

After a truly lovely dinner, of which I was able to eat only a third, I joined other passengers in the lounge to chat, soak up the Christmas ambiance, and listen to the relaxing music performed by their onboard musician, Indre. One of the passengers who stood out was a very old gentleman wearing a dark-green Biltmore Golden Pheasant fur-felt Tyrolean hat with a badger brush, which I had not seen in ages. When this very tall, skinny man, who used a mix of German and English to chatter rather incoherently with other passengers, started to try his luck with me, I instinctively moved away. The man did not look well. He seemed deadly sick. His dark-rimmed eyes looked hollow, the nose was extra-long and haggard, and the parchment-like skin on his face bordered on ashen. I could not look him in the face. Sorry. I think his name was Max.

After breakfast on November 24, I found a comfortable window spot in the lounge and enjoyed the scenic landscape, with its well-kept, terraced vineyards and an occasional castle, while we cruised through the lovely Wachau Valley, a twenty-five-mile stretch between Melk and Krems. The ship's program director spoke about the valley's importance for wines.

The MS *Adagio* arrived at Melk at 12:30, and an hour and a half later, the buses took off for our guided tour of Melk Abbey, which I had looked forward to, since I had never visited this famous baroque Benedictine abbey and the *Stiftskirche* (abbey church), perched high above the town of Melk on a rocky outcrop.

Melk is a historic town known for the dramatic 900-year-old Melk Abbey. This ornate structure began as a Roman border post, served as a tenth-century Babenberg fortress, and became a Benedictine monastery in 1089. The abbey, built in 1702–1736 by architect Jakob Prandlauer, was the inspiration for several details in Umberto Eco's novel The Name of the Rose, *including the description of an abbey being ravaged by fire, which happened to Melk Abbey in 1279 and 1683. The stately baroque edifice that stands today, with its twin towers and 208-foot-high dome, dates from its reconstruction in 1736.* (GCT)

I was a bit unhappy when it started to rain while we walked down the many steps into the courtyard of the abbey. The guide cut his lecture short so we could avoid standing in the downpour. As soon as I entered the abbey church, I was in awe of the frescoed walls and the marble sculptures, so typical of the baroque period. I was even more impressed when I stepped into the library, with two floors and a Troger ceiling. It holds some eighty thousand volumes of priceless works. After admiring the Marble Hall and glancing at the line of portraits in the Emperor's Gallery, I paused to look out of one of the large windows toward the Danube and wondered whether Napoleon had looked out the very same window when he campaigned against Austria with Melk as his headquarters. The view from up there is sublime!

I skipped walking down to see the small town of Melk, since it was raining so hard and I was anxious to return to the ship. I even neglected to take a picture of the abbey. Imagine that.

Today, Melk is also a prestigious coed monastery school with more than seven hundred students.

Salzburg

On November 25, our Thanksgiving, we arrived in Linz at 4:00 p.m. Being so close to my beloved Salzburg and having dreamed many times about seeing Mozart's birthplace surrounded by snowcapped mountains, I spent a mere $100 to satisfy my wish. The city was named (Salt Burg) after the barges that carried salt on the Salzach River. They had to pay a toll in the eighth century, a custom common for European communities located on rivers. – I was not disappointed. The mountains were white; Salzburg wore her most precious Christmas gown. Decorated and lighted Christmas trees filled every nook and cranny, and I was happy as a child exploring the many stalls, which displayed thousands of different ornaments from various alpine regions of Austria. After our guide had pointed out all the Mozart-related sites and others of which I have written previously, I made the most of our leisure time. We spent quite a bit of time in the Getreidegasse, known for Austrian shopping. I loved the intricate architectural details of this lane of shops and galleries, which were nestled under their skillfully crafted wrought-iron signs. The vaulted passageways leading to artisans' workshops and arcaded courtyards reminded me of their counterparts in Bern, Merano, and Bolzano. I stopped for a glass of *Glühwein* and eventually walked into the world-famous Christmas shop, Käthe Wohlfahrt, to fulfill a longtime wish. I bought a bright-red, wooden Advent wreath with angels sitting in the center, playing musical instruments. I think of Salzburg whenever it graces my table at Christmastime.

We returned to the ship at about 6:00 p.m., after a beautiful trip through the countryside. The snow had blanketed the trees, meadows, rooftops, and mountains. Cattle and horses were huddled together underneath shelters. It all seemed covered by a magic veil when, in the distance, the golden sun turned from orange to crimson red before disappearing on the horizon. The bus driver surprised us with *The Sound of Music* on the way home. Some were sleeping, but I stayed awake and loved every minute of it.

I also relished the Thanksgiving dinner on the MS *Adagio*, which included "Roasted Turkey with Red Wine Cranberry Sauce, Mashed Potatoes with Garlic and Mascarpone, Bread Stuffing with Apple and Chestnut, Maple Glazed Sweet Potatoes and Sautéed Green Beans and a dessert of Warm Delicious Apple Crumble with Vanilla Ice Cream" (GCT). Just to give you an idea. After dinner, we had a good time at karaoke in the festive lounge.

Germany

Passau

On Friday, November 26, the MS *River Adagio* arrived in Passau, Germany, at 10:30 a.m. Passau, in Lower Bavaria, is called the Dreiflüssestadt (City on Three Rivers) due to the confluence of the Rivers Danube, Ilz, and Inn.

June 8, 2013 – Footnote: Passau, at this moment, is dangerously flooded.

According to GCT, "The prince bishops of Passau made it their royal residence and capital of the largest Danube diocese. This elegant town has served as a German cultural and intellectual hub for centuries. Its principal historic sites include the impressive Bishop's Residenz, the 13th-century Town Hall, and the magnificent 17th-century St. Stephen's Cathedral, which boasts the world's largest church organ. The cathedral's original Gothic plan is still evident through the 17th-century reconstruction it received in the grand baroque style, with one of its most striking features being its gorgeous octagonal dome."

Our thoughtful guide made sure we saw all of the highlights listed in GCT's brochure, and since Passau was another German city that was still new to me, I was happy to finally see it in person, if only for a short period of time, that is, two and a half hours. St. Stephen's Cathedral was almost overloaded with baroque statuettes and colorful paintings on the ceilings, etc. I personally prefer the simpler Romanesque and Gothic cathedrals. Regardless, I found the Nibelungenhalle, from the Nazi era, almost offensively stark and the monument to the Jewish people murdered by the Nazis aesthetically puzzling. The city-hall tower was nice and the clock on time.

Even nicer was Passau's dazzling Christmas Market, located in front of the cathedral, which I visited after eating lunch on the ship and taking another close look at the cathedral's interior.

The Passauer Christmas Market turned out to be a special experience. One of the major pavilions displayed the most beautiful wood-carved ornaments, pyramids, candle arches, nutcrackers, smoke men, angels, etc. from Seiffen, situated in the Erzgebirge (Ore Mountains, Saxony). I immediately stepped inside and began a conversation with the young couple in charge. When I told them about my experience when visiting Seiffen in 1979 in connection with a grant to develop a course comparing the two Germanys (a research trip I have written about in Part I of my memoirs), they were quite excited. Who would have thought that some twenty years later, someone from Seiffen, East Germany, would appear in Passau, West Germany, and sell their goods, heretofore off-limits in the West? I pointed out to them some of the items in their display that the Seiffeners had given me when I visited.

After dinner, we were treated to a fascinating glassblowing demonstration. A father and son from a town nearby, who had fled to the Passau area from Thuringia, in the former East Germany, were blowing glass into the neatest sparkling ornaments, figurines, etc. and offered them for sale as well. Passau is known for its Glass Museum. It displays more than thirty thousand pieces. But I did not visit it. I asked the men whether they knew my former boyfriend, who had fled the Russians with his parents and opened a crystal glass factory in Volpriehausen, where my family lived as evacuees. But they did not know the Buders.

What a day that was: inadvertently, I overheard someone in the lounge talking about a passenger who was found dead in his bed that morning. It was Max, the felt-hat guy. I guess he had gotten his wish, to see his homeland once more before departing from this world. Why was I not surprised?!

We left Passau on Saturday, November 27, at 6:45 p.m. and attended a lecture on "German Christmas Traditions." After dinner, a couple of our program directors told Christmas tales, which I followed intently to see whether they matched my own, and in part they did.

Regensburg

The MS *River Adagio* docked in Regensburg – Germany's largest medieval city, spared during the war – on Saturday, November 28, at 10:30 a.m., and soon thereafter we were ready for the scheduled Regensburg City Walk. Since I have related a previous visit to Regensburg in Part I, I will skip it.

I did join the group on the walk to the church up on a hill, where a group of four male singers treated us to a lovely assortment of German Christmas carols. It was definitely getting colder outside, and I was overjoyed when it began to snow. Back on the ship, we were again greeted with a hot Christmas brew, which I took to the lounge. I headed directly to the table near the entrance and helped myself to an assortment of the tastiest Christmas cookies, which reminded me of old times. During my childhood and even for some time thereafter, we lived rather frugally. This was one time when I did not count calories. In retrospect, I should have gone to the Christmas Market of Thurn and Taxis, but since I had taken a private tour of that castle years ago, I decided to rest up for the next and final stop of this Christmas odyssey: Nuremberg.

We left Regensburg on November 29 at 11:00 a.m. and spent the day listening to various announcements regarding disembarkation procedure, an optional galley tour, and high tea in the lounge at 4:30 p.m., which would be followed by the captain's farewell drink at 6:00 p.m., the captain's farewell dinner at 6:30 p.m., and finally a fun show performed by the crew.

I had decided to participate in the included tours while the ship was docked in Nuremberg on Monday, November 29. I was ready to hop on the bus at 9:00 a.m. to see what the guide had to report about Nuremberg, another city familiar to me.

"Nuremberg, the second-largest city in Bavaria, is one of the most important cities of Germany's Franconia region. 13th-century walls surround this medieval city. Today the city's name evokes the notorious post–World War II war crimes trials. But throughout its history, Nuremberg has been known for its wonderful creativity and handicrafts – its toys and fancy metalwork are particularly famous. Nuremberg's Christkindlmarkt is Germany's most famous traditional Christmas market. Here a myriad of colorful stalls offer handmade Christmas decorations, toys, ceramics, glasswork, and candles. Food stalls tempt you with bratwurst, mulled wines, and sweets and pastries – including the famous Nuremberg gingerbread" (GCT). It is all true.

No, I did not join the optional Nation Confronts Its Past tour. I know more about that time than I care to remember. I have lived it!

Bamberg

My good friend Ursel Segebrecht had offered to pick me up in Nuremberg on Tuesday, November 30, 2010, at 10:00 a.m. I waited in the lounge. The ship was almost deserted. It was snowing outside, and reports came that the roads were rather slick. I myself had started to come down with a bad cold, and I felt rather anxious about inconveniencing my friend at this particular time. But what could I do but wait? And not long after 10:00 a.m., there she was. Ursel had found me after a hassle involving locating the correct pier. Someone had given her poor directions. It was all forgotten as soon as we sat in their nice, new Mercedes-Benz and headed toward Bamberg, where we arrived not long after noon.

As always, my good and longtime friends went out of their way to spoil me. Ursel cooked meals with a Bavarian touch, had baked cakes so we would not want for anything at coffee time, and offered a variety of beers and wines in the evening to drink with or after supper. We talked endlessly while the snow continued to pile up and sighed with relief when Bettina, who had taken a train from Berlin to see me, arrived long after midnight on Friday. Her train had been stranded for hours on the tracks, waiting for the snow to be removed. –

I loved watching the numerous little birds feed all day long at the big, round, wooden bird feeder on the terrace. Unfortunately my cold was getting worse, and Ursel insisted on taking me to their doctor, who confirmed what I was thinking: that I did not have the flu but a very nasty cold. I was given several over-the-counter medicines, which I swallowed religiously. I was worried about my coughing and sniffling when we all went to a wonderful concert at the Bamberger Symphoniker, so I was glad to get through it without sneezing. It was a most impressive performance in the new concert hall. I applauded enthusiastically and was only a bit sad that my friend Mark Kosower, who had spent four years with this orchestra as solo cellist, was no longer there. –

Ursel kindly chauffeured me around to several shops, especially the big Aldi store, to purchase some things to take home, and Wulf spent quite some time at the computer and eventually found an excellent train connection from Bamberg to Munich. All three took me to the train station early on the 6th, I think around 5:00 a.m., to bid me farewell ever so warmly, and I sighed with relief when I arrived at the airport in Munich in one piece. Despite all the snow, changing platforms, etc., I boarded my flight back to the good old USA, where I arrived on the same day. When I called my friends to inform them of my return and thank them once more, I was sad to hear that with the exception of Bettina, my cold was making the rounds in the Segebrecht household.

SWITZERLAND

In January 2008, I began to plan a visit to Berguen, Switzerland. My friends Rosi Bartke and Friedhelm Moerke from Hannover, whom I had befriended in 2002 during a stay at Hotel Erika in Dorf Tyrol, South Tyrol (Italy), had been raving for years about their annual visit to Berguen, where they rented their favorite vacation apartment. My friends were more than happy to assist me with my plans and, most of all, to recommend a good hotel in a perfect location, Sporthotel Berguen AG. I was overjoyed to discover they had a room with kitchen facilities for me from August 2 to August 23. In addition, I had convinced the Segebrechts, including Bettina, to join me for at least a few days during that time, and they were able to book rooms at the same hotel.

Berguen

Mr. Weber, the manager of the hotel, had kindly provided information about train connections from Zurich to Berguen. On August 1, I flew from Indy to Zurich via Philadelphia and London, and after a three-hour train ride from Zurich to Berguen, which involved changing platforms in Chur, I arrived punctually at 9:17 p.m. Mr. Weber picked me up in his SUV and took me to the hotel. It was dark by then, and I was glad to finally fall into my comfortable bed. I woke up the next morning after sunrise.

My room was quite large and reminded me vaguely of my studio in Cancún. Here, when opening the sliding glass doors to the balcony, instead of seeing the ocean, I was greeted by a majestic mountain range, dark-green pine trees, lush meadows, and a sparkling mountain stream, that is, the Albula River, rushing by, meandering through the valley, and lulling me asleep at night.

I could not have been happier. The hotel offered a fabulous breakfast buffet with tempting cold cuts, cheeses from the region, pound cake, hearty dark breads, crisp rolls, and marmalades. Different kinds of coffee, fruit juices, fresh fruits, and yogurts were plentiful as well. I love the European breakfasts and tend to eat more than at home, because I skip lunch when visiting Europe. The bonus at my hotel was that tables were also set up on the terrace. Whenever the weather was nice, I found a table out there with a view of the mountains. And to top it off, I could hear the bells around the necks of a group of cows grazing close to the hotel.

Right after breakfast, I went to get a firsthand look at my immediate surroundings. Only a few yards behind the hotel, a narrow path led through the meadow, over a bridge across the rumbling stream, and up into a pine forest. I took my time walking up the hilly path. I paused frequently to take pictures of different wildflowers growing along the trail and sat down on a stone bench across from a fenced-in patch of meadow on which light-brown cows were grazing and resting in the shade. Not a soul could be seen or heard – though, at one point, a little boy, about eight years old, came rushing down the narrow lane on his mountain bike. I greeted him; he stopped, we chatted for a few minutes, and he continued on his way to the village.

Berguen/Bravuogn (its German/Romansh double name), with a population of under five hundred, is a village, rather than a town, in an incredibly stunning alpine setting, some 1,400 meters above sea level, in the canton of Graubuenden, Switzerland. This Swiss gem was foreign to me until my German friends told me about it. This truly unspoiled alpine village lies off the beaten track, at the foot of the legendary Albula Pass, gateway to the Engadine. Wherever you turn your head, you discover a picture-perfect vista. A mountain paradise! I was thus not surprised to learn that Berguen was the filming location for the 1990s TV series *The Director* and that even before that, when I still lived in Germany and was an enthusiastic reader of the *Heidi* books, was the area chosen for production of the much-loved 1952 *Heidi* film adaptation, which I had been fortunate to see prior to leaving for the United States.

Upon my arrival at the Sporthotel, I found on the breakfast-nook table in my room a welcome package with greetings from my friends Rosi and Friedhelm. The package contained cookies, candies, and a whole bunch of brochures, into which my friends had inserted several pages of handwritten travel and hiking tips, enough to keep me going for longer than three weeks. I thought it was so nice. And to prove my sincere appreciation, I followed several of their suggestions.

Hardly a day went by when I did not walk down the main street of the village, which goes right through the heart of it, past a fenced-in meadow in which fat and healthy light-brown cows grazed, and past the noticeably picturesque Engadine houses. Each house was lavishly decorated with graffiti and frescoes and boasted unique little oriel or bay windows. They project outward without extending to the ground. Thus, a resident can check out the person ringing the bell at the front door below without opening the window and leaning out. I loved the flower boxes bursting with fat, dark-red geraniums beneath these fanciful windows. The majority of houses also had a small wooden or stone bench for two next to the main entrance. A pot of vibrant geraniums, giant begonias, or blue forget-me-nots often stood next to it. At the end of the main street you will find the old Roman Tower, more than one thousand years old. As the story goes, it had served as a refuge, as a place from which to defend the town, and when the railroad was being built, as a prison. On the side of the village road I noticed an occasional rectangular stone well with a pump, meant to provide a cool drink for anybody who was thirsty. I could hardly believe my eyes – and had to stop and take a picture – when I encountered a precious bunch of wild bluebells cropping up in the cracks of a 2' x 4' patch of gray cobblestone next to the sidewalk.

Not far from my hotel stood an old and very small Romanesque church or chapel. I noticed a somewhat faded fresco on the wall behind the altar. When I visited it for the first time, I just sat on one of the ancient wooden pews and took everything in for a while before going outside to check out the names on several tombstones in the small cemetery encircling the church. I was not surprised to find that the Swiss keep their graves just as beautifully decorated with flowers and groomed shrubs as the Germans do, and that they decorate much more simply than the Poles.

In the cemetery stood a comfortable gray stone bench on which I liked to sit and watch the bright-red trains of the famous Albula Railway, part of the Rhaetian Railway network, go by in the distance. I could never tire of watching the trains make a 360-degree turn, emerge from and disappear into a tunnel, and cross the famous Landwasser (Land Water) Viaduct. It is a genuine engineering miracle and a must-see for all train fanatics. If you want to see the entire miracle in miniature format, you must go to the local history museum. In addition to other displays that give you a glimpse into life in Berguen throughout its history, the museum has a captivating large model layout of the fabulous Albula route from Preda to Berguen. It is an aesthetically and intellectually stimulating adventure. Go for it!

By the way, a stroll on the path through the meadows and past nice Swiss houses with dark-brown, wood-flanked balconies, from which lush red geraniums cascade, will take you to Berguen's impressive Kurhaus, known for its art-nouveau lighting fixtures. It was built in 1906 and has been tastefully renovated to preserve its authentic historic charm. I have heard it is a place favored by families with children. – It is only a five-minute walk from the railroad station.

Bettina arrived in Berguen on Saturday, August 9. She had flown to Zurich, where her longtime friend Constantin now lived. He picked her up and drove her to Berguen. It was just wonderful to see both of them again, and after they settled in, I invited them out to dinner at the nice rustic hotel Weisses Kreuz, where we tasted some of the region's specialties and its beer. We talked endlessly about this and that and walked back to our hotel after dark. It was an uphill walk, easier for the youngsters than for me. On the way, Constantin stopped in front of a big zinc bucket full of blue-thistle bouquets. I had never seen these intriguingly beautiful flowers, grown by the locals in big fields, and it was so nice of Constantin to buy a big bouquet of these metallic-blue, shimmering, long-stemmed thistles for me. They greeted me for two weeks whenever I entered my room, and the maid was careful to keep the water fresh.

After breakfast on August 10, we climbed into Constantin's vintage Mercedes, ready to go. He had invited us on a scenic mountain trip on the Albula Pass to St. Moritz. We were happy to have a clear sky, and with each turn of the winding road, a new and spectacular panorama surprised us. Not much had changed on Lake St. Moritz, winter playground for the rich and famous, since my last visit. I needed to buy aspirin, and even those little pills cost a fortune. Since it was Sunday and the stores were closed, there was no reason to linger and window-shop and be depressed by the obscene prices.

Constantin returned to Berguen via Filisur, where Bettina and I climbed many steps to take a peek into a church, the name of which I have forgotten. I was more impressed, as I recall, by the vibrant orange begonias in a stone container next to someone's front door. I did not blame Constantin for declining to climb the steps. He drove us back by way of the Julia Pass, and once in Berguen, after a brief rest, I took the two out for a farewell dinner. Constantin had to leave in the morning to visit friends up in the mountains, so Bettina and I were left to plan activities for the week until he returned to take her back to Zurich.

We did not want to overdo it, and after Constantin's departure, Bettina and I took a not-too-strenuous hike on the Bahnhistorischer Lehrpfad (Historic Railroad Training Path), which took us from Preda – the train station closest to Berguen – to a lovely mountain lake. Our trail went through a forest of mostly deciduous trees and eventually ended at a small mountain lake, a truly idyllic spot. We sat on a bench and had our sandwiches. A flock of ducks, including little ones, was close to us, partially navigating the pond and partially waddling around on the shore. Bettina had fun throwing crumbs from her sandwich. What a treat! It was a peaceful spot. With the exception of a family with two toddlers on the opposite side of the lake, no other humans could be seen. – We did not hike around the lake. I was not in the mood for a long trek, because we had to cover quite a distance to return to Berguen, where we arrived after a two-hour hike, feeling pleasantly tired.

It was a bit overcast the next day, and we decided to take a look at Chur, capital of the canton Graubuenden, to be reached by a seventy-five-minute train ride through very scenic terrain. We walked through the old town to get a feel for the ambiance of this medieval town, untouched by the destruction of war so commonly in evidence in other European towns. We thought ourselves lucky to come upon a wedding at the Church of St. Martin. Though we were not allowed to go inside, we had ample opportunity to observe the guests who had gathered outside. I thought the navy-blue, highly polished VW Bug with a big, splashy bouquet of lush yellow sunflowers and white ribbons on the hood was so neat.

After exploring the town, we ended up on top of another hill, where a big cathedral, built in the late-Romanesque and Gothic styles between 1151 and 1272, stood and where another wedding, as well as the baptism of the couple's baby, was taking place. Unfortunately, we were again prevented from entering, but we got at least a sense of what Chur was like – where the men, it seemed, tend to marry the women after they give birth to their children.

A couple of days later, on a nice sunny day, Bettina and I hopped on the yellow post bus, a small van. It took us through gorgeous mountain country all the way up to Stugl, a small village between Berguen and Filisur. It was a heavenly spot, tranquil and harmonious. About one hundred feet up from the station, a tiny Evangelical chapel from the fourteenth century sat perched on a hill. We had to walk around it to find a door and were relieved when it opened. We admired a couple of fading murals, climbed the ladder to get a peek at the bell in the tower, and examined the few, well-kept graves outside. We found the spectacular mountain panorama from up there simply divine. We walked through the meadows, and instead of hiking up to the cottage where the *Heidi* film was made, we opted to walk down to Latsch, the next station in the direction of Berguen, in the blistering sun. In Latsch, we sat at a table beneath a sun umbrella, had a refreshing drink, and chatted with the proprietress, who posed for me. On the wall in their humble inn-restaurant was a very interesting display of pictures and photos that depicted scenes from the filming of the German version of the *Heidi* stories.

Before we knew it, it was time for Constantin to return to pick up Bettina. After a last hearty Swiss breakfast, we said our cordial goodbyes, and they returned to their own lives. And thus it goes . . .

No sooner had the two left than Bettina's parents, my good friends Wulf and Ursel, arrived from Bamberg in their new Mercedes. As always, it was a warm greeting, and in the evening, while enjoying a few glasses of red wine, we plotted when and what to see during their stay of four or five days. We decided on two major train trips on the highly recommended Bernina Express, one to Davos and another to Tirano, Italy.

Davos

A trip to Davos had been a lifelong dream. My longtime Jesuit friend had always talked about it in enthusiastic terms. He used to go to Davos frequently to undergo treatment at the world-famous sanatorium, which specialized in the treatment of tuberculosis. He knew one of the foremost specialists in Davos, who treated him for tuberculosis in one eye. Those who could afford it would spend extended periods of time at the sanatorium to convalesce or die. Davos is also known for hosting the annual World Economic Forum, usually in January, when the mountains and forests are covered with snow.

However, my fascination with Davos was in fact triggered by Thomas Mann's novel *The Magic Mountain*, which later earned him the Nobel Prize in Literature. While studying in Aix-en-Provence, I wrote a paper about the protagonist, Hans Castorp, who experienced a spiritual awakening while visiting a cousin who was being treated at the Waltzaner Sanatorium due to symptoms of tuberculosis. In essence, the novel suggests that people who undergo the illness are spiritually enriched by it whereas healthy people remain more or less shallow minded. Thomas Mann's wife, Katia, was diagnosed with tuberculosis, and when visiting her in 1912, he was so inspired that he began to write the novel. I was thrilled when my friends agreed to go with me to Davos. What greater honor than to walk with my longtime literary friends Professor Wulf and Dr. Ursel Segebrecht in Mann's footsteps in Davos, a mountain paradise located on the Landwasser River? As soon as we arrived, we

Fireball Lily

went to the information office, and Ursel asked for a map of the Thomas-Mann-Way, which we soon found. It started at the Waldhotel (formerly a woodland sanatorium) at 1,620 meters above sea level and ended at the Schatzalp, 1,880 meters above sea level. The incline was not too steep. The trail led through forested areas and past lush green meadows, and now and then we stopped to sit on a bench and look down on Davos or to read the signs at "literary stations," which provided information about the connections between Thomas Mann's works and Davos. The path ended behind Alpinum Schatzalp, the botanical garden.

Back in Davos, we treated ourselves to coffee and cake on the terrace of a nice restaurant. On the way to the train station, we took a look at the venue of the World Economic Forum, which did not really impress me. Upon arriving in Berguen, we agreed it was wonderful to have undertaken this comparatively brief but inspirational excursion.

Since Switzerland is famous for her trains, one is quite tempted to take advantage of a ride. It is so much more pleasant to sit in a beautiful panorama car of the Bernina Express than to drive through the mountains by car. After some coaxing, my friends accepted another invitation, this time to try out the Bernina Express from Berguen over Chur/Davos/St. Moritz to Tirano, in Northern Italy. It is a trip any mountain and nature lover should not miss. We were excited to take in the spectacular scenery and called each other's attention to this or that panorama, especially when peaks covered with the first snow – in August – came into view. After a few hours of travel through glacier terrain, we arrived in the sunny valley of Tirano – and could hardly believe it when we sighted palm trees in several courtyards.

ITALY

Tirano

Tirano has a population under ten thousand. It is the terminus of the Rhaetian Railway and the place where it meets up with the Italian State Railway, from Milan. We walked across the square between the two railroad stations and strolled leisurely through the streets and alleys of the small city, examining the uniqueness of the houses' facades. We found an ideal spot alongside the old city wall to take pictures and thought it was time for Berlusconi to invest some money here to prevent the town from slowly deteriorating. Ursel spotted an unoccupied bench in a shady place on the square, where we ate the sandwiches we had brought along. Since we did not have much time, we did not venture out to the Renaissance-style Madonna di Tirano Basilica to see the 1513 fresco depicting the appearance of the Blessed Virgin. Legend has it that on September 29, 1504, her vision appeared while the plague was ravishing Western Europe, and she told Mario Degli Omodei to build a sanctuary for travelers, which he did six months later. The basilica is popular with pilgrims. Our trip back to Berguen was just as pleasant as, and in a certain way even nicer than, the trip out. The setting sun cast a golden light over the mountaintops and let the occasional cascading mountain stream shimmer with a vibrant silver.

August 1, 2013 – Berlusconi was finally found guilty of tax fraud. Maybe now he can spend some of his billions to restore historic sites.

My friends had to return to Bamberg the next morning, right after breakfast. It was a sad and heartfelt goodbye. An hour after they left, the manager of the hotel knocked at my door and brought an assortment of Swiss cheeses the Segebrechts had unintentionally left behind. Too bad – Ursel had carefully selected these very tasty morsels at a store in Davos.

SWITZERLAND

Zermatt – Matterhorn

With all my friends gone, I began to seriously consider a quick trip with the highly recommended Glacier Express, which connected the two world-class resorts of Zermatt and St. Moritz. The brochure advertised this trip as "an adventurous 7 ½ hour journey crossing 291 bridges, 91 tunnels and the 6,708 feet high Oberalp Pass and one of the world's greatest train journeys." Given my penchant for mountain landscapes, how could I resist?! It was now or never. I just had to see the Matterhorn. Before I knew it, I stood at the counter in the Berguen train station and booked my round-trip train ticket, which was comparatively steep, so my credit card came in handy. My reservation for one night at the Jaeger Hotel in downtown Zermatt, however, was reasonably priced at $75.

With a couple days to wait for the Zermatt trip, I spent one day riding the miniature post bus once more to Stugle, just to enjoy the landscape. On the way, I chatted with a bunch of school kids who took this bus to commute between their school and the alpine pasture, which was their home. I learned that their life was very different from that of kids living in a village and attending a school nearby. Their days on the mountain farm meant helping with farming chores, which were at times quite challenging, especially when the closest neighbor's home could be reached only after a thirty-minute (or longer) hike through mountainous terrain. They had a lot of questions regarding my life in America, which I always enjoy talking about with youngsters in other countries and cultures.

The manager of the hotel very kindly dropped me off at the train station on the morning of my departure for Zermatt. I had to change platforms in Filisur and had no trouble finding my reserved seat in the panorama car. It was fabulous, like sitting in a moving glass house. This train is indeed the ultimate mode of transportation for this spectacular stretch of earth.

There are not enough superlatives to describe my emotional high. An added bonus was the company in the train. I had no trouble connecting with several of the international passengers. There was the Indian mother who was treating her son, a student in Geneva, to a trip and a French lady who was, like me, a world traveler. We conversed in French and English. Another couple, visiting from China, wanted to know where in China I had been, etc. The train went via Thusis, Chur, Disentis, and Brig. Whenever the Express passed a noteworthy spot, a commentary was made over a loudspeaker to keep us informed and entertained and give us a chance to snap a picture. In Disentis, which lies high in the Rhine Valley, I was able to get pictures of the church and town as well as one of the oldest Swiss Benedictine monasteries, with spectacular mountain ranges in the background.

Switzerland

As we approached the village of Zermatt, which has a population of five thousand, my mood started to change. With each mile, the panoramas were increasingly covered with fog. At first, the darkest clouds imaginable began to move in and cast their spell, first over the mountaintops and then gradually over the meadows in which cows were grazing and over the roofs and church steeples of the villages. Eventually, the rain poured down in buckets – or like cats and dogs, if you prefer. Our glass roof had no windshield wipers, and we saw nothing except the long faces of companion travelers. As soon as the train stopped in Zermatt, I got out and found a chauffeur with a cap that read "Hotel Jaegerhof." I got in, and a few minutes later he entered something resembling a courtyard and let me out at the so-called hotel. The lady at the dimly lit reception desk was very friendly, as was the cozy atmosphere of this very small – forty-five units or so – inn. I liked the rustic, quaint, intimate Swiss ambiance of the place. And as I was quite tired, it did not take me long to settle into my tiny room, which had a narrow oak single bed and a red-and-white-checkered down comforter, just as I had imagined. I even had a little TV and an oak wardrobe, and the shower room was very clean and sufficient. There was a long but narrow window from which I could see the wall of another house. I think it had stopped raining.

I fell asleep telling myself that the trip to Zermatt might have been in vain, like the one I took in New Zealand to see Mount Cook, where, after spending some $1,500, I saw nothing. – Well, I did like the very cozy bed. I woke up very early in the morning, peeked out the window, saw nothing but gray, and went back to bed. When my alarm went off at about 7:00 a.m., I got ready and went downstairs for breakfast. The room in which a fire was flickering in the fireplace was filling up with guests, and all were chattering happily. The ambiance of the room was warm and inviting and the breakfast buffet full of everything one might desire. The Swiss are not stingy when it comes to satisfying the palates of their customers. I quickly discovered why the guests were so animated. I had asked a lady at the table next to mine whether the rain had stopped. She told me in glowing terms that it had stopped indeed and that the Matterhorn was snow-white. After all, when it rains in the mountains, it turns to snow. I was so ecstatic about the news that all the guests joined in. The lady invited me to follow her to her room, where we stepped out on the balcony, from which I saw in the distance the snow-white Matterhorn. It was one of those extraordinary, exhilarating, and highly memorable experiences.

I did not have a lot of time, so I quickly finished my breakfast. I went outside and hurried down the street toward the bridge over the Matter Vispa River, fed by waters from the surrounding glaciers. From this bridge, where others were gathering, I saw the Matterhorn, 15,203 feet high, in all its glory, immaculate and majestic against a vibrant blue sky and bathed in a light-golden hue from the morning sun. – What a gorgeous photo it provided! I took a deep breath and got ready to return to the hotel to pick up my gear. My train was scheduled to depart at 9:13 a.m. The chauffeur let me out of the electric-powered vehicle at the train station, which was right downtown. I had enough time to walk around the big plaza in front of the station and take in the surrounding picture-perfect houses. Rarely had I seen such a profusion of crimson geraniums; they crowned the dark-brown balustrades of the balconies of the chalet-style houses, so endearing with their overhanging roofs. While I was busy taking photographs, I ran into the Chinese couple from the train and asked them to pose for me. Their formerly long faces were now smiling! We said good-bye. I boarded the train, and on the way back to Berguen, I was thrilled to see that a blanket of snow covered all the fabulous mountains, which had been hidden by clouds on our way to Zermatt. When I walked to my hotel from the train station in Berguen, I was overjoyed to see that the snow had also capped the mountains I had seen from the hotel balcony.

I was ready to return home. Three days later, on August 23, 2008, I landed safe and sound in Indianapolis with a head full of memories.

MEXICO

Cancún

On January 9, 2013, I was back in Cancún on the Sunset Lagoon at noon, greeted by pelicans, seagulls, a heron, a stray dolphin, and a baby crocodile. I was enchanted by yellow, orange, and crimson hibiscus, purple bougainvillea, and tall and slender palms laden with ripening coconuts. – My fascination with the exotic should by now be obvious to anybody who has plowed through my memoirs. Then – why did it take me so long to visit America's fiftieth state, hailed as a paradise? Well, I'll tell you.

When Doc and I honeymooned for three months in Mérida and Progreso, on the Yucatán Peninsula, we liked to relax in the shade of coconut palms on a white-sand beach. Each morning, we sipped the milk from a fresh coconut, and at times we reminisced about his time in Honolulu. When I mentioned that at some point I would love to visit the Army hospital of Fort Shafter, in Honolulu, where he had served as chief surgeon, he strongly objected: "I never want to go back there!" It was the place where he had become so sick that he was forced into early retirement from the Army. "Besides," he said, "you have the same white beaches, palm trees, tropical flora, and turquoise waters right here." He entertained the thought of possibly buying an oceanfront villa down there. Only nine months later, Doc left this world for another, unknown. I am certain he had no illusions about whereto. He was a realist. For his sake, I hope it was a realm unlike Hawaii.

Having traveled with Doc in 1956 to most states in the United States, having seen more of the world than most mortals, and still harboring a desire to return to Japan to see more of that beautiful and intriguing country, especially Hiroshima, I decided in early 2010 to take the plunge – I booked back-to-back trips with Grand Circle: Hawaiian Island Explorer (June 3 to June 14, 2010), an eleven-day ocean cruise with NCL on the MS *Pride of America*, followed by a three-week OAT trip, Japan's Cultural Treasures (June 21 to July 12).

One week prior to my departure from the States, the Japan voyage was canceled due to lack of participation. After a week of agonized thinking, I decided to sign up for the Japan trip scheduled to begin a week or so later. It meant extending my stay in Honolulu for six days at an additional expense of some $1,000, which I did not like, because Honolulu is sinfully expensive. Ultimately, though, I thought, "It's now or never."

HAWAII - ALOHA!

Honolulu – O'ahu

On June 3, 2010, I flew by way of Chicago to Honolulu, where a GCT guide greeted us and arranged transport to the Doubletree Alana Hotel in Waikiki, at which we spent a couple of days prior to embarkation. The next morning, I was more than ready to get a taste of Honolulu, capital of the Aloha State, on the island of O'ahu. Hawaii changed its status from US territory to the fiftieth state on August 21, 1959, that is, two years after Doc passed away. Located in the Central Pacific Ocean, it is the only US state made up entirely of islands as well as the northernmost island group of Polynesia. Remember, I had been to the Society Islands in 2000.

Hawaii was formerly known as the independent Kingdom of Hawaii. Thus, our first and major stop downtown was the Iolani Palace, built in 1882, in front of which stands the impressive statue of King Kamehameha, the last ruler of Hawaii. If you have time, you can visit the interior and get a glimpse of the opulence of a Hawaiian monarchic residence. The carefully restored palace is a national historic landmark and well worth a visit. The giant king, dressed in rich, golden armor, which shines against his dark-brown complexion, can be sighted from quite a distance. The grounds around the palace are meticulously manicured, so if you like tropical flowers, I spotted a nice variety not far from the king. – It struck me as a bit strange that all of this had become the property of America. Somehow, the entire state of Hawaii, way out in the North Pacific Ocean, thousands of miles removed from North America, seemed more unreal than Alaska and more like a country than a state.

There was no time for us to take a peek inside the palace, the Bishop Museum, or the Honolulu Art Museum. Sorry. I was not disappointed, because I had signed up for this trip mainly to get at least a glimpse of the scenic highlights of the archipelagos. I was happy as our bus headed toward the coast. The vistas that unfolded were simply stunning. I was genuinely moved at the first sight of Doc's Diamond Head. You could not miss this extinct volcano. Honolulu's landmark sticks out into the Pacific and dominates the landscape: majestic, striking, eternal. The coastline embracing the crater is just out of this world, rugged shores interspersed with white-sand beaches, accented by tall and slender coconut palms. All of this borders the azure waters of the Pacific, and to truly appreciate it you must explore it personally. Of course, what makes the panoramas so special are the whitecaps of the swells as they splash against the black lava rocks or lap gently upon the white-sand beaches, where they disappear in the sand. As I looked down, I imagined higher waves and skilled surfers, and I got excited whenever we passed tropical trees with rich purple, orange, white, or pink canopies, such as jacaranda and tiger's claw.

Hawaii – Aloha!

Hawaiian Island Explorer – MS *Pride of America*

Diamond Head looks most striking from a distance. Soon after I had embarked on the MS *Pride of America*, docked about a mile away, I stood mesmerized when I saw the rock shimmering golden in the setting sun. I had made it up to the fourteenth deck of the megaship, a seventy-thousand-gross-tonnage, 2,100-passenger monstrosity, which was just as glitzy and presumptuous as any of the floating palaces that crowd the oceans. This Americana-themed NCL ship was even more luxurious than the ships on which I had cruised the Baltic and the Bahamas a few years earlier. I had opted for a Hawaiian cruise because I was not in the mood to go island hopping by way of planes, small ships, or ferries. This kind of transportation was for lazy travelers such as I had become at the ripe old age of seventy-eight. When I observed the madness of the tourists on a couple of the decks below, I decided to look for a spot hidden away from the crowds. I was also glad that thanks to my Latitude status, I had been upgraded to a cabin with a balcony. I liked freestyle cruises, because I could eat whenever and wherever I wanted. I had some ten restaurants to choose from. Most importantly, I had ample opportunity to meet travelers from all walks of life. Early on, I had the most entertaining conversation with three female African-American ministers of one of the hundreds of esoteric religious sects in America. Though they made no efforts at conversion, they educated me a little. To be honest, I have forgotten what they believed in. I am sure it was Jesus. In the end, it did not matter. Kindness and respect is what counts.

Maui

Our first port stop, on day 4, was Kahuli, Maui. I had heard much praise of Maui and especially its soothing climate, which is due to the ever-present tropical trade winds and the lush tropical vegetation that bewitches its visitors. The beaches have been called "heavenly" and the seas "whale filled," although I did not see a single whale, because it was not the season. Yet Maui turned out to be incredibly gorgeous. I had signed up for a trip to the Haleakala Crater, which rises some ten thousand feet from the sea and is said to be the world's largest dormant volcano; it last erupted more than four hundred years ago. The view from the summit was dramatic: towering cinder cones, dry, porous rocks, and lush forest canopies spread out in an immense panorama, which reminded me somewhat of the Grand Canyon. Outside the visitor center, I was fascinated by the Haleakala Silver Sword. It is a long, silver-gray, pointed, pampas-like grass about a foot high. I had never seen this striking plant and could just imagine what Haleakala Mountain looked like when it was covered with this grass – that is, as if blanketed with snow. Though we did see the Haleakala Observatory from the visitor center, none in the group felt inclined to venture up to it. I had no idea that it occasionally snows on Haleakala! When Mark Twain visited the place in 1866, he wrote that Haleakala was "the sublimest spectacle I ever witnessed" (NCL). At the end of our tour, each of us was presented with a "House of the Sun" certificate signed by the superintendent of the National Park Service, stating that we had survived the "37-mile drive up from sea level to the summit of Haleakala volcano (10,023 ft./3,055 m), one of the greatest elevation gains in the shortest distance in the world!"

The next day, despite some warnings from passengers and the guide that the trip on the legendary Road to Hana is physically challenging, I was ready to go and shared the jeep with three cotravelers. The drive turned out to be quite a trip. It took the driver about three hours to navigate the mere thirty-seven-mile narrow road along the cliffs, which had numerous blind twists, turns, and dips. We traveled through tropical rainforests full of exotic flowers and past hidden waterfalls and extraordinarily beautiful seascape vistas of the Pacific. The rugged, black lava-flow coastline reminded me of the coastline of Easter Island and even that of the Galápagos. We were told the road had caused many car accidents, even fatalities, and that it was a favorite of cyclists. After walking around in the small, rustic town of Hana, which had a population of about seven hundred, we started down on the same road, enjoying the vistas once more. Unfortunately, we passed the scene of an accident. Someone in a group of cyclists on the way down from Hana had fallen off the cliff. The rest of the cyclists had stopped, and an ambulance had just arrived. Two men with medical gear were slowly descending the cliff to reach the fallen cyclist. We did not stop, but I hope the accident did not result in major injuries.

The accidents are predominantly the result of distracted drivers and cyclists. They are so captivated by the beautiful scenery that they forget to pay attention to the twists and drive or race too fast – and before they know it, an accident happens. I know all about it. I fell down a cliff while cycling in Switzerland when I was young. When I chatted later that evening with a couple in the dining room, the husband complemented me for not having attempted to tackle the road by renting a car, which they had done. He lamented that since he was driving, he saw very little of the beautiful scenery.

Big Island

Our next stop, on day 6, was Port Hilo, on the windward side of the Big Island. It is the "oldest port of entry with a population of 38,000, and the second largest city in Hawaii situated on the east coast of the Big Island (the Orchid Island). The Big Island is just that – *big*. It accounts for 63% of the state (about 4,000 square miles). Shipping and fishing business is significant, plus there's a campus for the University of Hawaii in Hilo. It is believed this was the first island to be inhabited by Polynesian voyagers from the Marquesas Islands, around 700 A.D. Hilo is America's wettest city, over 120 inches annually, and holds the record for the most rain in 24 hours (22.3 inches), set in 1979. Hilo is the gateway to Hawaii Volcanoes National Park, America's most exciting national park, where Kilauea Volcano has erupted every day since 1983" (NCL).

Though I had wished to see an active, hot, lava-spewing volcano in Hawaii, someone talked me out of taking the optional helicopter trip. That person claimed there was little activity in the volcano at that time. And so it goes. I was also told we would most likely see glowing lava flow from the deck of the ship later on, when passing the volcano at night. When the time came, I saw only a tiny glimmer of red, glowing lava falling into the ocean. We were all quite disappointed. I did not treat myself to the exotic-looking volcano cocktail, which the waiter offered us on a big tray. There was nothing to celebrate.

I enjoyed walking up and down Kamehameha Avenue alongside the beautiful, half-moon Hilo Bay with our ship in the distance, and I took a good look at the restored wooden Victorian-style buildings. I stopped at a shop where two attractive young women offered pearls for sale. A glass bowl was filled with oyster half shells and a pearl inside. – I stood for a while underneath a big shade tree and watched a coconut-palm-frond weaver make palm-leaf hats and baskets, and I wished later I had brought one home. I thought it was a rather ingenious way to make something worthwhile and pretty out of palm leaves. That's about all I experienced during this leisurely intermezzo at the Port of Hilo.

Kona

On day 7, our ship docked at Sleepy Kona, the port on the leeward side of the Big Island. Since I am neither a coffee drinker nor a coffee connoisseur, I did not know Kona is synonymous with great coffee and big fish. The NCL brochure had this to say about the Big Island and Kona: "The Big Island embodies what the Hawaiians call 'mana,' a sense of spirituality that is still apparent through acres of petroglyphs etched in the black lava landscape. About 20 miles south of Kona is Kealakekua Bay, the place where Captain James Cook arrived in 1778. He was honored as the Hawaiian god Lono, but less than a month later he was killed. Cook was searching for a northwest passage to England and came south to these islands seeking shelter from the winter months. . . . The Big Island's population is about 150,000. Most live in Hilo and what is called the Kohala-Kona coast. . . . More ethnic and cultural groups are represented in Hawaii than in any other state. Chinese laborers, who came to work in the sugar industry, were the first of the large groups of immigrants to arrive (starting in 1852), and Filipinos and Koreans were the last (after 1900). Other immigrant groups – including Portuguese, Germans, Japanese, and Puerto Ricans – came in the latter part of the 19th century. Intermarriage with other races has brought a further decrease in the number of pureblooded Hawaiians, who compromise a very small percentage of the population. Kailua-Kona lies at the base of Mt. Hualalai, which is 8,271 ft. tall and home of the Kona coffee trade, macadamia nuts, avocados, and citrus fruit."

I skipped the optional Kona trip and just walked around, soaking up the scenic atmosphere. The Kona coast, with its lava caves and jagged inlets, which are lapped by rough waves, reminded me again of Easter Island. I just love to watch the drama of the sea. I did check out one of the many coffee shops in Kona and was amazed at the exorbitant prices and the thousand varieties of coffee they offered. I shook my head in disbelief and went my way without taking a sip of Kona coffee.

Kauai

Nawiliwili Harbor, on the island of Kauai, where we spent days 8 and 9, was next on our itinerary. In general, organized tours follow an itinerary that builds up to a climactic finale. Though I thought Maui was incredibly scenic, once I got to know Kauai a bit better, and after looking over my volume of pictures, I could not but put Kauai a notch above Maui. I was constantly exclaiming, "Ah" and "Oh" and "How beautiful!" This place, due not least to the generous rainfall, boasts ultimate beauty and even tops that which I experienced on my trip to the Society Islands. It therefore comes as no surprise that this place has attracted many celebrities. Since 1933, some sixty films have been shot here, from *South Pacific* to all three *Jurassic Park* movies and the remake of *King Kong*.

Kauai's first settlers arrived around 500 A.D., approximately 500 years before the rest of the islands were settled. Through a succession of kings, the island prospered. Captain James Cook landed on Kaui first, coming ashore at Waimea in 1778. Kaui is also known for being the only island that resisted takeover attempts by King Kamehameha during his quest to unify the islands under one rule. The island remained an independent kingdom until 1810. Kauai is the smallest of the four major islands covering 552 square miles. (NCL)

The trip to Waimea Canyon, called the Grand Canyon of the Pacific by Mark Twain, in the heart of Kauai, turned out to be a most exciting journey through still more gorgeous scenery. The canyon, some ten miles long, one mile wide, and over three thousand feet deep, was a most dramatic sight to behold. I stopped at the various lookouts, admired the different colors of the layers of stone, had my picture taken, and was amazed that this geological wonder was part of the USA.

As the MS *Pride of America* left the Garden Island in the forenoon, I sat on my balcony for about an hour as we cruised along Kauai's Na Pali Coast, overwhelmed by the landscape. I marveled at the hanging valleys, jagged emerald mountain cliffs, and cascading waterfalls. On the balcony next to mine, leaning over the railing, was a family from Australia who had taken a helicopter trip to get a bird's-eye view of this natural wonder. I was a bit envious but had an idea of what it must have been like. I had taken trips by helicopter on other ventures, such as over Victoria Falls in Africa and Mount McKinley in Alaska.

Hawaii – Aloha!

Honolulu

Our ship docked in Honolulu Harbor in the early forenoon on June 14. We were transferred to the Doubletree Alana Hotel for the last night of the trip, before continuing home or, in my case, to Japan. I decided to stay at the Doubletree Alana despite the fact that they charged me quite a bit more than the rate GCT had paid. However, the young women at the reception desk were very nice and handed me a big chocolate cookie whenever I had reason to approach the desk for an inquiry. I also liked that I could see the ocean from my balcony, and more importantly, the hotel was within short walking distance of the Hilton Hawaiian Village, which claims to be located on the second-best beach in America. I am not sure I would agree. Nevertheless, it was nice – and it came at a substantial price. A couple I talked with in the very spacious, open lobby complained about the $20 per hour they had to pay for a lounge chair on the beach. I guarantee they would not have had enough lounge chairs to accommodate all the guests in the skyscraper hotel, because the beach itself could not have provided enough space. Curiously, I did not spot a single rooster on the beach. I saw plenty of cute, multicolored dwarf roosters, hens, and chicks running around in most of the parking areas on the Big Island.

Be that as it may, I loved walking on the flagstone walkways through the grounds of the Village Resort and spent quite a bit of time admiring the man-made waterfall built with huge boulders at the entrance. I took plenty of time to look at the tropical wildlife, such as gracious pink flamingos, green-, orange-, red-, and blue-feathered macaws perched on palm-tree branches, and huge black-and-white-spotted orange koi swimming around in ornamental ponds on which lotus flowers and sea roses, among other tropical water plants, were floating. The Polynesian and Asian artwork in the lobby deserved attention. If you have any doubt about America's wealth, take a look at this spot in Honolulu. – I did get a good picture of a just-married couple in the lobby. The bride, in a stunning white gown, was beaming. On the last day, I hung out on Waikiki Beach, where a surfing regatta was underway. Boys and girls as well as more mature guys were busily readying their surfboards for the competition – Do not be fooled, though, because there were more homeless people here (about six thousand) than in any other city in the United States. – Try to find an inexpensive restaurant. Impossible. A hamburger cost $8 and a banana $1. I have never lived more frugally than during those extra days in Honolulu.

The bus service in Honolulu was excellent. There was a hop-on, hop-off trolley one could ride free of charge, and when I discovered by accident that I could take a ride for several hours alongside the incredible beaches – to the Dole Pineapple Farms, Pearl Harbor, etc. – for a $1 senior fare, I took full advantage of it and had a lot of fun, even on the bus itself. I chatted with other tourists and on one ride sat next to a man who was obsessed with UFOs. He showed me a book he carried under his arm, which left no doubt in my mind that these saucers do exist. I did not know this believer cult has thousands of followers. I made sure to tell other Americans waiting for a bus to take advantage of the senior-citizen fare, and they all thanked me with a big smile – if they were over sixty. I had quite an interesting conversation with a student from England who was traveling with a backpack and planning to spend some nights on beaches. Good for him. I love the young for their spirit of adventure.

Pearl Harbor

I did not get off at the Dole Pineapple Farms, but one day I did spend a few hours at Pearl Harbor, Oʻahu. After checking my purse at the visitor center, I went to watch the film, a historic documentary of the events that took place at Pearl Harbor, starting with the fateful attack by the Japanese on December 7, 1941. It was this assault that launched the conflict with Japan and triggered America's active involvement in World War II. On that date, 1,177 US soldiers, including the crew on the USS *Arizona*, became the first casualties of the Pacific War. The narrative brought back many memories of my childhood, the bombings, Germany's devastation, the loss of our home, evacuation, and my strong desire to go to Hiroshima to help the victims of the atom bomb. As I walked around, reading the commentary for the various exhibits on the grounds, I reflected on the impact these epic events had on my own life. Without the war, I never would have come to America! I decided to ask a tourist to take a picture of me in front of the World War II Valor in the Pacific National Monument. The monument provides information about the events of the Pacific War, Pearl Harbor, the internment of Japanese-Americans, battles in the Aleutians, and the occupation of Japan. My visit to Pearl Harbor was important to me in view of the fact that I would complete the journey by going to Hiroshima only a few weeks later. I learned a lot! It was another moving experience, not unlike my visits to the concentration camps in Buchenwald and Auschwitz.

I did not go into the USS *Arizona* Memorial. I could no longer observe such atrocities of war. I saw the USS *Missouri* battleship from a distance. While waiting for the bus to return to the hotel, I chatted with a couple of soldiers who were stationed at Pearl Harbor. They liked staying there but appeared to be a tad homesick.

I had wanted to check out Fort Shafter, but gave it up when they told me the old hospital had been torn down and a new one built in its place. The last day in Honolulu, I took the bus – known as the beach bus to Hanauma Bay – to Diamond Head! As I left the bus, it felt good not to be surrounded by a bunch of tourists. The iconic Diamond Head, a registered natural landmark since 1968, was right in front of me. I just stood silent for a while and looked at the huge, world-famous volcanic crater – 3,520 feet in diameter, 760 feet to the summit – and wondered whether Doc, who had climbed such mountains as Mont Blanc and Mount Rainier, had climbed this rock when he lived directly across from it. I never asked him, but can say with near certainty that he did. – I walked around the park and watched a group of children, between seven and eight years old, play and picnic with their teachers.

I had brought my own lunch, so I enjoyed it on a bench on a walk alongside a white-sand beach next to the park. I never dreamed that one day I would sit next to Doc's Diamond Head and munch on a banana. And I wondered whether what I had heard was true, that is, that a couple of centuries earlier, British sailors saw the rock from afar and, because it glistened in the sunshine, mistakenly thought diamonds were buried in the soil. I whispered a gentle *aloha* – good-bye – to the hunk of stone and began to change gears. My thoughts turned to Tokyo, where I had last been eight years before.

JAPAN II

Tokyo – Déjà Vu

In the early afternoon on June 20, 2010, I boarded my plane (Delta) and had my last view of Diamond Head from my window seat, as I left the Aloha State for Tokyo, Japan, where we landed in the forenoon on June 21, at Narita International Airport. Just as I had promised, I was back. Since I had arranged my own travel, I was in charge of the transfer from the airport to Hotel Mets Shibuya. No problem. The Japanese are so well organized one would have to be an idiot not to understand what one is supposed to do. The hotel was about an hour away, and the transfer involved a change from bus to taxi at a central bus station. Along the way, I connected with a nice, young, English-speaking Japanese woman who made sure I got off at the right station. Hopefully, the young student from England, who sat on the other side of the aisle and kept falling asleep, eventually found the friend who had promised to pick her up at the bus terminal. – Everything in Japan is sinfully expensive. But instead of blowing some $240 for a taxi, I got away with spending less than $25. Not bad.

My room at the Mets Shibuya, close to the JR Shibuya Station in central Tokyo, was small and very neat, as expected. The breakfast, served at 7:00, before the welcome briefing given by our excellent OAT guide, Chieko Kikuchi, was just fine. – I never imagined all the brochures provided by OAT and its guides would come in so handy in writing my memoirs. They save me a lot of time and stress. Japan is especially challenging, because I took no notes, just pictures, and I never could have remembered all the names of the sites, temples, etc. on my own. Though my good friends and former neighbors Norm and Jeanne Overly, who lived for several years in Japan, might have helped me out, I would have been reluctant to bother them. And then there are Ellen and Pat Brantlinger, both retired IU professors (education and English), who were introduced to me by our mutual friends the Overlys because they had booked the same Japan trip. We connected happily at our first breakfast in Tokyo. (Unfortunately, the Brantlingers have been separated. Ellen, some ten years younger than I, suffered a heart attack and was taken from us to who knows where. It is hard to believe. Lesson learned: travel while you can, and carpe diem!)

Since Chieko went to the trouble of writing down what she told us about Japan's cultural treasures, I will copy it here, because I think it is good for my readers to know:

Japan is an island country in East Asia. Located in the Pacific Ocean, it lies to the east of China, Korea and Russia, stretching from the Sea of Okhotsk in the north to the East China Sea in the south. The characters that make up Japan's name mean "sun-origin," which is why Japan is sometimes identified as the "Land of the Rising Sun."

Japan II

Japan comprises over 3,000 islands, the largest of which are Honshu, Hokkaido, Kyushu and Shikoku, together accounting for 97% of land area. Most of the islands are mountainous, many volcanic; for example, Japan's highest peak, Mount Fuji, is a volcano. Japan has the world's tenth largest population, with about 128 million people. The greater Tokyo Area, which includes the capital city of Tokyo and several surrounding prefectures, is the largest metropolitan area in the world, with over 30 million residents.

Archaeological research indicates that people were living on the islands of Japan as early as the Upper Paleolithic period. The first written mention of Japan begins with brief appearances in Chinese history texts from the first century AD.

Influence from the outside world followed by long periods of isolation has characterized Japan's history. Since adopting its constitution in 1947, Japan has maintained a unitary constitutional monarchy with an emperor and an elected parliament, the Diet.

A major economic power, Japan has the world's second largest economy by nominal GDP. It is a member of the United Nations, G8, G4 and APEC, with the world's fifth largest defense budget. It is also the world's fourth largest exporter and sixth largest importer and a world leader in technology and machinery.

Our sightseeing tour of Tokyo started at 9:00 a.m., and though I had seen the Imperial Palace on my previous trip, I did not mind seeing it again. As in 2004, we were taken for a brief photo stop and let out on the Nijubashi (Double Bridge) to take pictures of the main residence of Japan's emperor. We could not see too much of the compound, but did get an idea of the rather sizeable complex of private residences, the museum and administrative offices, and the highly manicured, park-like surroundings. The palace is built on the site of the old, destroyed Edo castle. Its style is modernist, with distinct Japanese accents such as the hipped roof, beams, and columns.

Our visit to the Asakusa Kannon Temple, or Sensoji, Tokyo's largest Buddhist temple, was also a déjà vu for me. I had forgotten its history goes back to the seventh century, when according to legend a couple of local fishermen caught in their net a five-centimeter gilt-bronze statue in the Sumida River that resembled Kannon, the goddess of mercy, an event that eventually resulted in the construction of a shrine for the treasure. To reach the temple, we had to navigate the main entrance, that is, the Kaminari-mon (Thundergate), a nine-hundred-foot-long arcade flanked by numerous small shops selling traditional Japanese souvenirs, such as fans, masks, wooden *kokeshi* dolls, toys, oil-paper umbrellas, and Edo-style wigs. Tourist kitsch. Of course, the first thing that hits you is the huge red lantern hanging from the ceiling of the gate and the statues of the guardian gods Raijin (god of thunder) and Fujin (god of wind). I neglected to ask for a translation of the letters on the lantern, but knew that red stands for good luck, energy, heat, power, vitality, love, and other strong emotions. Next to the temple stands a five-storied pagoda supposedly containing some of the Buddha's ashes, and many people, mostly Japanese, were wafting incense over their bodies from a bronze incense burner. The worshippers believe the smoke will heal or prevent illness. I got another look at the Hozomon (Treasure-House Gate). A huge straw sandal was hung up on one side and guarded by scary-looking protector gods. It is the place where temporary markets, local festivals, and other events take place. I then made my way back through the crowds to the bus. – By the way, I could not view the tiny statue, because it is too sacred to be shown in public. Instead, visitors see a lavish mass of gilt and flowers. It goes without saying that we all adhered strictly to the etiquette required at the temple. We bowed our heads, lifted our hands in prayer when approaching or standing opposite a deity, and removed our shoes prior to stepping over the threshold to the inner sanctuary. If I were still a devout Catholic, all these theatrics would have guaranteed me a place in hell.

After the temple visit, we were dropped off in the Ginza (Silver Mint) district – the high-fashion center and site of upscale shops. I teamed up with a cotraveler whose name I have forgotten. She was a middle-aged, high-strung New Yorker, and she carried an umbrella that came in handy when it started to rain. Neither of us wanted to spend our leisure time in a restaurant. We were lucky. As soon as we stepped into one of the big department stores, we saw a scrumptious display of foods, such as cheeses, cookies, and chocolates. Beautiful young Japanese women wearing beige dresses with white aprons stood behind the counters and offered delectable samples of food and sweets. I chatted with them, and they were only too pleased to offer us samples of their goodies. We strolled through the store smilingly, thoroughly enjoying our free snacks and admiring the displays. The Japanese are masters at packaging their goods! I would not be surprised if the prices were yanked up considerably by the fancy wrapping. We bragged about our feast a bit at the welcome dinner in a local restaurant, and several in our group regretted not having thought of doing what we did. That's all I remember about the Ginza district. Nobody complained about not taking a special trip to Tokyo Tower, the tallest self-supporting steel tower in the world. Being 1,092 feet high and a replica of the Eiffel tower, it is a few feet higher than the Parisian original. So what! Why is it that big cities constantly compete over having the highest tower or building as their icon?

This trip involved a lot of luggage juggling. Right after dinner, I prepared an overnight bag for the next stop: two nights in Hakone. The rest was delivered to Kanazawa ahead of our arrival.

Hakone

On June 23, at 8:30 a.m., our bus took off for Hakone. Some of the landscape along the way looked familiar, but I could hardly wait to see Mount Fuji again. After a lunch stop, we headed toward my favorite mountain, absent the cherry blossoms. It became clear all too soon that the weather was not really in our favor. The first glimpse of Fuji was somewhat dismal, I thought. We could not drive up to the fifth station (at about 7,562 feet) and were let off at the Fuji visitor center instead. We all stared toward the summit and waited for the dark-gray clouds to drift away and afford us a brief view of the gray peak with patches of snow. We snapped pictures each time. I was careful not to gloat and rave about my first visit, in April 2004. I felt sorry for my cotravelers and, on the way down toward Hakone, coaxed the bus driver to stop a couple of times, that is, whenever it seemed we could get a better shot of the volcano. In the end, everybody was happy and content with our stop. I myself bought a nice, big color photo of the mountain with cherry blossoms at the visitor center to hang in my bedroom, just beneath Mount Everest and next to the Perito Moreno Glacier.

Chieko tried hard to teach us a few Japanese phrases on the way to the *ryokan*-style Gora Asahi Hotel, where we found ourselves suddenly immersed in true Japanese culture. The hotel was next to an *onsen* (hot spring), that is, a sulfurous volcanic "hell." It turned out to be quite an ordeal. My room reminded me of a scene in Puccini's opera *Madame Butterfly*, which I had seen at the Hannover Opera House years before. The floor was covered with tatami (rice-straw matting). A single, heavy, low rectangular table stood in the center, and futons, arranged by the *ryokan* staff, were laid out for us with sheets, coverlets, and extra blankets. I loved the sliding doors, which led to a sunroom. Known as shoji, the doors have translucent paper that filters the incoming light. The adjacent bathroom was incredibly curious and for me a first, because the toilet seat could be heated. Actually, there was a lot more to this supermodern and sanitary piece of essential equipment.

For dinner, we got dressed in our furnished *yukata* (a Japanese-style light cotton robe, similar to a kimono), put on the slippers, and took the elevator down to partake in a very tasty, typical Japanese-style meal. When it was time to get up the next morning, I discovered with dismay that my joints refused to function normally. I had to roll over toward the low table, about six feet away from my futon, in order to pull myself up. One of our cotravelers who was substantially heavier than I admitted that she had practiced getting up from the floor before coming on this trip.

There was no time for me to try out the hot springs before we took off for the sightseeing tour of Hakone. We took an aerial cableway, which was registered with the *Guinness Book of World Records*, to Owkudani Valley. The panoramic view from the cableway was commanding not only because of the scenic views and the volcanic activity, but also because it offered another choice view of Mount Fuji, which by then was out of the clouds. Thanks to a cloudless sky, our boat cruise across Lake Ashi, which sits 2,400 feet above sea level and is the result of the eruption of the old Hakone Volcano some three thousand years ago, turned out to be just wonderful. Equally wonderful was the view from the beautiful, upscale restaurant on Lake Ashi, where we were served a superb buffet-style lunch. Our table was next to the floor-to-ceiling windows, which provided a view of the divine Mount Fuji panorama, minus the snow. What more could you want?

Fireball Lily

On the way to the hotel, we stopped at Hamamatsu-ya, a wooden handicraft workshop, to attend a demonstration of the Hakone-Zaiku Marquetry manufacturing process. It was truly amazing to watch the intricate process in which the craftsmen created a multitude of artifacts from various woods. The skill involved the use of potter's wheels to make bowls, boxes, plates, trays, etc. of all sizes, enhanced by different inlays of wooden mosaic. The main colors of the thin, paper-like shavings from the juku tree were beige, tan, dark brown, and dark red, in chessboard design. I could not resist buying a 3"x 3" music box that played "Butterfly," which turned out to be not the aria of Puccini's opera, but a popular song in Japan.

Kanazawa

At 9:00 a.m. on June 25, after a second night on the futon, we were transferred by coach from the hotel to Odawara Station, where, for our first bullet-train ride, we boarded the Hikari-507 train to Nagoya, where we arrived some forty minutes later to change trains. At 11:48 a.m., the JR limited-express train Shirasagi-7 left Nagoya for Kanazawa, where we arrived at 2:51 p.m. The trains in Japan are incredibly fast and precise, supermodern, quiet, comfortable, and exciting to ride. The bullet train travels with lightning speed! Nevertheless, you do get a passing glimpse of the very Japanese countryside, that is, a patchwork-quilt pattern of rice fields in shades of yellow and green, broken up by wooded or mountainous terrain. I for one will never understand why our increasingly backward country seems unwilling to spend a few extra bucks to keep up with the rest of the world's advanced countries regarding mass transportation.

Taxis transferred us to the Kanazawa New Grand Hotel, where we stayed three nights. I was content with what we got and was in time the next morning for the Kanazawa sightseeing tour, with a first stop at Kenrokuen Garden. The guide assured us this garden was one of the three most beautiful gardens in Japan; it dates back to the seventeenth century and the feudal lords of Kaga. The major attributes of this garden are seclusion, spaciousness, antiquity, artifice, watercourses, and panoramas. Yes, it is a truly beautiful and artful work of strolling-style landscaping. I loved the pond and the Kotoji Lantern, a stone lantern with two legs that resembled a bridge on a koto; the Tea House, supported by stone legs and seeming to float on the Kasumga-ike Pond; and the Karasaki Matsu black-pine trees with their sprawling branches. I wished with all my heart that I could experience this oh-so-scenic spot in the winter! We understood why Kanazawa was a prosperous castle town between the sixteenth and eighteenth centuries and has been one of Japan's cultural centers ever since.

The following visit entailed a middle-class samurai house and a museum that also boasted a beautiful garden. It was definitely a first for me as well. I was not all that interested in the military nobility of preindustrial, feudal Japan, but entered the place with my innate curiosity. After all, it too is a part of this country's culture. I will copy below what my OAT brochure said about this particular place (I find it all a bit amusing):

This house, built in 1770, was originally 900 square meters on the premises of 2000 square meters. At the beginning of the Meiji era, about half of the house was demolished. However, it still retains many of the features of traditional samurai houses.
1) The arrangement of the rooms is made deliberately complicated to confuse enemies. There are few corridors and they are all separated.
2) The pillar at the side of the tokonoma or alcove in the guest room is cut halfway to make swords and spears easy to use.
3) The guest-room has an antechamber, where guards could wait in case of emergency.
4) All the wooden parts of the house are lacquered for protection.
5) The rooms have plain decoration without any paintings on fusuma (paper doors).
6) The ceiling of the tea-ceremony room is lower than the normal standard. This not only makes those sitting feel comfortable but also would have been a hindrance to the use of weapons.
7) The tea-ceremony room has more wall than usual, which makes you feel calm and peaceful with its dimming effect.

Yachiya Shuzo, a 377-year-old Japanese sake brewery located outside Kanazawa, was next on the list. I had my first taste of sake when a former boyfriend who had fought in the Korean War gave me a sake set as a gift. I thought it tasted rather bland compared to wine or beer. Again, we had to take off our shoes before entering the more or less dark and narrow place. The metal vat that, when in use, contained a mixture of rice, water, and koji, a special rice malt, was empty. But we were all given a tiny sip of sake before we were ushered out and put on our shoes. That is all I remember about the place. I knew it would be the first and last time I visited a sake brewery in Japan.

In the afternoon, we got a glimpse of the biggest of four *chaya* (geisha) districts in Kanazawa, which featured the old wooden structures. Unfortunately there was not enough time for us to be enchanted by dancing geishas. I was so fortunate to come upon several beautiful geishas, who posed for me during my stroll down the main street. I also sneaked into the entrance of one of the geisha houses, which had been renovated into a restaurant, to get at least a sense of what it used to be like. Our guide gave an excellent lecture about geishas, their historic background, the prerequisites for the occupation, and their training, skills, etc. Both physically and mentally, it is an extremely involved and challenging undertaking, pursued to the point of perfection. The geishas always remind me of china dolls, somewhat emotionless, enigmatic, and fragile. I have no ambition whatever of following in the footsteps of any one of them. Leave it to the Japanese to package their products for sale and appreciation, be they inanimate or human.

Chieko surprised us – I forget where, but it was probably in Kyoto – with a stop at a very upscale department store. The main floor was crammed full of spectators waiting for a kimono fashion show to take place. It was quite exciting, and I must say that at the end of the show, I walked away with a feeling of total satisfaction. I had seen some exceedingly gorgeous and exquisite kimonos. All of that for free. *Arigato*!

Before returning to the hotel, we had a chance to take a short walk through the Nagamachi Samurai District. Some twenty samurai residences still stood along the narrow street, and it seemed as though people were still living in some of them. Having visited the Terashima House earlier, we did not enter any houses in this particular district. I did not complain. It was hot and very tiring on that day. I talked our guide out of a visit to one of Kanazawa's gold-leaf producers. I own a vase with Kanazawa *haku*, that is, gold beaten into a paper-like sheet – the technique originated in China around 800 AD. It is used for decorating pottery, lacquer work, woven cloth, and Buddhist altars. I am sorry now for being selfish, because Ellen Brantlinger had really wanted to see it, and now she is dead.

On June 27, a Sunday, after a good night's rest, we assembled in the lobby for a day's trip by coach to Shirakawa-go and Gokayama, where we arrived an hour later. This was an optional trip, which I took because friends in the States had recommended it to me and I liked what OAT had to say about it:

Shirakawa and Gokayama are two mountain villages – and UNESCO World Heritage Sites – in the forested countryside outside of Kanasawa. Because of their relative isolation, these areas developed independently of Japanese society, resulting in a unique culture and lifestyle. In addition to creating their own dances, festivals, and traditions, residents developed a distinctive architectural style known as ghasso-zukuri. Characterized by steeply pitched thatched roofs that are both striking and elegant, these dwellings are considered to be some of the most efficient farmhouses in Japan – and we'll discover why upon enjoying a closer look. Then we'll visit a workshop to see how washi – a thick fibrous paper made from mulberry, cedar, and maple bark – is created. Afterwards, we'll head to Murakami House, which was built in 1578 and is the oldest gassho-style house in the area. (Gasshozukuri translates into "hands in a Buddhist prayer.") During our visit here, we'll learn more about the history and culture of Gokayama and enjoy a traditional dance performance. Later, we'll savor a traditional lunch of soba (buckwheat noodles) at a local restaurant, and learn the art of mochitsuki, or rice-making, with local people.

And we did all of that. The tour was exceptionally exciting and informative, as it was all new to me and unexpected. It was worth the $155. These rather rustic, dark-brown farmhouses, with their steep, rice-straw-covered thatched roofs, made without nails, reminded me vaguely of houses in rural Switzerland, Austria, and Norway. The roofs were designed in this way to stand up to heavy snowfall during the winter. I walked leisurely through the scenic village. It was so peaceful, and I was happy when I came upon a house where I bought a couple of unusual souvenirs: two brooms for dustpans. – The dance presentation at the Murakami House, as well as the rice-cake making at the Gassho-zukuri Folklore Park, was indeed unique, but I was ready to return to the hotel at the end of the tour, because the humidity and heat were beginning to bother me.

On June 28, after breakfast, we split up into small groups, and my group was taken by taxi to visit the home of Mr. and Mrs. Nakagawa, in Kanazawa, for tea. It was a highly interesting event. The house had three floors, and although the rooms were rather small, they provided enough space to accommodate the medium-sized Nakagawas. Noriko, the wife, was slender and tall and rather elegantly dressed. They were very proud of the various pieces of valuable art decorating the walls, and when we were shown a few of the dozen or more kimonos – gifts from the husband to his wife on various special occasions, wrapped in tissue paper and tucked away in separate sliding drawers along the wall – we all gasped in awe at their beauty. One lady in our group even put one on. She looked stunning. For tea, we sat around a *kotatsu* table, which was so unique. We sat on cushions placed on the floor, but our legs and feet rested in the opening underneath the table, where they have a heating device in the winter. At that table, before our time was up, Mr. Nakagawa wrote a special note for each one of us in Katakana. Mine translated as something like "in a lifetime, there is but one encounter." This sentiment is based on the philosophy of the tea ceremony. The note also bears my name and the Nakagawa's address. Well, the Japanese, just like everyone across the Asian world, love their tea. Our host gave all of us a nicely wrapped teacup. The cookies they served were good too. We all voiced great admiration when our hosts showed off their recently installed high-tech stainless-steel kitchen. Mr. Nakagawa took us down to his small store, where he sold sake, cookies, sweets, and a bunch of other goodies. I purchased a couple of sweets, which I munched on the way back to the hotel. How true: the visit to the Nakagawas was a once-in-a-lifetime encounter. – *Arigato*!

Taxis transferred us to the futuristic train station in Kanazawa, a marvel that integrates a traditional wooden temple gate into a glass-and-steel environment. A huge glass dome, built to prevent blockage from snowstorms, covers it. All the platforms are above street level, and the rolling stairs are so steep and high that riders feel they will end up somewhere in the sky. We arrived early enough to walk around and try out an escalator and were totally impressed. – At 1:55 p.m., the JR limited-express train Thunder Bird-26 sped from Kanazawa to Kyoto, where we arrived at 4:09 p.m. The taxi transferred us to the Hearton Hotel, close to the Nijo Castle and the Kyoto Imperial Palace, in central Kyoto, for a five-night stay.

Kyoto

"Kyoto was Japan's imperial capital from the 8th to the 19th centuries, and remains what is arguably the cultural heart of the country. There are a tremendous number of religious sites, including nearly 300 Shinto shrines and 1700 Buddhist temples. In fact, one of Japan's largest temples, the Chion-in, houses the country's largest bell, a bell so massive it requires 17 monks to ring. The striking architecture of

Kinkakujim, also known as the Golden Pavilion, dates from 1397, when it was built by the third Shogun of the Ashikaga Shogunate. The reflection of the pavilion on the water of the adjacent pond produces a breathtakingly beautiful and world-famous view" (OAT). Sorry, the OAT literature said nothing about the Kyoto Protocol, adopted to address climate change and signed in 1997.

On June 29, the Zen Buddhist temple Kinkakuji (aka Deer Garden Temple) was the first site on our schedule, and since the weather was perfect, this truly golden pavilion (it is coated with gold leaf) was a sight to behold. Just awesome – the reflection in the lake and its integration into the landscape is profoundly artistic and provides an unforgettable experience. Also unforgettable is the story behind the temple. Briefly, on "July 2, 1950, the pavilion, built in 1397 in Kinkaji architectural style, was burned down by a mentally sick novice monk. He survived a suicide attempt, spent 7 years in prison, and died in 1956 of tuberculosis. It was built by the third Shogun of the Ashikaga Shogunate" (Brochure). We were told the symbolic meaning of gold is the mitigation and purification of negative thoughts and feelings regarding death.

Nijo Castle, constructed between 1601 and 1603, has seventeen temples and other shrines to admire and is designated as a UNESCO World Heritage Site. "Although meant to represent power, it appears more a royal estate than a military post fortified with weapons. It was built by Tokugawa Ieyasu, founder of the Tokugawa shogunate, and became a meeting place for the shoguns. The largest building on the grounds is Ninomary Palace, intentionally built with floors that squeak so an intruder would be heard advancing through the room" (OAT).

After exploring most, but not all, of the buildings, I was ready for lunch at a local restaurant. But after that, we had two more stops to make. The first was Sanjusangendo Hall, built in the twelfth century and containing an impressive 1,001 statues of the thousand-armed Kannon Buddha. Honestly, by then I was almost exhausted and truly overwhelmed by the sight of all those Buddhas. By that time, I had seen so many Buddhas in China, Bhutan, Thailand, India, etc. that I was reaching a point of saturation when it came to Buddha statues – standing, sitting, or reclining, golden, bronze, or jade, laughing or meditating.

The second stop was Kiyomizu, an independent Buddhist temple founded in 778 and built in 1633 – again without the use of nails. Since it is built into a hill and is named after a waterfall within the complex, it goes without saying that the setting, comprised of several other shrines, including the ever-present pagoda, is truly beautiful. One of the main sites is the Kiyomizu stage. If you jump from it into the pond created by the Otowa waterfall, your wish will be granted. We were lucky enough to take a sip of water from the falls, but I completely forgot to wish for something. I was too busy taking a picture of a just-married young couple, who posed for me on the stage. The heat, as well as the constant ritual of climbing endless steps, taking my shoes off, and putting them on again, was slowly getting to me, and in retrospect

Japan II

I should have wished for the opportunity to visit the temple in the winter. The winter photos I saw later were out of this world.

I had no problem falling asleep that night.

On June 30, I readied myself for more temple torture, because I had signed up for the optional Nara and Fushimi Tour. OAT's description sounded tempting – do you agree?

This excursion takes us to the distinctive city of Nara, which was the capital of Japan before Kyoto. We will visit two UNESCO World Heritage Sites in Nara: Todaiji Temple and Kasuga Shinto Shrine. As we approach the Todaiji Temple, you will first be impressed by its massive size. It is said to be the largest wooden building in the world. It is also one of the major historic temples in Japan and contains valuable artifacts. Within this temple is one of the largest gilded bronze Buddha statues in existence. A charming feature of the park area is its free-roaming tame deer, which were traditionally regarded as the messengers of the Shinto god Kasuga. If you wish a close-up introduction to them, you can purchase biscuits to feed them, but be prepared to be very popular with these lovely creatures when you offer them food.

We also visit the Kasuga Shinto Shrine, dating back to AD 768. It is situated in the fields of the Mount Mikasa's foothills. These hills and the mountain are considered sacred because it is believed that a deity descended to the top of Mount Mikasa. After lunch at a local restaurant, we'll continue to the lovely town of Fushimi, one of Japan's most famous sake brewing districts. Our tour ends at Fushimi-inari, a shrine dedicated to the Shinto god of the harvest, particularly rice. Here, a series of some 10,000 vermilion torii *gates snakes along a woodland path for about 2.5 miles – a surreal sight that served as a backdrop in the film* Memoirs of a Geisha.

The trip, I must say, was well worth the $150.

As far as the deer are concerned, there were hundreds of them running around, and they pestered us so much I made a point of keeping my distance. I watched a deer pull the brochure a tourist was reading out of his hands and, while standing next to him, devour it bit by bit within seconds. How about that? I must say that the deer in my backyard are much better behaved. (I tested them, and they do not eat paper.) The *torii* gates leading to the Fushimi Inari Shrine were bright vermilion or China red – and so overwhelmingly impressive that I remember the gates more than the Buddha or the temple itself. Anyhow, if anybody reading this after my demise is curious, you can look at the 1,385 pictures I took on this trip and get an idea as to why some things will be remembered more than others.

On Thursday, July 1, at 8:30 a.m., another trip was scheduled. This one involved a tea ceremony and Zen meditation at Zuihoin Temple, one of twenty-two subtemples of the Daitokuji Monastery. Suffice it to say that the experience of drinking a cup of tea with a Zen master in silence was unique and soothing. We sat in a big hall on cushions on the floor, listening to the master. Chieko's translation of whatever it was he said was interesting, though I do not remember any specifics. Sorry. At the end, I was able to get up without too much trouble, because I had chosen my seat wisely, next to a post.

The temple garden was most unusual. "It was designed by Mirei Shigemori in the 1960s and is characterized by its vigorously raked sand, giving the impression of rough seas. The stone placement is equally vigorous, featuring numerous pointed stones. Whereas flat stones convey a calm and solid feeling, tall pointed stones project a strong and active mood. The combination of the vigorously raked 'waves' and the pointed stones infuses this garden with energy. The tiny bridge to the right is set very close to the sand and appears to be far away. The background hedges angle to the right in order to soften the right corner, clearly define the garden space and create a sense of intimacy when viewed from the veranda" (Brochure). Looking at the picture once more, I think I would have had a hard time coming to those interpretations on my own. One thing is clear: raking the gravel-like stones is definitely less troublesome than fertilizing, watering, and pulling weeds. But if I had to do it, I would go nuts.

I was genuinely looking forward to the next adventure. No temple – I am serious. Instead, our bus went through lovely countryside, with well-kept rice patches on both sides of the road. Occasionally, we spotted a Japanese wearing a brown coolie hat, bent down and working in a weedless rice paddy. After a forty-five-minute ride, we arrived in Kameoka, where we met some local farmers. We protected our shoes with a plastic guard and were handed a plastic bag. A man took us to a field where organic farming was practiced and where we picked various kinds of fresh produce before getting cleaned up to enter the Heki-tei, a three-hundred-year-old house where a famous samurai once lived. The Hioki family, whose ancestors were notable property owners in Kameoka, now owns the house. We gathered around tables arranged in a big square. In front of me was a sushi mat. Once we knew what to do, we helped ourselves to rice and various vegetables in order to prepare and eat our *makizushi* (rolled sushi). This too was a first for me. It was fun!

On July 2, our last day, I was glad to have skipped the optional Arashiyama and Japanese Gardens Tour. I was in no mood to traipse around more gardens, and as it turned out, it was a wise decision: not only did it rain cats and dogs the entire duration of the trip, but opting out allowed me to rest up for our dinner event that night.

Chieko really surprised us – especially the three IU professors – when she revealed that the dinner on July 2 would take place at Japan's second-oldest, and one of Asia's highest-ranking, educational institutions, Kyoto University. We learned that eight Nobel Prize laureates, in addition to numerous world-class researchers, were educated there. Our meal was served in one of the university's finest banquet rooms. The ambiance was elegant and made each one of us, I am sure, feel very special. After the meal I walked around and noticed a spacious faculty lounge with modern furnishings. Today, I wish I had bought one of their nice navy-blue sweatshirts in the gift shop, located not far from the dining room. Since it was summertime, many of the twenty thousand students, as well as many of the 2,860 professors, were absent.

According to the OAT brochure, "Kyoto University Clock Tower, designed by Goichi Takeda, professor and founder of the Department of Architecture in 1925, is their precious symbol. It is a place in which we might realize the internationalization of the arts and sciences, an exchange between every branch of learning, and an academic exchange between society and the university, thereby continuing the tradition and intellectual philosophy of Kyoto University."

Hiroshima

On July 4, some departed for the United States via Osaka, and those continuing to Hiroshima were taken by taxi to Kyoto Station, to leave on the JR bullet train Nozomi-15 at 10:29 a.m. We arrived in Hiroshima at 12:05 p.m. and, in the absence of taxis, walked some fifteen minutes in sweltering heat with our overnight bags, or in my case a rucksack, packed for three nights at the Hotel New Hiroden. Along the way, I grabbed a few of the paper fans handed out by guys in front of a department store. The heat index was approaching 90 degrees Fahrenheit, and the humidity was astronomical. But, no sweat, Hiroshima was my main reason for returning to Japan. Reports reached us that elderly people were dropping like flies from the heat.

Our sightseeing tour of Hiroshima, which we would explore by tram and on foot, began after a brief siesta. I could hardly believe I was finally there, the place I had longed to visit since the Bishop of Hiroshima, when visiting Hannover in 1952, delivered a sermon at St. Heinrich in which he pleaded so effectively for help for surviving victims of the atom bombs dropped on Hiroshima on August 6, 1945, partly to end World War II and partly to revenge the attack on the US naval base in Honolulu by the Imperial Japanese Navy. The Pearl Harbor attack, which occurred on December 7, 1941, killed 2,402 Americans, and the Hiroshima atom bomb eliminated between 90,000 and 166,000 people. An additional sixty to eighty thousand were killed by the bomb dropped on Nagasaki on August 9, 1945. No matter how one rationalizes these horrific acts, are not the victims human beings created equal before God? And those who believe in God and the Ten Commandments, including "thou shalt not kill," are guilty. There is no excuse.

I too am guilty – of not going into greater detail about the history of these senseless killings. Those who survive one war have no guarantee they won't die in the next. And if they live in America, the chances of being killed by a neighbor, a jealous husband, a relative, a thief, a member of a gang, or some nut are pretty good.

They purchased it because they intended to kill someone or something. Personally, I would rather be killed than kill.

Chieko took us first to the Peace Memorial Park, which was completed on April 1, 1954, that is, five weeks after my arrival in the United States. On the way, it was obvious that Hiroshima had risen from the ashes like a phoenix and was in that regard not unlike the many European cities that were decimated, my hometown Hannover included. My kind neighbors Norm and Jeanne Overly spent 1958–1963 as Baptist missionaries in Yokohama (now the second-largest city in Japan) and 1985–1986 in Hiroshima on the basis of a Fulbright missionary scholarship. They reported that during their stay, remnants of the destruction were still present.

The only such remnant I saw, or that we were shown, were the ruins of the Genbaku (Atomic Bomb) Dome, designated in 1996 as a UNESCO World Heritage Site. It is part of the Hiroshima Peace Memorial, and "Little Boy," the first atomic bomb, detonated almost directly above the dome. In case you are interested, my friends in Hannover told me that in the ruins of the Aegidienkirche, a church in Hannover bombed during World War II, a big bell hangs to commemorate the attack on Hiroshima, now a sister city of Hannover. The church was not rebuilt after the bombing of 1943, and it now symbolizes "a wish for peace."

In walking through the Peace Memorial Museum, where remnants of the bombing and accounts of survivors were displayed, I looked, paused, and reflected and, as in Buchenwald and Auschwitz, was overcome by a feeling of deep sadness and the as-yet-unanswered question, When will it ever end?

My heart broke when I stood in front of the Children's Peace Memorial in the park, where people from all over the world have placed folded paper cranes – origami – as offerings for harmony on our planet, and when I learned about two-year-old Sadako Sasaki. She is remembered for having folded a thousand origami cranes while dying, like many other children, of leukemia caused by radiation exposure. She made the cranes in the hope that the gods would grant her a wish if she folded a thousand of them. She was hospitalized in February 1955 and died on October 25, 1955, after having folded over one thousand origami cranes. Question: if God is so good, then why not save innocent children? I am still waiting for answers. In retrospect, had I come to Hiroshima instead of America in 1954, I might have been able to do more good – by cheering up some suffering children in Hiroshima instead of tending to the spoiled brats in Jones, Michigan.

Walking around the spacious park, I looked at the various sobering memorials, the statue of the girl stretching out her arms with a folded paper crane rising above her being the most memorable. Finally, I sat down on a bench by myself, reflecting until it was time to return to the bus.

Japan II

On Monday, July 5, we walked to the station and boarded a train that took us to Miyajima-guchi, from which a ferry took us to the Itsukushima Shinto Shrine, famous for its *torii* in the sea. Itsukushima is an island in the city of Hatsukaichi, in Hiroshima Prefecture.

It felt good to have a change of scenery. As our ferry approached the vermilion *torii* at ebb time, it was indeed a sight to behold, and the closer we came, the more pictures I snapped. On the back of my entrance ticket, it states, "Itsukushima Shrine was first built in 583, then rebuilt by Taifa-no-Kiyomori in 1168 on the same scale as it is today. A corridor of some 280 meters spans more than twenty buildings."

"The shrine was designated as a UNESCO World Heritage Site in December 1996. Miyajima has been worshipped as a divine island since ancient times. This is why the shrine was built on the seashore where the tide ebbs and flows. The contrast of the blue sea, green hills and the vivid vermilion-lacquered shrine is breathtakingly beautiful" (OAT). – I totally agree. It was so fascinating to see the gate, especially later in the day, when the tide rose and the gate seemed to float on the sea. Two other facts were unusual as well: all the buildings that make up the shrine are built in the water, and the shrine's halls and pathways are on stilts. As I strolled around the grounds, I came upon a wedding party and got another picture of a bride and groom in their beautiful wedding attire. I was surprised to see quite a few deer roaming freely on the park-like grounds, and in looking through my pictures just now, I am pleased to discover one of Ellen Brantlinger feeding a deer. Who would have believed then that her days were numbered? I will never forget the compliment she gave me when I was climbing steep temple steps in that godforsaken heat. She thought I was "very brave," especially since I was the oldest in the group and a solo traveler. I was seventy-eight, I think. – I admired Ellen for her deep social conscience.

We returned to the hotel at 5:30 p.m., and instead of looking for a restaurant, I munched on some fruit and yogurt left over from my breakfast. I liked to watch TV at night to catch up on the news and get an idea as to what interested the locals.

July 6 was our last sightseeing day in Hiroshima, and I had signed up for the Inland Sea Islands Tour for an additional $160, which was not cheap, but I knew I would never return in this life or the next, which I do not believe exists. I simply had to take advantage of the opportunity. Carpe diem!

Here is why:

The islands of the Inland Sea – the body of water separating the main Japanese islands of Honshu, Shikoku and Kyushu – are cherished by the Japanese for their beauty. After breakfast, we'll board a bus for Omishima Island, where we'll visit Tatara Shimanami Park and enjoy a magnificent view of the Inland Sea. Then we'll continue on to the Oyamazumi Shinto Shrine, dedicated to Oyamazumi-no-kami, the god of warriors and of

Fireball Lily

the sea. We will be welcomed by a 2,600-year-old camphor tree as we pass through the Torii gate. The spiritual atmosphere of this shrine is sure to leave a lasting impression. Then, traveling by taxi, we'll cross Tataraohashi Bridge to reach Ikuchijima Island. Here we visit the Ikuo Hirayama Museum of Art, which displays many works by world-famous Japanese painter Ikuo Hirayama, who was born and spent his boyhood on the island. Having experienced the tragedy of the A-bomb at Hiroshima, Hirayama created many works on the theme of peace. We also see the dazzling architecture of the Kosanji Temple, which was built by the Buddhist priest Kozo Kosanji (1891–1970) to honor his mother, and took more than 30 years to build. On the hill above the temple area is Miraishin no Oka (The Heights of Eternal Hope for the Future). This white marble sculpture garden – created by world-renowned artist Kazuto Kuetani – caps the entire hill. After lunch on your own, we depart for Mihara by speedboat, and then take a return train to Hiroshima. We'll arrive back at our hotel in the early evening. (OAT)

A taxi transferred us to the bus terminal, and at 8:08 a.m., our highway bus took us to Omishima Island via the Sanyo and Shimanami Kaido Highways. If they do not sound familiar to you, don't worry; they were new to me too.

All in all, the day we spent at the scheduled sites turned out to be a most enjoyable experience. It was a wonderful finale for the Japanese adventure. I felt especially rewarded by the quite stunning display of vibrant white and pink lotus flowers floating in the ponds surrounding the raised Kosanji temple. When I lived on the Croft, we had two ponds – Japanese style – where lotus flowers floated and big goldfish frolicked. How I wished Doc were alive so I could share with him this special exotic moment. On the train ride back from Mihara to Hiroshima, I was rewarded with another most memorable moment. Our seating was open, and I had a window seat opposite a partially handicapped man who pointed out exciting sights – mountains, bridges, and villages – whenever the train approached them. That was very kind. But then Chieko, who sat a few seats away, asked me to come and meet someone. She introduced me to the gentleman sitting next to her, who spoke Japanese only. Chieko said the man was exactly my age and, most importantly, a survivor of the A-bomb attack. At the time of the attack, he sat in a schoolroom some fifty miles away from Hiroshima and remembered the sky lighting up in a way he had never experienced before. Fortunately, he survived. I told him our house, too, had been bombed, that we also saw a red sky for many days from about one hundred miles away, and that I too had survived the horrors of World War II. In view of my own experiences concerning the Hiroshima disaster, I felt I could finally close that chapter. We shook hands, and Chieko took a picture of us two survivors. – I had come full circle and was ready to return home with an inner feeling of peace and harmony.

Our Western-style farewell dinner at the hotel was nice, as usual. We chatted animatedly, relished the tasty meal, and were glad we did not have to meet in the lobby until 11:00 a.m., instead of the usual 7:00 a.m. We walked to Hiroshima Station and boarded the train to Shin-Osaka, where we arrived at 12:58 p.m., in time to change trains to Kansai Kuko, Osaka, where the rest of our luggage awaited us and where we all took off for different places in the United States. – As far as I know, everyone arrived safe and sound at their desired destination.

A month after my return, on August 6, 2010, the Japanese news I watch on TV focused heavily on the anniversary of the A-bomb attack, bringing back once more my memories of the war. And then, some seven months later, the magnitude 9.03 Great East Japan earthquake, which triggered the mega-tsunami that devastated large areas along the east coast and killed thousands of innocent people, hit the country. Humans again succumbed to nuclear power when three reactors in the Fukushima Daiichi Nuclear Power Plant melted down. It makes you wonder, Why Japan?

Before I move on to my next trip, I must interject that Pope Benedict XVI made history by resigning his post, in my opinion the first sensible act in his papacy. I bet he was extremely glad to get out of the Vatican, that vipers' nest. – By the way, at one time during my travels, I was granted a private tour of the Sistine Chapel, the place where Francis held his inaugural mass on March 14, 2013, a day after he emerged as the new pope. A Jesuit named Francis! I always liked St. Francis, and I liked the Jesuits very much until I turned about fifty. By then I had gotten to know a few Jesuits very well, better than I knew many Catholics. They put on a good show of being "poor," if you wish. However, if you looked behind the scenes, you could not but wonder why they loved to be showered with expensive gifts, like the best wines and brandies, preferred to be invited to the best restaurants, asked for the finest vestments, enjoyed being taken in private planes to Switzerland, etc., and never offered to pick up the bill for a gourmet dinner when out with a female. I guarantee that none of the Jesuits I knew personally ever went to a prison to wash the feet of inmates. I hope the new pope's example will become a requirement for priests across the board. Unfortunately, I am not very optimistic that a dramatic change will take effect. – I wonder how many babies the Catholic clergy has fathered, and how many housekeepers of priests were more than just housekeepers. I knew of several.

Regardless, as soon as I returned home from Japan, I called up OAT and canceled my spot on the Ancient Kingdoms: Thailand, Laos, Vietnam & Cambodia trip, set to depart on October 23, 2010, and exchanged it for a river cruise on the Danube from Vienna, Austria, to Nuremberg, Germany, at Christmastime. Ellen, who took the Ancient Kingdoms trip a couple of years before, had mentioned it gets even hotter there than in Japan, that there, too, hundreds of temple steps had to be climbed, and that the humidity at times was almost unbearable. In retrospect, cancelling was probably a wise decision.

THE UNITED STATES' MAJESTIC NATIONAL PARKS

I returned from the 2010 Christmas cruise with a bad cold, which, fortunately, was gone by the time I went to Cancún, where I focused on my writing. I did not travel during 2011, with the exception of my annual trip to Cancún around Christmastime. Little by little, the travel bug started to bite again, so I began to sift more carefully through the GCT catalogs, and one day in May, I decided to sign up for the America's Majestic National Parks trip, scheduled for September 24 to October 11, 2012. Lucky me – I was able to use the last of my United Airlines frequent-flyer miles for a round trip from Indianapolis to Rapid City, South Dakota, and from Denver, Colorado, to Indianapolis.

If you have read Part I of my memoirs, aka my "novel," you may remember that in 1956, Doc, Maria, and I covered some 12,600 miles exploring the United States and Mexico by car and saw several of the major parks. I thought that at the ripe old age of eighty, it would be nice to return and see these and other parks once more. I was curious to see how much they had changed, if at all, since my previous visit, when I was only twenty-three. It would be a trip to five states – South Dakota, Wyoming, Utah, Arizona, and Colorado – and seven national parks – Mount Rushmore, Yellowstone, Grand Teton, Grand Canyon, Bryce Canyon, Monument Valley, and Zion. It was the last tour offered in 2012, and I was hoping both to see some snow in the mountains and that the temperatures would be more or less on the cool side.

South Dakota

Rapid City

I left Indianapolis on September 24 at 10:30 a.m., changed flights in Chicago, and landed in Rapid City at 1:20 p.m. I was fortunate; several other GCT travelers arrived on the same flight. I had no trouble hitching a free ride on the GCT transport bus from the airport to the Holiday Inn Rushmore Plaza, where I had a pleasant room for two nights. No, there were no futons, but king size beds and a huge bathroom. What would you expect? It is America. By the way, when I booked my free flight, I had a suspicion other GCT travelers might arrive on the same flight and that I would be able to hitch a free ride from the airport to the hotel, which otherwise I would have had to arrange for myself. By then, I knew the tricks – I had used them successfully on overseas trips as well.

On September 25, day 2, the bus trip started right after breakfast, and to my dismay I realized I had brought the wrong clothes. It was much warmer than I had anticipated. I had packed most of my cashmere sweaters and only two lightweight tops. Whatever – I was determined to get by with what I had, since there was not much time to go shopping. – On the way to the Crazy Horse Memorial, the bus driver took us on a brief trip to downtown Rapid City, the City of Presidents. We got excited the minute we saw the life-size bronze statues (there are forty of them) along the streets, corners, and sidewalks. That was really neat. I did not see Obama, because his statue had not yet arrived. We were told that the project began in 2000 and that the randomly spaced sculptures were privately funded. – Unfortunately, due to time constraints, we could not get out and take a closer look at each of the statues to appreciate their originality.

However, we were let out of the bus at the next surprise stop: Chapel in the Hills, dedicated on July 6, 1968, and located at the foot of the Black Hills, outside of Rapid City. This chapel, built of solid cedar, is a stave church similar to one I had seen when visiting Norway for the first time. We learned that this gem is a replica of the Borgund Stave Church in Norway and that the wood carvings are the work of the Norwegian wood-carvers Erik Fridstrom and Helge Christiansen of Rapid City. Sitting inside was a soothing experience, and walking around the park-like surroundings induced in me a feeling of calm and serenity. If you want to get away from the hustle and bustle of the city, or get married in peace and quiet, this is the ideal place. However, the time allocated for us to walk around would not have been sufficient for a wedding.

But we had more time at our next stop, Crazy Horse Memorial. Located in the Black Hills of South Dakota, of which I had never heard and which I did not see when I visited the area in 1956, it is the world's largest sculpture. "It is being constructed just 17 miles southwest of Mount Rushmore. Begun in 1948 by noted sculptor Korczak Ziolkowski at the request of Native Americans, the Memorial includes the Indian Museum of North America, the Native American Cultural Center, the sculptor's studio, and a 40,000-square-foot Orientation Center. The dramatic sculpture of the legendary chief astride his horse fulfills the wish of Lakota Chief Standing Bear spoken at the dedication of the statue in 1948: 'My fellow chiefs and I would like the white man to know that the red man has great heroes, too'" (GCT). Ziolkowski and his wife Ruth had ten children. He worked without pay until his death in 1982. This gigantic granite monument was under construction on privately held land. They were drilling, blasting, and bulldozing away at the monument each day, but judging by the model I saw in the museum, I doubt the project will be completed by the year 2020, as anticipated, unless they change their minds and accept some government funding. – I took an extra bus ride while there, and the guide claimed that when finished, the monument would be approximately six hundred feet wide and 550 feet tall. He also stated that Crazy Horse was captured and killed when his war party wiped out Custer and his men at Little Big Horn. Somehow, this gigantic rock reminded me of the Great Sphinx of Giza, near the Giza pyramids in Egypt.

Mount Rushmore

It became clear that a competition was going on between Mount Rushmore – the sixty-foot faces of George Washington, Abraham Lincoln, Thomas Jefferson, and Theodore Roosevelt – and the Crazy Horse Memorial as soon as I stood in front of the former, which supposedly symbolizes the American ideals of freedom and hope for all humanity. The sculptors were the Danish-American Gutzon Borglum and his son, Lincoln Borglum. The faces were completed between 1934 and 1939 with federal funding, which ran out after the architect's death in October 1941.

It was a rather emotional experience for me personally, because fifty-four years earlier, I had seen these faces with Doc standing next to me. The monument itself was the same, but the surroundings had changed dramatically. In '56, we parked the car in a nearby parking lot and walked over to the monument, where a handful of tourists had gathered. This time, the visit began in an imposing visitor center, which I approached together with many tourists on a new, long cement path flanked on both sides by flags, and we could even take an elevator down for easy access if we did not want to struggle up and down the many steps. I do not recall anybody telling me anything about the specifics in '56, unless I have forgotten. I was surprised I had first seen the monument only fifteen years after it was finished. At that time, I had no idea the monument was controversial – many claim it legitimizes racial superiority, and the sculptor himself was a member of the Ku Klux Klan. Of course, in '56 I had no idea what the Ku Klux Klan stood for. This time, I questioned the sincerity of Thomas Jefferson, coauthor of the Declaration of Independence, and the statement "all men are created equal." Jefferson acquired his wealth – as did Washington – with the help of slaves who labored in their cotton fields. – At that time, they were property and anything but free! I hope and pray that in due time, Obama's face will be carved into this mountain. To be honest, I liked Mount Rushmore better the first time, when the surroundings appeared more pristine. A woman my own age, who was strolling around the grounds and sat down on a bench next to me, felt the same way. She had first visited Mount Rushmore in 1956 – on her honeymoon. How about that?

I excused myself right after our welcome dinner and rested up for the following day, when we would travel from Rapid City to Sheridan, Wyoming, to see Devil's Tower.

Wyoming

It was a lovely morning when we climbed into our bus and traveled through the pine-clad mountains spread out on the Great Plains. Along the way, our guide talked a great deal about the Lakota Indians, who called the hills "black" because the dark pine trees that covered them looked black from a distance. The Lakota Indians were pushed around by the government due to Custer's Black Hills Expedition, when European-American miners, including mobs of gunslingers, gamblers, and outlaws, rushed to the area to look for gold. Get the idea? Sorry, but I will not launch into a discussion about the horrible massacres that have taken place over the years between the white races and the Native Americans. Besides, I had my own experience with my ex, who suddenly, before my eyes, turned into a full-fledged Cherokee.

Our goal was Devil's Tower. "Established in 1906, this is our first National Monument (1906 Theodore Roosevelt). The tower stands 1,267 feet above the Belle Fourche River – an almost vertical natural monolith; it's the remnant of an ancient volcano. Known by some northern plains tribes as *Mato Tipi* (Bear's Lodge), it is still a sacred site of worship for many Native Americans (Lakota, Cheyenne, Kiowa, Crow, etc.). You'll recognize the massive rock as the landing site of the alien space-craft in the popular film *Close Encounters of the Third Kind*" (GCT). Vaguely, this rock reminded me of Ayers Rock in Australia, mostly because it too was sacred territory for the aboriginals, or Maori. Of course, this chunk of stone cannot compete, in size or shape, with Ayers Rock in Australia. This specimen is a light-to-dark-gray igneous monolith, and to me it looks rather bizarre due to the hundreds of parallel vertical cracks (columns) in the outer layer. It is also a favorite among rock climbers. According to legend, when a human pursued by a great bear cried to the spirit world for aid, the ground below gave birth to the great tower. If you are in the vicinity of the rock, go and take a look at the "miracle."

Cody

On September 27, day 4, we left Sheridan, Wyoming, after breakfast and traveled to Cody to visit the Buffalo Bill Historical Center. The trip took us through majestic scenery – ranging from high-plains trails to badlands and canyons with magnificent gorges. I could not get enough of it and took it all in. I was feeling awestruck – until our bus driver warned us of some trouble with the coach. He slowed down considerably, tackling inclines with some difficulty, and when we were going downhill, I asked whether he had enough gasoline and whether the brakes would hold. My cotravelers responded with a nervous giggle, and when he pulled into a big parking lot at the foot of one of the hills thirty minutes later, we sighed with relief and complimented him on his expert driving skills. We split up, some of us taking pictures of the vast Wild West landscape and others trying a buffalo burger at Dirty Annie's, a diner welcoming hunters. I cornered a real hunk of a guy, a contractor who looked more like a cowboy, who was happy to have his picture taken standing on the porch in front of the diner. He was proud of his gun and the leather cover he'd made for his cell phone, which was decorated with a big, rough turquoise rock. He even gave me his phone number in case I wanted to contact him later. On the way back to the bus, I took a final picture of the modest house under construction, a creation of the very conservative Wyoming builder. As you can see, the bus trouble

Fireball Lily

turned out to be a welcome distraction. I did not mind arriving at the next hotel a couple of hours late. My old philosophy was again confirmed: everything negative will turn into a positive!

According to GCT, "Cody was founded by Buffalo Bill Cody in 1896, and is home to the Buffalo Bill Historical Center. Widely regarded as one of America's finest Western museums, the center advances knowledge about the American West through acquiring, exhibiting, and interpreting collections of artifacts and preserving their physical and contextual integrity. It features five internationally acclaimed museums under one roof – the Whitney Gallery of Western Art, the Buffalo Bill Museum, the Plains Indian Museum, the Cody Firearms Museum, and the Draper Museum of Natural History." It was a perfect opportunity to take in the history and culture of the lands we were en route to see. In particular, the fierce-looking stuffed buffalo, elk, and bear that confront you when you enter the museum will leave a lasting impression and put you on the lookout to catch one or more of these beasts in the open countryside. I took one look at the gun display and stopped right there. I asked the museum guard which guns I should see, and he took me to the display of the guns presented to our presidents. In talking to the gentleman, I discovered that he used to live in Three Rivers, Michigan, not far from Jones, the place to which I immigrated.

At that point, I had not heard of Buffalo Bill, who obviously had quite an influence on the West. Born in 1846 in Canada, William F. (Buffalo Bill) Cody was a colonel in the US Army between 1897 and 1899, made a name for himself as a bison hunter, and organized the *Buffalo Bill's Wild West* shows, which featured extravagant cowboy themes and entertained many people, including the rich and famous in Great Britain, Europe, and the United States.

This colorful fellow was also responsible for the construction of the Buffalo Bill Dam and the Shoshone Project, which we visited on September 28 on the way to West Yellowstone, Montana, where we would stop to see Yellowstone National Park.

"As the Union Pacific Railroad stretched across the Great Plains in the late 1860s, hundreds of pioneers sought their fortune in the unsettled territories of the West. As more and more settlers moved west to develop their homesteads, it became apparent that a dependable supply of water was needed. Buffalo Bill and his associates acquired from the State of Wyoming the right to take water from the Shoshone River to irrigate about 169,000 acres of land in the Bighorn Basin. – After surmounting enormous challenges, such as the deep granite canyon and the irregular flow of the Shoshone River, the project was completed in 1910. It was the Reclamation's first high concrete arch dam and the highest dam in the world at 325 feet. Because of its historical significance, Buffalo Bill Dam was added to the National Register of Historic Places in 1973. It is also a National Civil Engineering Landmark" (Brochure). I am always amazed when I see these engineering projects, which remind me of Hoover Dam and the Three Gorges Dam on the Yangtze – amazed at what men are willing to endure, mentally and physically, to bring such projects to completion.

After visiting Buffalo Bill Dam, we stopped at Mammoth Hot Springs for lunch on our own and got a first impression of the uniqueness of these limestone formations. The contrast between the multicolored stones and the steam from the hot springs' boiling water was fascinating to observe. I myself was more intrigued when I spotted a pair of bison grazing on a strip of grass beneath the trees lining the parking lot.

Yellowstone National Park

We spent the night at Best Western Desert Inn, and on September 29, day 6, we filed into our bus early to head to Yellowstone National Park. I was rather anxious to see Old Faithful again and wondered whether it would touch me the way it did when I saw it for the first time, in 1956.

"Yellowstone National Park is the first of America's national parks, set aside originally to preserve its remarkable geothermal formations – there are more geysers and hot springs here than in the rest of the world combined. The thundering falls of the great Yellowstone River have carved out a magnificent canyon. – Take in the natural phenomena of shooting geysers, and keep your eyes open for bighorn sheep, elk, coyote, grizzly, black bear, and other wildlife, in this park that remains 99% undeveloped – a true wilderness. You also stop at Firehole Falls, Midway Geyser Basin, and the Grand Canyon of Yellowstone. You'll also visit Old Faithful, the famed geyser that has been spouting an average of once every hour for one hundred years. During the Washburn-Langford-Doane Expedition in 1870, this famous geyser was officially given its name – the first in the park to don its own name" (GCT). That's it in a nutshell.

The brochure failed to mention that every now and then, we would pass long stretches of badly scorched pine forests. Thousands of long, charcoaled tree trunks resembled black spear tips reaching into the sky – it was an eerie ambiance, which gave way only when we passed lush, green patches of pines and golden aspens sparkling in the sun.

The area around Old Faithful was ever so much more developed than it was in 1956. The path leading up to the geyser was paved, and many long benches had been installed to allow the floods of visitors to sit while waiting for the big moment of the miracle's eruption (every 35–120 minutes). Each eruption lasts one and a half to five minutes and reaches 90–184 feet – exciting the onlookers and the photographers, who held their cameras ready to click. And so did I click my little Sony digital when the spectacle occurred, ever so faithfully – just as it did in 1956.

Thanks, Mother Nature! It was comforting to know some things in the world won't let you down.

On September 30, we departed West Yellowstone for Grand Teton National Park, taking the John D. Rockefeller Jr. Memorial Parkway. On the way, we stopped after sunrise for a last look at Old Faithful's miraculous eruption and proceeded to the Fountain Paint Pot area, where we walked around on boardwalks in the blistering sun and, quite puzzled and amazed, observed the numerous geysers, hot springs, mud pots, and fumaroles, that is, a conglomeration of hydrothermal formations. The entire area was steaming. I felt like I was walking on a huge lid covering hell, if you believe in it. No question about it, it was "damn hot" down there. For a bunch of elderly nuns who were younger than I, the walk uphill was too steamy. They stopped early on and sat down on a bench to catch their breath and rest.

We paused for lunch in a small Wild West town, formerly gold-rush territory, and while others hung out in restaurants eating hot dogs, bison burgers, or whatever, I found a perfect spot to sit down next to the entrance of a Native American souvenir shop. It was a sturdy bench made of glazed tree branches – it had a golden-brown finish and a carved Indian head in the back. The sun was shining, and I snacked on the banana and yogurt I had retrieved from the breakfast buffet in the hotel. A huge black bear, carved out of wood, stood next to the bench. Since I had not yet seen a living bear on this trip, this was just fine. As I sat there feeling happy and content, a young man came out of the store. He stopped right in front of me and said, "You have such a happy smile – keep it and share it with others." Suddenly, I felt warm inside. What a nice thing to say.

Grand Teton National Park

On September 30, day 7, we departed for Jackson Lake Lodge and Grand Teton National Park. It was a glorious day, with blue, cloudless skies and the sun shining bright. We stopped briefly at a rest area on a small lake, in the background of which stood the Grand Tetons, which were reflected in the water. I have loved these mountains since I first saw them in '56 and have enjoyed seeing them on TV so many times over the years. I was hoping they would be dusted with snow at this time of year. They were not, but it was all right – until I discovered, just when I was ready to snap my first photo, that my Sony was dead. I felt devastated and helpless and hoped the problem lay with the battery.

Our next stop was Jackson Lake Lodge, a grandiose lodge perched on a bluff on Jackson Lake, opposite the Teton Range, which is mirrored in the lake. Indeed, it is a picture-perfect panorama – even more beautiful than that at Chateau Lake Louise, in Alberta, Canada.

I searched the grounds for a place to picnic and found a secluded spot, a bench beneath big shade trees with a full view of the spectacular vista. I loved it. A few yards in front of me sat a motorcyclist eating his sandwich. I chatted with him, and it turned out to be a most exciting conversation. The young man, in his thirties, was from Stuttgart, Germany, the place where my late cousin Helga had been private secretary and foreign correspondent to the CEO of Mercedes-Benz and where my longtime friend Anneliese Loeser's father had founded the great Salamander leather and shoe factory, which they had to abandon when they sought refuge from the Nazis in the United States. The travel bug had bitten this biker a few years earlier. He quit his job, sold his possessions, and decided to travel the world by motorcycle. Incredibly, he had been to many of the places I had visited, including Patagonia, as far south as Ushuaia and the Torres del Paine. BMW had furnished him with a bike for this particular trip. Strangely enough, when I was in Patagonia, if you remember, I came upon a group of BMW motorcyclists. The coincidence somehow revived me from my Sony-blackout depression. I bought a bunch of panorama postcards, and as soon as we reached the Snow King Resort in Jackson Hole, I plugged in my battery charger to see whether it would do the trick. It worked, and I was happy!

With my Sony intact, I was good and ready the next morning to join the scenic Snake River tube trip. I hoped to get another chance to photograph the Tetons. Jeff, our guide, had assured me I would have that opportunity. We were transported by bus to the landing site. After paying for the trip, we were helped into our life-jacket gear as well as into the river-rafting tube. Everybody got a box lunch. We floated down the Snake River happily. A few times, the ride got a bit rough, and now and then our steering guide had to jump into the water and push us over a rocky spot. The scenery was gorgeous: we passed a couple of anglers and admired the golden aspen trees, which grew in bunches, their slender trunks white or silver, like the trunks of birch trees. But we did not come close to the Tetons. I ate a third of my ham sandwich while I entertained my four copassengers, the nuns who adored Obama.

As soon as we left the tube and were back on the rather shaky bus, I asked the driver, who sported a white beard as long as Santa Claus's and wore a wide-brimmed cowboy hat, if he knew anybody who would drive me back to the Tetons for fifty bucks. He himself was busy, but when he asked a guy who stood outside the bus, he was happy to oblige. We agreed he would pick me up at 6:00 p.m. in the lobby of my hotel.

I loved the room in the Snow King Resort – I had a balcony with a perfect view of the mountains. While relaxing, I suddenly became a bit worried, because nobody knew I had arranged for this evening outing. I took only $55 and the leftover sandwich, in case the guy got hungry. Jack, who also looked like a white-haired cowboy, because the front of his wide-brimmed hat almost covered his face, picked me up in the lobby at 6:00 p.m. sharp and half-lifted me into an almost-new SUV that belonged to his boss, who let him drive it now and then. I took it as a sign that I would be in good hands with this clean-shaven cowboy. I sat next to him and was happy as a lark as he sped along the highway. After some fifteen minutes, the Tetons appeared on the horizon. Jack told me I would see the Tetons in the light of the setting sun. I thought that would be just fine. It would definitely be a first for me! He drove off the highway after some twenty minutes and parked the vehicle in a small parking area, where another car had parked. A family with two children was picnicking while watching the sunset panorama. I was elated and snapped a bunch of pictures while a chipmunk watched me from four feet away.

Jack, a bachelor and fifty-six years old, had traveled quite a bit and white-water rafted on the Nenana River in Alaska, just as I had with Liesl in 1999. For ten years he had not owned a TV. When he told me to get back into the car, I did, and he drove eastward on some side roads toward who knows where, until I noticed about five or six cars parked ahead. It was dusk outside, and when I looked across the grasslands bordering the side road, I was stunned at what I saw. There was a big herd of sixty or more grazing bison. A couple of the humongous beasts were about to cross the road, and Jack cautioned me not to get out of the car. I took umpteen pictures and was more excited than I had been in a long time. Jack advanced some fifty yards, parked, and let me get out. We stepped into the meadow on the west side of the road, where at least four other guys were stationed with cameras on tripods, pointed west toward the heavenly panorama of the Tetons, with the sun setting behind the peaks and coloring the sky all shades of yellow, orange, vermillion, crimson, and burgundy. It seemed the colors were changing constantly. This was a photographer's mecca, a symphony of colors. Another herd of bison was in the foreground, grazing undisturbed. – When it began to get dark, Jack drove me away from the ultimate sunset and dropped me off at the hotel, at which point it was really dark. I thanked him profoundly, gave him the $55 I had stuck in my purse, and took the sandwich back to my room, because he did not want it.

In the lobby, I ran into Drs. Usha and Ramesh Bhalodi, my traveling friends from Hamilton, New York, but originally from India, and raved about my adventure. Ramesh was disappointed that I did not ask them to join me, but I had had no idea where to reach them. Besides, I was happy to go by myself. Ramesh took some ten thousand pictures on the trip. I had never met anybody who lugged around such a heavy camera – in addition to a couple of smaller ones, which his wife carried. I knew that like me, he had zoomed in on bison, elk, and other wildlife during our trip. But I also knew I was the only one in our group of forty or so who was lucky enough to see a virtual herd of bison with the Tetons and the setting sun in the background. I was happy to let those who asked to see the photos look at them. It was worth the fifty bucks.

This is what the GCT literature had to say about Jackson Hole: "Long before the pioneers came west the rock formations of the Grand Tetons presided over a traditional summer home for the Native Americans. When the early 'mountain men' ventured out this way, the area became a destination for hunters and fur-trappers. The first permanent settlers arrived in 1881, establishing Jackson Hole as a cattle-ranching center. The skiing industry took off here in the 1930s and Jackson Hole remains a winter sports mecca to this day. In the summer, this year-round resort offers hiking, river rafting, camping, and other outdoor activities." I had wanted to take a look at Jackson Hole for quite a while, because I liked the mountain scenes that aired on TV whenever the big bankers or the Fed met there. It was similar to the mountain scenes in Davos, Switzerland, that aired when the big financiers gathered on the other side of the Atlantic. I was content to have been to both hot spots, despite the missing snow scenes. I liked Jackson Hole more than Davos.

Utah

Salt Lake City

On October 2, day 9, our expert bus driver apologized that we had not yet seen snow on the mountains and headed toward Salt Lake City, Utah, another city I had not visited before and was anxious to see. I was curious to find out a bit more about Mitt Romney and what really makes him tick. One of my cotravelers, a moderate Republican, was not too crazy about the Mormons. He also feared the Tea Party would be their downfall, because they were low-IQers. I thought that was a keen observation, especially coming from a Republican.

The drive to the city that hosted the 2002 Winter Olympics was glorious. That is, the scenery was out of this world. We stopped for lunch on our own at an out-of-the-way truck stop. I made my way through some twenty parked 18-wheelers and located a tree stump in a field next to the paved lot. I sat down on the rough stump and pulled out my yogurt, a granola bar, and a banana, as well as a bottle of water to wash it down. When I got up again and walked toward our bus, I came upon a big, rough-looking trucker who was showing off the colorful parrot perched on his elbow. In his truck sat a tiny, dirty, white poodle or a poodle-like mutt. I found it all amusing enough to ask for his permission to photograph his ménage à trois. He gave me a big smile and told me to go and take a look at the zebra, a goat, a donkey, some chickens, and a couple of emaciated mutts in a fenced-in lot some fifty yards away. I sat down at a picnic table close to that pitiful zoo and was ready to forge ahead when I saw my group entering the bus.

It was a long trip through open valleys and mountain passes. We arrived at the Hampton Inn in Salt Lake City, Utah, in the early afternoon. Barely settled in, we were summoned to assemble in the lobby to embark on a walking tour of Temple Square, world headquarters of the Church of Jesus Christ of Latter-day Saints, or the LDS Church for short.

Temple Square contains a monument to Brigham Young and the "Three Witnesses Monument," honoring the three men who testified that an angel showed them the golden plates from which the Book of Mormon was translated. You'll marvel at the awesome Tabernacle, dedicated in 1893, and famous for its amazing acoustics and Mormon Tabernacle Choir. The massive Temple with its six spires dominates the square. (GCT)

The entire complex left no doubt that the Mormons knew how to impress. The grounds were covered with the most gorgeous and lush flowerbeds. The temple's architecture was monumental in appearance. After all, it is the Mormons' most sacred building. Three young girls, one Italian, one French, and one American, met us outside one of the buildings to introduce us to their faith. They continued after were entered, feeding us some far-fetched stories I found difficult to believe. When I dared to ask at one point whether they could prove what they just told us, the girl answered, "No, we just believe." Some of my cotravelers gave me dirty looks – just as in Moscow, when I asked a Russian lecturer about how many people Stalin had killed – but I did not let it bother me.

When traveling with my students abroad and while studying in France, I occasionally ran into a small group of Mormon elders (missionaries) who were doing their two-year stint abroad to persuade others to join the Mormon faith. Mitt Romney spent his two years as an elder in France, obviously to avoid being drafted to fight the Vietnamese. From all the reports I heard, during that time he lived comfortably in a palace or the like. I am sure it was not easy to persuade a French man to switch his religion from Catholicism to Mormonism, and I understand that some elders returned home rather depressed from the experience and that some left the faith because they stopped believing the stories they had to tell. All in all, it became clear to me that the Mormons pursue the rich. And years ago, they did not encourage African-Americans to convert. The fact that they kick you out if you do not tithe, in my opinion, is another reason not to join their faith. I left Salt Lake City fully confident that Mormonism was not my cup of tea. I felt sorry for those who had been bewitched by their leaders and was disappointed that instead of affording us a performance by their famous choir, they gave us a CD recording.

Bryce Canyon National Park

On October 3, day 10, we departed for Bryce Canyon National Park, another first for me. During our lunch break, I chatted with a friendly young man neatly attired in a dress shirt and necktie, who sat down next to me on a bench in front of the restaurant where others in my group had lunch. He turned out to be a young banker and a Mormon, and he was undecided about the upcoming election. I am sure of one thing: after I got through informing him about Romney and his corrupt dealings relating to Baines Capital and a bundle of other not-so-ethical doings, he would not vote for that scoundrel. I never give money to politicians, but I do my best to inform as many people as I can of the differences between the parties. Again and again, people have thanked me for educating them. Be that as it may, our next stop was just great, despite its association with Mormonism.

Bryce Canyon National Park is a collection of natural amphitheaters carved out of pink limestone and sandstone. Here, the force of rivers, rain, frost, and erosion has sculpted a myriad of whimsical rock formations called hoodoos. They are shaped in colorful spires, bridges, and arches that resemble a fairyland. Truly, it's a photographers' paradise. The Park itself contains majestic ponderosa pines and deep evergreen forests. It is named for a Mormon farmer, Ebenezer Bryce, who was one of the first settlers in the area. You will find it a spectacular place, and the high elevation of the Park gives it some of the best air quality in the country. (GCT)

I must say, this canyon was a huge surprise for me. Approaching the place was a mind-boggling experience; we drove through one of the arches and were struck by the fabulous pink rock formations alongside the winding road, which reached high into the blue sky. The hoodoos reminded me of the fairy chimneys in Cappadocia, Turkey. As I walked toward the rim of one of the canyons to take photographs, a strong wind suddenly threatened to push me forward. I quickly retreated to catch my breath and sat down on a nearby bench to chat with a group of Londoners, who claimed Zion National Park was even more spectacular.

That evening, we were treated to a big cowboy dinner at Ebenezer's Barn & Grill. I had never been to a place like it, but why not give it a try? Hundreds of tourists from around the globe were gathered there. We stood in line to pick up our dinner, which turned out to be very tasty. While waiting in line, I began a conversation with the guy in front of me, an Australian, and as we talked we discovered we had traveled to many of the same countries and places, including Antarctica. Back at the large, round table, where six more of my group sat, I could not help but overhear a bunch of Swiss tourists at a neighboring table speaking German. We tried to exchange some chitchat, but the music and singing began, and we all started to listen. I was so surprised at how good the cowboy entertainers were. Indeed, they were first rate and stuck to the harmony of the cowboy songs. Little by little, I got drawn into the Wild West ambiance, and I gave the musicians my genuine applause. It was an old Wild West show with lasso swinging, six-gun twirling, and sing-alongs. I liked it a lot, because it reminded me of a rodeo I had seen during my 1956 trip with Doc. It somehow stopped me from being too disappointed when the nuns, who had missed much of the show because they stayed back at the Best Western Hotel to watch the first Obama versus Romney debate, told me they were totally depressed and distraught. I was glad I had attended the cowboy shindig.

Zion National Park

On October 4, day 11, we stopped at Zion Lodge, in Zion National Park, for lunch. "Zion National Park encompasses the crossroads of the Mojave Desert, Colorado

Plateau, and Great Basin. You'll see where red desert rocks mingle with crystal rivers, aspen forests, and lush green canyons at this truly unique intersection of life zones. You'll want to pay close attention not just to the landscape, but also the sky – Zion is home to golden eagles, peregrine falcons, and the rare endangered California condor. – Natural hanging gardens and scenic views of Zion's most prominent mountain, the Great White Throne, line the path to Weeping Rock, where water seeps down the cliff and forms a veil of 'tears' spanning the rock alcove. Weeping Rock is the most popular of Zion's 14 trails, but the park is a destination for adventure seekers who come to rock-climb and hike The Narrows, an intense river trail that zigzags through glistening canyon walls" (GCT).

As I gazed up at the massive sandstone cliffs, shimmering in cream, pink, vermilion, and red against a brilliant blue sky, I had to agree with the Londoners. These formations were even more exuberant than those in Bryce Canyon. Again and again, I shouted, "Wow" and "How gorgeous." After a while, there are no words left to express your emotions. One looks speechlessly at these natural wonders. Indeed, America's natural wonders are nothing to sneeze at! I mean it. I can easily understand why the Mormons wanted to settle here and why the Ute Indians fought hard to keep their land.

While checking out the visitor center to find a comfortable spot to eat my lunch, I overheard a couple in their early fifties speaking German. I sat down on a couch opposite them and started a conversation. It turned out that this couple just loved the great parks of America. Every year, they vacationed for a month in the States, renting a car and making the rounds. When I told them a bit about my background and travels, they were quite impressed and could not believe I undertook such travels by myself. They vowed to look upon me as their role model. The wife worked in a senior-citizen home in Germany and assured me that not a single one of the seniors – many quite a bit younger than I – had either the courage or the health necessary to engage in such ambitious excursions. Well, it made me feel pretty good.

Arizona

Grand Canyon

On October 5, day 12, we traveled through the scenic Kaibab Plateau's meadows and its forest of dense ponderosa pine and mixed conifers to the North Rim of the Grand Canyon. I was anxious to see the North Rim, because in 1956 I had been to the South Rim. Our guide mentioned that the North Rim, situated eight thousand feet above sea level, is wilder and more pristine than the South Rim, which is visited by some five million tourists annually. I can assure you, when I was there in 1956, few people were visiting this powerful and inspiring canyon, carved by the Colorado River and recognized as one of the seven natural wonders of the world.

True enough, the North Rim, where we were treated to a good lunch in the Grand Canyon Lodge dining room and afforded incredible views thanks to the floor-to-ceiling windows, was not overrun with tourists. I ventured out along a narrow and rough path along the rim, but since it was a hot and sunny day, I decided not to go too far and instead sat down next to a couple of women in their fifties, who were relaxing in lounge chairs on the terrace of the lodge. The immense panorama that spread out before us was as breathtaking as it was in '56. It touched my senses profoundly, even though the coloration of the layers of stone seemed less distinct than I remembered. It was as though the stone was covered by a haze or a very thin veil. – I got excited when the woman I met was greeted by another, who had just returned from a seventeen-hour run around the lower rim. I forgot how many miles she covered – it was most likely the rim-to-rim stretch. She was excited, exhausted, and starving. I took a photo of the two and considered myself lucky to have run into this fifty-year-old female Grand Canyon rim runner. A group of these women come here once a year. If you are interested, you can rent a lovely rustic cabin on the grounds, with rocking chairs on the porch. I tried out a rocking chair just to get a sense of what it might be like. By the way, I read somewhere that it takes about four hours by bus to get from the North to the South Rim. Either way, if you are pressed for time, go and see the South Rim.

After this grandiose luncheon stop, we continued to Page, Arizona, and the Glen Canyon Recreation Area, crossing the Colorado River en route. This particular stretch was especially memorable, because the canyons, deserts, and spectacular cliffs we passed on the huge Navajo reservation were exceptionally dramatic. My Indian friend Ramesh was lucky enough to get a picture of a rare, endangered California condor right at the bridge over the Colorado River, at the Glen Canyon Dam. Wow!

We stayed at the Courtyard by Marriott in Page, where I went to bed early because I was coming down with a cold, just like others in my group. One of our passengers, about seventy years old, was missing the next morning, as was his wife. He had come on this trip despite being plagued by a very bad leg. He walked with a cane, and it was obvious to me he was in constant pain. – His leg had gotten infected, and he had to be flown home for immediate care in a hospital. I felt so sorry for him and his wife. I had engaged in a heated conversation with them about Notre Dame, their daughter's alma mater. I have voiced my opinion about this holy grail of academic institutions before and will therefore refrain from repeating my thoughts here. Too bad they had to miss the Antelope Canyon cruise on Lake Powell.

"Formed in 1963 with the construction of the Glen Canyon Dam, Lake Powell is 187 miles long, with almost 100 major side canyons, and a shoreline of more than 1,900 miles. Your boat cruise takes you through lovely scenery featuring dramatic rock formations soaring out of the water" (GCT). And it was just like that. The sights were out of this world. The boat snaked through the steep, polished, pink-rock canyons beneath a clear blue sky. As the lake narrowed, each sight seemed more gorgeous than the next. About two hundred passengers were on our boat, and it was a happy crowd, to say the least. We were told this was the most-photographed slot canyon in the American Southwest, and I believed it. The canyon actually has two separate sections, Upper Antelope Canyon, or the Crack, and Lower Antelope Canyon, or the Corkscrew.

I was glad I had allowed myself to be persuaded by Jeff, our guide, to sign up for the optional trip to "view the Canyon from another stunning vantage point – on land, in a nimble yet safe and comfortable vehicle. Ride to the canyon, where you will enjoy an easy walk through the canyon to see its awesome, natural sculptures of stone" (GCT). The Navajo also called this "spiral rock arches." – A couple of Native Americans picked us up at the Marriott. The vehicles were less substantial than I had imagined, and when I first laid eyes on them, I almost opted out of the trip. I was reluctant to get on the pickup truck, on which a few wooden benches had been installed for tourists. It was an open vehicle with a vinyl tarp hanging loosely above, in case of rain. Since I was the oldest, I think, and unattached, the nice Navajo Indian (who at one point informed me they do not like to be called "Indian") helped me climb into his SUV, where, after he had cleared away empty bottles and other stuff, I got to sit right next to him. I was so relieved, because the sun was beating down mercilessly on the desertlike Navajo reservation, and I doubted that even I would have survived the journey. I had a most engaging conversation with the Navajo while he drove toward the canyon. He seemed quite interested in my travel experience in Mongolia and my marriage to "Panther," my Cherokee ex. The Navajo had plenty to gripe about regarding the still-discriminatory treatment of his tribe, and I felt genuinely sorry, not so much for him, but for others on the reservation who were less fortunate.

After we finished the hike through this incredible canyon – it's hard to imagine that this too is a part of America – and after I had pleaded with the Navajo to help me take pictures inside the canyon, where I never knew at what angle to hold my Sony to get the right shot, he was happy to pose for a nice picture with me, for which we leaned against a rock at the end of the tunnel. Back at the hotel, he let me take a picture of a beautiful silver bracelet – some ten inches wide and decorated with big turquoise stones – which he wore proudly on his left wrist. Boy, were we lucky it did not rain that day. When it does rain, the flash floods rushing through the canyon tunnel are so fierce they are life-threatening. Indeed, we learned that in August 1997, eleven tourists, seven from France, one from Sweden, two from the United States, and one from the United Kingdom, were swept away by a flash flood and died.

On day 14, we ventured deep into Navajo country to experience the grandeur of Monument Valley. – "This rugged terrain may remind you of classic Western films. John Ford first used Monument Valley in his 1938 film *Stagecoach* starring John

Wayne, and it appeared in several of his subsequent films. The stunning weathered red sandstone buttes and windswept towers co-starred with 'The Duke' again in Ford's 1956 film, *The Searchers*. Experiencing it firsthand will give you a humbling picture of how vast and timeless this beautiful area is" (GCT). I had not seen any of the cited movies, but was nonetheless rather excited to ride through this panorama-rich terrain of America's Old West. The Monument Valley sights along the Utah–Arizona border were not completely foreign to me, as they are often used in commercials. I was glad we did not have to leave the bus too often for photo stops, because my cold was getting worse. My friend Usha suggested I start taking the antibiotic pills I had brought along, just in case. We stayed at the Best Western Plus Rio Grande Inn, and I had decided to skip the next sightseeing trip. At that point in time, I had seen so many pink sandstone formations I felt utterly saturated by them, despite the fact that each one was unique and extraordinary. I thought that if I saw another pink rock, I would scream!

Colorado

The next day, October 8, I decided against an optional trip to see the ancient cliff dwellings of Mesa Verde so I could just rest in my room in Durango, Colorado. Luckily, we were free to do as we pleased. "Durango was founded as a rail hub to service local mines and smelters. Many of the original pioneer buildings are still in use, and today you might visit the historic districts of Third or Main Avenue for insight into that period of American history. Durango was featured in the classic Western film *Butch Cassidy and the Sundance Kid*" (GCT).

On October 9, I felt ever so much better and was more than fit to participate in the ride on the Durango & Silverton Narrow Gauge Railroad, which took us to Silverton/Grand Junction. I had seen a documentary about the railroad not long before on Deutsche Welle–TV.

Today you travel through some of Colorado's untouched terrain aboard the coal-fired Narrow-Gauge Railroad, which connects the two Victorian towns of Durango and Silverton. Rolling on the rails through 45 miles of beautiful landscape in turn-of-the-century passenger cars you'll get a real feel for travel as it was in the 19th century. Arrive in Silverton, an old mining town, late morning. (GCT)

Coal-fired steam locomotives were not new to me, since I was raised and partially educated in pre- and postwar Germany. I had occasionally traveled on steam locomotives in other countries. Thus, this stretch, founded by the Denver & Rio Grande Railway in 1879, was just another railroad adventure to add to the list. But I admit that the scenery on the forty-five-mile stretch was simply out of this world. What made it extra special were the golden leaves of the many aspen trees growing in the rugged terrain of the San Juan Mountains and, below the tracks, the sparkling waters of the Animas River. What a treat!

After a good night at the Grand Vista Hotel in Grand Junction, Colorado, we took off on October 10, day 17, for the last stretch of our eighteen-day Wild West odyssey, during which we stayed in twelve different hotels, with seventeen breakfasts, four lunches, and seven dinners included. I managed to feed myself with random snacks throughout the trip. Whenever we were told we were "on our own" for lunch or dinner, I resorted to my reserves. Jeff, our guide, called me "the smart traveler." He also told me that during his twenty years as a tour guide, he never had a tourist who had traveled as much as I. I considered that quite a compliment. *Danke schön!*

We traveled through some of the Rockies' most beautiful mountain scenery. Colorado is without a doubt a state where I would not mind living. – In the fall, mile after mile of golden aspen trees, either singly or in clusters, lighten up the dark pine forests, and crystal-clear creeks snake through valleys of mountain ranges. They sparkle like silver ribbons in the bright sun.

Vail

Gore Creek flows through the center of Vail, which has a population of 5,300, sits at an elevation of some eight thousand feet, and is famous as an international ski resort. Near the creek, I had discovered the perfect spot to picnic while the others in the group feasted in their restaurant of choice. The creek was streaming merrily and glistening below me. I felt happy to be surrounded by such beautiful scenery. Vail Mountain reaches 8,120 feet, and if you like to ski, this is the place for you. My step-great-grandson Eric and his wife had recently gone skiing in Vail and just loved it. On this day, October 17, the place was more or less devoid of tourists, which was just wonderful.

Strolling around the town after my siesta, I came upon a fascinating souvenir shop, where I ended up buying a quaint little birdhouse made of driftwood and a little Gregorian chime made in Germany. When I attended boarding school with the Ursulines, I sang Gregorian chants in the church choir. That's why I bought this wind chime. While others bought food for their stomachs, I spent my money on food for the soul. The proceeds for these souvenirs supposedly benefit the Betty Ford Foundation. Nice.

Denver

We were treated to a good farewell dinner at the Red Lion Denver Southeast, where we said our good-byes. Some were dressed quite elegantly, and my Indian friends were decked out in true Indian garb, with dangling gold jewelry to match. I just had to take a picture of the two. They had been very caring and attentive throughout the trip and even called me after I had returned home to make sure I was all right. It was so kind of them to tell me they looked upon me as their role model and were convinced I would live a long and happy life. *Merci beaucoup!*

THE GRAND FINALE

As the reader of my memoirs well knows, music was my first love and has remained my life's most important touchstone. Anyone who lacks a true love and sensitivity for the art of all arts is only half a human being. – Thus, it is only fitting that I should end this magnum opus with a brief account of the last two Schubertiades I hosted at my residence, in 2007 and 2008.

I had kept in touch with several of my young musical friends over the years, despite my travels. Even before my second trip to Antarctica on the MV *Polar Star*, I had been in touch with Julien Quentin, who had become a highly accomplished pianist, and asked for his help in organizing a Schubertiade, which is by no means an easy undertaking. But, leave it to Julien, he eventually succeeded in booking two wonderful instrumentalists – Corey Cerovsek, violin, and Eric Jacobsen, cello – to perform with him on February 17, 2007, at 7:30 p.m. These internationally famous musicians, all of them in their early thirties, were to play works by Richard Strauss (Sonata for Cello and Piano in F Major, op. 6 [1883]), Gabriel Fauré (Sonata No. 1 for Violin and Piano in A Major, op. 13 [1875]), and Pyotr Ilyich Tchaikovsky (Trio for Piano, Violin, and Cello in A Minor, op. 50, "In Memory of a Great Artist" [1882]). Corey had been nominated for a Grammy award that year. I was so excited and grateful that they could squeeze in a concert at my humble abode. Corey, who studied under Josef Gingold, completed his doctoral coursework in mathematics and music at age eighteen, and performed on the "Milanollo" Stradivarius of 1728, once played by Niccolò Paganini, flew in from Paris. Eric, who studied under David Soyer and Harvey Shapiro at the Juilliard School and played a Bernardus Calcanius cello crafted in 1744, arrived from New York. And Julien, who earned degrees from Juilliard and IU, studied under Émile Naoumoff, György Sándor, György Sebők, and Nikita Magaloff, and performed as a regular at the famous Verbier Festival, came from Germany. After some serious consideration and upon Julien's advice, I decided to trade in my Knabe baby grand for a Yamaha baby grand.

The evening was once more a success. Lou Newman, who had graciously offered her condo to house the three artists during their stay in Bloomington, wrote a nice thank-you note (gold on black paper): "Well – another triumph for the Schubertiaden Queen!!" It made me smile. Equally nice was Ellen Michel's note: "Wow!!! Andreas and I had such a wonderful time the other night. What an incredible gift – to your humble neighbors, friends and to those extraordinary musicians. The experience of being so close to music that extraordinary was just magical. I was floating all day Sunday. Thank you! Ellen."

Instead of attempting to recapture, five years or so later, the mood that took hold of me at the time, I will take the easy way out and simply copy the correspondence between Corey and myself, from some four months after the event:

Dear Corey, you have probably forgotten about me by now. I assure you that I have not forgotten you and the wonderful evening February 17, which you together with Julien and Eric made so unforgettable. I apologize for not contacting you earlier, but as you may have sensed, the whole event was so exhilarating and enormous for me to digest that it took me an unusual long time to simmer down. How can I ever thank you, Julien and Eric enough for bringing so much joy into my life and into that of everybody who had gathered at my little house. Everybody was so overwhelmed and as some said "floating on air" yet the next day. I shall never forget the moment when the first note you played that evening on your magical violin was so indescribably beautiful that the woman sitting next to me grabbed my hand and squeezed it ever so tightly. It was so electrifying and incredible that two people simultaneously reacted to your play so strongly in the same way. The resonance to the evening was just wonderful. Friends, among those professional musicians, commented that it was the event in a decade and that they had not experienced anything of that "caliber" in a long time. I hope that after you returned to France your life continued to unfold as you wish and that nothing but happiness and success lies ahead. I cannot imagine it to be otherwise. You are such a great violinist of very rare talent and I know that the musical world will continue to look forward to your performances with great enthusiasm and excitement.

A couple of weeks ago I returned from a somewhat strenuous trip to Turkey (Istanbul, Ephesus, Kasudasi, Antalya and Cappadocia etc.). It was another great experience. The hikes in very rugged terrain were a bit strenuous at times, and I am glad I met the challenges. Well, I won't detain you. Just wanted you to know that I have not forgotten you and you can believe that I have raved to my friends here and abroad and on my trips about you and some are justifiably a bit envious. All will watch out for you in their respective countries. I'll attach a few photos from Turkey and am for now

fondly yours, Christa-Maria Beardsley.

A few days later, Corey responded as follows:

Dear Christa,

Not at all, not at all – it was a delightful evening we all spent together, and of course I remember it well!

You have no idea how happy it makes me to receive a note like this. We play in big halls all the time and of course the people duly applaud, but to know that simply in a modest living room one can create such happiness together with music really reaffirms to me what's important in what musicians do! You've brought a big smile to my face. :)

I'm glad you had such a great trip to Turkey! I've been three times so far and was also impressed by the people and sights. (Even though the last time I got a bit food poisoned and my pleasure was therefore a bit compromised!) The last time I played in Antalya at

The Grand Finale

a Roman amphitheater – the Tchaikovsky Concerto under the moon and stars. It was a magical experience.

Take care, thank you again for arranging that memorable evening at your home, and hope to see you again before long!

Corey

I think this sums it all up. I could hardly believe that only a few months earlier, I had walked around in the very same Roman amphitheater in Antalya where Corey had performed the Tchaikovsky Concerto under the stars. How exciting!

I was in the mood for another Schubertiade and hoped my longtime friend Mark Kosower, now married to Jee-Won Oh, would be able to perform. Mark and his wife had moved to Bamberg, Germany, where he was solo cellist with the Bamberg Symphony. We had stayed in touch, and I was hopeful that we could organize an evening around their busy concert schedule, which occasionally brought them to the States. As is so often the case in my life when I dream of something, this wish eventually came true. As my readers may recall, Mark played at my house shortly after he enrolled at the IU Jacobs School of Music, when he was seventeen or eighteen years old. I was ecstatic when Mark and Jee-Won told me they would love to come and play for us on October 31, 2008, at 7:30 p.m.

And play they did! My favorite music couple performed brilliantly, as always. This time, the repertoire consisted of Sonata in G Major, BWV 1027, by Johann Sebastian Bach (1685–1750), Songs and Dances, op. 84, by Alexander Tcherepnin (1899–1977), Sonata (1984) by Francis Poulenc (1899–1963), Sonata for Violoncello Solo (1953) by György Ligeti (1923–2006), and Sonata in A Major, op. 69, by Ludwig van Beethoven (1770–1827).

The response was once more overpowering. Standing ovations, bravos, and bravissimos resonated throughout my little house. I presented both Mark and Jee-Won with the usual long-stemmed dark-red rose and followed through with champagne and a rich buffet, which the thirty-five or so guests enjoyed. All were eager to congratulate the cellist, János Starker's and Joel Krosnick's student, and the pianist, Sebők's and Shigeo Neriki's student, whom by now they all knew quite well. It was like a homecoming for most of us and for some a final good-bye.

April 15, 2013 (Patriots' Day) – Today, two bombs exploded at 2:50 p.m. near the finish line of the annual Boston Marathon, killing three and injuring more than 170. The instigators were two brothers who emigrated from Chechen about ten years ago. The older brother died in a shootout, and the younger one survived but is in critical condition in the hospital.

I mention this incident because I started writing my memoirs shortly after the 9/11 attacks in 2001 and find it a bit strange that my own approach to the finish line coincides with another terrorist attack on America, the country to which I immigrated in 1954.

Back to my musicians. The bonds of friendship gradually strengthened. Since 2010, Mark and Jee-Won have lived in Cleveland, where Mark is principal cellist of the Cleveland Symphony Orchestra and on the faculty of the Cleveland Institute of Music. Mark and Jee-Won continue to perform internationally, both together and as soloists. Major music critics from around the globe are full of the highest praise. Since Mark's performances of Alberto Ginastera's cello concertos with the Bamberg Symphony have been recorded, South American concert halls have begun to pay attention, inviting him to perform the concertos with their orchestras.

I was pleased to finally acquaint Mark and Jee-Won with my longtime friends Professor Segebrecht and his wife, Ursel, who reside in Bamberg. And when the Cleveland Symphony Orchestra played at IU in 2011, Mark and Jee-Won arranged for me to briefly meet their famous and beloved music director, Franz Welser-Möst, during a break in their rehearsal. I had nicknamed the conductor "Apollo." When I mentioned it to him, he smiled and responded in German, "Andere haben mich auch so genannt" (Others have called me that as well). Coincidence or fate? You must agree that it was funny. – Since Franz Welser-Möst is also the music director at my favorite opera house, the Wiener Staatsoper, you can imagine how exciting the personal meeting was for me. *Danke und servus.*

***

Toward the end of my life, I decided to follow Plato's advice: "The unexamined life is not worth living." I have learned that traveling this path requires stamina, solitude, and guts. It brings tears as well as joy – and the realization that I have long forgiven many, yet not forgotten any.

The greatest reward of an examined life is a feeling of gratitude and peace, which flows from the knowledge that my life, in happiness and sorrow, in turmoil and calm, was worth living.

www.ingramcontent.com/pod-product-compliance
Lightning Source LLC
Chambersburg PA
CBHW030109240426
43661CB00031B/1348/J